Preface

The word *accounting* most often conjures up images of tedious figures, thick glasses, and headaches. However, the savvy businessperson realizes that accounting has come to be known as the *language of business* with good reason. Accounting conveys important financial information that is used in the management planning, control, and decision-making processes integral to achieving organizational objectives. Some command of this language is a necessity for those who wish to participate in these processes.

This text takes the reader through the basics: what accounting information is, what it means, and how it is used. Students examine financial statements and discover what they do and do not communicate. This knowledge will help them gain the decision-making and problem-solving abilities so crucial outside the academic environment. In short, this text is for the benefit of the many who simply want to know "what the numbers mean."

In 1989 the Accounting Education Change Commission was formed "to foster changes in the academic preparation of accountants consistent with the goal of improving their capabilities for successful professional careers." In Position Statement No. Two, "The First Course in Accounting," (June 1992) the commission stated:

> The primary objective of the first course in accounting is for students to learn about accounting as an information development and communication function that supports economic decision-making. The knowledge and skills provided by the first course in accounting should facilitate subsequent learning even if the student takes no additional academic work in accounting or directly related disciplines. For example, the course should help students perform financial analysis; derive information for personal or organizational decisions; and understand business, governmental, and other organizational entities.[1]

---

[1] Accounting Education Change Commission, Position Statement No. Two, "The First Course in Accounting" (Torrance, CA, 1992), p. 2.

Business Majors and Non-Business Majors

We believe that this text permits students to achieve this objective. Typical undergraduate business students are required to complete two entry-level accounting courses covering topics in financial and managerial accounting. The authors of this text believe that over the years, many of the textbooks used in those courses have become increasingly encyclopedic. The result has been the teaching of a great deal of accounting detail without having students obtain a "big picture" of financial statement and accounting information use. One of the objectives of this text is to provide that "big picture" while meeting the objective for a first course in accounting identified by the Accounting Education Change Commission. When supplemented with appropriate cases and other materials, this text can be used in both the financial accounting and managerial accounting entry-level courses taken by undergraduate business majors. Students who intend to pursue an accounting major will also have to learn the procedures of accounting, which can be taught in courses or with laboratory cases (e.g., practice sets) designed for those students. The majority of students in the entry-level courses will not become accounting majors. This text is aimed at helping them learn how to become effective users of accounting information while providing a solid foundation for those students who will pursue advanced study in accounting.

Many students whose academic interests are not in the business field can also benefit from exposure to accounting. These students, however, often have a restricted curriculum and may simply not be interested in investing two elective courses in acquiring some basic accounting tools. The structure of this text lends itself to a one-semester course that provides a basic understanding of accounting information. Students who could benefit from this approach include undergraduate majors in the following areas:

- Engineering
- Behavioral sciences
- Public administration
- Prelaw programs

MBA Students

Professionals in any of these broad disciplines are likely to be confronted with financial management issues early in their careers. In fact, accounting issues are likely to touch the majority of career paths open to a student today. MBA students who do not have a background in undergraduate business study or feel the need for a refresher course can use this text to gain or revive certain key business skills.

Organization and Approach

Chapter 1 presents a basic description of accounting and its evolution. Emphasis is placed on developments that have occurred to meet the needs of the users of accounting information and on dispelling the misconception that accounting standards are just a code of rules. The remainder of the text is divided into two major topic areas: financial accounting topics (Chapters 2 through 11) and managerial accounting topics (Chapters 12 through 16).

In presenting these two aspects of accounting, the **spiral approach** is used. In this teaching method, a general sketch is presented, and each chapter fills in a few of the finishing details until the reader possesses the full picture. The spiral approach is based on the belief that students can better navigate a subject matter if they are given a glimpse of the big picture first. Thus the objectives of the course are clear from the beginning, and the student can keep them in sight throughout the learning process.

Following this model, the first chapter of each section outlines the pertinent fundamental relationships and presents appropriate terminology so the student is given an overview before exposure to details. In the following chapters, the fundamentals are elaborated and developed until the picture is sufficiently fleshed out. The focus throughout the presentation is on understanding the meaning of the numbers in financial statements, their relationship to each other, and how they are used in evaluation, planning, and control. In taking the spiral approach, an instructor focuses on the function, not the formation, of the financial statements.

Highlights and Enhancements in This Edition

In this edition, every effort has been made to retain the straightforward style that has been a popular feature of prior editions. Wherever possible, technical details are avoided as a financial statement user approach is emphasized. End-of-chapter problem materials have been expanded and revised.

- **Chapter 1**—Two new Business in Practice boxes added; topics are Career Opportunities in Accounting and Business Ethics.

FASB Conceptual Framework section reworked, with a plain English explanation in the text and with quotes from the highlights in an exhibit.

The financial accounting portion (Chapters 2 through 11):

- **Chapter 2**—Getting the big picture.

A model of the accounting process and the role of financial statements.

The introduction of a schematic diagram that illustrates the interrelationship of various financial statements and facilitates understanding the effects of various transactions.

- **Chapter 3**—Introducing basic concepts.

Return on investment.

Return on equity.

Liquidity.

- **Chapter 4**—Understanding the method.

The bookkeeping system in general terms.

A powerful transaction analysis scheme featuring the "horizontal model," which builds on the schematic diagram presented in Chapter 2.

Introduction of journal entries and T-accounts with emphasis on the horizontal model as the way to understand the effect of transactions on the balance sheet and income statement.

A new Business in Practice box about computerized bookkeeping systems.

· **Chapters 5 through 10**—Examining the specifics.

The elements of the balance sheet, income statement, and statement of cash flows in relation to the schematic diagram.

The *unique* and valuable explication of Explanatory Notes in Chapter 10, crucial to understanding financial statements as a whole.

Knowledge of business practices as a foundation for an understanding of accounting for transactions.

A rewrite of the Business in Practice box about Internal Control in Chapter 5.

A new section about payroll taxes and other withholdings in Chapter 7.

A new section describing owners' equity for organizations other than corporations in Chapter 8.

A rewrite of the section about earnings per share reflecting FASB 128 in Chapter 9, updated with references to "Notes to the Consolidated Financial Statements" of Intel Corporation's annual report, and an expanded discussion of pension-related disclosures in Chapter 10.

· **Chapter 11**—Using the knowledge.

Financial statement analysis: from financial data to decision making.

Revised and updated coverage of the price/earning ratio, and expanded discussion of common size financial statements to include both vertical and horizontal analysis. Several new application-oriented problems added to the end of chapter materials.

The managerial accounting portion (Chapters 12–16):

· **Chapter 12**—Getting the big picture.

An introduction to cost accounting systems and cost classifications.

Diagrams of cost flow, cost systems, and cost behavior.

Exhibit 12–7 (Income Statement) added to the discussion of cost accounting systems to help students understand the link between financial and managerial accounting. New problem materials with income statement requirements were added to complement this addition.

· **Chapters 13 through 16**—Examining the specifics and putting them to use.

An in-depth look at the specific uses of cost data in the planning, control, and decision-making processes.

The relationship between cost data and other factors involved in these processes.

The operating leverage material moved to the end of Chapter 13 and problem materials highlighting the effects of operating leverage on a firm's operating income added.

Substantial revisions to the end-of-chapter materials made in Chapter 14, including the addition of comprehensive cash budgeting problems (14–11 and 14–12) and integrated sales/purchases/cash budgeting problems (14–13 and 14–14).

In Chapter 15, new references made to alternative measurement approaches to developing "standards" in both manufacturing and non-manufacturing environments, including organizational goals related to continual improvement, increased throughput, and reduced downtime.

In Chapter 16, a challenging case study using net present value analysis added to the problem materials (16–13) to emphasize the importance of professional judgment in the capital budgeting process.

Notable Features

Text

- **Business in Practice** boxes are used throughout the chapters to highlight and discuss various business practices and their financial statement impact. Understanding these business practices facilitates a more complete understanding of financial statements in general.

- **Learning Objectives** guide students conceptually by providing a framework for each chapter. In addition to being stated at the beginning of each chapter, each learning objective is shown in the margin at the beginning of the text material that relates to it.

WHAT DOES IT MEAN?

- **What Does It Mean** questions that permit the student to self-test her understanding of key points are presented at the end of related sections of each chapter. The answers are presented near the end of each chapter before the Exercises and Problems.

- **Chapter Summaries and Key Terms and Concepts** promote greater retention of important points and definitions.

- **The 1996 Annual Report of Intel Corporation** is presented in the Appendix. Frequent reference to this material is made in the financial accounting portion of the text. This real-world example piques student interest and gives students a hands-on experience. In addition, students are asked to obtain their own example of an actual annual report.

Intel

- **Updated End-of-Chapter Exercises and Problems** illustrate important concepts and applications. Problems that require the use of Intel Corporation financial statements and other financial information from the Appendix are identified with the Intel name shown here in the margin. The writing assignment logo, also shown in the margin, identifies questions requiring written answers.

Supplements

The supplements were prepared by the textbook authors.

For the Student

- **Study Guide and Working Papers** for student use includes several hundred matching, true/false, and multiple-choice review questions with annotated answers, and working papers laid out for all problems.
- **Student Supplement:** *Study Outlines, Solutions to Odd-Numbered Problems, and Ready Notes.* (Shrink-wrapped with text.) Study Outlines are copies of the Teaching Acetates (transparency masters), with space for students to take class notes. Solutions are provided for all odd-numbered problems. Even-numbered problems are usually similar to the preceding odd-numbered problem. Having the full solution (not just a check figure) of the preceding problem available as a model provides additional examples beyond those in the text, reinforces learning, minimizes frustration, and facilites the use of the text as self-study or Continuing Professional Educational resource. Ready Notes are copies of the Ready Shows (PowerPoint® slides) with space for students to take notes.

For the Instructor

- **Instructor's Manual, Solutions and Test Bank** featuring teaching/learning objectives, chapter outlines, teaching observations, exercise and problem solutions, quiz/exam questions, and take-home quizzes.
- **Teaching Acetates** provide instructors with a framework for chapter-by-chapter discussions. Some are figures lifted from the text, others simply organize the material under discussion.
- **Ready Shows,** prepared by Douglas Cloud of Pepperdine University, is a package of multimedia enhancement aids that uses PowerPoint® software to illustrate chapter concepts.
- **CompuTest,** an advanced-feature test generator, allows the user to add and edit questions; save and reload tests; create up to 99 different versions of each test; attach graphics to questions; import and export ASCII files; and select questions based on type, level of difficulty, or keyword. This software provides password protection of saved tests and question databases, and can run on a network.
- A **World Wide Web** site for this text is at ***http://www.mhhe.com/ business/accounting/marshall.*** Instructors and students are encouraged to visit this site and others for text updates and other information that may be helpful to both the teacher and students.

Additional Notes from the Authors

In this text, we have followed a pragmatic approach in explaining the information content and use of financial statements and financial data. Students should be encouraged to read *The Wall Street Journal* and other business publications regularly, and instructors should attempt to call students' attention to current developments relating to the course material.

In several places in the text, reference is made to World Wide Web sites, which students are encouraged to visit. Instructors are encouraged to suggest that students use this medium to reference real-world illustrations of the concepts presented in the text.

Users of the text are cautioned that accounting is not a spectator sport and that comprehension of the material does require actually working through the problems. Reviewing solutions to odd-numbered problems that are in the *Ready Notes and Solutions to Odd-Numbered Problems* without first attempting the problems will significantly dilute the learning process.

We hope the approach and scope of coverage in this text have achieved the previously identified objectives and, in addition, have filled the user's need. Any ideas for increasing the effectiveness of this text are welcome.

Acknowledgments

Although the approach to the material and the scope of coverage in this text are the results of our own conclusions, truly new ideas are rare. The authors whose textbooks we have used in the past have influenced many of our ideas for particular accounting and financial management explanations. Likewise, students and colleagues through the years have helped us clarify illustrations and teaching techniques. Many of the users of the first three editions—both teachers and students—have offered comments and constructive criticisms that have been encouraging and helpful. All of this input is greatly appreciated.

Support from the staff at McGraw-Hill Higher Education is greatly appreciated. In addition to the many activities crucial to publication and marketing, they surveyed adopters and non-adopters, and secured comprehensive reviews that have helped us with this revision. We are grateful to the following reviewers for their supportive comments and constructive criticisms.

Patrick Berry, Keller Graduate School, Atlanta
Ken Fowler, Mankato State University
Bill Francisco, Georgia Southern University
Betty Harper, Middle Tennessee State University
Timothy Hohmeier, Keller Graduate School, Oakbrook
Scott Monette, Keller Graduate School, Overland Park
Presha Neidermeyer, Union College

David H. Marshall
Wayne W. McManus

Brief Contents

Contents

7   Accounting for and Presentation of Liabilities   227

8   Accounting for and Presentation of Owners' Equity   267

9   The Income Statement and the Statement of Cash Flows   303

PART II

Managerial Accounting

Index of Business
in Practice Boxes

Accounting— Present and Past

The objective of this text is to present enough of the fundamentals of accounting to permit the nonaccountant to understand the financial statements of an organization operating in our society and to understand how financial information can be used in the management planning, control, and decision-making processes. Although usually expressed in the context of profit-seeking business enterprises, most of the material is equally applicable to not-for-profit social service and governmental organizations.

Accounting is sometimes called *the language of business,* and it is appropriate for people who are involved in the economic activities of our society—and that is just about everyone—to know at least enough of this language to be able to make decisions and informed judgments about those economic activities.

Learning Objectives

After studying this chapter you should understand:

1 The definition of *accounting.*

2 Who the users of accounting information are and why they find accounting information useful.

3 The variety of professional services that accountants provide.

4 The development of accounting from a broad historical perspective.

5 The role that the Financial Accounting Standards Board (FASB) plays in the development of financial accounting standards.

6 How financial reporting standards evolve.

7 The key elements of ethical behavior for a professional accountant.

8 The FASB's Conceptual Framework project.

9 The objectives of financial reporting for business enterprises.

10 The plan of the book.

What Is Accounting?

Objective 1
Understand the definition of *accounting.*

In a broad sense, **accounting** is the process of identifying, measuring, and communicating economic information about an organization for the purpose of making decisions and informed judgments. (Accountants frequently use the term **entity** instead of *organization* because it is more inclusive.)

This definition of accounting can be expressed schematically as follows:

Accounting is the process of:

Identifying
Measuring   Economic information   For decisions and
Communicating   about an entity   >   informed judgments

Who makes these decisions and informed judgments? Users of accounting information include the management of the entity or organization, the owners of the organization (who are frequently not involved in the management process), potential investors in and creditors of the organization, employees, and various federal, state, and local governmental agencies that are concerned with regulatory and tax matters. Exhibit 1–1 illustrates some of the users and uses of accounting information. Pause, and try to think of at least one other decision or informed judgment that each of these users might make from the economic information that could be communicated about an entity.

EXHIBIT 1–1   Users and Uses of Accounting Information

Objective 2
Understand who the users of accounting information are and why they find accounting information useful.

User	Decision/Informed Judgment Made
Management	When performing its functions of planning, directing, and controlling, management makes many decisions and informed judgments. For example, when considering the expansion of a product line, planning involves identifying and measuring costs and benefits; directing involves communicating the strategies selected; and controlling involves identifying, measuring, and communicating the results of the product line expansion during and after its implementation.
Investors	When considering whether or not to invest in the common stock of a company, **investors** use accounting information to help assess the amounts, timing, and uncertainty of future cash returns on their investment.
Creditors	When determining how much merchandise to ship to a customer before receiving payment, **creditors** assess the probability of collection and the risks of late (or non-) payment.
Employees	When planning for retirement, employees assess the company's ability to offer long-term job prospects and an attractive retirement benefits package.
SEC (Securities and Exchange Commission)	When reviewing for compliance with SEC regulations, analysts determine whether or not financial statements issued to investors fully disclose all required information.

Accounting information must be provided for just about every kind of organization. Accounting for business firms is what many people initially think of, but not-for-profit social service organizations, governmental units, educational institutions, social clubs, political committees, and other groups all require accounting for their economic activities.

Accounting is frequently perceived as something that others do, rather than as the process of providing information that supports decisions and informed judgments. Relatively few people actually become accountants, but almost all people use accounting information. The principal objective of this text is to help you become an informed user of accounting information, rather than to prepare you to become an accountant. However, the essence of this user orientation provides a solid foundation for those students who choose to become accounting majors.

If you haven't already experienced the lack of understanding or confusion that results from looking at one or more financial statements, you have been spared one of life's frustrations. Certainly during the course of your formal business education and early during your employment experience, you will be presented with financial data. Being an informed user means knowing how to use those data as information.

The following sections introduce the major areas of practice within the accounting discipline and help you to understand the types of work done by professional accountants within each of these broad categories. The Business in Practice discussion on page 6 highlights career opportunities in accounting.

WHAT DOES IT MEAN?

1. What does it mean to state that the accounting process should support decisions and informed judgments?

Financial Accounting

Objective 3
Understand the variety of professional services that accountants provide.

Financial accounting generally refers to the process that results in the preparation and reporting of financial statements for an entity. As will be explained in more detail, the financial statements present the financial position of an entity at a point in time, the results of the entity's operations for some period of time, the **cash flow** activities for the same period of time, and other information about the entity's financial resources, obligations, owners' interests, and operations.

Financial accounting is primarily externally oriented. The financial statements are directed to individuals who are not in a position to be aware of the day-to-day financial and operating activities of the entity. Financial accounting is also primarily concerned with the historical results of an entity's performance. Financial statements reflect what has happened in the past, and although readers may want to project past activities and their results into future performance, financial statements are not a clear crystal ball. Many corporate annual reports will make reference to the historical nature of financial accounting information to emphasize its importance to users. For instance, on pages 6 and 16 of Intel Corporation's 1996 Annual Report, which is reproduced in the Appendix, it is noted that, "Past performance does not guarantee future results." Users must make their own judgments about a firm's future prospects.

Bookkeeping procedures are used to accumulate the results of many of an entity's activities, and these procedures are part of the financial accounting process. Bookkeeping procedures have been thoroughly systematized using manual, mechanical, and computer techniques, and although these procedures support the financial accounting process, they are only a part of the process.

Financial accounting is done by accounting professionals who have generally earned a bachelor of science degree with a major in accounting. The financial accountant is employed by an entity to use her or his expertise, analytical skills, and judgment in the many activities that are necessary for the preparation of financial statements. The title **controller** is used to designate the chief accounting officer of a corporation. The controller is usually responsible for both the financial and managerial accounting functions (see below) of the organization. Sometimes the title *comptroller* (the Old English spelling) is used for this position.

An individual earns the **Certified Public Accountant (CPA)** professional designation by passing a comprehensive four-part examination taken over a two-day period. A uniform CPA exam is given nationally during May and November each year, although it is administered by individual states. Some states require that candidates have accounting work experience before sitting for the exam. About 40 states have enacted legislation increasing the educational requirements for CPA candidates from 120 semester hours of college study, or a bachelor's degree, to a minimum of 150 semester hours of college study to be eligible to take the exam. The American Institute of Certified Public Accountants (AICPA), the national professional organization of CPAs, has determined that an individual CPA wishing to become a member after the year 2000 must have met the 150-hour requirement. This increase in the educational requirements for becoming a CPA and for joining the AICPA reflects the increasing demands placed on accounting professionals to be both broadly educated and technically competent. Practicing CPAs work in all types of organizations, but as explained later, a CPA who expresses an auditor's opinion about an entity's financial statements must be licensed by the state in which she or he performs the auditing service.

Managerial Accounting/Cost Accounting

Managerial accounting is concerned with the use of economic and financial information to plan and control many of the activities of the entity and to support the management decision-making process. **Cost accounting** is a subset of managerial accounting that relates to the determination and accumulation of product, process, or service costs. Managerial accounting and cost accounting have a primarily internal orientation, as opposed to the primarily external orientation of financial accounting. Much of the same data used in or generated by the financial accounting process are used in managerial and cost accounting, but the data are more likely to be used in a future-oriented way, such as in the preparation of budgets. A detailed discussion of the similarities and differences between financial and managerial accounting is provided in Chapter 12 and highlighted in Exhibit 12–1.

Managerial accountants and cost accountants are professionals who have usually earned a bachelor of science degree with a major in accounting. Their work frequently involves close coordination with the production, marketing, and finance functions of the entity. The **Certified Management Accountant (CMA)** professional designation is earned by a management accountant/cost accountant who passes a broad four-part examination administered over a two-day period and who meets certain experience requirements.

Auditing—Public Accounting

Many entities have their financial statements reviewed by an independent third party. In most cases, an audit is required by securities laws if the stock or bonds of a company are owned and publicly traded by investors. **Public accounting** firms and individual CPAs provide this **auditing** service, which constitutes an important part of the accounting profession.

The result of an audit is the **independent auditor's report.** The report usually has three relatively brief paragraphs. The first paragraph identifies the financial statements that were audited, explains that the statements are the responsibility of the company's management, and states that the auditor's responsibility is to express an opinion about the financial statements. The second paragraph explains that the audit was conducted "in accordance with **generally accepted auditing standards**" and describes briefly what those standards require and what work is involved in performing an audit. The third paragraph contains the auditor's opinion, which is usually that the named statements "present fairly in all material respects" the financial position of the entity, and the results of its operations and cash flows for the identified periods "in conformity with **generally accepted accounting principles.**" This is an unqualified, or "clean," opinion. Occasionally the opinion will be qualified with respect to fair presentation, departure from generally accepted accounting principles, the auditor's inability to perform certain auditing procedures, or the firm's ability to continue as a going concern (i.e., as a viable economic entity). An unqualified opinion is not a clean bill of health about either the current financial condition of or the future prospects for the entity. Readers must reach their own judgments about these and other matters after studying the **annual report,** which includes the financial statements and the explanatory notes to the financial statements.

Auditors who work in public accounting are professional accountants who have usually earned at least a bachelor of science degree with a major in accounting. The auditor may work for a public accounting firm (a few firms have several thousand partners and professional staff) or as an individual practitioner. Most auditors seek and earn the CPA designation; the firm partner or individual practitioner who actually signs the audit opinion must be a licensed CPA in the state in which she or he practices. To be licensed, the CPA must satisfy the character, education, and experience requirements of the state.

To see an example of the independent auditors' report, refer to page 32 of the 1996 annual report of Intel Corporation, which is reproduced in the Appendix.

WHAT DOES IT MEAN?

2. What does it mean to work in public accounting?
3. What does it mean to be a CPA?

Internal Auditing

Organizations with many plant locations or activities involving many financial transactions employ professional accountants to do **internal auditing.** In many cases, the internal auditor performs functions much like those of the external auditor/public accountant, but perhaps on a smaller scale. For example, internal auditors may be responsible for reviewing the financial statements of a single plant or for analyzing the operating efficiency of an entity's activities. The qualifications of an internal auditor are similar to those of any other professional accountant. In addition to having the CPA and/or the CMA designation, the internal auditor may also have passed the examination to become a Certified Internal Auditor (CIA).

BUSINESS IN PRACTICE
Career Opportunities in Accounting

Because accounting is a profession, most entry-level positions require a bachelor of science degree with a major in accounting. Individuals are encouraged to achieve certification as quickly as feasible. Persons who work hard and smart can expect to attain high professional levels in their careers. The major employers of accountants include public accounting firms, industrial firms, government, and not-for-profit organizations.

Public Accounting

The work done by public accountants varies significantly depending on whether the employer is a local, regional, or international CPA firm. Small local firms concentrate on the bookkeeping, accounting, tax return, and financial planning needs of individuals and small businesses. These firms need "generalists" who are able to adequately serve in a variety of capacities. The somewhat larger, regional firms offer a broad range of professional services but concentrate on the performance of audits, corporate tax returns, and management advisory services. They often hire experienced financial and industry specialists to serve particular client needs, in addition to recruiting well qualified recent graduates.

The large, international CPA firms also perform auditing, tax, and consulting services. Their principal clients are large domestic and international corporations. As a result of the 1998 merger of Price Waterhouse and Coopers & Lybrand, forming the firm PricewaterhouseCoopers, the group of large, international CPA firms has been reduced to the "Big Five." The other four firms are Arthur Andersen, Deloitte & Touche, Ernst & Young, and KPMG Peat Marwick. These firms dominate the market in terms of total revenues, number of corporate audit clients, and number of offices, partners, and staff members. These international firms generally recruit outstanding graduates and highly experienced CPAs and encourage the development of specialized skills by their personnel.

Industrial Accounting

More accountants are employed in industry than in public accounting because of the vast number of manufacturing and merchandising firms of all

Business in Practice concluded

sizes. In addition to using the services of public accounting firms, all industrial firms employ cost and management accountants, as well as financial
accountants. Many accountants in industry started working in this environment right out of school; others got their start in public accounting as
auditors, but moved to industry after getting at least a couple of years of
experience.

Government and Not-for-Profit Accounting

Opportunities for accounting professionals in the governmental and not-for-
profit sectors of the economy are constantly increasing. In this country, literally thousands of state and local government reporting entities touch on
the lives of each and every citizen. Likewise, accounting specialists are employed by colleges and universities, hospitals, and voluntary health and welfare organizations such as the American Red Cross, the United Way, and
Greenpeace.

Governmental and Not-for-Profit Accounting

Governmental units at the municipal, state, and federal level and not-for-
profit entities such as colleges and universities, hospitals, and voluntary
health and welfare organizations require the same accounting functions to
be performed as do other accounting entities. Religious organizations, labor unions, trade associations, performing arts organizations, political par-
ties, libraries, museums, country clubs, and many other not-for-profit
organizations employ accountants with similar educational qualifications
as those employed in business and public accounting.

Income Tax Accounting

The growing complexity of federal, state, municipal, and foreign income
tax laws has led to a demand for professional accountants who are specialists in various aspects of taxation. Tax practitioners often develop spe-
cialties in the taxation of individuals, partnerships, corporations, trusts and
estates, or international tax law issues. These accountants work for corporations, public accounting firms, governmental units, and other entities.
Many tax accountants have bachelor's degrees and are CPAs; some are
attorneys as well.

How Has Accounting Developed?

Objective 4
Understand the
development of
accounting from a
broad historical
perspective.

Accounting has developed over time in response to the needs of users of
financial statements for financial information to support decisions and informed judgments such as those mentioned in Exhibit 1–1 and others that
you were challenged to identify. Even though an aura of exactness is conveyed by the numbers in financial statements, a great deal of judgment and

approximation is involved in determining the numbers to be reported. There isn't any "code of accounting rules" to be followed indiscriminately. Even though broad generally accepted principles of accounting do exist, different accountants may reach different but often equally legitimate conclusions about how to account for a particular transaction or event. A brief review of the history of the development of accounting principles may make this often confusing state of affairs a little easier to understand.

Early History

It is not surprising that evidence of record-keeping of economic events has been found in the earliest civilizations. Dating back to the clay tablets used by Mesopotamians of about 3000 B.C. to record tax receipts, accounting has responded to the information needs of users. In 1494, Luca Pacioli, a Franciscan monk and mathematics professor, published the first known text to describe a comprehensive double-entry bookkeeping system. Modern bookkeeping systems (as discussed in Chapter 4) have evolved directly from Pacioli's "method of Venice" system, which was developed in response to the needs of the Italian mercantile trading practices in that period.

The Industrial Revolution generated the need for large amounts of capital to finance the enterprises that supplanted individual craftsmen. This need resulted in the corporate form of organization marked by absentee owners, or investors, who entrusted their money to managers. It followed that investors required reports from the corporation managers showing financial position and results of operations. In mid-19th century England, the independent (external) audit function added credence to financial reports. As British capital was invested in a growing U.S. economy in the late 19th century, British chartered accountants and accounting methods came to the United States. However, no group was legally authorized to establish financial reporting standards. This led to alternative methods of reporting financial condition and results of operations, which resulted in confusion and, in some cases, outright fraud.

The Accounting Profession in the United States

Accounting professionals in this country organized themselves in the early 1900s and worked hard to establish certification laws, standardized audit procedures, and other attributes of a profession. However, not until 1932–1934 did the American Institute of Accountants (predecessor of today's American Institute of Certified Public Accountants—AICPA) and the New York Stock Exchange agree on five broad principles of accounting. This was the first formal accounting standard-setting activity. The accounting, financial reporting, and auditing weaknesses related to the 1929 stock market crash gave impetus to this effort.

The Securities Act of 1933 and the Securities Exchange Act of 1934 apply to securities offered for sale in interstate commerce. These laws had a significant effect on the standard-setting process because they gave the **Securities and Exchange Commission (SEC)** the authority to establish accounting principles to be followed by companies whose securities had to be registered with the SEC. The SEC still has this authority, but the standard-setting process has been delegated to other organizations over the years. Between 1939 and 1959 the Committee on Accounting Procedure of the American Institute of Accountants issued 51 *Accounting Research Bulletins* that dealt with accounting principles. This work was done without a common conceptual framework for financial reporting. Each bulletin dealt with a specific issue in a relatively narrow context, and alternative methods of reporting the results of similar transactions remained.

In 1959 the Accounting Principles Board (APB) replaced the Committee on Accounting Procedure as the standard-setting body. The APB was an arm of the AICPA, and although it was given resources and directed to engage in more research than its predecessor, its early efforts intensified the controversies that existed. The APB did issue 39 *Opinions* on serious accounting issues, but it failed to develop a conceptual underpinning for accounting.

Financial Accounting Standard Setting at the Present Time

Objective 5
Understand the role that the FASB plays in the development of financial accounting standards.

In 1973, as a result of congressional and other criticism of the accounting standard-setting process being performed by an arm of the AICPA, the **Financial Accounting Foundation** was created as a more independent entity. The Foundation established the **Financial Accounting Standards Board (FASB)** as the authoritative standard-setting body within the accounting profession. The FASB embarked on a project called the Conceptual Framework of Financial Accounting and Reporting and has issued six *Statements of Financial Accounting Concepts* through July 1998.

Concurrently with its conceptual framework project, the FASB has issued more than 130 *Statements of Financial Accounting Standards* that have established standards of accounting and reporting for particular issues, much like its predecessors did. Alternative ways of accounting for and reporting the effects of similar transactions still exist. In many aspects of financial reporting, the accountant still must use judgment in selecting between equally acceptable alternatives. In order to make sense of financial statements, one must understand the impact of the accounting methods used by a firm, relative to alternative methods that were not selected. Subsequent chapters will describe many of these alternatives and the impact that various accounting choices have on financial statements. For example, Chapter 5 discusses the effects of the first-in, first-out inventory cost flow assumption in comparison to the last-in, first-out and the weighted-average assumptions. Likewise, Chapter 6 discusses the difference between the straight-line and accelerated methods of depreciating long-lived assets. Although such terminology may not be meaningful to you at this time, you should understand that the FASB has sanctioned each of these alternative methods of accounting for inventory and depreciation, and that the methods selected can have a significant effect on a firm's reported profits.

The FASB does not set standards in a vacuum. An open, due process procedure is followed. The FASB invites input from any individual or organization who cares to provide ideas and viewpoints about the particular standard under consideration. Among the many professional accounting and financial organizations that regularly present suggestions to the FASB, in addition to the AICPA and the SEC, are the American Accounting Association, the Institute of Management Accountants, the Financial Executives Institute, and the Institute of Chartered Financial Analysts.

The point of this discussion is to emphasize that financial accounting and reporting practices are not codified in a set of rules to be mastered and blindly followed. Financial accounting and reporting have evolved over time in response to the changing needs of society, and they are still evolving. Your objective is to learn enough about the fundamentals of financial accounting and reporting practices to be neither awed nor confounded by the presentation of financial data.

Objective 6
Understand how financial reporting standards evolve.

WHAT DOES IT MEAN?

4. What does it mean to state that generally accepted accounting principles are not a set of rules to be blindly followed?

5. What does it mean when the Financial Accounting Standards Board issues a new *Statement of Financial Accounting Standards*?

Standards for Other Types of Accounting

Because managerial accounting/cost accounting is primarily oriented to internal use, it is presumed that internal users will know about the accounting practices being followed by their firms. As a result, the accounting profession has not regarded the development of internal reporting standards for use by management as an important issue. Instead, individual companies are generally allowed to self-regulate with respect to internal reporting matters. One significant exception is accounting for the cost of work done under government contracts. Over the years, various governmental agencies have issued directives prescribing the procedures to be followed by government contractors. During the 1970–1980 period, the **Cost Accounting Standards Board (CASB)** operated as a governmental body to establish standards applicable to government contracts. Congress abolished the CASB in 1981, although its standards remained in effect. In 1988, Congress reestablished the CASB as an independent body within the Office of Federal Procurement Policy and gave it authority to establish cost accounting standards for government contracts in excess of $500,000.

In the auditing/public accounting area, auditing standards are established by the Auditing Standards Board, a technical committee of the AICPA. The SEC has had input into this process, and over the years a number of auditing standards and procedures have been issued. One of the most important of these standards requires the auditor to be *independent* of the client whose financial statements are being audited. Yet auditors' judgment is still very important in the auditing process. Because of this, critics of the accounting profession often raise questions concerning the independence of CPA firms in the auditing process. Congressional committees have held hearings about the role of a company's auditing firm when the company has been involved in a major fraud or has gone bankrupt shortly after receiving an unqualified opinion. In 1987 the National Commission on Fraudulent Financial Reporting, a private-sector initiative sponsored by several professional associations, including the AICPA, issued recommendations designed to reduce further the already low incidence of fraudulent financial reporting. It is worth repeating here that an unqualified auditor's opinion does not constitute a clean bill of health about

---

EXHIBIT 1–2   **Web Sites for Accounting Organizations**

American Institute of Certified Public Accountants: http://www.aicpa.org

Financial Accounting Standards Board: http://www.rutgers.edu/accounting/raw/fasb/home.htm

Government Accounting Standards Board: http://www.rutgers.edu/accounting/raw/gasb/

Institute of Internal Auditors: http://www.rutgers.edu/accounting/raw/iia/

Institute of Management Accountants: http://panopticon.csustan.edu/ima/imafront.htm

International Accounting Standards Committee: http://www.iasc.org.uk

Securities and Exchange Commission: http://www.sec.gov

---

either the current financial condition of or the future prospects for the entity. It is up to the readers of the financial statements to reach their own judgments about these and other matters after studying the firm's annual report, which includes the financial statements and explanatory footnotes.

In 1984, the **Governmental Accounting Standards Board (GASB)** was established to develop guidelines for financial accounting and reporting by state and local governmental units. The GASB operates under the auspices of the Financial Accounting Foundation, which is also the parent organization of the FASB. The GASB is attempting to unify practices of the nation's many state and municipal entities, thus providing investors with a better means of comparing financial data of the issuers of state and municipal securities. In the absence of a GASB standard for a particular activity or transaction occurring in both the public and private sectors, governmental entities will continue to use FASB standards for guidance. Several GASB standards had been issued by the end of 1997.

The United States Internal Revenue Code and related regulations and the various state and local tax laws specify the rules to be followed in determining an entity's income tax liability. Although quite specific and complicated, the code and regulations provide rules of law to be followed. In income tax matters, accountants use their judgment and expertise to design transactions so that the entity's overall income tax liability is minimized. In addition, accountants prepare or help prepare tax returns and may represent clients whose returns are being reviewed or challenged by taxing authorities.

International Accounting Standards

Accounting standards in individual countries have evolved in response to the unique user needs and cultural attributes of each country. Thus, in spite of the development of a global marketplace, accounting standards in one country may differ significantly from those in another country. In 1973 the International Accounting Standards Committee (IASC) was formed by accountancy bodies in Australia, Canada, France, Germany, Japan, Mexico, the Netherlands, the United Kingdom and Ireland, and the United States to create and promote worldwide acceptance and observation of accounting and financial reporting standards. The IASC is a private organization based in London (in some ways similar to the FASB and GASB).

Although now supported by more than 80 nations, the development of uniform standards has been an almost impossible objective to achieve. One of the major challenges relates to a country's interest in protecting its local markets, where participants' interests are frequently quite different from entities involved in a global financial network. Countries throughout the world vary, for instance, in terms of the complexity of their capital markets, the need for disclosure of financial information, and the role of government oversight in the standard-setting process. Unfortunately, these nationalism issues are not the only obstacles confronting the IASC. The simple truth is that because the IASC is a private body, its pronouncements cannot be enforced. What is hoped for instead is that each country's accounting professional body will make and keep a "best efforts" pledge to move toward the acceptance of international standards.

Currently, the IASC is seeking methods of providing comparability between financial statements prepared according to the differing accounting standards of its member nations. This effort, often referred to as *harmonization,* involves both the elimination of inferior accounting methods that continue to exist today in many areas of the world and the limitation of alternative acceptable methods within the IASC's own standards. The development of a single set of international accounting standards to be applied by all countries is a long way off and may never be achieved in total. This makes it important to understand the standards of one's own country so that appropriate consideration can be given to financial statements prepared according to another country's standards. Exhibit 1–2 on page 11 has the addresses for various accounting organizations. You are encouraged to visit these sites for more information about each one.

WHAT DOES IT MEAN?

6. What does it mean that there are no generally accepted international accounting standards?

Ethics and the Accounting Profession

Objective 7
Understand the key elements of ethical behavior for a professional accountant.

One of the characteristics frequently associated with any profession is that those practicing the profession acknowledge the importance of an ethical code. This is especially important in the accounting profession because so much of an accountant's work involves providing information to support the informed judgments and decisions made by users of accounting information.

The American Institute of Certified Public Accountants (AICPA) and the Institute of Management Accountants (IMA) have both published ethics codes. The *Code of Professional Conduct,* most recently revised in 1988, was adopted by the membership of the AICPA. The organization's bylaws state that members shall conform to the rules of the Code or be subject to disciplinary action by the AICPA. Although it doesn't have the same enforcement mechanism, the IMA's *Standards of Ethical Conduct for Management Accountants* calls on management accountants to maintain the highest standards of ethical conduct as they fulfill their obligations to the organizations they serve, their profession, the public, and themselves.

Both codes of conduct identify integrity and objectivity as two of the key elements of ethical behavior for a professional accountant. Having

integrity means being honest and forthright in dealings and communications with others; **objectivity** means impartiality and freedom from conflict of interest. An accountant who lacks integrity and/or objectivity cannot be relied upon to produce complete and relevant information with which to make an informed judgment or decision.

Other elements of ethical behavior include independence, competence, and acceptance of an obligation to serve the best interests of the employer, the client, and the public. **Independence** is related to objectivity and is especially important to the auditor, who must be independent both in appearance and in fact. Having competence means having the knowledge and professional skills to adequately perform the work assigned. Accountants should recognize that the nature of their work requires an understanding of the obligation to serve those who will use the information communicated by them.

BUSINESS IN PRACTICE
Business Ethics

The level of concern about business ethics has been rising in recent years. An indication of the breadth of this concern is the development of the term *stakeholder* to refer to the many entities—owners, managers, employees, customers, suppliers, communities, and even competitors—who have a stake in the way an organization conducts its activities. Another indicator of this concern is that business ethics and corporate social responsibility issues are merging into a single broad area of interest.

This concern is international in scope and is attracting political attention. A key element of the winning Labor Party's platform in the 1997 British elections related to corporate responsibility. In the United States, President Clinton sponsored a conference on Corporate Citizenship that focused on the responsibility issue.

On a more localized level, it was reported that not long after his resignation as basketball coach at the University of North Carolina, Dean Smith met with a group that was concerned about the overseas workforce used to manufacture the brand of shoes used by the basketball team.

The Foreign Corrupt Practices Act of 1977 and 1991 additions to the Federal Sentencing Guidelines relating to an organization's responsibility for criminal acts perpetrated by employees have contributed to a management focus on ethical behavior. In 1987, a private sector commission, convened in response to perceived weaknesses with corporate financial reporting practices, recommended to the Securities and Exchange Commission that publicly owned corporations include in their annual report disclosures about how the company was fulfilling its responsibilities for achieving a broadly defined set of internal control objectives related to safeguarding assets, authorizing transactions, and reporting properly. (See the Business in Practice discussion of internal control in Chapter 5.) Although the SEC does not require them to do so, many companies do acknowledge this responsibility. The disclosure frequently refers to the company's code of conduct or ethics system. Within the accounting profession, it is generally accepted that an organization's integrity and ethical values bear directly on the effectiveness of its internal control system.

Business in Practice concluded

Researchers are beginning to demonstrate that well-constructed ethical and social programs can contribute to profitability by helping to attract customers, raise employee morale and productivity, and strengthen trust relationships within the organization.

It is never too early to understand and refine your own value system and to sharpen your awareness of the ethical dimensions of your activities. And don't be surprised if you are asked to literally "sign-on" to an employer's code of conduct.

The following World Wide Web sites reference other sites dealing with business ethics:

http://www.ethics.ubc.ca/resources/business
http://commfaculty.fullerton.edu/lester/ethics/ethics_list.html

---

In the recent past, there have been some highly publicized incidents involving allegations that accountants have violated their ethical codes by being dishonest, biased, and/or incompetent. The fact that some of these allegations have been proved true should not be used to condemn all accountants. The profession has used these rare circumstances to reaffirm that the public and the profession expect accountants to exhibit a very high level of ethical behavior. In this sense, are accountants really any different from those who are involved in any other endeavor?

WHAT DOES IT MEAN?

7. What does it mean to state that ethical behavior includes being objective and independent?

The Conceptual Framework

Objective 8
Understand the FASB's Conceptual Framework project.

Various accounting standards have existed for many years. But it wasn't until the mid-1970s that the FASB began the process of identifying a structure or framework of financial accounting concepts. New users of financial statements can benefit from an overview of these concepts because they provide the foundation for understanding financial accounting reports. The *Statements of Financial Accounting Concepts* that have been issued by the FASB through 1997 are:

Number	Title	Issue Date
1.	Objectives of Financial Reporting by Business Enterprises	November 1978
2.	Qualitative Characteristics of Accounting Information (Amended by Statement 6)	May 1980
3.	Elements of Financial Statements of Business Enterprises (Replaced by Statement 6)	December 1980
4.	Objectives of Financial Reporting by Nonbusiness Organizations	December 1980
5.	Recognition and Measurement in Financial Statements of Business Enterprises	December 1984
6.	Elements of Financial Statements	December 1985

These statements represent a great deal of effort by the FASB, and the progress made on this project has not come easily. The project was somewhat controversial at its inception because of the concern that trying to define the underlying concepts of accounting would inevitably have a significant impact on current generally accepted accounting principles and would be likely to result in major changes to financial reporting practices. Critics believe that, at best, this would have caused financial statement readers to become confused (or more confused than they already were) and, at the worst, could have disrupted financial markets and contractual obligations that were based on present financial reporting practices. The FASB recognized this concern and made the following assertions about the concepts statements:[1]

> Statements of Financial Accounting Concepts do not establish standards prescribing accounting procedures or disclosure practices for particular items or events, which are issued by the Board as Statements of Financial Accounting Standards. Rather, Statements in this series describe concepts and relations that will underlie future financial accounting standards and practices and in due course serve as a basis for evaluating existing standards and practices.
>
> Establishment of objectives and identification of fundamental concepts will not directly solve accounting and reporting problems. Rather, objectives give direction, and concepts are tools for solving problems.
>
> The Board itself is likely to be the most direct beneficiary of the guidance provided by the Statements in this series. They will guide the Board in developing accounting and reporting standards by providing the Board with a common foundation and basic reasoning on which to consider merits of alternatives.

"Highlights" of Concepts Statement No. 1— Objectives of Financial Reporting by Business Enterprises

Objective 9
Understand the objectives of financial reporting for business enterprises.

To set the stage more completely for your study of financial accounting, it is appropriate to have an overview of the "Highlights" of *Concepts Statement No. 1,* as contained in that statement. The "Highlights" are reproduced in Exhibit 1–3. Here is a summary overview.

Financial reporting is done for individual firms, or entities, rather than for industries or the economy as a whole and is aimed primarily at meeting the needs of external users of accounting information who would not otherwise have access to the firm's records. Investors, creditors, and financial advisors are the primary users who create the demand for accounting information. Financial reporting is designed to meet the needs of users by providing information that is relevant to making rational investment and credit decisions, and other informed judgments. The users of accounting information are assumed to be reasonably astute in business and financial reporting practices. However, each user reads the financial statements with her or his own judgment and biases and must be willing to take responsibility for her or his own decision making.

---

[1]Preface, *FASB Statement of Financial Accounting Concepts No. 6* (Stamford, CT, 1985). Copyright © the Financial Accounting Standards Board, High Ridge Park, Stamford, CT 06905, U.S.A. Excerpted with permission. Copies of the complete document are available from the FASB.

EXHIBIT 1–3   **"Highlights" of Concepts Statement No. 1—
Objectives of Financial Reporting by Business
Enterprises***

- Financial reporting is not an end in itself but is intended to provide information that is useful in making business and economic decisions.
- The objectives of financial reporting are not immutable—they are affected by the economic, legal, political, and social environment in which financial reporting takes place.
- The objectives are also affected by the characteristics and limitations of the kind of information that financial reporting can provide.
  - The information pertains to business enterprises rather than to industries or the economy as a whole.
  - The information often results from approximate, rather than exact, measures.
  - The information largely reflects the financial effects of transactions and events that have already happened.
  - The information is but one source needed by those who make decisions about business enterprises.
  - The information is provided and used at a cost.
- The objectives in this Statement are those of general purpose external financial reporting by business enterprises.
  - The objectives stem primarily from the needs of external users who lack the authority to prescribe the information they want and must rely on the information management communicates to them.
  - The objectives are directed toward the common interests of many users in the ability of an enterprise to generate favorable cash flows but are phrased using investment and credit decisions as a reference to give them focus. The objectives are intended to be broad, rather than narrow.
  - The objectives pertain to financial reporting and are not restricted to financial statements.
- The objectives state that:
  - Financial reporting should provide information that is useful to present and potential investors [stockholders] and creditors [lenders] and other users in making rational investment, credit, and similar decisions. The information should be comprehensible to those who have a reasonable understanding of business and economic activities and are willing to study the information with reasonable diligence.
  - Financial reporting should provide information to help present and potential investors and creditors and other users in assessing the amounts, timing, and uncertainty of prospective cash receipts from dividends or interest and the proceeds from the sale, redemption, or maturity of securities or loans. Since investors' and creditors' cash flows are related to enterprise cash flows, financial reporting should provide information to help investors, creditors, and others assess the amounts, timing, and uncertainty of prospective net cash inflows to the related enterprise.
  - Financial reporting should provide information about the economic resources of an enterprise, the claims to those resources (obligations of the enterprise to transfer resources to other entities and owners' equity), and the effects of transactions, events, and circumstances that change its resources and claims to those resources.
- "Investors" and "creditors" are used broadly and include not only those who have or contemplate having a claim to enterprise resources but also those who advise or represent them.

EXHIBIT 1–3 *(concluded)*

- Although investment and credit decisions reflect investors' and creditors' expectations about future enterprise performance, those expectations are commonly based at least partly on evaluations of past enterprise performance.
- The primary focus of financial reporting is information about earnings and its components.
- Information about enterprise earnings based on accrual accounting generally provides a better indication of an enterprise's present and continuing ability to generate favorable cash flows than information limited to the financial effects of cash receipts and payments.
- Financial reporting is expected to provide information about an enterprise's financial performance during a period and about how management of an enterprise has discharged its stewardship responsibility to owners.
- Financial accounting is not designed to measure directly the value of a business enterprise, but the information it provides may be helpful to those who wish to estimate its value.
- Investors, creditors, and others may use reported earnings and information about the elements of financial statements in various ways to assess the prospects for cash flows. They may wish, for example, to evaluate management's performance, estimate "earning power," predict future earnings, assess risk, or to confirm, change, or reject earlier predictions or assessments. Although financial reporting should provide basic information to aid them, they do their own evaluating, estimating, predicting, assessing, confirming, changing, or rejecting.
- Management knows more about the enterprise and its affairs than investors, creditors, or other "outsiders" and accordingly can often increase the usefulness of financial information by identifying certain events and circumstances and explaining their financial effects on the enterprise.

*The FASB cautions that these highlights are best understood in the context of the full Statement.
Source: "Highlights," *FASB Statement of Financial Accounting Concepts No. 1* (Stamford, CT, 1978). Copyright © the Financial Accounting Standards Board, High Ridge Park, Stamford, CT 06905, U.S.A. Excerpted with permission. Copies of the complete document are available from the FASB.

Most users are on the outside looking in. For its own use, management can prescribe the information it wants. Reporting for *internal* planning, control, and decision making need not be constrained by financial reporting requirements—thus, the concepts statements are not directed at internal (i.e., managerial) uses of accounting information.

Financial accounting is historical scorekeeping; it is not future oriented. Although the future is unknown, it is likely to be influenced by the past, and to the extent that accounting information provides a fair basis for the evaluation of past performance, it may be helpful in assessing an entity's future prospects. However, financial reports are not the sole source of information about an entity. For example, a potential employee might want to know about employee turnover rates, which are not disclosed in the financial reporting process. The information reported in financial accounting relates primarily to past transactions and events that can be measured in dollars and cents.

Financial accounting information is developed and used at a cost, and the benefit to the user of accounting information should exceed the cost of providing it.

Many of the objectives of financial reporting relate to the presentation of earnings and cash flow information. Investors and creditors are interested in making judgments about the firm's profitability and whether or not they are likely to receive payment of amounts owed to them. The user may ask, "How much profit did the firm earn during the year ended December 31, 1998?" or "What was the net cash inflow from operating the firm for the year?" Users understand that cash has to be received from somewhere before the firm can pay principal and interest to its creditors or dividends to its investors. A primary objective of financial reporting is to provide timely information about a firm's earnings and cash flow.

Financial reporting includes footnotes and other disclosures.

Accrual accounting—to be explained in more detail later—involves accounting for the effect of an economic activity, or transaction, on an entity when the activity has occurred, rather than when the cash receipt or payment takes place. Thus, the company for which you work reports a cost for your wages in the month in which you do the work, even though you may not be paid until the next month. Earnings information is reported on the accrual basis rather than the cash basis because past performance can be measured more accurately under accrual accounting. In the process of measuring a firm's accrual accounting earnings, some costs applicable to one year's results of operations may have to be estimated; for example, product warranty costs applicable to 1998 may not be finally determined until 2001. Reporting an approximately correct amount in 1998 is obviously preferable to recording nothing at all until 2001 when the precise amount is known.

In addition to providing information about earnings and cash flows, financial reporting should provide information to help users assess the relative strengths and weaknesses of a firm's financial position. The user may ask, "What economic resources does the firm own? How much does the firm owe? What caused these amounts to change over time?" Financial accounting does not attempt to directly measure the value of a firm. The numbers reported in a firm's financial statements do not change just because the market price of its stock changes.

Financial accounting standards are still evolving. In June 1997, the FASB issued Standard No. 130, which dealt with the reporting of "Comprehensive Income"—a topic that has been debated within the accounting profession for nearly two decades. With each new accounting standard, accounting procedures are modified to mirror new developments in the business world as well as current views and theories of financial reporting.

Students of accounting should be aware that the how-to aspects of accounting are not static; the accounting discipline is relatively young in comparison to other professions and is in constant motion. Perhaps the most important outcome of the conceptual framework project is the sense that the profession now has a blueprint in place that will carry financial reporting into the new millennium.

WHAT DOES IT MEAN?

8. What does it mean to state that the objectives of financial reporting given in *Statement of Financial Accounting Concepts No. 1* provide a framework for this text?

Objectives of Financial Reporting for Nonbusiness Organizations

At the outset of this chapter, it was stated that the material to be presented, although usually to be expressed in the context of profit-seeking business enterprises, would also be applicable to not-for-profit social service and governmental organizations. The FASB's "Highlights" of *Concepts Statement No. 4,* "Objectives of Financial Reporting by Nonbusiness Organizations," states: "Based on its study, the Board believes that the objectives of general purpose external financial reporting for government sponsored entities (for example, hospitals, universities, or utilities) engaged in activities that are not unique to government should be similar to those of business enterprises or other nonbusiness organizations engaged in similar activities."[2] *Statement 6* amended *Statement 2* by affirming that the qualitative characteristics described in *Statement 2* apply to the information about both business enterprises and not-for-profit organizations.

The objectives of financial reporting for nonbusiness organizations focus on providing information for resource providers (e.g., taxpayers to governmental entities and donors to charitable organizations), rather than investors. Information is provided about the economic resources, obligations, net resources, and performance of an organization during a period of time. Thus, even though nonbusiness organizations have unique characteristics that distinguish them from profit-oriented businesses, the information characteristics of the financial reporting objectives for each type of organization are similar.

It will be appropriate to remember the gist of the above objectives, as individual accounting and financial statement issues are encountered in subsequent chapters and are related to real-world situations.

Plan of the Book

Objective 10
Understand the plan of the book.

Part I of the book, Financial Accounting, includes Chapters 2 through 11. Chapter 2 describes financial statements, presents a model of how they are interrelated, and briefly summarizes key accounting concepts and principles. This is a "big picture" chapter; later chapters elaborate on most of the material introduced here. This chapter also includes four Business in Practice features. As you have seen from the features in this chapter, these are brief explanations of business practices that make some of the ideas covered in the text easier to understand.

Chapter 3 describes some of the basic interpretations of financial statement data that financial statement users make. Although a more complete

---

[2]*FASB, Statement of Financial Accounting Concepts No. 4* (Stamford, CT, 1980). Copyright © the Financial Accounting Standards Board, High Ridge Park, Stamford, CT 06905, U.S.A. Excerpted with permission. Copies of the complete document are available from the FASB.

explanation of financial statement elements is presented in subsequent chapters, understanding the basic relationships presented here permits better comprehension of the impact of alternative accounting methods discussed later. Chapter 11 presents a more comprehensive treatment of financial statement analysis, and some instructors will prefer presenting Chapter 3 material with that of Chapter 11.

Chapter 4 describes the bookkeeping process and presents a powerful transaction analysis model. Using this model, the financial statement user can understand the effect of any transaction on the statements, and many of the judgments based on the statements. You will not be asked to learn bookkeeping in this chapter.

Chapters 5 through 9 examine specific financial statement elements. Chapter 5 describes the accounting for short-term (i.e., *current*) assets, including cash, accounts and notes receivable, inventory, and prepaid items. Chapter 6 describes the accounting for long-term assets, including land, buildings and equipment, and a variety of intangible assets and natural resources. Chapter 7 discusses the accounting issues related to current and long-term liabilities, including accounts and notes payable, bonds payable, and deferred income taxes. Chapter 8 deals with the components of owners' equity, including common stock, preferred stock, retained earnings, and treasury stock. Chapter 9 presents a comprehensive view of the income statement and the statement of cash flows.

Chapter 10 covers the explanatory notes to the financial statements, and Chapter 11 concludes the financial accounting section with a detailed discussion of financial statement analysis. The financial accounting chapters frequently make reference to Intel Corporation's 1996 annual report, which is reproduced in the Appendix. You should refer to those financial statements and notes, as well as other company financial reports you may have, to get acquainted with actual applications of the issues being discussed in the text.

Part II of the book, Managerial Accounting, includes Chapters 12 through 16. Chapter 12 presents the "big picture" of managerial accounting and cost accounting. It contrasts these accounting classifications with financial accounting, introduces managerial accounting applications, and presents a lot of terminology. Chapter 13 focuses on cost behavior patterns by describing various applications of cost-profit-volume analysis, including the calculation of a firm's break-even point in units and sales dollars. Chapter 14 illustrates many aspects of a firm's operating budget, including the sales forecast, production and purchases budgets, and the cash budget. Performance reporting concepts and techniques are also discussed. Chapter 15 describes standard costing systems and the analysis of variances for raw materials, direct labor, and manufacturing overhead. Chapter 16 concludes the text with a demonstration of the payback, net present value, and internal rate of return techniques of making capital budgeting decisions.

The solutions to the odd-numbered problems of each chapter are provided for your convenience in the student supplement: *Study Outlines, Solutions to Odd-Numbered Problems, and Ready Notes* that accompanies this text. These problems serve as additional illustrations of the material presented in the chapters. Each even-numbered problem is similar to the problem that precedes it. We recommend that before working on an even-numbered problem you attempt to work out the preceding problem in writing, using the solution only to check your work unless you really don't know how to proceed.

Use each chapter's learning objectives, "What does it mean" questions, summary, and glossary of key terms and concepts to help manage your learning. With reasonable effort, you will achieve your objective of becoming an effective user of accounting information to support the related informed judgments and decisions you will make throughout your life.

Summary

Accounting is the process of identifying, measuring, and communicating economic information about an entity for the purpose of making decisions and informed judgments.

Users of financial statements include management, investors, creditors, employees, and government agencies. Decisions made by users relate, among other things, to entity operations, investment, credit, employment, and compliance with laws. Financial statements support these decisions because they communicate important financial information about the entity.

The major classifications of accounting include financial accounting, managerial accounting/cost accounting, auditing/public accounting, internal auditing, governmental and not-for-profit accounting, and income tax accounting.

Accounting has developed over time in response to the needs of users of financial statements for financial information. Financial accounting standards have been established by different organizations over the years. These standards are not a codified set of rules to be blindly followed; alternative methods of accounting for certain activities are used by different entities. Currently, the Financial Accounting Standards Board is the standard-setting body for financial accounting. Other organizations are involved in establishing standards for cost accounting, auditing, governmental accounting, and income tax accounting.

Integrity, objectivity, independence, and competence are several characteristics of ethical behavior for a professional accountant. High standards of ethical conduct are appropriate for all persons, but professional accountants have a special responsibility because so many people make decisions and informed judgments using information provided by the accounting process.

The Financial Accounting Standards Board has issued several *Statements of Financial Accounting Concepts* resulting from the conceptual framework project that has been under way in recent years. These statements describe concepts and relations that will underlie future financial accounting standards and practices, and will in due course serve as a basis for evaluating existing standards and practices.

"Highlights" of the concepts statement dealing with the objectives of financial reporting provide that financial information should be useful to investor and creditor concerns about the cash flows of the enterprise, the resources and obligations of the enterprise, and the profit of the enterprise. Financial accounting is not designed to measure directly the value of a business enterprise.

The objectives of financial reporting for nonbusiness enterprises are not significantly different from those for business enterprises, except that resource providers, rather than investors, are concerned about performance results, rather than profit.

The book starts with the big picture of financial accounting and then moves to some of the basic financial interpretations made from accounting data. An overview of the bookkeeping process is followed by a discussion of specific financial statement elements and explanatory notes to the financial statements. The financial accounting material ends with a chapter focusing on financial statement analysis and use of the data developed from analysis. The managerial accounting chapters focus on the development and use of financial information for managerial planning, control, and decision making.

Key Terms and Concepts

accounting (p. 2)   The process of identifying, measuring, and communicating economic information about an organization for the purpose of making decisions and informed judgments.

accrual accounting (p. 18)   Accounting that recognizes revenues and expenses as they occur, even though the cash receipt from the revenue or the cash disbursement related to the expense may occur before or after the event that causes revenue or expense recognition.

annual report (p. 5)   A document distributed to shareholders that contains the financial statements for the fiscal year of the reporting firm, together with the report of the external auditor's examination of the financial statements.

auditing (p. 5)   The process of reviewing the financial statements of an entity by an independent third party with the objective of expressing an opinion about the fairness of the presentation of the entity's financial position, results of operations, and changes in financial position. The practice of auditing is less precisely referred to as *public accounting.*

bookkeeping (p. 3)   Procedures that are used to keep track of financial transactions and accumulate the results of an entity's financial activities.

cash flow (p. 3)   Cash receipts or disbursements of an entity.

Certified Management Accountant (p. 5)   A professional designation earned by passing a broad, four-part examination administered over a two-day period and meeting certain experience requirements. Examination topics include economics and business finance; organization and behavior (including ethical considerations); public reporting standards, auditing, and taxes; internal reporting and analysis; and decision analysis, including modeling and information systems.

Certified Public Accountant (p. 4)   A professional designation earned by passing a comprehensive four-part examination taken over a two-day period. Examination topics include accounting theory and practice, income tax accounting, auditing, and business law.

controller (p. 4)   The job title of the person who is the chief accounting officer of an organization. The controller is usually responsible for both the financial and managerial accounting functions. Sometimes referred to as *comptroller.*

cost accounting (p. 4)   A subset of managerial accounting that relates to the determination and accumulation of product, process, or service costs.

Cost Accounting Standards Board (p. 10)   A group authorized by the U.S. Congress to establish cost accounting standards for government contractors.

creditor (p. 2)   An organization or individual who lends to the entity. Examples include suppliers who ship merchandise to the entity prior to receiving payment for their goods and banks that lend cash to the entity.

entity (p. 2)   An organization or individual, or a group of organizations or individuals, for which accounting is done.

financial accounting (p. 4)   Accounting that focuses on reporting financial position at a point in time and/or results of operations for a period of time.

Financial Accounting Foundation (p. 9)   An organization composed of people from the public accounting profession, businesses, and the public that is responsible for the funding of and appointing members to the Financial Accounting Standards Board.

Financial Accounting Standards Board (p. 9)   The body responsible for establishing generally accepted accounting principles.

generally accepted accounting principles (p. 5)   Pronouncements of the Financial Accounting Standards Board (FASB) and its predecessors that constitute appropriate accounting for various transactions used for reporting financial position and results of operations to investors and creditors.

generally accepted auditing standards (p. 5)   Standards for auditing that are established by the Auditing Standards Board of the American Institute of Certified Public Accountants.

Governmental Accounting Standards Board (p. 11)   Established by the Financial Accounting Foundation to develop guidelines for financial accounting and reporting by state and local governmental units.

independence (p. 13)   The personal characteristic of an accountant, especially an auditor, that refers to both appearing and being objective and impartial.

independent auditor's report (p. 5)   The report accompanying audited financial statements that explains briefly the auditor's responsibility and the extent of work performed. The report includes an opinion about whether the information contained in the financial statements is presented fairly in accordance with generally accepted accounting principles.

integrity (p. 13)   The personal characteristic of honesty, including being forthright in dealings and communications with others.

internal auditing (p. 6)   The practice of auditing within a company by employees of the company.

investor (p. 2)   An organization or individual who has an ownership interest in the firm. For corporations, referred to as *stockholder* or *shareholder*.

managerial accounting (p. 4)   Accounting that is concerned with the use of economic and financial information to plan and control many of the activities of an entity and to support the management decision-making process.

objectivity (p. 13)   The personal characteristic of impartiality, including freedom from conflict of interest.

public accounting (p. 5)   The segment of the accounting profession that provides auditing, income tax accounting, and management consulting services to clients.

Securities and Exchange Commission (p. 8)   A unit of the federal government that is responsible for establishing regulations and assuring full disclosure to investors about companies and their securities that are traded in interstate commerce.

Statements of Financial Accounting Standards (p. 9)   Pronouncements of the Financial Accounting Standards Board that constitute generally accepted accounting principles.

WHAT DOES IT MEAN?
ANSWERS

1. It means that accounting is a service activity that helps many different users of accounting information who use the information in many ways.

2. It means to perform professional services for clients principally in the areas of auditing, income taxes, and/or accounting systems evaluation and development.

3. It means that the individual has passed the examination to become a certified public accountant.

4. It means that generally accepted accounting principles sometimes permit alternative ways of accounting for identical transactions and that these principles are still evolving.

5. It means that the FASB has completed an extensive process of research and development, including receiving input from interested individuals and organizations, and has made an authoritative pronouncement that defines accounting and reporting for a specific activity or transaction.

6. It means that countries have not been able to agree on many accounting and reporting issues and that financial statements issued by an entity from another country must be carefully studied to determine how the statements differ from those issued by an entity from the reader's country.

7. It means that the individual is impartial, free from conflict of interest, and will not experience a gain from the activity in which she or he is involved.

8. It means that the accounting and financial reporting topics explained in the financial accounting part of this text should:

   a. Relate to external financial reporting.

   b. Support business and economic decisions.

   c. Provide information about cash flows.

   d. Focus on earnings based on accrual accounting.

   e. *Not* seek to directly measure the value of a business enterprise.

   f. Report information that is subject to evaluation by individual financial statement users.

Exercises and Problems

1–1. **Obtain an annual report.** Throughout this course, you will be asked to relate the material being studied to actual financial statements. After you complete this course, you will be able to use an organization's financial statements to make decisions and informed judgments about that organization. The purpose of this assignment is to provide the experience of obtaining a company's annual report. You may wish to refer to the financial statements in the report during the rest of the course.

Required:

a. Obtain the most recently issued annual report of a publicly owned manufacturing or merchandising corporation of your choice. Do not select a bank, insurance company, financial institution, or public utility. It would be appropriate to select a firm that you know something about or have an interest in. If you don't know the name or title of a specific individual to contact, address your request to the Shareholder Relations Department. Company addresses are available from several sources, including the following reference books in the library:

Standard & Poor's *Register of Corporations, Directors and Executives,* Vol. 1—Corporations.
Moody's *Handbook of Common Stocks.*
Standard & Poor's *Corporation Stock Market Encyclopedia.*
Moody's *Industrial Manual.*

b. Alternatively, you may be able to obtain an annual report via the Internet by typing http://www.firmname.com, or by using a search engine to locate your company's Web site, and then scanning your firm's home page for information about annual report ordering. By using Intel as your firm name, for example, you will discover that the most recent financial statements can be downloaded into Microsoft Excel files for subsequent manipulation.

c. As another alternative, you may wish to use *The Wall Street Journal*'s 24-hour, seven-day-a-week free Annual Report and Earnings Service. You can obtain annual reports and, if available, current quarterly information for many companies whose stock is traded on a major stock exchange. To order, call 1-800-654-2582 or visit http://www.icbinc.com. A full directory of participating companies is available on request.

LO 4

1–2. **Read and outline an article.** The accounting profession is frequently in the news, not always in the most positive light. The purpose of this assignment is to increase your awareness of an issue facing the profession.

Required:

Find, read, outline, and prepare to discuss a brief article from a general audience or business audience publication about accounting and/or the accounting profession. The article should have been published within the past 10 months and should relate to accounting or the accounting profession in general; it should not be about some technical accounting issue. The appropriate topical headings to use in the *Business Periodicals Index* or the computer-based retrieval system to which you have access are: accountants, accounting, and/or accounting (specific topic). You may find the *Accountant's Index* to be helpful if you are searching for a more specific topic.

LO 3

1–3. **Your ideas about accounting.** Write a paragraph describing your perceptions of what accounting is all about and the work that accountants do.

LO 10

1–4. **Your expectations for this course.** Write a statement identifying the expectations you have for this course.

LO 7

1–5. **Identify factors in an ethical decision.** Paul Alberga is an accountant for a local manufacturing company. Paul's good friend Chuck Haylock has been operating a retail sporting goods store for about a year. The store has been moderately successful, and Chuck needs a bank loan to help finance the next stage of his store's growth. He has asked Paul to prepare financial statements that the banker will use to help decide whether or not to grant the loan. Chuck has proposed that the fee he will pay for Paul's accounting work should be contingent upon his receiving the loan.

Required:

What factors should Paul consider when making his decision about whether or not to prepare the financial statements for Chuck's store?

LO 2

1–6. **Identify information used in making an informed decision.** Charlie and Maribelle Brown have owned and operated a retail furniture store for over 20 years. They have employed an independent CPA during this time to prepare various sales tax, payroll tax, and income tax returns, and financial statements for themselves and the bank from which they have borrowed money from time to time. They are considering selling the store but are uncertain about how to establish an asking price.

Required:

What type of information is likely to be included in the material prepared by the CPA that may help the Browns establish an asking price for the store?

PART I

Financial Accounting

Financial Statements and Accounting Concepts/Principles

Financial statements are the product of the financial accounting process. They are the means of communicating economic information about the entity to individuals who want to make decisions and informed judgments about the entity. Although each of the four principal financial statements has a unique purpose, they are interrelated, and all must be considered in order to get a complete financial picture of the reporting entity.

Users cannot make meaningful interpretations of financial statement data without understanding the concepts and principles that relate to the entire financial accounting process. It is also important for users to understand that these concepts and principles are broad in nature; they do not constitute a fixed set of rules, but instead serve as guidelines for the development of sound financial reporting practices.

Learning Objectives

After studying this chapter you should understand:

1 The kind of information reported on each financial statement and the way financial statements are related to each other.
2 What transactions are and the meaning and usefulness of the accounting equation.
3 The meaning of each of the captions on the financial statements illustrated in this chapter.
4 The broad, generally accepted concepts and principles that apply to the accounting process.
5 Several limitations of financial statements.
6 What a corporation's annual report is and why it is issued.
7 Business practices related to organizing a business, fiscal year, par value, and parent-subsidiary corporations.

Financial Statements

From Transactions to Financial Statements

An entity's financial statements are the end product of a process that starts with **transactions** between the entity and other organizations and individuals. Transactions are economic interchanges between entities; for example, a sale/purchase, or a receipt of cash by a borrower and the payment of cash by a lender. The flow from transactions to financial statements can be illustrated as follows:

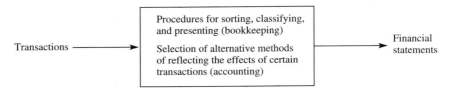

**WHAT
DOES IT
MEAN?**

1. What does it mean to say that there has been an accounting transaction between you and your school?

Transactions are summarized in **accounts,** and accounts are further summarized in the financial statements. In this sense, transactions can be seen as the bricks that build the financial statements. By learning about the form, content, and relationships among financial statements in this chapter, you will better understand the process of building those results—bookkeeping and transaction analysis—in Chapter 4 and subsequent chapters.

Current generally accepted accounting principles and auditing standards require that the financial statements of an entity show the following for the reporting period:

Financial position at the end of the period.

Earnings for the period.

Cash flows during the period.

Investments by and distributions to owners during the period.

The financial statements that satisfy these requirements are, respectively, the:

Balance sheet (or statement of financial position).

Income statement (or statement of earnings, or profit and loss statement, or statement of operations).

Statement of cash flows.

Statement of changes in owners' equity (or statement of changes in capital stock and/or statement of changes in retained earnings).

In addition to the financial statements themselves, the annual report will probably include several accompanying footnotes or explanations of the accounting policies and detailed information about many of the amounts and captions shown on the financial statements. These notes are designed to assist the reader of the financial statements by disclosing as much relevant supplementary information as the company and its auditors deem necessary and appropriate. For Intel Corporation, the notes to the

1996 financial statements are shown in the "Notes to Consolidated Financial Statements" section on pages 22–31 of the annual report in the Appendix. One of this text's objectives is to enable you to read, interpret, and understand financial statement footnotes. Chapter 10 describes the explanatory notes to the financial statements in detail.

Financial Statements Illustrated

Objective 1
Understand the kind of information reported on each financial statement and how the statements are related to each other.

Main Street Store, Inc., was organized as a corporation and began business during September 1998 (see Business in Practice—Organizing a Business). The company buys clothing and accessories from distributors and manufacturers, and sells these items from a rented building. The financial statements of Main Street Store, Inc., at August 31, 1999, and for the fiscal year (see Business in Practice—Fiscal Year) ended on that date are presented in Exhibits 2–1 through 2–4.

BUSINESS IN PRACTICE
Organizing a Business

There are three principal forms of business organization: proprietorship, partnership, and corporation.

A **proprietorship** is an activity conducted by an individual. Operating as a proprietorship is the easiest way to get started in a business activity. Other than the possibility of needing a local license, there aren't any formal prerequisites to beginning operations. Besides being easy to start, a proprietorship has the advantage, according to many people, that the owner is his or her own boss. A principal disadvantage of the proprietorship is that the owner's liability for business debts is not limited by the assets of the business. For example, if the business fails, and if, after using all available business assets to pay business debts, the business creditors are still owed money, the owner's personal assets can be claimed by business creditors. Another disadvantage is that the individual proprietor may have difficulty raising the money needed to provide the capital base that will be required if the business is to grow substantially. Because of the ease of getting started, every year many business activities begin as proprietorships.

The **partnership** is essentially a group of proprietors who have banded together. The unlimited liability characteristic of the proprietorship still exists, but with several partners the ability of the firm to raise capital may be improved. Income earned from partnership activities is taxed at the individual partner level; the partnership itself is not a tax-paying entity. Accountants, attorneys, and other professionals frequently operate their firms as partnerships. In recent years, many large professional partnerships, including the "Big Five" accounting firms, have been operating under *limited liability partnership* (LLP) rules, which shield individual partners from unlimited personal liability.

Most large businesses, and many new businesses, use the corporate form of organization. The owners of the corporation are called **stockholders.** They have invested funds in the corporation and received shares of **stock** as evidence of their ownership. Stockholders' liability is limited to the amount

Business in Practice concluded

invested; creditors cannot seek recovery of losses from the personal assets of stockholders. Large amounts of capital can frequently be raised by selling shares of stock to many individuals. It is also possible for all of the stock of a corporation to be owned by a single individual. A stockholder can usually sell his or her shares to other investors or buy more shares from other stockholders if a change in ownership interest is desired. A **corporation** is formed by having a charter and bylaws prepared and registered with the appropriate office in 1 of the 50 states. The cost of forming a corporation is usually greater than that of starting a proprietorship or forming a partnership. A major disadvantage of the corporate form of business is that corporations are tax-paying entities. Thus, any income distributed to shareholders is taxed first as income of the corporation and then a second time as income of the individual shareholders.

A form of organization that has been approved in many states is the *limited liability company.* For accounting and legal purposes, this type of organization is treated as a corporation even though some of the formalities of the corporate form of organization are not present. Shareholders of small corporations may find that banks and major creditors usually require the personal guarantees of the principal shareholders as a condition to granting credit to the corporation. Therefore, the limited liability of the corporate form may be, in the case of small corporations, more theoretical than real.

BUSINESS IN PRACTICE
Fiscal Year

A firm's **fiscal year** is the annual period used for reporting to owners, the government, and others. Many firms select the calendar year as their fiscal year, but other 12-month periods can also be selected. Some firms select a reporting period ending on a date when inventories will be relatively low or business activity will be slow because this facilitates the process of preparing financial statements.

Many firms select fiscal periods that relate to the pace of their business activity. Food retailers, for example, have a weekly operating cycle, and many of these firms select a 52-week fiscal year (with a 53-week fiscal year every five or six years so their year-end remains near the same date every year). Intel Corporation has adopted this strategy; note, on page 22 in the Appendix, that Intel's fiscal year ends on the last Saturday in December each year.

For internal reporting purposes, many firms use periods other than the month (e.g., 13 four-week periods). The firm wants the same number of operating days in each period so that comparisons between the same period of different years can be made without having to consider differences in the number of operating days in the respective periods.

As you look at these financial statements, you will probably have several questions concerning the nature of specific accounts and how the numbers are computed. For now, concentrate on the explanations and

---

EXHIBIT 2–1   Balance Sheet

MAIN STREET STORE, INC.
Balance Sheet
August 31, 1999

Assets		*Liabilities and Owners' Equity*	
Current assets:		Current liabilities:	
Cash...............	$ 34,000	Short-term debt	$ 20,000
Accounts receivable ...	80,000	Accounts payable	35,000
Merchandise			
inventory	170,000	Other accrued liabilities	12,000
Total current assets ..	$284,000	Total current	
Plant and equipment:		liabilities	$ 67,000
Equipment	40,000	Long-term debt	50,000
Less: Accumulated		Total liabilities	$117,000
depreciation........	(4,000)	Owners' equity	203,000
		Total liabilities and	
Total assets...........	$320,000	owners' equity........	$320,000

---

definitions that are appropriate and inescapable, and notice especially the characteristics of each financial statement. Many of your questions about specific accounts will be answered in subsequent chapters that explain the individual statements and their components in detail.

WHAT DOES IT MEAN?

2. What does it mean to refer to a balance sheet for the year ended August 31, 1999?

Explanations and Definitions

Balance Sheet

The **balance sheet** is a listing of the organization's assets, liabilities, and owners' equity *at a point in time.* In this sense, the balance sheet is like a snapshot of the organization's financial position, frozen at a specific point in time. The balance sheet is sometimes called the **statement of financial position** because it summarizes the entity's resources (assets), obligations (liabilities), and owners' claims (owners' equity). The balance sheet for Main Street Store, Inc., at August 31, 1999, the end of the firm's first year of operations, is illustrated in Exhibit 2–1.

Objective 2
Understand the meaning and usefulness of the accounting equation.

Notice the two principal sections of the balance sheet that are shown side by side: (1) assets and (2) liabilities and owners' equity. Observe that the dollar total of $320,000 is the same for each side. This equality is sometimes referred to as the **accounting equation** or the **balance sheet equation.** It is the equality, or balance, of these two amounts from which the term *balance sheet* is derived.

$$\text{Assets} = \text{Liabilities} + \text{Owners' equity}$$

$$\$320,000 = \$117,000 + \$203,000$$

Now some of those appropriate and inescapable definitions and explanations:

"**Assets** are probable future economic benefits obtained or controlled by a particular entity as a result of past transactions or events."[1] In brief, assets represent the amount of resources *owned* by the entity. Assets are frequently tangible; they can be seen and handled (e.g., cash, merchandise inventory, or equipment), or evidence of their existence can be observed (e.g., a customer's acknowledgment of receipt of merchandise and the implied promise to pay the amount due when agreed upon—an account receivable).

"**Liabilities** are probable future sacrifices of economic benefits arising from present obligations of a particular entity to transfer assets or provide services to other entities in the future as a result of past transactions or events."[2] In brief, liabilities are amounts *owed* to other entities. For example, the accounts payable arose because suppliers shipped merchandise to Main Street Store, Inc., and this merchandise will be paid for at some point in the future. In other words, the supplier has an "ownership right" in the merchandise until it is paid for and thus has become a creditor to the firm by supplying merchandise on account.

Owners' equity is the ownership right of the owner(s) of the entity in the assets that remain after deducting the liabilities. (A car or house owner uses this term when referring to his or her **equity** as the market value of the car or house less the loan or mortgage balance.) Owners' equity is sometimes referred to as **net assets.** This can be shown by re-arranging the basic accounting equation:

$$\text{Assets} - \text{Liabilities} = \text{Owners' equity}$$

$$\text{Net assets} = \text{Owners' equity}$$

Another term sometimes used when referring to owners' equity is **net worth.** However, this term is misleading because it implies that the net assets are "worth" the amount reported on the balance sheet as owners' equity. *Financial statements prepared according to generally accepted principles of accounting do not purport to show the current market value of the entity's assets, except in a few restricted cases.*

Objective 3
Understand the meaning of each of the captions on the financial statements illustrated in Exhibits 2–1 through 2–4.

3. What does it mean when a balance sheet has been prepared for an organization?

Each of the individual assets and liabilities reported by Main Street Stores, Inc., warrants a brief explanation. Each account (caption in the financial statements) will be discussed in more detail in later chapters. Your task at this point is to achieve a broad understanding of each account and to make sense of its classification as an asset or liability.

Cash represents cash on hand and in the bank or banks used by Main Street Store, Inc. If the firm had made any temporary cash investments in

---

[1]FASB, *Statement of Financial Accounting Concepts No. 6,* "Elements of Financial Statements" (Stamford, CT, 1985), para. 25. Copyright © by the Financial Accounting Standards Board, High Ridge Park, Stamford, CT 06905, U.S.A. Quoted with permission. Copies of the complete document are available from the FASB.
[2]Ibid., para. 35.

order to earn interest, these marketable securities would probably be shown as a separate asset because these funds are not as readily available as cash.

Accounts receivable represent amounts due from customers who have purchased merchandise on credit and who have agreed to pay within a specified period or when billed by Main Street Store, Inc.

Merchandise inventory represents the cost to Main Street Store, Inc., of the merchandise that it has acquired but not yet sold.

Equipment represents the cost to Main Street Store, Inc., of the display cases, racks, shelving, and other store equipment purchased and installed in the rented building in which it operates. The building is not shown as an asset because Main Street Store, Inc., does not own it.

Accumulated depreciation represents the portion of the cost of the equipment that is estimated to have been used up in the process of operating the business. Note that one-tenth ($4,000/$40,000) of the cost of the equipment has been depreciated. From this relationship, one might assume that the equipment is estimated to have a useful life of 10 years because this is the balance sheet at the end of the firm's first year of operations. **Depreciation** in accounting *is the process of spreading the cost of an asset over its useful life to the entity—it is not an attempt to recognize the economic loss in value of an asset because of its age or use.*

Short-term debt represents amounts borrowed, probably from banks, that will be repaid within one year of the balance sheet date.

Accounts payable represent amounts owed to suppliers of merchandise inventory that was purchased on credit and will be paid within a specific period of time.

Other **accrued liabilities** represent amounts owed to various creditors, including any wages owed to employees for services provided to Main Street Store, Inc., through August 31, 1999, the balance sheet date.

Long-term debt represents amounts borrowed from banks or others that will not be repaid within one year from the balance sheet date.

Owners' equity, shown as a single amount in Exhibit 2–1, is explained in more detail later in this chapter in the discussion of the statement of changes in owners' equity.

Notice that in Exhibit 2–1 some assets and liabilities are classified as "current." **Current assets** *are cash and those assets that are likely to be converted into cash or used to benefit the entity within one year,* and **current liabilities** *are those liabilities that are likely to be paid with cash within one year of the balance sheet date.* In this example, it is expected that the accounts receivable from the customers of Main Street Store, Inc., will be collected within a year and that the merchandise inventory will be sold within a year of the balance sheet date. This time-frame classification is important and, as will be explained later, is used in assessing the entity's ability to pay its obligations when they come due.

To summarize, the balance sheet is a listing of the entity's assets, liabilities, and owners' equity. A balance sheet can be prepared as of any date but is most frequently prepared as of the end of a fiscal reporting period (e.g., month-end or year-end). The balance sheet as of the end of one period is the balance sheet as of the beginning of the next period. This can be illustrated on a time line as follows:

```
        8/31/98          Fiscal 1999          8/31/99
          |                                     |
     Balance sheet                         Balance sheet
     A = L + OE                            A = L + OE
```

On the time line, Fiscal 1999 refers to the 12 months during which the entity carried out its economic activities.

Income Statement

The principal purpose of the **income statement,** or **statement of earnings** or **profit and loss statement,** or **statement of operations,** is to answer the question: "Did the entity operate at a **profit** for the period of time under consideration?" The question is answered by first reporting **revenues** from the entity's operating activities (e.g., selling merchandise) and then subtracting the costs and **expenses** incurred in generating those revenues and operating the entity. **Gains** and **losses** are also reported on the income statement. Gains and losses result from nonoperating activities, rather than from the day-to-day operating activities that generate revenues and expenses. The income statement reports results *for a period of time,* in contrast to the balance sheet focus on a single date. In this sense, the income statement is more like a movie than a snapshot; it depicts the results of activities that have occurred during a period of time.

The income statement for Main Street Store, Inc., for the year ended August 31, 1999, is presented in Exhibit 2–2. Notice that the statement starts with **net sales** (which are revenues) and that the various costs and expenses are subtracted to arrive at **net income** in total and per share of common stock outstanding. Net income is the profit for the period; if costs and expenses exceed net sales, a net loss results. The reasons for reporting net income or net loss per share of common stock outstanding, and the calculation of this amount, will be explained in Chapter 9.

EXHIBIT 2–2   Income Statement

MAIN STREET STORE, INC.
Income Statement
For the Year Ended August 31, 1999

Net sales	$1,200,000
Cost of goods sold	850,000
Gross profit	$ 350,000
Selling, general, and administrative expenses	311,000
Income from operations	$ 39,000
Interest expense	9,000
Income before taxes	$ 30,000
Income taxes	12,000
Net income	$ 18,000
Net income per share of common stock outstanding	$ 1.80

Now look at the individual captions on the income statement. Each warrants a brief explanation, which will be expanded in subsequent chapters. Your task at this point is to make sense of how each item influences the determination of net income.

Net sales represent the amount of sales of merchandise to customers, less the amount of sales originally recorded but that were canceled because the merchandise was subsequently returned by customers for one reason or another (wrong size, spouse didn't want it, and so on). The sales amount is frequently called *sales revenue,* or just *revenue.* Revenue results from selling a product or service to a customer.

Cost of goods sold represents the total cost of merchandise removed from inventory and delivered to customers as a result of sales. This is shown as a separate expense because of its significance, and because of the desire to show gross profit as a separate item.

Gross profit is the difference between net sales and cost of goods sold and represents the seller's maximum amount of "cushion" from which all other expenses of operating the business must be met before it is possible to have net income. Gross profit (sometimes referred to as *gross margin*) is shown as a separate item because it is significant to both management and nonmanagement readers of the income statement. The uses made of this amount will be explained in subsequent chapters.

Selling, general, and administrative expenses represent the operating expenses of the entity. In some income statements, these expenses will not be lumped together as in Exhibit 2–2 but will be reported separately for each of several operating expense categories, such as wages, advertising, and depreciation.

Income from operations represents one of the most important measures of the firm's activities. Income from operations (or operating income or earnings from operations) can be related to the assets available to the firm to obtain a useful measure of management's performance. A method of doing this is explained in Chapter 3.

Interest expense represents the cost of using borrowed funds. This item is reported separately because it is a function of how assets are financed, not how assets are used.

Income taxes is shown after all of the other income statement items have been reported because income taxes are a function of the firm's income before taxes.

Net income per share of common stock outstanding is reported as a separate item at the bottom of the income statement because of its significance in evaluating the market value of a share of common stock. This measure, which is often referred to as "earnings per share" or simply EPS, will be explained in more detail in Chapter 9.

To review, the income statement summarizes the entity's income- (or loss-) producing activities *for a period of time.* Transactions that affect the income statement will also affect the balance sheet. For example, a sale made for cash increases sales revenue on the income statement and increases cash, an asset on the balance sheet. Likewise, wages earned by employees during the last week of the current year to be paid early in the next year are an expense of the current year. These wages will be deducted from revenues in the income statement, and are considered a liability reported on the balance sheet at the end of the year. Thus, the income statement is a link between the balance sheets at the beginning and end of the year. How this link is made is explained in the next section, which describes the statement of changes in owners' equity. The time line presented earlier can be expanded as follows:

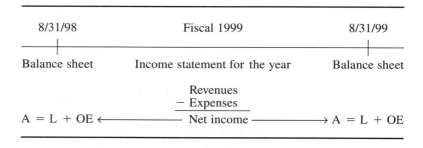

Statement of Changes in Owners' Equity

The **statement of changes in owners' equity,** or **statement of changes in capital stock** or **statement of changes in retained earnings,** like the income statement, has a *period of time* orientation. This statement shows the detail of owners' equity and explains the changes that occurred in the components of owners' equity during the year.

Exhibit 2–3 illustrates this statement for Main Street Store, Inc., for the year ended August 31, 1999. Remember that these are the results of Main Street Store's first year of operations, so the beginning-of-the-year balances are zero. On subsequent years' statements, the beginning-of-the-year amount is the ending balance from the prior year.

Notice that in Exhibit 2–3 owners' equity is made up of two principal components: **paid-in capital** and **retained earnings.** These items are briefly explained here and are discussed in more detail in Chapter 8.

EXHIBIT 2–3   Statement of Changes in Owners' Equity

MAIN STREET STORE, INC.
Statement of Changes in Owners' Equity
For the Year Ended August 31, 1999

Paid-In Capital:

Beginning balance	$ –0–
Common stock, par value, $10; 50,000 shares authorized,	
10,000 shares issued and outstanding	100,000
Additional paid-in capital	90,000
Balance, August 31, 1999	$190,000

Retained Earnings:

Beginning balance	$ –0–
Net income for the year	18,000
Less: Cash dividends of $.50 per share	(5,000)
Balance, August 31, 1999	$ 13,000
Total owners' equity	$203,000

Paid-in capital represents the total amount invested in the entity by the owners, in this case, the stockholders. When the stock issued to the owners has a **par value** (see Business in Practice—Par Value), there will usually be two categories of paid-in capital: common stock and additional paid-in capital.

BUSINESS IN PRACTICE
Par Value

Par value is a relic from the past that has, for all practical purposes, lost its significance. The par value of common stock is an arbitrary value assigned when the corporation is organized. Par value bears no relationship to the fair market value of a share of stock (except that a corporation may not issue its stock for less than par value). Many firms issue stock with a par value of a nominal amount, such as $1. Intel Corporation has taken this practice to an extreme by issuing stock with a $.001 par value. (See page 19 in the Appendix.) Because of investor confusion about the significance of par value, most states now permit corporations to issue no-par-value stock, which is in effect what Intel Corporation has accomplished. Some state laws permit a firm to assign a stated value to its no-par-value stock, in which case the stated value operates as a par value.

Common stock reflects the number of shares authorized by the corporation's charter, the number of shares that have been issued to stockholders, and the number of shares that are still held by the stockholders. When the common stock has a par value or stated value, the amount shown for common stock in the financial statements will always be the par value or stated value multiplied by the number of shares issued. If the common stock does not have a par value or stated value, the amount shown for common stock in the financial statements will be the total amount invested by the owners.

Additional paid-in capital is the difference between the total amount invested by the owners and the par value or stated value of the stock. (If no-par-value stock without a stated value is issued to the owners, there won't be any additional paid-in capital because the total amount paid in, or invested, by the owners will be shown as common stock.)

Retained earnings is the second principal category of owners' equity, and it represents the cumulative net income of the entity that has been retained for use in the business. **Dividends** are distributions of earnings that have been made to the owners, so these reduce retained earnings. If retained earnings has a negative balance, because cumulative losses and dividends have exceeded cumulative net income, this part of owners' equity is referred to as an *accumulated deficit,* or simply *deficit.*

Note that in Exhibit 2–3 the net income for the year of $18,000 added to retained earnings is the amount of net income reported in Exhibit 2–2. The retained earnings section of the statement of changes in owners' equity is where the link between the balance sheet and income statement is made. The time-line model is thus expanded and modified as follows:

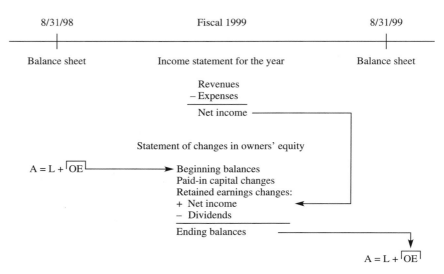

Notice that the total owners' equity reported in Exhibit 2–3 agrees with owners' equity shown on the balance sheet in Exhibit 2–1. Most balance sheets include the amount of common stock, additional paid-in capital, and retained earnings within the owners' equity section. Changes that occur in these components of owners' equity are likely to be shown in a separate statement so that users of the financial statements can learn what caused these important balance sheet elements to change.

Statement of Cash Flows

The purpose of the **statement of cash flows** is to identify the sources and uses of cash during the year. This objective is accomplished by reporting the changes in all of the other balance sheet items. Because of the equality that exists between assets and liabilities plus owners' equity, the total of the changes in every other asset and each liability and element of owners' equity will equal the change in cash. The statement of cash flows is described in detail in Chapter 9. For now, make sense of the three principal activity groups that cause cash to change, and see how the amounts on this statement relate to the balance sheet in Exhibit 2–1.

The statement of cash flows for Main Street Store, Inc., for the year ended August 31, 1999, is illustrated in Exhibit 2–4. Notice that this statement, like the income statement and statement of changes in owners' equity, is *for a period of time.* Notice also the three activity categories: operating activities, investing activities, and financing activities.

Cash flows from operating activities are shown first, and net income is the starting point for this measure of cash generation. Using net income also directly relates the income statement (see Exhibit 2–2) to the statement of cash flows. Next, items that affected net income but that did not affect cash are considered.

Depreciation expense is added back to net income because even though it was deducted as an expense in determining net income, *depreciation expense did not require the use of cash.* Remember—depreciation in accounting is the process of spreading the cost of an asset over its estimated useful life.

EXHIBIT 2–4   Statement of Cash Flows

MAIN STREET STORE, INC.
Statement of Cash Flows
For the Year Ended August 31, 1999

Cash Flows from Operating Activities:

Net income	$ 18,000
Add (deduct) items not affecting cash:	
Depreciation expense	4,000
Increase in accounts receivable	(80,000)
Increase in merchandise inventory	(170,000)
Increase in current liabilities	67,000
Net cash used by operating activities	$(161,000)

Cash Flows from Investing Activities:

Cash paid for equipment	$ (40,000)

Cash Flows from Financing Activities:

Cash received from issue of long-term debt	$ 50,000
Cash received from sale of common stock	190,000
Payment of cash dividend on common stock	(5,000)
Net cash provided by financing activities	$ 235,000
Net increase in cash for the year	$ 34,000

The increase in accounts receivable is deducted because this reflects sales revenues, included in net income, that have not yet been collected in cash.

The increase in merchandise inventory is deducted because cash was spent to acquire the increase in inventory.

The increase in current liabilities is added because cash has not yet been paid for the products and services that have been received during the current fiscal period.

Cash flows from investing activities shows the cash used to purchase long-lived assets. You should find the increase in equipment in the balance sheet (Exhibit 2–1), which shows the cost of the equipment owned at August 31, 1999. Since this is the first year of the firm's operations, the equipment purchase required the use of $40,000 during the year.

Cash flows from financing activities include amounts raised from the sale of long-term debt and common stock, and dividends paid on common stock. You should find each of these financing amounts in the balance sheet (Exhibit 2–1) or the statement of changes in owners' equity (Exhibit 2–3). For example, the $190,000 received from the sale of stock is shown on the statement of changes in owners' equity (Exhibit 2–3) as the increase in paid-in capital during the year.

The net increase in cash for the year of $34,000 is the amount of cash in the August 31, 1999, balance sheet. Check this out. This should make sense because the firm started in business during September 1998, so it had no cash to begin with.

The statement of cash flows results in a further expansion and modification of the time-line model that can be seen in the diagram that follows:

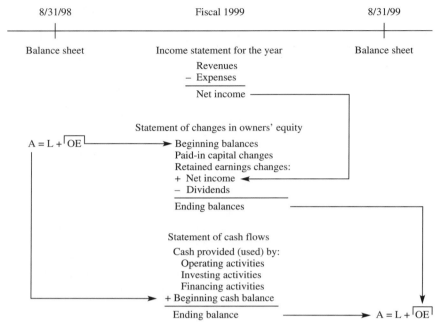

4. What does it mean when a business owner says that she needs to look at her firm's set of four financial statements to really understand financial position and results of operations?

5. What does it mean when a company that has a high net income doesn't have enough cash to pay its bills?

Comparative Statements in Subsequent Years

The financial statements presented on the previous pages for Main Street Store, Inc., show data as of August 31, 1999, and for the year then ended. Because this was the first year of the firm's operations, comparative financial statements are not possible. In subsequent years, however, comparative statements for the current and prior year should be presented so that users of the data can more easily spot changes in the firm's financial position and in its results of operations. Some companies present data for two prior years in their financial statements. Most companies will include selected data from their balance sheets and income statements for at least 5 years, and sometimes for up to 25 years, as supplementary information in their annual report to stockholders. Intel Corporation's 10-year financial summary, which appears on page 33 in the Appendix, illustrates the firm's dramatic growth.

Illustration of Financial Statement Relationships

Exhibit 2–5 uses the financial statements of Main Street Store, Inc., to illustrate the financial statement relationships just discussed. Note that in

EXHIBIT 2–5 Financial Statement Relationships

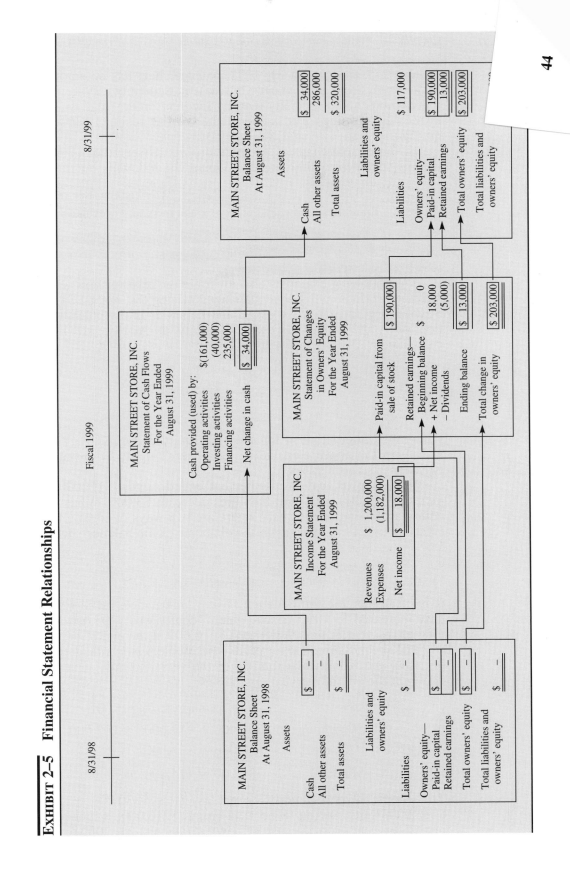

43

44

Exhibit 2–5, the August 31, 1998, balance sheet has no amounts because Main Street Store, Inc., started business in September 1998. As you study this exhibit, note especially that net income for the year was an increase in retained earnings and is one of the reasons retained earnings changed during the year.

In subsequent chapters, the relationship between the balance sheet and income statement will be presented using the following diagram:

Balance sheet	Income statement
Assets = Liabilities + Owners' equity ←	Net income = Revenues − Expenses

The arrow from Net income in the income statement to Owners' equity in the balance sheet is to indicate that net income affects retained earnings, which is a component of owners' equity.

The following examples also illustrate the relationships within and between the principal financial statements. Using the August 31, 1999, Main Street Store, Inc., data for assets and liabilities in the balance sheet equation of A = L + OE, owners' equity at August 31, 1999, can be calculated:

$$A = L + OE$$
$$\$320,000 = \$117,000 + OE$$
$$\$203,000 = OE$$

Remember, another term for owners' equity is *net assets*. This is shown clearly in the above calculation, as owners' equity is the difference between assets and liabilities.

Now suppose that during the year ended August 31, 2000, total assets increase $10,000, and total liabilities decrease $3,000. What was owners' equity at the end of the year? There are two ways of solving the problem. First, focus on the changes in the elements of the balance sheet equation:

$$A = L + OE$$

Change: $+10,000 = -3,000 + \text{?}$

It is clear that for the equation to stay in balance, owners' equity must have increased $13,000. Since owners' equity was $203,000 at the beginning of the year, it must have been $216,000 at the end of the year.

The second approach to solving the problem is to calculate the amount of assets and liabilities at the end of the year and then solve for owners' equity at the end of the year, as follows:

	A	=	L	+	OE
Beginning:	320,000	=	117,000	+	203,000
Change:	+10,000	=	−3,000	+	?
End:	330,000	=	114,000	+	?

The ending owners' equity or net assets is $330,000 − $114,000 = $216,000. Since ending owners' equity is $216,000, it increased $13,000 during the year from August 31, 1999, to August 31, 2000.

Assume that during the year ended August 31, 2000, the owners invested an additional $8,000 in the firm, and that dividends of $6,000 were declared. How much net income did the firm have for the year ended August 31, 2000? Recall that net income is one of the items that affects the retained earnings component of owners' equity. What else affects retained earnings? That's right—dividends. Since owners' equity increased from $203,000 to $216,000 during the year, and the items causing that change were net income, dividends, and the additional investment by the owners, the amount of net income can be calculated as follows:

Owners' equity, beginning of year	$203,000
Increase in paid-in capital from additional investment by owners	8,000
Net income	?
Dividends	−6,000
Owners' equity, end of year	$216,000

Solving for the unknown, net income is equal to $11,000.

An alternative solution to determine net income for the year involves focusing on just the *changes* in owners' equity during the year, as follows:

Increase in paid-in capital from additional investment by owners	8,000
Net income	?
Dividends	−6,000
Change in owners' equity for the year	$13,000

Again, solving for the unknown, net income is equal to $11,000.

The important points to remember here are:

1. The balance sheet shows the amount of assets, liabilities, and owners' equity at a point in time.
2. The balance sheet equation must always be in balance.
3. The income statement shows net income for a period of time.
4. The retained earnings component of owners' equity changes over a period of time as a result of the firm's net income (or loss) and dividends for that period of time.

WHAT DOES IT MEAN?

6. What does it mean to say that the balance sheet must be in balance after every transaction even though a lot of transactions affect the income statement?

Accounting Concepts and Principles

In order to understand the kinds of decisions and informed judgments that can be made from the financial statements, it is appropriate to have an understanding of some of the broad concepts and principles of accounting that have become generally accepted for financial accounting and reporting

Objective 4
Understand the broad, generally accepted concepts and principles that apply to the accounting process.

purposes. The terms *concepts* and *principles* are used interchangeably here. Some of these ideas relate directly to the financial accounting concepts introduced in Chapter 1, and others relate to the broader notion of generally accepted accounting principles. Again, it is important to recognize that these concepts and principles are more like practices that have been generally agreed upon over a period of time than hard and fast rules or basic laws such as those encountered in the physical sciences.

These concepts and principles can be related to the basic model of the flow of data from transactions to financial statements illustrated earlier, and as shown on page 47.

Concepts/Principles Related to the Entire Model

The basic accounting equation described earlier in this chapter is the mechanical key to the entire financial accounting process because the equation must be in balance after every transaction has been recorded in the accounting records. The method for recording transactions and maintaining this balance will be illustrated in Chapter 4.

Accounting entity refers to the entity for which the financial statements are being prepared. The entity can be a proprietorship, partnership, corporation, or even a group of corporations (see Business in Practice—Parent and Subsidiary Corporations). The entity for which the accounting is being done is defined by the accountant, and even though the entities may be related (e.g., an individual and the business he owns), the accounting is done for the defined entity.

The **going concern concept** refers to the presumption that the entity will continue to operate in the future—that it is not being liquidated. This

---

BUSINESS IN PRACTICE
Parent and Subsidiary Corporations

It is not unusual for a new corporation that wants to expand its operations to form a separate corporation to carry out its plans. In such a case the original corporation owns all of the stock of the new corporation; it has become the "parent" of a "**subsidiary.**" One parent may have several subsidiaries, and the subsidiaries themselves may be parents of subsidiaries. It is not necessary for the parent to own 100% of the stock of another corporation for the parent–subsidiary relationship to exist. If one corporation owns more than half of the stock of another, it is presumed that the majority owner can exercise enough control to create a parent–subsidiary relationship. When a subsidiary is not wholly owned, the other stockholders of the subsidiary are referred to as *minority* stockholders.

In most instances, the financial statements issued by the parent corporation will include the assets, liabilities, owners' equity, revenues, expenses, and gains and losses of the subsidiaries. Financial statements that reflect the financial position, results of operations, and cash flows of a parent and one or more subsidiaries are called *consolidated financial statements*.

continuity assumption is necessary because the amounts shown on the balance sheet for various assets do not reflect the liquidation value of those assets.

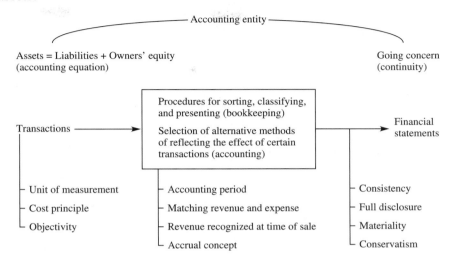

Concepts/Principles Related to Transactions

In the United States, the dollar is the *unit of measurement* for all transactions. No adjustment is made for changes in the purchasing power of the dollar. No attempt is made to reflect qualitative economic factors in the measurement of transactions.

The *cost principle* refers to the fact that transactions are recorded at their original cost to the entity as measured in dollars. For example, if a parcel of land were purchased by a firm for $8,600 even though an appraisal showed the land to be worth $10,000, the purchase transaction would be reflected in the accounting records, and the financial statements would report the land at its cost of $8,600. If the land is still owned and being used 15 years later, even though its market value has increased to $80,000, it continues to be reported in the balance sheet at its original cost of $8,600.

Objectivity refers to accountants' desire to have a given transaction recorded in the same way in all situations. This objective is facilitated by using the dollar as the unit of measurement and by applying the cost principle. However, as previously stressed, there are transactions for which the exercise of professional judgment could result in alternative recording results. These alternatives will be illustrated in subsequent chapters.

Concepts/Principles Related to Bookkeeping Procedures and the Accounting Process

These concepts/principles relate to the *accounting period,* that is, the period of time selected for reporting results of operations and changes in financial position. Financial position will be reported at the end of this period of time (and the balance sheet at the beginning of the period will probably be included with the financial statements). For most entities, the accounting period will be one year in length.

Matching revenue and expense is necessary if the results of the firm's operations are to reflect accurately its economic activities during the period. The **matching concept** does not mean that revenues and expenses for a period are equal. Revenue is not earned without effort (businesses do not receive birthday gifts), and expenses are the measure of the economic efforts exerted to generate revenues. A fair presentation of the results of a firm's operations during a period of time requires that all expenses incurred in generating that period's revenues be deducted from the revenues earned. This results in an accurate measure of the net income or net loss for the period. This seems like common sense, but as we shall see, there are alternative methods of determining some of the expenses to be recognized in any given period. This concept of matching revenue and expense is very important and will be referred to again and again as accounting practices are discussed in the following chapters.

Revenue is recognized at the time of sale, which is when title to the product being sold passes from the seller to the buyer or when the services involved in the transaction have been performed. Passing of legal ownership (title) is the critical event, not the cash payment from buyer to seller.

Accrual accounting uses the *accrual concept* and results in recognizing revenue at the point of sale and recognizing expenses as they are incurred, even though the cash receipt or payment occurs at another time or in another accounting period. Thus, many activities of the firm will involve two transactions: one that recognizes the revenue or expense and the other that reflects the receipt or payment of cash. It is the use of accrual procedures that accomplishes much of the matching of revenues and expenses because most transactions between business firms (and between many firms and individuals) involve purchase/sale at one point in time and cash payment/receipt at some other point in time.

The financial statement user relies on these concepts and principles related to the accounting period when making judgments and informed decisions about an entity's financial position and results of operations.

WHAT DOES IT MEAN?

7. What does matching of revenue and expense in the income statement mean?

8. What does the accrual concept mean?

Concepts/Principles Related to Financial Statements

Consistency in financial reporting is essential if meaningful trend comparisons are to be made using an entity's financial statements for several years. Thus, it is inappropriate for an entity to change from one generally accepted alternative of accounting for a particular type of transaction to another generally accepted method, unless both the fact that the change has been made and the effect of the change on the financial statements are explicitly described in the financial statements or the accompanying notes and explanations.

Full disclosure means that the financial statements and notes or explanations should include all necessary information to prevent a reasonably astute user of the financial statements from being misled. This is a tall order, one that the Securities and Exchange Commission has helped to define over the years. This requirement for full disclosure is one reason that the notes and explanations are usually considered an integral part of the financial statements.

Materiality means that absolute exactness, even if that idea could be defined, is not necessary in the amounts shown in the financial statements. Because of the numerous estimates involved in accounting, amounts reported in financial statements may be approximate, but they will not be "wrong" enough to be misleading. The financial statements of publicly owned corporations usually show amounts rounded to the nearest thousand, hundred thousand, or even million dollars. This rounding does not impair the information content of the financial statements and probably makes them easier to read. A management concept related to materiality is the cost–benefit relationship. Just as a manager would not spend $500 to get $300 worth of information, the incremental benefit of increased accuracy in accounting estimates is frequently not worth the cost of achieving the increased accuracy.

Conservatism in accounting relates to making judgments and estimates that result in lower profits and asset valuation estimates rather than higher profits and asset valuation estimates. Accountants try to avoid wishful thinking or pie-in-the-sky estimates that could result in overstating profits for a current period. This is not to say that accountants always look at issues from a gloom-and-doom viewpoint; rather, they seek to be realistic but are conservative when in doubt.

Limitations of Financial Statements

Objective 5
Understand several limitations of financial statements.

Financial statements report quantitative economic data; they do not reflect qualitative economic variables. Thus, the value to the firm of a management team or of the morale of the workforce is not included as a balance sheet asset because it cannot be objectively measured. Such qualitative attributes of the firm are frequently relevant to the decisions and informed judgments that the financial statement user is making, but they are not communicated in the financial statements.

As already emphasized, the cost principle requires assets to be recorded at their original cost. The balance sheet does not show the current market value or the replacement cost of the assets. Some assets are reported at the lower of their cost or market value, and in some cases market value may be reported parenthetically, but asset values are not increased to reflect current value. For example, the trademark of a firm has virtually no cost; its value has developed over the years as the firm has successfully met customers' needs. Thus, trademarks are usually excluded from the balance sheet listing of assets.

Estimates are used in many areas of accounting, and when the estimate is made, about the only fact known is that the estimate is probably not equal to the "true" amount. It is hoped that the estimate is near the "true" amount (the concept of materiality); it usually is. For example, recognizing depreciation expense involves estimating both the useful life to the entity of the asset being depreciated and the probable salvage value of the asset to the entity when it is disposed of. The original cost minus the salvage value is the amount to be depreciated or recognized as expense over the asset's life. Estimates must also be made to determine pension expense, warranty costs, and numerous other expense and revenue items to be reflected in the current year's income statement because they reflect the economic activity of the current year. These estimates also affect balance sheet accounts. So even though the balance sheet balances to the penny, do not be misled by this aura of exactness. Accountants do their best to make their estimates as accurate as possible, but estimates are still estimates.

The principle of consistency suggests that an entity should not change from one generally accepted method of accounting for a particular item to another generally accepted method of accounting for the same item. However, it is quite possible that two firms operating in the same industry may follow different methods. This means that *comparability* between firms may not be appropriate, or if comparisons are made, the effects of any differences between the accounting methods followed by the firms must be understood.

Related to the use of the original cost principle is the fact that financial statements are not adjusted to show the impact of inflation. Land acquired by a firm 50 years ago is still reported at its original cost, even though it may have a significantly higher current value because of inflation. Likewise, depreciation expense and the cost of goods sold—both significant expense elements of the income statement of many firms—reflect original cost, not replacement cost. This weakness is not significant when the rate of inflation is low, but the usefulness of financial statements is seriously impaired when the inflation rate rises to double digits. In 1980, the FASB began to require that large, publicly owned companies report certain inflation-adjusted data as supplementary information in the footnotes to the financial statements. In 1986, the FASB discontinued the requirement that this information be presented, but it encouraged further supplementary disclosures of the effects of inflation and changes in specific prices. This is a very controversial issue that will become more important if the rate of inflation rises significantly in the future.

Financial statements do not reflect **opportunity cost,** which is an economic concept relating to income forgone because an opportunity to earn income was not pursued. For example, if an individual or organization maintains a noninterest-bearing checking account balance that is $300 more than that required to avoid any service charges, the opportunity cost associated with that $300 is the interest that could otherwise be earned on the money if it had been invested. Financial accounting does not give formal recognition to opportunity cost; however, financial managers should be aware of the concept as they plan the utilization of the firm's resources.

WHAT DOES IT MEAN?   9. What does it mean when some investors state that a corporation's published financial statements don't tell the whole story about a firm's financial position and results of operations?

The Corporation's Annual Report

The annual report is the document distributed to shareholders that contains the reporting firm's financial statements for the fiscal year, together with

Objective 6
Understand what a corporation's annual report is and why it is issued.

the report of the external auditor's examination of the financial statements. The annual report document can be as simple as a transmittal letter from the president or chairman of the board of directors along with the financial statements, or as fancy as a glossy, 100-page booklet that showcases the firm's products, services, and personnel, as well as its financial results.

In addition to the financial statements described above and the explanatory comments (or footnotes or financial review) described more fully in Chapter 10, some other financial data are usually included in the annual report. Highlights for the year, including total revenues and net income, net income per share of common stock outstanding, and dividends paid during the year, appear inside the front cover or on the first page of the report. Intel Corporation has sprinkled various financial highlights throughout its 1996 annual report (see pages 1, 2, 6, 7, 16 and 17 in the Appendix). Most firms also include a historical summary of certain financial data for at least the past five years. This summary is usually located near the back of the annual report. Many of the specific aspects of Intel's annual report will be referred to in subsequent chapters.

Summary

Financial statements are used to communicate economic information for decisions and informed judgments.

The bookkeeping and accounting processes result in an entity's numerous transactions with other entities being reflected in the financial statements. The financial statements presented by an entity are the balance sheet, income statement, statement of changes in owners' equity, and statement of cash flows.

The balance sheet is a listing of the entity's assets, liabilities, and owners' equity at a point in time. Assets are probable future economic benefits (things or claims against others) controlled by the entity. Liabilities are amounts owed by the entity. An entity's owners' equity is the difference between its assets and liabilities. This relationship is known as the *accounting equation*. Current assets are cash and those assets likely to be converted to cash or used to benefit the entity within one year of the balance sheet date, such as accounts receivable and inventories. Current liabilities are expected to be paid within one year of the balance sheet date. The balance sheet as of the end of a fiscal period is also the balance sheet as of the beginning of the next fiscal period.

The income statement reports the results of the entity's operating activities for a period of time. Revenues are reported first, and costs and expenses are subtracted to arrive at net income or net loss for the period.

The statement of changes in owners' equity describes changes in paid-in capital and retained earnings during the period. Retained earnings are increased by the amount of net income and decreased by dividends to stockholders (and by any net loss for the period). It is through retained earnings that the income statement is linked to the balance sheet.

The statement of cash flows summarizes the impact on cash of the entity's operating activities, investing activities, and financing activities during the period. The bottom line of this financial statement is the change in cash from the amount shown in the balance sheet at the beginning of the period (e.g., fiscal year) to that shown in the balance sheet at the end of the period.

Financial statements are usually presented on a comparative basis so users can easily spot significant changes in an entity's financial position (balance sheet) and results of operations (income statement).

The financial statements are interrelated. Net income for the period (from the income statement) is added to retained earnings, a part of owners' equity (in the balance sheet). The statement of changes in owners' equity explains the difference between the amounts of owners' equity at the beginning and the end of the fiscal period. The statement of cash flows explains the change in the amount of cash from the beginning to the end of the fiscal period.

Accounting concepts and principles reflect generally accepted practices that have evolved over time. They can be related to a schematic model of the flow of data from transactions to the financial statements. Pertaining to the entire model are the accounting entity concept, the accounting equation, and the going concern concept.

Transactions are recorded in currency units (e.g., the U.S. dollar) without regard to purchasing power changes. Thus, transactions are recorded at an objectively determinable original cost amount.

The concepts and principles for the accounting period involve recognizing revenue when a sale of a product or service is made and then relating to that revenue all of the costs and expenses incurred in generating the revenue of the period. This matching of revenues and expenses is a crucial and fundamental concept to understand if accounting itself is to be understood. The accrual concept is used to implement the matching concept by recognizing revenues when earned and expenses when incurred, regardless of whether cash is received or paid in the same fiscal period.

The concepts of consistency, full disclosure, materiality, and conservatism relate primarily to financial statement presentation.

There are limitations to the information presented in financial statements. These limitations are related to the concepts and principles that have become generally accepted. Thus, subjective qualitative factors, current values, the impact of inflation, and opportunity cost are not usually reflected in financial statements. In addition, many financial statement amounts involve estimates. Permissible alternative accounting practices may mean that interfirm comparisons are not appropriate.

Corporations and other organizations include financial statements in an annual report that is made available to stockholders, employees, potential investors, and others interested in the entity. Refer to the financial statements on pages 18 to 21 of the Intel Corporation annual report in the Appendix, and refer to the financial statements of other annual report(s) you have, to see how the material discussed in this chapter is applied to real companies.

Key Terms and Concepts

account (p. 30)   A record in which transactions affecting individual assets, liabilities, owners' equity, revenues, and expenses are recorded.

account payable (p. 35)   A liability representing an amount payable to another entity, usually because of the purchase of merchandise or service on credit.

account receivable (p. 35)   An asset representing a claim against another entity, usually arising from selling goods or services on credit.

accounting equation (p. 33)   Assets = Liabilities + Owners' equity (A = L + OE). The fundamental relationship represented by the balance sheet and the foundation of the bookkeeping process.

accrual accounting (p. 48)   Accounting that recognizes revenues and expenses as they occur, even though the cash receipt from the revenue or the cash disbursement related to the expense may occur before or after the event that causes revenue or expense recognition.

accrued liabilities (p. 35)   Amounts that are owed by an entity on the balance sheet date.

accumulated depreciation (p. 35)   The sum of the depreciation expense that has been recognized over time. Accumulated depreciation is a contra asset that is subtracted from the cost of the related asset on the balance sheet.

additional paid-in capital (p. 39)   The excess of the amount received from the sale of stock over the par value of the shares sold.

assets (p. 34)   Probable future economic benefits obtained or controlled by an entity as a result of past transactions or events.

balance sheet (p. 33)   The financial statement that is a listing of the entity's assets, liabilities, and owners' equity at a point in time. Sometimes this statement is called the *statement of financial position*.

balance sheet equation (p. 33)   Another term for the *accounting equation*.

cash (p. 34)   An asset on the balance sheet that represents the amount of cash on hand and balances in bank accounts maintained by the entity.

common stock (p. 39)   The class of stock that represents residual ownership of the corporation.

corporation (p. 32)   A form of organization in which ownership is evidenced by shares of stock owned by stockholders; its features, for example, limited liability, make this the principal form of organization for most business activity.

cost of goods sold (p. 37)   Cost of merchandise sold during the period; an expense deducted from net sales to arrive at gross profit.

current assets (p. 35)   Cash and those assets that are likely to be converted to cash or used to benefit the entity within one year of the balance sheet date.

current liabilities (p. 35)   Those liabilities due to be paid within one year of the balance sheet date.

depreciation (p. 35)   The accounting process of recognizing that the cost of an asset is used up over its useful life to the entity.

depreciation expense (p. 40)   The expense recognized in a fiscal period for the depreciation of an asset.

dividend (p. 39)   A distribution of earnings to the owners of a corporation.

equity (p. 34)   The ownership right associated with an asset. See *owners' equity.*

expenses (p. 36)   Outflows or other using up of assets or incurring a liability during a period from delivering or producing goods, rendering services, or carrying out other activities that constitute the entity's major operations.

fiscal year (p. 32)   The annual period used for reporting to owners.

gains (p. 36)   Increases in net assets from incidental transactions that are not revenues or investments by owners.

going concern concept (p. 46)   A presumption that the entity will continue in existence for the indefinite future.

gross profit (p. 37)   The difference between net sales and cost of goods sold. Sometimes called *gross margin.*

income from operations (p. 37)   The difference between gross profit and operating expenses. Also referred to as *operating income.*

income statement (p. 36)   The financial statement that summarizes the entity's revenues, expenses, gains, and losses for a period of time, and reports the entity's results of operations for that period of time.

liabilities (p. 34)   Probable future sacrifices of economic benefits arising from present obligations of a particular entity to transfer assets or provide services to other entities in the future as a result of past transactions or events.

losses (p. 36)   Decreases in net assets from incidental transactions that are not expenses or distributions to owners.

matching concept (p. 48)   The concept that expenses incurred in generating revenues should be deducted from revenues earned during the period for which results are being reported.

merchandise inventory (p. 35)   Items held by an entity for sale to potential customers in the normal course of business.

net assets (p. 34)   The difference between assets and liabilities; also referred to as *owners' equity.*

net income (p. 36)   The excess of revenues and gains over expenses and losses for a fiscal period.

net income per share of common stock outstanding (p. 37)   Net income available to the common stockholders divided by the average number of shares of common stock outstanding during the period. Usually referred to as *earnings per share* or *EPS.*

net sales (p. 36)   Gross sales, less sales discounts and sales returns and allowances.

net worth (p. 34)   Another term for *net assets* or *owners' equity,* but not as appropriate because the term *worth* may be misleading.

opportunity cost (p. 50)   An economic concept relating to income forgone because an opportunity to earn income was not pursued.

owners' equity (p. 34)   The equity of the entity's owners in the assets of the entity. Sometimes called *net assets;* the difference between assets and liabilities.

paid-in capital (p. 38)   The amount invested in the entity by the owners.

par value (p. 39)   An arbitrary value assigned to a share of stock when the corporation is organized. Sometimes used to refer to the stated value or face amount of a security.

partnership (p. 32)   A form of organization indicating ownership by two or more individuals or corporations without the limited liability and other features of a corporation.

profit (p. 36)   The excess of revenues and gains over expenses and losses for a fiscal period; another term for *net income.*

profit and loss statement (p. 36)   Another term for the *income statement.*

proprietorship (p. 32)   A form of organization indicating individual ownership without the limited liability and other features of a corporation.

retained earnings (p. 38)   Cumulative net income that has not been distributed to the owners of a corporation as dividends.

revenues (p. 36)   Inflows of cash or increases in other assets, or settlement of liabilities during a period, from delivering or producing goods, rendering services, or performing other activities that constitute the entity's major operations.

statement of cash flows (p. 40)   The financial statement that explains why cash changed during a fiscal period. Cash flows from operating, investing, and financing activities are shown.

statement of changes in capital stock (p. 38)   The financial statement that summarizes changes during a fiscal period in capital stock and additional paid-in capital. This information may be included in the statement of changes in owners' equity.

statement of changes in owners' equity (p. 38)   The financial statement that summarizes the changes during a fiscal period in capital stock, additional paid-in capital, retained earnings, and other elements of owners' equity.

statement of changes in retained earnings (p. 38)   The financial statement that summarizes the changes during a fiscal period in retained earnings. This information may be included in the statement of changes in owners' equity.

statement of earnings (p. 36)   Another term for the *income statement;* it shows the revenues, expenses, gains, and losses for a period of time, and the entity's results of operations for that period of time.

statement of financial position (p. 33)   Another term for the *balance sheet;* a listing of the entity's assets, liabilities, and owners' equity at a point in time.

statement of operations (p. 36)   Another term for the *income statement.*

stock (p. 32)   The evidence of ownership of a corporation.

stockholders (p. 32)   The owners of a corporation's stock; sometimes called *shareholders.*

subsidiary (p. 46)   A corporation whose stock is more than 50 percent owned by another corporation.

transactions (p. 30)   Economic interchanges between entities that are accounted for and reflected in financial statements.

WHAT DOES IT MEAN?
ANSWERS

1. It means that there has been some sort of economic interchange; for example, you have agreed to pay tuition in exchange for classes.

2. It means the person doing this is really mixed up because the balance sheet presents data as of a point in time. It's a balance sheet *as of* August 31, 1999.

3. It means that the organization's financial position *at a point in time* has been determined and summarized.

4. It means that each individual financial statement provides unique information but focuses on only a part of the big picture, so all four statements need to be reviewed to achieve a full understanding of the firm's financial position and results of operations.

5. It means that revenues have been earned from selling product or providing services but that the accounts receivable from those revenues have not yet been collected—or if the receivables have been collected the cash has been used for some purpose other than paying bills.

6. It means that transactions affecting the income statement also affect the owners' equity section of the balance sheet as well as the asset and/or liability sections of the balance sheet.

7. It means that all expenses incurred in generating revenue for the period are subtracted from those revenues to determine net income. Matching does not mean that revenues equal expenses.

8. It means that revenues and expenses are recognized in the accounting period in which they are earned or incurred, even though cash is received or paid in a different accounting period.

9. It means that there may be both qualitative—for example, workforce morale—and quantitative—for example, opportunity cost—factors that are not reflected in the financial statements.

Exercises and Problems

LO 1, 3   **2–1.**   **Identify accounts by category and financial statement(s).** Listed below are a number of financial statement captions. Indicate in the spaces to the right of each caption the category of each item and the financial statement(s) on which the item can usually be found. Use the following abbreviations:

Category		Financial Statement	
Asset	A	Balance sheet	BS
Liability	L	Income statement	IS
Owners' equity	OE	Statement of changes	
Revenue	R	in owners' equity	SOE
Expense	E		
Gain	G		
Loss	LS		

Cash	_____	_____
Accounts payable	_____	_____
Common stock	_____	_____
Depreciation expense	_____	_____
Net sales	_____	_____
Income tax expense	_____	_____
Short-term investments	_____	_____
Gain on sale of land	_____	_____

Retained earnings   _____   _____
Dividends payable   _____   _____
Accounts receivable   _____   _____
Short-term debt   _____   _____

LO 1, 3   **2–2.**   **Identify accounts by category and financial statement(s).** Listed below are a number of financial statement captions. Indicate in the spaces to the right of each caption the category of each item and the financial statement(s) on which the item can usually be found. Use the following abbreviations:

Category		*Financial Statement*	
Asset	A	Balance sheet	BS
Liability	L	Income statement	IS
Owners' equity	OE	Statement of changes	
Revenue	R	in owners' equity	SOE
Expense	E		
Gain	G		
Loss	LS		

Accumulated depreciation _____   _____
Long-term debt _____   _____
Equipment _____   _____
Loss on sale of short-
  term investments _____   _____
Net income _____   _____
Merchandise inventory _____   _____
Other accrued liabilities _____   _____
Dividends paid _____   _____
Cost of goods sold _____   _____
Additional paid-in capital _____   _____
Interest income _____   _____
Selling expenses _____   _____

LO 1, 2   **2–3.**   **Understanding financial statement relationships.** The information presented below represents selected data from the December 31, 1999, balance sheets and the income statements for the year then ended for three firms.

	Firm A	*Firm B*	*Firm C*
Total assets, 12/31/99	$420,000	$540,000	$325,000
Total liabilities, 12/31/99	215,000	145,000	?
Paid-in capital, 12/31/99	75,000	?	40,000
Retained earnings, 12/31/99	?	310,000	?
Net income for 1999	?	83,000	113,000
Dividends declared and paid			
during 1999	50,000	19,000	65,000
Retained earnings, 1/1/99	78,000	?	42,000

Required:

Calculate the missing amounts for each firm.

LO 1, 2   2–4.   **Understanding financial statement relationships.** The information presented below represents selected data from the December 31, 1999, balance sheets and the income statements for the year then ended for three firms.

	Firm A	Firm B	Firm C
Total assets, 12/31/99	?	$435,000	$520,000
Total liabilities, 12/31/99	$80,000	?	205,000
Paid-in capital, 12/31/99	55,000	59,000	140,000
Retained earnings, 12/31/99	?	186,000	?
Net income for 1999	68,000	110,000	81,000
Dividends declared and paid during 1999	12,000	?	28,000
Retained earnings, 1/1/99	50,000	124,000	?

Required:
Calculate the missing amounts for each firm.

LO 1, 2   2–5.   **Calculate retained earnings.** From the data given below, calculate the retained earnings balance as of December 31, 1999.

Retained earnings, December 31, 1998	$311,800
Cost of equipment purchased during 1999	32,400
NI = Net loss for the year ended December 31, 1999	4,700
Dividends declared and paid in 1999	18,500
Decrease in cash balance from January 1, 1999, to December 31, 1999	13,600
Decrease in long-term debt in 1999	14,800

LO 1, 2   2–6.   **Calculate retained earnings.** From the data given below, calculate the retained earnings balance as of December 31, 1999.

Retained earnings, December 31, 2000	$210,300
Decrease in total liabilities during 2000	45,800
Gain on the sale of buildings during 2000	16,100
Dividends declared and paid in 2000	4,500
Proceeds from sale of common stock in 2000	49,400
Net income for the year ended December 31, 2000	22,600

LO 1, 2   2–7.   **Calculate dividends using the accounting equation.** At the beginning of its current fiscal year, Willie Corp.'s balance sheet showed assets of $12,400 and liabilities of $7,000. During the year, liabilities decreased by $1,200. Net income for the year was $3,000, and net assets at the end of the year were $6,000. There were no changes in paid-in capital during the year.

Required:
Calculate the dividends, if any, declared during the year. *(Hint: Set up an accounting equation for the beginning of the year, changes during the year, and at the end of the year. Enter known data and solve for the unknowns.)*

Here is a possible worksheet format:

				OE		
	A	=	L	+ PIC	+	RE
Beginning:		=		+		+
Changes:	___	=	___	+ ___	+	___
Ending:		=		+		+

LO 1, 2

2–8. **Calculate net income (or loss) using the accounting equation.** At the beginning of the current fiscal year, the balance sheet for Davis Co. showed liabilities of $320,000. During the year liabilities decreased by $18,000, assets increased by $65,000, and paid-in capital increased from $30,000 to $192,000. Dividends declared and paid during the year were $25,000. At the end of the year, owners' equity totaled $429,000.

Required:

Calculate net income (or loss) for the year. *(Hint: Set up an accounting equation for the beginning of the year, changes during the year, and at the end of the year. Enter known data and solve for the unknowns. Remember, net income [or loss] may not be the only item affecting retained earnings.)*

LO 1, 2

2–9. **Calculate cash available upon liquidation of business.** Circle-Square, Ltd., is in the process of liquidating and going out of business. The firm's balance sheet shows $22,800 in cash, inventory totaling $61,400, accounts receivable of $114,200, plant and equipment of $265,000, and total liabilities of $305,600. It is estimated that the inventory can be disposed of in a liquidation sale for 80 percent of its cost, all but 5 percent of the accounts receivable can be collected, and plant and equipment can be sold for $190,000.

Required:

Calculate the amount of cash that would be available to the owners if the accounts receivable are collected, the other assets are sold as described, and the liabilities are paid off in full.

LO 1, 2

2–10. **Calculate cash available upon liquidation of business.** Kimber Co. is in the process of liquidating and going out of business. The firm's accountant has provided the following balance sheet and additional information:

Assets

Assets		
Cash		$ 18,400
Accounts receivable		62,600
Merchandise inventory		114,700
Total current assets		$195,700
Land		$ 51,000
Buildings & equipment		343,000
Less: Accumulated depreciation		(195,000)
Total land, buildings, & equipment		199,000
Total assets		$394,700

Liabilities

Liabilities		
Accounts payable		$ 46,700
Notes payable		58,500
Total current liabilities		$105,200
Long-term debt		64,800

Owners' Equity

Common stock, no par	$110,000	
Retained earnings	114,700	
Total owners' equity		$224,700
Total liabilities and owners' equity		$394,700

It is estimated that the merchandise inventory can be disposed of in a liquidation sale for 85 percent of its cost, and all but 12 percent of the Accounts Receivable can be collected. Buildings and equipment can be sold at $40,000 above book value (the difference between original cost and accumulated depreciation shown on the balance sheet), and the land can be sold at its current appraisal value of $65,000. In addition to the liabilities included in the balance sheet, $2,400 is owed to employees for their work since the last pay period, and interest of $5,250 has accrued on notes payable and long-term debt.

Required:

a. Calculate the amount of cash that would be available to the stockholders if the accounts receivable are collected, the other assets are sold as described, and all liabilities and other claims are paid in full.

b. Briefly explain why the amount of cash available to stockholders (computed in part *a*) is different than the amount of total owners' equity shown in the balance sheet.

LO 1, 2, 3   **2–11.**   **Understanding and analyzing financial statement relationships—sales/service organization.** Pope's Garage had the following accounts and amounts in its financial statements on December 31, 1999. Assume that all balance sheet items reflect account balances at December 31, 1999, and that all income statement items reflect activities that occurred during the year then ended.

Accounts receivable	$ 33,000
Depreciation expense	12,000
Land	27,000
Cost of goods sold	90,000
Retained earnings	59,000
Cash	9,000
Equipment	71,000
Supplies	6,000
Accounts payable	23,000
Service revenue	20,000
Interest expense	4,000
Common stock	10,000
Income tax expense	12,000
Accumulated depreciation	45,000
Long-term debt	40,000
Supplies expense	14,000
Merchandise inventory	31,000
Sales revenue	140,000

Required:

a. Calculate the total current assets at December 31, 1999.

b. Calculate the total liabilities and owners' equity at December 31, 1999.

c. Calculate the earnings from operations (operating income) for the year ended December 31, 1999.

d. Calculate the net income (or loss) for the year ended December 31, 1999.

e. What was the average income tax rate for Pope's Garage for 1999?

f. If $16,000 of dividends had been declared and paid during the year, what was the January 1, 1999, balance of retained earnings?

LO 1, 2, 3   **2–12.** **Understanding and analyzing financial statement relationships—merchandising organization.** Gary's TV had the following accounts and amounts in its financial statements on December 31, 1999. Assume that all balance sheet items reflect account balances at December 31, 1999, and that all income statement items reflect activities that occurred during the year then ended.

Interest expense	$ 9,000
Paid-in capital	20,000
Accumulated depreciation	6,000
Notes payable (long term)	70,000
Rent expense	18,000
Merchandise inventory	210,000
Accounts receivable	48,000
Depreciation expense	3,000
Land	32,000
Retained earnings	225,000
Cash	36,000
Cost of goods sold	440,000
Equipment	18,000
Income tax expense	60,000
Accounts payable	23,000
Sales revenue	620,000

Required:

a. Calculate the difference between current assets and current liabilities for Gary's TV at December 31, 1999.

b. Calculate the total assets at December 31, 1999.

c. Calculate the earnings from operations (operating income) for the year ended December 31, 1999.

d. Calculate the net income (or loss) for the year ended December 31, 1999.

e. What was the average income tax rate for Gary's TV for 1999?

f. If $64,000 of dividends had been declared and paid during the year, what was the January 1, 1999, balance of retained earnings?

LO 1, 2, 3   **2–13.** **Prepare an income statement, balance sheet, and statement of changes in owners' equity; analyze results.** The following information was obtained from the records of Breanna, Inc.:

Accounts receivable	$ 10,000
Accumulated depreciation	52,000
Cost of goods sold	128,000
Income tax expense	8,000
Cash	65,000
Sales	200,000
Equipment	120,000
✕ Selling, general, and administrative expenses	$ 34,000
Common stock (9,000 shares)	90,000
Accounts payable	15,000

Retained earnings, 1/1/99	23,000
Interest expense	6,000
Merchandise inventory	37,000
Long-term debt	40,000
Dividends declared and paid during 1999	12,000

Except as otherwise indicated, assume that all balance sheet items reflect account balances at December 31, 1999, and that all income statement items reflect activities that occurred during the year ended December 31, 1999. There were no changes in paid-in capital during the year.

Required:

a. Prepare an income statement and statement of changes in owners' equity for the year ended December 31, 1999, and a balance sheet at December 31, 1999, for Breanna, Inc. Based on the financial statements that you have prepared for part *a,* answer the questions in parts *b–e* below. Provide brief explanations for each of your answers and state any assumptions you believe are necessary to ensure that your answers are correct.

b. What is the company's average income tax rate?

c. What interest rate is charged on long-term debt?

d. What is the par value per share of common stock?

e. What is the company's dividend policy (i.e., what proportion of the company's earnings are used for dividends)?

LO 1, 2, 3   **2–14.** **Prepare an income statement, balance sheet, and statement of changes in owners' equity; analyze results.** The following information was obtained from the records of Shae, Inc.:

Merchandise inventory	$ 44,000
Notes payable (long term)	50,000
Sales	150,000
Buildings and equipment	84,000
Selling, general, and administrative expenses	12,000
Accounts receivable	20,000
Common stock (7,000 shares)	35,000
Income tax expense	14,000
Cash	32,000
Retained earnings, 1/1/99	21,500
Accrued liabilities	3,000
Cost of goods sold	90,000
Accumulated depreciation	36,000
Interest expense	8,000
Accounts payable	15,000
Dividends declared and paid during 1999	6,500

Except as otherwise indicated, assume that all balance sheet items reflect account balances at December 31, 1999, and that all income statement items reflect activities that occurred during the year ended December 31, 1999. There were no changes in paid-in capital during the year.

Required:

a. Prepare an income statement and statement of changes in owners' equity for the year ended December 31, 1999, and a balance sheet at December 31, 1999, for Shae, Inc. Based on the financial statements that you have prepared for part *a,* answer the questions in parts *b–e* below. Provide brief explanations for each of your answers and state any assumptions you believe are necessary to ensure that your answers are correct.

b. What is the company's average income tax rate?

c. What interest rate is charged on long-term debt?

d. What is the par value per share of common stock?

e. What is the company's dividend policy (i.e., what proportion of the company's earnings are used for dividends)?

LO 1, 2, 3   **2–15.** **Calculate net income and cash flow information from balance sheet data; analyze results.** Presented below are the December 31, 1999 and 1998 comparative balance sheets for Garber, Inc., in summarized form.

	1999	*1998*
Cash	$ 50,000	$ 35,000
Production equipment (net of accumulated depreciation)	120,000	135,000
Total assets	$170,000	$170,000
Notes payable (long term)	$ 60,000	$ 65,000
Common stock	40,000	30,000
Retained earnings	70,000	75,000
Total liabilities and owners' equity	$170,000	$170,000

The following additional information is available:
1. No production equipment was purchased or sold during 1999.
2. Total revenue for 1999 was $120,000.
3. Dividends of $17,000 were declared and paid during 1999.

Required:

a. Calculate net income for the year ended December 31, 1999, and total expenses for the year. *(Hint: Prepare an analysis of the Retained Earnings account.)*

b. Complete the following summarized statement of cash flows for Garber, Inc., for the year ended December 31, 1999:

GARBER, INC.
Statement of Cash Flows
For the Year Ended December 31, 1999

Cash flows from operating activities	$
Cash flows from investing activities	
Cash flows from financing activities	(12,000)
Net increase in cash for the year	$
Cash balance, January 1, 1999	
Cash balance, December 31, 1999	$

c. Explain what caused the difference between the amount of net income computed in part *a* and the amount of cash flows from operating activities computed in part *b.*

d. Prepare a schedule to show how the ($12,000) cash flows from financing activities amount was determined. *(Hint: Review Exhibit 2–4.)*

e. In your opinion, is Garber, Inc., in a better or worse financial position at the end 1999, as compared to the beginning of 1999? Explain your reasoning.

LO 1, 2, 3   **2–16.   Calculate net income using summarized balance sheet and statement of cash flows data; analyze results and explain cash flow totals.** Presented below are the 1999 and 1998 comparative balance sheets, together with the statement of cash flows for the year ended December 31, 1999, for Swank, Inc. (in summarized form).

SWANK, INC.
Balance Sheets
December 31, 1999 and 1998

	1999	1998
Cash	$ 40,000	$ 50,000
Accounts receivable	60,000	30,000
Production equipment (net of		
accumulated depreciation)	220,000	240,000
Total assets	$320,000	$320,000
Accounts payable	$ 10,000	$ 25,000
Notes payable (long term)	80,000	120,000
Paid-in capital	50,000	40,000
Retained earnings	180,000	135,000
Total liabilities and owners' equity	$320,000	$320,000

SWANK, INC.
Statement of Cash Flows
For the Year Ended December 31, 1999

Cash flows from operating activities	$ 47,000
Cash flows from investing activities	0
Cash flows from financing activities	(57,000)
Net decrease in cash for the year	$(10,000)
Cash balance, January 1, 1999	50,000
Cash balance, December 31, 1999	$ 40,000

The following additional information is available:
1. No production equipment was purchased or sold during 1999.
2. Total revenue for 1999 was $250,000.
3. Dividends of $27,000 were declared and paid during 1999.

Required:

a. Calculate net income for the year ended December 31, 1999, and total expenses for the year. *(Hint: Prepare an analysis of the Retained Earnings account.)*

b. Prepare schedules that explain how the $47,000 cash flows from operating activities and the $(57,000) cash flows from financing activities amounts were determined. *(Hint: Review Exhibit 2–4.)*

c. Explain what caused the difference between the amount of net income computed in part *a* and the $47,000 of cash flows from operating activities.

d. In your opinion, is Swank, Inc., in a better or worse financial position at the end of 1999 than at the beginning of 1999? Explain your reasoning.

LO 1, 2   **2–17.   Transaction analysis—nonquantitative.** Indicate the effect of each of the following transactions on total assets, total liabilities, and total owners' equity. Use

+ for increase, − for decrease, and (NE) for no effect. The first transaction is provided as an illustration.

	Assets	Liabilities	Owners' Equity
a. Borrowed cash on a bank loan	+	+	NE
b. Paid an account payable			
c. Sold common stock			
d. Purchased merchandise inventory on account			
e. Declared and paid dividends			
f. Collected an account receivable			
g. Sold merchandise inventory on account at a profit			
h. Paid operating expenses in cash			
i. Repaid principal and interest on a bank loan			

LO 1, 2   **2–18.** **Transaction analysis—quantitative; analyze results.** Rick Hurd owns and operates Hurd's Furniture Emporium, Inc. The balance sheet totals for assets, liabilities, and owners' equity at August 1, 1999, are as indicated. Described below are several transactions entered into by the company throughout the month of August.

Required:

a. Indicate the amount and effect (+ or −) of each transaction on total assets, total liabilities, and total owners' equity, and then compute the new totals for each category. The first transaction is provided as an illustration.

	Assets	= Liabilities +	Owners' Equity
August 1, 1999, totals	$420,000	$345,000	$75,000
August 3, borrowed $15,000 in cash from the bank	+15,000	+15,000	
New totals	$435,000	$360,000	$75,000
August 7, bought merchandise inventory valued at $32,000 on account	+		
New totals	_____	_____	_____
August 10, paid $3,000 cash for operating expenses	−		
New totals	_____	_____	_____
August 14, received $30,000 in cash from sales of merchandise that had cost $21,000	+		
New totals	_____	_____	_____
August 17, paid $8,000 owed on accounts payable	−		
New totals	_____	_____	_____
August 21, collected $11,000 of accounts receivable	∅		
New totals	_____	_____	_____
August 24, repaid $10,000 to the bank plus $200 interest	−		
New totals	_____	_____	_____

> August 29, paid Rick Hurd a cash
>   dividend of $2,000 .... ———— ———— ————
>   New totals ....

   b. What was the amount of net income (or loss) during August? How much were total revenues and total expenses?

   c. What were the net changes during the month of August in total assets, total liabilities, and total owners' equity?

   d. Explain to Rick Hurd which transactions caused the net change in his owners' equity during August.

   e. Explain why dividend payments are not an expense, but interest is an expense.

   f. Explain why the money borrowed from the bank increased assets but did not increase net income.

   g. Explain why paying off accounts payable and collecting accounts receivable do not affect net income.

LO 1, 2, 4   **2–19.** **Complete the balance sheet.** A partially completed balance sheet for Blue Co., Inc., as of January 31, 2000, is presented below. Where amounts are shown for various items, the amounts are correct.

Assets		*Liabilities and Owners' Equity*	
Cash..................	$ 700	Note payable..............	$ ————
Accounts receivable	————	Accounts payable	3,400
Land..................	————		
Automobile.............	————	Total liabilities.........	$ ————
Less: Accumulated		Owners' equity	
depreciation..........	————	Common stock...........	$ 8,000
		Retained earnings.........	————
		Total owners' equity.....	$ ————
		Total liabilities +	
Total assets	$ ————	owners' equity...........	$ ————

Required:

Using the following data, complete the balance sheet.

   a. Blue Co.'s records show that current and former customers owe the firm a total of $4,000; $600 of this amount has been due for over a year from two customers who are now bankrupt.

   b. The automobile, which is still being used in the business, cost $9,000 new; a used car dealer's blue book shows that it is now worth $5,000. Management estimates that the car has been used for one-third of its total potential use.

   c. The land cost Blue Co. $7,000; it was recently assessed for real estate tax purposes at a value of $11,000.

   d. Blue Co.'s president isn't sure of the amount of the note payable, but he does know that he signed a note.

   e. Since the date Blue Co. was formed, net income has totaled $23,000, and dividends to stockholders have totaled $19,500.

LO 1, 2, 4   **2–20.** **Complete balance sheet using cash flow data.** Following is a partially completed balance sheet for Epsico, Inc., at December 31, 1999, together with comparative data for the year ended December 31, 1998. From the statement of cash flows for the year ended December 31, 1999, you determine that:

Net income for the year ended December 31, 1999, was $26.

Dividends paid during the year ended December 31, 1999, were $8.

Cash increased $8 during the year ended December 31, 1999.

The cost of new equipment acquired during 1999 was $15; no equipment was disposed of.

There were no transactions affecting the land account during 1999, but it is estimated that the fair market value of the land at December 31, 1999, is $42.→ ignore/no effect

Required:

Complete the balance sheet at December 31, 1999.

EPSICO, INC.
Balance Sheets
December 31, 1999 and 1998

Assets	1999	1998	Liabilities	1999	1998
Current assets:			Current liabilities:		
Cash	$ 38	$ 30	Note payable. . . .	$ 49	$ 40
Accounts receivable	126	120	Accounts payable.	123	110
Inventory	241	230			
Total current assets	$405	$ 380	Total current liabilities. . . .	$172	$150
			Long-term debt. .	$	$ 80
Land	$ 25	$ 25	**Owners' Equity**		
Equipment	390 ← 375 +15		Common stock	$200	$200
Less: Accumulated depreciation	(180)	(160)	Retained earnings		190
Total land & equipment	$ 235	$ 240	Total owners' equity	$	$390
			Total liabilities and owners' equity . . .	$	$620
Total assets	$640	$ 620			

LO 1, 2, 4 **2–21.** **Prepare balance sheet using statement of cash flows data.** Presented below is the statement of cash flows for Optico, Inc., for the year ended December 31, 1999, and the company's balance sheet at December 31, 1998.

OPTICO, INC.
Statement of Cash Flows
For the Year Ended December 31, 1999

Cash Flows from Operating Activities:

Net income	$ 37,000
Add (deduct) items not affecting cash:	
Depreciation expense	15,000
Decrease in accounts receivable	12,000
Increase in merchandise inventory	(14,000)
Decrease in short-term debt	(20,000)
Increase in accounts payable	7,000
Decrease in other accrued liabilities	(8,000)
Net cash provided by operating activities	$ 29,000

Cash Flows from Investing Activities:
Purchase of buildings . . . . $(40,000)

Cash Flows from Financing Activities:
Increase in long-term debt . . . . $ 18,000
Payment of cash dividend on common stock . . . . (12,000)
Net cash provided by financing activities . . . . $ 6,000
Net decrease in cash for the year . . . . $ (5,000)

OPTICO, INC.
Balance Sheet
December 31, 1998

Assets		*Liabilities and Owners' Equity*	
Current assets:		Current liabilities:	
Cash	$ 15,000	Short-term debt	$ 20,000
Accounts receivable	22,000	Accounts payable	13,000
Merchandise		Other accrued	
inventory	31,000	liabilities	17,000
Total current		Total current	
assets	$ 68,000	liabilities	$ 50,000
		Long-term debt	21,000
		Total liabilities	$ 71,000
Plant and equipment:			
Land	8,000	Owner's equity:	
Building	82,000	Common stock, no par	$ 10,000
Less: Accumulated		Retained earnings	41,000
depreciation	(36,000)		
	$ 54,000	Total owners'	
		equity	$ 51,000
		Total liabilities and	
Total assets	$122,000	owners' equity	$122,000

Required:
Using the information in the above financial statements, prepare the balance sheet for Optico, Inc., at December 31, 1999.

LO 1, 2, 4   **2–22.   Complete balance sheet and prepare retained earnings statement using statement of cash flows data.** Presented below is a statement of cash flows for Swords, Inc., for the year ended December 31, 1999. Also shown is a partially completed comparative balance sheet as of December 31, 1999, and 1998.

SWORDS, INC.
Statement of Cash Flows
For the Year Ended December 31, 1999

Cash Flows from Operating Activities:
Net income $20,000
Add (deduct) items not affecting cash:
Depreciation expense 12,000
Increase in accounts receivable . . . . (5,000)
Decrease in inventory 17,000
Decrease in short-term debt . . . . (6,000)
Decrease in notes payable . . . . (2,000)
Increase in accounts payable 11,000
Net cash provided by operating activities $47,000

Cash Flows from Investing Activities:
Purchase of buildings	$(70,000)
Proceeds from sale of land at its cost	2,000
Net cash used by investing activities	$(68,000)

Cash Flows from Financing Activities:
Proceeds from issuance of long-term debt	$ 18,000
Proceeds from issuance of common stock	22,000
Payment of cash dividends on common stock	(8,000)
Net cash provided by financing activities	$ 32,000
Net increase in cash for the year	$ 11,000

SWORDS, INC.
Balance Sheets
December 31, 1999, and 1998

	1999	1998
Assets		
Cash	$ 65,000	$
Accounts receivable	134,000	
Inventory		170,000
Total current assets	$	$
Land		10,000
Buildings		290,000
Less: Accumulated depreciation	(98,000)	
Total land and buildings	$	$
Total assets	$	$
Liabilities		
Short-term debt	$ 41,000	$
Notes payable	66,000	
Accounts payable		157,000
Total current liabilities	$	$
Long-term debt		75,000
Owners' Equity		
Common stock	$ 30,000	
Retained earnings		212,000
Total owners' equity	$	$
Total liabilities and owners' equity	$	$

Required:

a. Complete the December 31, 1999 and 1998, balance sheets.

b. Prepare a statement of changes in retained earnings for the year ended December 31, 1999.

LO 1, 3   **2–23. Understanding income statement relationships—Wal-Mart Stores, Inc.** Selected data from the January 31, 1997 and 1996 consolidated balance sheets and the income statements for the years then ended of Wal-Mart Stores, Inc., are presented below. All amounts are reported in millions.

	1997	1996
For the year ended January 31:		
Net sales and other income*	$106,146	$ 94,749
Cost of sales	83,663	74,564

Operating, selling, and general and administrative expenses	16,788	14,951
Interest costs	?	888
Income before income taxes	4,850	?
Provision for income taxes	?	1,606
Net income	$ 3,056	$?

*"Other income" amounted to $1,287 in 1997 and $1,122 in 1996.

a. Calculate the amount of Wal-Mart's gross profit for each year. Has gross profit as a percentage of sales changed significantly during the past year?

b. Calculate the amount of Wal-Mart's operating income for each year. Has operating income as a percentage of sales changed significantly during the past year?

c. After completing parts *a* and *b,* calculate the missing amounts for each year.

LO 1, 3   **2–24.   Understanding income statement relationships—Coca-Cola Enterprises, Inc.**
Selected data from the December 31, 1996 and 1995 consolidated balance sheets and the income statements for the years then ended of Coca-Cola Enterprises, Inc., are presented below. All amounts are reported in millions. *(Note: Coca-Cola Enterprises is the world's largest marketer and distributor of products of The Coca-Cola Company, which operates as a separate legal and accounting entity.)*

	1996	*1995*
For the year ended December 31:		
Net operating revenues	$ 7,921	$?
Cost of sales	?	4,267
Gross profit	3,025	2,506
Selling, general, and administrative expenses ...	?	2,038
Operating income	?	?
Interest expense, net	351	?
Income before income taxes	194	?
Income tax expense	?	63
Net income		
	$ 114	$ 82
Cash dividends declared	?	8
At December 31:		
Total assets	11,234	$?
Total liabilities	9,684	7,629
Total share—owners' equity	?	1,435
Reinvested earnings	237	144

a. Calculate the missing amounts for each year. *[Hint: Prepare an analysis of the reinvested (i.e., retained) earnings account for 1996.]*

b. What other balance sheet accounts do you suppose would explain the difference between the total share-owners' equity and reinvested earnings?

LO 1   **2–25.   Prepare a personal balance sheet.** Prepare a personal balance sheet for yourself as of today. Work at identifying your assets and liabilities; use rough estimates for the amounts associated with them.

Fundamental Interpretations Made from Financial Statement Data

Chapter 2 presented an overview of the financial statements that result from the financial accounting process. It is now appropriate to preview some of the interpretations made by financial statement users to support their decisions and informed judgments because understanding the uses of accounting information will make development of that information more meaningful. Current and potential stockholders are interested in making their own assessments about management's stewardship of the resources made available by the owners. For example, judgments about profitability will affect the investment decision. Creditors assess the entity's ability to repay loans and pay for products and services. These assessments about profitability and debt-paying ability involve interpreting the relationships among amounts reported in the financial statements. Most of these relationships will be referred to in subsequent chapters. They are introduced now to illustrate how management's financial objectives for the firm are quantified so that you may begin to understand what the numbers mean. Likewise, these concepts will prepare you to better understand the impact of alternative accounting methods on financial statements when accounting alternatives are explained in subsequent chapters.

   This chapter introduces some financial statement analysis concepts. Chapter 11, Financial Statement Analysis, is a comprehensive explanation of how to use financial statement data to analyze financial condition and results of operations. You will better understand topics in that chapter after you have studied the financial accounting material in Chapters 5 through 10.

Learning Objectives

After studying this chapter you should understand:

1 Why financial statement ratios are important.

2 The importance and calculation of return on investment.

3 The DuPont model, an expansion of the basic return on investment calculation, and the terms *margin* and *turnover*.

4 The significance and calculation of return on equity.

5 The meaning of liquidity and why it is important.

6 The significance and calculation of working capital, the current ratio, and the acid-test ratio.

7 How trend analysis can be used most effectively.

Financial Ratios and Trend Analysis

Objective 1
Understand why financial statement ratios are important.

The large dollar amounts reported on the financial statements of many companies, and the varying size of companies, make ratio analysis the only sensible method of evaluating various financial characteristics of a company. Students are frequently awed by the number of ratio measurements commonly used in financial management and are sometimes intimidated by the mere thought of calculating a ratio. Be neither awed nor intimidated! A ratio is simply the relationship between two numbers; the name of virtually every financial ratio describes the numbers to be related and usually how the ratio is calculated. As you study this material, concentrate on understanding why the ratio is considered important and work to understand the meaning of the ratio. If you do these things, you should avoid much of the stress associated with understanding financial ratios.

In most cases, a single ratio does not describe very much about the company whose statements are being studied. Much more meaningful analysis is accomplished when the *trend* of a particular ratio over several time periods is examined. Of course, consistency in financial reporting and in defining the ratio components is crucial if the trend is to be meaningful.

Most industry and trade associations publish industry average ratios based on aggregated data compiled by the association from reports submitted by association members. Comparison of an individual company's ratio with the comparable industry ratio is frequently made as a means of assessing a company's relative standing in its industry. However, comparison of a single observation for a company with that of the industry may not be very meaningful because the company may use a financial accounting alternative that is different from that used by the rest of the industry. **Trend analysis** results in a much more meaningful comparison because even though the data used in the ratio may have been developed under different financial accounting alternatives, internal consistency within each of the trends will permit useful trend comparisons.

Trend analysis is described later in this chapter, but a brief example now will illustrate the process. Suppose that a student's grade point average for last semester was 2.8 on a 4.0 scale. That GPA may be interesting, but it says little about the student's work. However, suppose you learn that this student's GPA was 1.9 four semesters ago, 2.3 three semesters ago, and 2.6 two semesters ago. The upward trend of grades suggests that the student is working "smarter and harder." This conclusion would be reinforced if you knew that the average GPA for all students in this person's class was 2.6 for each of the four semesters. You still don't know everything about the individual student's academic performance, but the comparative trend data do let you make a more informed judgment than was possible with just the grades from one semester.

WHAT DOES IT MEAN?

1. What does it mean to state that the trend of data is frequently more important than the data itself?

Return on Investment

Objective 2
Understand the importance and calculation of return on investment.

Imagine that you are presented with two investment alternatives. Each investment will be made for a period of one year, and each investment is equally risky. At the end of the year, you will get your original investment back, plus income of $75 from investment A and $90 from investment B. Which investment alternative would you choose? The answer seems so obvious that you believe the question is loaded, so you hesitate to answer—a sensible response. But why is this a trick question? A little thought should make you think of a question to which you need an answer before you can select between investment A and investment B. Your question? "How much money would I have to invest in either alternative?" If the amount to be invested is the same, for example, $1,000, then clearly you would select investment B because your income would be greater than that earned on investment A for the same amount invested. If the amount to be invested in investment B is more than that required for investment A, you would have to calculate the **rate of return** on each investment in order to choose the more profitable alternative.

Rate of return is calculated by dividing the amount of return (the income of $75 or $90 in the above example) by the amount of the investment. For example, using an investment of $1,000 for each alternative:

Investment A:

$$\text{Rate of return} = \frac{\text{Amount of return}}{\text{Amount invested}} = \frac{\$75}{\$1,000} = 7.5\%$$

Investment B:

$$\text{Rate of return} = \frac{\text{Amount of return}}{\text{Amount invested}} = \frac{\$90}{\$1,000} = 9\%$$

Your intuitive selection of investment B as the better investment is confirmed by the fact that its rate of return is higher than that of investment A.

It is important to remember that the example situation assumed the investments would be made for one year. Unless otherwise specified, rate of return calculations assume that the time period of the investment and return is one year.

The rate of return calculation is derived from the interest calculation that you probably learned many years ago. Recall that:

$$\text{Interest} = \text{Principal} \times \text{Rate} \times \text{Time}$$

Interest is the income or expense from investing or borrowing money.
Principal is the amount invested or borrowed.
Rate is the **interest rate** per year expressed as a percent.
Time is the length of time the funds are invested or borrowed, expressed in years.

Note that when time is assumed to be one year, that term of the equation becomes 1/1 or 1, and it disappears. Thus, the rate of return calculation is simply a rearranged interest calculation that solves for the annual interest rate.

Return to the example situation and assume that the amounts required to be invested are $500 for investment A and $600 for investment B. Now which alternative would you select on the basis of rate of return? You should have made these calculations:

Investment A:

$$\text{Rate of return} = \frac{\text{Amount of return}}{\text{Amount invested}} = \frac{\$75}{\$500} = 15\%$$

Investment B:

$$\text{Rate of return} = \frac{\text{Amount of return}}{\text{Amount invested}} = \frac{\$90}{\$600} = 15\%$$

All other things being equal (and they seldom are except in textbook illustrations), you would be indifferent with respect to the alternatives available to you because each has a rate of return of 15% (per year).

Rate of return and riskiness related to an investment go hand in hand. **Risk** relates to the range of possible outcomes from an activity. The wider the range of possible outcomes, the greater the risk. An investment in a bank savings account is less risky than an investment in the stock of a corporation because the investor is virtually assured of receiving her or his principal and interest from the savings account, but the market value of stock may fluctuate widely even over a short period of time. Thus, the investor anticipates a higher rate of return from the stock investment than from the savings account as compensation for taking on additional risk. Yet, the greater risk of the stock investment means that the actual rate of return earned could be considerably less (even negative) or much greater than the interest earned on the savings account. Market prices for products and commodities, as well as stock prices, reflect this basic risk/reward relationship. For now, understand that the higher the rate of return of one investment relative to another, the greater the risk associated with the higher return investment.

Rate of return is a universally accepted measure of profitability. Because it is a ratio, profitability of unequal investments can be compared, and risk/reward relationships can be evaluated. Bank advertisements for certificates of deposit feature the interest rate, or rate of return, that will be earned by the depositor. All investors evaluate the profitability of an investment by making a rate of return calculation.

Return on investment (ROI) is the label usually assigned to the rate of return calculation made using data from financial statements. This ratio is sometimes referred to as the *return on assets*. There are many ways of defining both the amount of return and the amount invested. For now, we use net income as the amount of return and use average total assets during the year as the amount invested. It is not appropriate to use total assets as reported on a single year-end balance sheet because that is the total at one point in time: the balance sheet date. Net income was earned during the entire fiscal year, so it should be related to the assets that were used during

EXHIBIT 3–1   **Condensed Balance Sheets and Income Statement of Cruisers, Inc., a Hypothetical Company**

CRUISERS, INC. Comparative Condensed Balance Sheets September 30, 1999 and 1998			CRUISERS, INC. Condensed Income Statement For the Year Ended September 30, 1999	
	1999	*1998*		
Current Assets:				
Cash and marketable securities	$ 22,286	$ 16,996	Net sales	$611,873
Accounts receivable	42,317	39,620	Cost of goods sold	428,354
Inventories	53,716	48,201	Gross margin	$183,519
Total current assets	$118,319	$104,817	Operating expenses	122,183
Other assets	284,335	259,903	Income from operations	$ 61,336
Total assets	$402,654	$364,720	Interest expense	6,400
Current liabilities	$ 57,424	$ 51,400	Income before taxes	$ 54,936
Other liabilities	80,000	83,000	Income taxes	20,026
Total liabilities	$137,424	$134,400	Net income	$ 34,910
Owners' equity	265,230	230,320		
Total liabilities and owners' equity	$402,654	$364,720	Earnings per share	$ 1.21

the entire year. Average assets used during the year are usually estimated by averaging the assets reported at the beginning of the year (the prior year-end balance sheet total) and assets reported at the end of the year. Recall from Chapter 2 that the income statement for the year is the link between the beginning and ending balance sheets. If seasonal fluctuations in total assets are significant (the materiality concept) and if quarter-end or month-end balance sheets are available, a more refined average asset calculation may be made.

The ROI of a firm is significant to most financial statement readers because it describes the rate of return management was able to earn on the assets that it had available to use during the year. Investors especially will make decisions and informed judgments about the quality of management and the relative profitability of a company based on ROI. Many financial analysts, these authors included, believe that ROI is the most meaningful measure of a company's profitability. Knowing net income alone is not enough; *an informed judgment about the firm's profitability requires relating net income to the assets used to generate that net income.*

Calculation of ROI is illustrated below, using data from the condensed balance sheets and income statement of Cruisers, Inc., a hypothetical company, which are presented in Exhibit 3–1:

From the firm's balance sheets:
Total assets, September 30, 1998 .... $364,720
Total assets, September 30, 1999 .... $402,654
From the firm's income statement for the year ended
September 30, 1999:
Net income .... $ 34,910

$$\text{Return on investment} = \frac{\text{Net income}}{\text{Average total assets}}$$

$$= \frac{\$34,910}{(\$364,720 + \$402,654)/2} = 9.1\%$$

Some financial analysts prefer to use income from operations (or earnings before interest and income taxes) and average operating assets in the ROI calculation. They believe that excluding interest expense, income taxes, and assets not used in operations provides a better measure of the operating results of the firm. With these refinements, the ROI formula would be:

$$\frac{\text{Return on}}{\text{investment}} = \frac{\text{Operating income}}{\text{Average operating assets}}$$

Other analysts will make similar adjustments to arrive at the amounts used in the ROI calculation. Consistency in the definition of terms is more important than the definition itself because the trend of ROI will be more significant for decision making than the absolute result of the ROI calculation for any one year. However, it is appropriate to understand the definitions used in any ROI results that you see.

WHAT DOES IT MEAN?

2. What does it mean to express economic performance as a rate of return?

3. What does it mean to say that return on investment (ROI) is one of the most meaningful measures of financial performance?

The DuPont Model, an Expansion of the ROI Calculation

Objective 3
Understand how to calculate and interpret margin and turnover using the DuPont model.

Financial analysts at E.I. DuPont de Nemours & Co. are credited with developing the **DuPont model,** an expansion of the basic ROI calculation, in the late 1930s. They reasoned that profitability from sales and utilization of assets to generate sales revenue were both important factors to be considered when evaluating a company's overall profitability. One popular adaptation of their model introduces total sales revenue into the ROI calculation as follows:

$$\frac{\text{Return on}}{\text{investment}} = \frac{\text{Net income}}{\text{Sales}} \times \frac{\text{Sales}}{\text{Average total assets}}$$

The first term, net income/sales, is **margin.** The second term, sales/average total assets, is **asset turnover,** or simply **turnover.** Of course, the sales quantities cancel out algebraically, but they are introduced to this version of the ROI model because of their significance. *Margin* emphasizes that from every dollar of sales revenue, some amount must work its way to the bottom line, net income, if the company is to be profitable. *Turnover* relates to the efficiency with which the firm's assets are used in the revenue-generating process.

Another quick quiz will illustrate the significance of turnover. Many of us look forward to a 40-hour-per-week job, generally thought of as five 8-hour days. Imagine a company's factory operating on such a schedule—one shift per day, five days per week. The question: What percentage of the available time is that factory operating? You may have answered 33% or one-third of the time, because eight hours is one-third of a day. But what about Saturday and Sunday? In fact, there are 21 shifts available in a week (7 days × 3 shifts per day), so a factory operating 5 shifts per week is only being used $5/21$ of the time—less than 25%! The factory is idle more than 75% of the time! And as you can imagine, many of the occupancy costs (real estate taxes, utilities, insurance) are incurred whether or not the plant is in use. This explains why many firms operate their plant on a two-shift, three-shift, or even seven-day basis rather than build additional plants—it allows them to increase their level of production and thereby expand sales volume without expanding their investment in assets. The higher costs associated with multiple-shift operations (e.g., late-shift premiums for workers and additional shipping costs relative to shipping from multiple locations closer to customers) will increase the company's operating expenses, thereby lowering net income and decreasing margin. Yet, the multiple-shift company's overall ROI will be higher if turnover is increased proportionately more than margin is reduced, which is likely to be the case.

Calculation of ROI using the DuPont model is illustrated below, using data from the financial statements of Cruisers, Inc., in Exhibit 3–1:

From the firm's balance sheets:
Total assets, September 30, 1998 . . . . $364,720
Total assets, September 30, 1999 . . . . $402,654
From the firm's income statement for
the year ended September 30, 1999:
Net sales $611,873
Net income . . . . $ 34,910

Return on investment = Margin × Turnover

$$= \frac{\text{Net income}}{\text{Sales}} \times \frac{\text{Sales}}{\text{Average total assets}}$$

$$= \frac{\$34,910}{\$611,873} \times \frac{\$611,873}{(\$364,720 + \$402,654)/2}$$

$$= 5.7\% \times 1.6$$

$$= 9.1\%$$

The significance of the DuPont model is that it has led top management in many organizations to consider utilization of assets, including keeping investment in assets as low as feasible, to be just as important to overall performance as generating profit from sales.

A rule of thumb useful for putting ROI in perspective is that average ROI, based on net income, for most American merchandising and manufacturing companies is between 7% and 10%. Average ROI based on operating income (earnings before interest and taxes) for the same set of firms is between 10% and 15%. Average margin, based on net income, ranges from about 7% to 10%. Using operating income, average margin ranges from 10% to 15%. Asset turnover is usually about 1.0 to 1.5 but often ranges as high as 3.0, depending upon the operating characteristics of the firm and its industry.

4. What does it mean when the straightforward ROI calculation is expanded by using margin and turnover?

Return on Equity

Objective 4
Understand how to calculate and interpret return on equity.

Recall that the balance sheet equation is:

$$\text{Assets} = \text{Liabilities} + \text{Owners' equity}$$

The return on investment calculation relates net income (perhaps as adjusted for interest, income taxes, or other items) to assets. Assets (perhaps adjusted to exclude nonoperating assets or other items) represent the amount invested to generate earnings. As the balance sheet equation indicates, the investment in assets can result from either amounts borrowed from creditors (liabilities) or amounts invested by the owners. Owners (and others) are interested in expressing the profits of the firm as a rate of return on the amount of owners' equity; this is called **return on equity (ROE),** and it is calculated as follows:

$$\text{Return on equity} = \frac{\text{Net income}}{\text{Average owners' equity}}$$

Return on equity is calculated using average owners' equity during the period for which the net income was earned for the same reason that average assets is used in the ROI calculation; net income is earned over a period of time, so it should be related to the owners' equity over that same period of time.

Calculation of ROE is illustrated below using data from the financial statements of Cruisers, Inc., in Exhibit 3–1:

From the firm's balance sheets:
  Total owners' equity, September 30, 1998 . . . . $230,320
  Total owners' equity, September 30, 1999 . . . . $265,230
From the firm's income statement for the year ended
  September 30, 1999: . . . .
    Net income . . . . $ 34,910

$$\text{Return on equity} = \frac{\text{Net income}}{\text{Average owners' equity}}$$

$$= \frac{\$34,910}{(\$230,320 + \$265,230)/2}$$

$$= \$34,910/\$247,775$$

$$= 14.1\%$$

A rule of thumb for putting ROE in perspective is that average ROE for most American merchandising and manufacturing companies has historically ranged from 10% to 15%. However, ROE results have improved dramatically in recent years due to America's longest-lasting postwar economic boom, which began in 1991. In the third quarter of 1997, average ROE was 16.8% for the 900 companies reported on in *Business Week*'s Corporate Scoreboard.[1]

Keep in mind that return on equity is a special-case application of the rate of return concept. ROE is important to current stockholders and prospective investors because it relates earnings to owners' investment, that is, the owners' equity in the assets of the entity. Adjustments to both net income and average owners' equity are sometimes made in an effort to improve the comparability of ROE results between firms, and some of these will be explained later in the text. For now, you should understand that both return on investment and return on equity are fundamental measures of the profitability of a firm, and that the data for making these calculations come from the firm's financial statements.

WHAT DOES IT MEAN?

5. What does it mean when return on equity is used to evaluate a firm's financial performance?

Working Capital and Measures of Liquidity

Objective 5
Understand the meaning of liquidity and why it is important.

Liquidity refers to a firm's ability to meet its current obligations and is measured by relating its current assets and current liabilities as reported on the balance sheet. **Working capital** is the excess of a firm's current assets over its current liabilities. Current assets are cash and other assets that are likely to be converted to cash within a year (principally accounts receivable and merchandise inventories). Current liabilities are those obligations that are expected to be paid within a year, including loans, accounts payable, and other accrued liabilities (such as wages payable, interest payable, and rent payable). Most financially healthy firms have positive working capital. Even though a firm is not likely to have cash on hand at any point in time equal to its current liabilities, it will expect to collect accounts receivable or sell merchandise inventory and then collect the resulting accounts receivable in time to pay the liabilities when they are scheduled for payment. Of course, in the process of converting inventories to cash, the firm will be purchasing additional merchandise for its inventory, and the suppliers will want to be assured of collecting the amounts due according to the previously agreed provisions for when payment is due.

Liquidity is measured in three principal ways:

1. Working capital = Current assets − Current liabilities

2. Current ratio = $\dfrac{\text{Current assets}}{\text{Current liabilities}}$

3. Acid-test ratio = $\dfrac{\text{Cash (including temporary cash investments)} + \text{Accounts receivable}}{\text{Current liabilities}}$

---

[1]Source: *Business Week,* November 17, 1997, page 151. Data: *Standard & Poor's Compustat,* a division of the McGraw-Hill Companies.

The dollar amount of a firm's working capital is not as significant as the ratio of its current assets to current liabilities because the amount can be misleading unless it is related to another quantity (e.g., how large is large?). Therefore, it is the *trend* of a company's **current ratio** that is most useful in judging its current bill-paying ability. The **acid-test ratio,** also known as the *quick ratio,* is a more conservative short-term measure of liquidity because merchandise inventories are excluded from the computation. This ratio provides information about an almost worst-case situation—the firm's ability to meet its current obligations even if none of the inventory can be sold.

Liquidity measure calculations are illustrated below using September 30, 1999, data from the financial statements of Cruisers, Inc., in Exhibit 3–1:

Objective 6
Understand the significance and calculation of working capital, the current ratio, and the acid-test ratio.

$$\text{Working capital} = \text{Current assets} - \text{Current liabilities}$$
$$= \$118,319 - \$57,424$$
$$= \$60,895$$

$$\text{Current ratio} = \frac{\text{Current assets}}{\text{Current liabilities}} = \frac{\$118,319}{\$57,424} = 2.1$$

$$\text{Acid-test ratio} = \frac{\text{Cash (including temporary cash investments)} + \text{Accounts receivable}}{\text{Current liabilities}}$$

$$= \frac{\$22,286 + \$42,317}{\$57,424}$$

$$= 1.1$$

As a general rule, a current ratio of 2.0 and an acid-test ratio of 1.0 are considered indicative of adequate liquidity. From these data, it can be concluded that Cruisers, Inc., has a high degree of liquidity; it should not have any trouble meeting its current obligations as they become due.

In terms of debt-paying ability, the higher the current ratio, the better. Yet an overly high current ratio can sometimes be a sign that the company has not made the most productive use of its assets. In recent years, many large, well-managed corporations have made efforts to streamline operations by reducing their current ratios to the 1.2–1.6 range, or even lower, with corresponding reductions in their acid-test ratios. Investments in cash, accounts receivable, and inventories are being minimized because these current assets tend to be the least productive assets employed by the company. For example, what kind of ROI is earned on accounts receivable or inventory? Very little, if any. Money freed up by reducing the investment in working capital items can be used to purchase new production equipment or to expand marketing efforts for existing product lines.

Remember, however, that judgments based on the results of any of these calculations using data from a single balance sheet are not as meaningful as the trend of the results over several periods. It is also important to note the composition of working capital and to understand the impact on the ratios of equal changes in current assets and current liabilities.

the following illustration shows, if a short-term bank loan were repaid just before the balance sheet date, working capital would not change (because current assets and current liabilities would each decrease by the same amount), but the current ratio (and the acid-test ratio) would change.

	Before Loan Repayment	*After $20,000 Loan Repaid*
Current assets	$200,000	$180,000
Current liabilities	100,000	80,000
Working capital	$100,000	$100,000
Current ratio	2.0	2.25

If a new loan were taken out just after the balance sheet date, the level of the firm's liquidity at the balance sheet date as expressed by the current ratio would have been overstated. Thus, liquidity measures should be viewed with a healthy dose of skepticism since the timing of short-term borrowings and repayments is entirely within the control of management.

Measures of liquidity are used primarily by potential creditors who are seeking to make a judgment about their prospects of being paid promptly if they enter into a creditor relationship with the firm whose liquidity is being analyzed (see Business in Practice—Establishing a Credit Relationship).

BUSINESS IN PRACTICE
Establishing a Credit Relationship

Most transactions between businesses, and many transactions between individuals and businesses, are credit transactions. That is, the sale of the product or provision of the service is completed some time before payment is made by the purchaser. Usually, before delivering the product or service, the seller wants to have some assurance that the bill will be paid when due. This involves determining that the buyer is a good **credit risk.**

Individuals usually establish credit by submitting to the potential creditor a completed credit application, which includes information about employment, salary, bank accounts, liabilities, and other credit relationships (e.g., charge accounts) established. Most credit grantors are looking for a good record of timely payments on existing credit accounts. This is why an individual's first credit account is usually the most difficult to obtain. Potential credit grantors may also check an individual's credit record as maintained by the credit bureau in the city in which the applicant lives or has lived.

Businesses seeking credit may follow a procedure similar to that used by individuals. Alternatively, they may provide financial statements and names of firms with which a credit relationship has been established. A newly organized firm may have to pay for its purchases in advance or on delivery **(COD)** until it has been in operation for several months. Then the seller may set a relatively low credit limit for sales on credit. Once a record is

> *Business in Practice concluded*
>
> established of having paid bills when due, the credit limit will be raised. After a firm has been in operation for a year or more, its credit history may be reported by the Dun & Bradstreet credit reporting service—a type of national credit bureau to which many companies subscribe. Even after a credit relationship has been established, it is not unusual for a firm to continue providing financial statements to its principal creditors.

The statement of cash flows is also useful in assessing the reasons for a firm's liquidity (or illiquidity). Recall that this financial statement identifies the reasons for the change in a firm's cash during the period (usually a year) by reporting the changes during the period in noncash balance sheet items.

WHAT DOES IT MEAN?

6. What does it mean to say that the financial position of the firm is liquid?

Illustration of Trend Analysis

Objective 7
Understand how trend analysis can be used most effectively.

Trend analysis of return on investment, return on equity, and working capital and liquidity measures is illustrated in the following tables and exhibits. The data in these illustrations come primarily from the financial statements in the 1996 annual report of Intel Corporation, reproduced in the Appendix.

The data in Table 3–1 come from the 10-year "financial summary" on page 33 of Intel's 1996 annual report and from balance sheets of prior annual reports. The data in Table 3–1 are presented graphically in Exhibits

TABLE 3–1   Intel Corporation (profitability* and liquidity data, 1996–1992)**

	1996	*1995*	*1994*	*1993*	*1992*
Margin (net income/net revenues)	24.7	22.0	19.9	26.1	18.3
Turnover (net revenues/average total assets)	1.01	1.03	0.92	0.90	0.81
ROI (net income/average total assets)	25.0	22.8	18.2	23.6	14.8
ROE (net income/average stockholders' equity)	35.6	33.3	27.3	35.5	21.6
Year-end position (in millions):					
Current assets	$13,684	$8,097	$6,167	$5,802	$4,691
Current liabilities	4,863	3,619	3,024	2,433	1,842
Working capital	$ 8,821	$4,478	$3,143	$3,369	$2,849
Current ratio	2.8	2.2	2.0	2.4	2.5

*Profitability calculations were made from the data presented in the 10-year financial summary.
**Liquidity calculations were made from the data presented in the balance sheets of this and prior annual reports.
Source: Intel Corporation, 1996 Annual Report, pp. 19, 33.

EXHIBIT 3–2   Intel Corporation, Return on Investment (ROI) and Return on Equity (ROE), 1992–1996

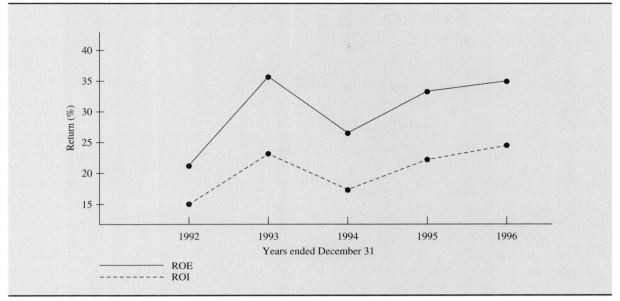

3–2 through 3–4. Note that the sequence of the years in the table is opposite from that of the years in the graphs. Tabular data are frequently presented so the most recent year is closest to the captions of the table. Graphs of time series data usually flow from left to right. In any event, it is necessary to notice and understand the captions of both tables and graphs.

The graph in Exhibit 3–2 illustrates that both ROI and ROE rose sharply in 1993, fell in 1994, recovered in 1995, and continued to move upward in 1996. Relative to other manufacturing companies, Intel's profitability measures were abnormally high during this period, reflecting the firm's continued dominance in the microprocessor industry. Intel's performance in 1996 was driven by a strong demand for its Pentium® and Pentium Pro® processors. Although it is difficult to sustain such high returns year after year, there is no end in sight to Intel's success. In 1996, the firm reported record revenues for the tenth consecutive year, reaching a new milestone of more than $20 billion. Intel also reported record earnings in 1996 for the seventh consecutive year.[2]

Exhibit 3–3 illustrates that margin jumped sharply in 1993 and returned to a more modestly rising trend from 1994 to 1996. Although turnover has not changed by much, it too has edged slightly upward, which is desirable. Ironically, Intel's continual growth in revenues has presented a major challenge for the firm in terms of its ability to increase asset turnover. Because of Intel's future growth opportunities, most of its earnings are reinvested in the business rather than being distributed to stockholders as dividends. Thus, assets (especially cash and short-term investments)

---

[2]See pages 6–7 and 33 in Intel's 1996 annual report in the Appendix.

Exhibit 3–3   **Intel Corporation, Margin and Turnover, 1992–1996**

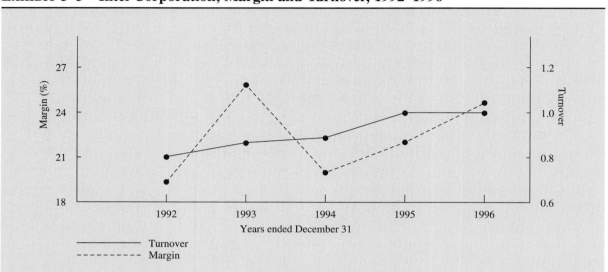

have expanded as rapidly as sales have grown—and since turnover expresses the relationship between assets and sales, it has not increased significantly.

Exhibits 3–2 and 3–3 illustrate a subtle point about graphical presentations. Note that the vertical axis scale of Exhibit 3–3 is about two and one-half times greater than that of Exhibit 3–2. That is, the vertical distance equal to 6 percentage points in Exhibit 3–3 is about equal to the vertical distance of 15 percentage points in Exhibit 3–2. Thus, the slope of the margin line in Exhibit 3–3 is steeper than if the graph had been constructed using the same scale as Exhibit 3–2, and so it looks like margin (in Exhibit 3–3) is changing at a much greater rate than the rates of return plotted in Exhibit 3–2. The visual message conveyed by a graph can be influenced by the scale selected. It is important to note the scale before jumping to a conclusion about the significance of the changes suggested by the slope of the lines on a graph.

The trend in Intel's liquidity position is clearly reflected by the steep upward slope of the working capital and current ratio graphs shown in Exhibit 3–4. Working capital has increased each year since 1992, and the current ratio has now fully recovered after falling from 1992 to 1994. Current assets have increased proportionately more than current liabilities since 1994, causing the current ratio to rise. A primary reason for this is that Intel's stockholders do not demand high dividend payments because the firm has been so profitable. Intel's ROE is much higher than the ROE its stockholders could earn by reinvesting their dividends in other firms. As a consequence, Intel has accumulated large amounts of working capital in excess of its immediate operating needs.

A potential investor in the common stock of Intel Corporation would probably be interested in the company's profitability compared to the industry within which it operates. Table 3–2 summarizes data taken from the

EXHIBIT 3–4   Intel Corporation, Working Capital and Current Ratio, 1992–1996

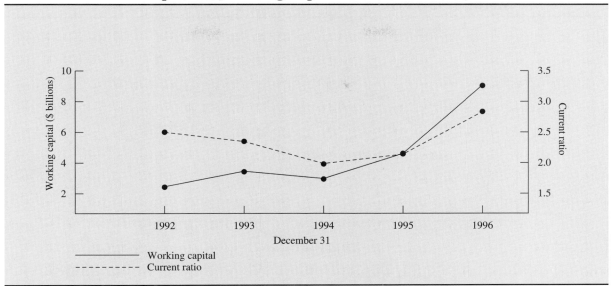

TABLE 3–2   Value Line Investment Survey (percentage earned on net worth, 1992–1996)

Intel Corporation and the Semiconductor Industry				
For the Year				
1996	*1995*	*1994*	*1993*	*1992*
Intel Corporation 30.6	28.8	27.7	30.4	19.8
Semiconductor industry 18.3	22.8	22.3	20.9	13.2

Source: Value Line Investment Survey, Part III, Vol. LIII, no. 7 (October 24, 1997), pp. 1052, 1061. Copyright © 1997 by Value Line Publishing, Inc. Reprinted by Permission; All Rights Reserved. Figures used are estimates. For subscription information to the Value Line Investment Survey please call (800) 833-0046.

Value Line Investment Survey, an investment advisory service. This data is graphed in Exhibit 3–5. Value Line classifies Intel Corporation in the semiconductor industry. Note that the Value Line calculations are based on net worth, a synonym for total owners' equity, and that the amounts are different from the return on common stockholders' equity reported in the 10-year summary of Intel's annual report and in Table 3–1. This definitional distinction will be clarified in a later chapter. Value Line's calculations exclude nonrecurring income statement items such as restructuring charges and the cumulative effect of changes in accounting. The story of the graph in Exhibit 3–5 is that the percentage earned on net worth of Intel Corporation has been improving at a greater rate than that of the industry since 1992.

All of the graphs presented in this chapter use an arithmetic vertical scale. This means that the distance between values shown on the vertical axis is the same. So if the data being plotted increase at a constant rate

Exhibit 3–5   Intel Corporation and Semiconductor Industry, Percentage Earned on Net Worth, 1992–1996

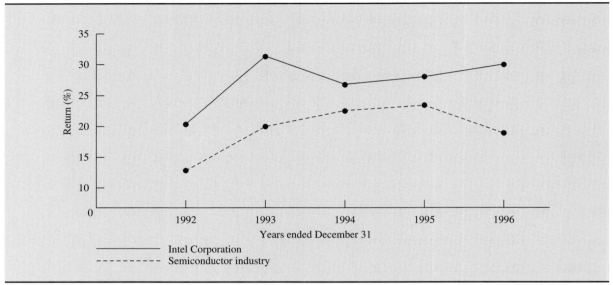

Data courtesy of Value Line Publishing, Inc.

over the period of time shown on the horizontal scale, the plot will be a line that curves upward more and more steeply. Many analysts prefer to plot data that will change significantly over time (a company's sales, for example) on a graph that has a logarithmic vertical scale. This is called a **semilogarithmic graph** because the horizontal scale is still arithmetic. The intervals between years, for example, will be equal. The advantage of a semilogarithmic presentation is that a constant rate of growth results in a straight-line plot. Exhibit 3–6 illustrates this point.

WHAT DOES IT MEAN?

7. What does it mean when the trend of a company's ROE is consistently higher by an approximately equal amount than the trend of ROE for the industry of which the company is a part?

Summary

Financial statement users express financial statement data in ratio format to facilitate making informed judgments and decisions. Users are especially interested in the trend of a company's ratios over time, and the comparison of the company's ratio trends with those of its industry as a whole.

The rate of return on investment is a universally accepted measure of profitability. Rate of return is calculated by dividing the amount of return, or profit, by the amount invested. Rate of return is expressed as an annual percentage rate.

Return on investment (ROI) is one of the most important measures of profitability because it relates the income earned during a period to the assets that were invested to generate those earnings. The DuPont model for calculating ROI expands the basic model by introducing sales to calculate margin (net income/sales) and asset turnover (sales/average assets);

EXHIBIT 3–6 Arithmetic versus Semilogarithmic Graphing Scale

Situation:
Cruisers, Inc., has experienced growth in sales over the past several years, as follows:

Year	Sales (in millions)
1994	$15.0
1995	19.5
1996	25.4
1997	32.9
1998	42.8
1999	55.6

Notice the difference in the visual images being portrayed when these data are plotted using graph paper having an arithmetic scale compared to graph paper having a semilogarithmic scale.

a. Arithmetic scale:

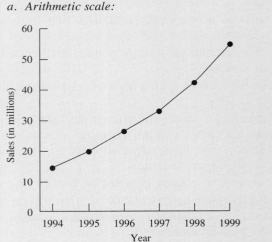

b. Semilogarithmic scale:

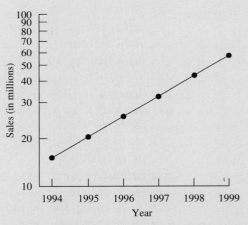

What is your conclusion about the rate of change in sales by looking at each graph? What is the actual rate of sales increase each year?

ROI equals margin × turnover. *Margin* describes the profit from each dollar of sales, and *turnover* expresses the sales-generating capacity (efficiency) of the firm's assets.

Return on equity (ROE) relates net income earned for the year to the average owners' equity for the year. This rate of return measure is important to current and prospective owners because it relates earnings to the owners' investment.

Creditors are interested in an entity's liquidity, that is, its ability to pay its liabilities when due. The amount of working capital, the current ratio, and the acid-test ratio are measures of liquidity. These calculations are made using the amounts of current assets and current liabilities reported on the balance sheet.

When ratio trend data are plotted graphically, it is easy to determine the significance of ratio changes and to evaluate a firm's performance. However, it is necessary to pay attention to how graphs are constructed because the visual image presented can be influenced by the scales used.

Key Terms and Concepts

acid-test ratio (p. 80)   The ratio of the sum of cash (including temporary cash investments) and accounts receivable to current liabilities. A primary measure of a firm's liquidity.

asset turnover (p. 76)   The quotient of sales divided by average assets for the year or other fiscal period.

COD (p. 81)   Cash on delivery, or collect on delivery.

credit risk (p. 81)   The risk that an entity to which credit has been extended will not pay the amount due on the date set for payment.

current ratio (p. 80)   The ratio of current assets to current liabilities. A primary measure of a firm's liquidity.

DuPont model (p. 76)   An expansion of the return on investment calculation to margin $\times$ turnover.

interest (p. 73)   The income or expense from investing or borrowing money.

interest rate (p. 73)   The percentage amount used, together with principal and time, to calculate interest.

liquidity (p. 79)   Refers to a firm's ability to meet its current financial obligations.

margin (p. 76)   The percentage of net income to net sales. Sometimes margin is calculated using operating income or other intermediate subtotals of the income statement. The term can also refer to the *amount* of gross profit, operating income, or net income.

principal (p. 73)   The amount of money invested or borrowed.

rate of return (p. 73)   A percentage calculated by dividing the amount of return on an investment for a period of time by the average amount invested for the period. A primary measure of profitability.

return on equity (p. 78)   The percentage of net income divided by average owners' equity for the fiscal period in which the net income was earned; frequently referred to as *ROE*. A primary measure of a firm's profitability.

return on investment (p. 74)   The rate of return on an investment; frequently referred to as *ROI*. Sometimes referred to as *return on assets*. A primary measure of a firm's profitability.

risk (p. 74)   A concept that describes the range of possible outcomes from an action. The greater the range of possible outcomes, the greater the risk.

semilogarithmic graph (p. 86)   A graph format in which the vertical axis is a logarithmic scale.

trend analysis (p. 72)   Evaluation of the trend of data over time.

turnover (p. 76)   The quotient of sales divided by the average assets for the year or some other fiscal period. A descriptor, such as total asset, inventory, or plant and equipment, usually precedes the turnover term. A measure of the efficiency with which assets are used to generate sales.

working capital (p. 79)   The difference between current assets and current liabilities. A measure of a firm's liquidity.

WHAT DOES IT MEAN?

ANSWERS

1. It means that almost everything is relative, so comparison of individual and group trends is important when making judgments about performance.

2. It means that the economic outcome, i.e., the amount of return, is related to the input, i.e., the investment, made to produce the return.

3. It means that investors and others can evaluate the economic performance of a firm, and make comparisons between firms, by using this ratio.

4. It means that a better understanding of ROI is achieved by knowing about the profitability from sales, i.e., margin, and the efficiency with which assets have been used, i.e., turnover, to generate sales.

5. It means that the focus is changed from return on total assets to return on the portion of total assets provided by the owners of the firm.

6. It means that the firm has enough cash, and/or is likely to soon collect enough cash to pay its liabilities that are now, or soon will be, due for payment.

7. It means that the company is following the industry; it does not necessarily mean that the company is doing better than the industry because the company's higher ROE may be caused by its use of different accounting practices than those used by other firms in the industry.

Exercises and Problems

LO 2

3–1. Compare investment alternatives. Two acquaintances have approached you about investing in business activities in which each is involved. Julie is seeking $560 and Sam needs $620. One year from now, your original investment will be returned, along with $50 income from Julie, or with $53 income from Sam. You can make only one investment.

Required:

a. Which investment would you prefer? Why?

b. What other factors should be considered before making either investment?

LO 2

3–2. Compare investment alternatives. A friend has $1,200 that has been saved from her part-time job. She will need her money, plus any interest earned on it, in six months and has asked for your help in deciding whether to put the money in a bank savings account at 5.5% interest or to lend it to Judy. Judy has promised to repay $1,240 after six months.

Required:

a. Calculate the interest earned on the savings account for six months.

b. Calculate the rate of return if the money is loaned to Judy.

c. Which alternative would you recommend? Explain your answer.

LO 2

3–3. Compare investment alternatives. You have two investment opportunities. One will have a 10% rate of return on an investment of $500; the other will have a 10.5% rate of return on principal of $550. You would like to take advantage of the higher yielding investment but have only $500 available.

Required:

What is the maximum rate of interest that you would pay to borrow the $50 needed to take advantage of the higher yield?

LO 2

3–4. Compare investment alternatives. You have accumulated $800 and are looking for the best rate of return that can be earned over the next year. A bank savings account will pay 6%. A one-year bank certificate of deposit will pay 8%, but the minimum investment is $1,000.

Required:

a. Calculate the amount of return you would earn if the $800 were invested for one year at 6%.

b. Calculate the net amount of return you would earn if $200 were borrowed at a cost of 15%, and then $1,000 were invested for one year at 8%.

c. Calculate the net rate of return on your investment of $800 if you accept the strategy of part *b*.

LO 3   **3–5.   ROI analysis using DuPont model.**

a. Firm A has a margin of 12%, sales of $600,000, and ROI of 18%. Calculate the firm's average total assets.

b. Firm B has net income of $78,000, turnover of 1.3, and average total assets of $950,000. Calculate the firm's sales, margin, and ROI.

c. Firm C has net income of $132,000, turnover of 2.1, and ROI of 7.37%. Calculate the firm's margin.

LO 3   **3–6.   ROI analysis using DuPont model.**

a. Firm D has net income of $27,900, sales of $930,000, and average total assets of $465,000. Calculate the firm's margin, turnover, and ROI.

b. Firm E has net income of $75,000, sales of $1,250,000, and ROI of 15%. Calculate the firm's turnover and average total assets.

c. Firm F has ROI of 12.6%, average total assets of $1,730,159, and turnover of 1.4. Calculate the firm's sales, margin, and net income.

LO 4   **3–7.   Calculate ROE.** At the beginning of the year, the net assets of Jansan Co. were $346,800. The only transactions affecting owners' equity during the year were net income of $42,300, and dividends of $12,000.

Required:

Calculate Jansan Co.'s return on equity (ROE) for the year.

LO 3, 4   **3–8.   Calculate margin, net income, and ROE.** For the year ended December 31, 1999, Metro, Inc., earned an ROI of 12%. Sales for the year were $12 million, and average asset turnover was 2.4. Average owners' equity was $3 million.

Required:

a. Calculate Metro's margin and net income.

b. Calculate Metro's return on equity.

LO 3   **3–9.   ROI analysis using DuPont model.** Charlie's Furniture Store has been in business for several years. The firm's owners have described the store as a "high-price, high-service" operation that provides lots of assistance to its customers. Margin has averaged a relatively high 32% per year for several years, but turnover has been a relatively low 0.4 based on average total assets of $800,000. A discount furniture store is about to open in the area served by Charlie's, and management is considering lowering prices in order to compete effectively.

Required:

a. Calculate current sales and ROI for Charlie's Furniture Store.

b. Assuming that the new strategy would reduce margin to 20%, and assuming that average total assets would stay the same, calculate the sales that would be required to have the same ROI as that currently earned.

LO 3   **3–10.   Applications of ROI using DuPont model; manufacturing versus service firm.** Manyops, Inc., is a manufacturing firm that has experienced strong competition in its traditional business. Management is considering joining the trend to the "service economy" by eliminating its manufacturing operations and concentrating on providing specialized maintenance services to other manufacturers. Management of Manyops, Inc., has had a target ROI of 15% on an asset base that has averaged $6 million. To achieve this ROI, average asset turnover of 2 was required. If the company shifts its operations from manufacturing to providing maintenance services, it is estimated that average assets will decrease to $1 million.

Required:

a. Calculate net income, margin, and sales required for Manyops, Inc., to achieve its target ROI as a manufacturing firm.

b. Assume that the average margin of maintenance service firms is 2.5%, and that the average ROI for such firms is 15%. Calculate the net income, sales, and asset turnover that Manyops, Inc., will have if the change to services is made, and the firm is able to earn an average margin and achieve a 15% ROI.

Intel

LO 3, 4, 6

3–11. **Calculate profitability measures using annual report data.** Using data from the financial statements of Intel Corporation in the Appendix, calculate:

a. ROI for 1996.

b. ROE for 1996.

c. Working capital at December 31, 1996, and December 31, 1995.

d. Current ratio at December 28, 1996, and December 30, 1995.

e. Acid-test ratio at December 28, 1996, and December 30, 1995.

Note: Visit www.intel.com to update this problem with data from the most recent annual report.

LO 3, 4, 6

3–12. **Calculate profitability and liquidity measures.** Presented below are the comparative balance sheets of Hames, Inc., at December 31, 1999, and 1998. Sales for the year ended December 31, 1999, totaled $580,000.

HAMES, INC.
Balance Sheets
December 31, 1999 and 1998

	1999	*1998*
Assets		
Cash	$ 21,000	$ 19,000
Accounts receivable	78,000	72,000
Merchandise inventory	103,000	99,000
Total current assets	$202,000	$190,000
Land	50,000	40,000
Plant and equipment	125,000	110,000
Less: Accumulated depreciation	(65,000)	(60,000)
Total assets	$312,000	$280,000
Liabilities		
Short-term debt	$ 18,000	$ 17,000
Accounts payable	56,000	48,000
Other accrued liabilities	20,000	18,000
Total current liabilities	$ 94,000	$ 83,000
Long-term debt	22,000	30,000
Total liabilities	$116,000	$113,000

Owners' Equity

Common stock, no par, 100,000 shares authorized, 40,000 and 25,000 shares issued, respectively	$ 74,000	$ 59,000
Retained earnings:		
Beginning balance	108,000	85,000
Net income for the year	34,000	28,000
Dividends for the year	(20,000)	(5,000)
Ending balance	$122,000	$108,000
Total owners' equity	$196,000	$167,000
Total liabilities and owners' equity	$312,000	$280,000

Required:

a. Calculate ROI for 1999.
b. Calculate ROE for 1999.
c. Calculate working capital at December 31, 1999.
d. Calculate the current ratio at December 31, 1999.
e. Calculate the acid-test ratio at December 31, 1999.

LO 3, 4, 6   **3–13.   Calculate and analyze liquidity measures.** Following are the current asset and current liability sections of the balance sheets for Freedom, Inc., at January 31, 1999, and 1998 (in millions).

	January 31, 1999	*January 31, 1998*
Current Assets		
Cash	$ 5	$ 2
Accounts receivable	3	6
Inventories	4	8
Other prepaids	2	2
Total current assets	$14	$18
Current Liabilities		
Note payable	$ 3	$ 3
Accounts payable	4	1
Other accrued liabilities	2	2
Total current liabilities	$ 9	$ 6

Required:

a. Calculate the current ratio and working capital at each balance sheet date.
b. Evaluate the firm's liquidity at each balance sheet date.
c. Assume that the firm operated at a loss during the year ended January 31, 1999. How could cash have increased during the year?

LO 6   **3–14.   Calculate and analyze liquidity measures.** Following are the current asset and current liability sections of the balance sheets for Calketch, Inc., at August 31, 1999, and 1998 (in millions).

	August 31, 1999	August 31, 1998
Current Assets		
Cash	$ 3	$ 6
Marketable securities	7	10
Accounts receivable	13	8
Inventories	18	8
Total current assets	$41	$32
Current Liabilities		
Note payable	$ 3	$ 8
Accounts payable	10	14
Other accrued liabilities	9	7
Total current liabilities	$22	$29

Required:

a. Calculate the current ratio and working capital at each balance sheet date.

b. Describe the change in the firm's liquidity from 1998 to 1999.

LO 6

3–15. Effect of transactions on working capital and current ratio. Management of Shady Co. anticipates that its year-end balance sheet will show current assets of $12,639 and current liabilities of $7,480 but is considering paying $3,850 of accounts payable before year-end, even though payment isn't due until later.

Required:

a. Calculate the firm's working capital and current ratio under each situation. Would you recommend early payment of the accounts payable? Why?

b. Assume that Shady Co. had negotiated a short-term bank loan of $5,000 that can be drawn down either before or after the end of the year. Calculate working capital and the current ratio at year-end under each situation, assuming that early payment of accounts payable is not made. When would you recommend that the loan be taken? Why?

LO 6

3–16. Effect of transactions on working capital and current ratio. Metro, Inc., had current liabilities at November 30 of $68,700. The firm's current ratio at that date was 1.8.

Required:

a. Calculate the firm's current assets and working capital at November 30.

b. Assume that management paid $15,300 of accounts payable on November 29. Calculate the current ratio and working capital at November 30 as if the November 29 payment had not been made.

c. Explain the changes, if any, to working capital and the current ratio that would be caused by the November 29 payment.

LO 3, 4, 6

3–17. Analysis of liquidity and profitability measures of Gateway 2000, Inc. The following summarized data (amounts in thousands) are taken from the December 31, 1996 and 1995 comparative financial statements of Gateway 2000, Inc., a direct marketer of personal computers (PCs) and PC-related products:

	1996	1995
For the Year Ended December 31:		
Net sales	$5,035,228	$3,676,328
Cost of goods sold	4,071,601	3,060,533
Operating income	356,094	249,008
Net income	$ 250,679	$ 172,981
At December 31:		
Cash and cash equivalents	$ 516,360	$ 169,429
Accounts receivable, net	449,723	405,283
Inventory	278,043	224,916
Other current assets	74,216	66,561
Property, plant, and equipment, net	242,365	170,263
Software costs, net	77,073	58,477
Other noncurrent assets	35,631	29,082
Total assets	$1,673,411	$1,124,011
Notes payable	$ 15,041	$ 13,564
Accounts payable	411,788	235,064
Accrued liabilities	190,762	108,976
Accrued royalties payable	125,270	123,385
Customer prepayments	16,574	16,397
Income taxes payable	40,334	27,905
Long-term obligations	7,244	10,805
Warranty and other liabilities	50,857	32,396
Common stock and additional paid-in capital	290,280	281,193
Retained earnings	524,712	274,033
Other stockholders' equity	549	293
Total liabilities and stockholders' equity	$1,673,411	$1,124,011

At December 31, 1994, total assets were $770,580 and total stockholders' equity was $376,035.

a. Calculate Gateway 2000, Inc.'s working capital, current ratio, and acid-test ratio at December 31, 1996 and 1995.

b. Calculate Gateway's ROE for the years ended December 31, 1996 and 1995.

c. Calculate Gateway's ROI, showing margin and turnover, for the years ended December 31, 1996 and 1995.

d. Evaluate the company's overall liquidity and profitability.

e. Gateway 2000, Inc., did not declare or pay any dividends during fiscal 1996 or fiscal 1995. What do you suppose is the primary reason for this?

LO 3, 4, 6   **3–18.**   **Analysis of liquidity and profitability measures of Motorola, Inc.** The following summarized data (amounts in millions) are taken from the December 31, 1996 and 1995 comparative financial statements of Motorola, Inc., a manufacturer of wireless communication devices, semiconductors, and advanced electronic systems.

	1996	1995
For the Year Ended December 31:		
Net sales	$27,973	$27,037
Manufacturing and other costs of sales	18,990	17,545
Operating income	1,960	2,931
Net earnings	$ 1,154	$ 1,781
At December 31:		
Cash and cash equivalents	$ 1,513	$ 725
Short-term investments	298	350
Accounts receivable, net	4,035	4,081
Inventory	3,220	3,528
Future income tax benefits	1,580	1,222
Other current assets	673	604
Property, plant, and equipment, net	9,768	9,356
Other assets	2,989	2,872
Total assets	$24,076	$22,738
Notes payable	$ 1,382	$ 1,605
Accounts payable	2,050	2,018
Accrued liabilities	4,563	4,170
Long-term debt	1,931	1,949
Deferred income taxes	1,108	968
Other liabilities	1,247	1,043
Common stock	1,780	1,774
Additional paid-in capital	1,672	1,750
Retained earnings	8,343	7,461
Total liabilities and stockholders' equity	$24,076	$22,738

At December 31, 1994, total assets were $17,495 and total stockholders' equity was $9,055.

a. Calculate Motorola, Inc.'s working capital, current ratio, and acid-test ratio at December 31, 1996 and 1995.

b. Calculate Motorola's ROE for the years ended December 31, 1996 and 1995.

c. Calculate Motorola's ROI, showing margin and turnover, for the years ended December 31, 1996 and 1995.

d. Evaluate the company's overall liquidity and profitability.

The Bookkeeping Process and Transaction Analysis

In order to understand how different transactions affect the financial statements and in turn make sense of the data on the financial statements, it is necessary to understand the mechanical operation of the bookkeeping process. The principal objectives of this chapter are to explain this mechanical process and to introduce a method of analyzing the effects of a transaction on the financial statements.

Learning Objectives

After studying this chapter you should understand:
1 The expansion of the basic accounting equation to include revenues and expenses.
2 How the expanded accounting equation stays in balance after every transaction.
3 How the income statement is linked to the balance sheet through owners' equity.
4 The meaning of the bookkeeping terms *journal, ledger, T-account, account balance, debit, credit,* and *closing the books.*
5 That the bookkeeping system is a mechanical adaptation of the expanded accounting equation.
6 How to analyze a transaction, prepare a journal entry, and determine the effect of a transaction on working capital.
7 The five questions of transaction analysis.

The Bookkeeping/Accounting Process

The bookkeeping/accounting process begins with **transactions** (economic interchanges between entities that are accounted for and reflected in financial statements) and culminates in the financial statements. This flow was illustrated in Chapter 2 as follows:

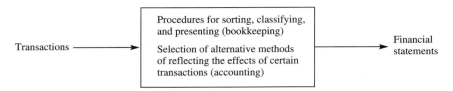

This chapter presents an overview of bookkeeping procedures. Your objective is not to become a bookkeeper but to learn enough about the mechanical process of bookkeeping so you will be able to determine the effects of any transaction on the financial statements. This ability is crucial to the process of making informed judgments and decisions from the financial statements. Bookkeepers (and accountants) use some special terms to describe the bookkeeping process, and you will have to learn these terms. The bookkeeping process itself is a mechanical process, however, and once you understand the language of bookkeeping, you will see that the process is quite straightforward.

The Balance Sheet Equation—A Mechanical Key

You now know that the balance sheet equation expresses the equality between an entity's assets and the claims to those assets:

$$\text{Assets} = \text{Liabilities} + \text{Owners' equity}$$

For present illustration purposes, let us consider a firm without liabilities. What do you suppose happens to the amounts in the equation if the entity operates at a profit? Well, assets (perhaps cash) increase, and if the equation is to balance (and it must), then clearly owners' equity must also increase. Yes, profits increase owners' equity, and to keep the equation in balance, assets will increase and/or liabilities will decrease. Every financial transaction that is accounted for will cause a change somewhere in the balance sheet equation, and the equation will remain in balance after every transaction.

Objective 1
Understand how the accounting equation is expanded to include revenues and expenses.

You have already seen that a firm's net income (profit) or loss is the difference between the revenues and expenses reported on its income statement (Exhibit 2–2). Likewise, you have seen that net income from the income statement is reported as one of the factors causing a change in the retained earnings part of the statement of changes in owners' equity (Exhibit 2–3). The other principal element of owners' equity is the amount of capital invested by the owners, that is, the paid-in capital of Exhibit 2–3. Given these components of owners' equity, it is possible to modify the basic balance sheet equation as follows:

$$\text{Assets} = \text{Liabilities} + \text{Owners' equity}$$

$$\text{Assets} = \text{Liabilities} + \text{Paid-in capital} + \text{Retained earnings}$$

$$\text{Assets} = \text{Liabilities} + \begin{array}{c}\text{Paid-in}\\\text{capital}\end{array} + \begin{array}{c}\text{Retained}\\\text{earnings}\\\text{(beginning}\\\text{of period)}\end{array} + \text{Revenues} - \text{Expenses}$$

To illustrate the operation of this equation and the effect of several transactions, study how the following transactions are reflected in Exhibit 4–1. Note that in the exhibit some specific assets and liabilities have been identified within those general categories, and columns have been established for each.

WHAT DOES IT MEAN?

1. What does it mean to determine "what kind of account" an account is?

Transactions

1. Investors organized the firm and invested $30. (In this example the broad category *Paid-In Capital* is used rather than *Common Stock* and, possibly, *Additional Paid-In Capital.* There isn't any beginning balance in Retained Earnings because the firm is just getting started.)
2. Equipment costing $25 was purchased for cash.
3. The firm borrowed $15 from a bank.
4. Merchandise costing $20 was purchased for inventory; $10 cash was paid and $10 of the cost was charged on account.
5. Equipment that cost $7 was sold for $7; $2 was received in cash, and $5 will be received later.
6. The $5 account receivable from the sale of equipment was collected.

Each column of the exhibit has been totaled after transaction (6). Does the total of all the asset columns equal the total of all the liability and owners' equity columns? (They'd better be equal!)

The firm hasn't had any revenue or expense transactions yet, and it's hard to make a profit without them, so the transactions continue:

7. Sold merchandise inventory that had cost $12 for a selling price of $20; the sale was made **on account** (that is, on credit), and the customer will pay later. Notice that in Exhibit 4–1 this transaction is shown on two lines; one reflects the revenue of $20 and the other reflects the expense, or cost of the merchandise sold, of $12.
8. Wages of $3 earned by the firm's employees are accrued. This means that the expense is recorded even though it has not yet been paid. The wages have been earned by employees (the expense has been incurred) and are owed but have not yet been paid; they will be paid in the next accounting period. The accrual is made in this period so that revenues and expenses of the current period will be matched (the matching concept), and net income will reflect the economic results of this period's activities.

Objective 2
Understand how the expanded accounting equation stays in balance after every transaction.

Again, each column of the exhibit has been totaled, and the total of all the asset columns equals the total of all the liability and owners' equity columns. If the accounting period were to end after transaction (8), the income statement would report net income of $5, and the balance sheet would show total owners' equity of $35. Simplified financial statements for Exhibit 4–1 data after transaction (8) are presented in Exhibit 4–2.

Exhibit 4–1   **Transaction Summary**

	Assets				=	Liabilities		+	Owners' equity			
Transaction	Cash	Accounts Receivable	Merchandise Inventory	Equipment	=	Notes Payable	Accounts Payable	+	Paid-In Capital	Retained Earnings	Revenue	− Expenses
1.	+30								+30			
2.	−25			+25								
3.	+15					+15						
4.	−10		+20				+10					
5.	+2	+5										
6.	+5	−5		−7								
Total	17	0	20	18	=	15	10	+	30	—	—	—
7. Revenues		+20									+20	
7. Expenses			−12									−12
8.							+3					−3
Total	17	20	8	18	=	15	13	+	30		+20	−15

+5

EXHIBIT 4–2   Financial Statements for Exhibit 4–1 Data

Objective 3
Understand how the income statement is linked to the balance sheet through owners' equity.

Exhibit 4–1 Data *Income Statement for* *Transactions (1) through (8)*		*Exhibit 4–1 Data* *Statement of Changes in* *Retained Earnings*	
Revenues	$20	Beginning balance	$ 0
Expenses	(15)	Net income	5
		Dividends	(0)
Net income	$ 5	Ending balance	$ 5

Exhibit 4–1 Data *Balance Sheet after Transaction (8)*			
Assets		**Liabilities & Owners' Equity**	
Cash	$17	Notes payable	$15
Accounts receivable.	20	Accounts payable	13
Merchandise inventory	8	Current liabilities.	$28
Current assets	$45		
Equipment.	18	Owners' equity:	
		Paid-in capital	$30
		Retained earnings	5
		Total owners' equity	$35
		Total liabilities &	
Total assets	$63	owners' equity	$63

Notice especially in Exhibit 4–2 how Net Income on the income statement gets into the balance sheet via the Retained Earnings section of owners' equity. In the equation of Exhibit 4–1, revenues and expenses were treated as a part of owners' equity to keep the equation in balance. For financial reporting purposes, however, revenues and expenses are shown in the income statement. In order to have the balance sheet balance, it is necessary that Net Income be reflected in the balance sheet, and this is done in Retained Earnings. If any retained earnings are distributed to the owners as a dividend, the dividend does not show on the income statement but is a deduction from retained earnings, shown in the statement of changes in retained earnings. This is because a dividend is not an expense (it is not incurred in the process of generating revenue). A dividend is a distribution of earnings to the owners of the firm.

What you have just learned is the essence of the bookkeeping process. Transactions are analyzed to determine which asset, liability, or owners' equity category is affected and how each is affected. The amount of the effect is recorded, the amounts are totaled, and financial statements are prepared.

Bookkeeping Jargon and Procedures

Because of the complexity of most business operations, and the frequent need to refer to past transactions, a bookkeeping system has evolved to facilitate the record-keeping process. The system may be manual or computerized, but the general features are virtually the same.

Objective 4
Understand the meaning of bookkeeping terms, such as *journal, ledger, T-account, account balance, debit, credit,* and *closing the books.*

Transactions are initially recorded in a **journal.** A journal (derived from the French word *jour,* meaning *day*) is a day-by-day, or chronological, record of transactions. Transactions are then recorded in—**posted** to—a **ledger.** The ledger serves the function of Exhibit 4–1, but rather than having a large sheet with a column for each asset, liability, and owners' equity category, there is an account for each category. In a manual bookkeeping system, each account is a separate page in a book much like a loose-leaf binder. Accounts are arranged in a sequence to facilitate the posting process. Usually the sequence is assets, liabilities, owners' equity, revenues, and expenses. A **chart of accounts** serves as an index to the ledger, and each account is numbered to facilitate the frequent written references that are made to it.

The account format that has been used for several hundred years looks like a "T." (In the following illustration, notice the T under the captions for Assets, Liabilities, and Owners' Equity.) On one side of the T, additions to the account are recorded, and on the other side of the T, subtractions are recorded. The **account balance** at any point in time is the arithmetic difference between the prior balance and the additions and subtractions. This is the same as in Exhibit 4–1 where the account balance shown after transactions (6) and (8) is the sum of the prior balance, plus the additions, minus the subtractions.

To facilitate making reference to account entries and **balances** (and to confuse neophytes), the left-hand side of a **T-account** is called the *debit* side, and the right-hand side of a T-account is called the *credit* side. In bookkeeping and accounting, **debit** and **credit** mean left and right, respectively, and nothing more (see Business in Practice—Bookkeeping Language in Everyday English). A record of a transaction involving a posting to the left-hand side of an account is called a *debit entry.* An account that has a balance on its right-hand side is said to have a *credit balance.*

BUSINESS IN PRACTICE
Bookkeeping Language in Everyday English

Many bookkeeping and accounting terms have found their way into the language, especially in the business context. *Debit* and *credit* are no exceptions to this, and some brief examples may stress the left–right definition. The terms *debit* and *credit* are used by banks to describe additions to or subtractions from an individual's checking account. For example, your account is credited for interest earned and is debited for a service charge or for the cost of checks that are furnished to you. From the bank's perspective, your account is a liability; that is, the bank owes you the balance in your account. Interest earned by your account increases that liability of the bank; hence, the interest is credited. Service charges reduce your claim on the bank—its liability to you—so those are debits. Perhaps because of these effects on a checking or savings account balance, many people think that debit is a synonym for bad, and that credit means good. In certain contexts these synonyms may be appropriate, but they do not apply in accounting.

Business in Practice concluded

A synonym for debit that is used in accounting is *charge*. To **charge** an account is to make a debit entry to the account. This usage carries over to the terminology used when merchandise or services are purchased on credit; that is, they are received now and will be paid for later. This arrangement is frequently called a *charge account* because from the seller's perspective, an asset (accounts receivable) is increasing as a result of the transaction, and assets increase with a debit entry. The fact that a credit card is used and that this is called a *credit transaction* may refer to the increase in the purchaser's liability.

An alternative to the credit card that merchants and banks are developing is the "debit card." This term is used from the bank's perspective because when a debit card is used at an electronic point-of-sale terminal, the purchaser's bank account balance will be immediately reduced by the amount of the purchase, and the seller's bank account balance will be increased. As you can imagine, consumers have been reluctant to switch from credit cards to debit cards because they would rather pay later than sooner for several reasons, not the least of which is that they may not have the cash until later.

Objective 5
Understand that the bookkeeping system is a mechanical adaptation of the expanded accounting equation.

The beauty of the bookkeeping system is that debit and credit entries to accounts, and account balances, are set up so that if debits equal credits, the balance sheet equation will be in balance. The key to this is that asset accounts will normally have a debit balance: Increases in assets are recorded as debit entries to these accounts, and decreases in assets are recorded as credit entries to these accounts. For liabilities and owners' equity accounts, the opposite will be true. To illustrate:

Assets		=	Liabilities		+	Owners' Equity	
Debit	*Credit*		*Debit*	*Credit*		*Debit*	*Credit*
Increases	Decreases		Decreases	Increases		Decreases	Increases
+	−		−	+		−	+
Normal balance				Normal balance			Normal balance

It is no coincidence that the debit and credit system of normal balances coincides with the balance sheet presentation illustrated earlier. In fact, the balance sheets illustrated so far have been presented in what is known as the *account format*. An alternative approach is to use the *report format*, in which assets are shown above liabilities and owners' equity.

Entries to revenue and expense accounts follow a pattern that is consistent with entries to other owners' equity accounts. Revenues are increases in owners' equity, so revenue accounts will normally have a credit balance and will increase with credit entries. Expenses are decreases in owners' equity, so expense accounts will normally have a debit balance and will increase with debit entries. Gains and losses are recorded like revenues and expenses, respectively.

The debit or credit behavior of accounts for assets, liabilities, owners' equity, revenues, and expenses is summarized in the following illustration:

Account Name *Account number*

Debit side	*Credit* side
Normal balance for:	Normal balance for:
Assets	Liabilities
Expenses	Owners' equity
	Revenues
Debit entries increase:	Credit entries increase:
Assets	Liabilities
Expenses	Owners' equity
	Revenues
Debit entries decrease:	Credit entries decrease:
Liabilities	Assets
Owners' equity	Expenses
Revenues	

Referring to the transactions that were illustrated in Exhibit 4–1, a bookkeeper would say that in transaction (1), which was the investment of $30 in the firm by the owners, Cash was debited—it increased—and Paid-in Capital was credited, each for $30. Transaction (2), the purchase of equipment for $25 cash, would be described as a $25 debit to Equipment and a $25 credit to Cash. Pretend that you are a bookkeeper and describe the remaining transactions of that illustration.

The bookkeeper would say, after transaction (8) has been recorded, that the Cash account has a debit balance of $17, the Note Payable account has a credit balance of $15, and the Expense account has a debit balance of $15. (There was only one expense account in the example; usually there will be a separate account for each category of expense and each category of revenue.) What kind of balance do the other accounts have after transaction (8)?

The journal was identified earlier as the chronological record of the firm's transactions. The journal is also the place where transactions are first recorded, and it is sometimes referred to as the *book of original entry*. The **journal entry** format is a useful and convenient way of describing the effect of a transaction on the accounts involved, and will be used in subsequent chapters of this text, so it is introduced now and is worth learning now.

The general format of the journal entry is:

Date	Dr. Account Name	Amount	
	Cr. Acccount Name		Amount

Notice these characteristics of the journal entry:

The date is recorded to provide a cross-reference to the transaction.

In many of our examples, a transaction reference number will be used instead of a date; the point is that a cross-reference is provided.

The name of the account to be debited and the debit amount are to the left of the name of the account to be credited and the credit amount. Remember, debit means *left* and credit means *right*.

The abbreviations *Dr.* and *Cr.* are used for *debit* and *credit*, respectively. These identifiers are frequently omitted from the journal entry to reduce writing time and because the indenting practice is universally followed and understood.

It is possible for a journal entry to have more than one debit account and amount, and/or more than one credit account and amount. The only requirement of a journal entry is that the total of the debit amounts equal the total of the credit amounts. Frequently, there will be a brief explanation of the transaction beneath the journal entry, especially if the **entry** is not self-explanatory.

The journal entry for transaction (1) of Exhibit 4–1 would appear as follows:

(1)	Dr. Cash	30	
	Cr. Paid-In Capital.................................		30
	To record investment in the firm by the owners.		

Technically, the journal entry procedure illustrated here is a *general journal entry*. Most bookkeeping systems also use specialized journals, but they are still books of original entry, recording transactions chronologically, involving various accounts, and resulting in entries in which debits equal credits. If you understand the basic general journal entry illustrated above, you will be able to understand a specialized journal if you ever see one.

Transactions generate **source documents,** such as an invoice from a supplier, a copy of a credit purchase made by a customer, a check stub, or a tape printout of the totals from a cash register's activity for a period. These source documents are the raw materials used in the bookkeeping process and support the journal entry.

The following flowchart illustrates the bookkeeping process that we have explored:

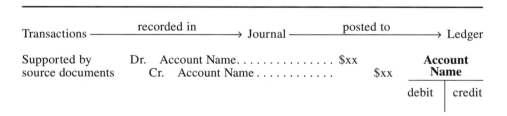

Although microcomputer technology has made it financially feasible for virtually all businesses to automate their accounting functions (see Business in Practice—Computerized Bookkeeping Systems), many small firms

BUSINESS IN PRACTICE
Computerized Bookkeeping Systems

A wide variety of bookkeeping software packages have been developed, ranging from systems focused primarily on budgeting and financial management for individuals, to complex, comprehensive, customized systems used by multinational corporations. The methodology for evaluating and

---

Business in Practice concluded

selecting a system should focus on the end-user's record-keeping processes, decision-making requirements, and informational needs. Once these have been specified, it can be determined which packages should be considered. Important elements to consider in the evaluation include the initial investment and ongoing costs, hardware and personnel requirements, supplier reliability and service levels, and conversion procedures in light of the user's existing accounting system.

In any computerized system, transaction information should be entered only once. For an individual, this may be when a check is written. For a business, this may be when an order is placed with a supplier or when an order is received from a customer. Once the initial transaction data have been entered, the system should be capable of performing all of the necessary bookkeeping steps that follow. More importantly, in today's business environment, the system should be able to use transaction data to develop information that supports the management planning, control, and decision-making processes.

Reviews of bookkeeping and accounting software packages appear regularly in computer and accounting periodicals. Product information, and even downloadable demos, are available at supplier web sites such as www.accpac.com and www.peachtree.com.

---

continue to rely upon manual processing techniques. Understanding basic bookkeeping terminology and appreciating how transactions are recorded will help you to understand any accounting software you may encounter.

WHAT DOES IT MEAN?

2. What does it mean when an account has a debit balance?

3. What does it mean to say that asset and expense accounts normally have debit balances?

4. What does it mean when a liability, owners' equity, or revenue account is credited?

Understanding the Effects of Transactions on the Financial Statements

Objective 6
Understand how to analyze a transaction, prepare a journal entry, and determine the effect of a transaction on working capital.

T-accounts and journal entries are models used by accountants to explain and understand the effects of transactions on the financial statements. These models are frequently difficult for a nonaccountant to use because one must know what kind of account (asset, liability, owners' equity, revenue, or expense) is involved, where in the financial statements (balance sheet or income statement) the account is found, and how the account is affected by the debit or credit characteristic of the transaction.

An alternative to the T-account and journal entry models that should be useful to you is the horizontal financial statement relationship model first introduced in Chapter 2. The **horizontal model** is as follows:

Balance sheet			Income statement		
Assets =	Liabilities +	Owners' equity	← Net income =	Revenues −	Expenses

The key to using this model is to keep the balance sheet in balance. The arrow from net income in the income statement to owners' equity in the balance sheet indicates that net income affects retained earnings, which is a component of owners' equity. For a transaction affecting both the balance sheet and income statement, the balance sheet will balance when the income statement effect on owners' equity is considered. In this model, the account name is entered under the appropriate financial statement category, and the dollar effect of the transaction on that account is entered with a plus or minus sign below the account name. For example, the journal entry shown earlier, which records the investment of $30 in the firm by the owners, would be shown in this horizontal model as follows:

Balance sheet			Income statement		
Assets =	Liabilities +	Owners' equity	← Net income =	Revenues −	Expenses
Cash		Paid-In Capital			
+30		+30			

To further illustrate the model's use, assume a transaction in which the firm paid $12 for advertising. The effect on the financial statements is:

Balance sheet			Income statement		
Assets =	Liabilities +	Owners' equity	← Net income =	Revenues −	Expenses
Cash					Advertising
−12					Expense
					−12

The journal entry would be:

```
Dr.  Advertising Expense...................................  12
     Cr.  Cash .........................................       12
```

Notice that in the horizontal model the amount of advertising expense is shown with a minus sign. This is because the expense reduces net income, which reduces owners' equity. A plus or minus sign is used in the context of each financial statement equation (A = L + OE, and NI = R − E). Thus, a minus sign for expenses means that net income is reduced (expenses are greater), not that expenses are lower.

It is possible that a transaction can affect two accounts in a single balance sheet or income statement category. For example, assume a transaction in which a firm receives $40 that was owed to it by a customer for services performed in a prior period. The effect of this transaction is shown as follows:

	Balance sheet			Income statement	
Assets =	Liabilities +	Owners' equity	← Net income =	Revenues −	Expenses
Cash +40					
Accounts Receivable −40					

The journal entry would be:

```
Dr.  Cash . . . . . . . . . . . . . . . . . . . . . . . . . . . . . . . . . . . . . . . . . . . . . .   40
     Cr.  Accounts Receivable . . . . . . . . . . . . . . . . . . . . . . . . . . . . . . .        40
```

It is also possible for a transaction to affect more than two accounts. For example, assume a transaction in which a firm provided $60 worth of services to a client, $45 of which was collected when the services were provided and $15 of which will be collected later. The effect on the financial statements is:

	Balance sheet			Income statement	
Assets =	Liabilities +	Owners' equity	← Net income =	Revenues −	Expenses
Cash +45				Service Revenues +60	
Accounts Receivable +15					

The journal entry would be:

```
Dr.  Cash . . . . . . . . . . . . . . . . . . . . . . . . . . . . . . . . . . . . . . . . . . . . . .   45
Dr.  Accounts Receivable . . . . . . . . . . . . . . . . . . . . . . . . . . . . . . . . . . .   15
     Cr.  Service Revenues . . . . . . . . . . . . . . . . . . . . . . . . . . . . . . . . . .        60
```

Recall that revenues and expenses from the income statement are increases and decreases, respectively, to owners' equity. Thus, the horizontal model and its two financial statement equations can be combined into the single equation:

$$Assets = Liabilities + Owners'\ equity + Revenues - Expenses$$

Note that the operational equal sign in the horizontal model is the one between assets and liabilities. You can check that a transaction recorded in the horizontal model keeps the balance sheet in balance by mentally (or actually) putting an equal sign between assets and liabilities as you use the model to record transaction amounts.

Spend some time now becoming familiar with the horizontal model (by working Problem 4–1, for example) so it will be easier for you to understand the effects on the financial statements of transactions that you will encounter later in this book, and in the "real world." As a financial statement user (as opposed to a financial statement preparer), you will find that the horizontal model is an easily used tool. With practice, you will also become proficient at understanding how an amount shown on either the balance sheet or income statement probably affected other parts of the financial statements when it was recorded.

WHAT DOES IT MEAN?

5. What does it mean when "the books are in balance"?

Adjustments/Adjusting Entries

After the end of the accounting period, the bookkeeper will probably have to record some **adjusting journal entries.** These entries are made to reflect accrual accounting in the financial statements. As discussed in Chapters 1 and 2, **accrual** accounting recognizes revenues and expenses as they occur, even though the cash receipt from the revenue or the cash disbursement related to the expense may occur before or after the event that causes revenue or expense recognition. Although prepared after the end of the accounting period (when all of the necessary information has been gathered) adjustments are dated and recorded as of the end of the period.

Adjustments result in revenues and expenses being reported in the appropriate fiscal period. For example, revenue may be *earned* in fiscal 1999 from selling a product or providing a service, and the customer/client may not pay until fiscal 2000. (Most firms pay for products purchased or services received within a week to a month after receiving the product or service.) It is also likely that some expenses *incurred* in fiscal 1999 will not be paid for until fiscal 2000. (Utility costs and employee wages are examples.) Alternatively, it is possible that an entity will receive cash from a customer/client for a product or service in fiscal 1998, and the product will not be sold or the service provided until fiscal 1999. (Subscription fees and insurance premiums are usually received in advance.) Likewise, the entity may pay for an item in fiscal 1998, but the expense applies to fiscal 1999. (Insurance premiums and rent are usually paid in advance.) These alternative activities are illustrated on the following time line:

Fiscal 1998	12/31/98	Fiscal 1999	12/31/99	Fiscal 2000
Cash received		Product sold or service provided and revenue earned		Cash received
Cash paid		Expense incurred		Cash paid

There are two categories of adjusting entries:

1. **Accruals**—Transactions for which cash has not yet been received or paid, but the effect of which must be recorded in the accounts in order to accomplish a matching of revenues and expenses, and accurate financial statements.

2. **Reclassifications**—The initial recording of a transaction, although a true reflection of the transaction at the time, does not result in assigning revenues to the period in which they were earned or expenses to the period in which they were incurred, so an amount must be reclassified from one account to another.

The first type of adjustment is illustrated by the accrual of wages expense and wages payable. For example, work performed by employees during March, for which they will be paid in April, results in wages expense to be included in the March income statement and a wages payable liability to be included in the March 31 balance sheet. To illustrate this accrual, assume that employees earned $60 in March that will be paid to them in April. Using the horizontal model, the **accrued** wages adjustment has the following effect on the financial statements:

Balance sheet	Income statement
Assets = Liabilities + Owners' equity ←	Net income = Revenues − Expenses
Wages Payable +60	Wages Expense −60

The journal entry would be:

| Dr. Wages Expense. . . . . | 60 | |
| Cr. Wages Payable. . . . . | | 60 |

Thus, the March 31 balance sheet will reflect the wages payable liability, and the income statement for March will include all of the wages expense incurred in March. Again, note that the recognition of the expense of $60 is shown with a minus sign because as expenses increase, net income and owners' equity (retained earnings) decrease. The balance sheet remains in balance after this adjustment because the $60 increase in liabilities is offset by the $60 decrease in owners' equity. When the wages are paid in April, both the Cash and Wages Payable accounts will be decreased; Wages Expense will not be affected by the cash payment entry because it was already affected when the accrual was made.

Similar adjustments are made to accrue revenues (e.g., for services performed but not yet billed or for interest earned but not yet received) and other expenses including various operating expenses, interest expense, and income tax expense.

The effect on the financial statements, using the horizontal model, of accruing $50 of interest income that has been earned but not yet received is shown as follows:

Balance sheet	Income statement
Assets = Liabilities + Owners' equity ←	Net income = Revenues − Expenses
Interest Receivable +50	Interest Income +50

The journal entry would be:

Dr. Interest Receivable	50	
Cr. Interest Income		50

An example of the second kind of adjustment is the reclassification for supplies. If the purchase of supplies at a cost of $100 during February was initially recorded as an increase in the Supplies (asset) account (and a decrease in Cash), the cost of supplies used during February must be removed from the asset account and recorded as Supplies Expense for February. Assuming that supplies costing $35 were used during February, the reclassification adjustment would be reflected in the horizontal model as follows:

Balance sheet	Income statement
Assets = Liabilities + Owners' equity ← Net income = Revenues − Expenses	
Supplies −35	Supplies Expense −35

The journal entry would be:

Dr. Supplies Expense	35	
Cr. Supplies.		35

Conversely, if the purchase of supplies during February at a cost of $100 was originally recorded as an increase in Supplies Expense for February, the cost of supplies still on hand at the end of February ($65, if supplies costing $35 were used during February) must be removed from the Supplies Expense account for February and recorded as an asset at the end of February. The reclassification adjustment for the $65 of supplies still on hand at the end of February would be reflected in the horizontal model as follows:

Balance sheet	Income statement
Assets = Liabilities + Owners' equity ← Net income = Revenues − Expenses	
Supplies +65	Supplies Expense +65

The journal entry would be:

Dr. Supplies	65	
Cr. Supplies Expense		65

What's going on here? Supplies costing $100 were originally recorded as an expense (a minus 100 in the expense column offset by a minus 100 of cash in the asset column). The expense for February should be only $35 because $65 of the supplies are still on hand at the end of February, so Supplies Expense is reduced to $35 by showing a plus 65 in the expense column. The model is kept in balance by increasing Supplies in the asset column by 65.

Adjustments for prepaid insurance (insurance premiums paid in a fiscal period before the insurance expense has been incurred) and revenues received in advance (cash received from customers before the service has been performed or the product has been sold) are also reclassification adjustments.

Generally speaking, every adjusting entry affects both the balance sheet and the income statement. That is, if one part of the entry—either the debit or the credit—affects the balance sheet, the other part affects the income statement. The result of adjusting entries is to make both the balance sheet at the end of the accounting period and the income statement for the accounting period more accurate. That is, asset and liability account balances are appropriately stated, all revenues earned during the period are reported, and all expenses incurred in generating those revenues are subtracted to arrive at net income. By properly applying the matching concept, the entity's ROI, ROE, and liquidity calculations will be valid measures of results of operations and financial position.

After the adjustments have been posted to the ledger accounts, account balances are determined. The financial statements are prepared using the account balance amounts, which are usually summarized to a certain extent. For example, if the company has only one ledger account for cash, the balance in that account is shown on the balance sheet as Cash. If the company has several separate selling expense accounts (e.g., Advertising Expense, Salesforce Travel Expense, and Salesforce Commissions), these account balances are added together to get the selling expense amount shown on the income statement.

This entire procedure is called **closing the books** and usually takes at least several working days to complete. At the end of the fiscal year for a large, publicly owned company, a period from 4 to 10 weeks may be required for this process because of the complexities involved, including the annual audit by the firm's public accountants.

It should be clear that the bookkeeping process itself is procedural, and that the same kinds and sequence of activities are repeated each fiscal period. These procedures and the sequence are system characteristics that make mechanization and computerization feasible. Mechanical bookkeeping system aids were developed many years ago. Today, there are a large number of computer programs that use transaction data as input and with minimum operator intervention complete the bookkeeping procedures and prepare financial statements. Accounting knowledge and judgment are as necessary as ever, however, to ensure that transactions are initially recorded in an appropriate manner, that required adjustments are made, and that the output of the computer processing is sensible.

WHAT DOES IT MEAN?

6. What does it mean that a revenue or expense must be accrued?
7. What does it mean when an adjusting entry should be made?

Transaction Analysis Methodology

Objective 7
Understand the five questions of transaction analysis.

The key to being able to understand the effect of any transaction on the financial statements is having the ability to analyze the transaction. **Transaction analysis methodology** involves answering five questions:

1. What's going on?
2. What accounts are affected?
3. How are they affected?
4. Does the balance sheet balance? (Do the debits equal the credits?)
5. Does my analysis make sense?

1. *What's going on?* To analyze any transaction, it is necessary to understand the transaction—that is, to understand the activity that is taking place between the entity for which the accounting is being done and the other entity involved in the transaction. This is why most elementary accounting texts, including this one, explain many business practices. It is impossible to understand the effect of a transaction on the financial statements if the basic activity being accounted for is not understood. One of your principal objectives is to learn about business activities.

2. *What accounts are affected?* This question is frequently answered by the answer to "What's going on?" because the specific account name is often included in that explanation. This question may also be answered by a process of elimination. First, think about whether one of the accounts is an asset, liability, owners' equity, revenue, or expense. From the broad category, it is usually possible to identify a specific account.

3. *How are they affected?* Answer this question with the word *increasing* or *decreasing* and then, if you are using the journal entry or T-account model, translate to *debit* or *credit*. Accountants learn to think directly in debit and credit terms after much more practice than you will probably have. Note that when using the horizontal model, the debit/credit issue is avoided.

4. *Does the balance sheet balance?* If the horizontal model is being used, it is possible to determine easily that the balance sheet equation is in balance by observing the arithmetic sign and amounts of the transaction. Remember that the operational equal sign in the model is between assets and liabilities. Alternatively, the journal entry for the transaction can be written, or T-accounts can be sketched, and the equality of the debits and credits can be verified. You know by now that if the balance sheet equation is not in balance, or if the debits do not equal the credits, your analysis of the transaction is wrong!

5. *Does my analysis make sense?* This is the most important question, and it involves standing back from the trees to look at the forest. You must determine whether the horizontal model effects or the journal entry that results from your analysis causes changes in account balances and the financial statements that are consistent with your understanding of what's going on. If the analysis doesn't make sense to you, go back to question number 1 and start again.

Application of this five-question transaction analysis routine is illustrated in Exhibit 4–3, which also illustrates the determination of the effect

EXHIBIT 4–3   Transaction Analysis

Situation:
On September 1, 1999 Cruisers, Inc., borrowed $2,500 from its bank; a note was signed that provided that the loan principal, plus interest, was to be repaid in 10 months.

Required:
a. Analyze the transaction and prepare a journal entry, or use the horizontal model, to record the transaction.
b. Describe the effect of the loan transaction on working capital and the current ratio of Cruisers, Inc.

Solution:
a. Analysis of transaction:
  What's going on? The firm signed a note at the bank and is receiving cash from the bank.
  What accounts are affected? Note Payable (a liability) and Cash (an asset).
  How are they affected? Note Payable is increasing and Cash is increasing.
  Does the balance sheet balance? Using the horizontal model, the effect of the loan transaction on the financial statements is:

Balance sheet	Income statement
Assets = Liabilities + Owners' equity ←	Net income = Revenues − Expenses

Cash   Note Payable
+2,500   +2,500

Yes, the balance sheet does balance; assets and liabilities each increased by $2,500. The journal entry for this transaction, in which debits equal credits, is:

Sept. 1, 1999	Dr. Cash	2,500	
	Cr. Note Payable		2,500
	Bank loan received.		

Does my analysis make sense? Yes, because a balance sheet prepared immediately after this transaction will show an increased amount of cash and the liability to the bank. The interest associated with the loan is not reflected in this entry because at this point Cruisers, Inc., has not incurred any interest expense, nor does the firm owe any interest; if the loan were to be immediately repaid, there would not be any interest due to the bank. Interest expense and the liability for the interest payable will be recorded as adjustments over the life of the loan.

  Let's get a preview of things to come by looking at how the interest would be accrued each month (the expense and liability have been incurred, but the liability has not yet been paid) and by looking at the ultimate repayment of the loan and accrued interest. Assume that the interest rate on the note is 12% (remember, an interest rate is an annual rate unless otherwise specified). Interest expense for one month would be calculated as follows:

$$\text{Annual interest} = \text{Principal} \times \text{Annual rate} \times \text{Time (in years)}$$

$$\text{Monthly interest} = \text{Principal} \times \text{Annual rate} \times \text{Time}/12$$

$$= \$2,500 \times .12 \times 1/12$$

$$= \$25$$

EXHIBIT 4–3   *(continued)*

It is appropriate that the monthly financial statements of Cruisers, Inc., reflect accurately the firm's interest expense for the month and its interest payable liability at the end of the month. To achieve this accuracy, the following adjusting entry would be made at the end of every month of the 10-month life of the note:

Each month-end	Dr. Interest Expense	25	
	Cr. Interest Payable		25
	To accrue monthly interest on bank loan.		

Using the horizontal model, the effect of this adjustment on the financial statements is:

Balance sheet	Income statement
Assets = Liabilities + Owners' equity ←	Net income = Revenues − Expenses
Interest Payable +25	Interest Expense −25
	(A reduction in net income, an increase in expenses)

Remember, a minus sign for expenses means that net income is reduced, not that expenses are reduced. As explained earlier, if the two financial statement equations are combined into the single equation

$$\text{Assets} = \text{Liabilities} + \text{Owners' equity} + \text{Revenues} - \text{Expenses}$$

the equation's balance will be preserved after each transaction or adjustment.

At the end of the 10th month, when the loan and accrued interest are paid, the following entry would be made:

June 30, 2000	Dr. Note Payable	2,500	
	Dr. Interest Payable	250	
	Cr. Cash		2,750
	Payment of bank loan and accrued interest.		

Using the horizontal model, the effect of this transaction on the financial statements is:

Balance sheet	Income statement
Assets = Liabilities + Owners' equity ←	Net income = Revenues − Expenses
Cash Note Payable	
−2,750 −2,500	
Interest Payable	
−250	

Apply the five questions of transaction analysis to both the monthly interest expense/interest payable accrual and to the payment. Also think about

---

EXHIBIT 4–3   *(concluded)*

the effect of each of these entries on the financial statements. What is happening to net income each month? What has happened to net income for the 10 months?

b. *Effect of the loan transaction on working capital and the current ratio:* Remember from the discussion in Chapter 3 that working capital is the arithmetic difference between current assets and current liabilities. Cash is a current asset. The note payable is a current liability because it is to be paid within a year. Because both current assets and current liabilities increased by the same amount when Cruisers, Inc., borrowed $2,500 from the bank, working capital was not affected. The current ratio is the ratio of current assets to current liabilities. Assuming that prior to this transaction the firm had positive working capital, its current ratio would have been greater than 1. Because both current assets and current liabilities have increased by the same amount, the proportionate increase in current assets is less than the proportionate increase in current liabilities. Therefore, the current ratio has decreased. This can be shown by calculating the current ratio using assumed amounts for current assets and current liabilities.

$$\text{Before: Current ratio} = \frac{\text{Current assets}}{\text{Current liabilities}} = \frac{\$10,000}{\$5,000} = 2.0$$

$$\text{After: Current ratio} = \frac{\text{Current assets}}{\text{Current liabilities}} = \frac{\$12,500}{\$7,500} = 1.7$$

You can test this conclusion using other assumed amounts for current assets and current liabilities before the transaction and then increasing each by the borrowed $2,500. If working capital had been negative prior to the transaction (an unusual situation because it reflects very low liquidity), the loan transaction would have increased the current ratio but still would not have affected the amount of working capital.

Query: What happened to working capital each month as interest expense was accrued? What happened to working capital when the loan and accrued interest were paid? What effects did these transactions/adjustments have on Cruisers, Inc.'s, current ratio, assuming that current assets were greater than current liabilities?

---

of a transaction on a firm's working capital. You are learning transaction analysis to better understand how the amounts reported on financial statements got there, which in turn will improve your ability to make decisions and informed judgments from those statements.

Transaction analysis methodology and knowledge about the arithmetic operation of a T-account can also be used to understand the activity that is recorded in an account. For example, assume that the Interest Receivable account shows the following activity for a month:

Interest Receivable

Beginning balance	2,400	Transactions	1,700
Month-end adjustment	1,300		
Ending balance	2,000		

What transactions caused the credit to this account? Since the credit to this asset account represents a reduction in the account balance, the question can be rephrased as: "What transaction would cause Interest Receivable to decrease?" The answer: receipt of cash from entities that owed this firm interest. The journal entry summarizing these transactions is:

Dr. Cash	1,700	
Cr. Interest Receivable.............................		1,700

What is the month-end adjustment that caused the debit to the account? The rephrased question is: "What causes Interest Receivable to increase?" The answer: accrual of interest income that was earned this month. The adjusting journal entry to record this accrual is:

Dr. Interest Receivable	1,300	
Cr. Interest Income		1,300

By using the horizontal model, the effect of this transaction and of the adjustment on the financial statements is:

Balance sheet	Income statement
Assets = Liabilities + Owners' equity ← Net income = Revenues − Expenses	

Transaction:
Cash
+1,700

Interest
Receivable
−1,700

Adjustment:
Interest	Interest
Receivable	Income
+1,300	+1,300

   The T-account format is a useful way of visualizing the effect of transactions and adjustments on the account balance. In addition, because of the arithmetic operation of the T-account (beginning balance +/− transactions and adjustments = ending balance), if all of the amounts except one are known, the unknown amount can be calculated.

   You should invest practice and study time to learn to use transaction analysis procedures and to understand the horizontal model, journal entries, and T-accounts because these are tools used in subsequent chapters to describe the impact of transactions on the financial statements. Although these models are part of the bookkeeper's "tool kit," you are not learning them to become a bookkeeper—you are learning them to become an informed user of financial statements.

WHAT DOES IT MEAN?

8. What does it mean to analyze a transaction?
9. What does it mean to use a T-account to determine what activity has affected the account during a period?

Summary

Financial statements result from the bookkeeping (procedures for sorting, classifying, and presenting the effects of a transaction) and accounting (the selection of alternative methods of reflecting the effects of certain transactions) processes. Bookkeeping procedures for recording transactions are built on the framework of the accounting equation (Assets = Liabilities + Owners' equity), which must be kept in balance.

The income statement is linked to the balance sheet through the retained earnings component of owners' equity. Revenues and expenses of the income statement are really subparts of retained earnings that are reported separately as net income (or net loss). Net income (or net loss) for a fiscal period is added to (or subtracted from) retained earnings at the beginning of the fiscal period in the process of determining retained earnings at the end of the fiscal period.

Bookkeeping procedures involve establishing an account for each asset, liability, owners' equity element, revenue, and expense. Accounts can be represented by a "T"; the left side is the debit side and the right side is the credit side. Transactions are recorded in journal entry format, which is:

Dr. Account Name	Amount
Cr. Account Name	Amount

The journal entry is the source of amounts recorded in an account. The ending balance in an account is the positive difference between the debit and credit amounts recorded in the account, including the beginning balance. Asset and expense accounts normally have a debit balance; liability, owners' equity, and revenue accounts normally have a credit balance.

The horizontal model is an easy and meaningful way of understanding the effect of a transaction on the balance sheet and/or income statement. The representation of the horizontal model is:

Balance sheet	Income statement
Assets = Liabilities + Owners' equity ←	Net income = Revenues − Expenses

The key to using this model is to keep the balance sheet in balance. The arrow from net income in the income statement to owners' equity in the balance sheet indicates that net income affects retained earnings, which is a component of owners' equity. For a transaction affecting both the balance sheet and income statement, the balance sheet will balance when the income statement effect on owners' equity is considered. In this model, the account name is entered under the appropriate financial statement category, and the dollar effect of the transaction on that account is entered with a plus or minus sign below the account name. The horizontal model can be shortened to the single equation:

Assets = Liabilities + Owners' equity + Revenues − Expenses

Adjusting journal entries describe accruals or reclassifications rather than transactions. Adjustments usually affect both a balance sheet account and an income statement account. Adjustments are part of accrual accounting, and they are required to achieve a matching of revenue and expense so that the financial statements reflect accurately the financial position and results of operations of the entity.

Transaction analysis is the process of determining how a transaction affects the financial statements. Transaction analysis involves asking and answering five questions:

1. What's going on?
2. What accounts are affected?
3. How are they affected?
4. Does the balance sheet balance? (Do the debits equal the credits?)
5. Does my analysis make sense?

Transactions can be initially recorded in virtually any way that makes sense at the time. Prior to the preparation of period-end financial statements, a reclassification adjustment can be made to reflect the appropriate asset/liability and revenue/expense recognition with respect to the accounts affected by the transaction (e.g., purchase of supplies) and subsequent activities (e.g., use of supplies).

Key Terms and Concepts

account balance (p. 102)   The arithmetic sum of the additions and subtractions to an account through a given date.

accrual (p. 109)   The process of recognizing revenue that has been earned but not collected, or an expense that has been incurred but not paid.

accrued (p. 110)   Describes revenue that has been earned and a related asset that will be collected, or an expense that has been incurred and a related liability that will be paid.

adjusting journal entry (p. 109)   A journal entry usually made during the process of "closing the books" that results in more accurate financial statements. Adjusting journal entries involve accruals and reclassifications.

balance (p. 102)   See *account balance.*

charge (p. 103)   In bookkeeping, a synonym for *debit.*

chart of accounts (p. 102)   An index of the accounts contained in a ledger.

closing the books (p. 112)   The process of posting transactions and adjustments to the ledger and preparing the financial statements.

credit (p. 102)   The right side of an account. A decrease in asset and expense accounts; an increase in liability, owners' equity, and revenue accounts.

debit (p. 102)   The left side of an account. An increase in asset and expense accounts; a decrease in liability, owners' equity, and revenue accounts.

entry (p. 105)   A journal entry or a posting to an account.

horizontal model (p. 106)   A representation of the balance sheet and income statement relationship that is useful for understanding the effects of transactions and adjustments on the financial statements. The model is:

Balance sheet	Income statement
Assets = Liabilities + Owners' equity	← Net income = Revenues − Expenses

journal (p. 102)   A chronological record of transactions.

journal entry (p. 104)   A description of a transaction in a format that shows the debit account(s) and amount(s) and credit account(s) and amount(s).

ledger (p. 102)   A book or file of accounts.

on account (p. 99)   Used to describe a purchase or sale transaction for which cash will be paid or received at a later date. A "credit" transaction.

post (p. 102)   The process of recording a transaction in the ledger using a journal as the source of the information recorded.

source document (p. 105)   Evidence of a transaction that supports the journal entry recording the transaction.

T-account (p. 102)   An account format with a debit (left) side and a credit (right) side.

transactions (p. 97)   Economic interchanges between entities that are accounted for and reflected in financial statements.

transaction analysis methodology (p. 113)   The process of answering five questions to ensure that a transaction is understood:

1. What's going on?
2. What accounts are affected?
3. How are they affected?
4. Does the balance sheet balance? (Do the debits equal the credits?)
5. Does my analysis make sense?

WHAT DOES IT MEAN?
ANSWERS

1. It means that you are being asked to determine whether the account is for an asset, liability, owners' equity element, revenue, or expense. Frequently, the account classification is included in the account title. In other cases, it is necessary to understand what transactions affect the account.

2. It means that the sum of the debit entries from transactions affecting the account, plus any beginning debit balance in the account, is larger than the sum of any credit entries from transactions affecting the account plus any beginning credit balance in the account.

3. It means that since the balance of these accounts is increased by a debit entry, an asset or expense account will usually have a debit balance.

4. It means that a transaction results in increasing the balance of this kind of account.

5. It means that the sum of all of the debit balances of accounts in the ledger equals the sum of all of the credit balances of accounts in the ledger.

6. It means that revenue has been earned by selling a product or providing a service, or that an expense has been incurred, but that cash has not been received—from a revenue—or paid—for an expense—so an account receivable or an account payable or some other liability must be recognized.

7. It means that a more accurate income statement—matching of revenue and expense—and a more accurate balance sheet will result from the accrual or reclassification accomplished by the adjusting entry.

8. It means that the effect of the transaction on the affected accounts is determined.

9. It means that by sketching a "T" and using arithmetic, if any three of the following are known—balance at the beginning of the period, total debits during the period, total credits during the period, or balance at the end of the period—the fourth can be calculated. The kinds of transactions or adjustments most likely to have affected the account are determined by knowing what the account is used for.

Exercises and Problems

LO 2, 6, 7   **4–1.**   **Record transactions and calculate financial statement amounts.** The transactions relating to the formation of Blue Co. Stores, Inc., and its first month of operations are shown below. Prepare an answer sheet with the columns shown. Record each transaction in the appropriate columns of your answer sheet. Show the amounts involved and indicate how each account is affected (+ or −). After all transactions have been recorded, calculate the total of assets, liabilities, and owners' equity at the end of the month and calculate the amount of net income for the month.

    a. The firm was organized and the owners invested cash of $8,000.

    b. The firm borrowed $5,000 from the bank; a short-term note was signed.

    c. Display cases and other store equipment costing $1,750 were purchased for cash. The original list price of the equipment was $900, but a discount was received because the seller was having a sale.

    d. A store location was rented, and $1,400 was paid for the first month's rent.

    e. Inventory of $15,000 was purchased; $9,000 cash was paid to the suppliers, and the balance will be paid within 30 days.

    f. During the first week of operations, merchandise that had cost $4,000 was sold for cash of $6,500.

    g. A newspaper ad costing $100 was arranged for; it ran during the second week of the stores's operations. The ad will be paid for in the next month.

    h. Additional inventory costing $4,200 was purchased; cash of $1,200 was paid, and the balance is due in 30 days.

    i. In the last three weeks of the first month, sales totaled $13,500, of which $9,600 was sold on account. The cost of the goods sold totaled $9,000.

    j. Employee wages for the month totaled $1,850; these will be paid during the first week of the next month.

    k. Collected a total of $3,160 from the sales on account recorded in transaction *i.*

    l. Paid a total of $4,720 of the amount owed to suppliers from transaction *e.*

Answer sheet:

Assets = Liabilities + Owners' equity

Transaction	Cash +	Accounts Receivable +	Merchandise Inventory +	Equipment =	Notes Payable +	Accounts Payable +	Paid-In Capital +	Retained Earnings +	Revenues −	Expenses

LO 2, 6, 7   **4–2.**   **Record transactions and calculate financial statement amounts.** The following are the transactions relating to the formation of Cardinal Mowing Services,

Inc., and its first month of operations. Prepare an answer sheet with the columns shown. Record each transaction in the appropriate columns of your answer sheet. Show the amounts involved and indicate how each account is affected (+ or −). After all transactions have been recorded, calculate the total of assets, liabilities, and owners' equity at the end of the month and calculate the amount of net income for the month.

a. The firm was organized and the owners invested cash of $600.

b. The company borrowed $900 from a relative of the owners; a short-term note was signed.

c. Two lawn mowers costing $480 each and a trimmer costing $130 were purchased for cash. The original list price of each mower was $610, but a discount was received because the seller was having a sale.

d. Gasoline, oil, and several packages of trash bags were purchased for cash of $90.

e. Advertising flyers announcing the formation of the business and a newspaper ad were purchased. The cost of these items, $170, will be paid in 30 days.

f. During the first two weeks of operations, 47 lawns were mowed. The total revenue for this work was $705; $465 was collected in cash and the balance will be received within 30 days.

g. Employees were paid $420 for their work during the first two weeks.

h. Additional gasoline, oil, and trash bags costing $110 were purchased for cash.

i. In the last two weeks of the first month, revenues totaled $920, of which $375 was collected.

j. Employee wages for the last two weeks totaled $510; these will be paid during the first week of the next month.

k. It was determined that at the end of the month the cost of the gasoline, oil, and trash bags still on hand was $30.

l. Customers paid a total of $150 due from mowing services provided during the first two weeks. The revenue for these services was recognized in transaction *f.*

Answer sheet:

Assets = Liabilities + Owners' equity

Transaction	Cash	+ Accounts Receivable	+ Supplies	+ Equipment	= Notes Payable	+ Accounts Payable	+ Paid-In Capital	+ Retained Earnings	+ Revenues	− Expenses

---

LO 6	**4–3.**	**Write journal entries.** Write the journal entry(ies) for each of the transactions of Problem 4–1.

LO 6	**4–4.**	**Write journal entries.** Write the journal entry(ies) for each of the transactions of Problem 4–2.

LO 2, 6, 7	**4–5.**	**Record transactions and adjustments.** Prepare an answer sheet with the column headings shown on the next page. Record the effect, if any, of the transaction entry or adjusting entry on the appropriate balance sheet category or on the income statement by entering the account name, amount, and indicating whether it is an addition (+) or subtraction (−). Column headings reflect the expanded balance sheet equation; items that affect net income should not be shown as affecting owners' equity. The first transaction is provided as an illustration. *Note: As an alternative to using the horizontal model format, you may write the journal entry for each transaction or adjustment.*

a. During the month, the Supplies (asset) account was debited $1,800 for supplies purchased. The cost of supplies actually used during the month was $1,400.

b. Paid an insurance premium of $480 for the coming year. Prepaid Insurance was debited.

c. Paid $3,200 of wages for the current month.

d. Received $250 of interest income for the current month.

e. Accrued $700 of commissions payable to sales staff for the current month.

f. Accrued $130 of interest expense at the end of the month.

g. Received $2,100 on accounts receivable accrued at the end of the prior month.

h. Purchased $600 of merchandise inventory from a supplier on account.

i. Paid $160 of interest expense for the month.

j. Accrued $800 of wages at the end of the current month.

k. Paid $500 of accounts payable.

Transaction/ Situation	Assets	Liabilities	Owners' Equity	Net Income
a.	Supplies −1,400			Supplies Exp. −1,400 *(Note: An increase to Supplies Expense decreases Net Income.)*

LO 2, 6, 7   **4–6.**   **Record transactions and adjustments.** Prepare an answer sheet with the column headings shown on the next page. Record the effect, if any, of the transaction entry or adjusting entry on the appropriate balance sheet category or on the income statement by entering the account name, amount, and indicating whether it is an addition (+) or subtraction (−). Column headings reflect the expanded balance sheet equation; items that affect net income should not be shown as affecting owners' equity. The first transaction is provided as an illustration. *Note: As an alternative to using the horizontal model format, you may write the journal entry for each transaction or adjustment.*

a. During the month, Supplies Expense was debited $1,800 for supplies purchased. The cost of supplies actually used during the month was $1,400.

b. During the month, the board of directors declared a cash dividend of $2,500, payable next month.

c. Employees were paid $2,100 in wages for their work during the first three weeks of the month.

d. Employee wages of $550 for the last week of the month have not been recorded.

e. Merchandise that cost $680 was sold for $1,420. Of this amount, $1,100 was received in cash and the balance is expected to be received within 30 days.

f. A contract was signed with a newspaper for a $200 advertisement; the ad ran during this month but will not be paid for until next month.

g. Revenues from services performed during the month totaled $5,100. Of this amount, $2,600 was received in cash and the balance is expected to be received within 30 days.

h. During the month, supplies were purchased at a cost of $220, and debited to the Supplies (asset) account. A total of $130 of supplies were used during the month.

i. Interest of $270 has been earned on a note receivable but has not yet been received.

j. Issued 400 shares of $10 par value common stock for $6,400 in cash.

Transaction/ Situation	Assets	Liabilities	Owners' Equity	Net Income
a.	Supplies +400			Supplies Exp. +400 *(Note: A decrease to Supplies Expense increases Net Income.)*

LO 2, 6, 7   **4–7.   Record transactions and adjustments.** Enter the following column headings across the top of a sheet of paper:

Transaction/ Situation	Assets	Liabilities	Owners' Equity	Net Income

Enter the transaction/situation number in the first column and show the effect, if any, of the transaction entry or adjusting entry on the appropriate balance sheet category or on the income statement by entering the amount and indicating whether it is an addition (+) or a subtraction (−). Column headings reflect the expanded balance sheet equation; items that affect net income should not be shown as affecting owners' equity. In some cases, only one column may be affected because all of the specific accounts affected by the transaction are included in that category. Transaction *a* has been done as an illustration. *Note: As an alternative to using the horizontal model, you may write the journal entry for each transaction or adjustment.*

a. Provided services to a client on account; revenues totaled $550.

b. Paid an insurance premium of $360 for the coming year. An asset, Prepaid Insurance, was debited.

c. Recognized insurance expense for one month from the above premium via a reclassification adjusting entry.

d. Paid $800 of wages accrued at the end of the prior month.

e. Paid $2,600 of wages for the current month.

f. Accrued $600 of wages at the end of the current month.

g. Received cash of $1,500 on accounts receivable accrued at the end of the prior month.

Transaction/ Situation	Assets	Liabilities	Owners' Equity	Net Income
a.	+550			+550

LO 2, 6, 7   **4–8.   Record transactions and adjustments.** Enter the following column headings across the top of a sheet of paper:

Transaction/ Situation	Assets	Liabilities	Owners' Equity	Net Income

Enter the transaction/situation number in the first column and show the effect, if any, of the transaction entry or adjusting entry on the appropriate balance sheet category or on the income statement by entering the amount and indicating whether it is an addition (+) or a subtraction (−). Column headings reflect the expanded balance sheet equation; items that affect net income should not be shown as affecting owners' equity. In some cases, only one column may be affected because all of the specific accounts affected by the transaction are included in that category. Transaction *a* has been done as an illustration. *Note: As an alternative to using the horizontal model, you may write the journal entry for each transaction or adjustment.*

a. During the month, Supplies Expense was debited $1,800 for supplies purchased. The cost of supplies actually used during the month was $1,400.

b. During the month, Supplies (asset) was debited $1,800 for supplies purchased. The total cost of supplies actually used during the month was $1,400.

c. Received $800 of cash from clients for services provided during the current month.

d. Paid $500 of accounts payable.

e. Received $300 of cash from clients for revenues accrued at the end of the prior month.

f. Received $900 of interest income accrued at the end of the prior month.

g. Received $1,200 of interest income for the current month.

h. Accrued $700 of interest income earned in the current month.

i. Paid $1,900 of interest expense for the current month.

j. Accrued $600 of interest expense at the end of the current month.

k. Accrued $2,500 of commissions payable to sales staff for the current month.

Transaction/ Situation	Assets	Liabilities	Owners' Equity	Net Income
a.	+400			+400

LO 2, 6, 7

4–9. Record transactions. Use the horizontal model, or write the journal entry, for each of the following transactions that occurred during the first year of operations at Kissick Co.

a. Issued 200,000 shares of $5-par-value common stock for $1,000,000 in cash.

b. Borrowed $500,000 from the Oglesby National Bank and signed a 12% note due in two years.

c. Incurred and paid $380,000 in salaries for the year.

d. Purchased $640,000 of merchandise inventory on account during the year.

e. Sold inventory costing $580,000 for a total of $910,000, all on credit.

f. Paid rent of $110,000 on the sales facilities during the first 11 months of the year.

g. Purchased $150,000 of store equipment, paying $50,000 in cash and agreeing to pay the difference within 90 days.

h. Paid the entire $100,000 owed for store equipment, and $620,000 of the amount due to suppliers for credit purchases previously recorded.

i. Incurred and paid utilities expense of $36,000 during the year.

j. Collected $825,000 in cash from customers during the year for credit sales previously recorded.

k. At year-end, accrued $60,000 of interest on the note due to Oglesby National Bank.

l. At year-end, accrued $10,000 of past-due December rent on the sales facilities.

LO 1

4–10. Prepare an income statement and balance sheet from transaction data.

a. Based on your answers to Problem 4–9, prepare an income statement (ignoring income taxes) for Kissick Co.'s first year of operations and a balance sheet as of the end of the year. *(Hint: You may find it helpful to prepare T-accounts for each account affected by the transactions.)*

b. Provide a brief written evaluation of Kissick Co.'s results from operations for the year and its financial position at the end of the year. In your opinion, what are the likely explanations for the company's net loss?

LO 3   **4–11.**   **Calculate retained earnings.** On February 1, 1999, the balance of the retained earnings account of Blue Power Corporation was $630,000. Revenues for February totaled $123,000, of which $115,000 was collected in cash. Expenses for February totaled $131,000, of which $108,000 was paid in cash. Dividends declared and paid during February were $12,000.

     Required:

Calculate the retained earnings balance at February 28, 1999.

LO 6, 7   **4–12.**   **Cash receipts versus revenues.** During the month of April, Macon Co. had cash receipts from customers of $79,000. Expenses totaled $52,000, and accrual basis net income was $14,000. There were no gains or losses during the month.

     Required:

    a. Calculate the revenues for Macon Co. for April.

    b. Explain why cash receipts from customers can be different from revenues.

LO 6, 7   **4–13.**   **Calculate income from operations and net income.** Selected information taken from the financial statements of Verbeke Co. for the year ended December 31, 1999, is presented below:

Gross profit	$412,000
General and administrative expenses	83,000
Net cash used by investing activities	106,000
Dividends paid	51,000
Extraordinary loss from an earthquake, net of tax savings of $25,000	61,000
Net sales	741,000
Advertising expense	76,000
Accounts payable	101,000
Income tax expense	83,000
Other selling expenses	42,000

    a. Calculate income from operations (operating income) for the year ended December 31, 1999. *(Hint: You may wish to review Exhibit 2–2.)*

    b. Calculate net income for the year ended December 31, 1999.

LO 6, 7   **4–14.**   **Calculate income from operations and net income.** Selected information taken from the financial statements of Graff Co. for the year ended December 31, 1999, is presented below:

Net cash provided by operations	$ 38,000
Cost of goods sold	131,000
Selling, general, and administrative expenses	45,000
Accounts payable	36,000
Extraordinary gain from early retirement of bonds, net of tax expense of $12,000	44,000
Research and development expenses	27,000
Net loss from discontinued operations, net of tax savings of $20,000	63,000
Provision for income taxes	17,000
Net sales	367,000
Interest expense	41,000

a. Calculate income from operations (operating income) for the year ended December 31, 1999. *(Hint: You may wish to review Exhibit 2–2.)*

b. Calculate net income for the year ended December 31, 1999.

LO 6, 7   **4–15.**   **Notes receivable—interest accrual and collection.** On April 1, 1999, Tabor Co. received a $6,000 note from a customer in settlement of a $6,000 account receivable from that customer. The note bore interest at the rate of 15% per annum, and the note plus interest was payable March 31, 2000.

Required:

a. Write the journal entry to record receipt of the note on April 1, 1999.

b. Write the journal (adjusting) entry to accrue interest at December 31, 1999.

c. Write the journal entry to record collection of the note and interest on March 31, 2000.

(Note: As an alternative to writing journal entries, use the horizontal model to show the transactions and adjustments.)

LO 6, 7   **4–16.**   **Notes payable—interest accrual and payment.** Proco had an account payable of $4,200 due to Shirmoo, Inc., one of its suppliers. The amount was due to be paid on January 31. Proco did not have enough cash on hand then to pay the amount due, so Proco's treasurer called Shirmoo's treasurer and agreed to sign a note payable for the amount due. The note was dated February 1, had an interest rate of 9% per annum, and was payable with interest on May 31.

Required:

Write the journal entry that would be appropriate for Proco to record on:

a. February 1, to show that the account payable had been changed to a note payable.

b. March 31, to accrue interest expense for February and March.

c. May 31, to record payment of the note and all of the interest due to Shirmoo.

(Note: As an alternative to writing journal entries, use the horizontal model to show the transactions and adjustments.)

LO 6, 7   **4–17.**   **Alternative adjusting entries—supplies.** On January 10, 1999, the first day of the spring semester, the cafeteria of The Defiance College purchased for cash enough paper napkins to last the entire 16-week semester. The total cost was $4,800.

Required:

a. Write the journal entry to record the purchase of the paper napkins, assuming that the purchase was initially recorded as an expense.

b. At January 31, it was estimated that the cost of the paper napkins used during the first three weeks of the semester totaled $950. Write the adjusting journal entry that should be made as of January 31 so that the appropriate amount of expense will be shown in the income statement for the month of January.

c. Write the journal entry to show the alternative way of recording the initial purchase of napkins.

d. Write the adjusting journal entry that would be appropriate at January 31 if the initial purchase had been recorded as in *c.*

e. Consider the effects that entries *a* and *b* would have on the financial statements of The Defiance College. Compare these effects to those that would be caused by entries *c* and *d.* Are there any differences between these alternative sets of entries on the:

1. Income statement for the month of January?

2. Balance sheet at January 31?

(Note: As an alternative to writing journal entries, use the horizontal model to show the transactions and adjustments.)

LO 6, 7   **4–18.   Alternative adjusting entries—rent.** Calco, Inc., rents its store location. Rent is $950 per month, payable quarterly in advance. On July 1, a check for $2,850 was issued to the landlord for the July–September quarter.

Required:

a. Write the journal entry to record the payment, assuming that all $2,850 is initially recorded as Rent Expense.

b. Write the adjusting journal entry that would be appropriate at July 31 if your entry in *a* had been made.

c. Write the journal entry to record the initial payment as Prepaid Rent.

d. Write the adjusting journal entry that would be appropriate at July 31 if your entry in *c* had been made.

e. Write the adjusting journal entry that would be appropriate at August 31 and September 30, regardless of how the initial payment had been recorded.

f. If you were supervising the bookkeeper, how would you suggest that the July 1 payment be recorded? Explain your answer.

(Note: As an alternative to writing journal entries, use the horizontal model to show the transactions and adjustments.)

LO 6, 7   **4–19.   Make corrections and adjustments to income statement and balance sheet.** Big Blue Rental Corp. provides rental agent services to apartment building owners. Big Blue Rental Corp.'s preliminary income statement for August, 1999, and its August 31, 1999, preliminary balance sheet, did not reflect the following:

a. Rental commissions of $200 had been earned in August but had not yet been received from or billed to building owners.

b. When supplies are purchased, their cost is recorded as an asset. As supplies are used, a record of those used is kept. The record sheet shows that $180 of supplies were used in August.

c. Interest on the note payable is to be paid on May 31 and November 30. Interest for August has not been accrued—that is, it has not yet been recorded. (The Interest Payable of $40 on the balance sheet is the amount of the accrued liability at July 31.) The interest rate on this note is 10%.

d. Wages of $130 for the last week of August have not been recorded.

e. The Rent Expense of $510 represents rent for August, September, and October, which was paid early in August.

f. Interest of $140 has been earned on notes receivable but has not yet been received.

g. Late in August, the board of directors met and declared a cash dividend of $1,400, payable September 10. Once declared, the dividend is a liability of the corporation until it is paid.

| | | Adjustments/Corrections | | |
BIG BLUE RENTAL CORP. **Income Statement—August**	*Preliminary*	*Debit*	*Credit*	*Final*
Commissions revenue	$ 4,500	$	$	$
Interest revenue	850			
Total revenue	$ 5,350	$	$	$
Rent expense	$ 510	$	$	$
Wages expense	1,190			
Supplies expense	—			
Interest expense	—			
Total expenses	$ 1,700	$	$	$
Net income	$ 3,650	$	$	$

BIG BLUE RENTAL CORP. Balance Sheet—August 31, 1999	Preliminary	Debit	Credit	Final
		Adjustments/Corrections		
Cash	$ 400	$	$	$
Notes receivable	13,000			
Commissions receivable	—			
Interest receivable	—			
Prepaid rent	—			
Supplies	650			
Total assets	$14,050	$	$	$
Accounts payable	$ 120	$	$	$
Notes payable	2,400			
Interest payable	40			
Wages payable	—			
Dividends payable	—			
Total liabilities	$ 2,560	$	$	$
Paid-in capital	$ 2,400	$	$	$
Retained earnings:				
Balance, August 1	$ 5,440	$	$	$
Net income	3,650			
Dividends	—			
Balance, August 31	$ 9,090	$	$	$
Total owners' equity	$11,490	$	$	$
Total liabilities and owners' equity	$14,050	$	$	$

Required:

Using the columns provided on the income statement and balance sheet for Big Blue Rental Corp., make the appropriate adjustments/corrections to the statements, and enter the correct amount in the Final column. Key your adjustments/corrections with the letter of the item in the above list. Captions/account names that you will have to use are on the statements. *(Hints: Use the five questions of transaction analysis. What is the relationship between net income and the balance sheet?)*

LO 6, 7   **4–20. Effects of adjusting entries.** A bookkeeper prepared the year-end financial statements of Giftwrap, Inc. The income statement showed net income of $16,400, and the balance sheet showed ending retained earnings of $83,000. The firm's accountant reviewed the bookkeeper's work and determined that adjusting entries should be made that would increase revenues by $3,000 and increase expenses by $5,700.

Required:

Calculate the amounts of net income and retained earnings after the above adjustments are recorded.

LO 6, 7   **4–21. Transaction analysis using T-accounts.** This exercise provides practice in understanding the operation of T-accounts and transaction analysis. For each situation, you must solve for a missing amount. Use a T-account for the balance sheet account, prepare journal entries for the information provided, and show the effect of each entry in the account. In each case, there is only one debit entry and one credit entry in the account during the month.

Example:
Accounts Payable had a balance of $3,000 at the beginning of the month and $2,700 at the end of the month. During the month, payments to suppliers amounted to $8,000. Calculate the purchases on account during the month.

Solution:

Accounts Payable						
Payment	8,000	Beginning balance	3,000			
		Purchase	? = 7,700			
		Ending balance	2,700			

Dr. Accounts
    Payable   8,000
  Cr. Cash   8,000
    Payments to suppliers.

Dr. Inventory   7,700
  Cr. Accounts
    Payable   7,700
    Purchases on account.

a. Accounts Receivable had a balance of $1,200 at the beginning of the month and $900 at the end of the month. Credit sales totaled $12,000 during the month. Calculate the cash collected from customers during the month, assuming that all sales were made on account.

b. The Supplies account had a balance of $540 at the beginning of the month and $730 at the end of the month. The cost of supplies used during the month was $2,340. Calculate the cost of supplies purchased during the month.

c. Wages Payable had a balance of $410 at the beginning of the month. During the month, $3,800 of wages were paid to employees. Wages Expense accrued during the month totaled $4,100. Calculate the balance of Wages Payable at the end of the month.

LO 6, 7

4–22.   T-account analysis. Answer these questions that are related to the Interest Payable T-account shown below:
a. What is the amount of the February 28 adjustment?
b. What account would most likely have been credited for the amount of the February transactions?
c. What account would most likely have been debited for the amount of the February 28 adjustment?
d. Why would this adjusting entry have been made?

Interest Payable			
February transactions	1,500	February 1 balance	1,200
		February 28 adjustment	?
		February 28 balance	2,100

4–23.   Effect of adjusting entries on net income. Assume that Cater Co.'s accountant neglected to record the payroll expense accrual adjusting entry at the end of October.

LO 6, 7

Required:
a. Explain the effect of this omission on net income reported for October.
b. Explain the effect of this omission on net income reported for November.
c. Explain the effect of this omission on total net income for the two months of October and November taken together.
d. Explain why the accrual adjusting entry should have been recorded as of October 31.

LO 6, 7   **4–24. Analyze several accounts using Intel Corporation annual report data.** Set up a horizontal model in the following format:

Intel	Assets			Liabilities	Revenues	Expenses	
	Cash and Cash Equivalents	Accounts Receivable, Net	Inventories	Accounts Payable	Net Revenues	Cost of Goods Sold	Marketing, General and Administrative Expenses
Beginning balance							
Net revenues							
Cost of goods sold							
Marketing, general and administrative expenses							
Purchases on account							
Collections of accounts receivable							
Payment of accounts payable							
Ending balance							

Required:

a. Enter the beginning (December 30, 1995) and ending (December 28, 1996) account balances for Accounts Receivable, Inventories, and Accounts Payable. Find these amounts on the balance sheet for Intel Corporation in the Appendix.

b. From the income statement for Intel Corporation for the year ended December 28, 1996, in the Appendix, record the following transactions in the model:

Net Revenues, assuming all revenues were made on account.

Cost of Goods Sold, assuming all costs were transferred from inventories.

Marketing, General and Administrative Expenses, assuming all of these expenses were accrued in the Accounts Payable liability account as they were incurred.

c. Assuming that the only other transactions affecting these balance sheet accounts were those described below, calculate the amount of each transaction:

Purchases of inventories on account.

Collection of accounts receivable.

Payment of accounts payable.

4–25. Capstone analytical problem for Chapters 2–4. Calculate liquidity and profitability measures and explain various financial statement relationships for a realty firm. DeBauge Realtors, Inc., is a realty firm owned by Jeff and Kristi DeBauge. The DeBauge family owns 100% of the corporation's stock. The

LO 6, 7

following summarized data (in thousands) are taken from the December 31, 1999, financial statements:

For the Year Ended December 31, 1999:

Commissions revenue	$142
Cost of services provided	59
Advertising expense	28
Operating income	$ 55
Interest expense	5
Income tax expense	16
Net income	$ 34

At December 31, 1999:

Cash and short-term investments	$ 30
Accounts receivable, net	40
Property, plant, and equipment, net	125
Total assets	$195
Accounts payable	$ 90
Income taxes payable	5
Notes payable (long term)	50
Paid-in capital	20
Retained earnings	30
Total liabilities and owners' equity	$195

At December 31, 1998, total assets were $205 and total owners' equity was $50. There were no changes in notes payable or paid-in capital during 1999.

Required:

a. What particular expense do you suppose accounts for the largest portion of the $59 cost of services provided?

b. The cost of services provided amount includes all operating expenses (i.e., selling, general, and administrative expenses) except advertising expense. What do you suppose the primary reason was for DeBauge Realtors, Inc., to separate advertising from other operating expenses?

c. Calculate the effective interest rate on the note payable for DeBauge Realtors, Inc.

d. Calculate the company's average income tax rate. *(Hint: You must first determine the earnings before taxes.)*

e. Calculate the amount of dividends declared and paid to Jeff and Kristi DeBauge during the year ended December 31, 1999. *(Hint: Do a T-account analysis of retained earnings.)* What is the company's dividend policy (i.e., what proportion of the company's earnings are distributed as dividends)?

f. DeBauge Realtors, Inc., was organized and operates as a corporation rather than a partnership. What is the primary advantage of the corporate form of business to a realty firm? What is the primary disadvantage of the corporate form?

g. Explain why the amount of income tax expense is different from the amount of income taxes payable.

h. Calculate the amount of working capital and the current ratio at December 31, 1999. Assess the company's overall liquidity.

i. Calculate ROI (including margin and turnover) and ROE for the year ended December 31, 1999. Explain why these single measures may not be very meaningful for this firm.

4–26.

LO 6, 7

Capstone analytical problem for Chapters 2–4. Calculate liquidity and profitability measures and explain various financial statement relationships for an excavation contractor. Gerrard Construction Co. is an excavation contractor. The following summarized data (in thousands) are taken from the December 31, 1999, financial statements:

For the Year Ended December 31, 1999:	
Net revenues	$1,610
Cost of services provided	570
Depreciation expense	325
Operating income	$ 715
Interest expense	190
Income tax expense	160
Net income	$ 365
At December 31, 1999:	
Cash and short-term investments	$ 140
Accounts receivable, net	490
Property, plant, and equipment, net	3,870
Total assets	$4,500
Accounts payable	$ 75
Income taxes payable	80
Notes payable (long term)	2,375
Paid-in capital	500
Retained earnings	1,470
Total liabilities and owners' equity	$4,500

At December 31, 1998, total assets were $4,100 and total owners' equity was $1,630. There were no changes in paid-in capital during 1999.

Required:

a. The cost of services provided amount includes all operating expenses (i.e., selling, general, and administrative expenses) except depreciation expense. What do you suppose the primary reason was for management to separate depreciation from other operating expenses? From a conceptual point of view, should depreciation be considered a "cost" of providing services?

b. Why do you suppose the amounts of depreciation expense and interest expense are so high for Gerrard Construction, Co.? To which specific balance sheet accounts should a financial analyst relate these expenses?

c. Calculate the company's average income tax rate. *(Hint: You must first determine the earnings before taxes.)*

d. Explain why the amount of income tax expense is different than the amount of income taxes payable.

e. Calculate the amount of total current assets. Why do you suppose this amount is so low, relative to total assets?

   f. Why doesn't the company have a Merchandise Inventory account?

   g. Calculate the amount of working capital and the current ratio at December 31, 1999. Assess the company's overall liquidity.

   h. Calculate ROI (including margin and turnover) and ROE for the year ended December 31, 1999. Assess the company's overall profitability. What additional information would you like to have to increase the validity of this assessment?

   i. Calculate the amount of dividends declared and paid during the year ended December 31, 1999. *(Hint: Do a T-account analysis of retained earnings.)*

CHAPTER 5

Accounting for and Presentation of Current Assets

Current assets include cash and those assets that are expected to be converted to cash or used up within one year, or an **operating cycle,** whichever is longer. An entity's operating cycle is the average time it takes to convert an investment in inventory back to cash. This is illustrated in the following diagram:

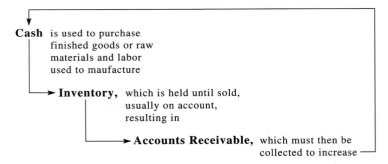

For most firms, the normal operating cycle is less than one year. As you learn more about each of the current assets discussed in this chapter, keep in mind that a shorter operating cycle permits a lower investment in current assets. This results in an increase in turnover, which in turn increases ROI. Many firms attempt to reduce their operating cycle and increase overall profitability by trying to sell inventory and collect accounts receivable as quickly as possible.

Current asset captions usually seen in a balance sheet are:

Cash.
Marketable (or Short-Term) Securities.
Accounts and Notes Receivable.
Inventories.
Prepaid Expenses or Other Current Assets.

Refer to the Consolidated Balance Sheets of Intel Corporation on page 19 of the Appendix. Note that Intel's current assets at December 28, 1996, total almost $13.7 billion and account for about 58% of the company's total assets. Look at the components of current assets. Notice that the largest current asset amounts are for Cash and Cash Equivalents, Short-Term Investments, and Accounts Receivable. Now refer to the balance sheets in other annual reports that you may have and examine the composition of current assets. Do they differ significantly from Intel's balance sheet? The objective of this chapter is to permit you to make sense of the current asset presentation of any balance sheet.

WHAT DOES IT MEAN?

1. What does it mean when an asset is referred to as a current asset?

Learning Objectives

After studying this chapter, you should understand:

1 What is included in the cash amount reported on the balance sheet.

2 The features of a system of internal control and why internal controls are important.

3 The bank reconciliation procedure.

4 How short-term marketable securities are reported on the balance sheet.

5 How accounts receivable are reported on the balance sheet, including the valuation allowances for estimated uncollectible accounts and estimated cash discounts.

6 How notes receivable and related accrued interest are reported on the balance sheet.

7 How inventories are reported on the balance sheet.

8 The alternative inventory cost-flow assumptions and their respective effects on the income statement and balance sheet when price levels are changing.

9 The impact of inventory errors on the balance sheet and income statement.

10 What prepaid expenses are and how they are reported on the balance sheet.

Cash

Objective 1
Understand what is included in the cash amount reported on the balance sheet.

The amount of cash reported on the balance sheet represents the cash that is available to the entity as of the close of business on the balance sheet date. This includes cash on hand in change funds, **petty cash** funds (see Business in Practice—Petty Cash Funds), undeposited cash receipts (including checks, money orders, and bank drafts), and the amount of cash available to the firm in its various bank accounts.

Since cash on hand or in checking accounts earns little if any interest, management of just about every organization will develop a cash management system to permit investment of cash balances not currently required for the entity's operation. The broad objective of the cash-management program is to maximize earnings by having as much cash as feasible invested for the longest possible time. Cash managers are usually interested

---

BUSINESS IN PRACTICE
Petty Cash Funds

Although most of a firm's cash disbursements should be made by check for security and record-keeping purposes, a petty cash fund could be used for small payments for which writing a check would be inconvenient. For example, postage due or **collect on delivery (COD)** charges or the cost of an urgently needed office supply item are often paid from the petty cash fund to avoid the delay and expense associated with creating a check.

The petty cash fund is an **imprest account,** which means that the sum of the cash on hand in the petty cash box and the receipts in support of disbursements (called *petty cash vouchers*) should equal the amount initially put in the petty cash fund.

Periodically (usually at the end of the accounting period), the petty cash fund is reimbursed in order to bring the cash in the fund back to the original amount. It is at this time that the expenses paid through the fund are recognized in the accounts.

The amount of the petty cash fund is included in the cash amount reported on the firm's balance sheet.

---

in minimizing investment risks, and this is accomplished by investing in U.S. Treasury securities, securities of agencies of the federal government, bank certificates of deposit, and/or commercial paper. (**Commercial paper** is like an IOU issued by a very creditworthy corporation.) Securities selected for investment will usually have a maturity date that is within a few months of the investment date and that corresponds to the time when the cash manager thinks the cash will be needed. *Cash equivalents* included with cash on the balance sheets of Intel Corporation are defined as "highly liquid investments with insignificant interest rate risk and with original maturities of three months or less" (see p. 22 in the Appendix).

Objective 2
Understand the features of a system of internal control and why internal controls are important.

In addition to an organization's cash management system, policies to minimize the chances of customer theft and employee embezzlement will also be developed. These are part of the **internal control system** (see Business in Practice—The Internal Control System), which is designed to help safeguard all of an entity's assets, including cash.

BUSINESS IN PRACTICE
The Internal Control System

Internal control is broadly defined as a process, established by an entity's board of directors, management, and other personnel, designed to provide reasonable assurance that objectives are achieved with respect to:

1. The effectiveness and efficiency of the operations of the organization.
2. The reliability of the organization's financial reporting.
3. The organization's compliance with applicable laws and regulations.

Business in Practice concluded

Internal controls relate to every level of the organization, and the tone established by the board of directors and top management establishes the control environment. Ethical considerations expressed in the organization's code of conduct and social responsibility activities are a part of this overall tone. Although the system of internal control is frequently discussed in the context of the firm's accounting system, it is equally applicable to every activity of the firm, and it is appropriate for everyone to understand the need for and significance of internal controls.

Internal control policies and procedures are sometimes classified as financial controls and administrative controls.

Financial controls include the series of checks and balances that remove from one person the sole involvement in a transaction from beginning to end. For example, most organizations require that checks be signed by someone other than the person who prepares them. The check signer is expected to review the documents supporting the disbursement and to raise questions about unusual items. Another internal control requires the credit manager who authorizes the write-off of an account receivable to have that write-off approved by another officer of the firm. Likewise, a bank teller or cashier who has made a mistake in initially recording a transaction must have a supervisor approve the correction.

Administrative controls are frequently included in policy and procedure manuals and are reflected in management reviews of reports of operations and activities. For example, a firm's credit policy might specify that no customer is to have an account receivable balance in excess of $10,000 until the customer has had a clean payment record for at least one year. The firm's internal auditors might periodically review the accounts receivable detail to determine whether or not this policy is being followed.

The system of internal control does not exist because top management thinks that the employees are dishonest. Internal controls provide a framework within which employees can operate, knowing that their work is being performed in a way that is consistent with the desires of top management. To the extent that temptation is removed from a situation that might otherwise lead to an employee's dishonest act, the system of internal control provides an even more significant benefit.

WHAT DOES IT MEAN?

2. What does it mean to have an effective system of internal control?

The Bank Reconciliation as a Control over Cash

Many transactions either directly or indirectly affect the receipt or payment of cash. For instance, a sale of merchandise on account normally leads to a cash receipt when the account receivable is collected. Likewise, a purchase of inventory on account results in a cash payment when the account payable is paid. In fact, cash (in one form or another) is eventually involved in the settlement of virtually all business affairs.

As a result of the high volume of cash transactions and the ease with which money can be exchanged, it is appropriate to design special controls to help safeguard cash. At a minimum, all cash received should be deposited in the entity's bank account at the end of each business day, and all cash payments (other than petty cash disbursements) should be made from the entity's bank account using prenumbered checks. Using this simple control system, a duplicate record of each cash transaction is automatically maintained—one by the entity and the other by the bank.

To determine the amount of cash available in the bank, it is appropriate that the Cash account balance as shown in the general ledger be reconciled with the balance reported by the bank. The **bank reconciliation** process, which you do (or should do) for your own checking account, involves bringing into agreement the account balance reported by the bank on the bank statement with the account balance in the ledger. The balances might differ for two reasons: timing differences and errors.

Timing differences arise because the entity knows about some transactions affecting the cash balance about which the bank is not yet aware, or the bank has recorded some transactions about which the entity is not yet aware. The most common timing differences involve:

Deposits in transit, which have been recorded in the entity's Cash account, but which have not yet been added to the entity's balance on the bank's records. From the entity's point of view, the deposit in transit represents cash on hand because it has been received.

Outstanding checks, which have been recorded as credits (reductions) to the entity's cash balance, but which have not yet been presented to the bank for payment. From the entity's point of view, outstanding checks should not be included in its cash balance because its intent was to disburse cash when it issued the checks.

Bank service charges against the entity's account, and interest income added to the entity's balance during the period by the bank. The bank service charge and interest income should be recognized by the entity in the period incurred or earned, respectively, since both of these items affect the cash balance at the end of the period.

NSF (not sufficient funds) checks, which are checks that have "bounced" from the maker's bank because the account did not have enough funds to cover the check. Because the entity that received the check recorded it as a cash receipt and added the check amount to the balance of its cash account, it is necessary to establish an account receivable for the amount due from the maker of the NSF check.

Errors, which can be made by either the firm or the bank, are detected in what may be a trial-and-error process if the book balance and bank balance do not reconcile after timing differences have been recognized. Finding errors is a tedious process involving verification of the timing difference amounts (e.g., double-checking the makeup and total of the list of outstanding checks), verifying the debits and credits to the firm's ledger account, and verifying the arithmetic and amounts included on the bank statement. If the error is in the recording of cash transactions on the entity's books, an appropriate journal entry must be made to correct the error. If the bank has made the error, the bank is notified but no change is made to the cash account balance.

There are a number of ways of mechanically setting up the bank reconciliation. The reverse side of the bank statement usually has a reconciliation format printed on it. Many computer-based bookkeeping systems contain a bank reconciliation module that can facilitate the bank reconciliation process. When the bank statement lists returned checks in numerical order, the process is made even easier. A simple and clear technique for setting up the reconciliation is illustrated in Exhibit 5–1.

EXHIBIT 5–1 A Bank Reconciliation Illustrated

Assumptions:
- The balance in the Cash account of Cruisers, Inc., at September 30 was $4,614.58.
- The bank statement showed a balance of $5,233.21 as of September 30.
- Included with the bank statement were notices that the bank had deducted a service charge of $42.76 and had credited the account with interest of $28.91 earned on the average daily balance.
- An NSF check for $35.00 from a customer was returned with the bank statement.
- A comparison of deposits recorded in the cash account with those shown on the bank statement showed that the September 30 deposit of $859.10 was not on the bank statement. This is not surprising because the September 30 deposit was put in the bank's night depository on the evening of September 30.
- A comparison of the record of checks issued with the checks returned in the bank statement showed that the amount of outstanding checks was $1,526.58.

Reconciliation as of September 30:

From Bank Records		*From Company Books*	
Indicated balance	$5,233.21	Indicated balance	$4,614.58
Add: Deposit in transit	859.10	Add: Interest earned	28.91
Less: Outstanding		Less: Service charge	(42.76)
checks	(1,526.58)	NSF check	(35.00)
Reconciled balance	$4,565.73	Reconciled balance	$4,565.73

The following adjusting journal entry would be made to adjust the balance in the company's general ledger account before reconciliation (the "Indicated balance") to the reconciled balance.

		Dr.	Cr.
Dr.	Service Charge Expense	42.76	
Dr.	Accounts Receivable	35.00	
Cr.	Interest Income		28.91
Cr.	Cash		48.85

Using the horizontal model, the effect of this adjustment on the financial statements is:

Balance sheet		Income statement	
Assets = Liabilities + Owners' equity	←	Net income = Revenues − Expenses	
Accounts Receivable + 35.00 Cash − 48.85		Interest Income + 28.91	Service Charge Expense − 42.76

EXHIBIT 5–1 *(concluded)*

> Alternatively, a separate adjusting journal entry could be made for each reconciling item. The amount from this particular bank account to be included in the cash amount shown on the balance sheet for September 30 is $4,565.73. There would not be an adjusting journal entry for the reconciling items that affect the bank balance because those items have already been recorded on the company's books.

WHAT DOES IT MEAN?

3. What does it mean to reconcile a bank account?

Short-Term Marketable Securities

As emphasized in the discussion of cash, a firm's ROI can be improved by developing a cash-management program that involves investing cash balances over and above those required for day-to-day operations in **short-term marketable securities.** An integral part of the cash management program is the forecast of cash receipts and disbursements (forecasting, or budgeting, is discussed in Chapter 14). Do you remember the cash equivalents and short-term investments that are part of Intel's current assets? Since investments with maturities of three months or less are classified as cash equivalents, Intel's "short-term investments" caption includes only those investments with maturities of greater than three months but less than one year. Recall from Chapter 2 that current assets are defined as *cash and those assets that are likely to be converted into cash or used to benefit the entity within one year.* Thus, any investments that mature beyond one year from the balance sheet date are reported as "long-term investments." Intel's annual report provides detailed notes and schedules regarding a broad variety of debt and equity securities and other financial arrangements that the company is involved in (see pp. 22, 24–26 in the Appendix). Although many of these specific investment arrangements are quite complicated and beyond the scope of this text, the accounting for them is usually straightforward.

Balance Sheet Valuation

Objective 4
Understand how short-term marketable securities are reported on the balance sheet.

Short-term marketable securities that will be held until they mature are reported in the balance sheet at the entity's *cost,* which is usually about the same as market value, because of their high quality and the short time until maturity. The majority of investments made by most firms are of this variety since the excess cash available for investment will soon be needed to meet working capital obligations. If an entity owns marketable securities that are not likely to be converted to cash within a few months of the balance sheet date, or securities that are subject to significant fluctuation in market value (like common and preferred stock), the balance sheet valuation and related accounting become more complex. Securities that may be traded or are available for sale are reported at *market value,* and any unrealized gain or loss is recognized. This is an application of the matching concept since the change in market value is reflected in the fiscal period in which it occurs. The requirement that some marketable securities be reported at market value is especially pertinent to banks and other entities in the financial industry.

The accounting for marketable securities can be seen in Intel's schedule of investments on page 24 in the Appendix. Note that separate columns are provided for the investment's cost, unrealized gains, unrealized losses, and estimated fair market value. Note also that the unrealized gains are largest for "preferred stock and other equity," and that little if any adjustment to the cost of debt securities is necessary because of their short time until maturity.

WHAT DOES IT MEAN?

4. What does it mean to invest cash in short-term marketable securities?

Interest Accrual

Of course, it is appropriate that interest income on short-term marketable securities be accrued as earned so that both the balance sheet and income statement more accurately reflect the financial position at the end of the period and results of operations for the period. The asset involved is called *Interest Receivable,* and *Interest Income* is the income statement account. The accrual is made with the following adjusting entry:

Dr. Interest Receivable	xx	
Cr. Interest Income		xx

The effect of the interest accrual on the financial statements is:

Balance sheet	Income statement
Assets = Liabilities + Owners' equity ←	Net income = Revenues − Expenses
+ Interest Receivable	+ Interest Income

The amount in the Interest Receivable account is combined with other receivables in the current asset section of the balance sheet.

WHAT DOES IT MEAN?

5. What does it mean when interest income from marketable securities must be accrued?

Accounts Receivable

Recall from the Intel Corporation balance sheet that Accounts Receivable is one of the largest current assets at December 28, 1996. Accounts receivable from customers for merchandise and services delivered are reported at **net realizable value**—the amount that is expected to be received from customers in settlement of their obligations. Two factors will cause this amount to be different from the amount of the receivable originally recorded: bad debts and cash discounts.

Bad Debts/Uncollectible Accounts

Objective 5
Understand how accounts receivable are reported on the balance sheet, including the valuation allowances for estimated uncollectible accounts and estimated cash discounts.

Whenever a firm permits its customers to purchase merchandise or services on credit, it knows that some of the customers will not pay. Even a thorough check of the potential customer's credit rating and history of payments to other suppliers will not assure that the customer will pay in the future. Although some bad debt losses are inevitable when a firm makes credit sales, internal control policies and procedures will exist in most firms to keep losses at a minimum and to ensure that every reasonable effort is made to collect all amounts that are due to the firm. Some companies, however, willingly accept high credit risk customers and know that they will experience high bad debt losses. These firms maximize their ROI by having a very high margin and requiring a down payment that equals or approaches the cost of the item being sold. Sales volume is higher than it would be if credit standards were tougher; thus, even though bad debts are relatively high, all or most of the product cost is recovered, and bad debt losses are more than offset by the profits from greater sales volume.

Based on recent collection experience, tempered by the current state of economic affairs of the industry in which a firm is operating, credit managers can estimate with a high degree of accuracy the probable **bad debts expense** (or **uncollectible accounts expense**) of the firm. Many firms estimate bad debts based upon a simplified assumption about the collectibility of all credit sales made during a period (percentage of sales method). Other firms perform a detailed analysis and aging of their year-end accounts receivable to estimate the net amount most likely to be collected (aging of receivables method). For instance, a firm may choose the following age categories and estimated collection percentages: 0–30 days (98%), 31–60 days (95%), 61–120 days (85%), and 121–180 days (60%). The firm may also have an administrative internal control policy requiring that all accounts more than six months overdue be immediately turned over to a collection agency. Such a policy is likely to increase the probability of collecting these accounts, facilitate the collection efforts for other overdue accounts, and reduce the overall costs of managing accounts receivable. The success of any bad debts estimation technique ultimately depends upon the careful application of professional judgment, using the best available information.

When the amount of accounts receivable estimated to be uncollectible has been determined, a **valuation adjustment** can be recorded to reduce the **carrying value** of the asset and recognize the bad debt expense. The adjusting entry is:

```
Dr.  Bad Debts Expense (or Uncollectible Accounts Expense) . . . . . .  xx
  Cr.  Allowance for Bad Debts (or Allowance for
       Uncollectible Accounts). . . . . . . . . . . . . . . . . . . . . . . . . . . . .      xx
```

The effect of this adjustment on the financial statement is:

Balance sheet	Income statement
Assets = Liabilities + Owners' equity ←	Net income = Revenues − Expenses

− Allowance
   for Bad Debts
	− Bad Debts
	   Expense

In bookkeeping language, the **Allowance for Uncollectible Accounts** or **Allowance for Bad Debts** account is considered a **contra asset** because it is reported as a subtraction from an asset in the balance sheet. The debit and credit mechanics of a contra asset account are the opposite of those of an asset account; that is, a contra asset increases with credit entries and decreases with debit entries, and it normally has a credit balance. The presentation of the Allowance for Bad Debts in the current asset section of the balance sheet (using assumed amounts) is:

Accounts receivable	$10,000
Less: Allowance for bad debts	(500)
Net accounts receivable	$ 9,500

or, as more commonly reported:

Accounts receivable, less allowance for bad debts of $500	$ 9,500

The Allowance for Bad Debts account communicates to financial statement readers that an estimated portion of the total amount of accounts receivable is expected to become uncollectible. So why not simply reduce the Accounts Receivable account directly for estimated bad debts? The problem with this approach is that the firm hasn't yet determined *which* customers will not pay—only that *some* will not pay. Before accounts receivable can be reduced, the firm must be able to identify which account needs to be written off as an uncollectible account. Throughout the year as accounts are determined to be uncollectible, they are written off against the allowance account with the following entry:

Dr. Allowance for Bad Debts.	xx	
Cr. Accounts Receivable		xx

The effect of this entry on the financial statement is:

Balance sheet	Income statement
Assets = Liabilities + Owners' equity ←	Net income = Revenues − Expenses

− Accounts
   Receivable
+ Allowance
   for Bad Debts	

Note that the **write-off** of an account receivable has no effect on the income statement, nor should it. The expense was recognized in the year in which the revenue from the transaction with this customer was recognized. The write-off entry removes from Accounts Receivable an amount that is never expected to be collected. Also note that the write-off of an account will not have any effect on the net accounts receivable reported on the balance sheet because both the asset (Accounts Receivable) and the contra asset (Allowance for Bad Debts) are affected the same way (each is reduced) by the same amount. Assume that $100 of the accounts receivable in the above example were written off. The balance sheet presentation would now be:

Accounts receivable	$9,900
Less: Allowance for bad debts	(400)
Net accounts receivable	$9,500

Providing for bad debts expense in the same year in which the related sales revenue is recognized is an application of the matching concept. The Allowance for Bad Debts (or Allowance for Uncollectible Accounts) account is a **valuation account,** and its credit balance is subtracted from the debit balance of Accounts Receivable to arrive at the amount of net receivables reported in the Current Asset section of the balance sheet. This procedure results in stating Accounts Receivable at the amount expected to be collected (i.e., net realizable value). If an appropriate allowance for bad debts is not provided, Accounts Receivable and net income will be overstated, and the ROI, ROE, and liquidity measures will be distorted. The amount of the allowance is usually reported parenthetically in the Accounts Receivable caption so financial statement users can make a judgment about the credit and collection practices of the firm.

WHAT DOES IT MEAN?

6. What does it mean that the Allowance for Bad Debts is a contra asset?

Cash Discounts

To encourage prompt payment, many firms permit their customers to deduct up to 2% of the amount owed if the bill is paid within a stated period—usually 10 days—of the date of the sale (usually referred to as the *invoice date*). Most firms' **credit terms** provide that if the invoice is not paid within the discount period, it must be paid in full within 30 days of the invoice date. This credit term is abbreviated as 2/10, n30. The 2/10 refers to the discount terms and the n30 means that the net amount of the invoice is due within 30 days. To illustrate, assume that Cruisers, Inc., has credit sales terms of 2/10, n30. On April 8, Cruisers, Inc., made a $5,000 sale to Mount Marina. Mount Marina has the option of paying $4,900 (5,000 − [2% × $5,000]) by April 18, or paying $5,000 on May 8.

Like most firms, Mount Marina will probably take advantage of the **cash discount** because it represents a high rate of return (see Business in Practice—Cash Discounts). The discount is clearly a cost to the seller because the selling firm will not receive the full amount of the account

---

BUSINESS IN PRACTICE
Cash Discounts

Cash discounts for prompt payment represent a significant cost to the seller and a benefit to the purchaser. Not only do they encourage prompt payment, they also represent an element of the pricing decision and will be considered when evaluating the selling prices of competitors.

Converting the discount to an annual return on investment will illustrate its significance. Assume that an item sells for $100, with credit terms of 2/10, n30. If the invoice is paid by the 10th day, a $2 discount is taken, and the payor (purchaser) gives up the use of the $98 paid for 20 days because the alternative is to keep the money for another 20 days and then pay $100 to the seller. In effect, by choosing not to make payment within the 10-day discount period, the purchaser is "borrowing" $98 from the seller for 20 additional days at a cost of $2. The return on investment for 20 days is $2/$98, or slightly more than 2%; however, there are 18 available 20-day periods in a year (360 days/20 days), so the annualized return on investment is over 36%! Very few firms are able to earn this high an ROI on their principal activities. For this reason, most firms have a rigidly followed internal control policy of taking all cash discounts possible.

One of the facts that credit rating agencies and credit grantors want to know about a firm when evaluating its liquidity and creditworthiness is whether or not the firm consistently takes cash discounts. If it does not, that is a signal that either the management doesn't understand their significance or that the firm can't afford to borrow money at a lower interest rate to earn the higher rate from the cash discount. Either of these reasons indicates a potentially poor credit risk.

Since the purchaser's benefit is the seller's burden, why do sellers allow cash discounts if they represent such a high cost? The principal reasons are to encourage prompt payment and to be competitive. Obviously, however, cash discounts represent a cost that must be covered for the firm to be profitable.

---

receivable resulting from the sale. The accounting treatment for estimated cash discounts is similar to that illustrated for estimated bad debts. Cash discounts on sales are usually subtracted from Sales in the income statement to arrive at the net sales amount that is reported because the discount is in effect a reduction of the selling price. On the balance sheet, it is appropriate to reduce Accounts Receivable by an allowance for cash discounts for the estimated cash discounts that will be taken by customers when they pay within the discount period. Estimated cash discounts are recognized in the fiscal period in which the sale is made, based on past experience with cash discounts taken.

Objective 6
Understand how notes receivable and related accrued interest are reported on the balance sheet.

Notes Receivable

If a firm has an account receivable from a customer who has developed difficulties paying its balance when due, the firm may convert that account receivable to a **note receivable.** The entry to reflect this transaction is:

```
Dr.  Notes Receivable ....................................  | xx |    |
   Cr.  Accounts Receivable...............................  |    | xx |
```

The effect of this entry on the financial statement is:

Balance sheet	Income statement
Assets = Liabilities + Owners' equity ←	Net income = Revenues − Expenses

− Accounts
  Receivable
+ Notes Receivable

One asset has been exchanged for another. Does the entry make sense?

A note receivable differs from an account receivable in several ways. A note is a formal document that includes specific provisions with respect to its maturity date (when it is to be paid), agreements or *covenants* made by the borrower (e.g., to supply financial statements to the lender or refrain from paying dividends until the note is repaid), identification of security or **collateral** pledged by the borrower to support the loan, penalties to be assessed if it is not paid on the maturity date, and most important, the interest rate associated with the loan. Although some firms assess an interest charge or service charge on invoice amounts that are not paid when due, this practice is unusual for regular transactions between firms. Thus, if an account receivable is not going to be paid promptly, the seller will ask the customer to sign a note so that interest can be earned on the overdue account.

Retail firms often use notes to facilitate sales transactions for which the initial credit period exceeds 60 or 90 days, such as an installment plan for equipment sales. In such cases, Notes Receivable (rather than Accounts Receivable) is increased at the point of sale, even though the seller may provide interest-free financing for a period of time.

Under other circumstances, a firm may lend money to another entity and take a note from that entity; for example, a manufacturer may lend money to a distributor that is also a customer or potential customer in order to help the distributor build its business. Such a transaction is another rearrangement of assets; Cash is decreased and Notes Receivable is increased.

Interest Accrual

If interest is to be paid at the maturity of the note (a common practice), it is appropriate that the holder of the note accrue interest income, usually on a monthly basis. This is appropriate because interest revenue has been earned, and accruing the revenue and increasing interest receivable results in more accurate monthly financial statements. The entry to do this is the same as that for interest accrued on short-term cash investments:

```
Dr.  Interest Receivable ....................................  | xx |    |
   Cr.  Interest Income .....................................  |    | xx |
```

The effect of this entry on the financial statements is:

Balance sheet	Income statement
Assets = Liabilities + Owners' equity	← Net income = Revenues − Expenses
+ Interest Receivable	+ Interest Income

This accrual entry reflects interest income that has been earned in the period, and increases current assets by the amount earned but not yet received.

Interest Receivable is frequently combined with Notes Receivable in the balance sheet for reporting purposes. Amounts to be received within a year of the balance sheet date are classified as current assets. If the note has a maturity date beyond a year, it will be classified as a noncurrent asset.

It is appropriate to recognize any probable loss from uncollectible notes and interest receivable just as is done for accounts receivable, and the bookkeeping process is the same. Cash discounts do not apply to notes, so there is no discount valuation allowance.

Inventories

Objective 7
Understand how inventories are reported on the balance sheet.

For service organizations, inventories consist mainly of office supplies and other items of relatively low value that will be used up within the organization, rather than being offered for sale to customers. As illustrated in Chapter 4, recording the purchase and use of supplies is a straightforward process, although adjusting entries are usually necessary to improve the accuracy of the accounting records.

For merchandising and manufacturing firms, the sale of inventory in the ordinary course of business provides the major, ongoing source of operating revenue. Cost of Goods Sold is usually the largest expense that is subtracted from Sales in determining net income, and not surprisingly, inventories represent the most significant current asset for many such firms. At Honda Motor Co., for example, inventories account for nearly 30% of the firm's current assets and 14% of total assets.[1] For Wal-Mart Stores, Inc., 88% of current assets and 40% of total assets are tied up in inventories.[2] For Intel, however, inventories represent only 9.5% of current assets and 5.4% of total assets.[3] Can you think of some possible explanations for these varying results? Obviously, not all firms (and not all industries) have the same inventory needs because of differences in their respective

---

[1]Data based on Honda Motor Co.'s 1996 Annual Report for the year ended March 31, 1996.

[2]Data based on Wal-Mart Stores, Inc.'s 1997 Annual Report for the year ended January 31, 1997.

[3]Data based on Intel Corporation's 1996 Annual Report for the year ended December 28, 1996.

products, markets, customers, and distribution systems. Moreover, some firms do a better job than others at managing their inventory by turning it over quickly to enhance ROI. What other factors might cause the relative size of inventories to vary among firms?

Although inventory management practices are diverse, the accounting treatment for inventory items is essentially the same for all firms. Just as warehouse bins and store shelves hold inventory until the product is sold to the customer, the inventory accounts of a firm hold the *cost* of a product until that cost is released to the income statement to be subtracted from (matched with) the revenue from the sale. The cost of a purchased or manufactured product is recorded as an asset and carried in the asset account until the product is sold (or becomes worthless or is lost or stolen), at which point the cost becomes an expense to be reported in the income statement. The cost of an item purchased for inventory includes not only the invoice price paid to the supplier, but also other costs associated with the purchase of the item such as freight and material handling charges. Cost is reduced by the amount of any cash discount allowed on the purchase. The income statement caption used to report this expense is Cost of Goods Sold (see Exhibit 2–2). The entries for purchase and sale transactions are:

Dr. Inventory	xx	
Cr. Accounts Payable (or Cash)		xx
Purchase (or manufacture) of inventory.		
Dr. Cost of Goods Sold.................................	xx	
Cr. Inventory..		xx
To transfer cost of item sold to income statement.		

These transactions are illustrated in the horizontal model as follows:

Balance sheet	Income statement
Assets = Liabilities + Owners' equity ← Net income = Revenues − Expenses	
Purchase of inventory: + Inven- + Accounts tory Payable	
Recognize cost of goods sold: −Inven- tory	− Cost of Goods Sold

Recognizing cost of goods sold is a process of accounting for the *flow of costs* from the Inventory (asset) account of the balance sheet to the Cost of Goods Sold (expense) account of the income statement. T-accounts can also be used to illustrate this flow of costs, as shown in Exhibit 5–2. Of course, the sale of merchandise also generates revenue, but *recognizing revenue is a separate transaction* involving Accounts Receivable (or Cash) and the Sales Revenue accounts. The following discussion focuses only on the accounting for the cost of the inventory sold.

EXHIBIT 5–2   Flow of Costs from Inventory to Cost of Goods Sold

Balance Sheet/Income Statement

Inventory (asset)		*Cost of Goods Sold (expense)*
Purchases of merchandise for resale increase inventory (credit to accounts payable or cash)	When merchandise is sold, the cost flows from the Inventory asset account to ⟶	the Cost of Goods Sold expense account

Inventory Cost-Flow Assumptions

Accounting for inventories is one of the areas in which alternative generally accepted practices can result in major differences between the assets and expenses reported by companies that might otherwise be alike in all respects. It is therefore important to study this material carefully in order to gain an appreciation of the impact of inventory method choices on a firm's financial statements.

The inventory accounting alternative selected by an entity relates to the assumption about how costs flow from the Inventory account to the Cost of Goods Sold account. There are four principal alternative **cost-flow assumptions:**

1. Specific identification.
2. Weighted-average.
3. First-in, first-out (FIFO) (pronounced FIE-FOE).
4. Last-in, first-out (LIFO) (pronounced LIE-FOE).

Objective 8
Understand the alternative inventory cost-flow assumptions and their respective effects on the income statement and balance sheet when price levels are changing.

It is important to recognize that these are *cost-flow assumptions,* and that FIFO and LIFO do not refer to the physical flow of product. Thus, it is possible for a firm to have a FIFO physical flow (a grocery store usually tries to accomplish this) and to use the LIFO cost-flow assumption.

The **specific identification** alternative links cost and physical flow. When an item is sold, the cost of that specific item is determined from the firm's records, and that amount is transferred from the Inventory account to Cost of Goods Sold. The amount of ending inventory is the cost of the items held in inventory at the end of the year. This alternative is appropriate for a firm dealing with specifically identifiable products, such as automobiles, that have an identifying serial number and are purchased and sold by specific unit. This assumption is not practical for a firm having a large number of inventory items that are not easily identified individually.

The **weighted-average** alternative is applied to individual items of inventory. It involves calculating the average cost of the items in the beginning inventory plus purchases made during the year. Then this average is used to determine the cost of goods sold and the carrying value of ending inventory. This method is illustrated in Exhibit 5–3. Notice that the average cost is not a simple average of the unit costs but is instead an average weighted by the number of units in beginning inventory and each purchase.

First-in, first-out, or **FIFO,** means more than first-in, first-out; it means that the first costs *in to inventory* are the first costs *out to cost of goods sold.* The first cost in is the cost of the inventory on hand at the beginning of the fiscal year. The effect of this inventory cost-flow assumption is to transfer to the Cost of Goods Sold account the oldest costs incurred for the quantity of merchandise sold and to leave in the Inventory

---

EXHIBIT 5–3 Inventory Cost-Flow Alternatives Illustrated

Situation:
On September 1, 1998, the inventory of Cruisers, Inc., consisted of five Model OB3 boats. Each boat had cost $1,500. During the year ended August 31, 1999, 40 boats were purchased on the dates and at the costs that follow. During the year, 37 boats were sold.

Date of Purchase	Number of Boats	Cost per Boat	Total Cost
September 1, 1998 (Beginning inventory) 5		$1,500	$ 7,500
November 7, 1998 8		1,600	12,800
March 12, 1999 12		1,650	19,800
May 22, 1999 10		1,680	16,800
July 28, 1999 6		1,700	10,200
August 30, 1999 4		1,720	6,880
Total of boats available for sale 45			$73,980
Number of boats sold 37			
Number of boats in August 31, 1999 inventory . . . 8			

Required:
Determine the ending inventory amount at August 31, 1999, and the cost of goods sold for the year then ended, using the weighted-average, FIFO, and LIFO cost-flow assumptions.

Solution:
a. Weighted-average cost-flow assumption:

$$\text{Weighted-average cost} = \frac{\text{Total cost of boats available for sale}}{\text{Number of boats available for sale}}$$

$$= \frac{\$73,980}{45}$$

$$= \$1,644 \text{ per boat}$$

Cost of ending inventory = $1,644 × 8 = $13,152
Cost of goods sold = $1,644 × 37 = $60,828

b. FIFO cost-flow assumption:
The cost of ending inventory is the cost of the eight most recent purchases:

4 boats purchased August 30, 1999 @ $1,720 ea =	$ 6,880
4 boats of July 28, 1999, purchase @ $1,700 ea =	6,800
Cost of 8 boats in ending inventory	$13,680

EXHIBIT 5–3   *(concluded)*

The cost of 37 boats sold is the sum of the costs for the first 37 boats purchased:

Beginning inventory	5 boats @	$1,500 =	$ 7,500
November 7, 1998 purchase	8 boats @	1,600 =	12,800
March 12, 1999 purchase	12 boats @	1,650 =	19,800
May 22, 1999 purchase	10 boats @	1,680 =	16,800
July 28, 1999 purchase*	2 boats @	1,700 =	3,400
Cost of goods sold			$60,300

*Applying the FIFO cost-flow assumption, the cost of two of the six boats purchased this date is transferred from Inventory to Cost of Goods Sold.

Note that the cost of goods sold could also have been calculated by subtracting the ending inventory amount from the total cost of the boats available for sale.

Total cost of boats available for sale	$73,980
Less cost of boats in ending inventory	(13,680)
Cost of goods sold	$60,300

c. LIFO *cost-flow assumption:*

The cost of ending inventory is the cost of the eight oldest purchases:

5 boats in beginning inventory @ $1,500 ea	=	$7,500
3 boats of November 7, 1998 purchase @ $1,600 ea =		4,800
Cost of 8 boats in ending inventory		$12,300

The cost of the 37 boats sold is the sum of costs for the last 37 boats purchased:

August 30, 1999 purchase	4 boats @	$1,720 =	$ 6,880
July 28, 1999 purchase	6 boats @	1,700 =	10,200
May 22, 1999 purchase	10 boats @	1,680 =	16,800
March 12, 1999 purchase	12 boats @	1,650 =	19,800
November 7, 1998 purchase*	5 boats @	1,600 =	8,000
Cost of goods sold			$61,680

*Applying the LIFO cost-flow assumption, the cost of five of the eight boats purchased this date is transferred from Inventory to Cost of Goods Sold.

Note that the cost of goods sold could also have been calculated by subtracting the ending inventory amount from the total cost of the boats available for sale.

Total cost of boats available for sale	$73,980
Less cost of boats in ending inventory	(12,300)
Cost of goods sold	$61,680

asset account the most recent costs of merchandise purchased or manufactured for the quantity in ending inventory. This cost-flow assumption is also illustrated in Exhibit 5–3.

Last-in, first-out, or **LIFO,** is an alternative cost-flow assumption opposite to FIFO. Remember, we are thinking about cost flow, not physical flow, and it is possible for a firm to have a FIFO physical flow (like the grocery store) and still use the LIFO cost-flow assumption. Under LIFO, the most recent costs incurred for merchandise purchased or manufactured are transferred to the income statement (as Cost of Goods Sold) when items are sold, and the inventory on hand at the balance sheet date is costed at the oldest costs, including those used to value the beginning inventory. This cost-flow assumption is also illustrated in Exhibit 5–3.

The way these cost-flow assumptions are applied depends on the inventory accounting system in use. The two systems—*periodic* and *perpetual*—are described later in this chapter. Exhibit 5–3 uses the periodic system.

To recap the results of the three alternatives presented in Exhibit 5–3:

Cost-Flow Assumption	Cost of Ending Inventory	Cost of Goods Sold
Weighted-average	$13,152	$60,828
FIFO	13,680	60,300
LIFO	12,300	61,680

Although the differences between amounts seem small in this illustration, under real-world circumstances with huge amounts of inventory the differences become large and are material (the materiality concept). Why do the differences occur? Because, as you have probably noticed, the cost of the boats purchased changed over time. If the cost had not changed, there would not have been any difference in the ending inventory and cost of goods sold among the three alternatives. But in practice, costs do change. Notice that the amounts resulting from the weighted-average cost-flow assumption are between those for FIFO and LIFO; this is to be expected. Weighted-average results will never be outside the range of amounts resulting from FIFO and LIFO.

The crucial point to understand about the inventory cost-flow assumption issue is the impact on cost of goods sold, operating income, and net income of the alternative assumptions. Although Intel's inventories are relatively small in comparison to total assets, this is not the case for many manufacturing and merchandising firms. For instance, the following statement appeared in the 1996 annual report for Armstrong World Industries, Inc.: "Approximately 57% in 1996 and 51% in 1995 of the company's total inventory is valued on a LIFO (last-in, first-out) basis. Such inventory values were lower than would have been reported on a total FIFO (first-in, first-out) basis, by $60.6 million at the end of 1996 and $62.4 million at year-end 1995." LIFO inventory values $60.6 million lower than FIFO means that cost of goods sold over the years has been $60.6 million higher and operating income has been $60.6 million lower than would have been the case under FIFO! To put this number in perspective, Armstrong World Industries, Inc.'s inventories at December 31, 1996, totaled $205.7 million, and retained earnings at that date totaled $1,222.6 million. The impact of LIFO on Armstrong World Industries, Inc.'s, financial position and results of operations has been significant, and this company is not unique (see Table 5–1). Clearly, Armstrong World Industries, Inc.'s ROI, ROE, and measures of liquidity have been impacted by the choice of inventory cost-flow assumption. Because of the importance of the inventory valuation to a firm's measures of profitability and liquidity, the impact of alternative

TABLE 5–1   Inventory Cost-Flow Assumptions Used by 600 Publicly Owned Industrial and Merchandising Corporations—1996

	Number of Companies
Methods:	
First-in, first-out (FIFO)	417
Last-in, first-out (LIFO)	332
Average cost	181
Other	37
Use of LIFO:	
All inventories	15
50% or more of inventories	178
Less than 50% of inventories	92
Not determinable	47
Companies using LIFO	332

Source: Reprinted with permission from *Accounting Trends and Techniques,* Table 2–8, copyright © 1997 by American Institute of Certified Public Accountants, Inc.

cost-flow assumptions must be understood if these measures are to be used effectively in making judgments and informed decisions—especially if comparisons are made between entities.

WHAT DOES IT MEAN?

7. What does it mean to identify the inventory cost-flow assumption?

The Impact of Changing Costs (Inflation/Deflation)

It is important to understand how the inventory cost-flow assumption used by a firm interacts with the direction of cost changes to affect both inventory and cost of goods sold. *In times of rising costs,* LIFO results in lower ending inventory and higher cost of goods sold than FIFO. These changes occur because the LIFO assumption results in most recent, and higher, costs being transferred to cost of goods sold. When purchase costs are falling, the opposite is true. These relationships are illustrated graphically in Exhibit 5–4.

The graphs in Exhibit 5–4 are helpful in understanding the relative impact on cost of goods sold and ending inventory when costs move in one direction. Of course, in the real world, costs rise and fall over time, and the impact of a strategy chosen during a period of rising costs will reverse when costs decline. Thus, in the mid-1980s some firms that had switched to LIFO during a prior inflationary period began to experience falling costs. These firms then reported higher profits under LIFO than they would have under FIFO.

The Impact of Inventory Quantity Changes

Changes in the quantities of inventory will have an impact on profits that is dependent on the cost-flow assumption used and the extent of cost changes during the year.

EXHIBIT 5–4 **Effect of Changing Costs on Inventory and Cost of Goods Sold under FIFO and LIFO**

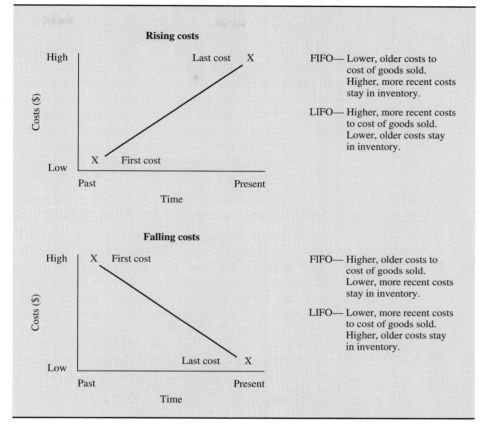

Under FIFO, whether inventory quantities rise or fall, the cost of the beginning inventory is transferred to Cost of Goods Sold because the quantity of goods sold during the year usually exceeds the quantity of beginning inventory. As previously explained, when costs are rising, costs of goods sold will be lower and profits will be higher than under LIFO. The opposite is true if costs fall during the year.

When inventory quantities rise during the year and LIFO is used, a "layer" of inventory value is added to the book value of inventories at the beginning of the year. If costs have risen during the year, LIFO results in higher cost of goods sold and lower profits than FIFO. The opposite is true if costs fall during the year.

When inventory quantities decline during the year and LIFO is used, the inventory value layers built up in prior years when inventory quantities were rising are now transferred to Cost of Goods Sold, with costs of the most recently added layer transferred first. The effect on Cost of Goods Sold and profits of LIFO versus FIFO depends on the costs in each value layer relative to current costs of inventory if FIFO is used. Generally, costs increase over time, so inventory reductions of LIFO layers result in lower cost of goods sold and higher profits than with FIFO—just the opposite of what you would normally expect under LIFO. This process is known as a

LIFO liquidation because the cost of old LIFO layers included in beginning inventory is removed or "liquidated" from the inventory account.

In recent years, many firms have sought to increase their ROI by reducing assets while maintaining or increasing sales and margin. Thus, turnover (sales/average assets) is increasing, with a resulting increase in ROI. When lower assets are achieved by reducing inventories in a LIFO environment, older and lower costs (from old LIFO layers) are released from inventory to cost of goods sold. Since revenues reflect current selling prices, which are independent of the cost-flow assumption used, profit is higher than it would be without a LIFO liquidation. In other words, net income can be increased by this unusual liquidation situation, whereby old LIFO inventory costs are matched with current sales revenues. Thus, ROI is boosted by both increased turnover and higher margin, but the margin effect occurs only in the year of the LIFO liquidation.

Selecting an Inventory Cost-Flow Assumption

What factors influence the selection of a cost-flow assumption? When rates of inflation were relatively low and the conventional wisdom was that they would always be low, most financial managers selected the FIFO cost-flow assumption because that resulted in slightly lower cost of goods sold and hence higher net income. Financial managers have a strong motivation to report higher, rather than lower, net income to the stockholders. However, when double-digit inflation was experienced, the higher net income from the FIFO assumption resulted in higher income taxes. (Federal income tax law requires that if the LIFO cost-flow assumption is used for reporting to stockholders, it must also be used for tax purposes. This tax requirement is a constraint that does not exist in other areas where alternative accounting methods exist.)

Rapidly rising costs result in **inventory profits,** or **phantom profits,** when the FIFO assumption is used because the release of older, lower costs to the income statement results in higher profits than if current costs were recognized. Since taxes must be paid on these profits and the cost of replacing the merchandise sold is considerably higher than the old cost, users of the financial statements can be misled about the firm's real economic profitability. To avoid inventory profits, many firms changed from FIFO to LIFO for at least part of their inventories during the years of high inflation. (Generally accepted accounting principles do not require that the same cost-flow assumption be used for all inventories.) This change to LIFO resulted in higher cost of goods sold than FIFO and lower profits, lower taxes, and (in the opinion of some analysts) more realistic financial reporting of net income. Note, however, that even though net income may better reflect a matching of revenues (which also usually rise on a per unit basis during periods of inflation) and costs of merchandise sold, the inventory amount on the balance sheet will be reported at older, lower costs. Thus, under LIFO, the balance sheet will not reflect current costs for items in inventory. This is consistent with the original cost concept and underscores the fact that balance sheet amounts do not reflect current values of most assets.

But what about consistency, the concept that requires whatever accounting alternative selected for one year be used for subsequent financial reporting? With respect to the inventory cost-flow assumption, the Internal Revenue Service permits a one-time, one-way change from FIFO to LIFO. Since tax reporting and financial reporting must be consistent in this area, firms must change from FIFO to LIFO for financial reporting also. If they do change methods, it is required that the effect of the change on both the balance sheet inventory amount and cost of goods sold be disclosed, so financial statement users can evaluate the impact of the change on the firm's financial position and results of operations.

Table 5–1 summarizes the methods used to determine inventory cost by 600 industrial and merchandising corporations whose annual reports are reviewed and summarized by the AICPA. It is significant that many companies use at least two methods, and that only 14 companies use LIFO for all inventories. The mix of inventory cost-flow assumptions used emphasizes the complex ramifications of selecting a cost-flow assumption.

WHAT DOES IT MEAN?

8. What does it mean to say that net income includes inventory profits?

Inventory Accounting System Alternatives

The system to account for inventory cost flow is very complex in practice because most firms have hundreds or thousands of inventory items. There are two principal **inventory accounting systems:** perpetual and periodic.

In a **perpetual inventory system,** a record is made of every purchase and every sale, and a continuous record of the quantity and cost of each item of inventory is maintained. Computers have made perpetual inventory systems feasible for an increasingly large number of small to medium-sized retail organizations that were forced in previous years to use periodic systems. Advances in the use of product bar coding and scanning devices at cash registers have lowered the costs of maintaining perpetual records. The accounting issues involved with a perpetual system are easy to understand (see Business in Practice—The Perpetual Inventory System) once you have learned how the alternative cost-flow assumptions are applied in a periodic system (refer to Exhibit 5–3 if you need a review).

BUSINESS IN PRACTICE
The Perpetual Inventory System

Under a perpetual inventory system, the cost-flow assumption used by the firm is applied on a day-to-day basis as sales are recorded, rather than at the end of the year (or month). This allows the firm to record increases to Cost of Goods Sold and decreases to Inventory on a daily basis. This makes sense from a matching perspective because the *sale* of inventory is what triggers the *cost* of goods sold. The following journal entries are recorded at the point of sale:

Dr.	Accounts Receivable (or Cash)	xx	
	Cr. Sales		xx
Dr.	Cost of Goods Sold	xx	
	Cr. Inventory		xx

Business in Practice concluded

The effects of these entries on the financial statements are:

Balance sheet	Income statement
Assets = Liabilities + Owners' equity ←	Net income = Revenues − Expenses

Record sale of goods:
+ Accounts   + Sales
   Receivable
   (or Cash)

Recognize cost of goods sold:
− Inventory   − Cost of
                                                    Goods
                                                    Sold

Thus, a continuous (or perpetual) record is maintained of the inventory account balance. Under FIFO, the periodic and perpetual systems will always produce the same results for ending inventory and cost of goods sold. Why would this be the case? Even though the FIFO rules are applied at different points in time—at the end of the year (or month) with periodic, and daily with perpetual—the first-in cost will remain in inventory until the next item of inventory is sold. Once first in, always first in, and costs flow from Inventory to Cost of Goods Sold based strictly on the chronological order of purchase transactions. The results are the same under either system because whenever the question "What was the first-in cost?" is asked (daily or monthly), the answer is the same.

Under LIFO, when the question "What was the last-in cost?" is asked, the answer will change each time a new item of inventory is purchased. In a perpetual system, the last-in costs must be determined on a daily basis so that cost of goods sold can be recorded as sales transactions occur; the cost of the most recently purchased inventory items are assigned to Cost of Goods Sold each day. But as soon as new items of inventory are purchased, the last-in costs are redefined accordingly. This differs from the periodic approach to applying the LIFO rules. In a periodic system, the last-in costs are assumed to relate only to those inventory items that are purchased toward the end of the year (or month), even though some of the sales transactions occurred earlier in the year (or month).

The weighted-average method becomes a "moving" average under the perpetual system. As with the LIFO method, when the question "What was the average cost of inventory?" is asked, the answer is likely to change each time new inventory items are purchased.

In a **periodic inventory system,** a count of the inventory on hand (taking a **physical inventory**) is made periodically—frequently at the end of the fiscal year—and the cost of the inventory on hand, based on the cost-flow assumption being used, is determined and subtracted from the sum of the beginning inventory and purchases to determine the cost of goods sold. This calculation is illustrated with the following **cost of goods sold model,** using data from the FIFO cost-flow assumption of Exhibit 5–3.

Beginning inventory	$ 7,500
Purchases	66,480
Cost of goods available for sale	$73,980
Less: Ending inventory	(13,680)
Cost of goods sold	$60,300

The examples in Exhibit 5–3 use the periodic inventory system. Although less detailed record keeping is needed for the periodic system than for the perpetual system, the efforts involved in counting and costing the inventory on hand are still significant.

Even when a perpetual inventory system is used, it is appropriate to periodically verify that the quantity of an item shown by the perpetual inventory record to be on hand is the quantity actually on hand. Bookkeeping errors and theft or mysterious disappearance will cause differences between the recorded and actual quantity of inventory items. When differences are found, it is appropriate to reflect these as inventory losses, or corrections to the inventory account, as appropriate. If the losses are significant, management would probably authorize an investigation to determine the cause of the loss and develop recommendations for strengthening the system of internal control over inventories.

This discussion of accounting for inventories has focused on the products available for sale to the entity's customers. A retail firm would use the term **merchandise inventory** to describe this inventory category; a manufacturing firm would use the term **finished goods inventory.** Besides finished goods inventory, a manufacturing firm will have two other broad inventory categories: raw materials and work in process. In a manufacturing firm, the **Raw Materials Inventory** account is used to hold the costs of raw materials until the materials are released to the factory floor, at which time the costs are transferred to the **Work in Process Inventory** account. Direct labor costs (wages of production workers) and factory overhead costs (e.g., factory utilities, maintenance costs for production equipment, and the depreciation of factory buildings and equipment) are also recorded in the Work in Process Inventory account. These costs, *incurred in making the product,* as opposed to costs of selling the product or administering the company generally, are appropriately related to the inventory items being produced and become part of the product cost to be accounted for as an asset (inventory) until the product is sold. Accounting for production costs is a large part of cost accounting, a topic that will be explored in more detail in Chapter 12.

Inventory Errors

Objective 9
Understand the impact of inventory errors on the balance sheet and income statement

Errors in the amount of ending inventory have a direct dollar-for-dollar effect on cost of goods sold and net income. This direct link between inventory amounts and reported profit or loss causes independent auditors, income tax auditors, and financial analysts to look closely at reported inventory amounts. The following T-account diagram illustrates this link:

Balance Sheet/Income Statement

Inventory (asset)	Cost of Goods Sold (expense)
Beginning balance Cost of goods purchased or manufactured Ending balance	Cost of goods sold ⟶ Cost of goods sold

The cost of goods sold model illustrated earlier expresses the same relationships depicted in the T-account diagram but in a slightly different manner. Shown below is a simplified income statement for the months of January and February, using the cost of goods sold model and assumed amounts:

	January	February
Sales	$6,000	$8,000
Cost of Goods Sold:		
Beginning inventory	$1,200	$ 900
Cost of goods purchased or manufactured	4,100	5,500
Cost of goods available for sale	$5,300	$6,400
Less: ending inventory	(900)	(1,400)
Cost of goods sold	(4,400)	(5,000)
Gross profit	$1,600	$3,000
Operating expenses	(600)	(1,000)
Net income (ignoring income taxes)	$1,000	$2,000

If the beginning balance of inventory and the cost of goods purchased or manufactured are accurate, an error in the ending inventory affects cost of goods sold (in the opposite direction). The amount of goods available for sale during the period must either remain on hand as ending inventory (asset) or flow to the income statement as cost of goods sold (expense). For example, if ending inventory for January is *understated* by $100 (i.e., ending inventory should have been $1,000) in the above example, then cost of goods sold for January will be *overstated* by $100. Do you agree that if ending inventory in January is $1,000, then cost of goods sold for January will be $4,300? Overstated cost of goods sold results in understated gross profit and net income. How much would these amounts be for January if the $100 error were corrected? (Note that sales and operating expenses are not affected by the error.)

The error will also affect cost of goods sold and net income of the subsequent period, but the effects of the error will be reversed because one period's ending inventory is the next period's beginning inventory. In our example, the beginning inventory for February should be $1,000, rather than $900. With understated beginning inventory, the cost of goods available for sale will also be understated by $100 (it should be $6,500). Assuming that ending inventory was valued correctly in February, then cost of goods sold will be understated by $100, which in turn will cause gross profit and net income to be overstated by $100. What are the correct amounts for these items in February? You should take some time to puzzle through these relationships.

When the periodic inventory system is used, a great deal of effort is made to have the inventory count and valuation be as accurate as possible because inventory errors can have a significant impact on both the balance sheet and the income statement for each period affected. You should note, however, that this type of error "washes out" over the two periods taken together (i.e., *total* net income is not affected by the error). Check this out by adding together the total net income for January and February before and after the error is corrected.

WHAT DOES IT MEAN?

9. What does it mean to say that an error in the ending inventory of one accounting period has an equal and opposite effect on the net income of the subsequent accounting period?

Balance Sheet Valuation at the Lower of Cost or Market

Inventory carrying values on the balance sheet are reported at the **lower of cost or market.** This reporting is an application of accounting conservatism. The "market" of lower of cost or market is generally the replacement cost of the inventory on the balance sheet date. If market value is lower than cost, then a loss is reported in the accounting period in which the decline in inventory value occurred. The loss is recognized because the decision to buy or make the item was costly, to the extent that the item could have been bought or manufactured at the end of the accounting period for less than its original cost.

The lower-of-cost-or-market determination can be made with respect to individual items of inventory, broad categories of inventory, or to the inventory as a whole. A valuation adjustment will be made to reduce the carrying value of inventory items that have become obsolete or that have deteriorated and will not be salable at normal prices.

Prepaid Expenses and Other Current Assets

Objective 10
Understand what prepaid expenses are and how they are reported on the balance sheet.

Other current assets are principally **prepaid expenses,** that is, expenses that have been paid in the current fiscal period but that will not be subtracted from revenue until a subsequent fiscal period. This is the opposite of an accrual and is referred to in accounting and bookkeeping jargon as a *deferral* or *deferred charge* (or *deferred debit* since *charge* is a bookkeeping synonym for *debit*). An example of a **deferred charge** transaction is a premium payment to an insurance company. It is standard business practice to pay an insurance premium at the beginning of the period of insurance coverage. Assume that a one-year casualty insurance premium of $1,800 is paid on November 1, 1999. At December 31, 1999, insurance coverage for two months has been received, and it is appropriate to recognize the cost of that coverage as an expense. However, the cost of coverage for the next 10 months should be deferred, that is, not shown as an expense but reported as **prepaid insurance,** an asset. Usual bookkeeping practice is to record the premium payment transaction as an increase in the Prepaid Insurance asset account and then to transfer a portion of the premium to the Insurance Expense account as the expense is incurred. The journal entries are:

Nov.	1	Dr. Prepaid Insurance	1,800	
		Cr. Cash................................		1,800
		Payment of one-year premium.		
Dec.	31	Dr. Insurance Expense......................	300	
		Cr. Prepaid Insurance.....................		300
		Insurance expense for two months incurred.		

With the horizontal model, this transaction and the adjustment affect the financial statements as follows:

Balance sheet	Income statement
Assets = Liabilities + Owners' equity ←	Net income = Revenues − Expenses

Payment of premium for the year:
Cash
− 1,800

Prepaid
Insurance
+ 1,800

Recognition of expense for two months:
Prepaid   Insurance
Insurance   Expense
− 300   − 300

The balance in the Prepaid Insurance asset account at December 31 would be $1,500, which represents the premium for the next 10 months' coverage that has already been paid and will be transferred to Insurance Expense over the next 10 months.

Other expenses that could be prepaid and included in this category of current assets include rent, office supplies, postage, and travel expense advances to salespeople and other employees. The key to deferring these expenses is that they can be objectively associated with a benefit to be received in a future period. Advertising expenditures are not properly deferred because it is not possible to determine objectively how much of the benefit of advertising occurred in the current period and how much of the benefit will be received in future periods. As with advertising expenditures, research and development costs are not deferred but are instead treated as expenses in the year incurred. The accountant's principal concerns are that the prepaid item be a properly deferred expense and that it will be used up, and become an expense, within the one-year time frame for classification as a current asset.

WHAT DOES IT MEAN?

10. What does it mean to defer an expense?

Deferred Tax Assets

Deferred income taxes arise from differences in the fiscal year in which revenues and expenses are recognized for financial accounting and income tax determination purposes. When an expense is recognized for financial accounting purposes in a fiscal year before the fiscal year in which it is deductible in the determination of taxable income, a **deferred tax asset** arises. Deferred tax assets commonly arise from employee benefit costs, accrued pension and postretirement benefits, bad debts and inventory obsolescence provisions, accrued warranty costs, and other current year expenses that are not deductible for income tax purposes until a later year. Deferred tax assets represent a reduction in the income tax liability of a future year when the expense will become deductible for tax purposes. If this benefit will be realized in the coming year, the deferred tax asset is a current asset; otherwise, it is a noncurrent asset.

As discussed in Chapter 7, **deferred tax liabilities** must also be reported by firms for the probable future tax consequences of events that have occurred up to the balance sheet date. As explained more thoroughly in Chapter 7, the effect of recognizing deferred tax assets and liabilities is to report as income tax expense an amount that is appropriate for the amount of earnings before income taxes, even though the amount of income taxes actually payable for the fiscal year is more or less than the income tax expense recognized. Accounting for deferred income taxes is a very complex issue that has caused a lot of debate within the accounting profession. For now, you should understand that there are a number of timing differences between the revenue and expense recognition practices of financial accounting and the regulations of income tax determination, and that deferred tax assets and liabilities are recorded to account for these differences.

Summary

This chapter has discussed the accounting for and the presentation of the following balance sheet current assets and related income statement accounts:

Balance sheet	Income statement
Assets = Liabilities + Owners' equity ←	Net income = Revenues − Expenses
Cash	
Marketable Securities	
Interest Receivable	Interest Income
Accounts Receivable	Sales Revenue
(Allowance for Bad Debts)	Bad Debts Expense
Inventory	Cost of Goods Sold
Prepaid Expenses	Operating Expenses
Deferred Tax Assets	Income Tax Expense

The amount of cash reported on the balance sheet represents the cash available to the entity as of the close of business on the balance sheet date. Cash available in bank accounts is determined by reconciling the bank statement balance with the entity's book balance. Reconciling items are caused by timing differences (such as deposits in transit or outstanding checks) and errors.

Petty cash funds are used as a convenience for making small disbursements of cash.

Entities temporarily invest excess cash in short-term marketable securities in order to earn interest income. Cash managers invest in short-term, low-risk securities that are not likely to have a widely fluctuating market value. Marketable securities that will be held until maturity are reported in the balance sheet at cost; securities that may be traded or are available for sale are reported at market value.

Accounts receivable are valued in the balance sheet at the amount expected to be collected. This valuation principle, as well as the matching concept, requires that the estimated losses from uncollectible accounts be recognized in the fiscal period in which the receivable arose. A valuation adjustment recognizing bad debts expense and using the Allowance for Bad Debts account is used to accomplish this. When an account receivable is determined to be uncollectible, it is written off against the allowance account.

Firms encourage customers to pay their bills promptly by allowing a cash discount if the bill is paid within a specified period such as 10 days. Cash discounts are classified in the income statement as a deduction from sales revenue. It is appropriate to reduce accounts receivable with an allowance for cash discounts, which accomplishes the same objectives associated with the allowance for bad debts.

Organizations have a system of internal control to promote the effectiveness and efficiency of the organization's operations, the reliability of the organization's financial reporting, and the organization's compliance with applicable laws and regulations.

Notes receivable usually have a longer term than accounts receivable, and they bear interest. The accounting for notes receivable is similar to that for accounts receivable.

Accounting for inventories involves selecting and applying a cost-flow assumption that determines the assumed pattern of cost flow from the Inventory asset account to the Cost of Goods Sold expense account. The alternative cost-flow assumptions are specific identification; weighted-average; first-in, first-out; and last-in, first-out. The assumed cost flow will probably differ from the physical flow of the product. When price levels change, different cost-flow assumptions result in different cost of goods sold amounts in the income statement and different Inventory account balances in the balance sheet. The cost-flow assumption used also influences the effect of inventory quantity changes on the balance in both Cost of Goods Sold and ending Inventory. Because of the significance of inventories in most balance sheets and the direct relationship between inventory and cost of goods sold, accurate accounting for inventories must be achieved if the financial statements are to be meaningful.

Prepaid expenses (or deferred charges) arise in the accrual accounting process. To achieve an appropriate matching of revenue and expense, amounts prepaid for insurance, rent, and other similar items should be recorded as assets (rather than expenses) until the period in which the benefits of such payments are received.

Deferred tax assets arise when an expense is recognized for financial accounting purposes in a year before it is deductible for income tax purposes.

Refer to the Intel Corporation balance sheet and related notes in the Appendix, and to other financial statements you may have, and observe how current assets are presented.

Key Terms and Concepts

administrative controls (p. 138)   Features of the internal control system that emphasize adherence to management's policies and operating efficiency.

allowance for uncollectible accounts (or **allowance for bad debts**) (p. 144)   The valuation allowance that results in accounts receivable being reduced by the amount not expected to be collected.

bad debts expense (or **uncollectible accounts expense**) (p. 143)   An estimated expense, recognized in the fiscal period of the sale, representing accounts receivable that are not expected to be collected.

bank reconciliation (p. 139)   The process of bringing into agreement the balance in the Cash account in the entity's ledger and the balance reported on the bank statement.

bank service charge (p. 139)   The fee charged by a bank for maintaining the entity's checking account.

carrying value (p. 143)   The balance of the ledger account (including related contra accounts, if any) of an asset, liability, or owners' equity account. Sometimes referred to as *book value.*

cash discount (p. 145)   A discount offered for prompt payment.

collateral (p. 147)   The security provided by a borrower that can be used to satisfy the obligation if payment is not made when due.

collect on delivery (COD) (p. 137)   A requirement that an item be paid for when it is delivered. Sometimes COD is defined as *"cash" on delivery.*

commercial paper (p. 137)   A short-term security usually issued by a large, creditworthy corporation.

contra asset (p. 144)   An account that normally has a credit balance that is subtracted from a related asset on the balance sheet.

cost-flow assumption (p. 150)   An assumption made for accounting purposes that identifies how costs flow from the inventory account to cost of goods sold. Alternatives include specific identification; weighted average; first-in, first-out; and last-in, first-out.

cost of goods sold model (p. 158)   The way to calculate cost of goods sold when the periodic inventory system is used. The model follows:

Beginning inventory
Purchases

Cost of goods available for sale

Less: Ending inventory

Cost of goods sold

credit terms (p. 145)   A seller's policy with respect to when payment of an invoice is due and what cash discount (if any) is allowed.

deferred charge (p. 161)   An expenditure made in one fiscal period that will be recognized as an expense in a future fiscal period. Another term for a *prepaid expense.*

deferred tax asset (p. 163)   An asset that arises because of temporary differences between when an item is recognized for book and tax purposes.

deferred tax liability (p. 163)   A liability that arises because of temporary differences between when an item is recognized for book and tax purposes.

deposit in transit (p. 139)   A bank deposit that has been recorded in the entity's cash account but that does not appear on the bank statement because the bank received the deposit after the date of the statement.

financial controls (p. 138)   Features of the internal control system that emphasize accuracy of bookkeeping and financial statements, and protection of assets.

finished goods inventory (p. 159)   The term used primarily by manufacturing firms to describe inventory ready for sale to customers.

first-in, first-out (FIFO) (p. 151)   The inventory cost-flow assumption that the first costs in to inventory are the first costs out to cost of goods sold.

imprest account (p. 137)   An asset account that has a constant balance in the ledger; cash and receipts or vouchers add up to the account balance. Used especially for petty cash funds.

internal control system (p. 136)   Policies and procedures designed to provide reasonable assurance that objectives are achieved with respect to:

1. The effectiveness and efficiency of the operations of the organization.
2. The reliability of the organization's financial reporting.
3. The organization's compliance with applicable laws and regulations.

inventory accounting system (p. 157)   The method used to account for the movement of items in to inventory and out to cost of goods sold. The alternatives are the periodic system and the perpetual system.

inventory profits (p. 156)   Profits that result from using the FIFO cost-flow assumption rather than LIFO during periods of inflation. Sometimes called *phantom profits.*

last-in, first-out (LIFO) (p. 152)   The inventory cost-flow assumption that the last costs in to inventory are the first costs out to cost of goods sold.

LIFO liquidation (p. 156)   Under the LIFO cost-flow assumption, when the number of units sold during the period exceeds the number of units purchased or made, at least some of the costs assigned to the LIFO beginning inventory are transferred to Cost of Goods Sold. As a result, outdated costs are matched with current revenues and *inventory profits* occur.

lower of cost or market (p. 161)   A valuation process that may result in an asset being reported at an amount less than cost.

merchandise inventory (p. 159)   The term used primarily by retail firms to describe inventory ready for sale to customers.

net realizable value (p. 142)   The amount of funds expected to be received upon sale or liquidation of an asset. For accounts receivable, the amount expected to be collected from customers after allowing for bad debts and cash discounts.

note receivable (p. 146)   A formal document (usually interest bearing) that supports the financial claim of one entity against another.

NSF (not sufficient funds) check (p. 139)   A check returned by the maker's bank because there were not enough funds in the account to cover the check.

operating cycle (p. 135)   The average time it takes a firm to convert an amount invested in inventory back to cash. For most firms, the operating cycle is measured as the average number of days to produce and sell inventory plus the average number of days to collect accounts receivable.

outstanding check (p. 139)   A check that has been recorded as a cash disbursement by the entity but that has not yet been processed by the bank.

periodic inventory system (p. 158)   A system of accounting for the movement of items in to inventory and out to cost of goods sold that involves periodically making a physical count of the inventory on hand.

perpetual inventory system (p. 157)   A system of accounting for the movement of items in to inventory and out to cost of goods sold that involves keeping a continuous record of items received, items sold, and inventory on hand.

petty cash (p. 136)   A fund used for small payments for which writing a check is inconvenient.

phantom profits (p. 156)   See *inventory profits*.

physical inventory (p. 158)   The process of counting the inventory on hand and determining its cost based on the inventory cost-flow assumption being used.

prepaid expenses (p. 161)   Expenses that have been paid in the current fiscal period but that will not be subtracted from revenues until a subsequent fiscal period. Usually a current asset. Another term for *deferred charge*.

prepaid insurance (p. 161)   An asset account that represents an expenditure made in one fiscal period for insurance that will be recognized as an expense in the subsequent fiscal period to which the coverage applies.

raw materials inventory (p. 159)   Inventory of materials ready for the production process.

short-term marketable securities (p. 141)   Investments made with cash not needed for current operations.

specific identification (p. 150)   The inventory cost-flow assumption that matches cost flow with physical flow.

valuation account (p. 145)   An account that reduces the carrying value of an asset to a net realizable value that is less than cost.

valuation adjustment (p. 143)   An adjustment that results in an asset being reported at a net realizable value that is less than cost.

weighted-average (p. 150)   The inventory cost-flow assumption that is based on an average of the cost of beginning inventory and the cost of purchases during the year, weighted by the quantity of items at each cost.

work in process inventory (p. 159)   Inventory account for the costs (raw materials, direct labor, and manufacturing overhead) of items that are in the process of being manufactured.

write-off (p. 145)   The process of removing an account receivable that is not expected to be collected from the Accounts Receivable account. Also used generically to describe the reduction of an asset and the related recognition of an expense.

WHAT DOES IT MEAN?
ANSWERS

1. It means that the asset is cash, or it is an asset that is expected to be converted to cash or used up in the operating activities of the entity within one year.

2. It means that from the Board of Directors down through the organization, the policies and procedures related to effectiveness and efficiency of operations, reliability of financial reporting, and compliance with laws and regulations are understood and followed.

3. It means that the balance in the Cash account in the ledger has been brought into agreement with the balance on the bank statement by recognizing timing differences and errors between transactions recorded in the ledger and those recorded by the bank.

4. It means that cash not immediately required for use by the entity is invested for awhile in order to earn interest and thus increase the entity's ROI and ROE.

5. It means that interest has not been received by the entity for part of the period for which funds have been invested even though the interest has been earned, so interest receivable and interest income are recognized by an adjusting entry.

6. It means that the estimate of accounts receivable that will not be collected is subtracted from the total accounts receivable because it isn't yet known which specific accounts receivable will not be collected.

7. It means to identify the method used to transfer the cost of an item sold from the Inventory asset account to the Cost of Goods Sold expense account in the income statement. This is different from the physical flow, which describes the physical movement of product from storeroom to customer. The alternative inventory cost-flow assumptions are FIFO, LIFO, weighted-average cost, and specific identification.

8. It means that because of applying a particular inventory cost-flow assumption, net income is higher or lower than what it would have been if an alternative cost-flow assumption had been used.

9. It means that an ending inventory error affects cost of goods sold on the income statement for two consecutive periods. Since ending inventory of one period is beginning inventory of the next period, the over/understatement of cost of goods sold in one period will be reversed in the next period.

10. It means to delay the income statement recognition of an expense until a future period to which it is applicable. Even though a cash payment has been made, the expense has not yet been incurred. An asset account is established for the prepaid expense.

Exercises and Problems

LO 3   **5–1. Bank reconciliation.** Prepare a bank reconciliation as of October 31 from the following information:
  a. The October 31 cash balance in the general ledger is $844.
  b. The October 31 balance shown on the bank statement is $373.
  c. Checks issued but not returned with the bank statement were No. 462 for $13, and No. 483 for $50.
  d. A deposit made late on October 31 for $450 is included in the general ledger balance but not in the bank statement balance.
  e. Returned with the bank statement was a notice that a customer's check for $75 that was deposited on October 25 had been returned because the customer's account was overdrawn.
  f. During a review of the checks that were returned with the bank statement, it was noted that the amount of Check No. 471 was $65 but that in the company's records supporting the general ledger balance, the check had been erroneously recorded as a payment of an account payable in the amount of $56.

LO 3   **5–2. Bank reconciliation.** Prepare a bank reconciliation as of January 31 from the following information:
  a. The January 31 balance shown on the bank statement is $1,860.
  b. There is a deposit in transit of $210 at January 31.
  c. Outstanding checks at January 31 totaled $315.
  d. Interest credited to the account during January but not recorded on the company's books amounted to $18.
  e. A bank charge of $6 for checks was made to the account during January. Although the company was expecting a charge, its amount was not known until the bank statement arrived.
  f. In the process of reviewing the canceled checks, it was determined that a check issued to a supplier in payment of accounts payable of $316 had been recorded as a disbursement of $361.
  g. The January 31 balance in the general ledger Cash account, before reconciliation, is $1,698.

LO 3   **5–3. Bank reconciliation adjusting entry.**
  a. Write the adjusting journal entry (or entries) that should be prepared to reflect the reconciling items of Problem 5–1 or show the reconciling items in a horizontal model.
  b. What is the amount of cash to be included in the October 31 balance sheet for the bank account reconciled in Problem 5–1?

LO 3   **5–4. Bank reconciliation adjusting entry.**
  a. Write the adjusting journal entry (or entries) that should be prepared to reflect the reconciling items of Problem 5–2 or show the reconciling items in a horizontal model.

b. What is the amount of cash to be included in the January 31 balance sheet for the bank account reconciled in Problem 5–2?

LO 3   **5–5.   Bank reconciliation—compute Cash account balance and bank statement balance before reconciling items.** Beckett Co. received its bank statement for the month ending June 30, 1999, and reconciled the statement balance to the June 30, 1999, balance in the Cash account. The reconciled balance was determined to be $4,800. The reconciliation recognized the following items:
1. Deposits in transit were $2,100.
2. Outstanding checks totaled $3,000.
3. Bank service charges shown as a deduction on the bank statement were $50.
4. An NSF check from a customer for $400 was included with the bank statement. The firm had not been previously notified that the check had been returned NSF.
5. Included in the canceled checks was a check actually written for $890. However, it had been recorded as a disbursement of $980.

Required:
a. What was the balance in Beckett Co.'s Cash account before recognizing any of the above reconciling items?
b. What was the balance shown on the bank statement before recognizing any of the above reconciling items?

LO 3   **5–6.   Bank reconciliation—compute Cash account balance and bank statement balance before reconciling items.** Branson Co. received its bank statement for the month ending May 31, 1999, and reconciled the statement balance to the May 31, 1999, balance in the Cash account. The reconciled balance was determined to be $3,100. The reconciliation recognized the following items:
1. A deposit made on May 31 for $1,700 was included in the Cash account balance but not in the bank statement balance.
2. Checks issued but not returned with the bank statement were No. 673 for $490 and No. 687 for $950.
3. Bank service charges shown as a deduction on the bank statement were $40.
4. Interest credited to Branson Co.'s account but not recorded on the company's books amounted to $24.
5. Returned with the bank statement was a "debit memo" stating that a customer's check for $320 that had been deposited on May 23 had been returned because the customer's account was overdrawn.
6. During a review of the checks that were returned with the bank statement, it was noted that the amount of check No. 681 was $160 but that in the company's records supporting the Cash account balance, the check had been erroneously recorded in the amount of $16.

Required:
a. What was the balance in Branson Co.'s Cash account before recognizing any of the above reconciling items?
b. What was the balance shown on the bank statement before recognizing any of the above reconciling items?

LO 5   **5–7.   Bad debts analysis—Allowance account.** On January 1, 1999, the balance in Tabor Co.'s Allowance for Bad Debts account was $13,400. During the first 11 months of the year, bad debts expense of $21,462 was recognized. The balance in the Allowance for Bad Debts account at November 30, 1999, was $9,763.

Required:
a. What was the total of accounts written off during the first 11 months? (*Hint: Make a T-account for the Allowance for Bad Debts account.*)

b. As the result of a comprehensive analysis, it is determined that the December 31, 1999, balance of the Allowance for Bad Debts account should be $9,500. Show, in general journal format, the adjusting entry required or show the adjustment in the horizontal model.

c. During a conversation with the credit manager, one of Tabor's sales representatives learns that a $1,230 receivable from a bankrupt customer has not been written off but was considered in the determination of the appropriate year-end balance of the Allowance for Bad Debts account balance. Write a brief explanation to the sales representative explaining the effect that the write-off of this account receivable would have had on 1999 net income.

LO 5   **5–8. Bad debts analysis—Allowance account.** On January 1, 1999, the balance in Kubera Co.'s Allowance for Bad Debts account was $1,210. During the year, a total of $3,605 of delinquent accounts receivable was written off as bad debts. The balance in the Allowance for Bad Debts account at December 31, 1999, was $1,450.

Required:

a. What was the total amount of bad debts expense recognized during the year? (*Hint: Make a T-account for the Allowance for Bad Debts account.*)

b. As a result of a comprehensive analysis, it is determined that the December 31, 1999, balance of Allowance for Bad Debts should be $4,300. Show, in general journal format or in the horizontal model, the adjusting entry required.

LO 5   **5–9. Bad debts analysis—Allowance account and financial statement effect.** The following is a portion of the current assets section of the balance sheets of Avanti's, Inc., at December 31, 1999 and 1998:

	12/31/99	12/31/98
Accounts receivable, less allowance for bad debts of $9,500 and $17,900, respectively	$173,200	$236,400

Required:

a. If $11,800 of accounts receivable were written off during 1999, what was the amount of bad debts expense recognized for the year? (*Hint: Use a T-account model of the allowance account, plug in the three amounts that you know, and solve for the unknown.*)

b. The December 31, 1999, Allowance account balance includes $3,100 for a past due account that is not likely to be collected. This account has *not* been written off. *If it had been written off,* what would have been the effect of the write-off on:

1. Working capital at December 31, 1999?
2. Net income and ROI for the year ended December 31, 1999?

c. What do you suppose was the level of Avanti's sales in 1999, compared to 1998? Explain your answer.

LO 5   **5–10. Bad debts analysis—Allowance account and financial statement effects.** The following is a portion of the current asset section of the balance sheets of HiROE Co., at December 31, 1999, and 1998:

	December 31, 1999	December 31, 1998
Accounts receivable, less allowance for uncollectible accounts of $9,000 and $3,000, respectively	151,000	117,000

Required:

a. Describe how the allowance amount at December 31, 1999, was most likely determined.

b. If bad debts expense for 1999 totaled $8,000, what was the amount of accounts receivable written off during the year? (*Hint: Use the T-account model of the allowance account, plug in the three amounts that you know, and solve for the unknown.*)

c. The December 31, 1999, Allowance account balance includes $3,500 for a past due account that is not likely to be collected. This account has *not* been written off. *If it had been written off,* what would have been the effect of the write off on:

    1. Working capital at December 31, 1999?

    2. Net income and ROI for the year ended December 31, 1999?

d. What do you suppose was the level of HiROE's sales in 1999, compared to 1998? Explain your answer.

e. Calculate the ratio of the Allowance for Uncollectible Accounts balance to the Accounts Receivable balance at December 31, 1998 and 1999. What factors might have caused the change in this ratio?

LO 5   **5–11.** **Analysis of accounts receivable and allowance for bad debts—determine beginning balances.** A portion of the current assets section of the December 31, 1999, balance sheet for Carr Co. is presented below.

Accounts receivable	$50,000	
Less: Allowance for bad debts	(7,000)	$43,000

The company's accounting records revealed the following information for the year ended December 31, 1999:

Sales (all on account)	$400,000
Cash collections from customers	410,000
Accounts written off	15,000
Bad debts expense (accrued at 12/31/99)	12,000

Required:

Using the information provided for 1999, calculate the net realizable value of accounts receivable at December 31, 1998, and prepare the appropriate balance sheet presentation for Carr Co., as of that point in time. (*Hint: Use T-accounts to analyze the Accounts Receivable and Allowance for Bad Debts accounts. Remember that you are solving for the beginning balance of each account.*)

LO 5   **5–12.** **Analysis of accounts receivable and allowance for bad debts—determine ending balances.** A portion of the current assets section of the December 31, 1998, balance sheet for Gibbs Co. follows.

Accounts receivable	$42,000	
Less: Allowance for bad debts	(6,000)	$36,000

The company's accounting records revealed the following information for the year ended December 31, 1999:

Sales (all on account)	$320,000
Cash collections from customers	290,000
Accounts written off	7,000
Bad debts expense (accrued at 12/31/99)	11,000

Required:

Calculate the net realizable value of accounts receivable at December 31, 1999, and prepare the appropriate balance sheet presentation for Gibbs Co., as of that point in time. *(Hint: Use T-accounts to analyze the Accounts Receivable and Allowance for Bad Debts accounts.)*

LO 5   **5–13.**   **Cash discounts—ROI.** Annual credit sales of Nadak Co. total $340 million. The firm gives a 2% cash discount for payment within 10 days of the invoice date; 90% of Nadak's accounts receivable are paid within the discount period.

Required:

a. What is the total amount of cash discounts allowed in a year?

b. Calculate the approximate annual rate of return on investment that Nadak Co.'s cash discount terms represent to customers who take the discount.

LO 5   **5–14.**   **Cash discounts—ROI.**

a. Calculate the approximate annual rate of return on investment of the following cash discount terms:

1. 1/15, net 30
2. 2/10, net 60
3. 1/10, net 90

b. Which of the above terms, if any, is not likely to be a significant incentive to the customer to pay promptly? Explain your answer.

LO 6   **5–15.**   **Notes receivable—interest accrual and collection.** Agrico, Inc., took a 10-month, 13.8% (annual rate), $4,500 note from one of its customers on June 15; interest is payable with the principal at maturity.

Required:

a. Write the entry, in general journal format, to record the interest earned by Agrico during its fiscal year ended October 31.

b. Write the entry, in general journal format, to record collection of the note and interest at maturity.

(Note: As an alternative to writing journal entries, use the horizontal model to show the interest accrual and collection.)

LO 6   **5–16.**   **Notes receivable—interest accrual and collection.** Decdos Co.'s assets include notes receivable from customers. During fiscal 1999, the amount of notes receivable averaged $46,800, and the interest rate of the notes averaged 9.2%.

Required:

a. Calculate the amount of interest income earned by Decdos Co. during fiscal 1999 and write a journal entry that accrues the income interest earned from the notes.

b. If the balance in the Interest Receivable account increased by $1,100 from the beginning to the end of the fiscal year, how much interest receivable was collected during the fiscal year? Write the journal entry to show the collection of this amount.

(Note: As an alternative to writing journal entries, use the horizontal model to show the interest accrual and collection.)

LO 7, 8   **5–17.   Cost-flow assumptions—FIFO and LIFO using a periodic system.** Mower-Blower Sales Co. started business on January 20, 1999. Products sold were snow blowers and lawn mowers. Each product sold for $350. Purchases during 1999 were:

	Blowers	Mowers
January 21	20 @ $200	
February 3	40 @ 195	
February 28	30 @ 190	
March 13	20 @ 190	
April 6		20 @ $210
May 22		40 @ 215
June 3		40 @ 220
June 20		60 @ 230
August 15		20 @ 215
September 20		20 @ 210
November 7	20 @ 200	

In inventory at December 31, 1999, were 10 blowers and 25 mowers. Assume the company uses a periodic inventory system.

Required:

a. What will be the *difference* between ending inventory valuation at December 31, 1999, and cost of goods sold for 1999, under the FIFO and LIFO cost-flow assumptions? *(Hint: Compute ending inventory and cost of goods sold under each method, and then compare results.)*

b. If the cost of mowers had increased to $240 each by December 1, and if management had purchased 30 mowers at that time, which cost-flow assumption is probably being used by the firm? Explain your answer.

LO 7, 8   **5–18.   Cost-flow assumptions—FIFO, LIFO, and weighted-average using a periodic system.** The following data are available for Sellco for the fiscal year ended on January 31, 1999:

Sales	800 units
Beginning inventory	250 units @ $4.00
Purchases, in chronological order	300 units @ $5.00
	400 units @ $6.00
	200 units @ $8.00

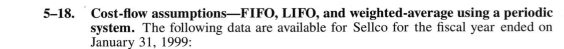

Required:

a. Calculate cost of goods sold and ending inventory under the following cost-flow assumptions (using a periodic inventory system):
  1. FIFO.
  2. LIFO.
  3. Weighted-average.

b. Assume that net income using the weighted-average cost-flow assumption is $14,500. Calculate net income under FIFO and LIFO.

LO 7, 8 **5–19. Cost-flow assumptions—FIFO and LIFO using periodic and perpetual systems.** The inventory records of Kuffel Co. reflected the following information for the year ended December 31, 1999:

Date	Transaction	Number of Units	Unit Cost	Total Cost
1/1	Beginning inventory....................	150	$30	$ 4,500
2/22	Purchase	70	33	2,310
3/7	Sale	(100)	—	—
4/15	Purchase	90	35	3,150
6/11	Purchase	140	36	5,040
9/28	Sale	(100)	—	—
10/13	Purchase	50	38	1,900
12/4	Sale	(100)	—	—
12/31	Goods available for sale................	500		$16,900

Required:

a. Assume that Kuffel Co. uses a periodic inventory system. Calculate cost of goods sold and ending inventory under FIFO and LIFO.

b. Assume that Kuffel Co. uses a perpetual inventory system. Calculate cost of goods sold and ending inventory under FIFO and LIFO.

c. Explain why the FIFO results for cost of goods sold and ending inventory are the same in your answers to parts *a* and *b*, but the LIFO results are different.

LO 7, 8 **5–20. Cost-flow assumptions—FIFO and LIFO using periodic and perpetual systems.** The inventory records of Cushing, Inc., reflected the following information for the year ended December 31, 1999:

	Number of Units	Unit Cost	Total Cost
Inventory, January 1	100	$13	$1,300
Purchases:			
May 30	160	15	2,400
September 28	200	16	3,200
Goods available for sale	460		$6,900
Sales:			
February 22	(70)		
June 11	(150)		
November 1	(190)		
Inventory, December 31	50		

Required:

a. Assume that Cushing, Inc., uses a periodic inventory system. Calculate cost of goods sold and ending inventory under FIFO and LIFO.

b. Assume that Cushing, Inc., uses a perpetual inventory system. Calculate cost of goods sold and ending inventory under FIFO and LIFO.

c. Explain why the FIFO results for cost of goods sold and ending inventory are the same in your answers to parts *a* and *b,* but the LIFO results are different.

d. Explain why the results from the LIFO periodic calculations in part *a* cannot possibly represent the actual physical flow of inventory items.

LO
7, 8

5–21.   LIFO versus FIFO—matching and balance sheet impact. Proponents of the LIFO inventory cost-flow assumption argue that this costing method is superior to the alternatives because it results in better matching of revenue and expense.

Required:

a. Explain why "better matching" occurs with LIFO.

b. What is the impact on the carrying value of inventory in the balance sheet when LIFO rather than FIFO is used during periods of inflation?

LO 7, 8

5–22.   LIFO versus FIFO—impact on ROI. Natco, Inc., uses the FIFO inventory cost-flow assumption. In a year of rising costs and prices, the firm reported net income of $120 and average assets of $600. If Natco had used the LIFO cost-flow assumption in the same year, its cost of goods sold would have been $20 more than under FIFO, and its average assets would have been $20 less than under FIFO.

Required:

a. Calculate the firm's ROI under each cost-flow assumption.

b. Suppose that two years later costs and prices were falling. Under FIFO, net income and average assets were $130 and $650, respectively. If LIFO had been used through the years, inventory values would have been $30 less than under FIFO, and current year cost of goods sold would have been $10 less than under FIFO. Calculate the firm's ROI under each cost-flow assumption.

LO 7

5–23.   Effects of inventory errors.

a. If the beginning balance of the Inventory account and the cost of items purchased or made during the period are correct, but an error resulted in overstating the firm's ending inventory balance by $5,000, how would the firm's cost of goods sold be affected? Explain your answer by drawing T-accounts for Inventory and Cost of Goods Sold and entering amounts that illustrate the difference between correctly stating and overstating the ending inventory balance.

b. If management wanted to understate profits, would ending inventory be understated or overstated? Explain your answer.

LO 7

5–24.   Effects of Inventory Errors. Following are condensed income statements for Uncle Bill's Home Improvement Center, for the years ended December 31, 1998, and 1997.

	1998	1997
Sales	$541,200	$523,600
Cost of Goods Sold:		
Beginning inventory	$ 91,400	$ 85,300
Cost of goods purchased	393,000	366,500
Cost of goods available for sale	$484,400	$451,800
Less: ending inventory	(79,800)	(91,400)
Cost of goods sold	(404,600)	(360,400)
Gross profit	$136,600	$163,200
Operating expenses	(103,700)	(94,700)
Net income (ignoring income taxes)	$ 32,900	$ 68,500

Uncle Bill was concerned about the operating results for 1998 and asked his recently hired accountant, "If sales increased in 1998, why was net income less than half of what it was in 1997?" In February of 1999, Uncle Bill got his answer, "The ending inventory reported in 1997 was overstated by $23,500 for merchandise that we were holding on consignment on behalf of Kirk's Servistar. We still keep some of their appliances in stock, but the value of these items was not included in the 1998 inventory count because we don't own them."

a. Recast the 1997 and 1998 income statements to take into account the correction of the 1997 ending inventory error.

b. Calculate the combined net income for 1997 and 1998 before the correction of the error and after the correction of the error. Explain to Uncle Bill why the error was corrected in 1998 before it was actually discovered in 1999.

c. What effect, if any, will the error have on net income and owners' equity in 1999?

LO 10   **5–25. Prepaid expenses—insurance.**

a. Write the journal entry to record the payment of a one-year insurance premium of $3,000 on March 1.

b. Write the adjusting entry that will be made at the end of every month to show the amount of insurance premium "used" that month.

c. Calculate the amount of prepaid insurance that should be reported on the August 31 balance sheet with respect to this policy.

d. If the premium had been $6,000 for a two-year period, how should the prepaid amount at August 31 of the first year be reported on the balance sheet?

e. Why are prepaid expenses reflected as an asset instead of being recorded as an expense in the accounting period in which the item is paid?

(Note: As an alternative to writing journal entries, use the horizontal model to show the premium payment and monthly adjustment.)

LO 10   **5–26. Prepaid expenses—rent.**
(Note: See Problem 7–11 for the related unearned revenue accounting.)
On September 1, 1998, Wenger Co. paid its landlord $4,200 in cash as an advance rent payment on its store location. The six-month lease period ends on February 28, 1999, at which time the contract may be renewed.

Required:

a. Use the horizontal model or write the journal entry to record the six-month advance rent payment on September 1, 1998.

b. Use the horizontal model or write the adjusting entry that will be made at the end of every month to show the amount of rent "used" during the month.

c. Calculate the amount of prepaid rent that should be reported on the December 31, 1998, balance sheet with respect to this lease.

d. If the advance payment made on September 1, 1998, had covered an 18-month lease period at the same amount of rent per month, how should Wenger Co. report the prepaid amount on its December 31, 1998, balance sheet?

LO 5, 6, 8   **5–27.** **Transaction analysis—various accounts.** Prepare an answer sheet with the column headings shown below. For each of the following transactions or adjustments, you are to indicate the effect of the transaction or adjustment on the appropriate balance sheet category and on net income by entering for each account affected the account name and amount and indicating whether it is an addition (+) or a subtraction (−). Transaction *a* has been done as an illustration. Net income is *not* affected by every transaction. In some cases, only one column may be affected because all of the specific accounts affected by the transaction are included in that category.

	Current Assets	Current Liabilities	Owners' Equity	Net Income
a. Accrued interest income of $15 on a note receivable	Interest Receivable + 15			Interest Income + 15

b. Determined that the Allowance for Bad Debts balance should be increased by $2,200.

c. Recognized bank service charges of $30 for the month.

d. Received $25 cash for interest accrued in a prior month.

e. Purchased five units of a new item of inventory on account at a cost of $35 each.

f. Purchased 10 more units of the above item at a cost of $38 each.

g. Sold eight of the items purchased (in *e* and *f* above), and recognized the cost of goods sold using the FIFO cost-flow assumption.

LO 5, 8, 10   **5–28.** **Transaction analysis—various accounts.** Prepare an answer sheet with the column headings shown on the next page. For each of the following transactions or adjustments, you are to indicate the effect of the transaction or adjustment on the appropriate balance sheet category and on net income by entering for each account affected the account name and amount and indicating whether it is an addition (+) or a subtraction (−). Transaction *a* has been done as an illustration. Net income is *not* affected by every transaction. In some cases, only one column may be affected because all of the specific accounts affected by the transaction are included in that category.

	Current Assets	Current Liabilities	Owners' Equity	Net Income
a. Accrued interest income of $15 on a note receivable				
	Interest Receivable + 15			Interest Income + 15

b. Determined that the Allowance for Bad Debts balance should be decreased by $1,600 because expense during the year had been overestimated.

c. Wrote off an account receivable of $720.

d. Received cash from a customer in full payment of an account receivable of $250 that was paid within the 2% discount period.

e. Purchased eight units of a new item of inventory on account at a cost of $20 each.

f. Purchased 17 more units of the above item at a cost of $19 each.

g. Sold 20 of the items purchased (in *e* and *f* above), and recognized the cost of goods sold using the LIFO cost-flow assumption.

h. Paid a one-year insurance premium of $240 that applied to the next fiscal year.

i. Recognized insurance expense related to the above policy during the first month of the fiscal year to which it applied.

LO 5, 6, 7   **5–29.   Transaction analysis—various accounts.** Prepare an answer sheet with the column headings shown below. For each of the following transactions or adjustments, you are to indicate the effect of the transaction or adjustment on the appropriate balance sheet category and on net income by entering for each account affected the account name and amount, and indicating whether it is an addition (+) or a subtraction (−). Transaction *a* has been done as an illustration. Net income is *not* affected by every transaction. In some cases, only one column may be affected because all of the specific accounts affected by the transaction are included in that category.

	Current Assets	Current Liabilities	Owners' Equity	Net Income
a. Accrued interest income of $15 on a note receivable				
	Interest Receivable + 15			Interest Income + 15

b. Recorded estimated bad debts in the amount of $700.

c. Wrote off an overdue account receivable of $520.

d. Converted a customer's $1,200 overdue account receivable into a note.

e. Accrued $48 of interest earned on the note (in *d* above).

f. Collected the accrued interest (in *e* above).

g. Recorded $4,000 of sales, 80% of which were on account.

h. Recognized cost of goods sold in the amount of $3,200.

LO 7, 8, 10   **5–30.** **Transaction analysis—various accounts.** Prepare an answer sheet with the column headings shown below. For each of the following transactions or adjustments, you are to indicate the effect of the transaction or adjustment on the appropriate balance sheet category and on net income by entering for each account affected the account name and amount and indicating whether it is an addition (+) or a subtraction (−). Transaction *a* has been done as an illustration. Net income is *not* affected by every transaction. In some cases, only one column may be affected because all of the specific accounts affected by the transaction are included in that category.

	Current Assets	Current Liabilities	Owners' Equity	Net Income
a. Accrued interest income of $15 on a note receivable	Interest Receivable + 15			Interest Income + 15

b. Inventory was acquired on account and recorded for $410.

c. It was later determined that the amount of inventory acquired on account (in *b* above) was erroneously recorded. The actual amount purchased was only $140. No payments have been made. Record the correction of this error.

d. Purchased 12 units of inventory at a cost of $20 each and then 8 more units of the same inventory item at $22 each.

e. Sold 15 of the items purchased (in *d* above) and recognized cost of goods sold using the LIFO cost-flow assumption.

f. Assume the same facts (in *e* above) except that the company uses the FIFO cost-flow assumption. Record the cost of goods sold.

g. Assume the same facts (in *e* above) except that the company uses the weighted-average cost-flow assumption. Record the cost of goods sold.

h. Paid $1,400 in cash as an advance rent payment for a short-term lease that covers the next four months.

i. Recorded an adjusting entry at the end of the first month (of *h* above) to show the amount of rent "used" in the month.

CHAPTER 6

Accounting for and Presentation of Property, Plant, and Equipment, and Other Noncurrent Assets

Noncurrent assets include land, buildings, and equipment (less accumulated depreciation); intangible assets such as leaseholds, patents, trademarks, and goodwill; and natural resources. The presentation of property, plant, and equipment, and other noncurrent assets on the Consolidated Balance Sheets of Intel Corporation on page 19 of the Appendix, appears straightforward. However, there are several business and accounting matters involved in understanding this presentation, and the objective of this chapter is to permit you to make sense of the noncurrent assets section of any balance sheet.

The primary issues related to the accounting for noncurrent assets are as follows:

1. Accounting for the acquisition of the asset.
2. Accounting for the use (depreciation) of the asset.
3. Accounting for maintenance and repair costs.
4. Accounting for the disposition of the asset.

Learning Objectives

After studying this chapter, you should understand:

1 How the cost of land, buildings, and equipment is reported on the balance sheet.

2 How the terms *capitalize* and *expense* are used with respect to property, plant, and equipment.

3 Alternative methods of calculating depreciation for financial accounting purposes, and the relative effect of each on the income statement (depreciation expense) and the balance sheet (accumulated depreciation).

4 Why depreciation for income tax purposes is an important concern of taxpayers and how tax depreciation differs from financial accounting depreciation.

5 The accounting treatment of maintenance and repair expenditures.

6 The effect on the financial statements of the disposition of noncurrent assets, either by abandonment, sale, or trade-in.

7 The difference between an operating lease and a capital lease.

8 The role of present value concepts in financial reporting and their usefulness in decision making.

9 The similarities in the financial statement effects of buying an asset compared to using a capital lease to acquire the rights to an asset.

10 The meaning of various intangible assets, how their values are measured, and how their costs are reflected in the income statement.

Land

Objective 1
Understand how the cost of land is reported on the balance sheet.

Land owned and used in the operations of the firm is shown on the balance sheet at its original cost. All ordinary and necessary costs the firm incurs to get the land ready for its intended use are considered part of original cost. These costs include the purchase price of the land, title fees, legal fees, and other costs related to the acquisition. If a firm purchases land with a building on it and razes the building so that a new one can be built to the firm's specifications, then the cost of the land, old building, and razing (less any salvage proceeds) all become the cost of the land and are *capitalized* (see Business in Practice—Capitalizing versus Expensing) because all of these costs were incurred to get the land ready for its intended use.

BUSINESS IN PRACTICE
Capitalizing versus Expensing

Objective 2
Understand how the terms *capitalize* and *expense* are used with respect to property, plant, and equipment.

An expenditure involves using an asset (usually cash) or incurring a liability to acquire goods, services, or other economic benefits. Whenever a firm buys something, it has made an expenditure. All expenditures must be accounted for as either assets (**capitalizing** an expenditure) or as expenses (**expensing** an expenditure). Although this jargon applies to any expenditure, it is most prevalent in discussions about property, plant, and equipment.

Expenditures should be capitalized if the item acquired will have an economic benefit to the entity that extends beyond the end of the current fiscal year. However, expenditures for preventative maintenance and normal repairs, even though they are needed to maintain the usefulness of the asset over a number of years, are expensed as incurred. The capitalize versus expense issue is resolved by applying the matching concept, under which costs incurred in generating revenues are subtracted from revenues in the period in which the revenues are earned.

When an expenditure is capitalized (or treated as a capital expenditure), plant assets increase. If the asset is depreciable—and all plant assets except land are depreciable—depreciation expense is recognized over the estimated useful life of the asset. If the expenditure is expensed, then the full cost is reflected in the current period's income statement. There is a broad gray

Business in Practice concluded

area between expenditures that are clearly capital and those that are obviously expenses. This gray area leads to differences of opinion that have a direct impact on the net income reported for a fiscal period.

The materiality concept (see Chapter 2) is often applied to the issue of accounting for capital expenditures. Generally speaking, most accountants will expense items that are not material. Thus, the cost of a $5 wastebasket may be expensed, rather than capitalized and depreciated, even though the wastebasket clearly has a useful life of many years and should theoretically be accounted for as a capital asset.

Another factor that influences the capitalize versus expense decision is the potential income tax reduction in the current year that results from expensing. Although depreciation would be claimed (and income taxes reduced) over the life of a capitalized expenditure, many managers prefer the immediate income tax reduction that results from expensing. This capitalize versus expense issue is another area in which accountants' judgments can have a significant effect on an entity's financial position and results of operations. Explanations in this text will reflect sound accounting theory. However, recognize that in practice there may be some deviation from theory.

WHAT DOES IT MEAN?

1. What does it mean to capitalize an expenditure?

Land acquired for investment purposes or for some potential future but undefined use is classified as a separate noncurrent and nonoperating asset. This asset is reported at its original cost. A land development company would treat land under development as inventory, and all development costs would be included in the asset carrying value. As lots are sold, the costs are transferred from inventory to cost of goods sold.

Because land is not "used up," no accounting depreciation is associated with land.

When land is sold, the difference between the selling price and cost will be a gain or loss to be reported in the income statement of the period in which the sale occurred. For example, if a parcel of land on which Cruisers, Inc., had once operated a plant is sold this year for a price of $140,000 and the land had cost $6,000 when it was acquired 35 years earlier, the entry would be:

Dr.	Cash	140,000		
	Cr.	Land		6,000
	Cr.	Gain on Sale of Land		134,000

The effect of this transaction on the financial statements is:

Balance sheet	Income statement
Assets = Liabilities + Owners' equity ←	Net income = Revenues − Expenses
Cash + 140,000 Land − 6,000	Gain on Sale of Land + 134,000

Since land is carried on the books at original cost, the unrealized holding gain that had gradually occurred was ignored from an accounting perspective by Cruisers, Inc., until it sold the land (and realized the gain). Thus, the financial statements for each of the years between purchase and sale would *not* have reflected the increasing value of the land. Instead, the entire $134,000 gain will be reported in this year's income statement. The gain will not be included with operating income; it will be highlighted in the income statement as a nonrecurring, nonoperating item, so financial statement users will not be led to expect a similar gain in future years.

The original cost valuation of land (and all other categories of noncurrent assets discussed in this chapter) is often criticized for understating asset values on the balance sheet and for failing to provide proper matching on the income statement. Cruisers, Inc., management would have known that its land was appreciating in value over time, but this appreciation would not have been reflected on the balance sheet. The accounting profession defends the *cost principle* based on its reliability, consistency, and conservatism. To record land at market value would involve appraisals or other subjective estimates of value that could not be verified until an exchange transaction (i.e., sale) occurred. Although approximate market value would be more relevant than original cost for decision makers, original cost is the basis for accounting for noncurrent assets. You should be aware of this important limitation of the noncurrent asset information shown in balance sheets.

WHAT DOES IT MEAN?

2. What does it mean to state that balance sheet values do not represent current fair market values of long-lived assets?

Buildings and Equipment

Cost of Assets Acquired

Objective 1
Understand how the cost of buildings and equipment is reported on the balance sheet.

Buildings and equipment are recorded at their original cost, which is the purchase price plus all the ordinary and necessary costs incurred to get the building or equipment ready to use in the operations of the firm. "Construction in Progress," or some similar description, is often used to accumulate the costs of facilities that are being constructed to the firm's specifications, until the completed assets are placed in service. Interest costs associated with loans used to finance the construction of a building are capitalized until the building is put into operation. Installation and shakedown costs (costs associated with adjusting and preparing the equipment to be used in production) incurred for a new piece of equipment should be capitalized. If a piece of equipment is made by a firm's own employees, all of the material, labor, and overhead costs that would ordinarily be recorded as inventory costs (were the machine being made for an outside customer) should be capitalized as equipment costs. Such costs are capitalized because they are directly related to assets that will be used by the firm over several accounting periods and are not related only to current period earnings.

Original cost is not usually difficult to determine, but when two or more noncurrent assets are acquired in a single transaction for a lump-sum purchase price, the cost of each asset acquired must be measured and recorded separately. In such cases, an allocation of the "basket" purchase price is made to the individual assets acquired based on relative appraisal values on the date of acquisition. Exhibit 6–1 illustrates this allocation process and the related accounting.

Depreciation for Financial Accounting Purposes

In financial accounting, depreciation is an application of the matching concept. The original cost of noncurrent assets represents the *prepaid* cost of

---

EXHIBIT 6–1   Basket Purchase Allocation Illustrated

Situation:
Cruisers, Inc., acquired a parcel of land, along with a building and some production equipment, from a bankrupt competitor for $200,000 in cash. Current values reported by an independent appraiser were: land, $20,000; building, $170,000; and equipment, $60,000.

Allocation of Acquisition Cost:

Asset	Appraised Value	Percent of Total*	Cost Allocation
Land	$ 20,000	8%	$200,000 × 8% = $ 16,000
Building	170,000	68%	$200,000 × 68% = 136,000
Equipment	60,000	24%	$200,000 × 24% = 48,000
	$250,000	100%	$200,000

*$20,000/$250,000 = 8%, $170,000/$250,000 = 68%, $60,000/$250,000 = 24%

Entry to Record the Acquisition:

Dr.	Land	16,000	
Dr.	Building.	136,000	
Dr.	Equipment	48,000	
	Cr. Cash.		200,000

Effect of the Acquisition on the Financial Statements:

Balance sheet	Income statement
Assets = Liabilities + Owners' equity ← Net income = Revenues − Expenses	

Land
+ 16,000

Building
+ 136,000

Equipment
+ 48,000

Cash
− 200,000

economic benefits that will be received in future years. To the extent that an asset is "used up" in the operations of the entity, a portion of the asset's cost should be subtracted from the revenues that were generated through the use of the asset. Thus, the depreciation process involves an allocation of the cost of an asset to the years in which the benefits of the asset are expected to be received. Depreciation is *not* an attempt to recognize a loss in market value or any difference between the original cost and replacement cost of an asset. In fact, the market value of noncurrent assets may actually increase as they are used—but "appreciation" is not presently recorded (as discussed in the land section of this chapter). Depreciation expense is recorded in each fiscal period with this adjusting entry:

Dr. Depreciation Expense..................................	xx	
Cr. Accumulated Depreciation		xx

The effect of this adjusting entry on the financial statements is:

Balance sheet	Income statement
Assets = Liabilities + Owners' equity ←	Net income = Revenues − Expenses
− Accumulated Depreciation	− Depreciation Expense

Accumulated depreciation is another contra asset, and the balance in this account is the cumulative total of all the depreciation expense that has been recorded over the life of the asset up to the balance sheet date. It is classified with the related asset on the balance sheet, as a subtraction from the cost of the asset. The difference between the cost of an asset and the accumulated depreciation on that asset is the **net book value** of the asset. The balance sheet presentation of a building asset and its related Accumulated Depreciation account (using assumed amounts) is:

Building	$100,000
Less: Accumulated depreciation	(15,000)
Net book value of building	$ 85,000

or, as more commonly reported:

Building, less accumulated depreciation of $15,000	$ 85,000

With either presentation, the user can determine how much of the cost has been recognized as expense since the asset was acquired—which would not be possible if the Building account was directly reduced for the amount depreciated each year. This is why a contra asset account is used for accumulated depreciation.

Note that cash is not involved in the depreciation expense entry. The entity's Cash account was affected when the asset was purchased or as it is being paid for if a liability was incurred when the asset was acquired. The fact that depreciation expense does not affect cash is important in understanding the statement of cash flows, which identifies the sources and uses of a firm's cash during a fiscal period.

There are several alternative methods of calculating depreciation expense for financial accounting purposes. Each involves spreading the amount to be depreciated, which is the asset's cost minus its estimated salvage value, over the asset's estimated useful life to the entity. The depreciation method selected will not affect the total depreciation expense to be recognized over the life of the asset; however, different methods will result in different patterns of depreciation expense by fiscal period. There are two broad categories of depreciation calculation methods: the straight-line methods and accelerated methods. Depreciation expense patterns resulting from these alternatives are illustrated in Exhibit 6–2.

WHAT DOES IT MEAN?

3. What does it mean to say that depreciation expense does not affect cash?

Accelerated depreciation methods result in greater depreciation expense and lower net income than straight-line depreciation during the early years of the asset's life. During the later years of the asset's life, annual depreciation expense using accelerated methods is less than it would be using straight-line depreciation, and net income is higher.

Objective 3
Understand the alternative methods of calculating depreciation for financial accounting purposes and the relative effect of each on the income statement and the balance sheet.

Which method is used, and why? For purposes of reporting to stockholders, most firms use the **straight-line depreciation method** because in the early years of an asset's life it results in lower depreciation expense and hence higher reported net income than accelerated depreciation. In later years, when accelerated depreciation is less than straight-line depreciation, *total* depreciation expense using the straight-line method will still be less than under an accelerated method if the amount invested in new assets has grown each year. Such a regular increase in depreciable assets is not unusual for firms that are growing, assuming that prices of new and replacement equipment are rising.

EXHIBIT 6–2   Depreciation Expense Patterns

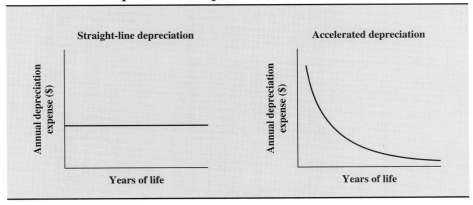

The specific depreciation calculation methods are:

Straight-line:
    Straight-line.
    Units of production.
Accelerated:
    Sum-of-the-years'-digits.
    Declining-balance.

Each of these depreciation calculation methods is illustrated in Exhibit 6–3.

EXHIBIT 6–3   Depreciation Calculation Methods

Assumptions:

Cruisers, Inc., purchased a molding machine at the beginning of 1998 at a cost of $22,000.

The machine is estimated to have a useful life to Cruisers, Inc., of five years, and an estimated salvage value of $2,000.

It is estimated that the machine will produce 200 boat hulls before it is worn out.

a. **Straight-line depreciation:**

$$\text{Annual depreciation expense} = \frac{\text{Cost} - \text{Estimated salvage value}}{\text{Estimated useful life}}$$

$$= \frac{\$22,000 - \$2,000}{5 \text{ years}}$$

$$= \$4,000$$

Alternatively, a straight-line depreciation rate could be determined and multiplied by the amount to be depreciated.

$$\text{Straight-line depreciation rate} = \frac{1}{\text{Life in years}} = \frac{1}{5} = 20\%$$

$$\text{Annual depreciation expense} = 20\% \times \$20,000 = \$4,000$$

b. **Units-of-production depreciation:**

$$\text{Depreciation expense per unit produced} = \frac{\text{Cost} - \text{Estimated salvage value}}{\text{Estimated total units to be made}}$$

$$= \frac{\$22,000 - \$2,000}{200 \text{ hulls}}$$

$$= \$100$$

Each year's depreciation expense would be $100 multiplied by the number of hulls produced.

c. **Sum-of-the-years'-digits depreciation:**

$$\text{Annual depreciation expense} = (\text{Cost} - \text{Estimated salvage value}) \times \frac{\text{Remaining life in years}}{\text{Sum-of-the-years' digits}}$$

$$1998 \text{ depreciation expense} = (\$22,000 - \$2,000) \times \frac{5 \text{ years}}{1 + 2 + 3 + 4 + 5}$$

$$= \$20,000 \times \frac{5}{15}$$

$$= \$6,667$$

EXHIBIT 6–3   *(concluded)*

Subsequent years' depreciation expense:

$$1999 \ldots \ldots \$20,000 \times \frac{4}{15} = \$\ 5,333$$

$$2000 \ldots \ldots \$20,000 \times \frac{3}{15} = \ \ 4,000$$

$$2001 \ldots \ldots \$20,000 \times \frac{2}{15} = \ \ 2,667$$

$$2002 \ldots \ldots \$20,000 \times \frac{1}{15} = \ \ 1,333$$

Total depreciation expense over 5 years = $20,000

d. **Declining-balance depreciation:**

Annual depreciation expense = Double the straight-line depreciation rate
× Asset's net book value at beginning of year

$$\text{Straight-line depreciation rate} = \frac{1}{\text{Life in years}} = \frac{1}{5} = 20\%$$

Double the straight-line depreciation rate is 40%.

Year	Net Book Value at Beginning of Year	Factor	Depreciation Expense for the Year	Accumulated Depreciation	Net Book Value at End of Year
1998	$22,000	× 0.4 =	$8,800	$ 8,800	$13,200
1999	13,200	× 0.4 =	5,280	14,080	7,920
2000	7,920	× 0.4 =	3,168	17,248	4,752
2001	4,752	× 0.4 =	1,901	19,149	2,851
2002	2,851	× 0.4 =	851*	20,000	2,000

*Depreciation expense at the end of the asset's life is equal to an amount that will cause the net book value to equal the asset's estimated salvage value.

Recap of depreciation expense by year and method:

Year	Straight-Line	Sum-of-the-Years'-Digits	Declining-Balance
1998	$ 4,000	$ 6,667	$ 8,800
1999	4,000	5,333	5,280
2000	4,000	4,000	3,168
2001	4,000	2,667	1,901
2002	4,000	1,333	851
Total	$20,000	$20,000	$20,000

Note that the total depreciation expense for the five years is the same for each method; it is the pattern of the expense that differs. Since depreciation is an expense, the effect on operating income of the alternative methods will be opposite; 1998 operating income will be highest if the straight-line method is used, and lowest if the declining-balance method is used.

Depreciation calculations using the straight-line, units of production, and sum-of-the-years'-digits methods involve determining the amount to be depreciated by subtracting the estimated salvage value from the cost of the asset. Salvage is considered in the declining-balance method only near the end of the asset's life when salvage value becomes the target for net book value.

TABLE 6–1 Depreciation Calculation Methods Used by 600 Publicly Owned Industrial and Merchandising Corporations—1996

	Number of Companies
Methods:	
Straight-line	575
Declining-balance	28
Sum-of-the-years'-digits	12
Accelerated method—not specified	48
Units of production	42
Other	12

Source: *Accounting Trends and Techniques,* Table 3–13, copyright © 1997 by American Institute of Certified Public Accountants, Inc. Reprinted with permission.

The declining-balance calculation illustrated in Exhibit 6–3 is known as *double-declining balance* because the depreciation rate used was double the straight-line rate. In some instances, the rate used is 1.5 times the straight-line rate; this is referred to as *150% declining-balance* depreciation. Whatever rate is used, a constant percentage is applied each year to the declining balance of the net book value.

Although many firms will use a single depreciation method for all of their depreciable assets, the consistency concept is applied to the depreciation method used for a particular asset acquired in a particular year. Thus, it is possible for a firm to use an accelerated depreciation method for some of its assets and the straight-line method for other assets. Differences can even occur between similar assets purchased in the same or different years. In order to make sense of the income statement and balance sheet, it is necessary to find out from the footnotes to the financial statements which depreciation methods are used (see p. 22 of the Intel annual report). Table 6–1 summarizes the depreciation methods used for stockholder reporting purposes by 600 large firms.

The estimates made of useful life and salvage value are educated guesses to be sure, but accountants, frequently working with engineers, are able to estimate these factors with great accuracy. A firm's experience and equipment replacement practices are considered in the estimating process. For income tax purposes (see Business in Practice—Depreciation for

Objective 4
Understand why depreciation for income tax purposes is an important concern of taxpayers and how tax depreciation differs from financial accounting depreciation.

BUSINESS IN PRACTICE
Depreciation for Income Tax Purposes

Depreciation is a deductible expense for income tax purposes. Although depreciation expense does not directly affect cash, it does reduce taxable income. Therefore, most firms would like to have deductible depreciation expense as large an amount as possible because this would mean lower

Business in Practice concluded

taxable income and lower taxes payable. The Internal Revenue Code has permitted taxpayers to use an accelerated depreciation calculation method for many years. Estimated useful life is generally the most significant factor (other than calculation method) affecting the amount of depreciation expense, and for many years this was a contentious issue between taxpayers and the Internal Revenue Service.

In 1981 the Internal Revenue Code was amended to permit use of the **Accelerated Cost Recovery System (ACRS),** frequently pronounced "acres," for depreciable assets placed in service after 1980. The ACRS rules simplified the determination of useful life and allowed rapid write-off patterns similar to the declining-balance methods, so most firms started using ACRS for tax purposes. Unlike the LIFO inventory cost-flow assumption (which, if selected, must be used for both financial reporting and income tax determination purposes), there is no requirement that "book" (i.e., financial statement) and tax depreciation calculation methods be the same. Most firms continued to use straight-line depreciation for book purposes.

ACRS used relatively short, and arbitrary, useful lives, and ignored salvage value. The intent was more to permit relatively quick "cost recovery" and thus encourage investment than it was to recognize traditional depreciation expense. For example, ACRS permitted the write-off of most machinery and equipment over three to five years.

However, in the Tax Reform Act of 1986, Congress changed the original ACRS provisions. The system is now referred to as the **Modified Accelerated Cost Recovery System (MACRS).** Recovery periods were lengthened, additional categories for classifying assets were created, and the method of calculating the depreciation deduction was specified. Cost recovery periods are specified based on the type of asset and its class life, as defined in the Internal Revenue Code. Most machinery and equipment is depreciated using the double-declining-balance method, but the 150% declining-balance method is required for some longer lived assets, and the straight-line method is specified for buildings.

In addition to the MACRS rules, small businesses benefit from a special relief provision that allows certain depreciable assets to be treated as immediate depreciation expense deductions as they are purchased. An annual election can be made to expense as much as $17,500 of the cost of qualifying depreciable property purchased for use in a trade or business, subject to certain limitations. The immediate deduction for expensed assets promotes administrative convenience by eliminating the need for extensive depreciation schedules for small purchases.

The use of ACRS for book depreciation was discouraged because of the arbitrarily short lives involved. MACRS lives are closer to actual useful lives, but basing depreciation expense for financial accounting purposes on tax law provisions, which are subject to frequent change, is not appropriate. Yet, many small to medium-sized business organizations yield to the temptation to do so. Such decisions are based on the inescapable fact that tax depreciation schedules must be maintained to satisfy Internal Revenue Service rules, and therefore the need to keep separate schedules for financial reporting is avoided.

Income Tax Purposes), the useful life of various depreciable assets is determined by the Internal Revenue Code, which also specifies that salvage values are to be ignored.

A number of technical accounting challenges must be considered when calculating depreciation in practice. These include part-year depreciation for assets acquired or disposed of during a year, changes in estimated salvage value and/or useful life after the asset has been depreciated for some time, and asset grouping to facilitate the depreciation calculation. These are beyond the scope of this text; your task is to understand the alternative calculation methods and the different effect of each on both depreciation expense in the income statement and accumulated depreciation (and net book value) on the balance sheet.

WHAT DOES IT MEAN?

4. What does it mean to use an accelerated depreciation method?

5. What does it mean to refer to the tax benefit of depreciation expense?

Maintenance and Repair Expenditures

Objective 5
Understand the accounting treatment of maintenance and repair expenditures.

Preventative maintenance expenditures and routine repair costs are clearly expenses of the period in which they are incurred. There is a gray area with respect to some maintenance expenditures, however, and accountants' judgments may differ. If a maintenance expenditure will extend the useful life or salvage value of an asset beyond that used in the depreciation calculation, it is appropriate that the expenditure be capitalized and that the new net book value of the asset be depreciated over the asset's remaining useful life.

In practice, most accountants will decide in favor of expensing rather than capitalizing for several reasons. Revising the depreciation calculation data is frequently time-consuming, with little perceived benefit. Because depreciation involves estimates of useful life and salvage value to begin with, revising those estimates without overwhelming evidence that they are significantly in error is an exercise of questionable value. For income tax purposes, most taxpayers would rather have a deductible expense now (expensing) rather than later (capitalizing and depreciating).

Because of the possibility that net income could be affected either favorably or unfavorably by inconsistent judgments about the accounting for repair and maintenance expenditures, auditors (internal and external) and the Internal Revenue Service usually look closely at these expenditures when they are reviewing the firm's reported results.

WHAT DOES IT MEAN?

6. What does it mean to prefer expensing maintenance and repair expenditures rather than capitalizing them?

Disposal of Depreciable Assets

When a depreciable asset is sold or scrapped, both the asset and its related accumulated depreciation account must be reduced by the appropriate amounts. For example, throwing out a fully depreciated piece of equipment, for which no salvage value had been estimated, would result in the following entry:

Objective 6
Understand the effect
on the financial
statements of the
disposition of
noncurrent assets by
sale or abandonment.

Dr. Accumulated Depreciation................................ xx	
Cr. Equipment.......................................	xx

Note that this entry does not affect *total* assets or any other parts of the financial statements.

Balance sheet	Income statement
Assets = Liabilities + Owners' equity ← Net income = Revenues − Expenses	

− Equipment
+ Accumulated
   Depreciation

When the asset being disposed of has a positive net book value, either because a salvage value was estimated or because it has not reached the end of its estimated useful life to the firm, a gain or loss on the disposal will result unless the asset is sold for a price that is equal to the net book value. For example, if equipment that cost $6,000 new has a net book value equal to its estimated salvage value of $900 and is sold for $1,200, the following entry will result:

Dr. Cash.....................................	1,200	
Dr. Accumulated Depreciation.....................	5,100*	
Cr. Equipment................................		6,000
Cr. Gain on Sale of Equipment		300
Sold equipment.		

*Net book value = Cost − Accumulated depreciation
      900 = 6,000 − Accumulated depreciation
Accumulated depreciation = 5,100

The effect of this entry on the financial statements is:

Balance sheet	Income statement
Assets = Liabilities + Owners' equity ← Net income = Revenues − Expenses	

Cash
+ 1,200

Accumulated
Depreciation
+ 5,100

Equipment
− 6,000

Gain on
Sale of Equipment
+ 300

Alternatively, assume that the above equipment had to be scrapped without any salvage value. The entry would be:

Dr. Accumulated Depreciation.....................	5,100	
Dr. Loss on Disposal of Equipment	900	
Cr. Equipment................................		6,000
Scrapped equipment.		

The effect of this entry on the financial statements is:

Balance sheet			Income statement		
Assets	= Liabilities +	Owners' equity	← Net income =	Revenues −	Expenses
Accumulated Depreciation + 5,100					Loss on Disposal of Equipment − 900
Equipment − 6,000					

The gain or loss on the disposal of a depreciable asset is, in effect, a correction of the total depreciation expense that has been recorded over the life of the asset. If salvage value and useful life estimates had been correct, the net book value of the asset would be equal to the **proceeds** (if any) received from its sale or disposal. Depreciation expense is never adjusted retroactively, so the significance of these gains or losses gives the financial statement user a basis for judging the accuracy of the accountant's estimates of salvage value and useful life. Gains or losses on the disposal of depreciable assets are not part of the operating income of the entity. If significant, they will be reported separately as elements of other income or expense. If not material, they will be reported with miscellaneous other income.

Trade-In Transactions

Objective 6
Understand the effect on the financial statements of asset trade-in transactions.

Frequently, an old asset is traded in on a similar new asset. In this kind of transaction, a trade-in allowance is determined by the seller of the new equipment. The trade-in allowance is then subtracted from the list price of the new asset to determine the amount of cash to be paid for it.

Assume that you have an old car to trade in on a new one. Which is more important to you: the trade-in allowance on the old car or the amount you have to pay to get the new car? Clearly, it is the amount you have to pay. If you focused on the trade-in allowance, an unscrupulous dealer could offer a trade-in allowance much greater than the market value of your old car, and then work from a list price for the new car that had been inflated by an even larger amount. Because trade-in allowances are not always determined objectively, using a trade-allowance as if it were the same thing as the proceeds from the sale of an asset could lead to a fictitious gain or loss.

For income tax purposes, a trade-in transaction results in neither a gain nor a loss to the entity trading in an old asset and acquiring a new asset. Generally accepted accounting principles provide for recognizing a loss, but not a gain, on a trade-in transaction involving similar assets (accounting conservatism). When no gain or loss is recognized, the cost of the new asset becomes the net book value of the old asset, plus the cash (or "boot," as in "I got the new car in exchange for my old car and $3,000 to boot.") paid and/or liability assumed in the transaction. The new asset cost, less estimated salvage value, will be depreciated over the estimated useful life to the entity of the new asset. Accounting for a trade-in transaction is illustrated in Exhibit 6–4.

If the trade-in transaction involves dissimilar assets, both generally accepted accounting principles and the Internal Revenue Code consider two

---

EXHIBIT 6–4 Trade-In Transaction Accounting Illustrated

Assumptions:

The cost of the old car was $9,300.

Accumulated depreciation on the old car is $8,100.

The new car list price is $12,800; a $2,600 trade-in allowance is given for the old car.

The buyer is going to pay $1,500 cash and sign a note for the $8,700 balance due to the new car dealer.

Accounting:

The entry to record this trade-in transaction for the buyer is:

Dr.	Accumulated Depreciation (on old car)	8,100	
Dr.	Automobiles (cost of new car)	11,400	
	Cr. Automobiles (cost of old car)		9,300
	Cr. Cash		1,500
	Cr. Note payable		8,700
	Trade of old car for new car.		

The effect of this transaction on the financial statements is shown below. Notice that the income statement is not affected.

Balance sheet	Income statement
Assets = Liabilities + Owners' equity ←	Net income = Revenues − Expenses

Accumulated   Note
Depreciation   Payable
(on old car)   + 8,700
+ 8,100

Automobiles (cost of new car)
+ 11,400

Automobiles (cost of old car)
− 9,300

Cash
− 1,500

Recap of Amounts:

New car list price	$12,800
Old car trade-in allowance	2,600
Amount required from buyer to get new car	$10,200
Amount paid in cash (boot)	1,500
Amount of note payable	$ 8,700
Net book value of old car ($9,300 − $8,100)	$ 1,200
Amount required from buyer to get new car	10,200
Cost of new car	$11,400

transactions to have occurred: the "sale" of the old asset and the purchase of a new asset. Thus, a gain or loss is recognized on the sale of the old asset, with the trade-in allowance being considered the proceeds from the sale. The cost of the new asset is the fair market value of the old asset plus the cash paid and/or liability incurred.

Assets Acquired by Capital Lease

Objective 7
Understand the difference between an operating lease and a capital lease.

Many firms will lease, or rent, assets rather than purchase them. An **operating lease** is an ordinary, frequently short-term, lease for the use of an asset that does not involve any attributes of ownership. For example, the renter (lessee) of a car from Hertz or Avis (the lessor) must return the car at the end of the lease term. Therefore, assets rented under an operating lease are not reflected on the lessee's balance sheet, and the rent expense involved is reported in the income statement as an operating expense.

A **capital lease** (or *financing lease*) results in the lessee (renter) assuming virtually all of the benefits and risks of ownership of the leased asset. For example, the lessee of a car from an automobile dealership may sign a noncancelable lease agreement with a term of five years requiring monthly payments sufficient to cover the cost of the car, plus interest and administrative costs. A lease is a capital lease if it has *any* of the following characteristics:

1. It transfers ownership of the asset to the lessee.
2. It permits the lessee to purchase the asset for a nominal sum at the end of the lease period.
3. The lease term is at least 75 percent of the economic life of the asset.
4. The **present value** (see Business in Practice—Present Value) of the lease payments is at least 90 percent of the fair value of the asset.

Objective 8
Understand the role of present value concepts in financial reporting and their usefulness in decision making.

BUSINESS IN PRACTICE
Present Value

Organizations and individuals are frequently confronted with the choice of paying for a purchase today or at a later date. Intuition suggests that all other things being equal, it would be better to pay later because in the meantime the cash could be invested to earn interest. This reflects the fact that money has value over time. Of course, other things aren't always equal, and sometimes the choice is between paying one amount—say $100—today, and a larger amount—say $110—a year later. Or in the opposite case, the choice may be between receiving $100 today or $110 a year from now. Present value analysis is used to determine which of these alternatives is financially preferable.

The present value concept is an application of compound interest—the process of earning interest on interest. If $1,000 is invested in a savings account earning interest at the rate of 10% compounded annually and if the account is left alone for four years, the results shown in the following table will occur:

Year	Principal at Beginning of Year	Interest Earned at 10%	Principal at End of Year
1	$1,000	$100	$1,100
2	1,100	110	1,210
3	1,210	121	1,331
4	1,331	133	1,464

This is an example of future value, and most of us think of a future amount when we think about compound interest. We understand that the future value of $1,000 invested for four years at 10% interest compounded annually is $1,464, because we are familiar with this aspect of the compound interest concept. This relationship can be illustrated on a time line as follows:

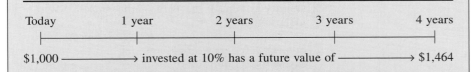

(There is a formula for calculating future value, and tables of future value factors are also available. Many computer program packages and business calculators include a future value function as well.)

Present value analysis involves looking at the same compound interest concept from the opposite perspective. Using data in the above table, you can say that the present value of $1,464 to be received four years from now, assuming an interest rate of 10% compounded annually, is $1,000. On a time-line representation, the direction of the arrow indicating the time perspective is reversed.

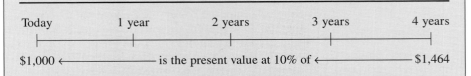

If someone owed you $1,464 to be paid four years from now, and if you were to agree with your debtor that 10 percent was a fair interest rate for that period of time, you would both be satisfied to settle the debt for $1,000 today. Or, alternatively, if you owed $1,464 payable four years from now, both you and your creditor would be satisfied to settle the debt for $1,000 today (still assuming agreement on the 10% interest rate). That is because $1,000 invested at 10% interest compounded annually will grow to $1,464 in four years. Stated differently, the future value of $1,000 at 10% interest in four years is $1,464, and the present value of $1,464 in four years at 10% is $1,000.

Business in Practice continued

Present value analysis involves determining the present amount that is equivalent to an amount to be paid or received in the future, recognizing that money does have value over time. The time value of money is represented by the interest that can be earned on money over an investment period. In present value analysis, **discount rate** is a term frequently used for *interest rate*. In the above example, the present value of $1,464, discounted at 10% for four years, is $1,000. Thus, the *time value of money* in this example is represented by the $464 in interest that is being charged to the borrower for the use of money over the four-year period.

Present value analysis does not directly recognize the effects of inflation, although inflationary expectations will influence the discount rate used in the present value calculation. Generally, the higher the inflationary expectations, the higher the discount rate used in present value analysis.

The above example deals with the present value of a *single amount* to be received or paid in the future. Some transactions involve receiving or paying the same amount each period for a number of periods. This sort of receipt or payment pattern is referred to as an **annuity.** The present value of an annuity is simply the sum of the present value of each of the annuity payment amounts.

There are formulas and computer program functions for calculating the present value of a single amount and the present value of an annuity. In all cases, the amount to be received or paid in the future, the discount rate, and the number of years (or other time periods) are used in the present value calculation. Table 6–2 presents factors for calculating the present value of $1 (single amount), and Table 6–3 gives the factors for the present value of an annuity of $1 for several discount rates and for a number of periods. Take a moment now to glance at these tables and learn how they are constructed. Notice that for any given number of periods, the factors shown in the annuity table represent cumulative totals of the factors shown in the present value of $1 table. Check this out by adding together the single amount factors for periods 1, 2, and 3 in the 4% column of Table 6–2 and comparing your result to the annuity factor shown for 3 periods at 4% in Table 6–3. In both cases, your answer should be 2.7751. Notice also (by scanning across the tables) that for any given number of periods, the higher the discount (interest) rate, the lower the present value. This makes sense when you remember that present values operate in the opposite manner as future values. The higher the interest rate, the greater the future value—and the lower the present value. Now scan down Table 6–2 and notice that for any given interest rate, the present value of $1 decreases as more periods are added. The same effects are also present in Table 6–3 but cannot be visualized because the annuity factors represent cumulative totals; yet for each additional period, a smaller amount is added to the previous annuity factor.

To find the present value of any amount, the appropriate factor from the table is multiplied by the amount to be received or paid in the future. Using the data from the initial example described above, we can calculate the present value of $1,464 to be received four years from now, based on a discount rate of 10 percent, as:

$$\$1,464 \times 0.6830 \text{ (from the 10\% column, four-period row of}$$
$$\text{Table 6–2)} = \$1,000 \text{ (rounded)}$$

Business in Practice continued

What is the present value of a lottery prize of $1,000,000, payable in 20 annual installments of $50,000 each, assuming a discount (interest) rate of 12 percent? The time-line representation of this situation is:

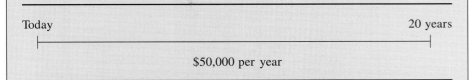

The present value of this annuity is calculated by multiplying the annuity amount ($50,000) by the annuity factor from Table 6–3. The solution is:

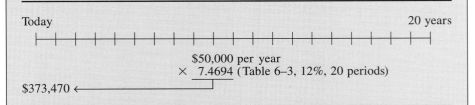

Although the answer of $373,470 shouldn't make the winner feel less fortunate, she certainly has not become an instant millionaire in present value terms. The lottery authority needs to deposit only $373,470 today in an account earning 12% interest in order to be able to pay the winner $50,000 per year for 20 years beginning a year from now. What is the present value of the same lottery prize assuming that 8% was the appropriate discount rate? What if a 16% interest rate was used? (Take a moment to calculate these amounts.) Imagine how the wife of The Born Loser comic strip character must have felt upon learning that he had won a million dollars—payable $1 per year for a million years! As these examples point out, the present value of future cash flows is directly affected by both the chosen discount rate and the relevant time frame.

Let's look at another example. Assume that you have accepted a job from a company willing to pay you a signing bonus, and you must now choose between three alternative payment plans. The plan A bonus is $3,000 payable today. The plan B bonus is $4,000 payable three years from today. The plan C bonus is three annual payments of $1,225 each (an annuity) with the first payment to be made one year from today. Assuming a discount rate of 8%, which bonus should you accept? The solution requires calculation of the present value of each bonus. Using the time-line approach:

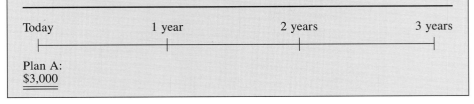

TABLE 6–2   Factors for Calculating the Present Value of $1

No. of Periods	Discount Rate									
	4%	6%	8%	10%	12%	14%	16%	18%	20%	22%
1	0.9615	0.9434	0.9259	0.9091	0.8929	0.8772	0.8621	0.8475	0.8333	0.8197
2	0.9246	0.8900	0.8573	0.8264	0.7972	0.7695	0.7432	0.7182	0.6944	0.6719
3	0.8890	0.8396	0.7938	0.7513	0.7118	0.6750	0.6407	0.6086	0.5787	0.5507
4	0.8548	0.7921	0.7350	0.6830	0.6355	0.5921	0.5523	0.5158	0.4823	0.4514
5	0.8219	0.7473	0.6806	0.6209	0.5674	0.5194	0.4761	0.4371	0.4019	0.3700
6	0.7903	0.7050	0.6302	0.5645	0.5066	0.4556	0.4104	0.3704	0.3349	0.3033
7	0.7599	0.6651	0.5835	0.5132	0.4523	0.3996	0.3538	0.3139	0.2791	0.2486
8	0.7307	0.6274	0.5403	0.4665	0.4039	0.3506	0.3050	0.2660	0.2326	0.2038
9	0.7026	0.5919	0.5002	0.4241	0.3606	0.3075	0.2630	0.2255	0.1938	0.1670
10	0.6756	0.5584	0.4632	0.3855	0.3220	0.2697	0.2267	0.1911	0.1615	0.1369
11	0.6496	0.5268	0.4289	0.3505	0.2875	0.2366	0.1954	0.1619	0.1346	0.1122
12	0.6246	0.4970	0.3971	0.3186	0.2567	0.2076	0.1685	0.1372	0.1122	0.0920
13	0.6006	0.4688	0.3677	0.2897	0.2292	0.1821	0.1452	0.1163	0.0935	0.0754
14	0.5775	0.4423	0.3405	0.2633	0.2046	0.1597	0.1252	0.0985	0.0779	0.0618
15	0.5553	0.4173	0.3152	0.2394	0.1827	0.1401	0.1079	0.0835	0.0649	0.0507
16	0.5339	0.3936	0.2919	0.2176	0.1631	0.1229	0.0930	0.0708	0.0541	0.0415
17	0.5134	0.3714	0.2703	0.1978	0.1456	0.1078	0.0802	0.0600	0.0451	0.0340
18	0.4936	0.3503	0.2502	0.1799	0.1300	0.0946	0.0691	0.0508	0.0376	0.0279
19	0.4746	0.3305	0.2317	0.1635	0.1161	0.0829	0.0596	0.0431	0.0313	0.0229
20	0.4564	0.3118	0.2145	0.1486	0.1037	0.0728	0.0514	0.0365	0.0261	0.0187
21	0.4388	0.2942	0.1987	0.1351	0.0926	0.0638	0.0443	0.0309	0.0217	0.0154
22	0.4220	0.2775	0.1839	0.1228	0.0826	0.0560	0.0382	0.0262	0.0181	0.0126
23	0.4057	0.2618	0.1703	0.1117	0.0738	0.0491	0.0329	0.0222	0.0151	0.0103
24	0.3901	0.2470	0.1577	0.1015	0.0659	0.0431	0.0284	0.0188	0.0126	0.0085
25	0.3751	0.2330	0.1460	0.0923	0.0588	0.0378	0.0245	0.0160	0.0105	0.0069
30	0.3083	0.1741	0.0994	0.0573	0.0334	0.0196	0.0116	0.0070	0.0042	0.0026
35	0.2534	0.1301	0.0676	0.0356	0.0189	0.0102	0.0055	0.0030	0.0017	0.0009
40	0.2083	0.0972	0.0460	0.0221	0.0107	0.0053	0.0026	0.0013	0.0007	0.0004
45	0.1712	0.0727	0.0313	0.0137	0.0061	0.0027	0.0013	0.0006	0.0003	0.0001
50	0.1407	0.0543	0.0213	0.0085	0.0035	0.0014	0.0006	0.0003	0.0001	0.0000

TABLE 6–3 **Factors for Calculating the Present Value of an Annuity of $1**

No. of Periods	Discount Rate									
	4%	*6%*	*8%*	*10%*	*12%*	*14%*	*16%*	*18%*	*20%*	*22%*
1	0.9615	0.9434	0.9259	0.9091	0.8929	0.8772	0.8621	0.8475	0.8333	0.8197
2	1.8861	1.8334	1.7833	1.7355	1.6901	1.6467	1.6052	1.5656	1.5278	1.4915
3	2.7751	2.6730	2.5771	2.4869	2.4018	2.3216	2.2459	2.1743	2.1065	2.0422
4	3.6299	3.4651	3.3121	3.1699	3.0373	2.9137	2.7982	2.6901	2.5887	2.4936
5	4.4518	4.2124	3.9927	3.7908	3.6048	3.4331	3.2743	3.1272	2.9906	2.8636
6	5.2421	4.9173	4.6229	4.3553	4.1114	3.8887	3.6847	3.4976	3.3255	3.1669
7	6.0021	5.5824	5.2064	4.8684	4.5638	4.2883	4.0386	3.8115	3.6046	3.4155
8	6.7327	6.2098	5.7466	5.3349	4.9676	4.6389	4.3436	4.0776	3.8372	3.6193
9	7.4353	6.8017	6.2469	5.7590	5.3282	4.9464	4.6065	4.3030	4.0310	3.7863
10	8.1109	7.3601	6.7101	6.1446	5.6502	5.2161	4.8332	4.4941	4.1925	3.9232
11	8.7605	7.8869	7.1390	6.4951	5.9377	5.4527	5.0286	4.6560	4.3271	4.0354
12	9.3851	8.3838	7.5361	6.8137	6.1944	5.6603	5.1971	4.7932	4.4392	4.1274
13	9.9856	8.8527	7.9038	7.1034	6.4235	5.8424	5.3423	4.9095	4.5327	4.2028
14	10.5631	9.2950	8.2442	7.3667	6.6282	6.0021	5.4675	5.0081	4.6106	4.2646
15	11.1184	9.7122	8.5595	7.6061	6.8109	6.1422	5.5755	5.0916	4.6755	4.3152
16	11.6523	10.1059	8.8514	7.8237	6.9740	6.2651	5.6685	5.1624	4.7296	4.3567
17	12.1657	10.4773	9.1216	8.0216	7.1196	6.3729	5.7487	5.2223	4.7746	4.3908
18	12.6593	10.8276	9.3719	8.2014	7.2497	6.4674	5.8178	5.2732	4.8122	4.4187
19	13.1339	11.1581	9.6036	8.3649	7.3658	6.5504	5.8775	5.3162	4.8435	4.4415
20	13.5903	11.4699	9.8181	8.5136	7.4694	6.6231	5.9288	5.3527	4.8696	4.4603
21	14.0292	11.7641	10.0168	8.6487	7.5620	6.6870	5.9731	5.3837	4.8913	4.4756
22	14.4511	12.0416	10.2007	8.7715	7.6446	6.7429	6.0113	5.4099	4.9094	4.4882
23	14.8568	12.3034	10.3711	8.8832	7.7184	6.7921	6.0442	5.4321	4.9245	4.4985
24	15.2470	12.5504	10.5288	8.9847	7.7843	6.8351	6.0726	5.4509	4.9371	4.5070
25	15.6221	12.7834	10.6748	9.0770	7.8431	6.8729	6.0971	5.4669	4.9476	4.5139
30	17.2920	13.7648	11.2578	9.4269	8.0552	7.0027	6.1772	5.5168	4.9789	4.5338
35	18.6646	14.4982	11.6546	9.6442	8.1755	7.0700	6.2153	5.5386	4.9915	4.5411
40	19.7928	15.0463	11.9246	9.7791	8.2438	7.1050	6.2335	5.5482	4.9966	4.5439
45	20.7200	15.4558	12.1084	9.8628	8.2825	7.1232	6.2421	5.5523	4.9986	4.5449
50	21.4822	15.7619	12.2335	9.9148	8.3045	7.1327	6.2463	5.5541	4.9995	4.5452

Business in Practice continued

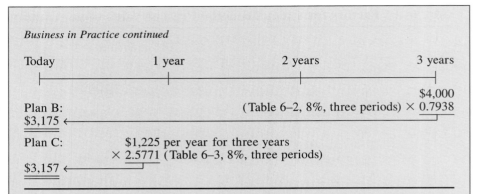

Today	1 year	2 years	3 years

$4,000

Plan B: (Table 6–2, 8%, three periods) × 0.7938

$3,175 ←

Plan C: $1,225 per year for three years

× 2.5771 (Table 6–3, 8%, three periods)

$3,157 ←

Bonus plan B has the highest present value and for that reason would be the plan selected based on present value analysis.

The frequency with which interest is compounded affects both future value and present value. You would prefer to have the interest on your savings account compounded monthly, weekly, or even daily, rather than annually, because you will earn more interest the more frequently compounding occurs. This is recognized in present value calculations by converting the annual discount rate to a discount rate per compounding period by dividing the annual rate by the number of compounding periods per year. Likewise, the number of periods is adjusted by multiplying the number of years involved by the number of compounding periods per year. For example, the present value of $1,000 to be received or paid six years from now, at a discount rate of 16% compounded annually, is $410.40 (the factor 0.4104 from the 16% column, six-period row of Table 6–2, multiplied by $1,000). If interest were compounded quarterly, or four times per year, the present value calculation uses the factor from the 4% column (16% per year/four periods per year), and the 24-period row (six years × four periods per year), which is 0.3901. Thus, the present value of $1,000 to be received or paid in six years, compounding interest quarterly, is $390.10. Using the time-line approach:

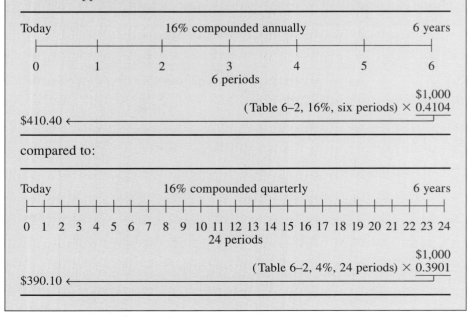

Today			16% compounded annually			6 years
0	1	2	3	4	5	6

6 periods

$1,000

(Table 6–2, 16%, six periods) × 0.4104

$410.40 ←

compared to:

Today	16% compounded quarterly	6 years

0 1 2 3 4 5 6 7 8 9 10 11 12 13 14 15 16 17 18 19 20 21 22 23 24

24 periods

$1,000

(Table 6–2, 4%, 24 periods) × 0.3901

$390.10 ←

You can make sense of the fact that the present value of a single amount is lower the more frequent the compounding by visualizing what you could do with either $410.40 or $390.10 if you were to receive the amount today rather than receiving $1,000 in six years. Each amount could be invested at 16%, but interest would compound on the $410.40 only once a year, while interest on the $390.10 would compound every three months. Even though you start with different amounts, you'll still have $1,000 after six years. Test your comprehension of this calculation process by verifying that the present value of an annual annuity of $100 for 10 years, discounted at an annual rate of 16% is $483.32, and that the present value of $50 paid every six months for 10 years, discounted at the same annual rate (which is an 8% semiannual rate) is $490.91. The present value of an annuity is greater the more frequent the compounding because the annuity amount is paid or received sooner than when the compounding period is longer.

Many of these ideas may seem complicated to you now, but your common sense will affirm the results of present value analysis. Remember that $1 in your hands today is worth more than $1 to be received tomorrow or a year from today. This explains why firms are interested in speeding up the collection of accounts receivable and other cash inflows. Of course, the opposite logic applies to cash payments, which explains why firms will defer the payment of accounts payable whenever possible. The prevailing attitude is, "We're better off with the cash in our hands than in the hands of our customers or suppliers." Several applications of present value analysis to business transactions will be illustrated in subsequent chapters. By making the initial investment of time now, you will understand these ideas more quickly later.

WHAT DOES IT MEAN?

7. What does it mean to say that money has value over time?
8. What does it mean to talk about the present value of an amount of money to be received or spent in the future?
9. What does it mean to receive an annuity?

Objective 9
Understand the similarities in the financial statement effects of buying an asset and using a capital lease to acquire the rights to an asset.

The economic impact of a capital lease isn't really any different from buying the asset outright and signing a note payable that will be paid off, with interest, over the life of the asset. Therefore, it is appropriate that the asset and related liability be reflected in the lessee's balance sheet. In the lessee's income statement, the cost of the leased asset will be reflected as depreciation expense, rather than rent expense, and the financing cost will be shown as interest expense.

Prior to an FASB standard issued in 1976, many companies did not record assets acquired under a capital lease because they did not want to reflect the related lease liability in their balance sheet. This practice was known as *off-balance-sheet financing* and was deemed inappropriate because the full disclosure concept was violated.

Assets acquired by capital lease are now included with purchased assets on the balance sheet. The amount recorded as the cost of the asset involved in a capital lease, and as the related lease liability, is the present value of the lease payments to be made, based on the interest rate used by the lessor to determine the periodic lease payments. The entries to record capital lease transactions are as follows:

1. Date of acquisition.

Dr. Equipment......................................	xx	
Cr. Capital Lease Liability.........................		xx

2. Annual depreciation expense.

Dr. Depreciation Expense	xx	
Cr. Accumulated Depreciation.....................		xx

3. Annual lease payments.

Dr. Interest Expense................................	xx	
Dr. Capital Lease Liability...........................	xx	
Cr. Cash.......................................		xx

The effects of these transactions on the financial statements using the horizontal model are shown below.

Balance sheet		Income statement	
Assets = Liabilities + Owners' equity	←	Net income = Revenues − Expenses	
1. Date of acquisition			
+ Equipment + Capital Lease Liability			
2. Annual depreciation expense:			
− Accumulated Depreciation		− Depreciation Expense	
3. Annual lease payment:			
− Cash − Capital Lease Liability		− Interest Expense	

The first entry shows the asset acquisition and the related financial obligation that has been incurred. The second shows depreciation expense in the same way it is recorded for purchased assets. The third shows the lease payment effect on cash, reflects the interest expense for the period on the amount that has been borrowed (in effect) from the lessor, and reduces the lease liability by what is really a payment on the principal of the loan from the lessor.

To illustrate the equivalence of capital lease payments and a long-term loan, assume that a firm purchased a computer system at a cost of $217,765 and borrowed the money by giving a note payable that had an annual interest rate of 10 percent and that required payments of $50,000 per year for six years. The purchase would be recorded using the following entry:

Dr. Computer Equipment	217,765	
Cr. Note Payable		217,765

Using the horizontal model, the following is the effect on the financial statements:

Balance sheet		Income statement
Assets = Liabilities + Owners' equity	←	Net income = Revenues − Expenses
Computer Equipment + 217,765	Note Payable + 217,765	

Each year, the firm will accrue and pay interest expense on the note, and make principal payments, as shown in the following table:

Year	*Principal Balance at Beginning of Year*	*Interest at 10%*	*Payment Applied to Principal ($50,000 − Interest)*	*Principal Balance at End of Year*
1	$217,765	$21,776	$28,224	$189,541
2	189,541	18,954	31,046	158,495
3	158,495	15,849	34,151	124,344
4	124,344	12,434	37,566	86,778
5	86,778	8,677	41,323	45,455
6	45,455	4,545	45,455	–0–

After six years, the note will have been fully paid.

If the firm were to lease the computer system and agree to make annual lease payments of $50,000 for six years instead of borrowing the money and buying the computer system outright, the financial statements should reflect the transaction in essentially the same way. This will happen because the present value of all of the lease payments (which include principal and interest) is $217,765. (From Table 6–3, in the 10% column and six-period row, the factor is 4.3553. This factor multiplied by the $50,000 annual lease payment is $217,765.) The entry at the beginning of the lease will be:

Dr. Computer Equipment	217,765
Cr. Capital Lease Liability......................	217,765

Using the horizontal model, the following is the effect on the financial statements:

Balance sheet		Income statement
Assets = Liabilities + Owners' equity	←	Net income = Revenues − Expenses
Computer Equipment + 217,765	Capital Lease Liability + 217,765	

Each year, the principal portion of the lease payment will reduce the capital lease liability, and the interest portion will be recognized as an expense. In addition, the computer equipment will be depreciated each year. Thus, liabilities on the balance sheet and expenses in the income statement will be the same as under the borrow and purchase alternative.

Again, the significance of capital lease accounting is that the economic impact of capital leasing isn't really any different from buying the asset outright; the impact on the financial statements shouldn't differ either.

WHAT DOES IT MEAN?

10. What does it mean to acquire an asset with a capital lease?

Intangible Assets

Objective 10
Understand the meaning of various intangible assets, how their values are measured, and how their costs are reflected in the income statement.

Intangible assets are long-lived assets that differ from property, plant, and equipment that has been purchased outright or acquired under a capital lease—either because the asset is represented by a contractual right or because the asset results from a purchase transaction but is not physically identifiable. Examples of the first type of intangible asset are leaseholds, patents, and trademarks; the second type of intangible asset is known as *goodwill.*

Just as the cost of plant and equipment is transferred to expense over time through accounting depreciation, the cost of most intangibles is also expensed over time. **Amortization,** which means spreading an amount over time, is the term used to describe the process of allocating the cost of an intangible asset from the balance sheet to the income statement. The cost of tangible assets is depreciated; the cost of intangible assets is amortized. The terms are different, but the process is the same. Most intangibles are amortized on a straight-line basis based on useful life to the entity but not for any period in excess of 40 years. Although an Accumulated Amortization account is sometimes used, amortization expense is usually recorded as a direct reduction in the carrying value of the related intangible asset. Thus, periodic amortization would be recorded as follows:

Dr. Amortization Expense	xx	
Cr. Intangible Asset.....................................		xx

The effect of this entry on the financial statements is:

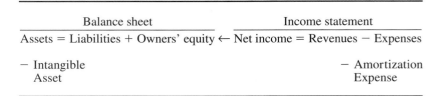

Balance sheet	Income statement
Assets = Liabilities + Owners' equity ←	Net income = Revenues − Expenses
− Intangible Asset	− Amortization Expense

Amortization expense is usually included with depreciation expense in the income statement. Note that neither depreciation expense nor amortization expense involves a cash disbursement; cash is disbursed when the asset is acquired or, if a loan is used to finance the acquisition, when the loan payments are made.

Leasehold Improvements

When the tenant of an office building makes modifications to the office space, such as having private offices constructed, the cost of these modifications is a capital expenditure to be amortized over their useful life to the tenant or over the life of the lease, whichever is shorter. The concept is the same as that applying to buildings or equipment, but the terminology is different. Entities that use rented facilities extensively, such as smaller shops or retail store chains that operate in shopping malls, may have a significant amount of **leasehold improvements.**

Patents, Trademarks, and Copyrights

A **patent** is a monopoly license granted by the government giving the owner control of the use or sale of an invention for a period of 17 years. A **trademark** (or trade name), when registered with the Federal Trade Commission, can be used only by the entity that owns it or by another entity that has secured permission from the owner. A trademark has an unlimited life, but it can be terminated by lack of use. A **copyright** is a protection granted to writers and artists that is designed to prevent unauthorized copying of printed or recorded material. A copyright is granted for a period of time equal to the life of the writer or artist, plus 50 years.

To the extent that an entity has incurred some cost in obtaining a patent, trademark, or copyright, that cost should be capitalized and amortized over its estimated remaining useful life to the entity or its statutory life, whichever is shorter. The cost of developing a patent, trademark, or copyright is not usually significant. Most intangible assets in this category arise when one firm purchases a patent, trademark, or copyright from another entity. An intangible that becomes very valuable because of the success of a product (e.g., "Coke") cannot be assigned a value and recorded as an asset while it continues to be owned by the entity that created it. In some cases, a firm will include a caption for trademarks, or another intangible asset, in its balance sheet and report a nominal cost of $1, just to communicate to financial statement users that it does have this type of asset.

License fees or royalties earned from an intangible asset owned by a firm are reported as operating revenues in the income statement. Likewise, license fees or royalty expenses incurred by a firm using an intangible asset owned by another entity are operating expenses.

Goodwill

Goodwill results from the purchase of one firm by another for a price that is greater than the fair market value of the net assets acquired. (Recall from Chapter 2 that net assets means total assets minus total liabilities.) Why would one firm be willing to pay more for a business than the fair market value of the inventory, plant, and equipment, and other assets being acquired? Because the purchasing firm does not see the transaction as the purchase of assets but instead evaluates the transaction as the purchase of *profits.* The purchaser will be willing to pay such an amount because the profits expected to be earned from the investment will generate an adequate return on the investment. If the firm being purchased has been able to earn a greater than average rate of return on its invested net assets, then the owners of that firm will be able to command a price for the firm that is greater than the fair market value of its net assets. This greater than average return may result from excellent management, a great location, unusual customer loyalty, a unique product or service, or some other factor.

When one firm purchases another, the purchase price is first assigned to the physical net assets acquired. The cost recorded for these net assets is their fair market value, usually determined by appraisal. This cost then becomes the basis for depreciating plant and equipment or for determining cost of goods sold if inventory is involved. To the extent that the total price exceeds the fair market value of the physical net assets acquired, the excess is recorded as goodwill. For example, assume that Cruisers, Inc., purchased a business by paying $1,000,000 in cash, and assuming a note payable liability of $100,000. The fair market value of the net assets acquired was $700,000, assigned as follows: Inventory, $250,000; Land, $150,000; Buildings, $400,000; and Notes Payable, $100,000. The entry would be:

Dr.	Inventory		250,000	
Dr.	Land		150,000	
Dr.	Buildings		400,000	
Dr.	Goodwill		300,000	
	Cr.	Notes Payable		100,000
	Cr.	Cash		1,000,000

The effect of this transaction on the financial statements is:

Balance sheet			Income statement		
Assets	= Liabilities	+ Owners' equity	← Net income	= Revenues	− Expenses
Inventory + 250,000	Notes Payable + 100,000				
Land + 150,000					
Buildings + 400,000					
Goodwill + 300,000					
Cash − 1,000,000					

Goodwill is an intangible asset, and it will be amortized over its expected economic life (which is the period that the expected higher-than-average rate of return will continue) or over 40 years, whichever is less. Accounting conservatism would suggest a period of much less than 40 years, but because it is difficult to determine objectively the economic life of goodwill, 40 years is a frequently used amortization period. Cruisers, Inc., would make the following entry to record goodwill amortization at the end of each year for the next 40 years:

Dr. Amortization Expense............................	7,500	
Cr. Goodwill		7,500

The effect of this adjustment on the financial statements is:

Balance sheet	Income statement
Assets = Liabilities + Owners' equity ←	Net income = Revenues − Expenses
Goodwill − 7,500	Amortization Expense − 7,500

Goodwill amortization expense has not been an allowable deduction for federal income tax purposes until recently. The Internal Revenue Code now allows goodwill and other intangibles purchased after 1993 to be amortized over a 15-year period. Despite this change in the tax law, most firms continue to use the 40-year amortization period for financial accounting purposes because it minimizes the expense reported in their income statements.

Goodwill cannot be recorded by a firm simply because its management believes that goodwill exists or even if the firm receives an offer to purchase it for more than the carrying value of its assets. Goodwill can only be recorded by a purchasing firm when an actual exchange takes place, and the purchase price exceeds the fair market value of the net assets acquired.

Another way of describing goodwill is to say that it is the present value of the greater-than-average earnings of the acquired firm, discounted for the period they are expected to last, at the acquiring firm's desired return on investment. That is, goodwill is the amount a firm is willing to pay now for expected future earnings that are greater than the earnings expected on the fair market value of the net assets acquired. In fact, when analysts at the acquiring firm are calculating the price to offer for the firm to be acquired, they use a lot of present value analysis.

Some critics suggest that goodwill is a fictitious asset that should be written off against the firm's retained earnings. Others point out that it is at best a "different" asset that must be carefully evaluated when it is encountered. However, if goodwill is included in the assets used in the return on investment calculation, the ROI measure will reflect management's ability to earn a return on this asset.

WHAT DOES IT MEAN?

11. What does it mean when goodwill results from the acquisition of another firm?

Natural Resources

Accounting for natural resource assets, such as coal deposits, crude oil reserves, timber, and mineral deposits, parallels that for depreciable assets.

Depletion, rather than depreciation, is the term for the using up of natural resources, but the concepts are exactly the same, even though depletion usually involves considerably more complex estimates.

For example, when a firm pays for the right to drill for oil or mine for coal, the cost of that right and the costs of developing the well or mine are capitalized. The cost is then reflected in the income statement as Depletion Expense, which is matched with the revenue resulting from the sale of the natural resource. Depletion is usually recognized on a straight-line basis, based on geological and engineering estimates of the quantity of the natural resource to be recovered. Thus, if $1 million was the cost of a mine that held an estimated 20 million tons of coal, the depletion cost would be $.05 per ton. In most cases, the cost of the asset is credited, or reduced directly, in the Depletion Expense entry instead of using an Accumulated Depletion account.

In practice, estimating depletion expense is very complex. Depletion expense allowed for federal income tax purposes frequently differs from that recognized for financial accounting purposes because the tax laws have, from time to time, been used to provide special incentives to develop natural resources.

Other Noncurrent Assets

Long-term investments, notes receivable that mature more than a year after the balance sheet date, and other noncurrent assets are included in this category. At such time as they become current (receivable within one year), they will be reclassified to the current asset section of the balance sheet. The explanatory footnotes, or financial review, accompanying the financial statements will include appropriate explanations about these assets if they are significant.

Summary

This chapter has discussed the accounting for and presentation of the following balance sheet noncurrent asset and related income statement accounts:

Balance sheet		Income statement
Assets = Liabilities + Owners' equity ←		Net income = Revenues − Expenses
Land		Gain on *or* Loss on Sale* Sale*
Purchased		Repairs and
Buildings/		Maintenance
Equipment		Expense
Leased	Capital	Interest
Buildings/	Lease	Expense
Equipment	Liability	

Balance sheet	Income statement
Assets = Liabilities + Owners' equity ←	Net income = Revenues − Expenses

(Accumulated . . . . Depreciation)	Depreciation Expense
Natural . . . . Resources	Depletion Expense
Intangible . . . . Assets	Amortization Expense

*For any noncurrent asset

Property, plant, and equipment owned by the entity are reported on the balance sheet at their original cost, less (for depreciable assets) accumulated depreciation.

Expenditures representing the cost of acquiring an asset that will benefit the entity for more than the current fiscal period are capitalized. Routine repair and maintenance costs are expensed in the fiscal period in which they are incurred.

Accounting depreciation is the process of spreading the cost of an asset to the fiscal periods in which the asset is used. Depreciation does not affect cash, nor is it an attempt to recognize a loss in the market value of an asset.

Depreciation expense can be calculated several ways. The calculations result in a depreciation expense pattern that is straight-line or accelerated. Straight-line methods are usually used for book purposes, and accelerated methods (based on the Modified Accelerated Cost Recovery System specified in the Internal Revenue Code) are usually used for income tax purposes.

When a depreciable asset is disposed of, both the asset and its related accumulated depreciation are removed from the accounts. A gain or loss results, depending on the relationship of any cash received in the transaction to the net book value of the asset disposed of.

When an asset is traded in on a similar asset, no gain or loss results. The cost of the new asset is the net book value of the old asset plus the cash paid and/or debt incurred to acquire the new asset.

When the use of an asset is acquired in a capital lease transaction, the asset and related lease liability are reported in the balance sheet. The cost of the asset is the present value of the lease payments, calculated using the interest rate used by the lessor to determine the periodic lease payments. The asset is depreciated, and interest expense related to the lease is recorded.

The present value concept recognizes that money does have value over time. The present value of an amount to be paid or received in the future is calculated by multiplying the future amount by a present value factor based on the discount (interest) rate and the number of periods involved. An annuity is a fixed amount to be paid or received each period for some number of periods. In the calculation of the present value of an annuity, the fixed periodic amount is multiplied by the appropriate factor. The present value concept is widely used in business and finance.

Intangible assets are represented by a contractual right or are not physically identifiable. The cost of intangible assets is spread over the useful life to the entity of the intangible asset and is called *amortization expense.* Intangible assets include leasehold improvements, patents, trademarks, copyrights, and goodwill. The cost of natural resources is recognized as *depletion expense,* which is allocated to the natural resources recovered.

Refer to the Intel Corporation balance sheet and related notes in the Appendix, and to other financial statements you may have, and observe how information about property, plant, and equipment, and other noncurrent assets is presented.

Key Terms and Concepts

Accelerated Cost Recovery System (ACRS) (p. 191)   The method prescribed in the Internal Revenue Code for calculating the depreciation deduction; applicable to the years 1981–1986.

accelerated depreciation method (p. 187)   A depreciation calculation method that results in greater depreciation expense in the early periods of an asset's life than in the later periods of its life.

amortization (p. 206)   The process of spreading the cost of an intangible asset over its useful life.

annuity (p. 198)   The receipt or payment of a constant amount over some period of time.

capital lease (p. 196)   A lease, usually long-term, that has the effect of financing the acquisition of an asset. Sometimes called a *financing lease.*

capitalizing (p. 182)   To record an expenditure as an asset as opposed to expensing the expenditure.

copyright (p. 207)   An intangible asset represented by the legally granted protection against unauthorized copying of a creative work.

declining-balance depreciation method (p. 189)   An accelerated depreciation method in which the declining net book value of the asset is multiplied by a constant rate.

depletion (p. 210)   The accounting process recognizing that the cost of a natural resource asset is used up as the natural resource is consumed.

discount rate (p. 198)   The interest rate used in a present value calculation.

expensing (p. 182)   To record an expenditure as an expense, as opposed to capitalizing the expenditure.

goodwill (p. 207)   An intangible asset arising from the purchase of a business for more than the fair market value of the net assets acquired. Goodwill is the present value of the expected earnings of the acquired business in excess of the earnings that would represent an average return on investment, discounted at the investor's required rate of return for the expected duration of the excess earnings.

intangible asset (p. 206)   A long-lived asset represented by a contractual right, or an asset that is not physically identifiable.

leasehold improvement (p. 207)   A depreciable asset represented by the cost of improvements made to a leasehold by the lessee.

Modified Accelerated Cost Recovery System (MACRS) (p. 191)   The method prescribed in the Internal Revenue Code for calculating the depreciation deduction; applicable to years after 1986.

net book value (p. 186)   The difference between the cost of an asset and the accumulated depreciation related to the asset. Sometimes called *carrying value.*

operating lease (p. 196)   A lease (usually short-term) that does not involve any attribute of ownership.

patent (p. 207)   An intangible asset represented by a government-sanctioned monopoly over the use of a product or process.

present value (p. 196)   The value now of an amount to be received or paid at some future date, recognizing an interest (or discount) rate for the period from the present to the future date.

proceeds (p. 194)   The amount of cash (or equivalent value) received in a transaction.

straight-line depreciation method (p. 187)   Calculation of periodic depreciation expense by dividing the amount to be depreciated by the number of periods over which the asset is to be depreciated.

sum-of-the-years'-digits depreciation (p. 188)   An accelerated depreciation method in which the amount to be depreciated is multiplied by a rate that declines each year.

trademark (p. 207)   An intangible asset represented by a right to the exclusive use of an identifying mark.

units of production depreciation method (p. 188)   A depreciation method based on periodic use and life expressed in terms of asset utilization.

WHAT DOES IT MEAN?
ANSWERS

1. It means that the expenditure is recorded as an asset rather than an expense. If the asset is a depreciable asset, depreciation expense will be recognized over the useful life—to the entity—of the asset.

2. It means that the assets are reported at their original cost, less accumulated depreciation if applicable. These book values are likely to be less than fair market values.

3. It means that cash is not paid out for depreciation expense. Depreciation expense results from spreading the cost of an asset to expense over the useful life—to the entity— of the asset. Cash is reduced when the asset is purchased or when payments are made on a loan that was obtained when the asset was purchased.

4. It means that relative to straight-line depreciation, more depreciation expense is recognized in the early years of an asset's life and less is recognized in the later years of an asset's life.

5. It means that because depreciation expense is deducted to arrive at taxable income, income taxes are lowered by the tax rate multiplied by the amount of depreciation expense claimed for income tax purposes.

6. It means that relative to a practice of capitalizing these expenditures, taxable income of the current year will be lower and that less time will be spent making depreciation expense calculations than if the expenditures were capitalized.

7. It means that money could be invested to earn a return—e.g., interest income—if it were invested for a period of time.

8. It means that the future amount has a value today that is equal to the amount that would have to be invested at a given rate of return to grow to the future amount. Present value is less than future value.

9. It means that the same amount will be received each period for a number of periods. For example, large lottery winnings are frequently received as an annuity, i.e., equal amounts over 20 years.

10. It means that rather than paying cash for the asset when it is acquired, or instead of borrowing funds to pay for the asset, the entity agrees to make payments to the lessor, or a finance company, of specified amounts over a specified period. The agreement is called a lease, but it is really an installment payment agreement.

11. It means that the acquiring firm paid more than the fair market value of the individual identifiable assets acquired because the potential for earning a return on its investment in the acquired firm as a going concern is greater than the rate of return that could be earned by investing in the individual assets.

Exercises and Problems

LO 1

6–1.   Basket purchase allocation. Dorsey Co. has expanded its operations by purchasing a parcel of land with a building on it from Bibb Co. for $90,000. The appraised value of the land is $20,000, and the appraised value of the building is $80,000.

Required:

a. Assuming that the building is to be used in Dorsey Co.'s business activities, what cost should be recorded for the land?

b. Explain why, for income tax purposes, management of Dorsey Co. would want as little of the purchase price as possible allocated to land.

c. Assuming that the building is razed at a cost of $10,000 so the land can be used for employee parking, what cost should Dorsey Co. record for the land?

d. Explain why Dorsey Co. allocated the cost of assets acquired based on appraised values at the purchase date rather than on the original cost of the land and building to Bibb Co.

LO 1

6–2.   Basket purchase allocation. Crow Co. purchased some of the machinery of Hare, Inc., a bankrupt competitor, at a liquidation sale for a total cost of $8,400. Crow's cost of moving and installing the machinery totaled $800. The following data are available:

Item	Hare's Net Book Value on the Date of Sale	List Price of Same Item If New	Appraiser's Estimate of Fair Value
Punch press	$5,040	$9,000	$6,000
Lathe	4,032	4,500	3,000
Welder	1,008	1,500	1,000

Required:

a. Calculate the amount that should be recorded by Crow Co. as the cost of each piece of equipment.

b. Which of the following alternatives should be used as the depreciable life for Crow Co.'s depreciation calculation? Explain your answer.

> The remaining useful life to Hare, Inc.
> The life of a new machine.
> The useful life of the asset to Crow Co.

LO 2 **6–3. Capitalizing versus expensing.** For each of the following expenditures, indicate the type of account (asset or expense) in which the expenditure should be recorded. Explain your answers.

a. $15,000 annual cost of routine repair and maintenance expenditures for a fleet of delivery vehicles.
b. $60,000 cost to develop a coal mine, from which an estimated 1 million tons of coal can be extracted.
c. $124,000 cost to replace the roof on a building.
d. $70,000 cost of a radio and television advertising campaign to introduce a new product line.
e. $4,000 cost of grading and leveling land so that a building can be constructed.

LO 2 **6–4. Capitalizing versus expensing.** For each of the following expenditures, indicate the type of account (asset or expense) in which the expenditure should be recorded. Explain your answers.

a. $200 for repairing damage that resulted from the careless unloading of a new machine.
b. $7,000 cost of designing and registering a trademark.
c. $1,400 in legal fees incurred to perform a title search for the acquisition of land.
d. $400 cost of patching a leak in the roof of a building.
e. $90,000 cost of salaries paid to the research and development staff.

LO 5 **6–5. Capitalizing versus expensing—effect on ROI and operating income.** During the first month of its current fiscal year, Green Co. incurred repair costs of $20,000 on a machine that had five years of remaining depreciable life. The repair cost was inappropriately capitalized. Green Co. reported operating income of $160,000 for the current year.

Required:

a. Assuming that Green Co. took a full year's straight-line depreciation expense in the current year, calculate the operating income that should have been reported for the current year.
b. Assume that Green Co.'s total assets at the end of the prior year and at the end of the current year were $940,000 and $1,020,000, respectively. Calculate ROI (based on operating income) for the current year using the originally reported data and for the current year using corrected data.
c. Explain the effect on ROI of subsequent years if the error is not corrected.

LO 5 **6–6. Capitalizing versus expensing—effect on ROI.** Early in January 1998, Tellco, Inc., acquired a new machine and incurred $10,000 of interest, installation, and overhead costs that should have been capitalized but were expensed. The company earned net income of $100,000 on average total assets of $800,000 for 1998. Assume that the total cost of the new machine will be depreciated over 10 years using the straight-line method.

Required:

a. Calculate the ROI for Tellco Inc., for 1998.

b. Calculate the ROI for Tellco Inc., for 1998, assuming that the $10,000 had been capitalized and depreciated over 10 years using the straight-line method. *(Hint: There is an effect on net income and average assets.)*

c. Given your answers to *a* and *b*, why would the company want to account for this expenditure as an expense?

d. Assuming that the $10,000 is capitalized, what will be the effect on ROI for 1999 and subsequent years, compared to expensing the interest, installation, and overhead costs in 1998? Explain your answer.

LO 3   **6–7.**   **Depreciation calculation methods.** Millco, Inc., acquired a machine that cost $80,000 early in 1999. The machine is expected to last for eight years, and its estimated salvage value at the end of its life is $8,000.

Required:

a. Using straight-line depreciation, calculate the depreciation expense to be recognized in the first year of the machine's life and calculate the accumulated depreciation after the fifth year of the machine's life.

b. Using declining-balance depreciation at twice the straight-line rate, calculate the depreciation expense for the third year of the machine's life.

c. Using sum-of-the-years'-digits depreciation, calculate the amount of accumulated depreciation after the fifth year of the machine's life. Compare this amount to the accumulated depreciation calculated in *a*.

d. What will be the net book value of the machine at the end of its eighth year of use before it is disposed of, under each depreciation method?

LO 3   **6–8.**   **Depreciation calculation methods.** Kleener Co. acquired a new delivery truck at the beginning of its current fiscal year. The truck cost $26,000 and has an estimated useful life of four years and an estimated salvage value of $4,000.

Required:

a. Calculate depreciation expense for each year of the truck's life using:
  1. Straight-line depreciation.
  2. Sum-of-the-years'-digits depreciation.
  3. Double-declining-balance depreciation.

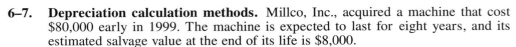

b. Calculate the truck's net book value at the end of its third year of use under each depreciation method.

c. Assume that Kleener Co. had no more use for the truck after the end of the third year and that at the beginning of the fourth year it had an offer from a buyer who was willing to pay $6,200 for the truck. Should the depreciation method used by Kleener Co. affect the decision to sell the truck?

LO 3   **6–9.**   **Straight-line and sum-of-the-years'-digits depreciation methods—partial year.** With respect to new assets, Misty Co.'s policy is to begin recording depreciation at the beginning of the month following the month in which the asset is acquired. On March 3, 1998, it acquired a machine costing $9,600. The machine has an estimated life of seven years and estimated salvage value of $1,200.

Required:

Calculate depreciation expense for calendar 1998 and 1999 using:
1. Straight-line depreciation.
2. Sum-of-the-years'-digits depreciation.

LO 3   **6–10.**   **Depreciation calculation methods—partial year.** Freedom Co. purchased a new machine on July 2, 1998, at a total installed cost of $44,000. The machine has an estimated life of five years and an estimated salvage value of $6,000.

Required:

a. Calculate the depreciation expense for each year of the *asset's life* using:
  1. Straight-line depreciation.
  2. Sum-of-the-years'-digits depreciation.
  3. Double-declining-balance depreciation.
  4. 150% declining-balance depreciation.
b. How much depreciation expense should be recorded by Freedom Co. for its fiscal year ended December 31, 1998, under each of the four methods? *(Note: The machine will have been used for one-half of its first year of life.)*
c. Calculate the accumulated depreciation and net book value of the machine at December 31, 1999, under each of the four methods.

LO 3   **6–11.   Identify depreciation methods used.** Grove Co. acquired a production machine on January 1, 1998, at a cost of $120,000. The machine is expected to have a four-year useful life, with a salvage value of $20,000. The machine is capable of producing 50,000 units of product in its lifetime. Actual production was as follows: 11,000 units in 1998; 16,000 units in 1999; 14,000 units in 2000; and 9,000 units in 2001.

  Shown below is the comparative balance sheet presentation of the *net book value* of the production machine at December 31 for each year of the asset's life, using four alternative depreciation methods (items *a–d*).

Production Machine, Net of Accumulated Depreciation

Depreciation Method?	At December 31			
	2001	*2000*	*1999*	*1998*
a. _____	$20,000	$30,000	$50,000	$80,000
b. _____	20,000	38,000	66,000	98,000
c. _____	20,000	20,000	30,000	60,000
d. _____	20,000	45,000	70,000	95,000

Required:

Identify the depreciation method used for each comparative balance sheet presentation shown above (items *a–d*). If a declining-balance method is used, be sure to indicate the percentage (150% or 200%). *(Hint: Read the balance sheet from right to left to determine how much has been depreciated each year. Remember that December 31, 1998, is the end of the first year.)*

LO 3   **6–12.   Identify depreciation methods used.** Moyle Co. acquired a machine on January 1, 1998, at a cost of $80,000. The machine is expected to have a five-year useful life, with a salvage value of $5,000. The machine is capable of producing 150,000 units of product in its lifetime. Actual production was as follows: 30,000 units in 1998; 20,000 units in 1999; 40,000 units in 2000; 25,000 units in 2001; and 35,000 units in 2002.

Required:

Identify the depreciation method used for each accumulated depreciation T–account listed below. If a declining-balance method is used, be sure to indicate the percentage (150% or 200%). *(Hint: What do the amounts shown for each year represent?)*

a.   **Accumulated Depreciation**

25,000	12/31/98
20,000	12/31/99
15,000	12/31/00
10,000	12/31/01
5,000	12/31/02

d.   **Accumulated Depreciation**

32,000	12/31/98
19,200	12/31/99
11,520	12/31/00
6,912	12/31/01
4,147	12/31/02

b.   **Accumulated Depreciation**

15,000	12/31/98
10,000	12/31/99
20,000	12/31/00
12,500	12/31/01
17,500	12/31/02

e.   **Accumulated Depreciation**

15,000	12/31/98
15,000	12/31/99
15,000	12/31/00
15,000	12/31/01
15,000	12/31/02

c.   **Accumulated Depreciation**

24,000	12/31/98
16,800	12/31/99
11,760	12/31/00
8,232	12/31/01
5,762	12/31/02

LO 3

6–13.   Partial-year depreciation calculations—straight-line and double-declining-balance methods. O'Sadnick Co. acquired a machine that cost $210,000 on July 1, 1998. The machine is expected to have a five-year useful life and an estimated salvage value of $20,000 at the end of its life. O'Sadnick Co. uses the calendar year for financial reporting. Depreciation expense for one-half of a year was recorded in 1998.

Required:

a. Using the straight-line depreciation method, calculate the depreciation expense to be recognized in the income statement for the year ended December 31, 2000, and the balance of the Accumulated Depreciation account as of December 31, 2000. *(Note: This is the third calendar year in which the asset has been used.)*

b. Using the double-declining-balance depreciation method, calculate the depreciation expense for the year ended December 31, 2000, and the net book value of the machine at that date.

LO 3

6–14.   Partial-year depreciation calculations—straight-line and double-declining-balance methods. Porter, Inc., acquired a machine that cost $360,000 on October 1, 1998. The machine is expected to have a four-year useful life and an estimated salvage value of $40,000 at the end of its life. Porter, Inc., uses the calendar year for financial reporting. Depreciation expense for one-fourth of a year was recorded in 1998.

Required:

a. Using the straight-line depreciation method, calculate the depreciation expense to be recognized in the income statement for the year ended December 31, 2000, and the balance of the Accumulated Depreciation account as of December 31, 2000. *(Note: This is the third calendar year in which the asset has been used.)*

b. Using the double-declining-balance depreciation method, calculate the depreciation expense for the year ended December 31, 2000, and the net book value of the machine at that date.

Intel LO 4 **6–15.** **Explain choice of depreciation method.** Find the discussion of depreciation methods used by Intel Corporation on page 22 of the annual report in the Appendix. Explain why the particular method is used for the purpose described. What method do you think the company uses for income tax purposes?

Intel LO 3 **6–16.** **Financial statement effects of depreciation methods.** Answer the following questions using data from the Intel Corporation Annual Report in the Appendix.

Required:

a. Calculate the ratio of the depreciation expense for 1996 reported on page 20 in the Consolidated Statements of Cash Flows to the cost (*not* net book value) of property, plant, and equipment reported in the December 28, 1996, balance sheet.

b. Based on the ratio calculated in part *a* and the depreciation method being used by Intel, what is the average useful life being used for its depreciation calculation?

c. Assume that the use of an accelerated depreciation method would have resulted in 50% more accumulated depreciation than reported at December 28, 1996, and that Intel's Retained Earnings account would have been affected by the entire difference. By what percentage would this have reduced the retained earnings amount reported at December 28, 1996?

LO 3 **6–17.** **Effect of depreciation on ROI.** Alpha, Inc., and Beta Co. are sheet metal processors that supply component parts for consumer product manufacturers. Alpha, Inc., has been in business since 1960 and is operating in its original plant facilities. Much of its equipment was acquired in the 1960s. Beta Co. was started two years ago and acquired its building and equipment then. Each firm has about the same sales revenue, and material and labor costs are about the same for each firm. What would you expect Alpha's ROI to be relative to the ROI of Beta Co.? Explain your answer. What are the implications of this ROI difference for a firm seeking to enter an established industry?

LO 3 **6–18.** **Financial statement effects of depreciation—straight-line versus accelerated methods.** Assume that a company chooses an accelerated method of calculating depreciation expense for financial statement reporting purposes for an asset with a 10-year life.

Required:

State the effect (higher, lower, no effect) of accelerated depreciation relative to straight-line depreciation on:

a. Depreciation expense in the first year.

b. The asset's net book value after two years.

c. Cash flows from operations (excluding income taxes).

LO 3, 6 **6–19.** **Determine depreciation method used and date of asset acquisition; record disposal of asset.** The balance sheets of Tully Corp. showed the following at December 31, 1999, and 1998:

	December 31, 1999	*December 31, 1998*
Machine, less accumulated depreciation of $42,000 at December 31, 1999, and $24,000 at December 31, 1998.	$28,000	$46,000

Required:

a. If there have not been any purchases or sales, or other transactions affecting this machine account since the machine was first acquired, what is the amount of depreciation expense for 1999?

b. Assume the same facts as in *a,* and assume that the estimated useful life of the machine is four years and the estimated salvage value is $10,000. Determine:
1. What the original cost of the machine was.
2. What depreciation method is apparently being used. Explain your answer.
3. When the machine was acquired.

c. Assume that the machine is sold on December 31, 1999, for $23,600. Use the horizontal model (or write the journal entry) to show the effect of the sale of the machine.

LO 3, 6　　**6–20.** **Determine depreciation method used and date of asset acquisition; record disposal of asset.** The balance sheets of HIROE, Inc., showed the following at December 31, 1999, and 1998:

	December 31, 1999	December 31, 1998
Equipment, less accumulated depreciation of $31,500 at December 31, 1999, and $22,500 at December 31, 1998	$40,500	$49,500

Required:

a. If there have not been any purchases or sales, or other transactions affecting this equipment account since the equipment was first acquired, what is the amount of the depreciation expense for 1999?

b. Assume the same facts as in *a* and assume that the estimated useful life of the equipment to HIROE, Inc., is eight years and that there is no estimated salvage value. Determine:
1. What the original cost of the equipment was.
2. What depreciation method is apparently being used. Explain your answer.
3. When the equipment was acquired.

c. Assume that this equipment account represents the cost of 10 identical machines. Calculate the gain or loss on the sale of one of the machines on January 2, 2000, for $4,500. Use the horizontal model (or write the journal entry) to show the effect of the sale of the machine.

LO 6　　**6–21.** **Asset trade-in transaction.** Nalco, Inc., traded in an old computer that had cost $85,000 several years ago for a new computer having a list price of $110,000. The old computer had a net book value of $21,000 at the time of the exchange, and a trade-in allowance of $12,000 was given. Nalco will pay cash for the balance.

Required:

a. Calculate the cost at which Nalco will record the new computer.

b. Use the horizontal model (or write the journal entry) to show the effect of the trade-in transaction.

LO 6　　**6–22.** **Asset trade-in transaction.** The company car owned by Charlie's Chili Co. is near the end of its life. The car cost $9,800 and has a net book value of $2,000. Charlie has approached two dealers who have made the following offers for the same new car model. Dealer A will allow a $2,900 trade-in allowance on the old car and sell Charlie a new car at its list price of $14,800. Dealer B isn't interested in taking the old car in trade; B's selling price for the new car is $13,000. If Charlie buys the new car from Dealer B, he'll be able to sell the old car outright for $900.

Required:
a. Which offer do you suggest Charlie accept? Explain your answer.
b. What caused the difference between the net book value of the old car and its trade-in allowance?
c. What caused the difference between the net book value of the old car and its cash selling value?
d. Assume that Charlie takes the trade-in allowance and pays for the new car in cash. Use the horizontal model (or write the journal entry) to record the trade-in transaction.

LO 6   **6–23.** **Asset trade-in transaction.** Printy, Inc., traded in an old machine that had cost $25,000 several years ago for a new machine having a list price of $40,000. At the time of the exchange, the Accumulated Depreciation account on the old machine had a balance of $18,000, before recognizing $2,000 of depreciation for the current year. A trade-in allowance of $3,600 was given for the old machine. Printy will pay cash for the balance.

Required:
a. Calculate the cost at which Printy will record the new machine.
b. Use the horizontal model (or write the journal entry) to show the effect of the trade-in transaction.
c. Assume that the cost of installation of the new machine was $700. How should Printy account for this cost? Explain your answer.

LO 6   **6–24.** **Asset trade-in transaction.** Callahan's Garage traded in an old hydraulic car lift that had cost $95,000 several years ago for a new lift having a $160,000 list price. At the time of the exchange, the Accumulated Depreciation account on the old lift had a balance of $63,000 before recognizing $4,000 of depreciation for the current year. A trade-in allowance of $35,000 was given for the old lift. Callahan's Garage will pay cash for the balance.

Required:
a. Calculate the cost at which Callahan's Garage will record the new car lift.
b. Use the horizontal model (or write the journal entry) to show the effect of the trade-in transaction.
c. Assume that the cost of removing the old lift was $2,000 and the cost of installing the new lift was $1,000. How should Callahan's Garage account for these costs? Explain your answer.

LO 7, 8, 9   **6–25.** **Accounting for capital leases.** On January 1, 1999, Carey, Inc., entered into a noncancellable lease agreement, agreeing to pay $3,500 at the end of each year for four years to acquire a new computer system having a market value of $10,200. The expected useful life of the computer system is also four years, and the computer will be depreciated on a straight-line basis with no salvage value. The interest rate used by the lessor to determine the annual payments was 14%. Under the terms of the lease, Carey, Inc., has an option to purchase the computer for $1 on January 1, 2003.

Required:
a. Explain why Carey, Inc., should account for this lease as a capital lease rather than an operating lease. *(Hint: Determine which of the four criteria for capitalizing a lease have been met.)*

b. Write the entry that Carey, Inc., should make on January 1, 1999. *(Hint: First determine the present value of future lease payments using Table 6–3.)* Round your answer to the nearest $10.

c. Write the entry that Carey, Inc., should make on December 31, 1999, to record the first annual lease payment of $3,500. *(Hint: Based on your answer to part b, determine the appropriate amounts for interest and principal.)* Do not round your answers.

d. What expenses (include amounts) should be recognized for this lease on the income statement for the year ended December 31, 1999?

e. Explain why the accounting for an asset acquired under a capital lease isn't really any different than the accounting for an asset that was purchased with money borrowed on a long-term loan.

(Note: As an alternative to writing journal entries, use the horizontal model to record the lease and first payment.)

LO 7, 8, 9   **6–26.   Accounting for capital leases versus purchased assets.** Ambrose Co. has the option of purchasing a new delivery truck for $28,200 in cash or leasing the truck for $6,100 per year, payable at the end of each year for six years. The truck also has a useful life of six years and will be depreciated on a straight-line basis with no salvage value. The interest rate used by the lessor to determine the annual payments was 8%.

Required:

a. Assume that Ambrose Co. purchased the delivery truck and signed a six-year, 8% note payable for $28,200 in satisfaction of the purchase price. Write the entry that Ambrose should make to record the purchase transaction.

b. Assume instead that Ambrose Co. agreed to the terms of the lease. Write the entry that Ambrose should make to record the capital lease transaction. *(Hint: First determine the present value of future lease payments using Table 6–3.)* Round your answer to the nearest $1.

c. Write the entry that Ambrose Co. should make at the end of the year to record the first annual lease payment of $6,100. *(Hint: Based on your answer to part b, determine the appropriate amounts for interest and principal.)* Do not round your answers.

d. What expenses (include amounts) should Ambrose Co. recognize on the income statement for the first year of the lease?

e. How much would the annual payments be for the note payable signed by Ambrose Co. in part *a?* *(Hint: Use the present value of an annuity factor from Table 6–3.)*

(Note: As an alternative to writing journal entries, use the horizontal model to record the lease and first payment.)

LO 8   **6–27.   Present value calculations.** Using a present value table, your calculator, or a computer program present value function, calculate the present value of:

a. A car down payment of $3,000 that will be required in two years, assuming an interest rate of 10%.

b. A lottery prize of $6 million to be paid at the rate of $300,000 per year for 20 years, assuming an interest rate of 10%.

c. The same annual amount as in *b,* but assuming an interest rate of 14%.

d. A capital lease obligation that calls for the payment of $8,000 per year for 10 years, assuming a discount rate of 8%.

LO 8, 9   **6–28.   Present value calculation—capital lease.** Renter Co. acquired the use of a machine by agreeing to pay the manufacturer of the machine $900 per year for

10 years. At the time the lease was signed, the interest rate for a 10-year loan was 12%.

Required:

a. Use the appropriate factor from Table 6–3 to calculate the amount that Renter Co. could have paid at the beginning of the lease to buy the machine outright.

b. What causes the difference between the amount you calculated in *a* and the total of $9,000 ($900 per year for 10 years) that Renter Co. will pay under the terms of the lease?

c. What is the appropriate amount of cost to be reported in Renter Co.'s balance sheet (at the time the lease was signed) with respect to this asset?

LO 8   **6–29.**   **Present value calculations—effects of compounding frequency, discount rates, and time periods.** Using a present value table, your calculator, or a computer program present value function, verify that the present value of $100,000 to be received in five years at an interest rate of 16%, compounded annually, is $47,610. Calculate the present value of $100,000 for each item *(a–f)* below using the same facts as above, except:

a. Interest is compounded semiannually.

b. Interest is compounded quarterly.

c. A discount rate of 12% is used.

d. A discount rate of 20% is used.

e. The cash will be received in three years.

f. The cash will be received in seven years.

LO 8   **6–30.**   **Present value calculations.** Using a present value table, your calculator, or a computer program present value function, answer the following questions:

Required:

a. What is the present value of nine annual cash payments of $4,000, to be paid at the end of each year using an interest rate of 6%?

b. What is the present value of $15,000 to be paid at the end of 20 years, using an interest rate of 18%?

c. How much cash must be deposited in a savings account as a single amount in order to accumulate $300,000 at the end of 12 years, assuming that the account will earn 10% interest?

d. How much cash must be deposited in a savings account (as a single amount) in order to accumulate $50,000 at the end of seven years, assuming that the account will earn 12% interest?

e. Assume that a machine was purchased for $60,000. Cash of $20,000 was paid, and a four-year, 8% note payable was signed for the balance.
1. How much is the equal annual payment of principal and interest due at the end of each year? Round your answer to the nearest $1.
2. What is the total amount of interest expense that will be reported over the life of the note? Round your answer to the nearest $1.
3. Use the horizontal model, or write the journal entries, to show the equal annual payments of principal and interest due at the end of each year.

LO 10   **6–31.**   **Goodwill effect on ROI.** Assume that fast-food restaurants generally provide an ROI of 15%, but that such a restaurant near a college campus has an ROI of 18% because its relatively large volume of business generates an above-average turnover (sales/assets). The replacement value of the restaurant's plant and equipment is $200,000. If you were to invest that amount in a restaurant elsewhere in town, you could expect a 15% ROI.

Required:

a. Would you be willing to pay more than $200,000 for the restaurant near the campus? Explain your answer.

b. If you purchased the restaurant near the campus for $240,000 and the fair value of the assets you acquired was $200,000, what balance sheet accounts would be used to record the cost of the restaurant?

LO 10   **6–32.   Goodwill—effect on ROI and operating income.** Goodwill arises when one firm acquires the net assets of another firm and pays more for those net assets than their current fair market value. Suppose that Target Co. had operating income of $60,000 and net assets with a fair market value of $200,000. Takeover Co. pays $300,000 for Target Co.'s net assets and business activities.

Required:

a. How much goodwill will result from this transaction?

b. Calculate the ROI for Target Co. based on its present operating income and the fair market value of its net assets.

c. Calculate the ROI that Takeover Co. will earn if the operating income of the acquired net assets continues to be $60,000. (Ignore goodwill amortization.)

d. Assume that Takeover Co. amortizes goodwill over a 40-year period. Use the horizontal model (or write the journal entry) to record the goodwill amortization for the first year.

e. What reasons can you think of to explain why Takeover Co. is willing to pay $100,000 more than fair market value for the net assets acquired from Target Co.?

LO 6, 9, 10   **6–33.   Transaction analysis—various accounts.** Prepare an answer sheet with the column headings shown below. For each of the following transactions or adjustments, indicate the effect of the transaction or adjustment on assets, liabilities, and net income by entering for each account affected the account name and amount, and indicating whether it is an addition (+) or a subtraction (−). Transaction *a* has been done as an illustration. Net income is *not* affected by every transaction. In some cases, only one column may be affected because all of the specific accounts affected by the transaction are included in that category.

	Assets	Liabilities	Net Income
a. Recorded $200 of depreciation expense.	Accumulated Depreciation − 200		Depreciation Expense − 200

b. Sold land that had originally cost $9,000 for $14,000 in cash.

c. Acquired a new machine under a capital lease. The present value of future lease payments, discounted at 10%, was $12,000.

d. Recorded the first annual payment of $2,000 for the leased machine (in *c* above).

e. Recorded a $6,000 payment for the cost of developing and registering a trademark.

f. Recognized periodic amortization for the trademark (in *e* above) using a 40-year useful life.

g. Sold used production equipment for $16,000 in cash. The equipment originally cost $40,000, and the accumulated depreciation account has an unadjusted balance of $22,000. It was determined that a $1,000 year-to-date depreciation entry must be recorded before the sale transaction can be recorded. Record the adjustment and the sale.

h. Traded in an old tractor plus $12,000 in cash for a new tractor having a $20,000 list price. The old tractor had cost $16,000 and had a net book value of $7,000 at the time of the exchange. A trade-in allowance of $8,000 was given for the old tractor.

LO 3, 5, 6, 10 **6–34.** **Transaction analysis—various accounts.** Prepare an answer sheet with the column headings shown below. For each of the following transactions or adjustments, you are to indicate the effect of the transaction or adjustment on assets, liabilities, and net income by entering for each account affected the account name and amount, and indicating whether it is an addition, (+) or a subtraction (−). Transaction *a* has been done as an illustration. Net income is *not* affected by every transaction. In some cases, only one column may be affected because all of the specific accounts affected by the transaction are included in that category.

	Assets	Liabilities	Net Income
a. Recorded $200 of depreciation expense.	Accumulated Depreciation − 200		Depreciation Expense − 200

b. Sold land that had originally cost $13,000 for $11,400 in cash.

c. Recorded a $68,000 payment for the cost of developing and registering a patent.

d. Recognized periodic amortization for the patent (in 2 above) using the maximum statutory useful life.

e. Capitalized $3,200 of cash expenditures made to extend the useful life of production equipment.

f. Expensed $1,800 of cash expenditures incurred for routine maintenance of production equipment.

g. Sold a used machine for $9,000 in cash. The machine originally cost $30,000 and had been depreciated for the first two years of its five-year useful life using the double-declining-balance method. *(Hint: You must compute the balance of the accumulated depreciation account before you can record the sale.)*

h. Purchased a business for $320,000 in cash. The fair market values of the net assets acquired were as follows: Land, $40,000; Buildings, $200,000; Equipment, $100,000; and Long-Term Debt, $70,000.

i. Recognized periodic amortization of goodwill from the purchase transaction (in *h* above) using a 40-year useful life.

CHAPTER 7

Accounting for and Presentation of Liabilities

Liabilities are obligations of the entity, or as defined by the FASB, "probable future sacrifices of economic benefits arising from present obligations of a particular entity to transfer assets or provide services to other entities in the future as a result of past transactions or events."[1] Note that liabilities are recorded only for *present* obligations that are the result of *past* transactions or events that will require the probable *future* sacrifice of resources. Thus, the following items would not yet be recorded as liabilities: (1) negotiations for the possible purchase of inventory, (2) increases in the replacement cost of assets due to inflation, and (3) contingent losses on unsettled lawsuits against the entity.

Most liabilities that meet the above definition arise because credit has been obtained in the form of a loan (notes payable) or in the normal course of business—for example, when a supplier ships merchandise before payment is made (accounts payable) or when an employee works one week not expecting to be paid until the next week (wages payable). As has been illustrated in previous chapters, many liabilities are recorded in the accrual process that matches revenues and expenses. The term *accrued expenses* is used on some balance sheets to describe these liabilities, but this is shorthand for *liabilities resulting from the accrual of expenses.* If you keep in mind that revenues and expenses are reported only on the income statement, you will not be confused by this mixing of terms. Current liabilities are those that must be paid or otherwise satisfied within a year of the balance sheet date; noncurrent liabilities are those that will be paid or satisfied more than a year after the balance sheet date. Liability captions usually seen in a balance sheet are:

Current Liabilities:
Accounts Payable
Short-Term Debt (Notes Payable)

---

[1]FASB, *Statement of Financial Accounting Concepts No. 6,* "Elements of Financial Statements" (Stamford, CT, 1985), para. 35. Copyright © by the Financial Accounting Standards Board, High Ridge Park, Stamford, CT 06905, U.S.A. Quoted with permission. Copies of the complete document are available from the FASB.

Current Maturities of Long-Term Debt
Unearned Revenue or Deferred Credits
Other Accrued Liabilities

Noncurrent Liabilities:
Long-Term Debt (Bonds Payable)
Deferred Income Taxes
Minority Interest in Subsidiaries

The order in which liabilities are presented within the current and noncurrent categories is a function of liquidity (i.e., how soon the debt becomes due) and management preferences.

Review the liabilities section of the Intel Corporation consolidated balance sheets on page 19 of the annual report in the Appendix. Note that most of these captions have to do with debt, accrued liabilities, and income taxes. The business and accounting practices relating to these items make up a major part of this chapter.

Some of the most significant and controversial issues that the FASB has addressed in recent years, including accounting for income taxes, accounting for pensions, and consolidation of subsidiaries, relate to the liability section of the balance sheet. A principal reason for the interest generated by these topics is that the recognition of a liability usually involves recognizing an expense as well. Expenses reduce net income, and lower net income means lower ROI. Keep these relationships in mind as you study this chapter.

Learning Objectives

After studying this chapter, you should understand:

1 The financial statement presentation of short-term debt and current maturities of long-term debt.

2 The difference between interest calculated on a straight basis and on a discount basis.

3 What unearned revenues are and how they are presented in the balance sheet.

4 The accounting for an employer's liability for payroll and payroll taxes.

5 The importance of making estimates for certain accrued liabilities and how these items are presented in the balance sheet.

6 What leverage is and how it is provided by long-term debt.

7 The different characteristics of a bond, which is the formal document representing most long-term debt.

8 Why bond discount or premium arises and how it is accounted for.

9 What deferred income taxes are and why they arise.

10 What minority interest is, why it arises, and what it means in the balance sheet.

Current Liabilities

Short-Term Debt

Objective 1
Understand the financial statement presentation of short-term debt and current maturities of long-term debt.

Most firms experience seasonal fluctuations during the year in the demand for their products or services. For instance, a firm like Cruisers, Inc., a manufacturer of small boats, is likely to have greater demand for its product during the spring and early summer than in the winter. In order to use its production facilities most efficiently, Cruisers, Inc., will plan to produce boats on a level basis during the year. This means that during the fall and winter seasons, its inventory of boats will be increased in order to have enough product on hand to meet spring and summer demand. In order to finance this inventory increase and be able to keep its payments to suppliers and employees current, Cruisers, Inc., will obtain a **working capital loan** from its bank. This type of short-term loan is made with the expectation that it will be repaid from the collection of accounts receivable that will be generated by the sale of inventory. The short-term loan usually has a **maturity date** specifying when the loan is to be repaid. Sometimes a firm will negotiate a **revolving line of credit** with its bank. The credit line represents a predetermined maximum loan amount, but the firm has flexibility in the timing and amount borrowed. There may be a specified repayment schedule or an agreement that all amounts borrowed will be repaid by a particular date. Whatever the specific loan arrangement may be, the borrowing is recorded by the following entry:

Dr. Cash...	xx	
Cr. Short-Term Debt................................		xx
Borrowed money from bank.		

The effect of this transaction on the financial statements is:

Balance sheet	Income statement
Assets = Liabilities + Owners' equity ←	Net income = Revenues − Expenses
+ Cash + Short-Term Debt	

The short-term debt resulting from this type of transaction is sometimes called a **note payable.** The note is a formal promise to pay a stated amount at a stated date, usually with interest at a stated rate, and sometimes secured by collateral.

Interest expense is associated with almost any borrowing, and it is appropriate to record interest expense for each fiscal period during which the money is borrowed. The alternative methods of calculating interest are explained in Business in Practice—Interest Calculation Methods.

Prime rate is the term frequently used to express the interest rate on short-term loans. The prime rate is established by the lender, presumably for its most creditworthy borrowers, but is in reality just a benchmark rate. The prime rate is raised or lowered by the lender in response to credit market forces. The borrower's rate may be expressed as "prime plus 1,"

Objective 2
Understand the difference between interest calculated on a straight basis and on a discount basis.

BUSINESS IN PRACTICE
Interest Calculation Methods

Lenders calculate interest on either a straight (simple interest) basis or on a discount basis. The straight calculation involves charging interest on the money actually available to the borrower for the length of time it was borrowed. Interest on a **discount loan** is based on the principal amount of the loan, but the interest is subtracted from the principal and only the difference is made available to the borrower. In effect, the borrower pays the interest in advance. Assume that $1,000 is borrowed for one year at an interest rate of 12%.

Straight Interest

The **interest calculation—straight basis** is made as follows:

$$\text{Interest} = \text{Principal} \times \text{Rate} \times \text{Time (in years)}$$
$$= \$1,000 \times 0.12 \times 1$$
$$= \$120$$

At the maturity date of the note, the borrower will repay the principal of $1,000 plus the interest owed of $120. The borrower's effective *interest rate*—the **annual percentage rate (APR)** is 12%:

$$\text{APR} = \text{Interest paid}/\text{Money available to use} \times \text{Time (in years)}$$
$$= \$120/\$1,000 \times 1$$
$$= 12\%$$

You should understand that this is another application of the present value concept described in Chapter 6. The amount of the liability on the date the money is borrowed is the present value of the amount to be repaid in the future, calculated at the effective interest rate—which is the rate of return desired by the lender. To illustrate, the amount to be repaid in one year is $1,120, the sum of the $1,000 principal plus the $120 of interest. From Table 6–2, the factor in the 12% column and one-period row is 0.8929; $1,120 × 0.8929 = $1,000 (rounded). These relationships are illustrated on the following time line:

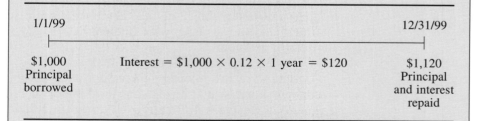

1/1/99		12/31/99
$1,000 Principal borrowed	Interest = $1,000 × 0.12 × 1 year = $120	$1,120 Principal and interest repaid

Discount

The **interest calculation—discount basis** is made as illustrated above, except that the interest amount is subtracted from the loan principal, and the borrower receives the difference. In this case, the loan proceeds would be $880 ($1,000 − $120). At the maturity of the note, the borrower will pay just the principal of $1,000 because the interest of $120 has already been paid—it was subtracted from the principal amount when the loan was obtained. These relationships are illustrated on the following time line:

1/1/99		12/31/99
$880 Proceeds	Interest = $1,000 × 0.12 × 1 year = $120	$1,000 Principal repaid

Because the full principal amount is not available to the borrower, the effective interest rate (APR) on a discount basis is much higher than the rate used in the lending agreement to calculate the interest:

$$\text{APR} = \text{Interest paid}/\text{Money available to use} \times \text{Time (in years)}$$

$$= \$120/\$880 \times 1$$

$$= 13.6\%$$

Applying present value analysis, the carrying value of the liability on the date the money is borrowed represents the amount to be repaid, $1,000, multiplied by the present value factor for 13.6% for one year. The factor is 0.8803, and although it is not explicitly shown in Table 6–2, it can be derived approximately by **interpolating** between the factors for 12% and 14%.

An *installment loan* is repaid periodically over the life of the loan, so only about half of the proceeds (on average) are available for use throughout the life of the loan. Thus, the effective interest rate is about twice that of a *term loan* requiring a lump-sum repayment of principal at the maturity date.

In the final analysis, it isn't important whether interest is calculated using the straight method or the discount method, or whether an installment loan or term loan is arranged; what is important is the APR, or effective interest rate. The borrower's objective is to keep the APR (which must be disclosed in accordance with federal truth in lending laws) to a minimum.

for example, which means that the interest rate for the borrower will be the prime rate plus 1 percent. It is quite possible for the interest rate to change during the term of the loan, in which case a separate calculation of interest is made for each period having a different rate.

For a loan on which interest is calculated on a straight basis, interest is accrued each period with the following entry:

Dr. Interest Expense	xx	
Cr. Interest Payable		xx
Accrued interest for period.		

The effect of this entry on the financial statement is:

Balance sheet	Income statement
Assets = Liabilities + Owners' equity ←	Net income = Revenues − Expenses
+ Interest Payable	− Interest Expense

Interest Payable is a current liability because it will be paid within a year of the balance sheet date. It may be disclosed in a separate caption or included with other accrued liabilities in the current liability section of the balance sheet.

For a loan on which interest is calculated on a discount basis, the amount of cash **proceeds** represents the initial carrying value of the liability. Using the data from the discount example in Business in Practice, the journal entry for the borrower is:

```
Dr.  Cash..........................................  880
Dr.  Discount on Short-Term Debt........................  120
    Cr.  Short-Term Debt ...............................        1,000
```

The effect of this entry on the financial statements is:

Balance sheet	Income statement
Assets = Liabilities + Owners' equity ←	Net income = Revenues − Expenses
Cash	Short-Term
+ 880	Debt
	+ 1,000
	Discount on
	Short-Term Debt
	− 120

The Discount on Short-Term Debt account is a **contra liability,** classified as a reduction of Short-Term Debt on the balance sheet. As interest expense is incurred, the Discount on Short-Term Debt is amortized as follows:

```
Dr.  Interest Expense.....................................  xx
    Cr.  Discount on Short-Term Debt.........................        xx
```

The effect of this entry on the financial statements is:

Balance sheet	Income statement
Assets = Liabilities + Owners' equity ←	Net income = Revenues − Expenses
+ Discount on Short-Term Debt	− Interest Expense

The amortization of the discount to interest expense affects neither cash nor interest payable. Net income decreases as interest expense is recorded, and the carrying value of short-term debt increases as the discount is amortized.

WHAT DOES IT MEAN?

1. What does it mean to borrow money on a discount basis?

Current Maturities of Long-Term Debt

When funds are borrowed on a long-term basis (a topic to be discussed later in this chapter), it is not unusual for principal repayments to be required on an installment basis; every year, a portion of the debt matures and is to be repaid by the borrower. Any portion of a long-term borrowing that is to be repaid within a year of the balance sheet date is reclassified from the noncurrent liability section of the balance sheet to the **Current Maturities of Long-Term Debt** account. These amounts are reported in the current liability section but separately from short-term debt because the liability arose from a long-term borrowing transaction. Interest payable on long-term debt is classified with other interest payable and may be combined with other accrued liabilities for reporting purposes.

Accounts Payable

Amounts owed to suppliers for goods and services that have been provided to the entity on credit are the principal components of **accounts payable.** Unlike accounts receivable, which are reported net of estimated cash discounts expected to be taken, accounts payable to suppliers that permit a cash discount for prompt payment are not usually reduced by the amount of the cash discount expected to be taken. This treatment is supported by the materiality concept because the amount involved is not likely to have a significant effect on the financial position or results of the operations of the firm. However, accounts payable for firms that record purchases net of anticipated cash discounts will be reported at the amount expected to be paid.

Purchase transactions for which a cash discount is allowed are recorded using either the *gross* or *net* method. The difference between the two is the timing of the recognition of cash discounts. The gross method results in recognizing cash discounts only when invoices are paid within the discount period. The net method recognizes cash discounts when purchases are initially recorded, under the assumption that all discounts will be taken; an expense is then recognized if a discount is not taken. An evaluation of these methods is provided in Business in Practice—Gross and Net Methods of Recording Purchases.

BUSINESS IN PRACTICE
Gross and Net Methods of Recording Purchases

Because cash discounts represent such a high return on investment (see Business in Practice—Cash Discounts in Chapter 5), most firms have a rigidly

---

Business in Practice concluded

followed internal control policy of taking all cash discounts possible. Thus, many firms use the net method, which assumes that cash discounts will be taken. Under the net method, if a discount is missed because an invoice is paid after the cash discount date, the expense Purchase Discounts Lost is recorded. This expense highlights in the financial statements the fact that a discount was missed, and management can then take the appropriate action to eliminate or minimize future missed discounts. Thus, the net method has the advantage of strengthening the firm's system of internal control because any breakdown in the policy of taking every possible cash discount is highlighted. The net method is easy to apply in practice because no special accounts are involved in recording payments made within the discount period—which is the usual case.

The gross method treats cash discounts taken by the firm as a reduction of the cost of goods sold reported in the income statement but does not report any cash discounts that were missed. Thus, management cannot so easily determine how well its internal control policy is being followed. Although the gross method involves more bookkeeping because the Purchase Discounts account is affected each time a cash discount is recorded, in practice many firms use the gross method.

To illustrate and contrast the gross and net methods of recording purchases on account, assume that a $1,000 purchase is made with terms 2/10, n30. The journal entries under each method are as follows:

	Method Used			
	Gross		*Net*	
1. Record purchase:				
Dr. Inventory	1,000		980	
Cr. Accounts Payable		1,000		980
2. Pay within the discount period:				
Dr. Accounts Payable	1,000		980	
Cr. Cash		980		980
Cr. Purchase Discounts		20		
3. Pay after the discount period:				
Dr. Purchase Discounts Lost			20	
Dr. Accounts Payable	1,000		980	
Cr. Cash		1,000		1,000

The financial statement effects of each method are:

Balance sheet	Income statement
Assets = Liabilities + Owners' equity ←	Net income = Revenues − Expenses

A. Gross method

1. Record purchase:

Inventory   Accounts
+ 1,000   Payable
           + 1,000

2. Pay within the discount period:

Cash   Accounts   Purchase
− 980   Payable   Discounts*
         − 1,000   + 20

*(A reduction of cost of goods sold)

3. Pay after the discount period:

Cash   Accounts
− 1,000   Payable
         − 1,000

B. Net method

1. Record purchase:

Inventory   Accounts
+ 980   Payable
           + 980

2. Pay within the discount period:

Cash   Accounts
− 980   Payable
         − 980

3. Pay after the discount period:

Cash   Accounts   Purchase
− 1,000   Payable   Discounts
         − 980   Lost
                                    − 20

Unearned Revenue or Deferred Credits

Objective 3
Understand what unearned revenues are and how they are presented in the balance sheet.

Customers often pay for services or even products before the service or product is delivered. An entity collecting cash in advance of earning the related revenue records an **unearned revenue,** or a **deferred credit,** which is included in current liabilities. Unearned revenues must then be allocated to the fiscal periods in which the services are performed or the products are delivered, in accordance with the matching concept. The accounting for revenue received in advance was discussed with adjusting entries in Chapter 4. To illustrate, assume that a magazine publisher requires a subscriber to pay in advance for a subscription. The entry to record this transaction is:

Dr.   Cash   xx
     Cr.   Unearned Subscription Revenue   xx

The adjusting entry to record the revenue earned during the fiscal period would be:

```
Dr.  Unearned Subscription Revenue . . . . . . . . . . . . . . . . . . . . . . . .  xx
    Cr.  Subscription Revenue . . . . . . . . . . . . . . . . . . . . . . . . . . . . .       xx
```

The financial statement effects of this transaction and adjustment are:

Balance sheet	Income statement
Assets = Liabilities + Owners' equity ←	Net income = Revenues − Expenses

Cash received with subscription:
+ Cash   + Unearned
           Subscription
           Revenue

Adjustment in fiscal period in which revenue is earned (magazines delivered):
    − Unearned   + Subscription
      Subscription   Revenue
      Revenue

As you think about this situation, you should understand that it is the opposite of the prepaid expense/deferred charge transaction described in Chapter 5 (see pages 161–163). In that kind of transaction, cash was *paid* in the current period, and *expense* was recognized in subsequent periods. Unearned revenue/deferred credit transactions involve the *receipt* of cash in the current period and the recognition of *revenue* in subsequent periods.

Deposits received from customers are also accounted for as deferred credits. If the deposit is an advance payment for a product or service, the deposit is transferred from a liability account to a revenue account when the product or service is delivered. Or, for example, if the deposit is received as security for a returnable container, when the container is returned the refund of the customer's deposit reduces (is a credit to) cash and eliminates (is a debit to) the liability.

Unearned revenues/deferred credits are usually classified with other accrued liabilities in the current liability section of the balance sheet.

Payroll Taxes and Other Withholdings

Objective 4
Understand the accounting for an employer's liability for payroll and payroll taxes.

The total wages earned by employees for a payroll period, including bonuses and overtime pay, is referred to as their **gross pay,** which represents the employer's Wages Expense for the period. From this amount, several *deductions* are subtracted to arrive at the **net pay** (i.e., *take-home pay*) that each employee will receive, which represents the employer's Wages Payable (or Accrued Payroll). The largest deductions are normally for federal and state income tax withholdings and **FICA tax** withholdings, but employees frequently make voluntary contributions for hospitalization insurance, contributory pension plans, union dues, the United Way, and a variety of other items. Employers are responsible for remitting payment to the appropriate entities on behalf of their employees for each amount withheld. Thus, a separate liability account (e.g., Federal Income Taxes Withheld) is normally used for each applicable item. The entry to record a firm's payroll obligation is:

Dr. Wages Expense (for gross pay).................................	xx
Cr. Wages Payable (or Accrued Payroll, for net pay)..........	xx
Cr. Withholding Liabilities (various descriptions).............	xx

The effect of this transaction on the financial statements is:

Balance sheet	Income statement
Assets = Liabilities + Owners' equity ←	Net income = Revenues − Expenses
+ Wages Payable + Withholding Liabilities	− Wages Expense

When the withholdings are paid, both cash and the appropriate withholding liability are reduced.

Most employers are also subject to federal and state *payroll taxes* based on the amount of compensation paid to their employees. These taxes, assessed directly against the employer, include federal and state unemployment taxes and the employer's share of FICA tax. Employer taxes are appropriately recognized when compensation expense is accrued. This involves recognizing payroll tax expense and a related liability. The entry to record a firm's payroll tax obligation is:

Dr. Payroll Tax Expense......................................	xx
Cr. Payroll Taxes Payable (or Accrued Payroll Taxes).........	xx

The effect of this transaction on the financial statements is:

Balance sheet	Income statement
Assets = Liabilities + Owners' equity ←	Net income = Revenues − Expenses
+ Payroll Taxes Payable	− Payroll Tax Expense

When the taxes are paid, both cash and the liability are reduced.

The liabilities for accrued payroll, payroll withholdings, and accrued payroll taxes are usually classified with other accrued liabilities in the current liability section of the balance sheet.

Other Accrued Liabilities

As discussed above, this caption normally includes the accrued payroll accounts as well as most unearned revenue/deferred credit accounts. Accrued property taxes, accrued interest (if not reported separately), estimated warranty liabilities, and other accrued expenses such as advertising and insurance obligations are often included in this description. This is another application of the matching principle. Each of these items represents an expense that has been incurred but not yet paid. The expense is recognized and the liability is shown so that the financial statements present a more complete summary of the results of operations (income statement) and financial position (balance sheet) than would be presented without the accrual.

Objective 5
Understand the importance of making estimates for certain accrued liabilities, and how these items are presented in the balance sheet.

To illustrate the accrual of property taxes, assume that Cruisers, Inc., operates in a city in which real estate tax bills for one year are not issued until April of the following year and are payable in July. Thus, an adjusting entry must be made to record the estimated property tax expense for the year. The adjusting entry is:

Dr. Property Tax Expense.	xx	
Cr. Property Taxes Payable		xx

The effect of this adjustment on the financial statements is:

Balance sheet	Income statement
Assets = Liabilities + Owners' equity ←	Net income = Revenues − Expenses
+ Property Taxes Payable	− Property Tax Expense

When the tax bill is received in April, the payable account must be adjusted to reflect the amount actually owed in July. The adjustment also affects the current year's property tax expense account. The liability and expense amounts reported in the previous year are not adjusted because the estimate was based on the best information available at the time.

A firm's estimated liability under product warranty or performance guarantees is another example of an accrued liability. It is appropriate to recognize the estimated warranty expense that will be incurred on a product in the same period in which the revenue from the sale is recorded. Although the expense and liability must be estimated, past experience and statistical analysis can be used to develop very accurate estimates. The following entries are made in the fiscal periods in which the product is sold and when the warranty is honored.

To accrue the estimated warranty liability in the fiscal period in which the product is sold, the entry is:

Dr. Warranty Expense.	xx	
Cr. Estimated Warranty Liability		xx

To record actual warranty cost in the fiscal period in which the warranty is honored, the entry is:

Dr. Estimated Warranty Liability	xx	
Cr. Cash (or Repair Parts Inventory)		xx

The effect of warranty accounting on the financial statements is:

Balance sheet	Income statement
Assets = Liabilities + Owners' equity ←	Net income = Revenues − Expenses

Fiscal period in which product is sold:
+ Estimated   − Warranty
Warranty   Expense
Liability

Fiscal period in which warranty is honored:
− Cash   − Estimated
  and/or   Warranty
  Repair   Liability
  Parts
  Inventory

One accrued liability that is usually shown separately, because of its significance, is the accrual for income taxes. The current liability for income taxes is related to the long-term liability for deferred taxes; both are discussed later in this chapter.

2. What does it mean to be concerned that an entity's liabilities are not understated?

Long-Term Liabilities

Long-Term Debt

Objective 6
Understand what leverage is and how it is provided by long-term debt.

A corporation's *capital structure* is the mix of debt and owners' equity that is used to finance the acquisition of the firm's assets. For many non-financial firms, **long-term debt** accounts for up to half of the firm's capital structure. One of the advantages of using debt is that interest expense is deductible in calculating taxable income, whereas dividends (distributions of earnings to stockholders) are not tax deductible. Thus, debt usually has a lower economic cost to the firm than owners' equity. For example, assume that a firm has an average tax rate of 30% and that it issues long-term debt with an interest rate of 10%. The firm's after-tax cost of debt is only 7%, which is probably less than the return sought by stockholders. Another reason for using debt is to obtain favorable **financial leverage.** Financial leverage refers to the difference between the rate of return earned on assets (ROI) and the rate of return earned on owners' equity (ROE). This difference results from the fact that the interest cost of debt is usually a fixed percentage, which is not a function of the return on assets. Thus, if the firm can borrow money at an interest cost of 10 percent and use that money to buy assets on which it earns a return greater than 10 percent, then the owners will have a greater return on their investment (ROE) than if they had provided all of the funds themselves. In other words, financial leverage relates to the use of borrowed money to enhance the return to owners. This is illustrated in Exhibit 7–1.

This simplified illustration shows positive financial leverage. If a firm earns a lower return on investment than the interest rate on borrowed funds, financial leverage will be negative and ROE will be less than ROI.

EXHIBIT 7–1   Financial Leverage

Assumptions:

Two firms have the same assets and operating income. Current liabilities and income taxes are ignored for simplification. The firm without financial leverage has, by definition, no long-term debt. The firm with financial leverage has a capital structure that is 40% long-term debt with an interest rate of 10%, and 60% owners' equity. Return on investment and return on equity are shown below for each firm.

Note that the return-on-investment calculation has been modified from the model introduced in Chapter 3. ROI is based on income from operations and total assets rather than net income and total assets. Income from operations (which is net income before interest expense) is used because the interest expense reflects a financing decision, not an operating result. Thus, ROI becomes an evaluation of the operating activities of the firm.

Firm without Leverage		*Firm with Leverage*	
Balance Sheet:		**Balance Sheet:**	
Assets	$10,000	Assets	$10,000
Liabilities	$ 0	Liabilities (10% interest)	$ 4,000
Owners' equity	10,000	Owners' equity	6,000
Total liabilities + owners' equity	$10,000	Total liabilities + owners' equity	$10,000
Income Statement:		**Income Statement:**	
Income from operations	$ 1,200	Income from operations	$ 1,200
Interest expense	0	Interest expense	400
Net income	$ 1,200	Net income	$ 800

ROI and ROE Calculation:

Return on investment (ROI = Income from operations/Assets)

$$ROI = \$1{,}200/\$10{,}000 \qquad\qquad ROI = \$1{,}200/\$10{,}000$$
$$= 12\% \qquad\qquad\qquad\qquad = 12\%$$

Return on equity (ROE = Net income/Owners' equity)

$$ROE = \$1{,}200/\$10{,}000 \qquad\qquad ROE = \$800/\$6{,}000$$
$$= 12\% \qquad\qquad\qquad\qquad = 13.3\%$$

Analysis:

In this case, ROI is the same for both firms because the operating results did not differ—each firm was able to earn 12% on the assets it had available to use. What differed was the way in which the assets were financed (i.e., capital structure). The firm with financial leverage has a higher return on owners' equity because it was able to borrow money at a cost of 10% and use the money to buy assets on which it earned 12%. Thus, ROE will be higher than ROI for a firm with positive financial leverage. The excess return on borrowed funds is the reward to owners for taking the risk of borrowing money at a fixed cost.

Financial leverage adds risk to the firm because if the firm does not earn enough to pay the interest on its debt, the debtholders can force the firm into bankruptcy.

Financial leverage is discussed in greater detail in Chapter 11. For now you should understand that the use of long-term debt with a fixed interest cost usually results in ROE being different from ROI. Whether financial leverage is good or bad for the stockholders depends on the relationship between ROI and the interest rate on long-term debt.

WHAT DOES IT MEAN?

3. What does it mean to say that financial leverage has been used effectively?

4. What does it mean that the more financial leverage a firm has the greater the risk to owners and creditors?

Recall the discussion and illustration of capital lease liabilities in Chapter 6. Lease payments that are due more than a year from the balance sheet date are included in long-term debt and recorded at the present value of future lease payments.

Objective 7
Understand the different characteristics of a bond.

Most long-term debt, however, is issued in the form of bonds. A **bond** or **bond payable** is a formal document, usually issued in denominations of $1,000. Bond prices, both when issued and later when they are bought and sold in the market, are expressed as a percentage of the bond's **face amount**—the principal amount printed on the face of the bond. A $1,000 face amount bond that has a market value of $1,000 is priced at 100. (This means 100 percent; usually the term *percent* is neither written nor stated.) A $1,000 bond trading at 102.5 can be purchased for $1,025; such a bond priced at 96 has a market value of $960. When a bond has a market value greater than its face amount, it is trading at a premium; the amount of the **bond premium** is the excess of its market value over its face amount. A **bond discount** is the excess of the face amount over market value.

WHAT DOES IT MEAN?

5. What does it mean to say that a bond is a fixed income investment?

Accounting and financial reporting considerations for bonds can be classified into three categories: the original issuance of bonds, the recognition of interest expense, and the accounting for bond retirements or conversions.

If a bond is issued at its face amount, the journal entry and the effect on the financial statements is straightforward:

```
Dr.  Cash..............................................  xx
     Cr.  Bonds Payable.....................................       xx
Issuance of bonds at face amount.
```

Balance sheet	Income statement
Assets = Liabilities + Owners' equity ←	Net income = Revenues − Expenses
+ Cash + Bonds Payable	

As was the case with short-term notes payable, the bonds payable liability is reported at the present value of amounts to be paid in the future with respect to the bonds, discounted at the return on investment desired by the lender (bondholder). For example, assume that a 10% bond with a 10-year maturity is issued to investors who desire a 10% return on their investment. The issuer of the bonds provides two cash flow components to the investors in the bonds: the annual interest payments and the payment of principal at maturity. Note that the interest cash flow is an annuity because the same amount is paid each period. Using present value factors from Tables 6–2 and 6–3, the present values are:

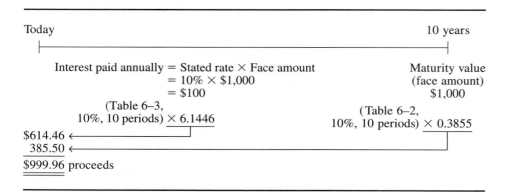

The present value of the liability is the sum of the discounted principal and interest payments. Except for a rounding difference in the present value factors, this sum is the same as the face amount of the bonds.

Because of the mechanics involved in a bond issue, there is usually a time lag between the establishment of the interest rate to be printed on the face of the bond and the actual issue date. During this time lag, market interest rates will fluctuate and the market rate on the issue date will probably differ from the **stated rate** (or **coupon rate**) used to calculate interest payments to bondholders. This difference in interest rates causes the proceeds (cash received) from the sale of the bonds to be more or less than the face amount; the bonds are issued at a premium or discount, respectively. The reason for this is illustrated in Exhibit 7–2.

Because bond premium or discount arises from a difference between the bond's stated interest rate and the market interest rate, it should follow that the premium or discount will affect the issuing firm's interest expense. Bond discount really represents additional interest expense to be recognized over the life of the bonds. The interest that will be paid (based on the stated rate) is less than the interest that would be paid if it were based on the market rate at the date the bonds were issued. Bond discount is a deferred charge that is amortized to interest expense over the life of the bond. The amortization increases interest expense over the amount actually paid to bondholders. Bond discount is classified in the balance sheet as a contra account to the Bonds Payable liability. Bond premium is a deferred credit that is amortized to interest expense, and its effect is to reduce interest expense below the amount actually paid to bondholders. Bond premium is classified in the balance sheet as an addition to the Bonds Payable liability. The journal entries to record the interest accrual, interest payment, and discount or premium amortization are as follows:

EXHIBIT 7–2   Bond Discount and Premium

Objective 8
Understand why bond discount or premium arises and how it is accounted for.

The interest paid by a borrower to its bondholders each period is fixed; that is, the same amount of interest (equal to the stated or coupon rate multiplied by the face amount of the bond) will be paid on each bond each period regardless of what happens to market interest rates. When an investor buys a bond, he or she is entitled to an interest rate that reflects market conditions at the time the investment is made. Because the amount of interest the investor is to receive is fixed, the only way the investor can earn an effective interest rate different from the stated rate is to buy the bond for more or less than its face amount (i.e., buy the bond at a premium or discount). In other words, since the stated interest rate cannot be adjusted, the selling price of the bond must be adjusted to reflect the changes that have occurred in market interest rates since the stated interest rate was established. As already illustrated, the amount the investor is willing to pay for the bond is the present value of the cash flows to be received from the investment, discounted at the investor's desired rate of return (i.e., the market interest rate).

Assumptions:
Cruiser's, Inc., issues a 10%, $1,000 bond when market interest rates are 12%. The bond will mature in eight years. Interest is paid semiannually.

Required:
Calculate the proceeds from the bond issue, and the premium or discount to be recognized.

Solution:
The solution involves calculating the present value of the cash flows to be received by the investor, discounted at the investor's desired rate of return, which is the market interest rate. There are two components to the cash flows: the semiannual interest payments and the payment of principal at maturity. Note that the interest is an annuity because the same amount is paid each period. Because the interest is paid semiannually, it is appropriate to recognize semiannual compounding in the present value calculation. This is accomplished by using the number of semiannual periods in the life of the bonds. Since the bonds mature in eight years, there are 16 semiannual periods. However, the interest rate per semiannual period is half of the annual interest rate. To be consistent, the same approach is used to calculate the present value of the principal. Thus, the solution uses factors from the 6% column (one-half the investors' desired ROI) and the 16-period row (twice the term of the bonds) of the present value tables. (If interest were paid quarterly, the annual ROI would be divided by 4, and the term of the bonds in years would be multiplied by 4.) Using present value factors from Tables 6–2 and 6–3, the present values are:

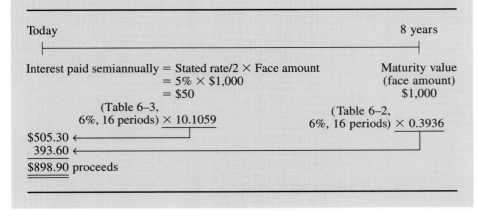

Today   8 years

Interest paid semiannually = Stated rate/2 × Face amount   Maturity value
                           = 5% × $1,000   (face amount)
                           = $50 $1,000

              (Table 6–3,   (Table 6–2,
           6%, 16 periods) × 10.1059   6%, 16 periods) × 0.3936

$505.30 ←
 393.60 ←
$898.90 proceeds

EXHIBIT 7–2   *(concluded)*

The proceeds received by Cruisers, Inc., as well as the amount invested by the buyer of the bond, are the sum of the present value of the interest payments and the present value of the principal amount. Since this sum is less than the face amount, the bond is priced at a discount.

This illustration demonstrates two important points about the process of calculating the proceeds from a bond issue:

1. The *stated interest rate* of the bond is used to calculate the amount of interest paid each payment period; this is the annuity amount used in the calculation of the present value of the interest.
2. The *market interest rate* (or the investors' desired ROI), adjusted for the compounding frequency, is the discount rate used in the present value calculations.

In this illustration, the market interest rate is higher than the bond's stated interest rate; thus, the investor would pay sufficiently less than the face amount of the bond, such that the $50 to be received each six months and the $1,000 to be received at maturity will provide a market rate of return.

The issuance of the $1,000 bond by Cruisers, Inc., will be recorded with the following entry:

Dr. Cash	898.90	
Dr. Discount on Bonds Payable	101.10	
Cr. Bonds Payable		1,000.00
Issued bond at a discount.		

The effect of this entry on the financial statements is:

Balance sheet	Income statement
Assets = Liabilities + Owners' equity ←	Net income = Revenues − Expenses
Cash Bonds Payable	
+ 898.90 + 1,000	
Discount on	
Bonds Payable	
− 101.10	

If market rates are less than the stated interest rate on the bond, the opposite will be true (i.e., the investor will be willing to pay a premium over the face amount of the bond). Use the above model to prove to yourself that if the market interest rate is 12%, then a 13% stated rate, $1,000 face amount, 10-year bond on which interest is paid semiannually would be issued for $1,057.34 (i.e., the bond would be issued at a premium of $57.34).

This exhibit illustrates the fundamental reason for bonds being issued for a price (or having a market value) that is different from the face amount. The actual premium or discount is a function of the magnitude of the difference between the stated interest rate of the bond and the market interest rate, and the number of years to maturity because present value factors reflect the time value of money. For any given difference between the bond's stated interest rate and the market interest rate, the closer a bond is to maturity, the smaller the premium or discount will be.

Interest accrual (each fiscal period, perhaps monthly):

```
Dr.   Interest Expense .......................................  xx
      Cr.   Interest Payable ..................................       xx
```

Interest payment (periodically, perhaps semiannually):

```
Dr.   Interest Payable .......................................  xx
      Cr.   Cash ............................................       xx
```

Amortization of discount (each time interest is accrued):

```
Dr.   Interest Expense .......................................  xx
      Cr.   Discount on Bonds Payable...........................       xx
```

Amortization of premium (each time interest is accrued):

```
Dr.   Premium on Bonds Payable ............................  xx
      Cr.   Interest Expense ..................................       xx
```

The effects of these transactions on the financial statements are:

Balance sheet	Income statement
Assets = Liabilities + Owners' equity ←	Net income = Revenues − Expenses

Interest accrual (each fiscal period, perhaps monthly):

+ Interest Payable	− Interest Expense

Interest payment (periodically, perhaps semiannually):

− Cash − Interest Payable	

Amortization (each time interest is accrued):

Discount:

+ Discount on Bonds Payable	− Interest Expense (An increase in interest expense)

Premium:

− Premium on Bonds Payable	+ Interest Expense (A reduction in interest expense)

Discount or premium is usually amortized on a straight-line basis over the life of the bonds because the amounts involved are often immaterial. However, it is more appropriate to use a compound interest method that results in amortization related to the carrying value (face amount plus unamortized premium or minus unamortized discount) of the bonds. Using the compound interest method, amortization is smallest in the first year of the bonds' life, and it increases in subsequent years.

Bonds payable are reported on the balance sheet at their carrying value. Sometimes this amount is referred to as the **book value** of the bonds. As discount is amortized over the life of a bond, the carrying value of the bond increases. At the maturity date, the bond's carrying value is equal to its face amount because the bond discount has been fully amortized. Likewise, as premium is amortized, the carrying value of the bond decreases until it equals the face amount at maturity. Thus, when bonds are paid off (or retired) at maturity, the journal entry is:

```
Dr.  Bonds Payable ....................................... xx
    Cr.  Cash ............................................         xx
Retirement of bonds at maturity.
```

The effect of this transaction on the financial statements is:

Balance sheet	Income statement
Assets = Liabilities + Owners' equity ←	Net income = Revenues − Expenses
− Cash − Bonds Payable	

Most bonds are **callable bonds;** this means the issuer may pay off the bonds before the scheduled maturity date. Bonds will be called if market interest rates have dropped below the rate being paid on the bonds and the firm can save interest costs by issuing new bonds at a lower rate. Or if the firm has cash that will not be needed in operations in the immediate future, it can redeem the bonds and save more interest expense than could be earned (as interest income) by investing the excess cash. A **call premium** is usually paid to bondholders if the bond is called; that is, bondholders receive more than the face amount of the bond because they must reinvest the proceeds, usually at a lower interest rate than was being earned on the called bonds.

If the bonds are called or redeemed prior to maturity, it is appropriate to write off the unamortized balance of premium or discount as part of the transaction. Since a call premium is usually involved in an early retirement of bonds, a loss on the retirement will usually be recognized—although a gain on the retirement is possible. The journal entry to record an early retirement of $100,000 face amount bonds having a book value of $95,000 by redeeming them for a total payment of $102,000 is:

```
Dr.  Bonds Payable.............................. 100,000
Dr.  Loss on Retirement of Bonds...................   7,000
    Cr.  Cash.....................................          102,000
    Cr.  Discount on Bonds Payable ................            5,000
```

The effect of this transaction on the financial statements is:

Balance sheet		Income statement
Assets = Liabilities + Owners' equity ←		Net income = Revenues − Expenses
Cash Bonds Payable		Loss on Retirement of Bonds
− 102,000 − 100,000		− 7,000
Discount on Bonds Payable + 5,000		

The loss or gain on the retirement of the bonds is reported as an extraordinary item (explained in more detail in Chapter 9) in the income statement. The loss or gain is not considered part of operating income or interest expense. The firm is willing to retire the bonds and recognize the loss because it will save, in future interest expense, more than the loss incurred.

A discussion of bonds involves quite a bit of specialized terminology, and although it all doesn't have to be mastered to understand the financial statement impact of bond transactions, it is relevant to understanding bonds.

The contract between the issuer of the bonds and the bondholders is the **bond indenture,** and it is frequently administered by a third party, the **trustee of bonds**—often a bank trust department. Bonds are issued in one of two forms: **registered bonds** and **coupon bonds.**

The name and address of the owner of a registered bond is known to the issuer, and interest payments are mailed to the bondholder on a quarterly or semiannual basis, as called for in the indenture. The owner of a coupon bond is not known to the issuer; the bondholder receives interest by clipping a coupon on the interest payment date and depositing it in her or his bank account. The coupon is then sent to the trustee and is honored as though it were a check. Coupon bonds are no longer issued because federal income tax regulations have been changed to require interest payers to report the name and social security number of payees, but coupon bonds issued prior to that regulation are still outstanding.

Bonds are also classified according to the security, or collateral, that is pledged by the issuer. **Debenture bonds** (or **debentures**) are bonds that are secured only by the general credit of the issuer. **Mortgage bonds** are secured by a lien against real estate owned by the issuer. **Collateral trust bonds** are secured by the pledge of securities or other intangible property.

Another classification of bonds relates to when the bonds mature. **Term bonds** require a lump-sum repayment of the face amount of the bond at the maturity date. **Serial bonds** are repaid in installments. The installments may or may not be equal in amount; the first installment is usually scheduled for a date several years after the issuance of the bonds. **Convertible bonds** may be converted into stock of the issuer corporation at the option of the bondholder. The number of shares of stock into which a bond is convertible is established when the bond is issued, but the conversion feature may not become effective for several years. If the stock price has risen substantially while the bonds have been outstanding, bondholders may elect to receive shares of stock with the anticipation that the stock will be worth more than the face amount of the bonds when the bonds mature.

The specific characteristics, the interest rate, and the maturity date are usually included in a bond's description. For example, you may hear or read about long-term debt described as Cruiser, Inc.'s, 12% convertible debentures due in 2008, callable after 1999 at 102, or its 12.5% First Mortgage Serial Bonds with maturities from 1998 to 2008.

WHAT DOES IT MEAN?

6. What does it mean when a bond is called a debenture bond?

7. What does it mean when bond market values change in the opposite direction from market interest rate changes?

8. What does it mean when a bond is issued at a premium?

Deferred Income Taxes

Deferred income taxes are provided for temporary differences between income tax and financial statement recognition of revenues and expenses. Deferred tax liabilities are normally long-term, and represent income taxes that are expected to be paid more than a year after the balance sheet date. For many firms, deferred income taxes are one of the most significant liabilities shown on the balance sheet. These amounts arise from the accounting process of matching revenues and expenses; a liability is recognized for the probable future tax consequences of events that have taken place up to the balance sheet date. For example, some revenues that have been earned and recognized for accounting (book) purposes during the current fiscal year may not be taxable until the following year. Likewise, some expenses (such as depreciation) may be deductible for tax purposes before they are recorded in determining book income. These temporary differences between book income and taxable income cause deferred tax liabilities that are postponed until future years.

The most significant temporary difference item resulting in a deferred income tax liability for most firms relates to depreciation expense. As previously explained, a firm may use straight-line depreciation for financial reporting and use the Modified Accelerated Cost Recovery System (prescribed by the Internal Revenue Code) for income tax determination. Thus, depreciation deductions for tax purposes are taken earlier than depreciation expense is recognized for book purposes. Of course, this temporary difference will eventually reverse; over the life of the asset, the same total amount of book and tax depreciation will be reported. To calculate the amount of the current liability to be recorded as Income Taxes Payable, the company's actual tax liability is determined each year. Income tax expense is based on book income before income taxes. The difference between income tax expense (usually called *provision for income taxes*) and income taxes payable is deferred income taxes. Although the calculations involved are complicated, the adjusting journal entry to accrue income taxes when an increase in the deferred income tax liability is required is straightforward:

```
Dr.  Income Tax Expense.....................................  xx
     Cr.  Income Taxes Payable...............................       xx
     Cr.  Deferred Income Taxes..............................       xx
     To accrue current and deferred income taxes.
```

The effect of this adjustment on the financial statements is:

Balance sheet	Income statement
Assets = Liabilities + Owners' equity ←	Net income = Revenues − Expenses
+ Income Taxes Payable	− Income Tax Expense
+ Deferred Income Taxes	

If income tax rates do not decrease, the deferred income tax liability of most firms will increase over time. As firms grow, more and more depreciable assets are acquired, and price-level increases cause costs for (new) replacement assets to be higher than the cost of (old) assets being replaced. Thus, the temporary difference between book and tax depreciation grows each year because the excess of book depreciation over income tax depreciation for older assets is more than offset by the excess of tax depreciation over book depreciation for newer assets. Accordingly, some accountants have questioned the appropriateness of showing deferred taxes as a liability since in the aggregate the balance of this account has grown larger and larger for many firms and therefore never seems to actually become payable. They argue that deferred tax liabilities—if recorded at all—should be recorded at the present value of future cash flows discounted at an appropriate interest rate. Otherwise, the amounts shown on the balance sheet will overstate the obligation to pay future taxes.

Most deferred income taxes result from the temporary difference between book and tax depreciation expense, but there are other temporary differences as well. As discussed in Chapter 5, when the temporary difference involves an expense that is recognized for financial accounting purposes before it is deductible for tax purposes, a deferred tax asset can arise. For example, an estimated warranty liability is shown on the balance sheet and warranty expense is reported in the income statement in the year the firm sells a warranted product, but the tax deduction is not allowed until an actual warranty expenditure is made. Because this temporary difference will cause taxable income to be lower in future years, a deferred tax asset is reported. As illustrated in Table 7–1, the number of companies reporting deferred tax assets has increased dramatically in recent years, while fewer companies are now reporting deferred tax liabilities. (Some firms may have both but offset one against the other for financial reporting purposes.) This overall trend is attributable to a number of corporate tax law changes that have made it increasingly difficult for firms to deduct accrued expenses for tax purposes until actual cash payments are made.

The accounting for deferred tax items is an extremely complex issue that has caused a great deal of debate within the accounting profession. Major changes in accounting for deferred income taxes have occurred in recent years as accounting standards have evolved in response to the needs of financial statement users.

TABLE 7–1 **Trends in Reporting Frequency of "Deferred Income Taxes" by Year and Category for 600 Publicly Owned Industrial and Merchandising Corporations**

Year	Current Assets	Noncurrent Assets	Current Liabilities	Noncurrent Liabilities
1983	120	13	67	504
1989	155	17	43	494
1992	247	95	33	451
1996	378	172	47	411

Source: *Accounting Trends and Techniques,* Tables 2–11, 2–19, 2–25, and 2–29, copyright © 1984, 1990, 1993, and 1997, by American Institute of Certified Public Accountants, Inc. Reprinted with permission.

WHAT DOES IT MEAN?

9. What does it mean when a company has a deferred income tax liability?

Other Long-Term Liabilities

Frequently included in this balance sheet category are obligations to pension plans and other employee benefit plans, including deferred compensation and bonus plans. Expenses of these plans are accrued and reflected in the income statement of the fiscal period in which the benefit is earned by the employee. Because benefits are frequently conditional upon continued employment, future salary levels, and other factors, actuaries and other experts estimate the expense to be reported in a given fiscal period. The employer's pension expense will also depend on the ROI earned on funds invested in the pension or other benefit plan trust accounts over a period of time. Because of the large number of significant factors that must be estimated in the expense and liability calculations, accounting for pension plans is a complex topic that has been controversial over the years. In 1985, the FASB issued an accounting standard to increase the uniformity of accounting for pensions. One of the significant provisions of the standard requires the recognition of a minimum liability on the balance sheet if the fair market value of the pension plan assets is less than the accumulated benefit obligation to pension plan participants.

An issue closely related to pensions is the accounting for postretirement benefit plans other than pensions. These plans provide medical, hospitalization, life insurance, and other benefits to retired employees. The cost of these plans was generally reported as an expense in the fiscal period in which payments were made to the plans that provide the benefits, and an entity's liabilities under these plans were not reflected in the balance sheet. After several years of study and quite a bit of controversy, in 1992 the FASB issued a standard that requires the recognition of the accumulated liability and accrual of costs during the employees' working years when the benefits are earned. Thus, the concept of matching revenues and expenses is to be applied on the same basis as for pension plans. One major difference between pension plans and other postretirement benefit plans is that very few firms had funded their other postretirement benefit plans. This means that the liabilities to be recognized are very large—in some cases more than half of a firm's owners' equity. The FASB standard gives firms the choice of recognizing the expense and accumulated liability all at once or deferring the expense and recognizing it over 20 years (or the remaining service life of the covered employees, if longer).

Another item included with other long-term liabilities of some firms is the estimated liability under lawsuits in progress, and/or product warranty programs. The liability is reflected at its estimated amount, and the related expense is reported in the income statement of the period in which the expense was incurred or the liability was identified. Sometimes the term *reserve* is used to describe these items, as in "reserve for product warranty claims." However, the term *reserve* is misleading because this amount refers to an estimated liability, not an amount of money that has been set aside to meet the liability.

The last caption in the long-term liability section of many balance sheets is **minority interest in subsidiaries.** A subsidiary is a corporation

Objective 10
Understand what minority interest is, why it arises, and what it means in the balance sheet.

that is more than 50 percent owned by the firm for which the financial statements have been prepared. (See Business in Practice—Parent and Subsidiary Corporations in Chapter 2 for more discussion about a subsidiary.) The financial statements of the parent company and its subsidiaries are combined through a process known as *consolidation*. The resulting financial statements are referred to as the **consolidated financial statements** of the parent and its subsidiary(ies). In consolidation, most of the assets and liabilities of the parent and subsidiary are added together. Reciprocal amounts (e.g., a parent's account receivable from a subsidiary and the subsidiary's account payable to the parent) are eliminated, or offset. The parent's investment in the subsidiary (an asset) is offset against the owners' equity of the subsidiary. Minority interest arises if the subsidiary is not 100 percent owned by the parent company because the parent's investment will be less than the owners' equity of the subsidiary. Minority interest is the equity of the other (i.e., minority) stockholders in the owners' equity of the subsidiary. This amount does not represent what the parent company would have to pay to acquire the rest of the stock of the subsidiary, nor is it a liability in the true sense of the term. The minority interest reported on a consolidated balance sheet is included because the subsidiary's assets and liabilities (except those eliminated to avoid double counting) have been added to the parent company's assets and liabilities, and the parent's share of owners' equity of the subsidiary is included in consolidated owners' equity. To keep the balance sheet in balance, the equity of the minority stockholders in the owners' equity of the subsidiary must be shown.

Although usually included with noncurrent liabilities, some accountants believe that minority interest should be shown as a separate item between liabilities and owners' equity because this amount is not really a liability of the consolidated entity.

Summary

This chapter has discussed the accounting for and presentation of the following liabilities and related income statement accounts. Contra liabilities and reductions of expense accounts are shown in parentheses.

Balance sheet	Income statement
Assets = Liabilities + Owners' equity ←	Net income = Revenues − Expenses
Current Liabilities:	
Short-Term Debt	Interest Expense
(Discount on Short-Term Debt)	Interest Expense
Accounts Payable	(Purchase Discounts) or: Purchase Discounts Lost
Unearned Revenue	Revenue

Balance sheet	Income statement
Assets = Liabilities + Owners' equity ← Net income = Revenues − Expenses	

Other Accrued . . . . Liabilities	Various Expenses
Long-Term Liabilities:	
Bonds Payable	Interest Expense
(Discount on. . . . . Bonds Payable)	Interest Expense
Premium on . . . . Bonds Payable	(Interest Expense)
Deferred Income . . . . Taxes	Income Tax Expense

Liabilities are obligations of the entity. Most liabilities arise because funds have been borrowed or an obligation is recognized as a result of the accrual accounting process. Current liabilities are those that are expected to be paid within a year of the balance sheet date. Noncurrent, or long-term, liabilities are expected to be paid more than a year after the balance sheet date.

Short-term debt, such as a bank loan, is obtained to provide cash for seasonal buildup of inventory. The loan is expected to be repaid when the inventory is sold and the accounts receivable from the sale are collected. The interest cost of short-term debt is sometimes calculated on a discount basis. Discount results in a higher annual percentage rate than straight interest because the discount is based on the maturity value of the loan, and the proceeds available to the borrower are calculated as the maturity value minus the discount. Discount is recorded as a contra liability and is amortized to interest expense. The amount of discounted short-term debt shown as a liability on the balance sheet is the maturity value minus the unamortized discount.

Long-term debt principal payments that will be made within a year of the balance sheet date are classified as a current liability.

Accounts payable represents amounts owed to suppliers of inventories and other resources. Some accounts payable are subject to a cash discount if paid within a time frame specified by the supplier. The internal control system of most entities will attempt to encourage adherence to the policy of taking all cash discounts offered.

Unearned revenue and other deferred credits, and other accrued liabilities arise primarily because of accrual accounting procedures that result in the recognition of expenses in the fiscal period in which they are incurred. Many of these liabilities are estimated because the actual liability isn't known when the financial statements are prepared.

Long-term debt is a significant part of the capital structure of many firms. Funds are borrowed, rather than invested by the owners, because the firm expects to take advantage of the financial leverage associated with debt. If borrowed money can be invested to earn a higher return (ROI) than the interest cost, the return on the owners' investment (ROE) will be greater than ROI. However, the opposite is also true. Leverage adds to the risk associated with an investment in an entity.

Long-term debt is frequently issued in the form of bonds payable. Bonds have a stated interest rate (that is almost always a fixed percentage), a face amount or principal, and a maturity date when they must be paid. Because the interest rate on a bond is fixed, changes in the market rate of interest result in fluctuations in the market value of the bond. As market interest rates rise, bond prices fall, and vice versa. The market value of a bond is the present value of the interest payments and maturity value, discounted at the market interest rate. When bonds are issued and the market rate at the date of issue is different from the stated rate of the bond, a premium or discount results. Both bond premium and discount are amortized to interest expense over the life of the bond. Premium amortization reduces interest expense below the amount of interest paid. Discount amortization increases interest expense over the amount of interest paid. A bond is sometimes retired before its maturity date because market interest rates have dropped significantly below the stated interest rate of the bond. Early retirement of bonds can result in a gain but usually results in a loss.

Deferred income taxes result from temporary differences between book and taxable income. The most significant temporary difference is caused by the different depreciation expense calculation methods used for each purpose. The amount of deferred income tax liability is the amount of income tax expected to be paid in future years, based on tax rates expected to apply in future years multiplied by the total amount of temporary differences.

Other long-term liabilities may relate to pension obligations, other postretirement benefit plan obligations, warranty obligations, or estimated liabilities under lawsuits in process. Also included in this caption in the balance sheet of some companies is the equity of minority stockholders in the net assets of less than wholly owned subsidiaries, all of whose assets and liabilities are included in the entity's consolidated balance sheet.

Refer to the Intel Corporation balance sheet and related notes in the Appendix, and to other financial statements you may have, and observe how information about liabilities is presented.

Key Terms and Concepts

account payable (p. 233)   A liability representing an amount payable to another entity, usually because of the purchase of merchandise or a service on credit.

annual percentage rate (APR) (p. 230)   The effective (true) annual interest rate on a loan.

bond or **bond payable** (p. 241)   A long-term liability with a stated interest rate and maturity date, usually issued in denominations of $1,000.

bond discount (p. 241)   The excess of the face amount of a bond issued over the market value of a bond or the proceeds of the issue.

bond indenture (p. 247)   The formal agreement between the borrower and investor(s) in bonds.

bond premium (p. 241)   The excess of the market value of a bond or the proceeds of a bond issue over the face amount of a bond or the bonds issued.

book value (p. 245)   The balance of the ledger account (including related contra accounts, if any), for an asset, liability, or owners' equity account. Sometimes referred to as *carrying value.*

callable bonds (p. 246)   Bonds that can be redeemed by the issuer, at its option, prior to the maturity date.

call premium (p. 246)   An amount paid in excess of the face amount of a bond when the bond is repaid prior to its established maturity date.

collateral trust bond (p. 247)   A bond secured by the pledge of securities or other intangible property.

consolidated financial statements (p. 251)   Financial statements resulting from the combination of parent and subsidiary company financial statements.

contra liability (p. 232)   An account that normally has a debit balance that is subtracted from a related liability on the balance sheet.

convertible bonds (p. 247)   Bonds that can be converted to preferred or common stock of the issuer, at the bondholder's option.

coupon bond (p. 247)   A bond for which the owner's name and address are not known by the issuer and/or trustee. Interest is received by clipping interest coupons that are attached to the bond and submitting them to the issuer.

coupon rate (p. 242)   The rate used to calculate the interest payments on a bond. Sometimes called the *stated rate.*

current maturity of long-term debt (p. 233)   Principal payments on long-term debt that are scheduled to be paid within one year of the balance sheet date.

debenture bonds or debentures (p. 247)   Bonds secured by the general credit of the issuer.

deferred credit (p. 235)   An account with a credit balance that will be recognized as a revenue (or as an expense reduction) in a future period. See *unearned revenue.*

deferred income taxes (p. 248)   A long-term liability that arises because of temporary differences between when an item (principally depreciation expense) is recognized for book purposes and tax purposes.

discount loan (p. 230)   A loan on which interest is paid at the beginning of the loan period.

face amount (p. 241)   The principal amount of a bond.

FICA tax (p. 236)   Federal Insurance Contribution Act tax used to finance federal programs for old-age and disability benefits (social security) and health insurance (Medicare).

financial leverage (p. 239)   The use of debt (with a fixed interest rate) that causes a difference between return on investment and return on equity.

gross pay (p. 236)   The total earnings of an employee for a payroll period.

interest calculation—discount basis (p. 230)   Interest calculation in which the interest (called *discount*) is subtracted from the principal to determine the amount of money (the proceeds) made available to the borrower. Only the principal is repaid at the maturity date because the interest is, in effect, prepaid.

interest calculation—straight basis (p. 230)   Interest calculation in which the principal is the amount of money made available to the borrower. Principal and interest are repaid by the borrower at the maturity date.

interpolating (p. 231)   A mathematical term to describe the process of *interpreting* and *relating* two factors from a (present value) table to approximate a third factor not shown in the table.

long-term debt (p. 239)   A liability that will be paid more than one year from the balance sheet date.

maturity date (p. 229)   The date when a loan is scheduled to be repaid.

minority interest in subsidiaries (p. 250)   An account that arises in the preparation of consolidated financial statements when some subsidiaries are less than 100 percent owned by the parent company.

mortgage bond (p. 247)   A bond secured by a mortgage on real estate.

net pay (p. 236)   Gross pay less payroll deductions; the amount the employer is obligated to pay to the employee.

note payable (p. 229)   Usually a short-term liability that arises from issuing a note; a formal promise to pay a stated amount at a stated date, usually with interest at a stated rate and sometimes secured by collateral.

prime rate (p. 229)   The interest rate charged by banks on loans to large and most creditworthy customers; a benchmark interest rate.

proceeds (p. 232)   The amount of cash received in a transaction.

registered bond (p. 247)   A bond for which the owner's name and address are recorded by the issuer and/or trustee.

revolving line of credit (p. 229)   A loan on which regular payments are to be made, but which can be increased to a predetermined limit as additional funds must be borrowed.

serial bond (p. 247)   A bond that is to be repaid in installments.

stated rate (p. 242)   The rate used to calculate the amount of interest payable on a bond. Sometimes called the *coupon rate.*

term bond (p. 247)   A bond that is to be repaid in one lump sum at the maturity date.

trustee of bonds (p. 247)   The agent who coordinates activities between the bond issuer and the investor in bonds.

unearned revenue (p. 235)   A liability arising from receipt of cash before the related revenue has been earned. See *deferred credit.*

working capital loan (p. 229)   A short-term loan that is expected to be repaid from collections of accounts receivable.

WHAT DOES IT MEAN?
ANSWERS

1. It means that interest on the loan is subtracted from the principal of the loan and it is the difference that is actually made available for the borrower's use.

2. It means that if liabilities are understated it is most likely that expenses are also understated, and if that is true net income is overstated.

3. It means that borrowed funds have been invested to earn a greater rate of return than the interest rate being paid on the borrowed funds.

4. It means that if the firm cannot earn a greater rate of return than the interest rate being paid on borrowed funds, its chances of not being able to repay the debt and of going bankrupt are greater than if it had less financial leverage.

5. It means that the interest rate used to calculate interest on the bond is fixed and does not change as market interest rates change.

6. It means that the bond is secured by the general credit of the issuer, not specific assets.

7. It means that as market interest rates rise, the value of the fixed interest return on the bond falls, and so the market value of the bond falls.

8. It means that the bond has been issued for more than its face amount because the stated interest rate is greater than the market interest rate on the issue date.

9. It means that the firm's deductions for income tax purposes have been greater than expenses subtracted in arriving at net income for book purposes, so when tax deductions become less than book expenses more income tax will be payable than income taxes based on book net income.

Exercises and Problems

LO 2

7–1. Notes payable—discount basis. On April 15, 1999, Arbyco, Inc., obtained a six-month working capital loan from its bank. The face amount of the note signed by the treasurer was $300,000. The interest rate charged by the bank was 9%. The bank made the loan on a discount basis.

Required:
a. Calculate the loan proceeds made available to Arbyco and use the horizontal model (or write the journal entry) to show the effect of signing the note and the receipt of the cash proceeds on April 15, 1999.
b. Calculate the amount of interest expense applicable to this loan during the fiscal year ended June 30, 1999.
c. What is the amount of the current liability related to this loan to be shown in the June 30, 1999, balance sheet?

LO 2

7–2. Notes payable—discount basis. On August 1, 1999, Colombo Co.'s treasurer signed a note promising to pay $240,000 on December 31, 1999. The proceeds of the note were $232,000.

Required:
a. Calculate the discount rate used by the lender.
b. Calculate the effective interest rate (APR) on the loan.
c. Use the horizontal model (or write the journal entry) to show the effects of:
   1. Signing the note and the receipt of the cash proceeds on August 1, 1999.
   2. Recording interest expense for the month of September.
   3. Repaying the note on December 31, 1999.

LO 4

7–3. Other accrued liabilities—payroll taxes. At March 31, 1999, the end of the first year of operations at Grencon, Inc., the firm's accountant neglected to accrue payroll taxes of $4,800 that were applicable to payrolls for the year then ended.

Required:
a. Use the horizontal model (or write the journal entry) to show the effect of the accrual that should have been made as of March 31, 1999.
b. Determine the income statement and balance sheet effects of not accruing payroll taxes at March 31, 1999.

c. Assume that when the payroll taxes were paid in April 1999, the payroll tax expense account was charged. Assume that at March 31, 2000, the accountant again neglected to accrue the payroll tax liability, which was $5,000 at that date. Determine the income statement and balance sheet effects of not accruing payroll taxes at March 31, 2000.

LO 5 **7–4. Other accrued liabilities—real estate taxes.** Spartan Co. operates in a city in which real estate tax bills for one year are issued in May of the subsequent year. Thus, tax bills for 1998 are issued in May 1999 and are payable in July 1999.

Required:

a. Explain how the amount of tax expense for calendar 1998 and the amount of taxes payable (if any) at December 31, 1998, can be determined.

b. Use the horizontal model (or write the journal entry) to show the effect of accruing 1998 taxes of $7,200 at December 31, 1998.

c. Assume that the actual tax bill, received in May 1999 was for $7,470. Use the horizontal model (or write the journal entry) to show the effects of this adjustment to the amount previously accrued.

d. Spartan Co.'s real estate taxes have been increasing at the rate of 10% annually. Determine the income statement and balance sheet effects of not accruing 1998 taxes at December 31, 1998 (assuming that taxes in *b* are not accrued).

LO 5 **7–5. Other accrued liabilities—advertising allowance.** Assume that Blueco Button Co. offered its customers, which are primarily retail fabric stores, an advertising allowance equal to 5% of the amount of purchases from Blueco during December if the retail store would spend the money for advertising in January. Blueco's sales in December totaled $2,700,000, and it was expected that 60% of those sales were made to retailers who would take advantage of the advertising allowance offer.

Required:

Use the horizontal model (or write the journal entry) to show the effect of the accrual (if any) that should be made as of December 31 with respect to the advertising allowance offer.

LO 5 **7–6. Other accrued liabilities—interest.** *(Note: This is an analytical assignment involving the interpretation of financial statement disclosures.)* A review of the accounting records at Corless Co. revealed the following information concerning the company's liabilities that were outstanding at December 31, 1999, and 1998, respectively:

Debt (thousands)	*1999*	*Year-End Interest Rate*	*1998*	*Year-End Interest Rate*
Short-term debt:				
Working capital loans	$125	12%	$ 95	11%
Current maturities of long-term debt	40	10%	40	10%
Long-term debt:				
Debenture bonds due in 2019	200	14%	200	14%
Serial bonds due in equal annual installments	120	10%	160	10%

Required:

a. Corless Co. has not yet made an adjusting entry to accrue the interest expense related to its *working capital loans* for the year ended December 31, 1999. Assume that the amount of interest to be accrued can be accurately estimated using an average-for-the-year interest rate applied to the average liability balance. Use the horizontal model (or write the journal entry) to record the effect of the 1999 interest accrual for working capital loans.

b. Note that the dollar amount and interest rate of the *current maturities of long-term debt* have not changed from 1998 to 1999. Does this mean that the $40,000 amount owed at the end of 1998 still has not been paid as of December 31, 1999? *(Hint: Explain your answer with reference to other information provided in the problem.)*

c. Assume that the *debenture bonds* were originally issued at their face amount. However, the market rate of interest for bonds of similar risk has decreased significantly in recent years and is 11% at December 31, 1999. If the debenture bonds were both callable by Corless Co. and convertible by its bondholders, which event is more likely to occur? Explain your answer.

d. Assume the same facts as in part c above. Would the market value of Corless Co.'s debenture bonds be more than or less than the $200,000 reported amount? Is this good news or bad news to the management of Corless Co.?

e. When the *Serial Bonds* account decreased during the year, what other account was affected, and how was it affected? Use the horizontal model (or write the journal entry) to record the effect of this transaction.

LO 5

7–7.   Other accrued liabilities—warranties. Kohl Co. provides warranties for many of its products. The January 1, 1999, balance of the Estimated Warranty Liability account was $35,200. Based on an analysis of warranty claims during the past several years, this year's warranty provision was established at 0.4% of sales. During 1999, the actual cost of servicing products under warranty was $15,600, and sales were $3,600,000.

Required:

a. What amount of Warranty Expense will appear on Kohl Co.'s income statement for the year ended December 31, 1999?

b. What amount will be reported in the Estimated Warranty Liability account on the December 31, 1999, balance sheet?

LO 5

7–8.   Other accrued liabilities—warranties. Prist Co. had not provided a warranty on its products, but competitive pressures forced management to add this feature at the beginning of 1999. Based on an analysis of customer complaints made over the past two years, the cost of a warranty program was estimated at 0.2% of sales. During 1999, sales totaled $4,600,000. Actual costs of servicing products under warranty totaled $12,700.

Required:

a. Use the horizontal model (or a T-account of the Estimated Warranty Liability) to show the effect of having the warranty program during 1999.

b. What type of accrual adjustment should be made at the end of 1999?

c. Describe how the amount of the accrual adjustment could be determined.

LO 3

7–9.   Unearned revenues—customer deposits. Coolfroth Brewing Company distributes its products in an aluminum keg. Customers are charged a deposit of $50 per keg; deposits are recorded in the Keg Deposits account.

Required:

a. Where on the balance sheet will the Keg Deposits account be found? Explain your answer.

b. Use the horizontal model (or write the journal entry) to show the effect of giving a refund to a customer.

c. A keg-use analyst who works for Coolfroth estimates that 200 kegs for which deposits were received during the year will never be returned. What accounting, if any, would be appropriate for the deposits associated with these kegs?

LO 3   **7–10.**   **Unearned revenues—ticket sales.** Kirkland Theater sells season tickets for six events at a price of $42. For the 1999 season, 1,200 season tickets were sold.

Required:

a. Use the horizontal model (or write the journal entry) to show the effect of the sale of the season tickets.

b. Use the horizontal model (or write the journal entry) to show the effect of presenting an event.

c. Where on the balance sheet would the account balance representing funds received for performances not yet presented be classified?

LO 3   **7–11.**   **Unearned revenues—rent.** *(Note: See Problem 5–26 for the related prepaid expense accounting.)* On September 1, 1999, Naumann Co. collected $4,200 in cash from its tenant as an advance rent payment on its store location. The six-month lease period ends on February 28, 2000, at which time the contract may be renewed.

Required:

a. Use the horizontal model (or write the journal entries) to record the effects of the following items for Naumann Co.:

  1. The six months of rent collected in advance on September 1, 1999.

  2. The adjustment that will be made at the end of every month to show the amount of rent "earned" during the month.

b. Calculate the amount of unearned rent that should be shown on the December 31, 1999, balance sheet with respect to this lease.

c. If the advance collection received on September 1, 1999, had covered an 18-month lease period at the same amount of rent per month, how should Naumann Co. report the unearned rent amount on its December 31, 1999, balance sheet?

LO 3   **7–12.**   **Unearned revenues—subscription fees.** Hayes Co. publishes a monthly newsletter for retail marketing managers and requires its subscribers to pay $30 in advance for a one-year subscription. During the month of September 1999, Hayes Co. sold 200 one-year subscriptions and received payments in advance from all new subscribers. Only 70 of the new subscribers paid their fees in time to receive the September newsletter; the other subscriptions began with the October newsletter.

Required:

a. Use the horizontal model (or write the journal entries) to record the effects of the following items:

  1. Subscription fees received in advance during September 1999.

  2. Subscription revenue earned during September 1999.

b. Calculate the amount of subscription revenue earned by Hayes Co. during the year ended December 31, 1999, for these 200 subscriptions.

Optional continuation of Problem 7–12—life-time subscription offer. *(Note: This is an analytical assignment involving the use of present value tables and accounting estimates. Only the first sentence in problem 7–12 applies to this continuation of the problem.)* Hayes Co. is now considering the possibility of offering a life-time membership option to its subscribers. Under this proposal, subscribers could receive the monthly newsletter throughout their life by paying a flat fee of $360. The one-year subscription rate of $30 would continue to apply to new and existing subscribers who choose to subscribe on an annual basis. Assume that the average age of Hayes Co.'s current subscribers is 38, and their life expectancy is 78 years. Hayes Co.'s average interest rate on long-term debt is 12%.

  c. Using the information above, determine whether it would be profitable for Hayes Co. to sell life-time subscriptions. *(Hint: Calculate the present value of a life-time membership for an average subscriber using the appropriate table in Chapter 6.)*

  d. What additional factors should Hayes Co. consider in determining whether or not to offer a life-time membership option? Explain your answer as specifically as possible.

LO 4   **7–13.   Other accrued liabilities—Payroll.** The following summary data for the payroll period ended on November 14, 1998, are available for Brac Construction, Ltd.:

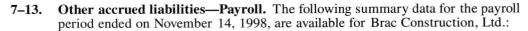

Gross pay	?
FICA tax withholdings	?
Income tax withholdings	$13,760
Medical insurance contributions	1,120
Union dues	640
Total deductions	21,640
Net pay	58,360

Required:
  a. Calculate the missing amount and then determine the FICA tax withholding percentage.
  b. Use the horizontal model (or write the journal entry) to show the effects of the payroll accrual.

LO 4   **7–14.   Other accrued liabilities—Payroll and payroll taxes.** The following summary data for the payroll period ended December 27, 1998, are available for Cayman Coating Co.:

Gross pay	$96,000
FICA tax withholdings	?
Income tax withholdings	15,360
Group hospitalization insurance	1,920
Employee contributions to pension plan	?
Total deductions	28,176
Net pay	?

Additional information:

  • FICA tax rates are 7.65% on the first $70,000 of each employee's annual earnings and 1.45% on any earnings in excess of $70,000. However, no employees had accumulated earnings for the year in excess of the $70,000 limit. The FICA tax rates are levied against *both* employers and employees.

  • The federal and state unemployment compensation tax rates are 0.8% and 5.4%, respectively. These rates are levied against the employer for the first $7,000 of each employee's annual earnings. Only $15,000 of the gross pay amount for the December 27, 1998, pay period was owed to employees who were still under the annual limit.

Required:

Assuming that Cayman Coating Co.'s payroll for the last week of the year is to be paid on January 3, 1999, use the horizontal model (or write the journal entry) to record the effects of the December 27, 1998, entries for:

a. Accrued payroll.

b. Accrued payroll taxes.

LO 8   **7–15.**   **Bonds payable—record issuance and premium amortization.** Gramm Co. issued $1 million face amount of 11% 20-year bonds on April 1, 1999. The bonds pay interest on an annual basis on March 31 each year.

Required:

a. Assume that market interest rates were slightly lower than 11% when the bonds were sold. Would the proceeds from the bond issue have been more than, less than, or equal to the face amount? Explain.

b. Independent of your answer to part *a,* assume that the proceeds were $1,080,000. Use the horizontal model (or write the journal entry) to show the effect of issuing the bonds.

c. Calculate the interest expense that Gramm Co. will show with respect to these bonds in its income statement for the fiscal year ended September 30, 1999, assuming that the premium of $80,000 is amortized on a straight-line basis.

LO 8   **7–16.**   **Bonds payable—record issuance and discount amortization.** Coley Co. issued $5 million face amount of 9% 10-year bonds on June 1, 1999. The bonds pay interest on an annual basis on May 31 each year.

Required:

a. Assume that the market interest rates were slightly higher than 9% when the bonds were sold. Would the proceeds from the bond issue have been more than, less than, or equal to the face amount? Explain.

b. Independent of your answer to part *a,* assume that the proceeds were $4,940,000. Use the horizontal model (or write the journal entry) to show the effect of issuing the bonds.

c. Calculate the interest expense that Coley Co. will show with respect to these bonds in its income statement for the fiscal year ended September 30, 1999, assuming that the discount of $60,000 is amortized on a straight-line basis.

LO 8   **7–17.**   **Bonds payable—calculate market value.** On August 1, 1991, Jane Investor purchased $5,000 of Huber Co.'s 10% 20-year bonds at face amount. Huber Co. has paid the semiannual interest due on the bonds regularly. On August 1, 1999, market rates of interest had fallen to 8%, and Jane is considering selling the bonds.

Required:

Using the present value tables in Chapter 6, calculate the market value of Jane's bonds on August 1, 1999.

LO 8   **7–18.**   **Bonds payable—calculate market value.** On March 1, 1994, Joe Investor purchased $7,000 of White Co.'s 8% 20-year bonds at face amount. White Co. has paid the annual interest due on the bonds regularly. On March 1, 1999, market interest rates had risen to 12%, and Joe is considering selling the bonds.

Required:

Using the present value tables in Chapter 6, calculate the market value of Joe's bonds on March 1, 1999.

LO 7   **7–19.** **Bonds payable—convertible.** O'Kelley Co. has outstanding $2 million face amount of 12% bonds that were issued on January 1, 1990, for $2 million. The 20-year bonds were issued in $1,000 denominations and mature on December 31, 2009. Each $1,000 bond is convertible at the bondholder's option into 5 shares of $10 par value common stock.

Required:

a. Under what circumstances would O'Kelley Co.'s bondholders consider converting the bonds?

b. Assume that the market price of O'Kelley Co.'s common stock is now $215 and that a bondholder elects to convert 400 $1,000 bonds. Use the horizontal model (or write the journal entry) to show the effect of the conversion on O'Kelley Co.'s financial statements.

LO 7   **7–20.** **Bonds payable—callable.** Riley Co. has outstanding $4 million face amount of 15% bonds that were issued on January 1, 1987, for $3,900,000. The 20-year bonds mature on December 31, 2006, and are callable at 102 (i.e., they can be paid off at any time by paying the bondholders 102% of the face amount).

Required:

a. Under what circumstances would Riley Co. managers consider calling the bonds?

b. Assume that the bonds are called on December 31, 1999. Use the horizontal model (or write the journal entry) to show the effect of the retirement of the bonds. *(Hint: Calculate the amount paid to bondholders, then determine how much of the bond discount would have been amortized prior to calling the bonds, and then calculate the gain or loss on retirement.)*

LO 8   **7–21.** **Bonds payable—various issues.** Doran Co. issued $40 million face amount of 11% bonds when market interest rates were 11.14% for bonds of similar risk and other characteristics.

Required:

a. How much interest will be paid annually on these bonds?

b. Were the bonds issued at a premium or discount? Explain your answer.

c. Will the annual interest expense of these bonds be more than, equal to, or less than the amount of interest paid each year? Explain your answer.

LO 8   **7–22.** **Bonds payable—various issues.** Howard Stone Co. issued $25 million face amount of 9% bonds when market interest rates were 8.92% for bonds of similar risk and other characteristics.

Required:

a. How much interest will be paid annually on these bonds?

b. Were the bonds issued at a premium or discount? Explain your answer.

c. Will the annual interest expense on these bonds be more than, equal to, or less than the amount of interest paid each year? Explain your answer.

LO 8   **7–23.** **Bonds payable—calculate issue price and amortize discount.** On January 1, 1999, Drennen, Inc., issued $3 million face amount of 10-year, 14% stated rate bonds when market interest rates were 12%. The bonds pay semiannual interest each June 30 and December 31, and mature on December 31, 2008.

Required:

a. Using the present value tables in Chapter 6, calculate the proceeds (issue price) of Drennen, Inc.'s, bonds on January 1, 1999, assuming that the bonds were sold to provide a market rate of return to the investor.

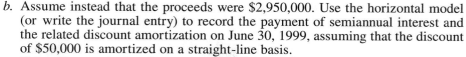
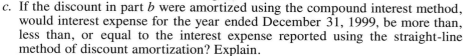

b. Assume instead that the proceeds were $2,950,000. Use the horizontal model (or write the journal entry) to record the payment of semiannual interest and the related discount amortization on June 30, 1999, assuming that the discount of $50,000 is amortized on a straight-line basis.

c. If the discount in part *b* were amortized using the compound interest method, would interest expense for the year ended December 31, 1999, be more than, less than, or equal to the interest expense reported using the straight-line method of discount amortization? Explain.

LO 8

7–24. **Bonds payable—calculate issue price and amortize premium.** On January 1, 1999, Learned, Inc., issued $6 million face amount of 20-year, 14% stated rate bonds when market interest rates were 16%. The bonds pay interest semiannually each June 30 and December 31, and mature on December 31, 2008.

Required:

a. Using the present value tables in Chapter 6, calculate the proceeds (issue price) of Learned, Inc.'s, bonds on January 1, 1999, assuming that the bonds were sold to provide a market rate of return to the investor.

b. Assume instead that the proceeds were $6,200,000. Use the horizontal model (or write the journal entry) to record the payment of semiannual interest and the related premium amortization on June 30, 1999, assuming that the premium of $200,000 is amortized on a straight-line basis.

c. If the premium in part *b* were amortized using the compound interest method, would interest expense for the year ended December 31, 1999, be more than, less than, or equal to the interest expense reported using the straight-line method of premium amortization? Explain.

d. In reality, the difference between the stated interest rate and the market rate would be substantially less than 2%. The dramatic difference in this problem was designed so that you could use present value tables to answer part *a*. What causes the stated rate to be different from the market rate, and why is the difference likely to be much less than depicted in this problem?

LO 6 **7–25.** **Financial leverage.** Describe the risks associated with financial leverage.

LO 6 **7–26.** **Financial leverage.** A firm that issues long-term debt that has a cost of 10% and that can be invested at an ROI of 12% is using financial leverage. What effect will this leverage have on the firm's ROE relative to having the same amount of funds invested by the owners?

LO 9 **7–27.** **Deferred income tax liability.** The difference between the amounts of book and tax depreciation expense, as well as the desire to report income tax expense that is related to book income before taxes, causes a long-term deferred income tax liability to be reported on the balance sheet. The amount of this liability reported on the balance sheets of many firms has been increasing over the years, creating the impression that the liability will never be paid. Why has the amount of the deferred income tax liability risen steadily for many firms?

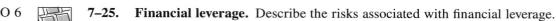

Intel **LO 9** **7–28.** **Deferred income tax liability—annual report data.** Refer to the Intel Corporation Annual Report in the Appendix.

Required:

a. Using data from the December 28, 1996, balance sheet, calculate the percentage of the deferred tax liabilities to total owners' equity. Is the deferred income tax amount material?

b. Find the "Provision for taxes" note on pages 26–27. What amount of the "deferred tax liabilities" relates to the difference between book and tax depreciation for 1996?

c. Some financial analysts maintain that the deferred tax liability should be considered as part of owners' equity, rather than as a liability, for purposes of evaluating the relationship between debt and equity, and calculating return on equity. Why might analysts do this?

LO 4, 5, 8   **7–29.**   **Transaction analysis—various accounts.** Enter the following column headings across the top of a sheet of paper.

Transaction/ Adjustment	Current Assets	Current Liabilities	Long-Term Debt	Net Income

Enter the transaction/adjustment letter in the first column and show the effect, if any, of each of the transactions/adjustments on the appropriate balance sheet category or on the income statement by entering the amount and indicating whether it is an addition (+) or a subtraction (−). You may also write the journal entries to record each transaction/adjustment.

a. Wages of $867 for the last three days of the fiscal period have not been accrued.

b. Interest of $170 on a bank loan has not been accrued.

c. Interest on bonds payable has not been accrued for the current month. The company has outstanding $240,000 of 8.5% bonds.

d. The discount related to the above bonds has not been amortized for the current month. The current month amortization is $50.

e. Product warranties were honored during the month; parts inventory valued at $830 was sent to customers making claims, and cash refunds of $410 were also made.

f. During the fiscal period, advance payments from customers totaling $1,500 were received and recorded as sales revenues. The items will not be delivered to the customers until the next fiscal period. Record the appropriate adjustment.

LO 4, 5, 8   **7–30.**   **Transaction analysis—various accounts.** Enter the following column headings across the top of a sheet of paper.

Transaction/ Adjustment	Current Assets	Current Liabilities	Long-Term Debt	Net Income

Enter the transaction/adjustment letter in the first column, and show the effect, if any, of each of the transactions/adjustments on the appropriate balance sheet category or on the income statement by entering the amount and indicating whether it is an addition (+) or a subtraction (−). You may also write the journal entries to record each transaction/adjustment.

a. Wages of $768 accrued at the end of the prior fiscal period were paid this fiscal period.

b. Real estate taxes of $2,400 applicable to the current period have not been accrued.

c. Interest on bonds payable has not been accrued for the current month. The company has outstanding $360,000 of 7.5% bonds.

d. The premium related to the above bonds has not been amortized for the current month. The current month amortization is $70.

e. Based on past experience with its warranty program, it is estimated that warranty expense for the current period should be 0.2% of sales of $918,000.

f. Analysis of the company's income taxes indicates that taxes currently payable are $76,000 and that the deferred tax liability should be increased by $21,000.

LO 1, 2, 5, 8, 9

7–31. **Transaction analysis—various accounts.** Enter the following column headings across the top of a sheet of paper.

Transaction/ Adjustment	Current Assets	Noncurrent Assets	Current Liabilities	Noncurrent Liabilities	Owners' Equity	Net Income

Enter the transaction/adjustment letter in the first column and show the effect, if any, of each transaction/adjustment on the appropriate balance sheet category or on net income by entering for each category affected the account name and amount, and indicating whether it is an addition (+) or a subtraction (−). Items that affect net income should *not* also be shown as affecting owners' equity. You may also write the journal entries to record each transaction/adjustment.

a. Income tax expense of $700 for the current period is accrued. Of the accrual, $200 represents deferred income taxes.

b. Bonds payable with a face amount of $5,000 are issued at a price of 99.

c. Of the proceeds from the above bonds, $3,000 is used to purchase land for future expansion.

d. Because of warranty claims, finished goods inventory costing $64 is sent to customers to replace defective products.

e. A three-month, 12% note payable with a face amount of $20,000 was signed. The bank made the loan on a discount basis.

f. The next installment of a long-term serial bond requiring an annual principal repayment of $35,000 will become due within the current year.

LO 5, 8

7–32. **Transaction analysis—various accounts.** Enter the following column headings across the top of a sheet of paper.

Transaction/ Adjustment	Current Assets	Noncurrent Assets	Current Liabilities	Noncurrent Liabilities	Owners' Equity	Net Income

Enter the transaction/adjustment letter in the first column and show the effect, if any, of each transaction/adjustment on the appropriate balance sheet category or on net income by entering for each category affected the account name and amount, and indicating whether it is an addition (+) or a subtraction (−). Items that affect net income should *not* also be shown as affecting owners' equity. You may also write the journal entries to record each transaction/adjustment.

a. Recorded the financing (capital) lease of a truck. The present value of the lease payments is $32,000; the total of the lease payments to be made is $58,000.

b. Paid, within the discount period, an account payable of $1,500 on which terms were 1/15, n30. The purchase had been recorded at the gross amount.

c. Issued $7,000 of bonds payable at a price of 102.

d. Adjusted the estimated liability under a warranty program by reducing previously accrued warranty expense by $2,500.

e. Retired bonds payable with a carrying value of $3,000 by calling them at a redemption value of 101.

f. Accrued estimated health care costs for retirees; $24,000 is expected to be paid within a year and $310,000 is expected to be paid in more than a year.

Accounting for and Presentation of Owners' Equity

Owners' equity is the claim of the entity's owners to the assets shown in the balance sheet. Another term for owners' equity is *net assets,* which is assets minus liabilities. Neither the liabilities nor the elements of owners' equity are specifically identifiable with particular assets, although certain assets may be pledged as collateral for some liabilities.

The specific terminology used to identify owners' equity will depend on the form of the entity's legal organization. For an individual proprietorship, the term **proprietor's capital,** or *capital,* perhaps combined with the owner's name, is frequently used. For example, in the balance sheet of a single proprietorship owned by Lorna Myers, owner's equity would be labeled Lorna Myers, Capital. For a partnership, **partners' capital** is the term used, and sometimes the capital account balance of each partner is shown on the balance sheet. In both proprietorships and partnerships, no distinction is made between invested (or paid-in) capital and retained earnings (or earned capital).

Because the corporate form of organization is used for firms that account for most of the business activity in our economy, this text focuses on corporation owners' equity. As explained in Chapter 2, there are two principal components of corporation owners' equity: paid-in capital and retained earnings. The financial statements of many small businesses that use the corporate form of organization are likely to show in owners' equity only capital stock (which is paid-in capital) and retained earnings. However, as shown by the stockholders' equity section of the Consolidated Balance Sheets of Intel Corporation on page 19 of the Appendix, the owners' equity section can become quite complex. The owners' equity section of the balance sheets in other annual reports that you have may appear equally complex. Owners' equity captions usually seen in a balance sheet are:

1. Paid-in capital:
   a. Common stock
   b. Preferred stock (optional)
   c. Additional paid-in capital
2. Retained earnings (Accumulated deficit if negative)

EXHIBIT 8–1   Owners' Equity Section of Racers, Inc., Balance Sheets at August 31, 1999, and 1998

	August 31	
	1999	*1998*
Owners' equity:		
Paid-in capital:		
Preferred stock, 6%, $100 par value, cumulative, callable at $102, 5,000 shares authorized, issued, and outstanding	$ 500,000	$ 500,000
Common stock, $2 par value, 1,000,000 shares authorized, 244,800 shares issued at August 31, 1999, and 200,000 shares issued at August 31, 1998	489,600	400,000
Additional paid-in capital	3,322,400	2,820,000
Total paid-in capital	$4,312,000	$3,720,000
Retained earnings	2,828,000	2,600,000
Less: Common stock in treasury, at cost; 1,000 shares at August 31, 1999	(12,000)	—
Total owners' equity	$7,128,000	$6,320,000

3. Cumulative foreign currency translation adjustment
4. Less: Treasury stock

The objective of this chapter is to permit you to make sense of the owners' equity presentation of any balance sheet. You will also learn about many characteristics of owners' equity that are relevant to personal investment decisions. A brief overview of personal investing is provided as an appendix to this chapter. For the purposes of our discussion, the owners' equity section of the balance sheets of Racers, Inc., in Exhibit 8–1 will be explained.

Learning Objectives

After studying this chapter, you should understand:

1 The characteristics of common stock, and how common stock is presented in the balance sheet.

2 What preferred stock is, what its advantages and disadvantages to the corporation are, and how it is presented in the balance sheet.

3 The accounting for a cash dividend, and the dates involved in dividend transactions.

4 What stock dividends and stock splits are, and why each is used.

5 What treasury stock is, why it is acquired, and how treasury stock transactions affect owners' equity.

6 What the cumulative foreign currency translation adjustment is, and why it appears in owners' equity.

7 How owners' equity transactions for the year are reported in the financial statements.

Paid-In Capital

The captions shown in the paid-in capital category of owners' equity (i.e., common stock, preferred stock, and additional paid-in capital) represent amounts invested in the corporation by stockholders and are sometimes referred to as *contributed capital*. On the other hand, the retained earnings (or earned capital) category of owners' equity represents the entity's cumulative earnings (i.e., net income over the life of the entity) less any dividends paid. Naturally, stockholders are interested in the relationship between paid-in capital and retained earnings. The higher the Retained Earnings account balance relative to paid-in capital amounts, the better—because retained earnings reflect, in part, management's ability to earn a return on invested (paid-in) amounts. However, a large retained earnings balance may also lead stockholders to pressure management and the board of directors to pay higher dividends. Remember to keep the distinction between paid-in capital and retained earnings in mind when interpreting the owners' equity section of any balance sheet.

Common Stock

Objective 1
Understand the characteristics of common stock and how common stock is presented in the balance sheet.

As already explained, **common stock** (called **capital stock** at times, especially when no other classes of stock are authorized) represents residual ownership. Common stockholders are the ultimate owners of the corporation; they have claim to all assets that remain in the entity after all liabilities and preferred stock claims (described in the next section) have been satisfied. In the case of bankruptcy or forced liquidation, this residual claim may not have any value because the liabilities and preferred stock claims may exceed the amount realized from the assets in liquidation. In this severe case, the liability of the common stockholders is limited to the amount they have invested in the stock; common stockholders cannot be forced by creditors and/or preferred stockholders to invest additional amounts to make up their losses. In the more positive (and usual) case, common stockholders prosper because the profits of the firm exceed the fixed claims of creditors (interest) and preferred stockholders (preferred dividends). All of these profits accrue to common stockholders—there is no upper limit to the value of their ownership interest. Of course, it is the market value of common stock that reflects the profitability (or lack thereof) and ultimate dividend-paying capability of the corporation. However, as residual owners, common stockholders are not entitled to receive any specific dividend amount and may not receive any dividends at all in some years.

Common stockholders have the right and obligation to elect members to the corporation's board of directors. The election process can take one of two forms, as described in Business in Practice—Electing Directors. The board of directors hires corporate officers, and the officers execute strategies for achieving corporate objectives. Some officers may also be directors **(inside directors),** but current practice is to have most boards made up primarily of **outside directors** (individuals not employed by the firm) who can bring an outside viewpoint to the considerations and deliberations of the board.

BUSINESS IN PRACTICE
Electing Directors

Directors are elected by a **cumulative voting** procedure or on a slate basis. Under cumulative voting, each stockholder is entitled to cast a number of votes equal to the number of shares owned multiplied by the number of directors to be elected. Thus, if five directors are to be elected, the owner of 100 shares of common stock is entitled to 500 votes: all 500 can be cast for one candidate or 100 can be cast for each of five candidates or they can be cast in any combination between these extremes. In **slate voting,** the common stockholder is entitled to one vote for each share owned, but each vote is for an entire slate of candidates.

In most cases, the voting method doesn't affect the outcome. A committee of the board of directors nominates director candidates (equal to the number of directors to be elected), a proxy committee made up of members of the board seeks proxies from the stockholders, and the required number of nominees are duly elected. Occasionally, however, an outside group challenges the existing board; under these circumstances, the election can be exciting. Each group nominates director candidates and solicits stockholder votes. Under slate voting, the successful group will be the one that gets a majority of the vote; that group's entire slate will be elected. Of course, controlling 50.1% of the voting shares will ensure success. Under cumulative voting, however, it is possible for a minority group of stockholders to concentrate their votes on one or two of their own candidates, thus making it easier to secure representation on the board of directors. For example, if five directors are to be elected, the votes of approximately 17% of the outstanding common stock are required to elect one director.

Many people, especially proponents of corporate democracy, favor cumulative voting. Some states require corporations organized under their laws to have cumulative voting for directors. Yet, corporations often prefer to maintain a slate voting practice because this method makes getting a seat on the board more difficult for corporate raiders and others. Another tactic designed to reduce an outsider's chance of securing a director position is to provide for rolling terms. For example, for a nine-member board, three directors will be elected each year for a three-year term. Thus, even with cumulative voting, the votes of many more shares are required to elect one director than would be required if all nine directors are elected each year.

Common stockholders must also approve changes to the corporate charter (for example, when the number of shares of stock authorized is changed so that additional shares can be sold to raise more capital) and may have to approve transactions such as mergers or divestitures.

Common stock can have **par value** or can be of a no-par-value variety. When it is used, par value is usually a nominal amount assigned to each share when the corporation is organized. In today's business world, par value has virtually no financial reporting or economic significance with respect to common stock. In most states, the par value of the issued shares represents the **legal capital** of the corporation. Most state corporation laws provide that stock with par value cannot be issued for a price less than par value, and they provide that total owners' equity cannot be reduced to less than legal capital by dividends or the purchase from stockholders of previously issued shares of stock. If the stock has par value, the amount reported in the balance sheet will be the par value multiplied by the number of shares issued. Any difference between par value and the amount realized from the sale of the stock is recorded as additional paid-in capital. Some firms assign a **stated value** to the common stock, which is essentially par value by another name. If a firm issues true no-par-value stock, then the total amount received from the sale of the shares is recorded as common stock. Intel takes an interesting approach; by using a par value of $.001 per share, its common stock is essentially treated as no-par-value stock because amounts for common stock and capital in excess of par value are combined and reported on the balance sheet as one amount (see page 19 in the Appendix).

A survey of the annual reports for 1996 of 600 publicly owned merchandising and manufacturing companies indicated that only 65 companies had no-par-value common stock. Of those 65 companies, 8 had an assigned or stated value per share.[1]

To illustrate the sale of common stock, assume that during the year ended August 31, 1999, Racers, Inc., sold 40,000 additional shares of its $2 par value common stock at a price of $13 per share. The journal entry to record this transaction was:

Dr.	Cash (40,000 shares × $13)	520,000	
Cr.	Common Stock (40,000 shares × $2)		80,000
Cr.	Additional Paid-In Capital (40,000 shares $11) ...		440,000

The effect of this stock issue on the financial statements of Racers, Inc., was:

Balance sheet	Income statement
Assets = Liabilities + Owners' equity ←	Net income = Revenues − Expenses
Cash + 520,000 (40,000 shares × $13)	Common Stock + 80,000 (40,000 shares × $2) Additional Paid-In Capital + 440,000 (40,000 shares × $11)

Refer to Exhibit 8–1 and notice that common stock and additional paid-in capital increased during 1999 (the remaining portion of these increases will be explained in the stock dividends section of this chapter).

On the balance sheet the number of shares *authorized, issued,* and *outstanding* will be disclosed. The number of **authorized shares** is stated in the corporate charter that is filed with the state according to its laws regarding corporate organization. This represents the maximum number of

---

[1]AICPA, *Accounting Trends and Techniques* (New York, 1997), Table 2–33.

shares that the corporation is legally approved to issue; increases in the number of authorized shares requires shareholder approval. The number of **issued shares** is the number of shares of stock that have actually been transferred from the corporation to shareholders. Issued shares are ordinarily *sold* to stockholders for cash, although it is possible to issue stock in exchange for other assets or for services. The number of **outstanding shares** will differ from the number of issued shares if the firm has **treasury stock.** As explained in more detail later in this chapter, treasury stock is a firm's own stock that has been acquired by the firm from stockholders. The relationship between these terms and the balance sheet disclosure required for each is summarized in Exhibit 8–2. The difference between the number of shares authorized and the number of shares issued represents the potential for additional shares to be issued. The common stock of many firms has a **preemptive right,** which gives present shareholders the right to purchase shares from any additional share issuances in proportion to their present percentage of ownership. The preemptive right is usually most significant in smaller, closely held corporations (i.e., those with only a few stockholders) in which existing stockholders want to prevent their ownership interest from being diluted. Even though they are not ordinarily bound by a preemptive right provision, many large corporations offer existing stockholders the right to purchase additional shares when more capital is needed. This maintains stockholder loyalty and can be a relatively inexpensive way to raise capital.

WHAT DOES IT MEAN?

1. What does it mean when common stock is referred to as part of paid-in capital?

2. What does it mean when the common stock of a corporation has a par value?

3. What does it mean when a corporation has treasury stock?

EXHIBIT 8–2   Balance Sheet Disclosure for Shares of Stock

Terminology	Number of Shares Disclosed	Dollar Amount Disclosed
Shares authorized	Number specified in the corporate charter (maximum approved to be issued)	None
Shares issued	Number of shares that have been issued to stockholders (usually by sale)	Number of shares × par or stated value or If no par or stated value, total amount received from sale of shares
Shares outstanding	Number of shares still held by stockholders (shares issued less treasury shares)	None
Treasury stock	Number of issued shares purchased by the corporation from stockholders and not formally retired	Cost of treasury stock owned by corporation

Preferred Stock

Preferred stock is a class of paid-in capital that is different from common stock, in that preferred stock has several debt-like features and a limited claim on assets in the event of liquidation. Also, in most cases, preferred stock does not have a voting privilege. (Common stock represents residual equity—it has claim to all assets remaining after the liabilities and preferred stock claims have been met in the liquidation of the corporation.) Historically, preferred stock has been viewed as having less risk than common stock. In the early years of the Industrial Revolution, when firms sought to raise the large amounts of capital required to finance factories and railroads, investors were more willing to acquire preferred stock in a firm than take the risks associated with common stock ownership. As firms have prospered and many investors have experienced the rewards of common stock ownership, preferred stock has become a less significant factor in the capital structure of many manufacturing, merchandising, and service-providing firms. However, utilities and financial corporations continue to issue preferred stock.

The preferences of preferred stock, relative to common stock, relate to dividends and to the priority of claims on assets in the event of liquidation of the corporation or redemption of the preferred stock. A **dividend** is a distribution of the earnings of the corporation to its owners. The dividend requirement of preferred stock must be satisfied before a dividend can be paid to the common stockholders. Most preferred stock issues call for a quarterly or semiannual dividend, which must be kept current if there is to be a dividend on the common stock. The amount of the dividend is expressed in dollars and cents or as a percentage of the par value of the preferred stock. As shown in Exhibit 8–1, the preferred stock of Racers, Inc., is referred to as "6%, $100 par value." This means that each share of preferred stock is entitled to an annual dividend of $6 (6% × $100). The same dividend result could have been accomplished by creating a $6 cumulative preferred stock. The terms of the stock issue will specify whether the dividend is to be paid at the rate of $1.50 per quarter, $3 semiannually, or $6 annually.

Preferred stock issues, including that of Racers, Inc., usually provide a **cumulative dividend,** which means that if a dividend payment is not made, missed dividends (or dividends *in arrears*) must be paid subsequently before any dividend can be paid to the common stockholders. Occasionally, preferred stock issues have **participating dividends,** which means that after the common stockholders have received a specified dividend, any further dividends are shared by the preferred and common stockholders in a specified ratio. Calculation of preferred stock dividend amounts is illustrated in Exhibit 8–3.

A preferred stock issue's claim on the assets in the event of liquidation **(liquidating value)** or redemption **(redemption value)** is an amount specified at the time the preferred stock is issued. If the preferred stock has a par value, the liquidating value or redemption value is usually equal to the par value or the par value plus a slight premium. If the preferred stock has no par value, then the liquidating value or redemption value is a stated amount. In either case, the claim in liquidation must be fulfilled before the common stockholders receive anything. However, once the liquidating

---

EXHIBIT 8–3   Illustration of Preferred Stock Dividend Calculation

---

Case 1

6%, $100 par value cumulative preferred stock, 50,000 shares authorized, issued, and outstanding. Dividend payable semiannually, no dividends in arrears.

Semiannual preferred dividend amount:

$$6\% \times \$100 \times 50{,}000 \text{ shares outstanding} \times \tfrac{1}{2} \text{ year} = \$150{,}000$$

Case 2

$4.50, $75 par value cumulative preferred stock, 50,000 shares authorized and issued, 40,000 shares outstanding (there are 10,000 shares of treasury stock). Dividend payable quarterly, no dividends in arrears.

Quarterly preferred dividend amount:

$$\$4.50 \times 40{,}000 \text{ shares outstanding} \times \tfrac{1}{4} \text{ year} = \$45{,}000$$

Case 3

8%, $50 par value cumulative preferred stock, 100,000 shares authorized, 60,000 shares issued, 54,000 shares outstanding (there are 6,000 shares of treasury stock). Dividend payable annually. Dividends were not paid in prior two years.

Dividend required in current year to pay dividends in arrears and current year's preferred dividend:

$$8\% \times \$50 \times 54{,}000 \text{ shares outstanding} \times 3 \text{ years} = \$648{,}000$$

Case 4

$2, $25 par value cumulative participating preferred stock, 30,000 shares authorized, 25,000 shares issued and outstanding. Dividend payable annually. Dividends were not paid in the prior two years. After preferred stockholders are paid for arrears and their current year preference, common stockholders receive a base dividend of $2 per share. Preferred and common stockholders are to share equally on a per share basis in any additional dividends. The company has 100,000 shares of common stock outstanding, and dividends for the year total $410,000.

	Preferred	Common	Remaining Balance
Allocation:			
Total amount declared			$410,000
Pay preferred dividends in arrears			
($2 × 25,000 shares × 2 years)	$100,000		310,000
Pay current year's preferred dividend			
($2 × 25,000 shares)	50,000		260,000
Pay common stock base dividend			
($2 × 100,000 shares)		$200,000	60,000
Allocate $60,000 available for			
participation*	12,000	48,000	0
Total dividends paid	$162,000	$248,000	

*25,000 preferred shares/125,000 total shares = 20% × $60,000 = $12,000.
100,000 common shares/125,000 total shares = 80% × $60,000 = $48,000.

---

claim is met, the preferred stockholders will not receive any additional amounts.

Callable preferred stock is redeemable (usually at a slight premium over par or liquidating value) at the option of the corporation. **Convertible preferred stock** may be exchanged for common stock of the corporation at the option of the stockholder at a conversion rate (e.g., six shares of common stock for each share of preferred stock) established when the preferred stock is authorized. For many firms, the call and conversion features of preferred stock cannot be exercised for a number of years after the authorization (or issue) date of the stock; such restrictions are specified in the stock certificate. Note in Exhibit 8–1 that the preferred stock of Racers, Inc., is callable at a price of $102.

You have probably noticed that preferred stock has some of the same characteristics as bonds payable. Exhibit 8–4 summarizes the principal similarities and differences of the two. The tax deductibility of interest expense causes many financial managers to prefer debt to preferred stock. After all, they reason, if a fixed amount is going to have to be paid out regularly, it might as well be in the form of deductible interest rather than nondeductible preferred dividends. (As explained in Chapter 7, the after-tax cost of bonds paying 10% interest is only 7% for a corporation with an average tax rate of 30%.) Most investors also prefer bonds because the interest owed to them is a fixed claim that must be paid, but preferred stock dividends may be skipped, even though any arrearage may have to be paid before dividends can be paid on common stock. Of 600 publicly owned industrial and merchandising companies whose annual reports for 1996 were reviewed by the AICPA, 472 had no preferred stock outstanding.[2]

From the creditors' point of view, preferred stock reduces the risk associated with financial leverage (introduced in Chapter 7). Financial firms (such as banks, insurance companies, and finance companies) and utilities frequently have a significant portion of their owners' equity represented

---

EXHIBIT 8–4 **Comparison of Preferred Stock and Bonds Payable**

Preferred Stock	*Bonds Payable*
Similarities	
Dividend is (usually) a fixed claim to income.	Interest is a fixed claim to income.
Redemption value is a fixed claim to assets.	Maturity value is a fixed claim to assets.
Is usually callable and may be convertible.	Is usually callable and may be convertible.
Differences	
Dividend may be skipped, even though it usually must be caught up if dividends are to be paid on the common stock.	Interest must be paid or firm faces bankruptcy.
No maturity date.	Principal must be paid at maturity.
Dividends are not an expense and are not deductible for income tax purposes.	Interest is a deductible expense for income tax purposes.

---

[2]Ibid., Table 2–32.

by preferred stock. This is because a significant proportion of the capital requirements of these firms is provided by investors who prefer the relative security of preferred stock rather than debt and/or common stock.

The balance sheet disclosures for preferred stock include:

The par value and dividend rate (or the amount of the annual dividend requirement).

The liquidating or redemption value.

The number of shares authorized by the corporate charter.

The number of shares issued.

The number of shares outstanding.

Any difference between the number of shares issued and the number of shares outstanding is caused by shares held in the firm's treasury, or treasury stock. In addition, the amount of any preferred dividends that have been missed (that are in arrears) will be disclosed.

4. What does it mean when a corporation has preferred stock?

Additional Paid-In Capital

As has already been illustrated, **additional paid-in capital** is an owners' equity category that reflects the excess of the amount received from the sale of preferred or common stock over par value. (Remember that the amount in the Common or Preferred Stock account is equal to the par value multiplied by the number of shares issued, or the total amount received from the sale of no-par-value stock.) The Additional Paid-In Capital account is also used for other relatively uncommon capital transactions that cannot be reflected in the Common or Preferred Stock accounts or that should not be reflected in Retained Earnings. **Capital in excess of par value** (or stated value) and *capital surplus* are terms sometimes used to describe additional paid-in capital. The latter term was widely used many years ago before the term *surplus* fell into disfavor because of its connotation as something "extra" and because uninformed financial statement readers might think that this amount was somehow available for dividends.

To summarize and emphasize, the paid-in capital of a corporation represents the amount invested by the owners, and if par value stock is involved, paid-in capital includes par value and additional paid-in capital. If no-par-value stock is issued, paid-in capital represents the owners' investment.

Retained Earnings

The **retained earnings** account reflects the cumulative earnings of the corporation that have been retained for use in the business rather than disbursed to the stockholders as dividends. *Retained earnings is not cash!* Retained earnings is increased by the firm's net income, and the accrual basis of accounting results in a net income amount that is different from the cash increase during a fiscal period. To the extent that operating results increase cash, that cash may be used for operating, investing, or financing activities.

Virtually the only factors affecting retained earnings are net income or loss reported on the income statement and dividends. (Remember that all revenue, expense, gain, and loss accounts reported on the income statement are indirect changes to the Retained Earnings account on the balance sheet. As these items are recorded throughout the year, retained earnings is, in effect, increased for revenues and gains and decreased for expenses and losses.) Under certain very restricted circumstances, generally accepted accounting principles permit direct adjustments of retained earnings for the correction of errors (referred to as *prior period adjustments*). For example, if a firm neglected to include a significant amount of inventory in its year-end physical count and this error was not discovered until the following year, a direct adjustment to inventory and retained earnings would be appropriate. However, new information about an estimate made in a prior year (e.g., for depreciation or bad debts) does not warrant a direct entry to retained earnings because the amounts reported would have reflected the best information available at the time. Accounting principles emphasize that the income statement is to reflect all transactions affecting owners' equity, except for the following:

1. Dividends to stockholders (which are a reduction in retained earnings).
2. Transactions involving the corporation's own stock (which are reflected in the paid-in capital section of the balance sheet).
3. A cumulative foreign currency translation adjustment (which is accounted for in a separate owners' equity account, as will be explained later in this chapter).
4. Unrealized gain or loss, net of related income taxes, on certain marketable securities that are reported at market value rather than cost.
5. Prior period adjustments for the correction of errors.

If the retained earnings account has a negative balance because cumulative losses and dividends have exceeded cumulative net income, this account is referred to as an **accumulated deficit**.

Cash Dividends

Objective 3
Understand the accounting for a cash dividend and the dates involved in a dividend transaction.

In order for a corporation to pay a cash dividend, it must meet several requirements: The firm must have retained earnings, the board of directors must declare the dividend, and the firm must have enough cash to pay the dividend. If the firm has agreed in a bond indenture or other contract to maintain certain minimum standards of financial health (e.g., a current ratio of at least 1.8:1), the dividend must not cause any of these measures to fall below their agreed-upon level. From both the corporation's and the stockholders' perspectives, there are several key dates related to the dividend (see Business in Practice—Dividend Dates). Once the board of directors has declared the dividend, it becomes a legally enforceable liability of the corporation. The journal entries to record the declaration and subsequent payment of a cash dividend are as follows:

On the declaration date:		
Dr. Retained Earnings.	xx	
Cr. Dividends Payable.		xx

BUSINESS IN PRACTICE
Dividend Dates

Three dates applicable to every dividend are the declaration date, the record date, and the payment date. In addition, there will be an ex-dividend date applicable to companies whose stock is publicly traded. There is no reason that the declaration, record, and payment dates for a closely held company couldn't be the same date.

The **declaration date** is the date on which the board of directors declares the dividend. The **record date** is used to determine who receives the dividend; the person listed on the stockholder records of the corporation on the record date is considered the owner of the shares. The owner of record is the person to whom the check is made payable and mailed to on the **payment date.** If shares have been sold but the ownership change has not yet been noted on the corporation's records, the prior owner (the one in the records) receives the dividend (and may have to settle with the new owner, depending upon their agreement with respect to the dividend). The **ex-dividend date** relates to this issue of who receives the dividend. When the stock of a publicly traded company is bought or sold, the seller has a settlement period of three business days in which to deliver the stock certificate. The buyer also has three business days to pay for the purchase. Thus, the stock trades "ex-dividend" three business days before the record date to give the corporation a chance to increase the accuracy of its ownership records. On the ex-dividend date, the stock trades without the dividend (i.e., the seller retains the right to receive the dividend if the stock is sold on or after the ex-dividend date). If the stock is sold before the ex-dividend date, then the buyer is entitled to receive the dividend. All other things being equal, the price of the stock in the market falls by the amount of the dividend on the ex-dividend date.

There is no specific requirement dealing with the number of days that should elapse between the declaration, record, and payment dates for publicly traded stocks. It is not unusual for two to four weeks to elapse between each date.

On the payment date:
Dr. Dividends Payable xx
   Cr. Cash xx

The effects on the financial statements of these entries are:

Balance sheet			Income statement		
Assets = Liabilities + Owners' equity			← Net income = Revenues − Expenses		
Declaration date:					
	+ Dividends	− Retained			
	Payable	Earnings			
Payment date:					
− Cash	− Dividends				
	Payable				

Note that *dividends are not an expense* and do not appear on the income statement. Dividends are a distribution of earnings of the corporation to its stockholders and are treated as a direct reduction of retained earnings. If a balance sheet is dated between the date the dividend is declared and the date it is paid, the Dividends Payable account will be included in the current liability section of the balance sheet.

5. What does it mean when a corporation's board of directors has declared a cash dividend?

Stock Dividends and Stock Splits

Objective 4
Understand what stock dividends and stock splits are, and why each is used.

In addition to a cash dividend, or sometimes instead of a cash dividend, a corporation may issue a **stock dividend.** A stock dividend is the issuance of additional shares of common stock to the existing stockholders in proportion to the number of shares each currently owns. It is expressed as a percentage; for example, a 5% stock dividend would result in the issuance of 5% of the previously issued shares. A stockholder who owns 100 shares would receive 5 additional shares of stock, but her proportionate ownership interest in the firm would not change. (Fractional shares are not issued, so an owner of 90 shares would receive 4 shares and cash equal to the market value of half of a share.)

The motivation for a stock dividend is usually to maintain the loyalty of stockholders when the firm does not have enough cash to pay (or increase) the cash dividend. Although many stockholders like to receive a stock dividend, such a distribution is not income to the stockholders. To understand why there is no income to stockholders, the impact of the stock dividend must be understood from the issuing corporation's point of view. A stock dividend does not cause any change in either assets or liabilities; therefore, it cannot affect *total* owners' equity. However, additional shares of stock are issued, and the common stock account must reflect the product of the number of shares issued multiplied by par value. Because the issuance of shares is called a *dividend,* it is also appropriate for retained earnings to be reduced. The amount of the reduction in retained earnings is the number of dividend shares issued multiplied by the market price per share. Any difference between market price and par value is recorded in the Additional Paid-In Capital account. If the shares are without par value, then the Common Stock account is increased by the market value of the dividend shares issued.

To illustrate the effects of a stock dividend transaction, assume that during the year ended August 31, 1999, Racers, Inc., issued a 2% stock dividend on its $2 par value common stock when the market price was $15 per share. Refer back to Exhibit 8–1 and assume further that the stock dividend occurred at some point after the additional 40,000 shares of common stock had been issued. Thus, a total of 4,800 dividend shares were issued (2% × 240,000 shares previously issued). The journal entry to record this transaction was:

Dr. Retained Earnings...............................	72,000	
Cr. Common Stock		9,600
Cr. Additional Paid-In Capital....................		62,400

Using the horizontal model, the effect of the financial statements was:

Balance sheet		Income statement
Assets = Liabilities + Owners' equity	←	Net income = Revenues − Expenses

Retained Earnings
(4,800 shares × $15)
− 72,000
Common Stock
(4,800 shares × $2)
+ 9,600
Additional Paid-In
Capital
(4,800 shares × $13)
+ 62,400

Note that the stock dividend affects *only* the owners' equity of the firm. **Capitalizing retained earnings** is the term sometimes used to refer to the effect of a stock dividend transaction because the dividend results in the permanent transfer of some retained earnings to paid-in capital. The income statement is not affected because the transaction is between the corporation and its stockholders (who own the corporation); no gain or loss can result from a capital transaction.

If the stock dividend percentage is more than 20 to 25%, only the par value or stated value of the additional common shares issued is transferred from retained earnings to common stock.

What happens to the market value of a share of stock when a firm issues a stock dividend? Is the share owner any wealthier? As already explained, nothing happens to the firm's assets, liabilities, or earning power as a result of the stock dividend; therefore, the *total* market value of the firm should not change. Since more shares of stock are now outstanding and the total market value of all the shares remains the same, the market value of each share will drop. This is why the stock dividend does not represent income to the stockholder. However, under some circumstances the market value per share of the common stock will not settle at its theoretically lower value. This will be true especially if the cash dividend per share is not adjusted to reflect the stock dividend. Thus, if the firm had been paying a cash dividend of $1.00 per share before the stock dividend, and the same cash dividend rate is continued, there has been an effective increase in the dividend rate, and the stock price will probably rise to reflect this.

Sometimes the managers of a firm want to lower the market price of the firm's common stock by a significant amount because they believe that a stock trading in a price range of $20 to $50 per share is a more popular investment than a stock priced at more than $50 per share. A **stock split** will accomplish this objective. A stock split involves issuing additional shares to existing stockholders and, if the stock has a par value, reducing the par value proportionately. For example, if a firm had 60,000 shares of $10 par value stock outstanding, with stock trading in the market at a price of $80 per share, a 4-for-1 stock split would involve issuing 3 additional shares to each stockholder for each share owned. Then the stockholder who had owned 200 shares would receive an additional 600 shares, bringing the total shares owned to 800. As in the case of a stock dividend, nothing has happened to the assets or liabilities of the firm, so nothing can happen to owners' equity. The total market value of the company would not change, but the market price of each share would fall. (Compare the results of 60,000 shares × $80 to 240,000 shares × $20.) There is no accounting entry required for a stock split. However, the common stock caption of owners' equity indicates the drop in par value per share and the proportionate increase in the number of shares authorized, issued, and outstanding. If the corporation has used no-par-value stock, only the number of shares changes.

Sometimes a stock split is accomplished in the form of a very large (e.g., 100 percent) stock dividend. As explained earlier, when this happens only the par or stated value of the additional shares issued is transferred from retained earnings to the common stock account. There is no adjustment to the par value of the stock.

WHAT DOES IT MEAN?

6. What does it mean when a corporation's board of directors has declared a stock dividend on the common stock?
7. What does it mean when a corporation has a stock split?

Treasury Stock

Objective 5
Understand what treasury stock is, why it is acquired, and how treasury stock transactions affect owners' equity.

Many corporations will, from time to time, purchase shares of their own stock. Any class of stock that is outstanding can be acquired as treasury stock. Rather than being retired, this stock is held for future use for employee stock purchase plans, acquisitions of other companies, or even to be resold for cash if additional capital is needed. Sometimes treasury stock is acquired as a defensive move to thwart a takeover by another company, and frequently a firm buys treasury stock with excess cash because the market price is low and the company's own stock is thought to be a good investment. Whatever the motivation, the purchase of treasury stock is in effect a partial liquidation of the firm because the firm's assets are used to reduce the number of shares of stock outstanding. For this reason, treasury stock is not reflected in the balance sheet as an asset; it is reported as a contra owners' equity account (i.e., treasury stock is deducted from the sum of paid-in capital and retained earnings).

Because treasury stock transactions are capital transactions (between the corporation and its stockholders), the income statement is never affected by the purchase or sale of treasury stock. When treasury stock is acquired, it is recorded at cost. When treasury stock is sold or issued, any difference between its cost and the consideration received is recorded in the Additional Paid-In Capital account. As can be seen in Exhibit 8–1, Racers, Inc., purchased 1,000 shares of its own common stock at a total cost of $12,000 during the year ended August 31, 1999. The journal entry to record this purchase was:

Dr. Treasury Stock	12,000	
Cr. Cash		12,000
Purchase of 1,000 shares of treasury stock at a cost of $12 per share.		

The effect of this transaction on the financial statements was:

Balance sheet		Income statement
Assets = Liabilities + Owners' equity	←	Net income = Revenues − Expenses
Cash − 12,000	Treasury Stock (A contra owners' equity account) − 12,000	

If 500 shares of this treasury stock were sold at a price of $15 per share in fiscal 2000, the journal entry to record the sale would be:

```
Dr.  Cash . . . . . . . . . . . . . . . . . . . . . . . . . . . . . . . . . . . . . . . .   7,500
    Cr.  Treasury Stock. . . . . . . . . . . . . . . . . . . . . . . . . . . . . .           6,000
    Cr.  Additional Paid-In Capital. . . . . . . . . . . . . . . . . . . . . .           1,500
Sale of 500 shares of treasury stock at a price of
$15 per share.
```

The effect of this transaction on the financial statements would be:

Balance sheet		Income statement
Assets = Liabilities + Owners' equity	←	Net income = Revenues − Expenses
Cash + 7,500	Treasury Stock + 6,000 Additional Paid-In Capital + 1,500	

Cash dividends are not paid on treasury stock. However, stock dividends are issued on treasury stock, and stock splits affect treasury stock. For many firms, the dollar amount reported for treasury stock represents a significant reduction in total owners' equity. Because treasury stock purchases are recorded at the market price per share, it is not uncommon to find a negative amount reported for total paid-in capital. Why? Let's say that 1,000 shares of common stock were issued in 1974 at the prevailing market price of $15 per share. These shares remained outstanding until 1998, when 300 shares were purchased as treasury stock for $80 per share. The $15,000 historical cost of common stock would now be offset by a $24,000 reduction for treasury stock. Many successful real-world companies, such as The Reader's Digest Association, 3M, and Tandy, reported negative total paid-in capital in 1996 because of the presence of recently purchased treasury stock. The primary culprit in this accounting anomaly is the cost principle.

You should understand that cash dividends are not paid on treasury stock because the company cannot pay a dividend to itself. However, stock dividends are issued on treasury stock, and stock splits affect treasury stock. What this means, in practical terms, is that cash dividends are based on the number of shares outstanding, while stock dividends and stock splits are based on the number of shares previously issued.

Cumulative Foreign Currency Translation Adjustment

Objective 6
Understand what the cumulative foreign currency translation adjustment is and why it appears in owners' equity.

When the financial statements of a foreign subsidiary are consolidated with those of its U.S. parent company, the financial statements of the subsidiary, originally expressed in the currency of the country in which it operates, must be converted to U.S. dollars. The conversion process is referred to as *foreign currency translation*. Because of the mechanics used in the translation process and because exchange rates fluctuate over time, a debit or credit difference between the translated value of the subsidiary's assets and liabilities and the translated value of the subsidiary's owners' equity arises in the translation and consolidation process. Prior to 1983, this debit or credit difference was reported as a loss or gain in the consolidated income statement. Because of large gyrations in exchange rates, a firm might have reported a large translation gain in one year and an equally large translation loss in the next year. The translation gain or loss had a material effect on reported results but did not have a significant economic impact because the gain or loss was never actually realized. The difference between the value of the subsidiaries as measured in U.S. dollars versus foreign currency units will *never* be converted to cash unless the foreign subsidiaries are sold. Therefore, the FASB issued an accounting standard that requires firms to report the translation gain or loss as a separate account within owners' equity rather than as a gain or loss in the income statement. The effect of this accounting standard was to make reported net income more meaningful and to highlight as a separate item in owners' equity the cumulative translation adjustment. To the extent that exchange rates of the U.S. dollar rise and fall relative to the foreign currencies involved, the amount of this **cumulative foreign currency translation adjustment** will fluctuate over time. This treatment of the translation adjustment is consistent with the going concern concept because as long as the entity continues to operate with foreign subsidiaries, the translation adjustment will not be realized.

Reporting Changes in Owners' Equity Accounts

Objective 7
Understand how owners' equity transactions for the year are reported in the financial statements.

It is appropriate that the reasons for changes to any owners' equity account during a fiscal period be presented in the balance sheet, in a separate statement of changes in owners' equity, or in the footnotes or financial review accompanying the financial statements. One possible format for a statement of changes in owners' equity is presented for Racers, Inc., in Exhibit 8–5. (Amounts for net income and dividends on common stock are assumed. You should prove to yourself the amount of the cash dividends on the preferred stock.) Alternative formats may be used.

Even if there are no changes to the paid-in capital accounts and there is no treasury stock or foreign subsidiary, an analysis of retained earnings is presented. This can be done in a separate statement, as illustrated for Racers, Inc., in Exhibit 8–6, or by appending the beginning balance,

EXHIBIT 8–5   Statement of Changes in Owners' Equity

RACERS, INC.
Statement of Changes in Owners' Equity
For the Year Ended August 31, 1999

	Preferred Stock		Common Stock		Additional Paid-In Capital $	Retained Earnings $	Common Treasury Stock	
	No. of Shares	$	No. of Shares	$			No. of Shares	$
Balance, August 31, 1998	5,000	500,000	200,000	400,000	2,820,000	2,600,000	—	—
Sale of common stock			40,000	80,000	440,000			
Purchase of common treasury stock							1,000	12,000
Net income						390,000		
Cash dividends:								
Preferred stock						(30,000)		
Common stock						(60,000)		
Stock dividend:								
2% on 240,000 shares when market value was $15 per share			4,800	9,600	62,400	(72,000)		
Balance, August 31, 1999	5,000	500,000	244,800	489,600	3,322,400	2,828,000	1,000	12,000

284

EXHIBIT 8–6   Statement of Changes in Retained Earnings

RACERS, INC.
Statement of Changes in Retained Earnings
For the Year Ended August 31, 1999

Retained earnings balance, beginning of year	$2,600,000
Add: Net income	390,000
Less: Cash dividends:	
Preferred stock	(30,000)
Common stock	(60,000)
2% stock dividend on common stock	(72,000)
Retained earnings balance, end of year	$2,828,000

dividend, and ending balance information to the bottom of the income statement, which then becomes a combined statement of income and retained earnings.

Note that Intel Corporation presents Consolidated Statements of Stockholders' Equity on page 21 of its 1996 Annual Report. What approach is used in the other annual reports that you have?

Owners' Equity for Other Types of Entities

Proprietorships and Partnerships

The discussion in this chapter has focused on owners' equity of corporations. Neither proprietorships nor partnerships (single and multiple-owner unincorporated businesses, respectively) issue stock, and a distinction between invested capital and retained earnings is not usually made. Owners' equity of these firms is usually referred to as capital, as in "Michael Jordan, Capital" in the case of a proprietorship, or as "Partners' Capital" in the case of a partnership. For a small partnership, the capital account balance of each partner may be listed separately in the balance sheet. For a partnership with many partners, the capital interest of each may be expressed in "units" or "shares" representing proportional interest, but these shares do not carry the same legal rights as capital stock of a corporation. In fact, partnership shares are frequently used *only* for profit and loss distribution purposes; each partner ordinarily has an equal voice in the management of the firm. The partnership agreement will specify how the profits and losses of the partnership are to be allocated to individual partners. Distributions to the owner or owners during the year, including any salaries paid to the proprietor or partners, are treated as reductions of owners' equity rather than expenses. These amounts are frequently accumulated in a "drawing" account, which is similar to the dividends account for a corporation. The statement of changes in owners' equity for the year reports the beginning capital balance, additional capital investments, net income of loss for the year, and capital withdrawals (drawings) to arrive at the ending capital balance.

Not-for-Profit and Governmental Organizations

These types of organizations do not have owners who have *direct* financial interests in the entity. The financial reporting requirements are therefore focused on resource providers (such as taxpayers or donors), rather than investors. Owners' equity in these organizations is referred to as *fund balance*. Because individual resource providers do not have specific claims against the organization's assets, capital accounts are inappropriate, and net income is not reported for most funds. There is usually an operating (or current) fund, and there are frequently several restricted funds for enhancing accountability for certain assets. For example, a university would account for tuition income and operating expenses in its current fund. Money that is donated for student scholarships is accounted for in a restricted fund to help ensure that it is used for its intended purpose. Other funds frequently used are an endowment fund, loan fund, plant fund, and debt retirement fund. The transactions that affect these funds are nonoperating in nature, and specific accountability is required. The statement of owners' equity is called the "statement of changes in fund balances," which summarizes the activities of each fund. Changes during the year include the excess (or deficiency) of operating revenues over (under) operating expenses, increases from contributions, grants, or other support, decreases from nonoperating transactions, and transfers to and from other funds. This statement is similar in purpose and content to the statement of owners' equity of a corporation and is just as easy to understand.

Summary

This chapter has described the accounting for and presentation of the following owners' equity accounts. (Note that, except for the fact that net income is added to retained earnings, transactions affecting owners' equity do not affect the income statement.)

Balance sheet	Income statement
Assets = Liabilities + Owners' equity ←	Net income = Revenues − Expenses

Paid-In Capital:
Preferred Stock
Common Stock
Additional Paid-
   In Capital
Retained   ← Net Income
   Earnings
Cumulative Foreign
   Currency Translation
   Adjustment
(Treasury Stock)

Owners' equity is also referred to as *net assets*. For single proprietorships and partnerships, the term *capital* is frequently used instead of owners' equity. For a corporation, the components of owners' equity are paid-in capital, retained earnings, treasury stock, and possibly the cumulative foreign currency translation adjustment and/or an unrealized loss on certain marketable securities.

Paid-in capital always includes common stock and may include preferred stock and additional paid-in capital. Common stock represents the basic ownership of the corporation. Common stock may have a par value or may be no par value. Additional paid-in capital represents the difference between the par (or stated) value of common stock issued and the total amount paid in to the corporation when the stock was issued. Additional paid-in capital is sometimes given the more descriptive caption "capital in excess of par (or stated) value." If no-par-value common stock has no stated value, the total amount paid in to the corporation when the stock was issued is reported as the dollar amount of common stock. The principal right and obligation of the common stockholders is to elect the board of directors of the corporation. Voting for directors can be on either a cumulative basis or a slate basis.

Preferred stock is different from common stock in that preferred has a prior claim to dividends and a prior claim on assets when the corporation is liquidated. In most cases, preferred stock does not have a voting privilege. Preferred stock is in some respects similar to bonds payable. However, the most significant difference between the two is that interest on bonds is a tax-deductible expense, and dividends on preferred stock are a nondeductible distribution of the corporation's earnings.

Retained earnings represents the cumulative earnings reinvested in the business. If earnings are not reinvested, they are distributed to stockholders as dividends. Retained earnings is not cash. The Retained Earnings account is increased by net income and decreased by dividends (and by a net loss).

Dividends are declared by the board of directors and paid to owners of the stock on the record date. Although cash dividends can be paid with any frequency, quarterly or semiannual dividend payments are most common in practice. Stock dividends represent the issuance of additional shares of stock to stockholders in proportion to the number of shares owned on the record date. Stock dividends do not affect the assets, liabilities, or total owners' equity of the firm but do result in the transfer of an amount of retained earnings to paid-in capital. Stock dividends are expressed as a percentage of the number of predividend shares issued and that percentage is usually relatively small (i.e., less than 20%).

Stock splits also involve issuing additional shares of stock to stockholders in proportion to the number of shares owned on the record date—but usually result in at least doubling the number of shares held by each stockholder. Stock splits are expressed as a ratio of the number of shares held after the split to the number held before the split (e.g., 2 for 1). The reason for (and effect of) a stock split is to reduce the market value per share of the stock.

Treasury stock is the corporation's own stock that has been purchased from stockholders and is being held in the treasury for future reissue. Treasury stock is reported as a contra owners' equity account. When treasury stock is reissued at a price different from its cost, no gain or loss is recognized, but paid-in capital is affected.

The cumulative foreign currency translation adjustment is an amount reported in owners' equity of corporations having foreign subsidiaries. The adjustment arises in the process of translating the financial statements of subsidiaries (expressed in foreign currency units) to U.S. dollars. Because exchange rates can fluctuate widely, net income could be distorted if this adjustment were reported in the income statement. To avoid this distortion, the adjustment is reported in owners' equity.

Owners' equity captions usually seen in a balance sheet are:

1. Paid-in capital:
   a. Common stock
   b. Preferred stock (optional)
   c. Additional paid-in capital
2. Retained earnings (Accumulated deficit if negative)
3. Cumulative foreign currency translation adjustment
4. Less: Treasury stock

It is possible that a firm may have only common stock (sometimes called *capital stock*) and retained earnings as components of owners' equity.

Changes in owners' equity are usually reported in a comprehensive statement that summarizes the changes of each element of owners' equity. However, if there have not been significant changes in paid-in capital accounts, a statement of changes in retained earnings may be presented by itself. Sometimes the statement of changes in retained earnings is combined with the income statement.

Proprietorships, partnerships, and not-for-profit organizations report changes in owners' equity using terminology unique to each type of entity. In the final analysis, the purpose of this statement for these entities is the same as for corporations: to explain the change in net assets of the entity during the reporting period.

Refer to Intel Corporation's balance sheets and the statements of stockholders' equity in the Appendix, and to other financial statements you may have, and observe how information about owners' equity is presented.

APPENDIX

PERSONAL INVESTING

An exciting milestone in every individual's financial life is the beginning of a personal investment program in stocks, bonds, and other securities. A number of questions about one's capability to accept the risks involved must be answered before an investment plan is put into action; it is appropriate for most people to consult a trusted financial advisor to help them understand and answer those questions and to establish a sensible plan.

One investment medium appropriate for many people is an investment company, or mutual fund. Investors purchase shares of the mutual fund, which uses the money received from investors to purchase shares of common stock, preferred stock, and/or bonds. In essence, each investor owns a share of the portfolio of securities owned by the mutual fund. Shares in some mutual funds are purchased through a registered representative employed by a brokerage firm, and in other cases the investor purchases shares directly from the mutual fund. You should understand that not all mutual funds are alike in their operating and investing objectives. Thus, an individual investor should carefully define her own objectives and *then* select a fund that invests in a portfolio of securities consistent with her own views. Whether dealing through a broker or directly with the mutual fund, an investor will receive a prospectus that describes the fund, its operating and investment policies, and the risks to which an investment is exposed.

An alternative method of investing is to make direct purchases of specific corporate securities. This is usually done by opening an account with a brokerage firm, although an employee can invest in the stock of her own employer through a 401(k) plan without having to go through a broker. By taking this approach, the investor has direct ownership of individual stocks and bonds, rather than an interest in a portfolio of securities owned by a mutual fund. A prospectus describing the securities purchased and risks involved is *not* furnished when an investor acquires previously issued shares traded on a stock exchange or in the over-the-counter market.

A full discussion of investment characteristics, risks, and alternatives is beyond the scope of this book. It is appropriate to have an understanding of the terminology, concepts, and financial reporting practices described here before starting an investment program. An interesting and informative way to begin is with *The Wall Street Journal's* free publication 'How to Read Between the Lines." Copies are available to students and educators by calling 1-800-JOURNAL, or by visiting the Web at "http://info.wsj.com/circ."

Key Terms and Concepts

accumulated deficit (p. 277)   Retained earnings with a negative (debit) balance.

additional paid-in capital (p. 276)   The excess of the amount received from the sale of stock over the par (or stated) value of the shares sold.

authorized shares (p. 271)   The number of shares of a class of stock authorized by the corporation's charter. The maximum number of shares the corporation can legally issue.

callable preferred stock (p. 274)   Preferred stock that can be redeemed by the corporation at its option.

capital in excess of par value (p. 276)   Another term for *additional paid-in capital.*

capital stock (p. 269)   The generic term for stock issued by a corporation.

capitalizing retained earnings (p. 280)   The transfer of retained earnings to paid-in capital that occurs when a stock dividend is declared.

common stock (p. 269)   The class of stock that represents residual ownership of the corporation.

convertible preferred stock (p. 274)   Preferred stock that can be converted to common stock of the corporation at the option of the stockholder.

cumulative dividend (p. 273)   A feature of preferred stock that requires that any missed dividends be paid before dividends can be paid on common stock.

cumulative foreign currency translation adjustment (p. 283)   A component of owners' equity arising from the translation of foreign subsidiary financial statements included in the consolidated financial statements.

cumulative voting (p. 270)   A system of voting for the directors of a firm in which the number of votes that can be cast for one or more candidates is equal to the number of shares of stock owned multiplied by the number of directors to be elected.

declaration date (p. 278)   The date a dividend is declared by the board of directors.

dividend (p. 273)   A distribution of earnings to the owners of a corporation.

ex-dividend date (p. 278)   The date on and after which the buyer of a publicly traded stock will not receive a dividend that has been declared.

inside director (p. 269)   A member of the firm's board of directors who is also an officer or employee of the firm.

issued shares (p. 272)   The number of shares of a class of stock that has been issued (usually sold) to stockholders.

legal capital (p. 270)   The amount associated with the capital stock that has been issued by a corporation. Legal capital is generally the par value or stated value of the shares issued.

liquidating value (p. 273)   The stated claim of preferred stock in the event the corporation is liquidated. Sometimes called *redemption value.*

outside director (p. 269)   A member of the firm's board of directors who is not also an officer or employee of the firm.

outstanding shares (p. 272)   The number of shares of a class of stock held by stockholders.

par value (p. 270)   An arbitrary value assigned to a share of stock when the corporation is organized. Sometimes used to refer to the stated value or face amount of a security.

participating dividend (p. 273)   A feature of preferred stock that provides a right to preferred stockholders to receive additional dividends at a specified ratio after a base amount of dividends has been paid to common stockholders.

partners' capital (p. 267)   The owners' equity in a partnership.

payment date (p. 278)   The date a dividend is paid.

preemptive right (p. 272)   The right of a stockholder to purchase shares from any additional share issuances in proportion to the stockholder's present percentage of ownership.

preferred stock (p. 273)   The class of stock representing an ownership interest with certain preferences relative to common stock, usually including a priority claim to dividends.

proprietor's capital (p. 267)   The owners' equity of an individual proprietorship.

record date (p. 278)   The date used to determine the stockholders who will receive a dividend.

redemption value (p. 273)   The stated claim of preferred stock in the event the corporation is liquidated. Sometimes called *liquidating value.*

retained earnings (p. 276)   Cumulative net income that has not been distributed to the owners of a corporation as dividends.

slate voting (p. 270)   A system of voting for the directors of a firm in which votes equal to the number of shares owned are cast for a single slate of candidates.

stated value (p. 271)   An arbitrary value assigned to shares of no-par-value stock.

stock dividend (p. 279)   A distribution of additional shares to existing stockholders in proportion to their existing holdings. The additional shares issued usually amount to less than 20% of the previously issued shares.

stock split (p. 280)   A distribution of additional shares to existing stockholders in proportion to their existing holdings. The additional shares issued usually amount to 100 percent or more of the previously issued shares.

treasury stock (p. 272)   Shares of a firm's stock that have been reacquired by the firm.

WHAT DOES IT MEAN?
ANSWERS

1. It means that common stock has been issued to stockholders in exchange for their investment of capital in the corporation. The capital has not been earned; it has been paid-in by the owners.

2. It means that an arbitrary amount has been assigned as a value for each share of common stock. This arbitrarily assigned value has no effect on the market value of each share of common stock.

3. It means that the corporation has reacquired from stockholders some previously issued shares of stock.

4. It means that the corporation has issued some stock that has many characteristics similar to those of bonds. Relative to common stock, preferred stock has a priority claim to dividends and to the assets in the event of liquidation.

5. It means that the corporation has retained earnings from its operations, and cash that the directors want to distribute to the stockholders.

6. It means that the corporation has retained earnings from its operations and that the directors want to transfer some of the retained earnings to paid-in capital rather than distribute cash to the stockholders.

7. It means that the corporation's board of directors wants to lower the market value of each share of common stock. This occurs because the corporation doesn't receive anything for the additional shares issued, so the total market value of the company is split among more shares than were outstanding before the stock split.

Exercises and Problems

8–1. **Review problem—calculate net income.** At the beginning of the current fiscal year, the balance sheet of Bublitz, Inc., showed owners' equity of $520,000. During the year, liabilities increased by $21,000 to $234,000, paid-in capital increased by $40,000 to $175,000, and assets increased by $260,000. Dividends declared and paid during the year were $55,000.

Required:

Calculate net income or loss for the year. *(Hint: Set up the accounting equation for beginning balances, changes during the year, and ending balances, and then solve for missing amounts.)*

	A	=	L	+	PIC	+	RE
							OE
Beginning	$	=		+		+	
Changes		=		+		+	
Ending		=		+		+	

8–2.   Review problem—calculate net income. At the beginning of the current fiscal year, the balance sheet of Olson Co. showed liabilities of $219,000. During the year, liabilities decreased by $36,000, assets increased by $77,000, and paid-in capital also increased by $10,000 to $190,000. Dividends declared and paid during the year were $62,000. At the end of the year, owners' equity totaled $379,000.

Required:

Calculate net income or loss for the year, using the same format as shown above in Problem 8–1.

8–3.   Review problem—calculate retained earnings. From the data given below, calculate the Retained Earnings balance as of December 31, 1999.

Retained earnings, December 31, 1998	$346,400
Cost of buildings purchased during 1999	41,800
Net income for the year ended December 31, 1999	56,900
Dividends declared and paid in 1999	32,500
Increase in cash balance from January 1, 1999, to December 31, 1999	23,000
Increase in long-term debt in 1999	44,600

8–4.   Review problem—calculate retained earnings. From the data given below, calculate the Retained Earnings balance as of December 31, 1999.

Retained earnings, December 31, 2000	$122,600
Net decrease in total assets during 2000	18,700
Net increase in accounts receivable in 2000	4,300
Dividends declared and paid in 2000	16,800
Proceeds from issuance of bonds during 2000	44,200
Net loss for the year ended December 31, 2000	11,500

LO 1

8–5.   Common stock balance sheet disclosure. The balance sheet caption for common stock is:

Common stock, $5 par value, 2,000,000 shares authorized, 1,400,000 shares issued, 1,250,000 shares outstanding	$?

Required:

a. Calculate the dollar amount that will be presented opposite this caption.

b. Calculate the total amount of a cash dividend of $.15 per share.

c. What accounts for the difference between issued shares and outstanding shares?

LO 1

8–6. Common stock—calculate issue price and dividend amount. The balance sheet caption for common stock is:

Common stock without par value, 4,000,000 shares authorized,
   800,000 shares issued, and 720,000 shares outstanding $2,600,000

Required:

a. Calculate the average price at which the shares were issued.

b. If these shares had been assigned a stated value of $1 each, show how the above caption would be different.

c. If a cash dividend of $.18 per share were declared, calculate the total amount of cash that would be paid to stockholders.

d. What accounts for the difference between issued shares and outstanding shares?

LO 2

8–7. Preferred stock—calculate dividend amounts. Calculate the annual cash dividends required to be paid for each of the following preferred stock issues:

a. $3.75 cumulative preferred, no par value; 200,000 shares authorized, 161,522 shares issued. (The treasury stock caption of the stockholders' equity section of the balance sheet indicates that 43,373 shares of this preferred stock issue are owned by the company.)

b. 6%, $40 par value preferred, 100,000 shares authorized, 85,400 shares issued, and 73,621 shares outstanding.

c. 11.4% cumulative preferred, $100 stated value, $104 liquidating value; 50,000 shares authorized, 43,200 shares issued, 37,600 shares outstanding.

LO 2

8–8. Preferred stock—calculate dividend amounts. Calculate the cash dividends required to be paid for each of the following preferred stock issues:

a. The semiannual dividend on 9% cumulative preferred, $60 par value; 10,000 shares authorized, issued, and outstanding.

b. The annual dividend on $2.40 cumulative preferred, 100,000 shares authorized, 60,000 shares issued, 53,200 shares outstanding. Last year's dividend has not been paid.

c. The quarterly dividend on 13.2% cumulative preferred, $100 stated value, $103 liquidating value, 60,000 shares authorized, 52,000 shares issued and outstanding. No dividends are in arrears.

LO 2

8–9. Preferred stock—calculate dividend amounts. Anderco, Inc., did not pay dividends on its $6.50, $50 par value, cumulative preferred stock during 1997 or 1998. Since 1992, 22,000 shares of this stock have been outstanding. Anderco, Inc., has been profitable in 1999 and is considering a cash dividend on its common stock that would be payable in December 1999.

Required:

Calculate the amount of dividends that would have to be paid on the preferred stock before a cash dividend could be paid to the common stockholders.

LO 2

8–10. Preferred stock—calculate dividend amounts. Poorco, Inc., did not pay dividends in 1997 or 1998, even though 45,000 shares of its 8.5%, $70 par value cumulative preferred stock were outstanding during those years. The company has 263,000 shares of $2.50 par value common stock outstanding.

Required:

a. Calculate the annual dividend per share obligation on the preferred stock.

b. Calculate the amount that would be received by an investor who has owned 200 shares of preferred stock and 450 shares of common stock since 1996 if a $.25 per share dividend on the common stock is paid at the end of 1999.

LO 1, 2

8–11. Common and preferred stock—issuances and dividends. Homestead Oil Corp. was incorporated on January 1, 1998, and issued the following stock, for cash:

800,000 shares of no-par common stock were authorized. 150,000 shares were issued on January 1, 1998, at $19 per share.

200,000 shares of $100 par value, 9.5% cumulative, preferred stock were authorized, and 60,000 shares were issued on January 1, 1998, at $122 per share.

Net income for the years ended December 31, 1998, and 1999, was $1,300,000 and $2,800,000, respectively.

No dividends were declared or paid during 1998. However, on December 28, 1999, the board of directors of Homestead declared dividends of $1,800,000, payable on February 12, 2000, to holders of record as of January 19, 2000.

Required:

a. Use the horizontal model (or write the journal entry) to show the effects of:
1. The issuance of common stock and preferred stock on January 1, 1998.
2. The declaration of dividends on December 28, 1999.
3. The payment of dividends on February 12, 2000.

b. Of the total amount of dividends declared during 1999, how much will be received by preferred shareholders?

LO 1, 2

8–12. Common and preferred stock—issuances and dividends. Permabilt Corp. was incorporated on January 1, 1998, and issued the following stock, for cash:

1,200,000 shares of no-par common stock were authorized. 350,000 shares were issued on January 1, 1998, at $23 per share.

400,000 shares of $100 par value, 10.5% cumulative, preferred stock were authorized, and 140,000 shares were issued on January 1, 1998, at $132 per share.

Net income for the years ended December 31, 1998, 1999, and 2000, was $5,250,000, $7,450,000, and $8,700,000, respectively.

No dividends were declared or paid during 1998 or 1999. However, on December 17, 2000, the board of directors of Permabilt Corp. declared dividends of $6,200,000, payable on February 9, 2001, to holders of record as of January 4, 2001.

Required:

a. Use the horizontal model (or write the journal entry) to show the effects of:
1. The issuance of common stock and preferred stock on January 1, 1998.
2. The declaration of dividends on December 17, 2000.
3. The payment of dividends on February 9, 2001.

b. Of the total amount of dividends declared during 2000, how much will be received by preferred shareholders?

LO 3 **8–13.** **Dividend dates—market price effects.** Blanker, Inc., has paid a regular quarterly cash dividend of $.50 per share for several years. The common stock is publicly traded. On February 21 of the current year, Blanker's board of directors declared the regular first-quarter dividend of $.50 per share payable on March 30 to stockholders of record on March 15.

Required:

As a result of this dividend action, state what would you expect to happen to the market price of the common stock of Blanker, Inc., on each of the following dates. Explain your answers.
a. February 21.
b. March 12.
c. March 15.
d. March 30.

LO 3 **8–14.** **Ex-dividend date—market price effect.** Find and review the Dividend News section of an issue of *The Wall Street Journal* that is at least one week old. Find the list of stocks that will trade ex-dividend a few days later. From the stock listings in *The Wall Street Journal* on the ex-dividend date, determine what happened to the market price of the stock on the ex-dividend date. Does this price action make sense? Explain your answer.

LO 3 **8–15.** **Requirements for declaring dividends.** Knight, Inc., expects to incur a loss for the current year. The chairman of the board of directors wants to have a cash dividend so that the company's record of having paid a dividend during every year of its existence will continue. What factors will determine whether or not the board can declare a dividend?

Intel LO 3 **8–16.** **Interpret dividend information from an annual report.** Refer to the Intel Corporation Annual Report in the Appendix. From the table of quarterly financial information on page 37 and the Ten-Year Financial Summary on page 33, find the information relating to cash dividends on common stock.

Required:

a. How frequently are cash dividends paid?
b. What has been the pattern of the cash dividend amount per share relative to the pattern of earnings per share? How can this be possible for a company as successful as Intel?
c. Calculate the rate of change in the annual dividend per share for each of the four years from 1993 through 1996.

LO 4 **8–17.** **Cash dividends versus stock dividends.** Under what circumstances would you (as an investor) prefer to receive cash dividends rather than stock dividends? Under what circumstances would you prefer stock dividends to cash dividends?

LO 4 **8–18.** **Calculate stock dividend shares and cash dividend amounts.** Assume that you own 200 shares of Blueco, Inc., common stock and that you currently receive cash dividends of $.84 per share per year.

Required:

a. If Blueco, Inc., declared a 5% stock dividend, how many shares of common stock would you receive as a dividend?
b. Calculate the cash dividend per share amount to be paid after the stock dividend that would result in the same total cash dividend (as was received before the stock dividend).

    c. If the cash dividend remained at $.84 per share after the stock dividend, what per share cash dividend amount without a stock dividend would have accomplished the same total cash dividend?

    d. Why would a company have a dividend policy of paying a $.10 per share cash dividend and issuing a 5% stock dividend every year?

LO 4   **8–19.**   **Effects of a stock split.** Assume that you own 100 shares of common stock of a company and the company has a 2-for-1 stock split when the market price per share is $40.

    Required:

    a. How many shares of common stock will you own after the stock split?

    b. What will probably happen to the market price per share of the stock?

LO 4   **8–20.**   **Stock splits versus stock dividends.** Assume that you own 75 shares of common stock of a company, that you have been receiving cash dividends of $3 per share per year, and that the company has a 4-for-3 stock split.

    Required:

    a. How many shares of common stock will you own after the stock split?

    b. What new cash dividend per share amount will result in the same total dividend income as you received before the stock split?

    c. What stock dividend percentage could have accomplished the same end result as the 4-for-3 stock split?

LO 5   **8–21.**   **Treasury stock transactions.** On May 4, 1999, Docker, Inc., purchased 800 shares of its own common stock in the market at a price of $18.25 per share. On September 11, 1999, 600 of these shares were sold in the open market at a price of $19.50 per share. There were 36,200 shares of Docker common stock outstanding prior to the May 4 purchase of treasury stock. A $.35 per share cash dividend on the common stock was declared and paid on June 15, 1999.

    Required:

    Use the horizontal model (or write the journal entry) to show the effect on Docker's financial statements of:

    a. The purchase of the treasury stock on May 4.

    b. The declaration and payment of the cash dividend on June 15.

    c. The sale of the treasury stock on September 11.

LO 5   **8–22.**   **Treasury stock transactions.** On January 1, 1998, Metco, Inc., had issued and outstanding 287,300 shares of $2 par value common stock. On March 15, 1998, Metco, Inc., purchased for its treasury 2,200 shares of its common stock at a price of $37.50 per share. On August 10, 1998, 700 of these treasury shares were sold for $42 per share. Metco's directors declared cash dividends of $.60 per share during the second quarter and again during the fourth quarter, payable on June 30, 1998, and December 31, 1998, respectively. A 2% stock dividend was issued at the end of the year. There were no other transactions affecting common stock during the year.

    Required:

    a. Use the horizontal model (or write the journal entry) to show the effect of the treasury stock purchase on March 15, 1998.

    b. Calculate the total amount of the cash dividends paid in the second quarter.

    c. Use the horizontal model (or write the journal entry) to show the effect of the sale of the treasury stock on August 10, 1998.

    d. Calculate the total amount of cash dividends paid in the fourth quarter.

    e. Calculate the number of shares of stock issued in the stock dividend.

LO 1, 2, 4, 5   **8–23.**   **Transaction analysis—various accounts.** Enter the following column headings across the top of a sheet of paper:

Trans-action	Cash	Other Assets	Liabil-ities	Paid-In Capital	Retained Earnings	Treasury Stock	Net Income

Enter the transaction letter in the first column and show the effect (if any) of each of the following transactions on each financial statement category by entering a plus (+) or minus (−) sign in the appropriate column. Do not show items that affect net income in the retained earnings column. You may also write the journal entries to record each transaction.

a. Sold 4,100 shares of $50 par value 9% preferred stock at par.

b. Declared the annual dividend on the preferred stock.

c. Purchased 650 shares of preferred stock for the treasury at $54 per share.

d. Issued 2,000 shares of $1 par value common stock in exchange for land valued at $113,000.

e. Sold 300 shares of the treasury stock purchased in transaction *c* for $58 per share.

f. Split the common stock 2 for 1.

LO 1, 2, 4, 5   **8–24.**   **Transaction analysis—various accounts.** Enter the following column headings across the top of a sheet of paper:

Trans-action	Cash	Other Assets	Liabil-ities	Paid-In Capital	Retained Earnings	Treasury Stock	Net Income

Enter the transaction letter in the first column and show the effect (if any) of the transaction on each financial statement category by indicating whether it is an addition (+) or subtraction (−) in the appropriate column. Do not show items that affect net income in the retained earnings column. You may also write the journal entries to record these transactions. You should assume that the transactions occurred in the same chronological sequence as indicated.

a. Sold 2,600 shares of $10 par value preferred stock at $12.50 per share.

b. Declared the annual cash dividend of $3.20 per share on common stock. There were 9,200 shares of common stock issued and outstanding throughout the year.

c. Issued 3,200 shares of $10 par value preferred stock in exchange for a building when the market price of preferred stock was $14 per share.

d. Purchased 150 shares of preferred stock for the treasury at a price of $16 per share.

e. Sold 70 shares of the preferred stock held in treasury (see *d* above) for $17 per share.

f. Declared and issued a 15% stock dividend on the $1 par value common stock when the market price per share was $45.

LO 1, 2, 4, 5   **8–25.**   **Transaction analysis—various accounts.** Enter the following column headings across the top of a sheet of paper:

Trans-action	Cash	Other Assets	Liabil-ities	Paid-In Capital	Retained Earnings	Treasury Stock	Net Income

Enter the transaction letter in the first column and show the effect (if any) of each of the following transactions on each financial statement category by entering a plus (+) or minus (−) sign and the amount in the appropriate column. Do not show items that affect net income in the retained earnings column. You may also write the journal entries to record these transactions. You should assume that the transactions occurred in this chronological sequence and that 40,000 shares of previously issued common stock remain outstanding. *(Hint: Remember to consider appropriate effects of previous transactions.)*

a. Sold 5,000 previously unissued shares of $1 par value common stock for $18 per share.

b. Issued 1,000 shares of previously unissued 8% cumulative preferred stock, $40 par value, in exchange for land and a building appraised at $40,000.

c. Declared and issued the annual cash dividend on the preferred stock issued in transaction *b.*

d. Purchased 250 shares of common stock for the treasury at a total cost of $4,750.

e. Declared a cash dividend of $.15 per share on the common stock outstanding.

f. Sold 130 shares of the treasury stock purchased in transaction *d* at a price of $20 per share.

g. Declared and issued a 3% stock dividend on the common stock when the market value per share of common stock was $21.

h. Split the common stock 3 for 1.

LO 1, 2, 4, 5   **8–26.**   **Transaction analysis—various accounts.** Enter the following column headings across the top of a sheet of paper:

Trans-action	Cash	Other Assets	Liabil-ities	Paid-In Capital	Retained Earnings	Treasury Stock	Net Income

Enter the transaction letter in the first column and show the effect (if any) of the transaction on each financial statement category by indicating whether it is an addition (+) or subtraction (−) and showing the amount in the appropriate column. Do not show items that affect net income in the retained earnings column. You may also write the journal entries to record these transactions. You should assume that the transactions occurred in the same chronological sequence as indicated and that no stock had been previously issued. *(Hint: Remember to consider appropriate effects of previous transactions.)*

a. Issued 500 shares of $100 par value preferred stock at par.

b. Issued 800 shares of $100 par value preferred stock in exchange for land that had an appraised value of $102,000.

c. Issued 23,000 shares of $5 par value common stock for $11 per share.

d. Purchased 4,500 shares of common stock for the treasury at $13 per share.

e. Sold 2,000 shares of the treasury stock purchased in transaction *d* for $14 per share.

f. Declared a cash dividend of $1.75 per share on the preferred stock outstanding, to be paid early next year.

g. Declared and issued a 5% stock dividend on the common stock when the market price per share of common stock was $15.

LO 1, 2, 3, 5, 7   **8–27.**   **Comprehensive problem—calculate missing amounts, dividends, total shares, and per share information.** Allyn, Inc., has the following owners' equity section in its November 30, 1999, balance sheet:

Paid-in capital:	
12% preferred stock, $60 par value, 1,500 shares authorized, issued, and outstanding	$?
Common stock, $8 par value, 100,000 shares authorized, ____?____ shares issued	240,000
Additional paid-in capital on common stock	540,000
Additional paid-in capital from treasury stock	13,000
Retained earnings	97,000
Less: Treasury stock, at cost (2,000 shares of common)	(18,000)
Total stockholders' equity	$?

Required:

a. Calculate the amount of the total annual dividend requirement on preferred stock.

b. Calculate the amount that should be shown on the balance sheet for preferred stock.

c. Calculate the number of shares of common stock that are issued and the number of shares of common stock that are outstanding.

d. On January 1, 1999, the firm's balance sheet showed common stock of $210,000 and additional paid-in capital on common stock of $468,750. The only transaction affecting these accounts during 1999 was the sale of some common stock. Calculate the number of shares that were sold and the selling price per share.

e. Describe the transaction that resulted in the additional paid-in capital from treasury stock.

f. The retained earnings balance on January 1, 1999, was $90,300. Net income for the past 11 months has been $24,000. Preferred stock dividends for all of 1999 have been declared and paid. Calculate the amount of dividends on common stock during the first 11 months of 1999.

LO 1, 2, 3, 4, 5, 7   **8–28.**   **Comprehensive problem—calculate missing amounts, issue price, net income, and dividends; interpret stock dividend and split.** Bacon, Inc., has the following owners' equity section in its May 31, 1999, comparative balance sheets:

	May 31, 1999	April 30, 1999
Paid-in capital:		
Preferred stock, $120 par value, 8%, cumulative, 50,000 shares authorized, 40,000 shares issued and outstanding	$ 4,800,000	$ 4,800,000
Common stock, $6 par value, 300,000 shares authorized, 200,000 and 190,000 shares issued, respectively	?	1,140,000
Additional paid-in capital	8,400,000	8,240,000
Retained earnings	6,950,000	6,812,000
Less: Treasury common stock, at cost; 9,000 shares and 8,500 shares, respectively	(830,000)	(816,000)
Total stockholders' equity	$?	$20,176,000

Required:

a. Calculate the amount that should be shown on the balance sheet for common stock at May 31, 1999.

b. The only transaction affecting additional paid-in capital during the month of May was the sale of additional common stock. At what price per share were the additional shares sold?

c. What was the average cost per share of the common stock purchased for the treasury during the month?

d. During May, dividends on preferred stock equal to one-half of the 1999 dividend requirement were declared and paid. There were no common dividends declared or paid in May. Calculate net income for May.

e. Assume that on June 1 the board of directors declares a cash dividend of $.42 per share on the outstanding shares of common stock. The dividend will be payable on July 15 to stockholders of record on June 15.

1. Calculate the total amount of the dividend.
2. Explain the impact this action will have on the June 30 balance sheet, and on the income statement for June.

f. Assume that on June 1 the market value of the common stock is $36 per share and that the board of directors declares a 3% stock dividend on the issued shares of common stock. Use the horizontal model (or write the journal entry) to show the issuance of the stock dividend.

g. Assume that instead of the stock dividend described in *f* above, the board of directors authorizes a 3-for-1 stock split on June 1 when the market price of common stock is $36 per share.
1. What will be the par value, and how many shares of common stock will be authorized after the split?
2. What will be the market price per share of common stock after the split?
3. How many shares of common stock will be in the treasury after the split?

h. By how much will total stockholders' equity change as a result of:
1. The stock dividend described in part *f*?
2. The stock split described in part *g*?

LO 1, 2, 5, 7   **8–29.**   **Analytical problem (part one)—calculate missing owners' equity amounts for 1998.** *(Note: The information presented in this problem is also used for Problem 8–30. For now, you can ignore the 1999 column in the balance sheet; all disclosures presented below relate to the June 30, 1998, balance sheet.)* DeZurik Corp. had the following owners' equity section in its June 30, 1998, balance sheet (in thousands, except share and per share disclosures):

(Disclosures)	Amounts at June 30	
	1999	*1998*
Paid-in capital:		
Preferred stock, $4.50, $___?___ par value, cumulative, 50,000 shares authorized, 24,000 shares issued and outstanding	_____	$ 1,440
Common stock, $5 par value, 1,000,000 shares authorized, 820,000 shares issued, 750,000 shares outstanding	_____	_____
Additional paid-in capital on common stock	_____	5,740
Retained earnings	_____	_____
Less: Treasury common stock, at cost, ___?___ shares	_____	_____
Total owners' equity	$16,542	$15,000

Required:

a. Calculate the par value per share of preferred stock and determine the preferred stock dividend percentage.

b. Calculate the amount that should be shown on the balance sheet for common stock at June 30, 1998.

c. What was the average issue price of common stock as of the June 30, 1998, balance sheet?

d. How many shares of treasury stock does DeZurik Corp. own at June 30, 1998?

e. Assume that the treasury shares were purchased for $18 per share. Calculate the amount that should be shown on the balance sheet for treasury stock at June 30, 1998.

f. Calculate the retained earnings balance at June 30, 1998, after you have completed parts *a–e* above. *(Hint: Keep in mind that treasury stock is a contra account.)*

g. (Optional) Review the solutions to parts *a–f* of this problem in the student supplement: *Study Outlines, Solutions to Odd-Numbered Problems, and Ready Notes* to this book. Assume that the retained earnings balance on July 1, 1997, was $4,800 (in thousands) and that net income for the year ended June 30, 1998, was $288 (in thousands). The 1998 preferred dividends were paid in full, and no other dividend transactions were recorded during the year. Verify that the amount shown in the solution to part *f* is correct. *(Hint: Prepare a statement of retained earnings, or do a T-account analysis to determine the June 30, 1998, balance.)*

LO 1, 2, 4, 5, 7

8–30. **Analytical problem (part two)—prepare owners' equity amounts and disclosures for 1999 using transaction information.** *(Note: You should review the solution to Problem 8–29 in the student supplement:* Study Outlines, Solutions to Odd-Numbered Problems and Ready Notes *before attempting to complete this problem.)* The transactions affecting the owners' equity accounts of DeZurik Corp. for the year ended June 30, 1999, are summarized below:

1. 80,000 shares of common stock were issued at $14.25 per share.
2. 20,000 shares of treasury (common) stock were sold for $18 per share.
3. Net income for the year was $320 (in thousands).
4. The fiscal 1999 preferred dividends were paid in full. Assume that all 24,000 shares were outstanding throughout the year ended June 30, 1999.
5. A cash dividend of $0.20 per share was declared and paid to common stockholders. Assume that transactions (1) and (2) above occurred before the dividend was declared.
6. The preferred stock was split 2 for 1 on June 30, 1999. *(Note: This transaction had no effect on transaction (4) above.)*

Required:

a. Calculate the *dollar amounts* that DeZurik Corp. would report for each owners' equity caption on its June 30, 1999, balance sheet after recording the transaction information described above. Note that total owners' equity at June 30, 1999, is provided as a check figure.

(Hint: To determine the retained earnings balance, begin with the June 30, 1998, balance of $4,980 (in thousands) as determined in Problem 8–29, then make adjustments for the effects of transactions (3–5) above.)

b. Indicate how the owners' equity *disclosures* for DeZurik Corp. would change for the June 30, 1999, balance sheet, as compared to the disclosures shown in Problem 8–29 for the 1998 balance sheet.

c. What was the average issue price of common stock as of the June 30, 1999, balance sheet?

CHAPTER 9

The Income Statement and the Statement of Cash Flows

The income statement answers some of the most important questions that users of the financial statements have: What were the financial results of the entity's operations for the fiscal period? How much profit (or loss) did the firm have? Are sales increasing relative to cost of goods sold and other operating expenses? Many income statement accounts were introduced in Chapters 5–8 when transactions also affecting asset and liability accounts were explained. However, because of the significance of the net income figure to managers, stockholders, potential investors, and others, it is appropriate to focus on the form and content of this financial statement.

The income statement of Intel Corporation is on page 18 of the annual report in the Appendix. This page of the annual report has been reproduced as Exhibit 9–1. Note that comparative statements for the years

EXHIBIT 9–1 Income Statement

INTEL CORPORATION
Consolidated Statements of Income
(dollars in millions)

Three Years Ended December 28, 1996	1996	1995	1994
Net revenues	**$20,847**	**$16,202**	**$11,521**
Cost of sales	9,164	7,811	5,576
Research and development	1,808	1,296	1,111
Market, general and administrative	2,322	1,843	1,447
Operating costs and expenses	13,294	10,950	8,134
Operating income	**$ 7,553**	**$ 5,252**	**$ 3,387**
Interest expense	(25)	(29)	(57)
Interest income and other, net	406	415	273
Income before taxes	**7,934**	**5,638**	**3,603**
Provision for taxes	2,777	2,072	1,315
Net income	**$ 5,157**	**$ 3,566**	**$ 2,288**
Earnings per common and common equivalent share	**$ 5.81**	**$ 4.03**	**$ 2.62**
Weighted average common and common equivalent shares outstanding	**888**	**884**	**874**

ended on the last Saturday in December of 1996, 1995, and 1994 are presented. This permits the reader of the statement to assess quickly the recent trend of these important data.

As you might expect, Intel's income statement starts with "net revenues" (sales); what in popular jargon is referred to as the *bottom line,* or "net income" is really the third line from the bottom of the statement. In between, subtotals are provided for "operating income" and "income before taxes." Can you determine how much "gross profit" Intel earned in 1996? Although not reported as a separate subtotal, this amount is the difference between net revenues and cost of sales, or a whopping $11,683 million! The significance of the last two lines of the statement will be discussed later in this chapter. The principal objective of the first part of this chapter is to permit you to make sense of any income statement.

The second part of this chapter explores the statement of cash flows in more detail than presented in Chapter 2. Remember that this statement explains the change in the entity's cash from the beginning to the end of the fiscal period by summarizing the cash effects of the firm's operating, investing, and financing activities during the period.

Intel's comparative statements of cash flows are presented on page 20 of the Appendix for each of the past three years. Notice that the subtotal captions describe the activities—operating, investing, and financing—that caused cash to be provided and used during these years. Pay more attention to these three "big-picture" items than to the detailed captions and amounts within each category. Notice, however, that Intel uses a substantial amount of cash each year to purchase property, plant, and equipment (an investing activity) and to repurchase and retire common stock (a financing activity). As explained later, these are both signs of a financially healthy firm—especially if the firm can cover these payments from its cash flows provided by operating activities. Did Intel do this for each year presented?

The income statement and statement of cash flows report what has happened for a *period of time* (usually, but not necessarily, for the fiscal year ended on the balance sheet date). The balance sheet, remember, is focused on a single *point in time*—usually the end of the fiscal year—but one can be prepared as of any date.

**WHAT
DOES IT
MEAN?**

1. What does it mean when net income is referred to as the "bottom line"?

Learning Objectives

After studying this chapter, you should understand:

1 What revenue is and what the two criteria are that permit revenue recognition.

2 How cost of goods sold is determined under both perpetual and periodic inventory accounting systems.

3 The significance of gross profit (or gross margin) and how the gross profit (or gross margin) ratio is calculated and used.

4 The principal categories and components of "other operating expenses" and how these items are reported on the income statement.

5 What "income from operations" includes and why this income statement subtotal is significant to managers and financial analysts.

6 The components of the earnings per share calculation and the reasons for some of the refinements made in that calculation.

7 The alternative income statement presentation models.

8 The unusual items that may appear on the income statement, including:

Discontinued operations.
Extraordinary items.
Minority interest in earnings of subsidiaries.

9 The purpose and general format of the statement of cash flows.

10 The difference between the direct and indirect methods of presenting cash flows from operating activities.

11 Why the statement of cash flows is significant to financial analysts and investors who rely on the financial statements for much of their evaluative data.

Income Statement

Revenues

Objective 1
Understand what revenue is and what the two criteria are that permit revenue recognition.

The FASB defines **revenues** as "inflows or other enhancements of assets of an entity or settlements of its liabilities (or a combination of both) from delivering or producing goods, rendering services, or other activities that constitute the entity's ongoing major or central operations."[1] In its simplest and most straightforward application, this definition means that when a firm sells a product or provides services to a client or customer and receives cash, creates an account receivable, or satisfies an obligation, the firm has revenue. Most revenue transactions fit this simple and straightforward situation. Revenues are generally measured by the amount of cash received or expected to be received from the transaction. If the cash is not expected to be received within a year, then the revenue is usually measured by the present value of the amount expected to be received.

In *Concepts Statement No. 5* the FASB expands upon the above definition of revenues to provide guidance in applying the fundamental criteria involved in recognizing revenue. To be recognized, revenues must be realized or realizable, and earned. Sometimes one of these criteria is more important than the other.

Realization means that the product or service has been exchanged for cash, claims to cash, or an asset that is readily convertible to a known amount of cash or claims to cash. Thus the expectation that the product or service provided by the firm will result in a cash receipt has been fulfilled.

Earned means that the entity has completed, or substantially completed, the activities it must perform to be entitled to the revenue benefits

---

[1]FASB, *Statement of Financial Accounting Concepts No. 6,* "Elements of Financial Statements" (Stamford, CT, 1985), para. 78. Copyright © by the Financial Accounting Standards Board, High Ridge Park, Stamford, CT 06905, U.S.A. Quoted with permission. Copies of the complete document are available from the FASB.

(i.e., the increase in cash or some other asset, or the satisfaction of a liability).

The realization and earned criteria for recognizing revenue are usually satisfied when the product or merchandise being sold is delivered to the customer or when the service is provided. Thus revenue from selling and servicing activities is commonly recognized when the sale is made, which means when the product is delivered or when the service is provided to the customer. The typical entry would be as follows:

Dr.	Cash (or Accounts Receivable)............................	xx	
Cr.	Sales (or Service Revenue)		xx

The effect of this transaction on the financial statements is:

Balance sheet	Income statement
Assets = Liabilities + Owners' equity ←	Net income = Revenues − Expenses

+ Cash, or
    Accounts
    Receivable
	+ Sales, or
	    Service
	    Revenue

An example of a situation in which the *earned* criterion is more significant than the realization criterion is the magazine publishing company that receives cash at the beginning of a subscription period. In this case, revenue is recognized as earned by delivery of the magazine. On the other hand, if a product is delivered or a service is provided without any expectation of receiving cash or satisfying a liability (i.e., when a donation is made), there is no revenue to be recognized because the *realization* criterion has not been fulfilled.

When revenues are related to the use of assets over a period of time—such as the renting of property or the lending of money—they are earned as time passes and are recognized based on the contractual prices that had been established in advance.

Some agricultural products, precious metals, and marketable securities have readily determinable prices and can be sold without significant effort. Where this is the case, revenues (and some gains or losses) may be recognized when production is completed or when prices of the assets change. These are unusual situations, however, and exceptions to the rule that an arms-length exchange (i.e., sales transaction) must occur to meet the realization and earned criteria.

Due to the increasing complexity of many business activities and other newly developed transactions, a number of revenue recognition problems have arisen over the years. Therefore, the FASB and its predecessors within the American Institute of Certified Public Accountants have issued numerous pronouncements about revenue recognition issues for various industries and transactions. As a result, revenue recognition is straightforward an overwhelming proportion of the time. However, since they are the key to the entire income statement, revenues that are misstated (usually on the high side) can lead to significantly misleading financial statements.

Accordingly, management and internal auditors often design internal control procedures to help promote the accuracy of the revenue recognition process of the firm.

Sales is the term used to describe the revenues of firms that sell purchased or manufactured products. In the normal course of business, some sales transactions will be subsequently voided because the customer returns the merchandise for credit or for a refund. In some cases, rather than have a shipment returned (especially if it is only slightly damaged or defective, and is still usable by the customer), the seller will make an allowance on the amount billed and reduce the account receivable from the customer for the allowance amount. If the customer has already paid, a refund is made. These **sales returns and allowances** are accounted for separately for internal control and analysis purposes but are subtracted from the gross sales amount to arrive at **net sales**. In addition, if the firm allows cash discounts for prompt payment, total cash discounts are also subtracted from gross sales for reporting purposes. A fully detailed income statement prepared for use within the company might have the following revenue section captions:

Sales	$
Less: Sales returns and allowances	( )
Less: Cash discounts on sales	( )
Net sales	$

Net sales, or net revenues, is the first caption usually seen in the income statement of a merchandising or manufacturing company (as illustrated in Exhibit 9–1). Many companies provide a detailed calculation of the net sales amount in the accompanying notes or financial review section of the annual report.

Firms that generate significant amounts of revenue from providing services in addition to (or instead of) selling a product will label the revenue source appropriately in the income statement. Thus, a leasing company might report Rental and service revenues as the lead item on its income statement, or a consulting service firm might show Fee revenues, or simply Fees. If a firm has several types of revenue, the amount of each could be shown if each amount is significant and is judged by the accountant to increase the usefulness of the income statement.

From a legal perspective, the sale of a product involves the passing of title (i.e., ownership rights) in the product from the seller to the purchaser. The point at which title passes is usually specified by the shipment terms (see Business in Practice—Shipping Terms). This issue becomes especially significant in two situations. The first involves shipments made near the end of a fiscal period. The shipping terms will determine whether revenue is recognized in the period in which the shipment was made or in the subsequent period when the shipment is received by the customer. Achieving an accurate "sales cutoff" may be important to the accuracy of the financial statements if the period-end shipments are material in amount. The second situation relates to any loss or damage of the merchandise

BUSINESS IN PRACTICE
Shipping Terms

Many products are shipped from the seller to buyer instead of being picked up by the buyer at the time of sale. **Shipping terms** define the owner of products while they are in transit. **FOB destination** and **FOB shipping point** are the terms used. (FOB means *free on board* and is jargon that has carried over from the days when much merchandise was shipped by boat.) When an item is shipped FOB destination, the seller owns the product until it is accepted by the buyer at the buyer's designated location. Thus title to merchandise shipped FOB destination passes from seller to buyer when the merchandise is received by the buyer. FOB shipping point means that the buyer accepts ownership of the product at the seller's shipping location.

Shipping terms also describe which party to the transaction is to *incur* the shipping cost. The *seller* incurs the freight cost for shipments made FOB destination; the *buyer* incurs the cost of shipments made FOB shipping point. *Payment* of the freight cost is another issue, however. The freight cost for products shipped **freight prepaid** is paid by the seller: when a shipment arrives **freight collect**, the buyer pays the freight cost. Ordinarily, items shipped FOB destination will have freight prepaid, and items shipped FOB shipping point will be shipped freight collect. However, depending on freight company policies or other factors, an item having shipping terms of FOB destination may be shipped freight collect, or vice versa. If this happens, the firm paying the freight subsequently collects the amount paid to the freight company from the other firm, which *incurred* the freight cost under the shipping terms.

while it is in transit from the seller to the buyer. The legal owner of the merchandise, as determined by the shipping terms, is the one who suffers the loss. Of course, this party may then seek to recover the amount of the loss from the party responsible for the damage (usually a third-party shipping company).

For certain sales transactions, a firm may take more than a year to construct the item being sold (for example, a shipbuilder or a manufacturer of complex custom machinery). In these circumstances, delaying revenue recognition until the product has been delivered may result in the reporting of misleading income statement information for a number of years. Because these items are being manufactured under a contract with the buyer that specifies a price, it is possible to recognize revenue (and costs and profits) under what is known as the **percentage-of-completion method.** If, based on engineers' analyses and other factors, 40 percent of a job has been completed in the current year, 40 percent of the expected revenue (and 40 percent of the expected costs) will be recognized in the current year.

Companies should disclose any unusual revenue recognition methods, such as the percentage-of-completion method, in the notes or financial review accompanying the financial statements. Because profits will be directly affected by revenue, the user of the financial statements must be alert to, and understand the effect of, any revenue recognition method that differs from the usual and generally accepted practice of recognizing revenue when the product or service has been delivered to the customer.

Gains, which are increases in an entity's net assets resulting from incidental transactions or nonoperating activities, are usually not included with revenues at the beginning of the income statement. Gains are reported as other income after the firm's operating expenses have been shown and income from operations has been reported. Interest income is an example of an "other income" item. The reporting of gains will be explained in more detail later in this chapter.

Expenses

The FASB defines **expenses** as "outflows or other using up of assets or incurrences of liabilities (or a combination of both) from delivering or producing goods, rendering services, or carrying out other activities that constitute the entity's ongoing major or central operations."[2] Some expenses (cost of goods sold is an example) are recognized concurrently with the revenues to which they relate. This is another application of the **matching principle,** which has been previously described and emphasized. Some expenses (administrative salaries, for example) are recognized in the period in which they are incurred because the benefit of the expense is used up simultaneously or soon after incurrence. Other expenses (depreciation, for example) result from an allocation of the cost of an asset to the periods that are expected to benefit from its use. In each of these categories, expenses are recognized in accordance with the matching principle because they are incurred to support the revenue-generating process. The amount of an expense is measured by the cash or other asset used up to obtain the economic benefit it represents. When the outflow of cash related to the expense will not occur within a year, it is appropriate to recognize the present value of the future cash flow as the amount of the expense.

Most of the time, the identification of expenses to be recognized in the current period's income statement is straightforward. Cost of goods sold, compensation of employees, uncollectible accounts receivable, utilities consumed, and depreciation of long-lived assets are all examples. In other cases (research and development costs and advertising expense, for example), the impact of the expenditure on the revenues of future periods is not readily determinable. For these types of expenditures, there is no sound method of matching the expenditure with the revenues that may be earned over several periods. To avoid the necessity of making arbitrary allocations, all advertising and R&D expenditures are recorded as expenses in the period incurred. This approach is justified by the objectivity and conservatism concepts.

Other types of expense involve complex recognition and measurement issues: Income tax expense and pension expense are just two examples. Recall the discussion of these topics in Chapter 7 when the liabilities related to these expenses were discussed.

---

[2]Ibid., para. 80.

Losses, which are decreases in an entity's net assets resulting from incidental transactions or nonoperating activities, are not included with expenses. Losses are reported after income from operations, as discussed later in this chapter.

The discussion of expenses in this chapter follows the sequence in which expenses are presented in most income statements.

Cost of Goods Sold

Cost of goods sold is the most significant expense for many manufacturing and merchandising companies. Recall from your study of the accounting for inventories in Chapter 5 that the **inventory cost-flow assumption** (FIFO, LIFO, weighted-average) being used by the firm affects this expense. **Inventory shrinkage,** the term that describes inventory losses from obsolescence, errors, and theft, is usually included in cost of goods sold unless the amount involved is material. In that case, the inventory loss would be reported separately as a loss after operating income has been reported.

Objective 2
Understand how cost of goods sold is determined under both perpetual and periodic inventory systems.

Determination of the cost of goods sold amount is a function of the inventory cost-flow assumption and the inventory accounting system (periodic or perpetual) used to account for inventories. Recall that under a perpetual system, a record is made of every purchase and every sale, and a continuous record of the quantity and cost of each item is maintained. When an item is sold, its cost (as determined according to the cost-flow asusmption) is transferred from the inventory asset to the cost of goods sold expense with the following entry:

| Dr.   Cost of Goods Sold . . . . | xx | |
| Cr.   Inventory . . . . | | xx |

The effect of this entry on the financial statements is:

Balance sheet	Income statement
Assets = Liabilities + Owners' equity ←	Net income = Revenues − Expenses
− Inventory	− Cost of Goods Sold

The key point about a perpetual inventory system is that cost is determined when the item is sold. As you can imagine, a perpetual inventory system requires much data processing but can give management a great deal of information about which inventory items are selling well and which are not. Advances in point of sale technologies (such as standard bar code scanners used by retail stores) have allowed even small merchandising firms to achieve perpetual inventories. Some systems are even tied in with the firms' suppliers so that when inventory falls to a certain level, a reorder is automatically placed. Under any type of perpetual system, regular counts of specific inventory items will be made on a cycle basis during the year, and actual quantities on hand will be compared to the computer record of the quantity on hand. This is an internal control procedure designed to determine whether the perpetual system is operating accurately and to trigger an investigation of significant differences.

In a periodic inventory system, a count of the inventory on hand (taking a physical inventory) is made periodically—frequently at the end of a fiscal year—and the cost of inventory on hand (determined according to the cost-flow assumption) is determined. This cost is then subtracted from the sum of the cost of the beginning inventory (i.e., the ending inventory of the prior period) and the cost of the merchandise purchased during the current period. (For a manufacturing firm the cost of goods manufactured—discussed in Chapter 12—rather than purchases, is used.) This **cost of goods sold model** is illustrated below using 1996 data from the Intel Corporation financial statements in the Appendix. Can you find the inventory amounts in the Appendix? The amounts for net purchases and goods available for sale have been forced in the model. All amounts are in millions of dollars.

Cost of beginning inventory	$ 2,004
+ Net purchases	8,453
= Cost of goods available for sale	$10,457
− Cost of ending inventory	(1,293)
= Cost of goods sold	$ 9,164

The amounts shown for cost of goods sold, inventory, and net purchases include the price paid to the supplier, plus all ordinary and necessary costs related to the purchase transaction (such as freight and material handling charges). Cost is reduced by the amount of any cash discount allowed on the purchase. When the periodic inventory system is used, freight charges, purchases discounts, and **purchases returns and allowances** (the purchaser's side of the sales return and allowance transaction) are usually recorded in separate accounts, and each account balance is classified with purchases. Thus the net purchases amount is made up of the following:

Purchases	$
Add: Freight charges	
Less: Purchase discounts	( )
Less: Purchase returns and allowances	( )
Net purchases	$

Although the periodic system may require a less complicated record-keeping system than the perpetual system, the need to take a complete physical inventory to determine accurately the cost of goods sold is a disadvantage. Also, although it can be estimated or developed from special analysis, inventory shrinkage (losses from theft, errors, etc.) is not really known when the periodic system is used because these losses are included in the total cost of goods sold.

Note that selling and administrative expenses (discussed later in the Other Operating Expense section of this chapter) are *not* included as part of cost of goods sold!

Gross Profit or Gross Margin

The difference between sales revenue and cost of goods sold is **gross profit,** or **gross margin.** Using data from Exhibit 9–1, the income statement for Intel Corporation to this point is:

INTEL CORPORATION
Consolidated Statements of Income
(dollars in millions)

Three Years Ended December 28, 1996	*1996*	*1995*	*1994*
Net revenues	$20,847	$16,202	$11,521
Cost of sales	9,164	7,811	5,576
Gross profit	$11,683	$ 8,391	$ 5,945

Objective 3
Understand the significance of gross profit and how the gross profit ratio is calculated and used.

When the amount of gross profit is expressed as a percentage of the sales amount, the resulting **gross profit ratio** (or **gross margin ratio**) is an especially important statistic for managers of merchandising firms. The calculation of the gross profit ratio for Intel Corporation for 1996 is illustrated in Exhibit 9–2.

Because the gross profit ratio is a measure of the amount of each sales dollar that is available to cover operating expenses and profit, one of its principal uses by the manager is to estimate whether or not the firm is operating at a level of sales that will lead to profitability in the current period. The manager knows from past experience that if the firm is to be profitable, a certain gross profit ratio and level of sales must be achieved. Sales can be determined on a daily basis from cash register tapes or sales invoice records, and that amount can then be multiplied by the estimated gross profit ratio to determine the estimated gross profit amount. This amount can be related to estimated operating expenses to estimate the firm's income from operations. In many cases, just knowing the amount of sales is enough to be able to estimate whether or not the firm has reached profitability. This is especially true for firms that have virtually the same

EXHIBIT 9–2   Gross Profit Ratio

INTEL CORPORATION
Gross Profit Ratio—1996
(dollars in millions)

Net sales (or net revenues) $20,847
Cost of goods sold (or cost of sales) 9,164
Gross profit (or gross margin) $11,683

Gross profit ratio = Gross profit/Net sales

= $11,683/$20,847

= 56%

gross profit ratio for every item sold. However, if the gross profit ratio differs by class of merchandise, and it usually does, then the proportion of the sales of each class to total sales (the **sales mix**) must be considered when estimating total gross profit. For example, if Intel has a 60% gross profit ratio on microprocessors, chipsets, and motherboards, and a 40% gross profit ratio on networking and communications products, and the sales mix changes frequently, then the sales of both product categories must be considered to estimate total gross profit anticipated for any given month.

The gross profit ratio can be used to estimate cost of goods sold and ending inventory for periods in which a physical inventory has not been taken. As illustrated in Exhibit 9–3, this is the process used to estimate the amount of inventory lost in a fire, flood, or other natural disaster. Note that the key to the calculation is the estimated gross profit ratio. Many firms prepare quarterly (or monthly) income statements for internal reporting purposes and use this estimation technique to avoid the cost and business interruptions associated with an inventory count.

Another important use of the gross profit ratio is to set selling prices. If the manager knows the gross profit ratio required to achieve profitability at a given level of sales, the cost of the item can be divided by the complement of the gross profit ratio (or the cost of goods sold ratio) to determine the selling price. This is illustrated in Exhibit 9–4. Of course, competitive pressures, the manufacturer's recommended selling price, and other factors will also influence the price finally established, but the desired gross profit ratio and the item's cost are frequently the starting points in the pricing decision.

EXHIBIT 9–3   **Using the Gross Profit Ratio to Estimate Ending Inventory and Cost of Goods Sold**

Assumptions:
A firm expects to have a gross profit ratio of 30% for the current fiscal year. Beginning inventory is known because it is the amount of the physical inventory taken at the end of the prior fiscal year. Net sales and net purchases are known from the accounting records of the current fiscal period.

The model (with assumed known data entered):

Net sales	$100,000	100%
Cost of goods sold:		
Beginning inventory	$ 19,000	
Net purchases	63,000	
Cost of goods available for sale	$ 82,000	
Less: Ending inventory	?	
Cost of goods sold	$?	
Gross profit	$?	30%

Calculation of Estimated Ending Inventory:

Gross profit = 30% × $100,000 = $30,000

Cost of goods sold = $100,000 − $30,000 = $70,000

Ending inventory = $82,000 − $70,000 = $12,000

EXHIBIT 9–4   Using Desired Gross Profit Ratio to Set Selling Price

Assumption:
A retail store's cost for a particular carpet is $8 per square yard. What selling price per square yard should be established for this product if a 20% gross profit ratio is desired?

$$\text{Selling price} = \text{Cost of product}/(1 - \text{Desired gross profit ratio})$$

$$= \$8/(1 - 0.2)$$

$$= \$10$$

Proof:

Calculated selling price	$10 per square yard
Cost of product	8 per square yard
Gross profit	$ 2

$$\text{Gross profit ratio} = \text{Gross profit}/\text{Selling price}$$

$$= \$2/\$10$$

$$= 20\%$$

The gross profit ratio required to achieve profitability will vary among firms as a result of their operating strategies. For example, a discount store seeks a high sales volume and a low level of operating expenses, so a relatively low gross profit ratio is accepted. A boutique, on the other hand, has a relatively low sales volume and higher operating expenses and needs a relatively high gross profit ratio to achieve profitability.

Even though gross profit and the gross profit ratio are widely used internally by the managers of the firm, many companies (such as Intel) do not present gross profit as a separate item in their published income statements. However, cost of goods sold is usually shown as a separate item. Thus, the user of the income statement can make the calculation for comparative and other evaluation purposes.

Other Operating Expenses

Objective 4
Understand the principal categories and components of "other operating expenses" and how these items are reported on the income statement.

The principal categories of other **operating expenses** frequently reported on the income statement are:

Selling expenses.
General and administrative expenses.
Research and development expenses.

These categories can be combined in a variety of ways for financial reporting purposes. For instance, Intel uses two categories, "Research and development" and "Marketing, general and administrative" expenses.

The financial statement footnotes, or financial review, will sometimes provide detailed disclosure of the nature and amount of expense items that are combined with others in the income statement. However, management often reports certain operating expenses as separate items to highlight their significance. Common examples include repairs and maintenance, research and development, and advertising. Total depreciation and amortization expense is frequently reported as a separate item on the income statement (or disclosed in the explanatory notes) because these expenses do not result in the disbursement of cash. The total of depreciation and amortization expense also appears in the statement of cash flows, as will be illustrated later in this chapter.

Income from Operations

Objective 5
Understand what "income from operations" includes and why this income statement subtotal is significant to managers and financial analysts.

The difference between gross profit and operating expenses represents **income from operations** (or **operating income**), as shown in the following partial income statement from Exhibit 9–1:

INTEL CORPORATION
Consolidated Statements of Income
(dollars in millions)

Three Years Ended December 28, 1996	*1996*	*1995*	*1994*
Net revenues	$20,847	$16,202	$11,521
Cost of sales	9,164	7,811	5,576
Research and development	1,808	1,296	1,111
Market, general and administrative	2,322	1,843	1,447
Operating costs and expenses	13,294	10,950	8,134
Operating income	$ 7,553	$ 5,252	$ 3,387

Although only an intermediate subtotal on the income statement, income from operations is frequently interpreted as the most appropriate measure of management's ability to utilize the firm's operating assets. Income from operations *excludes* the effects of interest expense, interest income, gains and losses, income taxes, and other nonoperating transactions. Thus, many investors prefer to use income from operations data (rather than net income data) to make a "cleaner" assessment of the firm's profitability trend. As discussed in Chapter 3, income from operations is frequently used in the return on investment calculation, which relates operating income to average operating assets.

Although operating income is commonly used as a proxy for net income, investors must pay careful attention to the items that are included in the determination of this important subtotal. In recent years, for example, many firms have reported items such as "restructuring charges" and "asset impairment losses" as operating expenses because the corporate downsizing efforts that lead to such write-offs have been occurring more frequently. Yet, other firms report these items in the "other income and expenses" category, which is shown as a *nonoperating* item. Of course, it is also permissible (and quite common) to simply subtract total expenses from total revenues to arrive at net income without indicating a separate amount for income from operations.

Managers of those firms that do not report income from operations as a separate item believe that other income and expense items (i.e., gains and losses) should receive as much attention in the evaluation process as revenues and expenses from the firm's principal operations. After all, nonoperating items do exist and do affect overall profitability. There is no single best presentation for all firms; this is another area in which the accountant's judgment is used to select among equally acceptable financial reporting alternatives.

Other Income and Expenses

Other income and expenses are reported after income from operations. These nonoperating items include interest expense, interest income, gains, and losses.

Interest expense is the item of other income and expenses most frequently identified separately. Most financial statement users want to know the amount of this expense because it represents a contractual obligation that cannot be avoided. As discussed in Chapter 7, interest expense is associated with financial leverage. The more a firm borrows, the more interest expense it incurs, and the higher its financial leverage. Although this may lead to a greater ROE for stockholders, it also increases the riskiness of their investment.

Interest income earned from excess cash that has been temporarily invested is not ordinarily subtracted from interest expense. Interest income is reported as a separate item if it is material in amount relative to other nonoperating items. The full disclosure principle is applied to determine the extent of the details reported in this section of the income statement. Significant items that would facilitate the reader's understanding of net income or loss are separately identified, either in the statement itself or in the footnotes or financial review. Items that are not significant are combined in an "other" or "miscellaneous" category. Examples of nonoperating gains or losses are those resulting from litigation, the sale or disposal of depreciable assets (including plant closings), and inventory obsolescence losses.

Income before Income Taxes and Income Tax Expense

The income statement usually has a subtotal labeled **"Income before income taxes,"** followed by the caption "Income taxes" or "Provision for income taxes" and the amount of this expense. Some income statements do not use the "Income before income taxes" caption; income taxes are simply listed as another expense in these statements. There will almost always be a footnote or financial review disclosure of the details of the income tax expense calculation.

WHAT DOES IT MEAN?

2.   What does it mean to look at the trend of the major subtotals on an income statement?

Net Income and Earnings per Share

Net income (or net loss), sometimes called *the bottom line,* is the arithmetic sum of the revenues and gains minus the expenses and losses. Because net income increases retained earnings, which is a necessary prerequisite to dividends, stockholders and potential investors are especially interested in net income. Reinforce your understanding of information presented in the income statement by referring again to Exhibit 9–1, and by studying the structure of income statements in other annual reports you may have.

Objective 6
Understand the components of the earnings per share calculation and the reasons for some of the refinements made in that calculation.

To facilitate interpretation of net income (or loss), it is also reported on a per share of common stock basis. As a result of an FASB statement issued in 1997, the reporting of earnings per share (EPS) data changed for periods ending after December 15, 1997. Required to be reported are **basic earnings per share** and, if the firm has issued stock options or convertible securities (long-term debt or preferred stock that is convertible into common stock), **diluted earnings per share.** Basic EPS and diluted EPS (if appropriate) are presented for both income from continuing operations or income before extraordinary items (discussed later in this chapter) and for net income. Basic earnings per share is calculated by dividing net income by the average number of shares of common stock outstanding during the year. There are two principal complications in the calculation that should be understood. First, a weighted-average number of shares of common stock is used. This is sensible because if shares are issued early in the year, the proceeds from their sale have been used longer in the income-generating process than the proceeds from shares issued later in the year. The weighting basis usually used is the number of months each block of shares has been outstanding. The weighted-average calculation is illustrated in Exhibit 9–5.

The other complication in the EPS calculation arises when a firm has preferred stock outstanding. Remember that preferred stock is entitled to its dividend before dividends can be paid on common stock. Because of this prior claim to earnings, the amount of the preferred stock dividend requirement is subtracted from net income to arrive at the numerator in the calculation of earnings per share of common stock outstanding. Recall that dividends are not expenses, so the preferred stock dividend requirement is

---

EXHIBIT 9–5 **Weighted-Average Shares Outstanding Calculation**

Assumptions:

On September 1, 1998, the beginning of its fiscal year, Cruisers, Inc., had 200,000 shares of common stock outstanding.

On January 3, 1999, 40,000 additional shares were issued for cash.

On June 25, 1999, 15,000 shares of common stock were acquired as treasury stock (and are no longer outstanding).

Weighted-Average Calculation:

Period	Number of Months	Number of Shares Outstanding	Months × Shares
9/1–1/3	4	200,000	800,000
1/3–6/25	6	240,000	1,440,000
6/25–8/31	2	225,000	450,000
Totals	12		2,690,000

Weighted-average number of shares outstanding = 2,690,000/12

= 224,167

not shown as a deduction in the income statement. To illustrate the basic EPS calculation, assume that Cruisers, Inc., had net income of $1,527,000 for the year ended August 31, 1998, and had 80,000 shares of a 7%, $50 par value preferred stock outstanding during the year. Using the weighted-average number of shares of common stock outstanding from Exhibit 9–5, the earnings per share of common stock would be calculated as follows:

Net income	$1,527,000
Less preferred stock dividend requirement	
(7% × $50 par value × 80,000 shares outstanding)	280,000
Net income available for common stock	$1,247,000

$$\text{Basic earnings per share of common stock outstanding} = \frac{\text{Net income available for common stock}}{\text{Weighted-average number of shares of common stock outstanding}}$$

$$= \$1,247,000/224,167$$

$$= \$5.56$$

Because of their significance, earnings per share amounts are reported on the income statement just below the amount of net income. The presentation of Intel's earnings per share shown in Exhibit 9–1 does not reflect the new reporting requirements because that income statement was issued before the most recent FASB pronouncement on EPS became effective.

As stated above, in addition to the basic earnings per share, a firm may be required to report *diluted earnings per share.* If the firm has issued long-term debt or preferred stock that is convertible into common stock, it is possible that the conversion of the debt or preferred stock could result in a reduction of basic earnings per share of common stock outstanding. This can happen because the increase in net income available for common stock (if interest expense is reduced, or preferred dividends are not required) is proportionately less than the number of additional common shares issued in the conversion. If a firm has a stock option plan (see Chapter 10), the issuance of additional shares pursuant to the plan has the potential of reducing basic earnings per share. Other incentive and financing arrangements may also require issuance of additional shares, which may also have the effect of reducing basic earnings per share. The reduction in basic earnings per share of common stock is referred to as **dilution.** The effect of the potential dilution is reported on the income statement by showing diluted earnings per share of common stock as well as basic earnings per share.

The income statement presentation of net income and EPS is shown below. Data are from the previous Cruisers, Inc. illustrations, which have no discontinued operations or extraordinary items, with an assumed diluted earnings per share amount.

Net income	$1,527,000
Basic earnings per share of common stock	$ 5.56
Diluted earnings per share of common stock	$ 4.98

If there are any *unusual items* on the income statement (discussed later in this chapter), the per share amount of each item is disclosed, and EPS is the sum of EPS before the unusual items and the per share amounts of the unusual items. This is done for both basic and diluted EPS data.

WHAT DOES IT MEAN?

3. What does it mean when earnings per share are subject to dilution?

Income Statement Presentation Alternatives

Objective 7
Understand the alternative income statement presentation models.

There are two principal alternative presentations of income statement data: the **single-step format** and the **multiple-step format.** These are illustrated in Exhibit 9–6, using hypothetical data for Cruisers, Inc., for fiscal years 1998 and 1999. (Examples of the unusual items that may appear on the income statement will be discussed in the next section of this chapter and illustrated in Exhibit 9–7.)

You may notice an inconsistency in the use of parentheses in the single-step and multiple-step formats in Exhibit 9–6. No parentheses are used in the single-step format; the user is expected to know by reading the captions which items to add and which to subtract in the calculation of net

EXHIBIT 9–6   Income Statement Format Alternatives

I. Single-step format

CRUISERS, INC., AND SUBSIDIARIES
Consolidated Income Statement
For the Years Ended August 31, 1999, and 1998
(000 omitted)

	1999	1998
Net sales	$77,543	$62,531
Cost of goods sold	48,077	39,870
Selling expenses	13,957	10,590
General and administrative expenses	9,307	7,835
Interest expense	3,378	2,679
Other income (net)	385	193
Minority interest (explained later)	432	356
Income before taxes	$ 2,777	$ 1,394
Provision for income taxes	1,250	630
Net income	$ 1,527	$ 764
Basic earnings per share of common stock	$ 5.56	$ 2.42

EXHIBIT 9–6   *(concluded)*

II. Multiple-step format

CRUISERS, INC., AND SUBSIDIARIES
Consolidated Income Statement
For the Years Ended August 31, 1999, and 1998
(000 omitted)

	1999	1998
Net sales	$77,543	$62,531
Cost of goods sold	48,077	39,870
Gross profit	$29,466	$22,661
Selling, general, and administrative expenses	23,264	18,425
Income from operations	$ 6,202	$ 4,236
Other income (expense):		
Interest expense	(3,378)	(2,679)
Other income (net)	385	193
Minority interest	(432)	(356)
Income before taxes	$ 2,777	$ 1,394
Provision for income taxes	1,250	630
Net income	$ 1,527	$ 764
Basic earnings per share of common stock	$ 5.56	$ 2.42

The principal difference between these two formats is that the multiple-step format provides subtotals for gross profit and income from operations. As previously discussed, each of these amounts is useful in evaluating the performance of the firm, and proponents of the multiple-step format believe that it is appropriate to highlight these amounts.

income. In the multiple-step format the caption for "Other income (expense)" indicates that *in this section of the statement,* items without parentheses are added and items in parentheses are subtracted. In other parts of the statement the caption indicates the arithmetic operation. With either format, the statement reader must be alert to make sense of the information presented in the statement.

The recent trend has been for more companies to use the multiple-step income statement format. A survey of the annual reports for 1996 of 600 publicly owned industrial and merchandising companies indicated that only 185 companies continued to use the single-step format (as compared to 232 companies in the 1989 survey, and 314 in 1983).[3] This trend apparently reflects the increasing complexity of business activities and the demand for more detailed information.

Objective 8
Understand the meaning and significance of each of the unusual items that may appear on the income statement.

Unusual Items Sometimes Seen on an Income Statement

One of the ways that investors and potential investors use the income statement is to predict probable results of future operations from the results of

---

[3]AICPA, *Accounting Trends and Techniques* (New York, 1997, 1990, and 1984), Table 3–2.

EXHIBIT 9–7 **Income Statement Presentation of Unusual Items**
(continued from Exhibit 9–6)

Under either the single-step or multiple-step format (see Exhibit 9–6), the "Income before taxes" caption would be shown as "Income *from continuing operations* before taxes," and the rest of the income statement would appear as follows:

	1999	*1998*
. . . .		
Income from continuing operations before taxes	$2,777	$1,394
Provision for income taxes	1,250	630
Income from continuing operations	$1,527	$ 764
Discontinued operations, net of income taxes:		
Loss from operations	(162)	—
Loss on disposal	(79)	—
Loss from discontinued operations	$ (241)	—
Earnings before extraordinary item	$1,286	$ 764
Extraordinary item:		
Gain on termination of pension plan, net of income taxes	357	—
Net income	$1,643	$ 764
Basic earnings per share of common stock outstanding:		
Continuing operations	$ 5.56	$ 2.42
Discontinued operations:		
Loss from operations	(.72)	—
Loss on disposal	(.35)	—
Extraordinary item	1.59	—
Net income	$ 6.08	$ 2.42

Note: The cumulative effect of a change in accounting principle would appear after extraordinary items, and would be reported net of tax. EPS disclosure would also be required.

current operations. Nonrecurring transactions that have an effect on the predictive process are highlighted and reported separately from the results of recurring transactions. The reporting of unusual items also facilitates users' comparisons of net income for the current year with that of prior years. Two of the more frequently encountered unusual items relate to discontinued operations and extraordinary items. Other captions sometimes seen on an income statement relate to the cumulative effect of a change in the application of an accounting principle or to the earnings of subsidiaries. *When any of these items affect income tax expense, the amount disclosed in the income statement is the amount of the item net of the income tax effect.* Each of these unusual items is discussed in the following paragraphs.

Discontinued Operations
When a segment, or major portion of a business, is disposed of, it is appropriate to disclose separately the impact that the discontinued operation has had on the current operations of the firm. This separate disclosure is made to help users of the financial statements understand how future

income statements may differ because the firm will be operating without the disposed business segment. This is accomplished by reporting the income or loss, after income taxes, of the discontinued operation separately after a subtotal amount labeled **income from continuing operations.** (Income from continuing operations is the income after income taxes of continuing operations.) By reporting discontinued operations as a separate item, net of taxes, all of the effects of the discontinued business segment are excluded from the revenues, expenses, gains, and losses of continuing operations. This presentation is illustrated in Exhibit 9–7. Note that earnings per share data are also reported separately for discontinued operations. If Cruisers, Inc. had issued dilutive securities or stock options, diluted EPS data would also have been reported.

WHAT DOES IT MEAN?

4.   What does it mean when income or loss from discontinued operations is shown in the income statement?

Extraordinary Items

A transaction that is unusual in nature and occurs infrequently qualifies for reporting as an **extraordinary item** if the amount involved has a significant after-tax income statement effect. The reason for such separate reporting is to emphasize that the item is extraordinary and that the income statements for subsequent years are not likely to include this kind of item. Examples of extraordinary items are gains or losses from early repayment of long-term debt, pension plan terminations, some litigation settlements, and utilization of tax loss carryforwards (see Business in Practice—Tax Loss Carryovers).

BUSINESS IN PRACTICE
Tax Loss Carryovers

The Internal Revenue Code provides that a business that experiences an operating loss in any year can offset that loss against profits that have been earned in the past or that may be earned in the future. Accordingly, the firm can recover the income taxes that were paid in the past or escape taxation on the future profits. Generally speaking, losses can be carried back 3 years, and carried forward 15 years. To illustrate, assume the following pattern of operating income and losses for a firm that began business in 1995:

	1995	1996	1997	1998	1999
Operating income/(loss)	$50,000	$30,000	$(100,000)	$(40,000)	$70,000

The corporation would have paid taxes in 1995 and 1996 based on its income in those years. In 1997, no taxes would be payable because the firm operated at a loss. Under the **tax loss carryover** rules, $50,000 of the 1997 loss would be carried back to 1995, and $30,000 of the 1997 loss would be carried back to 1996, and the taxes previously paid in each of those years would be refunded to the corporation. The remaining $20,000 of "unused"

Business in Practice concluded

loss from 1997 would be carried forward, to be offset against profits of the next 15 years. No taxes would be payable in 1998 because of the loss in that year, but there would be no carryback of that loss because the 1997 carryback absorbed the 1995 and 1996 profits; the 1998 loss would be carried forward. In 1999, the $70,000 of profits would be reduced by the $20,000 loss carryforward from 1997 and the $40,000 loss carryforward from 1998, so only $10,000 of 1999 profits would be subject to tax.

In the income statement, it is desirable to relate income tax expense, or recovery of income taxes previously paid, to results from operations. Thus, for the firm in the example, income tax expense for 1995 and 1996 would be reported in the usual way, as illustrated below. In the 1997 income statement, the income tax refund from 1995 and 1996 would be shown as an income tax recovery, or negative tax expense. The potential income tax reduction in the future from the carryforward is not reflected in the financial statements because it will not be realized unless profits are earned in the future. The 1998 income statement will not show either expense or potential future reduction of income taxes. The 1999 income statement will reflect income tax expense based on pre-tax income of $70,000; then, the tax reduction because of the $60,000 of loss carryover would be reported as an extraordinary item in 1999.

The income tax expense (recovery) for each year would be reported as follows, assuming an income tax rate of 40%:

	1995	1996	1997	1998	1999
Operating income (loss) before taxes	$50,000	$30,000	$(100,000)	$(40,000)	$70,000
Income tax expense (recovery)	20,000	12,000	(32,000)	—	28,000
Net income (loss)	$30,000	$18,000	$ (68,000)	$(40,000)	
Earnings before extraordinary item					$42,000
Extraordinary item: Utilization of tax loss carryforward					24,000
Net income					$66,000

When an extraordinary item is reported, basic and diluted (if applicable) earnings per share of common stock outstanding are reported for income before the extraordinary item, for the extraordinary item, and for net income (after the extrordinary item). This presentation is also illustrated in Exhibit 9–7. For basic EPS, it is assumed that Cruisers, Inc. has no dilutive securities or stock options.

Minority Interest in Earnings of Subsidiaries

As explained in Chapter 7, the financial statements of a subsidiary are consolidated with those of the parent even though the parent owns less than 100% of the stock of the subsidiary. The consolidated income statement includes all of the revenues, expenses, gains, and losses of the subsidiary. However, only the parent company's equity in the subsidiary's earnings is included in consolidated net income. The minority share owners' equity in the subsidiary's earnings is reported in the consolidated income statement as a deduction from income after income taxes when this minority interest is significant. When the **minority interest in the earnings of the subsidiary** is not significant, this deduction is included with other income and expense.

Cumulative Effect of a Change in Accounting Principle

A change from one generally accepted principle or method to another (from straight-line to accelerated depreciation, for example) is permitted only if there has been a change promulgated by a standard-setting body (such as the FASB) or if the change can be justified by the entity based on its current economic circumstances. The cumulative effect of the change on the reported net income of prior years, net of any income tax effect, is reported in the income statement for the year of the change. This amount is reported at the bottom of the income statement, after income from continuing operations and any other unusual items. Income statements of prior years that are presented for comparative purposes are not revised to reflect the change; however, the effect that the change would have had on those years is disclosed in the explanatory notes to the financial statements (see Chapter 10). An exception to this procedure occurs for some changes mandated by the FASB, for which restatement of prior years' financial statements is required. In these cases, the cumulative effect of the change is reflected in the beginning retained earnings balance of the earliest year presented in the comparative financial statements.

Statement of Cash Flows

Content and Format of the Statement

Objective 9
Understand the purpose and general format of the statement of cash flows.

The **statement of cash flows** is a relatively new financial statement that illustrates the way accounting evolves to meet the requirements of users of financial statements. The importance of understanding the cash flows of an entity has been increasingly emphasized over the years. The accrual basis income statement is not designed to present cash flows from operations, and except for related revenues and expenses, it shows no information about cash flows from investing and financing activities.

In the early 1960s, some companies began presenting information about changes in balance sheet items. In 1963 the Accounting Principles Board of the AICPA recommended that this statement be called the *statement of source and application of funds*. The term *funds* usually meant working capital (i.e., current assets minus current liabilities), and this statement explained the change in working capital that had occurred between the dates of the balance sheets presented in the annual report. In 1971 the Accounting Principles Board made the statement mandatory and gave it the title "Statement of Changes in Financial Position." In 1987, the FASB issued a standard requiring the presentation of a statement of cash flows, which has replaced the statement of changes in financial position.

The primary purpose of the statement of cash flows is to provide relevant information about the cash receipts and cash payments of an enterprise during a period.[4] The statement shows why cash (including short-term investments that are essentially equivalent to cash) changed during the period by reporting net cash provided or used by operating activities, investing activities, and financing activities.

Cash Flows from Operating Activities

Objective 10
Understand the difference between the direct and indirect methods of presenting cash flows from operating activities.

There are two alternative approaches to presenting the operating activities section of the statement of cash flows: the *direct-method presentation* and the *indirect-method presentation*. The direct method involves listing each major class of cash receipts transactions and cash disbursements transactions for each of the three activity areas. The operating activity transactions include cash received from customers, cash paid to merchandise or raw material suppliers, cash paid to employees for salaries and wages, cash paid for other operating expenses, cash payments of interest, and cash payments for taxes. A direct-method statement of cash flows is illustrated in Section I of Exhibit 9–8. *Notice that under the direct method, each of the captions reported on the statement explains how much cash was received or paid during the year for that item.* For this reason, the FASB standard encourages enterprises to use the direct method.

The indirect method explains cash flows from operating activities by explaining the change in each of the noncash operating accounts in the balance sheet. A statement of cash flows prepared this way shows net income as the first source of operating cash. However, net income is determined on the accrual basis and must be adjusted for revenues and expenses that do not affect cash. The most significant noncash income statement item is usually total depreciation and amortization expense. Recall the journal entries to record these items:

Dr. Depreciation Expense.................................. xx	
Cr. Accumulated Depreciation	xx

and

Dr. Amortization Expense xx	
Cr. Intangible Asset...................................	xx

The effects of these transactions on the financial statements are:

Balance sheet	Income statement
Assets = Liabilities + Owners' equity ←	Net income = Revenues − Expenses
− Accumulated Depreciation	− Depreciation Expense

and

---

[4]FASB, *Statement of Financial Accounting Standards No. 95,* "Statement of Cash Flows" (Stamford, CT, 1987), para. 4. Copyright © by the Financial Accounting Standards Board, High Ridge Park, Stamford, CT 06905, U.S.A. Quoted with permission. Copies of the complete document are available from the FASB.

EXHIBIT 9–8 **Statement of Cash Flows**

I. Direct method

CRUISERS, INC., AND SUBSIDIARIES
Consolidated Statements of Cash Flows
For the Years Ended August 31, 1999, and 1998
(000 omitted)

	1999	1998
Cash Flows from Operating Activities:		
Cash received from customers	$14,929	$13,021
Cash paid to suppliers	6,784	8,218
Payments for compensation of employees	2,137	1,267
Other operating expenses paid	1,873	1,002
Interest paid	675	703
Taxes paid	1,037	532
Net cash provided by operating activities	$ 2,423	$ 1,299
Cash Flows from Investing Activities:		
Proceeds from sale of land	$ —	$ 200
Investment in plant and equipment	(1,622)	(1,437)
Net cash used for investing activities	$ (1,622)	$ (1,237)
Cash Flows from Financing Activities:		
Additional long-term borrowing	$ 350	$ 180
Payment of long-term debt	(268)	(53)
Purchase of treasury stock	(37)	(26)
Payment of dividends on common stock	(363)	(310)
Net cash used for financing activities	$ (318)	$ (209)
Increase (Decrease) in cash	$ 483	$ (147)
Cash balance, August 31, 1998, and 1997	276	423
Cash balance, August 31, 1999, and 1998	$ 759	$ 276
Reconciliation of Net Income and		
Net Cash Provided by Operating Activities:		
Net income	$ 1,390	$ 666
Add (Deduct) items not affecting cash:		
Depreciation expense	631	526
Minority interest	432	356
Gain on sale of land	—	(110)
Increase in accounts receivable	(30)	(44)
Increase in inventories	(21)	(168)
Increase in current liabilities	16	66
Other (net)	5	7
Net cash provided by operating activities	$ 2,423	$ 1,299

Balance sheet	Income statement
Assets = Liabilities + Owners' equity	← Net income = Revenues − Expenses

− Intangible   − Amortization
  Asset   Expense

EXHIBIT 9–8 *(concluded)*

II. Indirect method

CRUISERS, INC., AND SUBSIDIARIES
Consolidated Statements of Cash Flows
For the Years Ended August 31, 1999, and 1998
(000 omitted)

	1999	1998
Cash Flows from Operating Activities:		
Net income	$ 1,390	$ 666
Add (Deduct) items not affecting cash:		
Depreciation expense	631	526
Minority interest	432	356
Gain on sale of land	—	(110)
Increase in accounts receivable	(30)	(44)
Increase in inventories	(21)	(168)
Increase in current liabilities	16	66
Other (net)	5	7
Net cash provided by operating activities	$ 2,423	$ 1,299
Cash Flows from Investing Activities:		
Proceeds from sale of land	$ —	$ 200
Investment in plant and equipment	(1,622)	(1,437)
Net cash used for investing activities	$ (1,622)	$ (1,237)
Cash Flows from Financing Activities:		
Additional long-term borrowing	$ 350	$ 180
Payment of long-term debt	(268)	(53)
Purchase of treasury stock	(37)	(26)
Payment of dividends on common stock	(363)	(310)
Net cash used for financing activities	$ (318)	$ (209)
Increase (Decrease) in cash	$ 483	$ (147)
Cash balance, August 31, 1998, and 1997	276	423
Cash balance, August 31, 1999, and 1998	$ 759	$ 276

Because the depreciation and amortization expense amounts do not affect cash, these items are added back to net income to determine more accurately the amount of cash generated from operations. Other income statement items that need to be considered in a similar way are:

- Income tax expense not currently payable (i.e., deferred income taxes resulting from temporary differences in the recognition of revenues and expenses for book and tax purposes).
- Gains or losses on the sale or abandonment of assets. The *proceeds* from the sale, not the gain or loss, affect cash. Losses are added back to net income, and gains are subtracted from net income. The sale proceeds are reported as an investing activity, described below.
- Increases (or decreases) to interest expense that result from the amortization of discount (or premium) on bonds payable. Discount amortization is added back to net income, and premium amortization is subtracted from net income.

Changes in the noncash operating accounts must also be shown. Thus increases in current assets and decreases in current liabilities are reported as operating uses of cash. Conversely, decreases in current assets and increases in current liabilities are reported as operating sources of cash. An indirect-method statement of cash flows is illustrated in Section II of Exhibit 9–8.

Note that the difference between the two methods is in the presentation of cash flows from operating activities. When the direct-method format is used, a separate schedule reconciling net income reported on the income statement with net cash provided by operating activities is required. This reconciliation is in the form of the indirect-method presentation of net cash provided by operating activities. A survey of the 1996 annual reports of 600 publicly owned merchandising and manufacturing companies indicated that 589 firms used the indirect-method presentation, while only 11 companies used the direct-method presentation.[5] Business in Practice—Understanding Cash Flow Relationships—Indirect Method explains the cash flow relationships under the indirect method in more detail.

BUSINESS IN PRACTICE
Understanding Cash Flow Relationships— Indirect Method

As indicated by the AICPA study, most firms report the statement of cash flows using the indirect method. Most statements of changes in financial position prepared prior to 1988 also used the indirect method. The primary reason for this preference is that no separate accounting procedures are needed for companies to accumulate cash flows data when the indirect method is used. The statement of cash flows is normally prepared using balance sheet and income statement data, and other information readily available in the company's accounting records. However, the operating activities information reported under the direct method is not so readily determinable, and the cost of generating this information can be prohibitive.

The primary objective of the operating activities section of the statement of cash flows (indirect method) is to determine the net cash provided by operating activities. Although net income is determined on an accrual basis, it is ordinarily the most accurate proxy for operating cash flows and thus serves as the starting point in the calculation of this important amount. *Note, however, that none of the adjustments shown in the operating activities section (indirect method) explain how much cash was actually received or paid during the year!* The only operating activity items that convey independent meaning are the amounts shown for net income and net cash provided by operating activities. Review the operating activities section of Exhibit 9–8 for the indirect method. Notice, for example, that accounts receivable increased during both years presented. Does this explain how much cash was received from the collection of accounts receivable during these years? (No, but the direct method shows these amounts.) Once you understand this, the

---

[5]AICPA, *Accounting Trends and Techniques.* (New York, 1997), Table 5–3.

adjustment process for the indirect method can be thought of in a rather mechanical fashion.

Net income is initially assumed to generate operating cash, and this assumption is then adjusted for the effects of noncash (or nonoperating) income statement items. As already explained, the amounts shown for depreciation and amortization expense will be added back to net income each year because cash is never paid for these expenses. Similar adjustments would be made to remove the effects of noncash revenues or to remove the effects of most nonoperating transactions included in net income. Once these income statement adjustments are made, the current (i.e., *operating*) accounts on the balance sheet must be analyzed to determine their effects on cash during the year. To simplify the analysis, assume that all changes in account balances from the beginning to the end of the year are attributable to cash transactions. If inventory (a current asset) increased during the year, then cash must have decreased (to pay for the increase in inventory). The assumed transaction would be:

Dr.	Inventory...	xx	
	Cr. Cash		xx

Likewise, if short-term debt (a current liability) increased during the year, then cash must have increased (for the receipt of the loan proceeds), as follows:

Dr.	Cash	xx	
	Cr. Short-Term Debt		xx

The financial statement effects of these assumed transactions would be:

Balance sheet	Income statement
Assets = Liabilities + Owners' equity ←	Net income = Revenues − Expenses

Increase in the Inventory account balance:
+ Inventory
− Cash

Increase in the Short-Term Debt account balance:
+ Cash   + Short-Term
       Debt

In a similar way, decreases in current asset accounts are assumed to increase cash (for example, the collection of an accounts receivable), and decreases in current liability accounts are assumed to decrease cash (for example, the payment of an account payable). Of course, these are only assumptions, but by assuming that cash is involved on the opposite side of every transaction, you will understand the nature of each of the adjustments made within the operating activities section of the statement of cash flows.

Cash Flows from Investing and Financing Activities

Investing activities relate primarily to the purchase and sale of noncurrent assets. Cash is often used for the acquisition of assets such as land, buildings, or equipment during the year (these investments are sometimes called *capital additions*). Investments in debt or equity securities of other entities are also shown as investing uses. Likewise, cash received from the sale of noncurrent assets is shown as an investing source of cash.

Financing activities relate primarily to changes during the year in noncurrent liabilities (such as bonds payable) and in owners' equity accounts. Thus, the issuance of bonds or common stock will result in a financing source of cash, and the retirement of bonds will be reported as a financing use. Cash dividends and treasury stock transactions are also reported as financing activities because they affect owners' equity.

Interpreting the Statement of Cash Flows

Objective 11
Understand why the statement of cash flows is significant to financial analysts and investors.

The statement of cash flows focuses on cash receipts and cash payments during the period, so the first question to be answered is: "Did the company's cash balance increase or decrease during the year?" The answer is usually found near the bottom of the statement. In the annual report of a publicly owned corporation, comparative statements for the most recent and prior two years will be presented, and the change in each of the three years can be noted. If the change in the cash balance during a year has been significant (more than 10% of the beginning cash balance), the financial statement user will try to understand the reasons for the change by focusing on the relative totals of each of the three categories of cash flows—operating activities, investing activities, and financing activities. Even if the change in the cash balance during a year is not significant, the relationship between these broad categories will be observed.

A firm should have a positive cash flow provided by operating activities. If operating activities do not generate cash, the firm will have to seek outside funding to finance its day-to-day activities, as well as its investment requirements. Although negative cash flow from operating activities might apply to a firm just starting up, it would be a sign of possible financial weakness for a mature company.

Virtually all financially healthy firms have growth in revenues as a financial objective. This growth usually requires increasing capacity to manufacture or sell products, or provide services. Thus, a principal investing activity is the acquisition of plant and equipment. The total cash used for investing activities is compared to the total cash provided by operating activities. If cash provided by operating activities exceeds cash used for investing activities, the indication is that the firm is generating the cash it needs to finance its growth, and that is probably positive. If the cash used for investing activities exceeds the cash provided by operating activities, the difference will have to be provided by financing activities or come from the cash balance carried forward from the prior year. This is not necessarily negative because investment requirements in any one year may be unusually high. If, however, cash used for investing activities exceeds cash provided by operating activities year after year, and the difference is provided from financing activities, a question about the firm's ability to generate additional funds from financing activities must be raised.

Financing activities include the issue and repayment of debt, the sale of stock and purchase of treasury stock, and the payment of dividends on stock (although some companies report cash dividends separately in the reconciliation of beginning and ending cash). For most companies, it would be desirable to have the cash dividend covered by the excess of cash provided from operating activities over cash used for investing activities.

After the big picture of the entity's cash flows has been obtained, it may be necessary to look at the details of each category of cash flows for clues that will explain the overall change. For example, if cash flows provided by operating activities are less than cash used for investing activities or if operating cash flows are decreasing even though profits are increasing, it may be that accounts receivable and/or inventories are increasing at a higher rate than sales. This is a signal that the firm may have liquidity problems that would not necessarily be reflected by the change in working capital, the current ratio, or the acid-test ratio. These liquidity measures include other items besides cash, and the firm's inability to collect its accounts receivable and/or sell its inventory may artificially increase current assets and distort these relationships. Of course, other interpretations of this same trend might also be possible, but the trend itself might not have been observed without a careful analysis of cash flow data.

The details of an entity's investing activities frequently describe its growth strategy. Besides investing in more plant and equipment, some firms acquire capacity by purchasing other companies or by investing in the securities of other companies. Occasionally a firm will sell some of its plant and equipment, in which case cash is provided. The reasons for and consequences of such a sale of assets are of interest to the financial statement user.

To illustrate these interpretation techniques, refer to Intel's Consolidated Statements of Cash Flows on page 20 in the annual report in the Appendix. Note that a large add back is made to net income each year for depreciation since no out-of-pocket costs are incurred for this expense. Note also that the net cash provided by operating activities exceeded net income in all three years, even though accounts receivable increased each year due to the firm's sales growth. Net cash provided by operating activities also exceeded the cash used for investing activities in all three years— a relationship generally considered desirable. Intel invested considerable amounts in property, plant, and equipment each year, and its purchases of available-for-sale investments exceeded the total maturities and sales of these items in 1995 and 1996. In all three years, financing activities resulted in a net use of cash. The company's repurchase and retirement of common stock have been significant. In relative terms, debt transactions and dividend payments have been immaterial. Cash dividends were paid each year, but Intel's stockholders seem to prefer that most earnings be reinvested to enhance future growth. The overall picture for Intel is good; net cash provided by operating activities is covering all of the firm's investing and financing requirements and is creating a surplus of cash for new investment opportunities.

The statement of cash flows provides useful information for owners, managers, employees, suppliers, potential investors, and others interested in the economic activities of the entity. This statement provides information that is difficult, if not impossible, to obtain from the other three financial statements alone.

5. What does it mean when the statement of cash flows shows a negative amount of cash provided by operating activities?

6. What does it mean when cash used for investing activities is greater than cash generated from operating activities?

Summary

This chapter has described the income statement and the statement of cash flows. The income statement summarizes the results of the firm's profit-generating or loss-generating activities for a fiscal period. The statement of cash flows explains the change in the firm's cash from the beginning to the end of the fiscal period by summarizing the cash effects of the firm's operating, investing, and financing activities during the period.

Revenues are reported at the beginning of the income statement. Revenues result from the sale of a product or the provision of a service, not necessarily from the receipt of cash. The revenues of most manufacturing and merchandising firms are called *sales.* Net sales, which is gross sales minus sales returns and allowances and cash discounts, is usually the first caption of the income statement. Service entities will describe the source of their revenues (e.g., rental fees or consulting fees).

Expenses are subtracted from revenues in the income statement. A significant expense for many firms is cost of goods sold. The actual calculation of cost of goods sold is determined by the system used to account for inventories. With a perpetual inventory system, cost can be determined and recognized when a product is sold. With a periodic inventory system, cost of goods sold is calculated at the end of the fiscal period using beginning and ending inventory amounts, and the purchases (or cost of goods manufactured) amount. Sometimes cost of goods sold is reported separately and subtracted from net sales to arrive at gross profit or gross margin in what is called a multiple-step income statement presentation. Other firms will include cost of goods sold with operating expenses in a single-step income statement presentation.

Gross profit (or gross margin) is frequently expressed as a ratio. The gross profit ratio can be used to monitor profitability, set selling prices, and estimate ending inventory and cost of goods sold.

Selling, general, and administrative expenses are the costs of operating the firm. They are deducted from gross profit to arrive at operating income, an important measure of management performance.

Interest expense is usually shown as a separate item in the other income and expense category of the income statement. Other significant gains or losses will also be identified.

Income before income taxes is frequently reported as a subtotal before income tax expense is shown, because taxes are a function of all items reported to this point in the income statement.

Net income, or net earnings, is reported in total and on a per share of outstanding common stock basis. If there is potential dilution from convertible debt, convertible preferred stock, or stock options, diluted earnings per share will also be reported.

To facilitate users' comparisons of net income with that of prior years, and to provide a basis for future expectations, income or loss from discontinued operations and extraordinary items are reported separately in the income statement and on a per share basis.

The determination of cash flows from operating activities is essentially a conversion of the accrual accounting income statement to a cash basis income statement. The principal reasons net income doesn't affect cash directly are that not all accounts receivable from sales are collected in the fiscal period of the sale and not all of the expenses reported in the income statement result in the disbursement of cash in the fiscal period in which the expenses are incurred.

Investing activities include purchases of plant and equipment, investments in other companies, and possibly the sale of noncurrent assets.

Financing activities include issuance and redemption of bonds and stock, including treasury stock transactions, and cash dividends on stock.

The statement of cash flows shows the change in cash during the year and reports cash provided from or used by operating activities, investing activities, and financing activities.

There are two presentation formats for the statement of cash flows. The difference between the two is primarily in the presentation of cash flows from operating activities. Most entities use the indirect method.

Interpretation of the statement of cash flows involves observing the relationship between the three broad categories of cash flows (operating activities, investing activities, and financing activities) and the change in the cash balance for the year. It is desirable to have cash provided from operating activities that is equal to or greater than cash used for investing activities, although large investment requirements in any one year may cause a reduction in the beginning-of-the-year cash balance. Cash can also be raised from financing activities to offset large investment requirements. The detailed activities of each cash flow category will be reviewed to assess their effect on the overall cash position of the firm. The statement of cash flows provides important information that is not easily obtained from the other financial statements.

Refer to the income statement and statement of cash flows for Intel Corporation in the Appendix, and to these statements in other annual reports you may have, to observe content and presentation alternatives.

Key Terms and Concepts

basic earnings per share (p. 317)   Net income available to common stockholders divided by the weighted average number of shares of common stock outstanding during the period.

cost of goods sold (p. 310)   Cost of merchandise sold during the period; an expense deducted from net sales to arrive at gross profit.

cost of goods sold model (p. 311)   The formula for calculating cost of goods sold by adding beginning inventory and purchases and subtracting ending inventory.

diluted earnings per share (p. 317)   An amount less than basic earnings per share that assumes that additional shares of common stock have been issued pursuant to convertible debt, convertible preferred stock, and/or stock option plans.

dilution (p. 318)   The reduction in "earnings per share of common stock" that may occur if convertible securities are actually converted to common stock and/or if additional shares of common stock are issued pursuant to a stock option plan.

earned (p. 305)   A revenue recognition criterion that relates to completion of the revenue-generating activity.

expenses (p. 309)   Outflows or other using up of assets or incurrences of liabilities during a period from delivering or producing goods, rendering services, or carrying out other activities that constitute the entity's major operations.

extraordinary item (p. 322)   A gain or loss from a transaction that is both unusual in nature and occurs infrequently; it is reported separately in the income statement.

FOB destination (p. 308)   The shipping term that means that title passes from seller to buyer when the merchandise arrives at its destination.

FOB shipping point (p. 308)   The shipping term that means that title passes from seller to buyer when the merchandise leaves the seller's premises.

freight collect (p. 308)   A freight payment alternative meaning that freight is payable when the merchandise arrives at its destination.

freight prepaid (p. 308)   A freight payment alternative meaning that freight is paid by the shipper.

gains (p. 309)   Increases in net assets from incidental transactions and other events affecting an entity during a period except those that result from revenues or investments by owners.

gross margin (p. 312)   Another term for *gross profit.*

gross margin ratio (p. 312)   Another term for *gross profit ratio.*

gross profit (p. 312)   The difference between net sales and cost of goods sold. Sometimes called *gross margin.*

gross profit ratio (p. 312)   The ratio of gross profit to net sales. Sometimes called *gross margin ratio.*

income before income taxes (p. 316)   An income statement subtotal on which income tax expense is based.

income from continuing operations (p. 322)   An income statement subtotal that is presented before income or loss from discontinued operations.

income from operations (p. 315)   The difference between gross profit and operating expenses. Also called *operating income.*

inventory cost-flow assumption (p. 310)   The application of FIFO, LIFO, weighted-average, or specific identification procedures to determine the cost of goods sold.

inventory shrinkage (p. 310)   Inventory losses resulting from theft, deterioration, and record-keeping errors.

losses (p. 310)   Decreases in net assets from incidental transactions and other events affecting an entity during a period except those that result from expenses or distributions to owners.

matching principle (p. 309)   The concept that expenses incurred in generating revenues should be "matched" against revenues earned during some period of time, usually one year, in determining net income or loss for the period.

minority interest in earnings of subsidiary (p. 324)   An income statement item representing the minority stockholders' share of the earnings of a subsidiary that have been included in the consolidated income statement.

multiple-step format (p. 319)   An income statement format that includes subtotals for gross profit, operating income, and income before taxes.

net income (p. 316)   The excess of revenues and gains over expenses and losses for a fiscal period.

net sales (p. 307)   Gross sales, less sales discounts and sales returns and allowances.

operating expenses (p. 314)   Expenses, other than cost of goods sold, incurred in the day-to-day activities of the entity.

operating income (p. 315)   The difference between gross profit and operating expenses. Also referred to as *earnings from operations.*

other income and expenses (p. 316)   An income statement category that includes interest expense, interest income, and gain or loss items not related to the principal operating activities of the entity.

percentage-of-completion method (p. 308)   A method of recognizing revenue based on the completion percentage of a long-term construction project.

purchases returns and allowances (p. 311)   Reductions in purchases from products returned to the supplier or adjustments in the purchase cost.

realization (p. 305)   A revenue recognition criterion that relates to the receipt of cash or a claim to cash in exchange for the product or service.

revenues (p. 305)   Inflows of cash or increases in other assets, or settlement of liabilities, during a period from delivering or producing goods, rendering services, or performing other activities that constitute the entity's major operations.

sales (p. 307)   Revenues resulting from the sale of product.

sales mix (p. 313)   The proportion of total sales represented by various products or categories of products.

sales returns and allowances (p. 307)   Reductions in sales from product returns or adjustments in selling price.

shipping terms (p. 308)   The description of the point at which title passes from seller to buyer.

single-step format (p. 319)   An income statement format that excludes subtotals such as gross profit and operating income.

statement of cash flows (p. 324)   The financial statement that explains why cash changed during a fiscal period. Cash flows from operating, investing, and financing activities are shown in the statement.

tax loss carryover (p. 322)   A loss for tax purposes for the current year that can be carried back or forward to offset taxable income of other years.

WHAT DOES IT MEAN?
ANSWERS

1. It means that although net income is not the literal bottom line on the income statement, many financial statement users consider it the most important amount on the income statement.

2. It means that to have the "big picture" of the entity's results, one must look at more than the amounts opposite one or two captions. It is especially important to be aware of unusual items that may appear on the income statement.

3. It means that additional shares of common stock may be issued because of the existence of convertible bonds, convertible preferred stock, or stock options. Issuance of shares for these items could cause a reduction of earnings per share of common stock and a reduction in the market value of the common stock.

4. It means that future income statements will not be affected by the results of the discontinued operations and that by highlighting this item it should be possible for a financial statement user to make adjustments when anticipating future results for the firm.

5. It means that the firm has not generated cash from its operations—a situation that should not exist for long. In order to keep operating, the firm will need to have generated cash from investing or financing activities, and/or used cash on hand at the beginning of the reporting period.

6. It means that during the year, the firm may have made some significant investments financed by creditors or owners and/or used cash on hand at the beginning of the reporting period.

Exercises and Problems

LO 1   **9–1.   Calculate earned revenues.** Big Blue University has a fiscal year that ends on June 30. The 1999 summer session of the university runs from June 9 through July 28. Total tuition paid by students for the summer session amounted to $112,000.

Required:

a. How much revenue should be reflected in the fiscal year ended June 30, 1999? Explain your answer.

b. Would your answer to *a* be any different if the university had a tuition refund policy that stated that no tuition would be refunded after the end of the third week of summer session classes? Explain your answer.

LO 1   **9–2.   Calculate earned revenues.** Kirkland Theater sells season tickets for six events at a price of $42. In pricing the tickets, the planners assigned the leadoff event a value of $10 because the program was an expensive symphony orchestra. The last five events were priced equally; 1,200 season tickets were sold for the 1999 season.

Required:

a. Calculate the theater's earned revenue after the first three events have been presented.

b. About 95% of the season ticket holders attended the first event. Subsequent events were attended by about 80% of the season ticket holders. To what extent, if any, should the attendance data impact revenue recognition? Explain your answer.

LO 2   **9–3.**   **Effects of inventory error.** If the ending inventory of a firm is overstated by $50,000, by how much and in what direction (overstated or understated) will the firm's operating income be misstated? *(Hint: Use the cost of goods sold model, enter hypothetically "correct" data, and then reflect the ending inventory error and determine the effect on cost of goods sold.)*

LO 2   **9–4.**   **Effects of inventory error.** Assume that the ending inventory of a merchandising firm is overstated by $40,000.

Required:

a. By how much and in what direction (overstated or understated) will the firm's cost of goods sold be misstated?

b. If this error is not corrected, what effect will it have on the subsequent period's operating income?

c. If this error is not corrected, what effect will it have on the total operating income of the two periods (i.e., the period in which there is an error and the subsequent period) combined?

 Intel LO 2, 3   **9–5.**   **Calculate gross profit ratio and cost of goods sold.** Refer to the consolidated statements of income on page 18 of the Intel Corporation Annual Report in the Appendix.

a. Calculate the gross profit ratio for each of the past three years.

b. Assume that Intel's net revenues for the first four months of 1997 totaled $7.8 billion. Calculate an estimated cost of goods sold and gross profit for the four months.

LO 2, 3   **9–6.**   **Calculate gross profit, cost of goods sold, and selling price.** MBI, Inc., had sales of $37.9 million for fiscal 1999. The company's gross profit ratio for that year was 22.6%.

Required:

a. Calculate the gross profit and cost of goods sold for MBI, Inc., for fiscal 1999.

 b. Assume that a new product is developed, and that it will cost $485 to manufacture. Calculate the selling price that must be set for this new product if its gross profit ratio is to be the same as the average achieved for all products for fiscal 1999.

c. From management's viewpoint, what would you do with this information?

LO 5   **9–7.**   **Operating income versus net income.** If you were interested in evaluating the profitability of a company and could have only limited historical data, would you prefer to know operating income or net income for the past five years? Explain your answer.

Intel LO 5   **9–8.**   **Operating income versus net income.** Refer to the Ten-Year Financial Summary on page 33 of the Intel Corporation Annual Report in the Appendix.

Required:

 Compare the trend of the operating income data with the trend of net income data from 1992 through 1996. Which series of data is more meaningful? Explain your answer.

LO 5   **9–9.**   **Calculate operating income and net income.** The following information is available from the accounting records of Manahan Co. for the year ended December 31, 1999:

Net cash provided by financing activities	$112,000
Dividends paid	18,000
Extraordinary loss from flood, net of taxes of $35,000	105,000
Income tax expense	26,000
Other selling expenses	13,000
Net sales	644,000
Advertising expense	45,000
Accounts receivable	62,000
Cost of goods sold	368,000
General and administrative expenses	143,000

Required:

a. Calculate the operating income for Manahan Co. for the year ended December 31, 1999.

b. Calculate the company's net income for 1999.

LO 5   **9–10. Calculate operating income and net income.** The following information is available from the accounting records of Spenser Co. for the year ended December 31, 1999:

Selling, general, and administrative expenses	$ 51,000
Accounts payable	85,000
Extraordinary gain from early retirement of bonds, net of tax expense of $28,000	104,000
Research and development expenses	37,000
Loss from discontinued operations net of tax savings of $5,000	16,000
Provision for income taxes	74,000
Net sales	579,000
Interest expense	64,000
Net cash provided by operations	148,000
Cost of goods sold	272,000

Required:

a. Calculate the operating income for Spenser Co. for the year ended December 31, 1999.

b. Calculate the company's net income for 1999.

LO 3   **9–11. Use gross profit ratio to calculate inventory loss.** Franklin Co. has experienced gross profit ratios for 1998, 1997, and 1996 of 33%, 30%, and 31%, respectively. On April 3, 1999, the firm's plant and all of its inventory were destroyed by a tornado. Accounting records for 1999, which were available because they were stored in a protected vault, showed the following:

Sales from January 1 thru April 2	$142,680
January 1 inventory amount	63,590
Purchases of inventory from January 1 thru April 2	118,652

Required:

Calculate the amount of the insurance claim to be filed for the inventory destroyed in the tornado. *(Hint: Use the cost of goods sold model and a gross profit ratio that will result in the largest claim.)*

LO 3   **9–12.** **Use gross profit ratio to calculate inventory loss.** On April 8, 1999, a flood destroyed the warehouse of Stuco Distributing Co. From the waterlogged records of the company, management was able to determine that the firm's gross profit ratio had averaged 29% for the past several years and that the inventory at the beginning of the year was $17,350. It was also determined that during the year until the date of the flood, sales had totaled $32,700 and purchases totaled $21,860.

Required:

Calculate the amount of inventory loss from the flood.

LO 7   **9–13.** **Calculate basic EPS.** Ringemup, Inc., had net income of $473,400 for its fiscal year ended October 31, 1999. During the year the company had outstanding 38,000 shares of $4.50, $50 par value preferred stock, and 105,000 shares of common stock.

Required:

Calculate the basic earnings per share of common stock for fiscal 1999.

LO 7   **9–14.** **Calculate basic EPS, and explain the EPS effect of convertible preferred.** Thrifty Co. reported net income of $745,000 for its fiscal year ended January 31, 1999. At the beginning of that fiscal year, 240,000 shares of common stock were outstanding. On October 31, 1998, an additional 40,000 shares were issued. No other changes in common shares outstanding occurred during the year. During the year the company paid the annual dividend on the 30,000 shares of 5%, $40 par value preferred stock that were also outstanding the entire year.

Required:

a. Calculate basic earnings per share of common stock for the year ended December 31, 1999.

b. If Thrifty Co.'s preferred stock was convertible into common stock, what additional calculation would be required?

LO 10   **9–15.** **Accrual to cash flows.** For each of the items below, calculate the cash sources or cash uses that should be recognized on the statement of cash flows for Baldin Co. for the year ended December 31, 1999.

a. Sales on account (all are collectible) amounted to $760,000, and accounts receivable decreased by $24,000. How much cash was collected from customers?

b. Income tax expense for the year was $148,000, and income taxes payable decreased by $34,000. How much cash was paid for income taxes?

c. Cost of goods sold amounted to $408,000, accounts payable increased by $19,000, and inventories increased by $14,000. How much cash was paid to suppliers?

d. The net book value of buildings increased by $240,000. No buildings were sold, and depreciation expense for the year was $190,000. How much cash was paid to purchase buildings?

LO 10   **9–16.** **Cash flows to accrual.** For each of the items below, calculate the amount of revenue or expense that should be recognized on the income statement for Pilkey Co. for the year ended December 31, 1999.

a. Cash collected from customers during the year amounted to $812,000, and accounts receivable increased by $45,000. How much were sales on account for the year ended December 31, 1999?

    b. Cash payments for income taxes during the year were $210,000, and income taxes payable increased by $41,000. How much was income tax expense?

    c. Cash paid to suppliers during the year amounted to $678,000, accounts payable decreased by $32,000, and inventories decreased by $14,000. How much was cost of goods sold?

    d. The net book value of buildings increased by $150,000. No buildings were sold, and a new building costing $270,000 was purchased during the year. How much was depreciation expense?

LO 10   **9–17.**   **Cash flows from operations—indirect method.** The financial statements of Simon Co. include the following items (amounts in thousands):

	For the Year Ended December 31, 1999	
Income Statement		
Net income	$420	
Depreciation and amortization expense	320	

	At December 31	
	1999	*1998*
Balance Sheets		
Accounts receivable	$125	$170
Inventory	170	150
Accounts payable	80	90
Income taxes payable	50	15

Required:

    a. Calculate the net cash flow provided by operations for Simon Co. for the year ended December 31, 1999.

    b. Explain why net income is different from the net cash provided by operations.

LO 10   **9–18.**   **Prepare a statement of cash flows—indirect method.** The financial statements of Stein Co. included the following information for the year ended December 31, 1999 (amounts in millions):

Depreciation and amortization expense	$130
Cash dividends declared and paid	165
Purchase of equipment	410
Net income	192
Beginning cash balance	60
Common stock issued	74
Sale of building (at book value)	106
Accounts receivable increase	8
Ending cash balance	20
Inventory decrease	19
Accounts payable increase	22

Required:
Complete the following statement of cash flows, using the indirect method:

STEIN CO.
Statement of Cash Flows
For the Year Ended December 31, 1999

Cash Flows from Operating Activities:
Net income . . . . $ 192
Add (deduct) items not affecting cash:

_____ . . . .
_____ . . . .
_____ . . . .
_____ . . . .

Net cash provided (used) by operating activities . . . . $

Cash Flows from Investing Activities:

_____ . . . .
_____ . . . .

Net cash provided (used) by investing activities . . . . $

Cash Flows from Financing Activities:

_____ . . . .
_____ . . . .

Net cash provided (used) by financing activities . . . . $
Net increase (decrease) in cash for the year . . . . $
Cash balance, January 1, 1999   60
Cash balance, December 31, 1999 . . . . $ 20

LO 10   **9–19   Cash flows from operating, investing, and financing activities—direct method.** The following information is available from Reding Co.'s accounting records for the year ended December 31, 1999 (amounts in millions):

Cash dividends declared and paid	$ 340
Interest and taxes paid	90
Collections from customers	1,350
Payment of long-term debt	220
Purchase of land and buildings	170
Cash paid to suppliers and employees	810
Issuance of preferred stock	300
Proceeds from the sale of equipment	40

Required:
a. Calculate net cash provided (used) by operating activities for Reding Co. for the year ended December 31, 1999.
b. Calculate net cash provided (used) by investing activities.
c. Calculate net cash provided (used) by financing activities.
d. Calculate the net increase (decrease) in cash for the year.

LO 10   **9–20.   Cash flows from operating, investing, and financing activities—direct method.** The following information is available from Gray Co.'s accounting records for the year ended December 31, 1999 (amounts in millions):

Cash dividends declared and paid	$ 140
Retirement of bonds payable at maturity	80
Interest and taxes paid	60
Issuance of common stock	220
Proceeds from the sale of land	50
Collections from customers	1,270
Cash paid to suppliers and employees	*(a)*
Purchase of buildings and equipment	*(b)*

Required:

a. The net cash provided by operating activities for Gray Co. for the year ended December 31, 1999, is $490 million. Calculate the cash paid to suppliers and employees.

b. The increase in cash for the year was $100 million. Calculate the amount of cash used to purchase buildings and equipment. *(Hint: Set up a model of the statement of cash flows to determine the net cash provided (used) by investing activities, and then solve for the missing amount.)*

Intel LO 6, 7 **9–21.** **Income statement format and EPS disclosures.** Refer to the consolidated statements of income on page 18 of the Intel Corporation Annual Report in the Appendix and answer the following questions:

a. Does Intel use the single-step format or the multiple-step format? Which format do you prefer? Explain your answer.

b. Refer to the earnings per common and common equivalent share data on page 18 and the related note disclosures on page 23. Explain why this disclosure is appropriate.

Intel LO 11 **9–22.** **Statement of cash flows analysis.** Refer to the consolidated statements of cash flows on page 20 of the Intel Corporation Annual Report in the Appendix.

Required:

a. Identify the three most significant sources of cash from operating activities during 1996. How much of a cash source amount do these items represent?

b. What were the firm's investing activities during 1996, and how much cash did they use or generate?

c. Identify the two most significant financing activities during 1996. What was the net effect on cash of these items?

d. What was the amount of dividends paid during 1996?

LO 10, 11   **9–23.** **Statement of cash flows analysis.** Refer to the statement of cash flows in the annual report you have obtained either as a result of completing Exercise 1–1 or otherwise.

Required:

a. Which method, direct or indirect, is used in the statement?

b. List the principal sources and uses of cash for this firm.

c. Evaluate the change in cash. Has the firm generated most of its cash requirements from operations, or has it had to borrow extensively? Have its uses of cash been balanced between investment and dividends?

d. Has the cash balance been increasing or decreasing? What seem to be the implications of this pattern for dividends?

LO 3, 5, 7, 8   **9–24.** **Income statement analysis.** Refer to the income statement in the annual report you have obtained either as a result of completing Exercise 1–1 or otherwise.

Required:

a. Which method, single step or multiple step, is used in the statement?
b. Calculate the gross profit ratio for the years reported.
c. Is operating income increasing or decreasing for the years reported?
d. Does the company report any unusual items? If so, what are the effects of these items on net income and earnings per share?

LO 10, 11   **9–25.** **Complete balance sheet and prepare a statement of cash flows.** Presented below is a partially completed balance sheet for Hoeman, Inc., at December 31, 1999, together with comparative data for the year ended December 31, 1998. From the statement of cash flows for the year ended December 31, 1999, you determine that:

> Net income for the year ended December 31, 1999, was $94,000.
>
> Dividends paid during the year ended December 31, 1999, were $67,000.
>
> Accounts receivable decreased $10,000 during the year ended December 31, 1999.
>
> The cost of new buildings acquired during 1999 was $125,000.
>
> No buildings were disposed of during 1999.
>
> The land account was not affected by any transactions during the year, but the fair market value of the land at December 31, 1999, was $178,000.

HOEMAN, INC.
Comparative Balance Sheets
At December 31, 1999, and 1998

	1999	1998
Assets		
Current assets:		
Cash	$ 52,000	$ 46,000
Accounts receivable		134,000
Inventory	156,000	176,000
Total current assets	$	$ 356,000
Land	$	140,000
Buildings		290,000
Less: Accumulated depreciation	(120,000)	(105,000)
Total land and buildings	$	325,000
Total assets	$	$ 681,000
Liabilities		
Current liabilities:		
Note payable	$ 155,000	$ 124,000
Accounts payable		197,000
Total current liabilities	$ 322,000	$ 321,000
Long-term debt	$	$ 139,000
Owners' Equity		
Common stock	$ 50,000	$ 45,000
Retained earnings		176,000
Total owners' equity	$	$ 221,000
Total liabilities and owners' equity	$	$ 681,000

Required:

a. Complete the December 31, 1999, balance sheet. *(Hint: Long-term debt is the last number to compute to make the balance sheet balance.)*

b. Prepare a statement of cash flows for the year ended December 31, 1999, using the indirect method.

LO 10, 11   **9–26.   Complete balance sheet and prepare a statement of changes in retained earnings.** Presented below is a statement of cash flows for Hartford, Inc., for the year ended December 31, 1999. Also shown is a partially completed comparative balance sheet as of December 31, 1999, and 1998.

HARTFORD, INC.
Statement of Cash Flows
For the Year Ended December 31, 1999

Cash Flows from Operating Activities:

Net income	$ 9,000
Add (deduct) items not affecting cash:	
Depreciation expense	45,000
Decrease in accounts receivable	23,000
Increase in inventory	(7,000)
Increase in short-term debt	5,000
Increase in notes payable	12,000
Decrease in accounts payable	(6,000)
Net cash provided by operating activities	$ 81,000

Cash Flows from Investing Activities:

Purchase of equipment	$(50,000)
Purchase of buildings	(48,000)
Net cash used by investing activities	$(98,000)

Cash Flows from Financing Activities:

Cash used for retirement of long-term debt	$(25,000)
Proceeds from issuance of common stock	10,000
Payment of cash dividends on common stock	(3,000)
Net cash used by financing activities	$(18,000)
Net decrease in cash for the year	$(35,000)

HARTFORD, INC.
Comparative Balance Sheets
At December 31, 1999, and 1998

	1999	1998
Assets		
Current assets:		
Cash	$	$ 88,000
Accounts receivable		73,000
Inventory	56,000	
Total current assets	$	$
Land	$	$ 40,000
Buildings and equipment	260,000	
Less: Accumulated depreciation		(123,000)
Total land, buildings, and equipment	$	$
Total assets	$	$

	1999	1998
Liabilities		
Current liabilities:		
Short-term debt	$ 32,000	$
Notes payable		36,000
Accounts payable		29,000
Total current liabilities	$	$
Long-term debt	$ 85,000	$
Owners' Equity		
Common stock	$ 40,000	$
Retained earnings		
Total owners' equity	$	$
Total liabilities and owners' equity ..	$	$

Required:

a. Complete the December 31, 1999, and 1998, balance sheets.
b. Prepare a statement of changes in retained earnings for the year ended December 31, 1999.

LO 10, 11 **9–27.** **Prepare balance sheet and retained earnings statement using statement of cash flows data.** Presented below is a statement of cash flows for Harris, Inc., for the year ended December 31, 1999, and the firm's balance sheet at December 31, 1998.

HARRIS, INC.
Statement of Cash Flows
For the Year Ended December 31, 1999

Cash Flows from Operating Activities:	
Net income	$ 13,000
Add (deduct) items not affecting cash:	
Depreciation expense	29,000
Increase in accounts receivable	(6,000)
Decrease in merchandise inventory	30,000
Decrease in short-term debt	(4,000)
Decrease in notes payable	(9,000)
Increase in accounts payable	3,000
Net cash provided by operating activities	$ 56,000
Cash Flows from Investing Activities:	
Purchase of buildings	(90,000)
Proceeds from sale of land at its cost	7,000
Net cash used by investing activities	$(83,000)
Cash Flows from Financing Activities:	
Proceeds from issuance of long-term debt	15,000
Proceeds from issuance of common stock	8,000
Payment of cash dividends on common stock	(5,000)
Net cash used by financing activities	$ 18,000
Net decrease in cash for the year	$ (9,000)

HARRIS, INC.
Balance Sheet
December 31, 1998

Assets

Cash	$ 15,000
Accounts receivable	61,000
Merchandise inventory	76,000
Total current assets	$152,000
Land	34,000
Buildings	118,000
Less: Accumulated depreciation	(72,000)
Total land and buildings	80,000
Total assets	$232,000

Liabilities

Short-term debt	$ 16,000
Notes payable	33,000
Accounts payable	58,000
Total current liabilities	$107,000
Long-term debt	50,000

Owners' Equity

Common stock, no par	$ 20,000
Retained earnings	55,000
Total owners' equity	$ 75,000
Total liabilities and owners' equity	$232,000

Required:

a. Using the above information, prepare the balance sheet for Harris, Inc., at December 31, 1999.

b. Prepare a statement of changes in retained earnings for the year ended December 31, 1999.

LO 10, 11   **9–28.**   **Prepare statement of cash flows using balance sheet data.** Presented below are comparative balance sheets for Millco, Inc., at January 31 and February 28, 1999.

MILLCO, INC.
Balance Sheets
January 31 and February 28, 1999

	February 28	January 31
Assets		
Cash	$ 42,000	$ 37,000
Accounts receivable	64,000	53,000
Merchandise inventory	81,000	94,000
Total current assets	$187,000	$184,000
Plant and equipment:		
Production equipment	166,000	152,000
Less: Accumulated depreciation	(24,000)	(21,000)
Total assets	$329,000	$315,000

	February 28	January 31
Liabilities		
Short-term debt	$ 44,000	$ 44,000
Accounts payable	37,000	41,000
Other accrued liabilities	21,000	24,000
Total current liabilities	$102,000	$109,000
Long-term debt	33,000	46,000
Total liabilities	$135,000	$155,000
Owners' Equity		
Common stock, no par value, 40,000 shares authorized, 30,000 and 28,000 shares issued, respectively	$104,000	$ 96,000
Retained earnings:		
Beginning balance	$ 64,000	$ 43,000
Net income for month	36,000	29,000
Dividends	(10,000)	(8,000)
Ending balance	$ 90,000	$ 64,000
Total owners' equity	$194,000	$160,000
Total liabilities and owners' equity	$329,000	$315,000

Required:

Prepare a statement of cash flows that explains the change that occurred in cash during the month. You may assume that the change in each balance sheet amount is due to a single event (e.g., the change in the amount of production equipment is *not* the result of both a purchase and sale of equipment). *(Hints: What is the purpose of the statement of cash flows? How is this purpose accomplished?)*

Use the space to the right of the January 31 data to enter the difference between the February 28 and January 31 amount of each balance sheet item; these are the amounts that will be in your solution.

Explanatory Notes and Other Financial Information

Objective 1
Understand that the explanatory notes are an integral part of the financial statements.

Because of the complexities related to financial reporting and because of the number of alternative generally accepted accounting principles that can be used, **explanatory notes to the financial statements** are included as an integral part of the financial statements. As explained in Chapter 2, the full disclosure concept means that companies are required to report all necessary information to prevent a reasonably astute user of the financial statements from being misled. The explanatory notes, or **financial review**, are referred to on each individual financial statement and are presented immediately following the financial statements. In the Intel Corporation annual report in the Appendix, the notes to the consolidated financial statements are on pages 22 through 31.

At first glance, the notes to the financial statements can appear quite intimidating because they frequently require more pages than the financial statements themselves, contain a great deal of detailed information, and include much financial management terminology. However, the reader cannot fully understand the financial statements without referring to the notes.

Financial statements of companies whose securities are publicly traded must be audited by independent auditors, and the annual report of such a company must include disclosures required by the Securities and Exchange Commission. An understanding of the auditors' report and a review of the other disclosures lead to a more complete picture of a company's financial condition, results of operations, and cash flows.

The principal objective of this chapter is to permit you to make sense of the explanatory notes and other financial information found in most corporate annual reports.

Learning Objectives

After studying this chapter you should understand:

1 That the explanatory notes are an integral part of the financial statements; the notes provide detailed disclosure of information needed

by users wishing to gain a full understanding of the financial statements.

2 The kinds of significant accounting policies that are explained in the notes.

3 The nature and content of disclosures relating to:
   Accounting changes.
   Business combinations.
   Contingencies and commitments.
   Events subsequent to the balance sheet date.
   Impact of inflation.
   Segment information.

4 The role of the Securities and Exchange Commission, and some of its reporting requirements.

5 Why a statement of management's responsibility is included with the notes.

6 The significance of management's discussion and analysis of the firm's financial condition and results of operations.

7 What is included in the five-year (or longer) summary of financial information.

8 The meaning and content of the independent auditors' report.

General Organization

The explanatory notes that refer to specific financial statement items are generally presented in the same sequence as the financial statements and in the same sequence that items appear within the individual statements. The financial statement sequence is usually:

1. Income statement.
2. Balance sheet.
3. Statement of cash flows.

Placement of the statement of changes in owners' equity usually depends on the complexity of that statement. If paid-in capital has not changed during the year, a statement of changes in retained earnings may be presented following the income statement and may even be combined with it because net income is the principal item affecting retained earnings. If there have been several capital stock transactions during the year, a full statement of changes in owners' equity, which includes changes in retained earnings, would be presented separately following the balance sheet. Some companies present the statement of changes in owners' equity as part of the notes or financial review.

In addition to the notes or financial review, many annual reports include a narrative section called **management's discussion and analysis**. This is a description of the firm's activities for the year, including comments about its financial condition and results of operations. Also included in most annual reports is a comparative summary of key financial data for several years. Both of these components can be quite helpful to users of the annual report.

1. What does it mean when a note at the bottom of the financial statements states: "The accompanying notes are an integral part of these statements"?

Explanatory Notes (or Financial Review)

Significant Accounting Policies

Objective 2
Understand the kinds of significant accounting policies that are explained in the notes.

As emphasized in earlier chapters, management must make a number of choices among alternative accounting practices that are generally acceptable. Because these choices differ among firms, disclosure of the specific practices being followed by any given firm is necessary for readers to make sense of that firm's financial statements. Users also need information about **significant accounting policies** in order to make intelligent comparisons of the financial position and results of operations of different firms in the same industry. The following discussion highlights the importance of many of these accounting policy disclosures. The comments in italics refer to the 1996 Annual Report of Intel Corporation in the Appendix.

Depreciation method—The method (straight-line, units-of-production, sum-of-the-years'-digits, or declining-balance) being used for financial reporting purposes and the range of useful lives assumed for broad categories of asset types are usually disclosed. The amount of depreciation expense may also be disclosed in the notes, although it is also reported in the statement of cash flows as an add back to net income. *Intel generally uses straight-line depreciation for financial reporting purposes (see p. 22 in Appendix). How much depreciation and amortization expense did Intel report for 1996? (This amount is reported in the statement of cash flows on p. 20.)*

Inventory valuation method—The method (weighted-average, FIFO, or LIFO) being used is disclosed. If different methods are being used for different categories of inventory, the method used for each category is disclosed. When LIFO is used, a comparison of the cumulative difference in the balance sheet inventory valuation under LIFO, with what it would have been under FIFO, is usually disclosed. *Intel's inventories are presented on a FIFO basis (see p. 22); its work in process inventory at December 28, 1996, exceeded the combined amount invested in raw materials, purchased parts, and finished goods.*

Basis of consolidation—A brief statement confirms the fact that the consolidated financial statements include the financial data of all subsidiaries—or if not, why not.

Income taxes—A reconciliation of the statutory income tax rate (presently about 35%) with the effective tax rate (indicated by the firm's income tax expense as a percentage of pre-tax income) is provided. Reasons for this difference include tax credits (e.g., for investment in new plant and equipment) and other special treatment given certain items for income tax purposes. This disclosure is especially pertinent for firms having a substantial business presence in a foreign country. In Japan, for example, the normal corporate income tax rate is 52%. Because of the tax loss carryover rules (see Business in Practice—Tax Loss Carryovers in Chapter 9), the effective tax rate can differ from the statutory rate for a firm that has reported a net loss in a recent year. Intel reports its effective tax rate for each of the past three years (see p. 26). You can verify these calculations by dividing the "Provision for taxes" reported on the income statement by the "Income before taxes." Try this with the income statement data reported on page 18.

An explanation is also made of the deferred taxes resulting from differences between the fiscal year in which an expense (or revenue) is reported for book purposes and the fiscal year in which it is reported for tax purposes. As already discussed, the principal factor in deferred taxes is the use of straight-line depreciation for book purposes and accelerated depreciation for tax purposes. However, many firms also report significant deferred tax amounts for a variety of other items (as discussed in Chapter 7). *Intel reports a detailed table of deferred income tax assets and liabilities for the past two years (see p. 26). Notice that the deferred tax assets partially offset the deferred tax liabilities related to depreciation methods (and other liability items).*

Employee benefits—The cost of employee benefit plans included as an expense in the income statement will be disclosed. The significant actuarial assumptions made with respect to funding pension plans may be discussed, and certain estimated future pension liabilities may be disclosed. The key to understanding the funded status of a defined-benefit pension plan is to compare the *projected benefit obligation* (i.e., the present value of expected future payments to retirees) to the *fair market value of plan assets* that are currently held in the pension fund. With some adjustments, the difference between these two amounts represents the **prepaid pension cost** (an asset, if overfunded) or the **accrued pension cost** (a liability, if underfunded). *Intel reports the funded status of its U.S. and foreign plans in separate schedules on page 29 in the Appendix. Which plan is overfunded? Which is underfunded?*

An additional schedule is provided to show the components of **net pension expense** for each of the past three years, if this amount is material. Several elements of pension expense will be reported, including the current service cost, prior service cost, interest cost of the projected benefit obligation, and the actual return on plan assets. The latter item is treated as a reduction of pension expense because future funding requirements will decrease as income is earned on invested assets. Current and prior service costs represent the actuarially determined cost to provide future pension benefits based on employees' earnings and service in the current and prior years, respectively. Although the accounting for pension plans is complex, these key items are easy to identify in the schedules provided by most firms. *Intel provides a "Net pension expense" schedule for its foreign defined-benefit plans (see p. 29) but does not disclose these details for its U.S. plans because the amounts involved are immaterial.*

Amortization of intangible assets—If the balance sheet includes the intangible asset goodwill, the method of amortizing this intangible asset and the amount of amortization expense recorded in the current year will be disclosed. The maximum amortization period allowed by generally accepted accounting principles is 40 years, but many firms use a shorter period. As discussed in Chapter 6, accounting for goodwill is a sticky problem for accountants.

Earnings per share of common stock—An explanation of the calculation will be provided, perhaps including the details of the calculation of the weighted-average number of shares outstanding and the adjustments to net income for preferred stock dividends. The potential dilution of the earnings per share (EPS) figure resulting from convertible bonds or convertible preferred stock if conversions had taken place during the year, and the potential dilution from stock option plans will also be explained. *Intel describes its EPS calculation process in a brief footnote on page 23.*

Stock option and stock purchase plans—Many firms have a **stock option plan** under which officers and key employees are given an option to buy a certain number of shares of stock *at some time in the future,* but at a price equal to the market value of the stock when the option is granted. The stock option presumably provides an incentive to increase the profitability of the firm so that the stock price will rise. Then, when the option is exercised, the owner has an immediate profit that is in effect additional compensation for a job well done. *Intel reports that 84.4 million option shares were outstanding at the end of 1996. The $29.96 average exercise price of the outstanding option shares (see table on page 27) was substantially less than the market value per share of common stock, which ranged from $95.44 to $137.50 during the fourth quarter of 1996 (reported in the Ten-Year Financial Summary on p. 33).*

Under a *stock purchase plan* the employees can purchase shares of the company's common stock at a slight discount from market value. The objective is to permit the employees to become part owners of the firm and thus to have more of an owner's attitude about their jobs and the company. *Intel has an employee stock participation plan, in which "eligible employees may purchase shares of Intel's Common stock at 85% of fair market value at specific predetermined dates" (see p. 28).*

From the employees' point of view, stock option and stock purchase plans are usually good fringe benefits. From the investors' point of view, the shares that are issuable under these plans represent potential dilution of equity. Thus the nature of these plans is described, and the potential dilution is disclosed.

Details of Other Financial Statement Amounts

Many firms will include in the explanatory notes the details of amounts that are reported as a single item in the financial statements. For example, details may be provided for: the amount of research and development expenses included in a broader operating expense category on the income statement, the details of the "other income" category of the income statement, or details of the cost and accumulated depreciation of plant and equipment that are reported in total on the balance sheet. Long-term debt, frequently reported as a single amount on the balance sheet, is usually made up of several obligations. A descriptive listing of the obligations, including a schedule of the principal payments required for each of the next five years, is usually reported. The extent of such detail to be reported is decided by the financial officers of the firm and is generally based on their judgment of the benefit of such detail to the broad user audience that will receive the financial statements. In some cases disclosure requirements of the Securities and Exchange Commission and the desire to conform the stockholders' report with the report required to be filed with the SEC (see Business in Practice—Reporting to the Securities and Exchange Commission) result in these details.

BUSINESS IN PRACTICE
Reporting to the Securities and Exchange Commission

Objective 4
Understand the role of the SEC and some of its reporting requirements.

The Securities and Exchange Commission (SEC) was created by the Securities and Exchange Act of 1934 to administer the provisions of that act and the Securities Act of 1933. Subsequently, Congress assigned to the SEC the authority and responsibility for administering other securities laws. Securities issued by corporations (principally stocks and bonds) that are offered for sale to more than a very few investors must be registered with the SEC. The basic objective of this registration is to provide to potential investors a full and fair disclosure of the securities being issued, the issuer's business activities and financial position, and an explanation of the use to be made of the proceeds of the security issue. Registration does not result in a "seal of approval" or a guarantee against loss. It is up to investors to decide whether or not their objectives are likely to be achieved. Registration is required for additional issues of previously unregistered securities (for example, if the corporation wants to raise capital by selling additional shares of stock) and for issues of newly created securities (for example, bonds that will be offered to the public). A **prospectus** summarizing the complete registration statement must be provided to investors prior to or concurrently with their purchase of the security. A prospectus is provided by the company or the broker through whom the securities are being sold.

Registered securities can be traded publicly on a stock exchange or in the over-the-counter market. Firms that issue these securities are required to file an annual report with the SEC. This report is referred to as *Form 10-K*. The requirements of Form 10-K have had a significant impact on the scope of material included in the annual report to stockholders. Most companies include in their annual report to stockholders all of the financial statement information required in the Form 10-K.

Form 10-K requires some information not usually found in the financial statements, including data about executive compensation and ownership of

> *Business in Practice concluded*
>
> voting stock by directors and officers. This information is also included in the *proxy statement* sent to stockholders along with the notice of the *annual meeting* and a description of the items expected to be acted upon by the stockholders at that meeting. Stockholders who do not expect to attend the annual meeting are invited to return a **proxy**. Although the proxy gives another person (usually a director of the corporation) the right to vote the stockholder's shares, the owner can indicate her/his preference for how the shares are to be voted on the indicated issues.
>
> The registration statement, prospectus, Form 10-K, and proxy statement are public documents, and copies can be obtained from the corporation, or from the SEC. Try the web site of the corporation in which you are interested, or access the Electronic Data Gathering, Analysis and Retrieval (EDGAR) system on the SEC's web site at http://www.sec.gov/edgarhp.htm

Other Disclosures

Accounting Change

Objective 3
Understand the nature and content of various note disclosures.

An **accounting change** is a change in an accounting principle that has a material effect on the comparability of the current period financial statements with those of prior periods. The effects of recently adopted accounting changes must be disclosed. For example, if a firm changes its inventory cost-flow assumption from FIFO to LIFO, this fact and the dollar effect of the change on both the income statement and balance sheet must be disclosed. Likewise, a change in depreciation methods, a change in the method of accounting for pension costs, or any other change having a significant effect on the financial statements must be disclosed.

Sometimes, the accounting change is the result of an FASB pronouncement. The most common change reported in the AICPA survey of the 1996 annual reports of 600 corporations was of this variety and involved the impairment of long-lived assets.[1]

Business Combinations

If the firm has been involved in a **business combination** (i.e., a merger, acquisition, or disposition), the transaction(s) involved will be described and the effect on the financial statements will be explained. Recall that in the case of the disposition of part of the business, the income statement will segregate the impact on the current year's results of discontinued operations.

Most mergers and acquisitions are accounted for using **purchase accounting**. Under purchase accounting, the assets acquired are recorded by the acquiring company at their *fair market value* at the date of acquisition. Any amount paid for the acquired assets (or company) in excess of the fair market value of the assets is recorded as goodwill—an intangible asset that is then amortized to expense over a period of time. An alternative accounting method, **pooling of interests accounting**, can be used in certain

---

[1]AICPA, *Accounting Trends and Techniques* (New York, 1997), Table 1–8.

circumstances. Under pooling, the assets acquired are recorded by the acquiring company at the *book value* at which they are carried by the acquired company. Likewise, the stock issued in the merger is recorded at the book value of the acquired company, not the market value of the shares issued. This accounting alternative eliminates any necessity for goodwill but usually results in the acquired assets being recorded by the acquiring company at less than fair market value. The notes will explain the accounting method used in the merger or acquisition. In the AICPA survey of the 1996 annual reports of 600 corporations, 256 firms reported business combinations under the purchase method, while only 32 firms reported poolings of interests.[2]

Contingencies and Commitments

It is not unusual for a firm to be involved in litigation, the results of which are not known when the financial statements are prepared. If the firm is denying liability in a lawsuit in which it is a defendant, it is appropriate to disclose the fact of the lawsuit to readers of the financial statements. Of course, the concept of matching revenue and expense requires the recognition of any anticipated cost of verdicts that the company expects to have to pay. An expense or a loss and a related liability should be reported in the period affected. Even if the lawsuit is one that management and legal counsel believe will not result in any liability to the company, the fact of the potential loss and liability should be disclosed. The nature of the legal action, the potential damages, and a statement to the effect that the claims against the company are not likely to be sustained are included in the notes. *Intel's "Contingencies" footnote briefly describes several lawsuits pending against the company, none of which (in the opinion of management and internal counsel) will have a material adverse effect on the company's financial position or overall trends in results of operations. Included among these lawsuits is a "groundwater cleanup" claim brought under the California and U.S. Superfund statutes in which Intel and two other companies may be held jointly and severally liable for the sites in question (see p. 30).*

In some cases, a firm or one of its subsidiaries may act as a guarantor of the indebtedness of another entity. In such cases, it is appropriate for the amount of the potential liability and a brief description of the circumstances to be disclosed in the notes. If the firm has made commitments to purchase a significant amount of plant and equipment or has committed to pay significant amounts of rent on leased property for several years into the future, these commitments will be disclosed. This is because the commitment is like a liability but is not recorded on the balance sheet because the actual purchase transaction has not yet occurred. *Intel's "Commitments" footnote indicates that it had committed approximately $1.6 billion for the construction of property, plant, and equipment at December 28, 1996. The company also discloses its "minimum rental expense commitments" under noncancelable operating leases for each year from 1997 to 2002 (see p. 30).*

---

[2]AICPA, *Accounting Trends and Techniques* (New York, 1997), Table 1–10.

A firm may have quite a few other kinds of **contingencies** and **commitments**. Most will have a negative impact on the financial position of the firm or its results of operations if they materialize. The purpose of disclosing these items is to provide full disclosure to the user of the financial statements.

Events Subsequent to the Balance Sheet Date

If, subsequent to the balance sheet date, a significant event occurs that has a material impact on the balance sheet or income statement, it is appropriate to provide an explanation of the probable impact of the subsequent event on future financial statements. Examples of such significant events include the issuance of a large amount of long-term debt, the restructuring of long-term debt, the issuance of a large amount of capital stock, the sale of a significant part of the company's assets, and the agreement to enter into a business combination. *Intel's 1996 annual report makes reference to a two-for-one stock split that was approved by the Board of Directors in January, 1997, subject to stockholder approval of an increased number of authorized shares at the company's annual meeting in May, 1997. None of the share, per share, or dollar amounts shown in the 1996 annual report were restated for the 1997 stock split (see p. 23).*

Impact of Inflation

It has been emphasized that the financial statements do not reflect the impact of inflation. The original cost concept and the objectivity principle result in assets being recorded at their historical cost to the entity, based on current dollars at the time the transactions are initially recorded. In 1979, because of the significant inflation that the United States had experienced in the prior decade, the FASB required large companies to report certain inflation-adjusted data in the explanatory notes to the financial statements. This was done on a trial basis for a period of five years. In effect, the income statement, earnings per share of common stock, and total net assets were adjusted based on two methods of reflecting the impact of changing prices: a price index method and a current replacement cost method. The effect of each of these methods was usually to reduce reported earnings because higher amounts would be reported for depreciation expense and cost of goods sold. Depreciation expense was greater than recorded because asset values had increased. For firms that used the FIFO cost-flow assumption, cost of goods sold also increased because inventory replacement costs were higher than the historical cost used in traditional accounting. Firms that used LIFO did not experience as much of a cost of goods sold increase because LIFO releases more current costs to the income statement. Net assets were generally increased significantly under each method of reflecting inflation. In 1986, the FASB rescinded the requirement, and now firms are merely encouraged to report the effects of inflation.

Reporting the effects of inflation is a controversial and complex area of accounting. If the economy experiences high rates of inflation in the future, efforts to reflect the impact of inflation directly in the financial statements are likely to be renewed.

Segment Information

Most large corporations operate in several lines of business and in several international geographic areas. In addition, some firms have major customers (frequently the U.S. government) that account for a significant part of the total business. A **business segment** is a group of the firm's business activities that have a common denominator. The components of each business segment are identified and defined by management. Segments may reflect the company's organizational structure, manufacturing processes, product-line groups, or industries served. The required disclosure of segment, geographic, and major customer information is designed to permit the financial statement user to make judgments about the impact on the firm of factors that might influence specific lines of business, geographic areas, or specific major customers.

Data shown for each segment include sales to unaffiliated customers, operating profit, capital expenditures, depreciation and amortization expense, and identifiable assets. Note that from these data it is possible to make a DuPont model return-on-investment calculation and to prepare for each segment a simple statement of cash flows showing cash flows from operating activities (net income plus depreciation expense), minus cash used for investing activities (capital expenditures). This simple statement of cash flows omits financing activities (such as long-term debt and dividend transactions), but it does highlight the principal cash flows related to each segment. Although these segment measures cannot be combined to equal the total company's ROI or cash flows (because assets and expenses applicable to the corporation as a whole have not been arbitrarily allocated to segments), segment trends over time can be determined. Business segment data are not disclosed by Intel because the company operates predominately in one segment (microcomputer components and related products).

Sales to unaffiliated customers, operating profits, and identifiable assets are also reported by geographic areas in which the firm operates. For example, the areas in the geographic breakdown used by many firms with international operations are the United States, Europe, Africa, Pan America, and the Pacific. ROI calculations can also be made based on geographic areas, but cash flow information cannot be approximated because the required geographic disclosures do not include capital expenditures or depreciation and amortization expense.

If a firm has a major customer that accounts for more than 10% of its total sales, it is appropriate to disclose this fact to the financial statement user so that a judgment can be made about the influence of this customer on the firm's continued profitability.

Management's Statement of Responsibility

Objective 5
Understand why a statement of management's responsibility is included with the notes.

Many firms include in the explanatory notes **management's statement of responsibility**, which explains that the responsibility for the financial statements lies with the management of the firm, not the external auditors/ certified public accountants who express an opinion about the fairness with which the financial statements present the financial condition and results of operations of the company. The statement of responsibility usually refers to the firm's system of internal controls, the internal audit function, the

audit committee of the board of directors, and other policies and procedures designed to ensure that the company operates at a high level of ethical conduct. The survey of the 1996 annual reports of 600 publicly owned
merchandising and manufacturing companies showed that 356 companies
included this kind of management report.[3] Intel does not include a management's statement of responsibility in its report.

Management's Discussion and Analysis

Objective 6
Understand the
significance of
management's
discussion and
analysis of the firm's
financial condition
and results of
operations.

For many years, the Securities and Exchange Commission has required
companies that must file a Form 10-K annual report with the Commission
to include in the report a discussion by management of the firm's activities
during the year, and its financial condition and results of operations. This
discussion is being included in more and more annual reports to stockholders. Management's discussion and analysis should enhance disclosure to
the public of information about the corporation. It is a part of the annual
report that should be read by current and potential investors. In the Intel
Corporation report in the Appendix, management's discussion and analysis
of financial condition and results of operations are on pages 34 through 36.

**WHAT
DOES IT
MEAN?**

2. What does it mean to state that management's discussion and analysis are essential to understanding the firm's activities and financial
statements?

Five-Year (or Longer) Summary of Financial Data

Objective 7
Understand what is
included in the
summary of financial
information.

Most corporate annual reports will present a summary of financial data for
at least the five most recent years. Many firms report these data for longer
periods, and at least one firm reports for every year since it was organized.
Included in the summary are key income statement data or even the entire
income statement in condensed form. In addition to amounts, significant
ratios such as earnings as a percentage of sales, average assets, and average
owners' equity may also be included. Earnings and dividends per share,
the average number of shares outstanding each year, and other operating
statistics may be reported. Year-end data from the balance sheet such as
working capital; property, plant, and equipment (net of accumulated depreciation); long-term debt; and owners' equity are usually reported. Book
value per share of common stock and the year-end market price of common stock are frequently reported. When stock dividends or stock splits
have occurred, the per share data of prior years are adjusted retroactively
so that the per share data are comparable.

As an illustration of the adjustment of per share data for stock dividends or stock splits, assume that Cruisers, Inc., reported basic earnings
per share and cash dividends per share of $4.50 and $2.00, respectively,
for fiscal 1997. Assume also that in 1998 the firm had a 2-for-1 stock split.
In the annual report for 1998, earnings and dividends for 1997 should
reflect the fact that because of the split there are now twice as many shares

---

[3]AICPA, *Accounting Trends and Techniques* (New York, 1997), p. 589.

of common stock outstanding as there were when 1997 amounts were first reported. Therefore, in the 1998 annual report, 1997 basic earnings per share and dividends per share will be reported at $2.25 and $1.00, respectively. Assume further that in 1999 Cruisers had a 10% stock dividend that resulted in 110 shares outstanding for every 100 shares that were outstanding before the stock dividend. The 1999 annual report will report 1997 basic earnings per share and dividends per share as $2.05 ($2.25/1.10) and $.91 ($1.00/1.10), respectively. Diluted earnings per share data (if required to be reported) would also be adjusted.

The **five-year summary** is not included in the scope of the outside auditors' work, nor does their opinion relate to the summary. Therefore, the summary appears in the annual report *after* the outside auditors' opinion. Likewise, the summary is not a part of the explanatory notes to the financial statements; it is a supplementary disclosure. Intel's annual report includes a ten-year financial summary on page 33.

WHAT DOES IT MEAN?

3. What does it mean to review the trends in the **five-year (or longer) summary** of financial data?

Independent Auditors' Report

Objective 8
Understand the meaning and content of the independent auditors' report.

The independent auditors' report is a brief (usually three paragraphs), often easily overlooked report that relates to the financial statements and the accompanying explanatory notes. The SEC requires an audit of the financial statements of a publicly owned company. Many privately owned firms will have an audit of their financial statements to support their bank loan negotiations.

The independent auditors' report for Intel Corporation (which is on page 32 of the annual report in the Appendix) is reproduced in Exhibit 10–1. This report format has been standardized by the Auditing Standards Board of the AICPA and is almost universal. Note that Intel received an *unqualified,* or "clean" audit opinion, meaning that its financial statements were "present[ed] fairly, in all material respects . . . in conformity with generally accepted accounting principles." This is by far the most commonly presented opinion in annual reports because most firms would prefer to make the necessary "auditor-suggested adjustments" to financial statement amounts and footnote disclosures than to receive a *qualified* audit opinion.

The report is usually addressed to the board of directors and stockholders of the corporation. The first paragraph, or *introductory paragraph,* identifies the financial statements that were audited and briefly describes the responsibilities of both management and the auditors with respect to the financial statements. It is important to note here that management is responsible for the financial statements; the auditors' task is to express an opinion about them.

The second paragraph is the *scope paragraph,* and it describes the nature and extent of the auditors' work. Note that their concern is with obtaining reasonable assurance about whether the financial statements are free of material misstatements and that their work involves tests. Auditors give no guarantee that the financial statements are free from fraudulent

EXHIBIT 10–1   Independent Auditors' Report

The Board of Directors and Stockholders
Intel Corporation

We have audited the accompanying consolidated balance sheets of Intel Corporation as of December 28, 1996, and December 30, 1995, and the related consolidated statements of income, stockholders' equity, and cash flows for each of the three years in the period ended December 28, 1996. These financial statements are the responsibility of the Company's management. Our responsibility is to express an opinion on these financial statements based on our audits.

We conducted our audits in accordance with generally accepted auditing standards. Those standards require that we plan and perform the audit to obtain reasonable assurance about whether the financial statements are free of material misstatements. An audit includes examining, on a test basis, evidence supporting the amounts and disclosures in the financial statements. An audit also includes assessing the accounting principles used and significant estimates made by management, as well as evaluating the overall financial statement presentation. We believe that our audits provide a reasonable basis for our opinion.

In our opinion, the consolidated financial statements referred to above present fairly, in all material respects, the consolidated financial position of Intel Corporation at December 28, 1996, and December 30, 1995, and the consolidated results of its operations and its cash flows for each of the three years in the period ended December 28, 1996, in conformity with generally accepted accounting principles.

Ernst & Young LLP

San Jose, California
January 13, 1997

transactions or from the effects of errors. Remember that the accuracy of the financial statements is the responsibility of management, not of the auditors. However, generally accepted auditing standards do require extensive audit procedures as a means of obtaining reasonable assurance that the financial statements are free from material misstatements.

The third paragraph is the *opinion paragraph,* and in that sense it is the most important. The benchmark for fair presentation is generally accepted accounting principles. Again, note the reference to materiality. If, during the course of the audit, the auditor determines that the financial statements taken as a whole do not "present fairly," the auditor will require a change in the presentation or withdraw from the audit. The latter action is very rare.

The name of the auditing firm, sometimes presented as a facsimile signature, and the date of the report are shown. The date of the report is the date the audit work was completed, and a required audit procedure is to review transactions subsequent to the balance sheet date up to the date of the report. As discussed earlier in this chapter, unusual transactions that occur during this period must be disclosed in the financial statements or in the explanatory notes.

Occasionally, the auditors' report will include an explanatory paragraph that describes a situation that does not affect fair presentation but that should be disclosed to keep the financial statements from being misleading. Items that require additional explanation include the following:

1. Basing the opinion in part on the work of another auditor.
2. Uncertainties about the outcome of certain events that would have affected the presentation if the outcome could be estimated.
3. Substantial doubt about the entity's ability to continue as a going concern.
4. A material change between periods in an accounting principle or its method of application.

The auditor can issue a qualified opinion if the scope of the audit was restricted and essential audit work could not be performed or if there is a material departure from generally accepted accounting principles that affects only part of the financial statements. The reason for the qualification is explained in the report, and the opinion about fair presentation is restricted to the unaffected parts of the financial statements. Qualified opinions rarely occur in practice.

It is appropriate for the financial statement reader to review the independent auditors' report and determine the effect of any departure from the standard report.

WHAT DOES IT MEAN?

4. What does it mean to say that the auditors have given a clean opinion about the financial statements?

Financial Statement Compilations

Accounting firms also perform services for client organizations whose debt and equity securities are not publicly traded (and whose financial statements are not required to be audited). Many small businesses use an outside accounting firm to prepare the necessary tax returns and to assemble financial information into conventional financial statements. The accounting firm may prepare financial statements to submit to banks and other major suppliers for purposes of obtaining commercial credit. Since the accounting firm is not engaged in an audit, it is necessary that a report be issued that clearly communicates to the user that the accounting firm is not providing any form of assurance as to the fairness of the financial statements. Such a report, called a *compilation report,* is shown in Exhibit 10–2.

The user of the financial statements should be aware that the compilation means exactly what it says. If the firm's need for capital is great and it borrows substantial amounts from its bank, it is not uncommon for the bank to reject compilations and insist on financial statements that have been audited by an independent accountant. Having an audit will usually cause the firm's accounting costs to rise significantly.

Summary

Explanatory notes to the financial statements are an integral part of the statements. These notes, sometimes called the *financial review,* result from

---

EXHIBIT 10–2   Compilation Report

The Board of Directors and Shareholders,
Cruisers, Inc.:

We have compiled the accompanying balance sheet of Cruisers, Inc., as of December 31, 1998, and the related statements of income and retained earnings and cash flows for the year then ended, in accordance with standards established by the American Institute of Certified Public Accountants.

A compilation is limited to presenting in the form of financial statements information that is the representation of management. We have not audited or reviewed the accompanying financial statements and, accordingly, do not express an opinion or any other form of assurance on them.

Management has elected to omit substantially all of the disclosures required by generally accepted accounting principles. If the omitted disclosures were included in the financial statements, they might influence the user's conclusions about Cruisers, Inc.'s financial condition, results of operations, cash flows, and changes in financial position. Accordingly, these financial statements are not designed for those who are not informed about such matters.

(Accounting firm's signature, address, and date)

---

the application of the full disclosure concept discussed in Chapter 2. The notes disclose details of amounts summarized for financial statement presentation, explain which permissible alternative accounting practices have been used by the entity, and provide detailed disclosure of information needed to have a full understanding of the financial statements.

Accounting policies disclosed include the depreciation method, inventory cost-flow assumption, and basis of consolidation. Accounting for the entity's income taxes, employee benefits, and amortization of intangible assets is described. Details of the calculation of earnings per share of common stock are sometimes provided. There is a discussion of employee stock option and stock purchase plans. The materiality concept is applied to the extent of each of these disclosures.

If there have been changes in the accounting for a material item, the consistency concept requires disclosure of the effect of the change on the financial statements. Sometimes accounting or reporting changes are required by new FASB standards.

There is a full discussion of any business combinations in which the entity has been involved.

Significant contingencies and commitments, such as litigation or loan guarantees, as well as significant events that have occurred since the balance sheet date, are described. This is a specific application of the full disclosure concept.

The impact of inflation on the historical cost amounts used in the financial statements may be reported, although this information is not currently required to be shown.

Segment information summarizes some financial information for the principal activity areas of the firm. The intent of this disclosure is to permit judgment about the significance to the entity's overall results of its activities in certain business segments and geographic areas.

The financial statements are the responsibility of management, not the auditors, and management's statement of responsibility acknowledges this. This acknowledgment usually includes a reference to the system of internal control.

Management's discussion and analysis of the firm's financial condition and results of operations provide an important and useful summary of the firm's activities.

Although not usually a part of the explanatory notes to the financial statements, most annual reports do include a summary of key financial data for a period of several years. This summary permits financial statement users to make trend evaluations easily.

The independent auditors' report includes their opinion about the fair presentation of the financial statements in accordance with generally accepted accounting principles and calls attention to special situations. Auditors do not guarantee that the company will be profitable, nor do they give assurance that the financial statements are absolutely accurate.

The Securities and Exchange Commission is responsible for administering federal securities laws. One of its principal concerns is that investors have full disclosure about securities and the companies that issue them. The reporting requirements of the SEC have led to many of the disclosures contained in corporate annual reports.

Refer to the notes to the consolidated financial statements in the Intel Corporation annual report in the Appendix and to the comparable part of other annual reports that you may have. Observe the organization of this part of the financial statements and the comprehensive explanation of the material discussed. Read management's discussion and analysis of the firm's financial condition and results of operations. Find the summary of key financial data for several years and evaluate the trends disclosed for sales, profits, total owners' equity, and other items reported in the summary. The next chapter will describe and illustrate some of the ways of analyzing financial statement data to support the informed judgments and decisions made by users of financial statements.

Key Terms and Concepts

accounting change (p. 355)   A change in the application of an accounting principle.

accrued pension cost (p. 352)   A liability representing the estimated amount by which a company's defined-benefit pension plan is *underfunded,* based on certain actuarial assumptions. Normally reported in a detailed schedule in the financial review section of an annual report.

business combination (p. 355)   A merger between two or more firms, or the purchase of one firm by another.

business segment (p. 358)   A group of the firm's similar business activities; most large firms have several segments.

commitment (p. 357)   A transaction that has been contractually agreed to but that has not yet occurred and is not reflected in the financial statements.

contingency (p. 357)   An event that has an uncertain but potentially significant effect on the financial statements.

explanatory notes to the financial statements (p. 349)   An integral part of the financial statements that contains explanations of accounting policies and descriptions of financial statement details.

financial review (p. 349)   Another name for the footnotes to the financial statements.

five-year (or longer) summary (p. 360)   A summary of key financial data included in an organization's annual report; it is not a financial statement included in the scope of the independent auditor's report.

management's discussion and analysis (p. 350)   A narrative description of the firm's activities for the year, including comments about its financial condition and results of operations.

management's statement of responsibility (p. 358)   A discussion included in the explanatory notes to the financial statements describing management's responsibility for the financial statements.

net pension expense (p. 352)   The estimated annual cost of providing pension-related benefits to current and former employees, based on certain actuarial assumptions. Normally reported in a detailed schedule in the financial review section of an annual report.

pooling of interests accounting (p. 355)   A method of accounting for the acquisition of another company that results in the book values of the acquired company's assets and liabilities being recorded by the acquiring company.

prepaid pension cost (p. 352)   An asset representing the estimated amount by which a company's defined-benefit pension plan is *overfunded,* based on certain actuarial assumptions. Normally reported in a detailed schedule in the financial review section of an annual report.

prospectus (p. 354)   A summary of the characteristics of a security being offered for sale, including a description of the business and financial position of the firm selling the security.

proxy (p. 355)   An authorization given by a stockholder to another person to vote the shares owned by the stockholder.

purchase accounting (p. 355)   A method of accounting for the purchase of another company that records as the cost of the investment the fair market value of the cash and/or securities paid, less the liabilities assumed in the transaction.

significant accounting policies (p. 351)   A brief summary or description of the specific accounting practices followed by the entity.

stock option plan (p. 353)   A plan for compensating key employees by providing an option to purchase a company's stock at a future date at the market price of the stock when the option is issued (granted).

WHAT DOES IT MEAN?
ANSWERS

1. It means that to understand the financial statements it is necessary to review the related notes to learn about the accounting policies that were followed, details of summary amounts reported in the financial statements, and unusual or significant transactions that affected the financial statements.

2. It means that this part of the annual report contains information that adds substance to the amounts reported in the financial statements.

3. It means that a picture of the firm's recent financial history can be readily obtained by reviewing these data and using them in various calculations (ROI, ROE) if those results are not included in the summary.

4. It means that in the opinion of an independent third party, the financial statements present fairly in all material respects, in accordance with generally accepted accounting principles, the financial position, results of operations, and cash flows of the entity for the period. It does not mean that there have not been any fraudulent transactions, that the company has been given an absolute "clean bill of health," or that investors are guaranteed that they will not suffer losses from investing in the company's securities.

Exercises and Problems

Intel LO 1 **10–1.** **Scan the financial review and read other annual report disclosures.** Refer to the Intel Corporation annual report for 1996 in the Appendix. Find and scan the financial review (notes to consolidated financial statements). Read management's statement of responsibility, the independent auditors' report, and management's discussion and analysis of financial condition and results of operations.

LO 5   **10–2.** **Read and interpret management's statement of responsibility.** Find and read management's statement of responsibility in the annual report that you obtained as a result of completing Exercise 1–1. Identify the principal topics covered in that statement. Are there other topics that you believe would be appropriate to have included in the statement? Explain your answer.

Intel LO 3 **10–3.** **Calculate ROI for geographic areas.** Refer to the geographic area information on page 31 of the Intel Corporation annual report in the Appendix. Calculate ROI, using the DuPont model to show margin and turnover, for the United States, Europe, Japan, and Asia-Pacific for 1996.

LO 3   **10–4.** **Calculate ROI for business segments; analyze results—Dow Jones & Company.** Refer to the business segment data shown below (in thousands), from the 1996 annual report of Dow Jones & Company, publisher of *The Wall Street Journal*:

	Business Publishing	*Financial Information Services*	*Community Newspapers*	*Corporate*	*Consolidated*
Revenues					
1996	$1,214,336	$ 979,745	$287,511		$2,481,592
1995	1,049,462	961,398	272,901		2,283,761
1994	961,417	837,392	252,168		2,090,977
Operating Income					
1996	159,418	155,848	43,766	$(22,052)	336,980
1995	95,509	197,015	32,987	(21,470)	304,041
1994	157,429	183,135	36,166	(18,413)	358,317
Identifiable Assets					
1996	635,615	1,607,971	223,860	292,185	2,759,631
1995	587,032	1,598,041	229,515	184,112	2,598,700
1994	482,633	1,608,538	198,985	155,610	2,445,766

a. Explain why the operating income shown in the "Corporate" column is negative each year.
b. Based on an "eyeballing" of the data, can you identify any significant trends in the consolidated totals? Are there any notable trends in the data for specific business segments?
c. Using the DuPont model to show margin and turnover, calculate ROI for each of the three business segments for 1996.
d. Looking only at the data for the "Business Publishing" segment, would you think the ROI in 1996 is up or down, relative to 1995? What about the "Financial Information Services" segment? Explain your answers.
e. Why would Dow Jones invest the majority of its assets in "Financial Information Services" if this segment provides the lowest ROI?

LO 7   **10–5.   Effects of stock split and stock dividend on EPS.**
a. For the year ended December 31, 1997, Finco, Inc., reported earnings per share of $3.12. During 1998 the company had a 3-for-1 stock split. Calculate the 1997 earnings per share that will be reported in Finco's 1998 annual report for comparative purposes.
b. During 1999 Finco had a 2-for-1 stock split. Calculate the 1997 earnings per share that will be reported in Finco's 1999 annual report for comparative purposes.
c. If Finco had issued a 10% stock dividend in 1998 and did not have a stock split, calculate the 1997 earnings per share that will be reported in Finco's 1998 annual report for comparative purposes.

LO 7   **10–6.   Calculate EPS and effect of stock split on EPS.** During the year ended December 31, 1999, Gluco, Inc., split its stock on a 3-for-1 basis. In its annual report for 1998, the firm reported net income of $925,980 for 1998, with an average 268,400 shares of common stock outstanding for that year. There was no preferred stock.

Required:
a. What amount of net income for 1998 will be reported in Gluco's 1999 annual report?
b. Calculate Gluco's earnings per share for 1998 that would have been reported in the 1998 annual report.
c. Calculate Gluco's earnings per share for 1998 that will be reported in the 1999 annual report for comparative purposes.

LO 7   **10–7   Calculate EPS reported before stock split and stock dividend.** During the fiscal year ended September 30, 1999, Rentco, Inc., had a 2-for-1 stock split and a 5% stock dividend. In its annual report for 1999, the company reported earnings per share for the year ended September 30, 1998, on a restated basis, of $.60.

Required:
Calculate the originally reported earnings per share for the year ended September 30, 1998.

LO 7   **10–8.   Calculate EPS and dividends per share before stock split.** For several years Dorcel, Inc., has followed a policy of paying a cash dividend of $.40 per share and having a 10% stock dividend. In the 1999 annual report, Dorcel reported restated earnings per share for 1997 of $.90.

Required:
a. Calculate the originally reported earnings per share for 1997.
b. Calculate the restated cash dividend per share for 1997 reported in the 1999 annual report for comparative purposes.

LO 8 **10–9. Interpret auditors' opinion.** It is impossible for an auditor to "guarantee" that a company's financial statements are free of all error because the cost to the company to achieve absolute accuracy (even if that were possible) and the cost of the auditor's verification would be prohibitively expensive. How does the auditors' opinion recognize this absence of absolute accuracy?

LO 8 **10–10. Interpret auditors' opinion.** To what extent is the auditors' opinion an indicator of a company's future financial success and future cash dividends to stockholders?

Intel LO 2, 7 **10–11. Understanding footnote disclosures and financial summary data.** This problem is based on the 1996 annual report of Intel Corporation in the Appendix.

Find in the Ten-Year Financial Summary, or calculate, the following data:
a. Net revenues in 1989.
b. Gross profit in 1992.
c. Difference between operating income and net income in 1994.
d. Year(s) in which net income decreased as compared to the previous year.

Find the following data for 1996 in the Notes to the Consolidated Financial Statements:
e. Potential obligation under put warrants.
f. Amount of short-term and long-term debt.
g. Total assets invested in operations outside the United States.
h. Amount committed for the construction of property, plant, and equipment.
i. Amount of available-for-sale securities classified as cash equivalents.
j. Gross profit for the third quarter of 1996.
k. Amount of interest income earned.

Intel LO 2, 7 **10–12. Understanding footnote disclosures and financial summary data.** This problem is based on the 1996 annual report of Intel Corporation in the Appendix.

Find in the Ten-Year Financial Summary, or calculate, the following data:
a. Percentage of R&D relative to net revenues in 1996.
b. Amount by which property, plant, and equipment *decreased* during 1996 (i.e., for depreciation, asset sales, and similar transactions).
c. Year in which stockholders' equity grew by the greatest amount over the previous year.
d. Change in total liabilities from 1990 to 1996.

Find the following data for 1996 in the Notes to the Consolidated Financial Statements:
e. Amount of work-in-process inventory.
f. Amount of interest expense capitalized as a component of construction costs.
g. Amount of operating income earned in Europe.
h. The company's effective tax rate.
i. Cost and estimated fair value of investments held in corporate bonds.
j. Market price range of common stock for the fourth quarter of 1996.
k. Amount of current and deferred taxes incurred from foreign operations.

LO 2 **10–13. Find various accounting policy disclosures.** Refer to the financial statement footnotes or financial review section of the annual report you have obtained either as a result of completing Exercise 1–1 or otherwise. Read the "significant accounting policy" footnote disclosures and answer the following questions:
Required:

a. What are the principal components included in the firm's receivables (or accounts and notes receivable, or trade receivables)?

b. What inventory valuation method(s) are being used for financial reporting purposes? How much more would ending inventory be if it were reported on a total FIFO basis? *(Hint: This disclosure is sometimes referred to as the "LIFO Reserve.")*

c. Does the firm report a reconciliation of the statutory income tax rate with the effective tax rate? If so, what are these rates, and what are the principal temporary differences that caused them to differ?

d. Does the firm have an employee stock purchase plan, an employee stock ownership plan (ESOP), or other restrictive stock plans? If so, describe the key characteristics of these plans from the perspective of a common stockholder.

e. Have any significant subsequent events occurred since the balance sheet date? If so, describe the effects that these items will have on future financial statements.

LO 2 **10–14. Find various accounting policy disclosures.** Refer to the financial statement footnotes or financial review section of the annual report you have obtained either as a result of completing Exercise 1–1 or otherwise. Read the "significant accounting policy" footnote disclosures and answer the following questions:

Required:

a. Do the financial statements report information about consolidated subsidiaries? Does the firm have any nonconsolidated subsidiaries?

b. What are the principal components included in the firm's cash (or cash and equivalents, or cash and short-term investments)?

c. What depreciation method(s) are being used for financial reporting purposes? How much total depreciation and amortization expense did the firm report?

d. Does the firm have any stock options outstanding? If so, how many option shares are exercisable at the end of the year?

e. Does the firm have any significant contingencies or commitments that have not been reported as liabilities on the balance sheet? If so, describe the potential effects of these items from the perspective of a common stockholder.

CHAPTER 11

Financial Statement Analysis

The process of interpreting an entity's financial statements can be facilitated by certain ratio computations, and if one entity's financial condition and results of operations are to be compared to those of another entity, ratio analysis of the financial statements is essential. In Chapter 3 you learned about some of the fundamental interpretations made from financial statement data. The importance of financial statement ratios and the significance of *trends* in the ratio results were explained. The calculation of return on investment (ROI) and the use of the DuPont model, which recognizes margin and turnover in the ROI calculation, were described. In addition, the calculation and significance of return on equity (ROE) and the liquidity measures of working capital, current ratio, and acid-test ratio were explained. It would be appropriate for you to review Chapter 3 if you don't thoroughly understand these analytical tools. In Chapters 5 through 10 you learned about the business and accounting aspects of almost all of the transactions that an entity may experience. The effects of these transactions on the financial statements were described and explained. Your understanding of the accounting process and the alternative choices that management must make for financial reporting purposes will permit you to make sense of an entity's financial statements. This chapter builds on the material presented in Chapter 3 and provides a comprehensive discussion of financial statement analysis concepts. The objective of this chapter is to expand your ability to read and interpret financial statements so that you can make decisions and informed judgments about an entity's financial condition and results of operations.

WHAT DOES IT MEAN?

1. What does it mean to use the trend of financial statement ratios to compare the financial position and results of operations of one firm with another firm?

Learning Objectives

After studying this chapter, you should understand:

1 How liquidity measures can be influenced by the inventory cost-flow assumption used.

2 How suppliers and creditors use a customer's payment practices to judge liquidity.

3 The influence of alternative inventory cost-flow assumptions and depreciation methods on turnover ratios.

4 How the number of days' sales in accounts receivable and inventory are used to evaluate the effectiveness of the management of receivables and inventory.

5 The significance of the price/earnings ratio in the evaluation of the market price of a company's common stock.

6 How dividend yield and the dividend payout ratio are used by investors to evaluate a company's common stock.

7 What financial leverage is and why it is significant to management, creditors, and owners.

8 What book value per share of common stock is, how it is calculated, and why it is not a very meaningful amount for most companies.

9 How common size financial statements can be used to evaluate a firm's financial position and results of operations over a number of years.

10 How operating statistics using physical, or nonfinancial, data can be used to help management evaluate the results of the firm's activities.

Financial Statement Analysis Ratios

The ratios used to facilitate the interpretation of an entity's financial position and results of operations can be grouped into four categories that have to do with:

1. Liquidity.
2. Activity.
3. Profitability.
4. Debt, or financial leverage.

Liquidity Measures

Objective 1
Understand how liquidity measures can be influenced by the inventory cost-flow assumption used.

The liquidity measures of working capital, current ratio, and acid-test ratio were discussed in Chapter 3. One point that deserves reemphasis is the **effect of the inventory cost-flow assumption on working capital.** The balance sheet carrying value of inventories will depend on whether the weighted-average, FIFO, or LIFO assumption is used. In periods of rising prices, a firm using the FIFO cost-flow assumption will report a relatively higher asset value for inventories than a similar firm using the LIFO cost-flow assumption. Thus, even though the firms may be similar in all other respects, they will report different amounts of working capital, and they will have different current ratios. Therefore, a direct comparison of the liquidity of the two firms by using these measures is not possible. To ease this reporting difficulty, many firms using the LIFO method will disclose a *LIFO reserve* amount in the explanatory footnotes (or financial review) section of their annual reports. The LIFO reserve is the difference between the inventory valuation as reported on the LIFO basis and the amount that would have been reported under the FIFO basis. For example, American Greetings Corporation disclosed a LIFO reserve of $89 million in its 1997 annual report, which would have increased the firm's reported inventory of greeting cards by more than 30%. Of course, the differences caused by the LIFO-FIFO selection are often less dramatic for firms operating in other industries, as suggested by the LIFO reserves disclosed in 1996 by Sherwin-Williams (15% of reported inventory), and Quaker-Oats (5%). Intel Corporation's inventories are reported on a basis that approximates FIFO (see page 22 in the Appendix).

Even more significant to suppliers or potential suppliers/creditors of the firm than the aggregate working capital or liquidity ratios is the firm's current and recent payment experience. Suppliers/creditors want to know whether or not the firm is paying its bills promptly. One indication of this is whether or not all cash discounts for prompt payment (e.g., for payment terms of 2/10, net 30) are being taken. Information about current and recent payment practices can be obtained by contacting other suppliers or credit bureaus and by reviewing Dun & Bradstreet reports (see Business in Practice—Credit Rating and Financial Analysis Services).

Objective 2
Understand how suppliers and creditors use a customer's payment practices to judge liquidity.

BUSINESS IN PRACTICE
Credit Rating and Financial Analysis Services

To help potential creditors and investors evaluate the financial condition and investment prospects of companies, a credit rating and financial analysis industry has developed. Firms in this industry gather and report data about individual companies, industries, segments of the economy, and the economy as a whole.

Credit rating firms such as Dun & Bradstreet and credit bureaus collect data from companies (and individuals) and their creditors, and sell credit history data to potential suppliers and others. These firms usually have a rating system and assign a credit risk value based on that system. A company or individual being reported on can request to see the data in their file so that erroneous data can be eliminated or corrected.

The financial statements of larger firms whose stock or bonds have been issued to the public are analyzed and reported on by firms such as Standard & Poor's Corporation or Moody's Investors Service, Inc. A rating is assigned to bonds to reflect the rating firm's assessment of the risk associated with the security. The ratings range from AAA to C, or no rating at all for a speculative bond. Summary financial statements, ratio calculation results, and bond ratings are published in manuals that are available in many libraries. In addition to rating bonds, these firms and many others (such as Value Line Publishing, Inc., and stock brokerage firms) evaluate the common and preferred stock issues of publicly owned companies. They report summary financial data and trends in key ratios, along with their opinions about the investment prospects for the stocks. A potential investor will likely use reports from one or more of these sources as well as the company's annual report to support the investment decision.

2. What does it mean to assess the liquidity of an entity?

Activity Measures

The impact of efficient use of assets on the firm's return on investment was explained in Chapter 3, in the discussion of the asset turnover component of the DuPont model (ROI = Margin × Turnover). Activity measures focus primarily on the relationship between asset levels and sales (i.e., turnover). Recall that the general model for calculating turnover is:

$$\text{Turnover} = \text{Sales/Average assets}$$

Recall also that average assets are used in the turnover calculation (rather than year-end assets) because the amount invested is compared to sales, which are generated over a period of time. The average assets amount is ordinarily determined by using the balance sheet amounts reported at the beginning and end of the period; however, if appropriate and available, monthly or quarterly balance sheet data can be used in the calculation. Turnover is frequently calculated for:

Accounts receivable.

Inventories.

Plant and equipment.

Total operating assets.

Total assets.

Objective 3
Understand the influence of alternative inventory cost-flow assumptions and depreciation methods on turnover ratios.

Alternative inventory cost-flow assumptions and depreciation methods will affect the comparability of turnover between companies. For example, a company using LIFO and an accelerated depreciation method would report lower amounts for inventory and net book value of depreciable assets than would a company using FIFO and the straight-line method. Although the sales volume of the two companies may be identical, the company reporting lower asset values would show a higher asset turnover. Of more significance than intercompany or company–industry comparisons as of a given date is the trend of turnover for the company relative to the trend of turnover for other companies or the industry. Even if the company's turnover data are not directly comparable to industry data because of accounting method choices, the patterns exhibited in the respective trends can be compared accurately.

When calculating inventory turnover, some analysts substitute the cost of goods sold amount for the sales amount in the calculation because inventories are reported at cost, not at selling prices. This approach eliminates distortions that could be caused by sales mix changes between product categories with different gross profit ratios or mark-up percentages. Even if sales is used in the numerator consistently, the inventory turnover trend will not be significantly affected unless there are major relative mark-up differences and major sales mix changes.

Some analysts use the cost of plant and equipment rather than the net book value (cost minus accumulated depreciation) when calculating plant and equipment turnover. This removes the impact of different depreciation calculation methods and may make intercompany and industry turnover data more comparable. This may be an illusory improvement, however, because the assets of each firm are reported at original cost, not current value or replacement cost. If they were acquired over different periods of time, the cost data are not likely to be comparable.

Exhibit 11–1 illustrates some turnover calculations for Intel Corporation, with data from the company's 1996 annual report. Calculation results are not usually carried beyond one decimal place because aggregate financial statement data are being used, and the accuracy implied by additional decimal places is not warranted.

Two other activity measures that permit assessment of the efficiency of asset management are the **number of days' sales in accounts receivable** and the **number of days' sales in inventory.** The sooner that accounts receivable can be collected, the sooner cash is available to use in the business or to permit temporary investment, and the less cash needs to be borrowed for prompt payment of liabilities. Likewise, the lower that inventories can be maintained relative to sales, the less inventory needs to

---

EXHIBIT 11–1 Intel Corporation, Asset Turnover Calculations Illustrated

Accounts receivable turnover for 1996 ($ millions):

Sales (net revenues) for 1996	$20,847
Accounts receivable (net) 12/28/96	3,723
Accounts receivable (net) 12/30/95	3,116

$$\text{Accounts receivable turnover} = \frac{\text{Sales}}{\text{Average accounts receivable}}$$

$$= \frac{\$20,847}{(\$3,723 + \$3,116)/2}$$

$$= 6.1 \text{ times}$$

Inventory turnover for 1996 ($ millions):

Cost of goods sold for 1996	$ 9,164
Inventories, 12/28/96	1,293
Inventories, 12/30/95	2,004

$$\text{Inventory turnover} = \frac{\text{Cost of goods sold}}{\text{Average inventories}}$$

$$= \frac{\$9,164}{(\$1,293 + \$2,004)/2}$$

$$= 5.6 \text{ times}$$

Plant and equipment turnover for 1996 ($ millions):

Sales (net revenues) for 1996	$20,847
Plant and equipment (net) at 12/28/96	8,487
Plant and equipment (net) at 12/30/95	7,471

$$\text{Plant and equipment turnover} = \frac{\text{Sales}}{\text{Average plant and equipment}}$$

$$= \frac{\$20,847}{(\$8,487 + \$7,471)/2}$$

$$= 2.6 \text{ times}$$

be financed with debt or owners' equity, and the greater the return on investment. However, the risk of having minimum inventories is that an unanticipated increase in demand or a delay in receiving raw materials or finished product can result in an out-of-stock situation that may result in lost sales. Inventory management is a very important activity for many firms, and many quantitative and operational techniques have been developed to assist in this activity. The just-in-time (JIT) inventory management system was pioneered by some Japanese firms and has been adopted by many firms in this country. The primary objective of a JIT system is to keep the investment in inventories at a minimum by forecasting needs and having suppliers deliver components as they are needed in the production process.

Objective 4
Understand how the number of days' sales in accounts receivable and inventory are used to evaluate the effectiveness of the management of receivables and inventory.

Each of the number of days' sales calculations involves calculating an average day's sales (or cost of sales) and dividing that average into the year-end balance sheet amount. A 365-day year is usually assumed for the average day's sales (or cost of sales) calculation. As in the calculation of inventory turnover, it is more appropriate to use cost of sales data in the days' sales in inventory calculation. Year-end asset values are used instead of average amounts because the focus here is on the number of days' sales (or cost of sales) in the ending balance sheet amounts. The results of these calculations can also be referred to, for receivables, as the average collection period for accounts receivable, or the number of days' sales outstanding; and for inventories, as the average sales period for inventories. It must be stressed again that the inventory cost-flow assumption will influence the result of the inventory activity calculations. Exhibit 11–2 illustrates these calculations for Intel Corporation for 1996.

Again, in evaluating the firm's operating efficiency it is the trend of these calculation results that is important. A single year's days' sales in receivables or inventory is not very useful. Intel Corporation's 65.2 days' sales in accounts receivable wouldn't make much sense if its credit terms are a combination of 2/10, net 30, and net 30 (without a discount), as is the case for many manufacturing firms. However, this result may be consistent with management's expectations if Intel's credit terms generally allow for a longer payment period. Or perhaps certain concessions are granted to major customers (e.g., original equipment manufacturers) to enhance the market penetration of Intel's microprocessors, chipsets, and motherboards. In any event, it is difficult to assess the job performance of Intel's credit managers without knowing about the firm's credit policies and the details of its accounts receivable balance by customer category. If the calculation were based on 260 business days in the year (52 weeks of five days each), the average age of the accounts receivable works out to 46.4 days, which is more reasonable. In fact, if the credit manager wanted to know how many days' sales were in receivables at any time, the most accurate result could be determined by doing the following:

1. Obtaining the daily sales amounts for the period ending with the date of the total accounts receivable.
2. Adding the daily sales amounts (working backward by day) until the sum equals the total accounts receivable.
3. Counting the number of days' sales that had to be included to reach this total.

EXHIBIT 11–2   Intel Corporation, Number of Days' Sales Calculations Illustrated

---

Number of days' sales in accounts receivable ($ millions):
Sales (net revenues) for 1996 .... $20,847
Accounts receivable (net) at 12/28/96 3,723

$$\text{Average day's sales} = \frac{\text{Annual sales}}{365}$$

$$= \$20{,}847/365$$

$$= \$57.115$$

$$\text{Days' sales in accounts receivable} = \frac{\text{Accounts receivable}}{\text{Average day's sales}}$$

$$= \$3{,}723/\$57.115$$

$$= 65.2 \text{ days}$$

The result of this calculation can also be expressed as the average age of accounts receivable, the number of days' sales outstanding, or the average collection period for accounts receivable.

Number of days' sales in inventory ($ millions):
Cost of goods sold for 1996 .... $ 9,164
Inventories at 12/28/96 1,293

$$\text{Average day's cost of goods sold} = \frac{\text{Annual cost of goods sold}}{365}$$

$$= \$9{,}164/365$$

$$= \$25.107$$

$$\text{Days' sales in inventory} = \frac{\text{Inventory}}{\text{Average day's cost of goods sold}}$$

$$= \$1{,}293/\$25.107$$

$$= 51.5 \text{ days}$$

The result of this calculation can also be expressed as the average age of the inventory, or the average sales period for inventory.

Because of the different operating characteristics of various industries, rules of thumb for activity measures are difficult to develop. In general, the higher the turnover or the fewer the number of days' sales in accounts receivable and inventory, the greater the efficiency. Again, it should be emphasized that the answer from any financial statement analysis calculation is not important by itself; the *trend* of the result over time is most meaningful. An increase in the age of accounts receivable, an increase in inventory relative to sales, or a reduction in plant and equipment turnover are all early warning signs that the liquidity and profitability of a firm may be weakening.

**WHAT
DOES IT
MEAN?**

3. What does it mean to assess the activity measures of an entity?
4. What does it mean to state that total asset turnover has improved?

Profitability Measures

Two of the most significant measures of profitability, *return on investment* and *return on equity,* were explained and illustrated in Chapter 3. Each of these measures relates net income, or an income statement subtotal (e.g., operating income), to an element of the balance sheet. Operating income, which excludes other income and expense (principally interest expense) and income taxes, is frequently used in the ROI calculation because it is a more direct measure of the results of management's activities than is net income. Interest expense is a function of the board of directors' decisions about capital structure (the relationship between debt and owners' equity); income taxes are a function of the tax laws. Thus, ROI based on operating income becomes an evaluation of the operating activities of the firm. The balance sheet elements for these calculations are average total assets (or average operating assets) for ROI, and average common stockholders' equity for ROE. You know enough about accounting principles and how financial statement data are developed to have some healthy skepticism about the relationship of these rates of return to what a "true" rate of return based on real economic profit related to fair market values would be.

Of course, the problem is that there is no agreement among managers, accountants, or financial analysts about what constitutes real economic profit or how to objectively determine fair market values of the balance sheet data. In addition, the unique characteristics of individual companies and industries make the development of benchmark or target profitability ratios difficult if not impossible. Although many valid exceptions exist, a very broad rule of thumb useful for putting ROI in perspective is that average ROI, based on net income, for most American merchandising and manufacturing companies, is between 7% and 10%. Average ROI based on operating income (earnings before interest and taxes) for the same set of firms is between 10% and 15%. Average margin, based on net income, ranges from about 7% to 10%. Using operating income, average margin ranges from 10% to 15%. Asset turnover is usually about 1.0 to 1.5. A rule of thumb useful for putting ROE in perspective is that average ROE, for most American merchandising and manufacturing companies, is between 12% and 20%. Do not draw firm conclusions based on these rules of thumb. Profitability evaluations are likely to be more valid when they are based on the *trend* of one company's ROI and ROE relative to the *trend* of industry and competitors' rates of return.

WHAT DOES IT MEAN?

5. What does it mean when ROI has decreased even though net income has increased?

6. What does it mean to use the DuPont model to help explain a decrease in ROI?

The **price/earnings ratio,** or simply the P/E ratio, is calculated by dividing the market price of a share of common stock by the earnings per share of common stock (discussed in detail in Chapter 9). Subsequent to December 15, 1997, diluted earnings per share has usually been used in the P/E ratio calculation. The P/E ratio is used extensively by investors to evaluate the market price of a company's common stock relative to that of other companies and relative to the market as a whole. **Earnings multiple** is another term for the price/earnings ratio. This term merely reflects the fact that the market price of stock is equal to the earnings per share multiplied by the P/E ratio. The following calculation illustrates this concept using data for Intel Corporation, as of December 28, 1996:

$$\frac{\text{Price/earnings ratio}}{\text{(or earnings multiple)}} = \frac{\text{Market price of common stock}}{\text{Earnings per share of common stock}}$$

$$= \frac{\$131.00^*}{\$5.81^\dagger}$$

$$= 22.5$$

Objective 5
Understand the significance of the price/earnings ratio in the evaluation of the market price of a company's stock.

To understand the significance of the P/E ratio, think about the reason an individual invests in the common stock of a company. The obvious objective is to "make money" (i.e., to achieve the investor's desired return on the investment). It is anticipated that return on investment will be realized in two ways: (1) the firm will pay cash dividends and (2) the market price of the firm's stock will increase. The change in market value is usually called a *capital gain* or *loss*. A number of factors can cause the market price to change. One of the most significant of these is the prospect for future cash dividends. Both present and future cash dividends are a function of earnings. So in a very real sense the market price of a company's common stock reflects investors' expectations about the firm's future earnings. The greater the probability of increased earnings, the more investors are willing to pay for a claim to those earnings. Relating market price and earnings per share in a ratio is a way to express investors' expectations without confusing the issue by focusing on just market price per share. To illustrate, assume the following market price per share of common stock for each of two companies:

	Company A	Company B
Market price per share	$45.00	$63.00

Based on market price alone, the tempting conclusion is that the stock of Company B is more expensive than the stock of Company A. However, when earnings per share are considered, the table looks like this:

	Company A	Company B
Market price per share	$45.00	$63.00
Diluted earnings per share	$ 1.80	$ 3.50

---

*Approximated using Intel's $137.50 high market price for 1996 from the quarterly data shown on page 37 in the Appendix, and by reading the "stock price trading ranges" graph on page 6, which indicates that the year-end closing price was slightly lower.

†Bottom of consolidated statements of income on page 18 of 1996 annual report in the Appendix. *Note that Intel's EPS for the year ended December 28, 1996, predates the change in the EPS calculation mandated by the FASB in 1997, discussed in Chapter 9.*

The price/earnings ratio can now be calculated by dividing the market price per share by the earnings per share:

	Company A	Company B
Market price per share	$\dfrac{\$45.00}{\$1.80} = 25$	$\dfrac{\$63.00}{\$3.50} = 18$
Diluted earnings per share		

Company A's stock is more expensive because investors are willing to pay 25 times earnings for it, but they will pay only 18 times earnings for Company B. In essence, investors are showing that they expect greater future earnings growth and dividend payments from Company A than from Company B; therefore, they are willing to pay relatively more for a given amount of current earnings.

The price/earnings ratio, or earnings multiple, is one of the most important measures used by investors to evaluate the market price of a firm's common stock. This is one reason that earnings per share is reported prominently on the face of the income statement. As explained in Chapter 9, the effect of extraordinary items and potential dilution of EPS from any convertible long-term debt and/or convertible preferred stock, and stock options, is also disclosed separately on the income statement. It is usually the diluted earnings per share amount that is used to calculate the P/E ratio associated with a company's stock. Because of its significance, the P/E ratio is disclosed in the stock listing tables of *The Wall Street Journal* and other periodicals. Although the above illustration of the P/E ratio calculation was based on earnings for the past year, analysts sometimes use expected future earnings per share and the current market price in the calculation in order to evaluate the prospects for changes in the stock's market price. Another approach to forecast market price is to use expected future earnings per share and the current (or expected future) earnings multiple. It should be noted, however, that the P/E ratio applies only to common stock. Since the preferred stock dividend does not fluctuate as earnings change, it would not be meaningful to calculate a preferred stock P/E ratio.

A rule of thumb for putting the price/earnings ratio in perspective is that for the common stocks of most merchandising and manufacturing companies, average P/E ratios have historically ranged from 12 to 18. However, P/E ratios have increased dramatically in recent years, reflecting an underlying confidence among investors in U.S. equity markets. In the third quarter of 1997, the average P/E ratio for the 900 companies included in *Business Week*'s Corporate Scoreboard was 23.[1] Of course, it is difficult to predict whether or not such high earnings multiples will be sustainable in the long run. What is clear is that the rise in U.S. stock market prices throughout the 1990s outpaced the earnings growth reported by American businesses, thus driving P/E ratios higher. (Visit www.businessweek.com

---

[1]Source: *Business Week,* November 17, 1997, page 151. Data: *Standard & Poor's Compustat,* a division of The McGraw-Hill Companies.

to find the most recent "Corporate Scoreboard" and the All-Industry Composite data reported at the top of the data table.)

Despite these changes, the interpretation of P/E ratios for individual firms is fairly straightforward. An above-average P/E ratio indicates that the common stock price is high relative to the firm's current earnings, probably because investors anticipate relatively favorable future developments, such as increased earnings per share or higher dividends per share. Low P/E ratios usually indicate poor earnings expectations. Keep in mind, however, that P/E ratios are significantly influenced by the company's reported earnings. For example, assume that Cruisers, Inc., reported earnings per share of $2.42 in 1998 and $5.56 in 1999, as illustrated in Exhibit 9–6. Assume also that the year-end market price per share of common stock was $40 in 1998 and $60 in 1999. Thus, the P/E ratio for Cruisers, Inc., would have fallen from 16.5 ($40/$2.42) to 10.8 ($60/$5.56) even though net income nearly doubled (from $764,000 in 1998 to $1,527,000 in 1999) and the market price per share of common stock increased by 50%, in just one year! In this type of situation, the relatively low P/E ratio at the end of 1999 would probably reflect investors' recognition that 1999 earnings were exceptionally high relative to the company's recent experience. Although the market price per share has increased significantly, it has not adjusted as quickly as earnings have grown. What this demonstrates is that the P/E ratio should not be the sole, or even principal, consideration in an investment decision. Financial analysts might consider a low P/E ratio for a well-established company an indicator that the company's stock warrants further analysis.

WHAT DOES IT MEAN?

7. What does it mean when the price/earnings ratio of a firm's common stock is significantly higher than the P/E ratio for the overall stock market?

Objective 6
Understand how dividend yield and the dividend payout ratio are used by investors to evaluate a company's common stock.

Another ratio used by both common stock investors and preferred stock investors is the **dividend yield.** This is calculated by dividing the annual dividend by the current market price of the stock. This calculation is illustrated here, again using Cruisers, Inc., per share data for the year ended August 31, 1999 (as shown in Chapter 9):

$$\text{Dividend yield} = \frac{\text{Annual dividend per share}}{\text{Market price per share of stock}}$$

Dividend yield on:

$$\text{Common stock} = \frac{\$1.98}{\$60.00} = 3.3\%$$

$$\text{Preferred stock} = \frac{\$3.50}{\$56.00^*} = 6.25\%$$

The dividend yield would be compared to the yield available on alternative investments to help the investor evaluate the extent to which her investment

---

*Arbitrarily selected for illustration purposes.

objectives were being met. In many cases, investors will accept a low current dividend yield from a common stock if they believe that the firm is reinvesting the earnings retained for use in the business at a relatively high ROI because investors anticipate that future earnings will permit higher future dividends. In the case of preferred stock, investors will compare the yield to that available on other fixed income investments with comparable risk to determine whether or not to continue holding the preferred stock as an investment. You may have noticed that the dividend yield on Cruisers, Inc.'s preferred stock is lower than the 7% stated dividend rate on its $50 par value preferred stock (refer to the EPS illustration on page 318 in Chapter 9). Since preferred dividends are linked to the par value per share, the dividend yield for preferred shareholders decreases as the market price per share increases. The average dividend yield on common stocks has historically been in the range of 3% to 6%, although it was near 2% in early 1998 because dividends had not kept pace with the rise in common stock prices during 1996 and 1997. For preferred stocks, the yield is usually somewhat greater, in the range of 5% to 8%.

WHAT DOES IT MEAN?

8. What does it mean when the dividend yield on a firm's common stock is less than the average dividend yield for all common stocks?

Another ratio involving the dividend on common stock is the **dividend payout ratio.** This ratio, computed by dividing the dividend per share of common stock by the earnings per share of common stock (usually diluted earnings per share), reflects the dividend policy of the company. Most firms have a policy of paying dividends that are a relatively constant proportion of earnings (e.g., 40 to 50%, or 10 to 15%). Knowing the dividend payout ratio permits the investor to project dividends from an assessment of the firm's earnings prospects. Cruisers, Inc.'s dividend payout for fiscal 1999 would be computed as follows (data from Chapter 9):

$$\text{Dividend payout ratio} = \frac{\text{Annual dividend per share}}{\text{Earnings per share}}$$

$$= \$1.98/\$5.56$$

$$= 35.6\%$$

Most firms try to avoid having significant fluctuations in the amount of the cash dividend per share because investors prefer to be relatively assured of the dividend amount. Therefore, very few firms use the payout ratio as the sole, or even the principal, determinant of the dividend amount. To help communicate its dividend policy to the stockholders, a firm refers to its dividends in two ways: **Regular dividends** are the stable, or gradually changing, periodic (i.e., quarterly, semiannual, or annual) dividends; **extra dividends** are larger dividends that may be declared and paid after an especially profitable year. The significance of the extra dividend is that it indicates to stockholders that they should not expect to receive the larger amount every year.

As a rule of thumb, the dividend payout ratio for most merchandising and manufacturing companies is usually in the range of 30% to 50%. Keep in mind, however, that this range can vary significantly—especially when a firm has a low (or even negative) earnings year but wishes to maintain its dividend per share amount.

From the preferred stockholders' point of view, the ratio of net income to the total preferred stock dividend requirement indicates the margin of safety of the preferred dividend. If net income is less than three or four times the preferred dividend requirement and has been falling over time, the preferred stockholders would become concerned about the firm's ability to generate enough earnings and cash to be able to pay the preferred dividend. This **preferred dividend coverage ratio** for Cruisers, Inc., for fiscal 1999 (data from Chapter 9) was a somewhat healthy 5.5, calculated as follows:

$$\frac{\text{Preferred dividend}}{\text{coverage ratio}} = \frac{\text{Net income}}{\text{Preferred dividend requirement}}$$

$$= \frac{\$1,527,000}{\$280,000}$$

$$= 5.5 \text{ times}$$

Financial Leverage Measures

Objective 7
Understand what financial leverage is and why it is significant to management, investors, and creditors.

Financial leverage (frequently called just *leverage*) refers to the use of debt (and, in the broadest context of the term, preferred stock) to finance the assets of the entity. Leverage adds risk to the operation of the firm because if the firm does not generate enough cash to pay principal and interest payments, creditors may force the firm into bankruptcy. However, because the cost of debt (i.e., interest) is a fixed charge regardless of the amount of earnings, leverage also magnifies the return to the owners (ROE) relative to the return on assets (ROI). The magnification effect of financial leverage is illustrated in Exhibit 11–3.

As Exhibit 11–3 illustrates, borrowing money at an interest rate that is less than the rate of return that can be earned on that money increases (or magnifies) the return on owners' equity. This makes common financial sense; who wouldn't borrow money at a 9% interest cost if the money could be invested to earn more than 9%? Of course, if the return on investment were less than the cost of borrowing, the result would be a reduction of owners' equity (a loss) at best, and bankruptcy at worst. This is the risk of leverage—the magnification works both ways! Highly leveraged firms or individuals (i.e., those with lots of debt relative to owners' equity) are exposed to the risk of losses or bankruptcy if the return on investment falls below the cost of borrowing. This does happen in economic recessions and industry business cycles. Accordingly, most nonfinancial firms try to limit the debt in their capital structure to no more than 50% of total capital (debt plus owners' equity).

The effect of leverage can be seen in the graphs of Exhibit 3–2 (see p. 83), on which are plotted ROI and ROE for Intel Corporation, for the period 1992–1996. Notice that ROE is significantly higher than ROI for each year presented. Debt and preferred stock provide leverage because the interest cost (or dividend rate) is fixed. When debt is issued, the

---

EXHIBIT 11–3   Financial Leverage Illustrated

I. Without financial leverage:

Assume the following balance sheet and income statement:

Balance Sheet		Income Statement	
Assets.................	$10,000	Earnings before interest and taxes.................	$2,000
		Interest.................	0
Liabilities...............	$ 0	Earnings before taxes.......	$2,000
Owners' equity	10,000	Income taxes (40%)........	$ 800
Total L + OE............	$10,000	Net income..............	$1,200

$$\text{Return on investment (assets) before interest and taxes} = \text{Earnings before interest and taxes/Total assets}$$

$$= \$2,000/\$10,000$$

$$= 20\%$$

$$\text{Return on equity, after taxes} = \text{Net income/Owners' equity}$$

$$= \$1,200/\$10,000$$

$$= 12\%$$

Return on investment measures the efficiency with which management has used the operating assets to generate operating income. Note that the return on investment calculaton is based on earnings before interest and taxes (operating income) and total assets, rather than net income and total assets. Earnings before interest and taxes (operating income) is used because the interest expense reflects a financing decision, not an operating result, and income taxes are beyond the control of operating management. Thus, ROI becomes an evaluation of the operating activities of the firm.

Return on equity measures the rate of return that net income provides to the owners.

ROI and ROE differ only because income taxes have been excluded from ROI but have been included in ROE.

II. With financial leverage:

Assume the following balance sheet and income statement:

Balance Sheet		Income Statement	
Assets.................	$10,000	Earnings before interest and taxes.................	$2,000
		Interest.................	360
Liabilities (9% interest)	$ 4,000	Earnings before taxes.......	$1,640
Owners' equity	6,000	Income taxes (40%)........	$ 656
Total L + OE............	$10,000	Net income..............	$ 984

$$\text{Return on investment (assets) before interest and taxes} = \text{Earnings before interest and taxes/Total assets}$$

$$= \$2,000/\$10,000$$

$$= 20\%$$

EXHIBIT 11–3   *(concluded)*

Return on equity, after taxes = Net income/Owners' equity

= $984/$6,000

= 16.4%

The use of financial leverage has not affected ROI: financial leverage refers to how the assets are financed, not how efficiently the assets are used to generate operating income.

The use of financial leverage has caused the ROE to increase from 12% to 16.4% because ROI (20%) exceeds the cost of the debt (9%) used to finance a portion of the assets.

interest rate is set and remains unchanged for the life of the debt issue. If the interest rate on the debt were to fluctuate as a function of the firm's ROI, or as a result of inflation or deflation in the economy, the magnification of ROE would be diminished or eliminated.

Another feature of debt illustrated in Exhibit 11–3 is the deductibility of interest as an expense in determining income subject to income taxes. The after-tax cost of debt is its interest rate multiplied by the complement of the firm's tax rate. In this example, the assumed tax rate is 40%, so the after-tax cost of the debt is 9% $\times$ (1 − 0.40) = 5.4%. Since preferred stock dividends are not deductible as an expense, financial managers prefer to use debt, rather than preferred stock, as the source of fixed-cost capital.

Two **financial leverage measures,** the debt ratio and the debt/equity ratio, are used to indicate the extent to which a firm is using financial leverage. Each ratio expresses the relationship between debt and equity in a slightly different manner. The **debt ratio** is the ratio of total liabilities to the total of liabilities and owners' equity. The **debt/equity ratio** is the ratio of total liabilities to total owners' equity. Thus, a debt ratio of 50% would be the same as a debt/equity ratio of 1 (or 1:1). To illustrate these ratios, assume the following *capital structure* (i.e., right-hand side of the balance sheet) for a firm:

Liabilities	$ 40,000
Owners' equity	60,000
Total L + OE	$100,000

$$\text{Debt ratio} = \frac{\text{Total liabilities}}{\text{Total liabilities and owners' equity}}$$

$$= \frac{\$40,000}{\$100,000}$$

$$= 40\%$$

$$\text{Debt/Equity ratio} = \frac{\text{Total liabilities}}{\text{Total owners' equity}}$$

$$= \frac{\$40,000}{\$60,000}$$

$$= 66.7\%$$

As already indicated, most nonfinancial firms will usually have a debt ratio below 50%—a debt/equity ratio of less than 1—because of the risk associated with having a greater proportion of debt in the capital structure. However, many firms have been forced into unusually high financial leverage positions in recent years in order to survive competitive pressures (see Business in Practice—The Leveraged Buyout).

BUSINESS IN PRACTICE
The Leveraged Buyout

The mid- and late-1980s was a period of relatively high corporate ownership rearrangement activity featuring friendly and unfriendly mergers and acquisitions, as well as leveraged buyouts. In a merger or acquisition one firm acquires another, either by issuing stock of the surviving company to the stockholders of the firm being acquired (usually a merger) or by buying the stock of the company being acquired by paying cash (and sometimes other securities) to the stockholders of the other firm. This is a *takeover*. Changes in top management and operations of the acquired company frequently result. A leveraged buyout is a transaction in which the present top management of a publicly held firm buys the stock of the nonmanagement stockholders, and the firm becomes "privately owned" (i.e., its shares are no longer traded in the public market). Neither management nor the operations of the firm change significantly. Some firms that have been takeover targets have "gone private" through a leveraged buyout in order to avoid being acquired by another firm.

The leveraged buyout transaction gets its label from the fact that the company goes heavily into debt in order to obtain the funds needed to buy the shares of the public stockholders. In many cases the debt ratio will be substantially higher than is usually considered prudent, but investors are willing to invest in the firm's bonds because of their confidence in management's proven ability to operate the firm profitably.

The debt issued in a leveraged buyout is usually considered speculative or high risk (the term *junk bond* has been applied to much of it). Investors are often concerned about the impact of a major economic recession on the ability of these firms to meet their interest and principal payment requirements. During the recession of the early 1990s, many firms were forced into bankruptcy or mergers with other firms, and some of the firms that survived were forced to sell off many of their assets. Other financially healthier firms took advantage of rising stock market values to realign their capital structure by selling stock (going public again) and using the proceeds to reduce high-cost long-term debt.

Since the deferred income tax liability and most of an entity's current liabilities are not interest bearing, many financial analysts exclude these items from the numerator of the debt ratio and the debt/equity ratio. This allows analysts to get a better sense of what proportion of the entity's capital structure is financed by long-term, interest-bearing debt. Other liabilities that do not add risk to the entity's operations, such as minority interest, may also be excluded from these calculations.

Holders of a company's long-term debt will frequently want to know the **times interest earned ratio** for the firm. This measure is similar to the preferred dividend coverage ratio previously explained; it shows the relationship of earnings before interest and taxes (operating income) to interest expense. The greater the ratio, the more confident the debtholders can be about the firm's prospects for continuing to have enough earnings to cover interest expense, even if the firm experiences a decline in the demand for its products or services. Using data from the Cruisers, Inc., income statement for fiscal 1999, as shown in Exhibit 9–6, the calculation of times interest earned is:

Earnings before income taxes	$2,777 million
Add back interest expense	3,378 million
Earnings before interest and taxes	$6,155 million

$$\text{Times interest earned} = \frac{\text{Earnings before interest and taxes}}{\text{Interest expense}}$$

$$= \$6,155/\$2,777$$

$$= 2.2 \text{ times}$$

The debtholders of Cruisers, Inc. would be concerned about the company's ability to continue to earn enough to cover its interest expense. As a general rule of thumb, a times interest earned ratio of 5 or higher is considered by creditors to indicate a relatively low risk that a firm will not be able to pay interest in the future. (Refer to Intel's income statement on page 18 in the Appendix to verify an amazing times interest earned of 318.4 for 1996.)

WHAT DOES IT MEAN?

9. What does it mean to state that a firm is highly leveraged?

10. What does it mean that the more financial leverage a firm has the greater the risk to owners and creditors?

Objective 8
Understand what book value per share of common stock is and why it is not a very meaningful amount for most companies.

Other Analytical Techniques

Book Value per Share of Common Stock

The **book value per share of comon stock** is a frequently cited ratio in the financial press that can be easily misunderstood by investors who do not carefully interpret its meaning. Book value per share is calculated by dividing the total common stockholders' equity by the number of shares of common stock outstanding. If there is preferred stock in the capital structure of the firm, the liquidating value of the preferred stock is subtracted from total owners' equity to get the common stockholders' equity. *Net asset value per share of common stock* is another name for this measure.

The following illustration using data as of December 28, 1996, for Intel Corporation, illustrates the calculation (in millions of dollars):

$$\text{Book value per share of common stock} = \frac{\text{Common stockholders' equity}}{\text{Number of shares of common stock outstanding}}$$

$$= \frac{\$16{,}872 \text{ million*}}{821 \text{ million*}}$$

$$= \$20.55$$

Because total common stockholders' equity reflects the application of generally accepted accounting principles and the specific accounting policies that have been selected, book value per share is not a number that can be meaningfully compared to the market value per share of stock for most companies, especially if the market value is greater than the book value (which is usually the case). For Intel, the 1996 year-end market price per share was approximately $131.00, which was obviously unrelated to its $20.55 book value per share. Although book value per share is not a very useful measure most of the time, you should be aware of how it is calculated and understand its limitations.

WHAT DOES IT MEAN?

11. What does it mean to state that a company's book value per share of common stock is less than its market value per share of common stock?

Common Size Financial Statements

Objective 9
Understand how common size financial statements can be used to evaluate a firm's financial position and results of operations over a number of years.

When comparing and evaluating the operating results of a company over a number of years, many analysts like to express the balance sheet and income statement in a percentage format. This type of presentation is a **common size statement.** To prepare a common size balance sheet, each asset is expressed as a percentage of total assets, and each liability and owners' equity amount is expressed as a percentage of that total. For the income statement sales is set at 100%, and each item on the income statement is expressed as a percentage of sales. This type of percentage analysis makes spotting trends in the composition of balance sheet and income statement items much easier than looking at dollar amounts. For example, inventories that represent an increasing percentage of total assets may indicate a weakness in inventory control procedures. An increase in the ratio of cost of goods sold to sales (which would be a decrease in the gross profit ratio) would indicate that management is either unable or unwilling to increase selling prices in response to cost increases, thus causing downward

---

*From stockholders' equity section of consolidated balance sheets, page 19 of 1996 annual report in the Appendix.

pressure on operating income. Of course, a well-designed graphical display of key balance sheet and income statement percentage data can also greatly help a reader interpret the data.

Exhibit 11–4 presents common size income statements for Intel Corporation for each of the years 1992 through 1996. When analyzing common size financial statement data, you should look first at the "big picture" items, and make quick comparisons from year to year. Notice, for example, that total operating costs and expenses represented only 61.4% of net revenues (i.e., sales) in 1993, which was a five-year low. As a result, operating income, income before taxes, and net income each showed a five-year high in 1993, but the provision for taxes was also at a high point. This was an exceptional year, even for Intel. However, the opposite was true for each of these items in 1992 when total operating costs and expenses were 74.5% of net revenues. Check this out by scanning across each of the lines shown in bold print in Exhibit 11–4. As you do this, you should also notice the direct relationship between income before taxes and the provision for taxes in each year. This relationship makes sense; when earnings as a percent of sales are high, so are taxes. In fact, if you visualize the trends in operating income and net income without considering the 1993 data, you can see that earnings as a percent of sales increased in each year since 1992. These trends are remarkable when considering that sales grew from $5,844 million in 1992 to $20,847 million in 1996. What it means is that *earnings growth* was even more rapid than *sales growth* during this period. (This reflects operating leverage, discussed in Chapter 13.)

A line-by-line analysis of a company's common size data will often reveal additional information in support of the reader's basic interpretation of major trends. For example, the percentages shown for Intel's research

EXHIBIT 11–4   Common Size Income Statements

INTEL CORPORATION
Common Size Income Statements
For the Five Years Ended December 28, 1996

	1996	1995	1994	1993	1992
Net revenues	**100.0%**	**100.0%**	**100.0%**	**100.0%**	**100.0%**
Cost of sales	44.0	48.2	48.4	37.0	43.8
Research and development	8.7	8.0	9.6	11.1	13.3
Marketing, general and administrative	11.1	11.4	12.6	13.3	17.4
Operating costs and expenses	63.8	67.6	70.6	61.4	74.5
Operating income	**36.2**	**32.4**	**29.4**	**38.6**	**25.5**
Interest expense	−0.1	−0.2	−0.5	−0.6	−0.9
Interest income and other, net	1.9	2.6	2.4	2.2	2.3
Income before taxes	**38.0**	**34.8**	**31.3**	**40.2**	**26.9**
Provision for taxes	13.3	12.8	11.4	14.1	8.6
Net income	**24.7%**	**22.0%**	**19.9%**	**26.1%**	**18.3%**

and development, and marketing, general and administrative expense categories both decreased substantially from 1992 to 1996. This doesn't necessarily mean that management became less committed to R&D and marketing efforts. In reality, the actual dollar amounts for these expenditures increased significantly from year to year, but—again—not as quickly as Intel's sales growth. Interest expense also decreased each year, although the amounts were not material. These are all good signs, and each of these trends helps to explain the overall trend that shows net income increasing as a percent of sales.

As mentioned at the beginning of this section, common size balance sheets can also be prepared using total assets as 100%. For any given year, each of the individual asset, liability, and owners' equity captions would be compared to total assets to determine its relative percentage. This process, illustrated in Exhibit 11–4 with Intel's income statement data, is often referred to as *vertical* common size analysis because each financial statement is examined from top to bottom on an annual basis. It is likewise possible, and often useful, to prepare *horizontal* common size financial statements. With horizontal analysis, several years' financial data are stated in terms of a base year. The amount reported for *each* item on the income statement or balance sheet in the base year is equal to 100%, and the amounts reported for all subsequent years are stated as a percentage of this base. To illustrate, consider the tremendous sales and earnings growth that Intel has enjoyed in recent years:

	1996	1995	1994	1993	1992
Net revenues (millions)	$20,847	$16,202	$11,521	$8,782	$5,844
Net income (millions)	5,157	3,566	2,288	2,295	1,067

In Intel's case, it is easy to see that both trends are extraordinary (although net income fell slightly in 1994). Unfortunately, these raw data do not answer all of the questions you may have. For example, how rapidly have sales been increasing, and has net income kept pace with sales? Horizontal analysis answers these questions directly:

	1996	1995	1994	1993	1992
Net revenues (i.e., sales)	357%	277%	197%	150%	100%
Net income (i.e., earnings)	483%	334%	214%	215%	100%

Even though net income slipped a bit in 1994, earnings grew more quickly than sales for each year presented (as compared to the base year). If you were to prepare Intel's entire income statement on a horizontal basis, you would also find that sales have grown at a higher rate than expenses have, as suggested above in the discussion of Exhibit 11–4.

WHAT DOES IT MEAN?

12. What does it mean to prepare common size financial statements?

Other Operating Statistics

Physical measures of activity, rather than the financial measures included in the financial statements, are frequently useful. For example, reporting sales in units provides a perspective that may be hidden by price changes when only sales dollars are reported. Or reporting the total number of employees (or employees by division or department) may be more useful for some purposes than reporting payroll costs.

Many analysts combine physical and financial measures to develop useful statistics to show trends or make comparisons between firms. For example, sales dollars per employee and operating income per employee each indicate a type of productivity measure. Plant operating expenses per square foot of plant space or gross profit per square foot of selling space might also be useful indicators of efficiency. There is no "cookbook" of quantitative measures for management to follow; the challenge is to understand the firm's objectives and procedures, and then to develop measurement and reporting techniques to help people accomplish their goals.

WHAT DOES IT MEAN?

13. What does it mean to use more than financial ratios to evaluate a company's position and/or performance?

Summary

Financial statement analysis using ratio measurements and trend analysis assists the user of financial statements in making informed judgments and decisions about the entity's financial condition and results of operations. Keep in mind, however, that an analysis of an entity's financial data should be tempered somewhat by the fact that all of the data reviewed are historical information. As a result, the analyst is making decisions about future events based primarily on past events. Without diminishing the value of financial ratio computations, it must be recognized that they do little to foretell the future. Therefore, the analyst must give due consideration to many other factors before making a decision about the entity.

Rate of return calculations in general, and the return on investment (ROI) and return on equity (ROE) measures in particular, are essential in evaluating profitability. These measures were discussed in detail in Chapter 3.

The trend of a ratio over time contains much more information than a single ratio at one point in time. Trend comparisons between the entity and broad industry averages are also useful.

Creditors especially are interested in the entity's liquidity. Working capital and the calculation of the current ratio and acid-test ratio were also discussed in Chapter 3.

Because alternative accounting methods affect financial statement data differently, it is important that readers know which alternatives (e.g., FIFO versus LIFO for inventory) have been used in the financial statements being analyzed.

Activity measures reflect the efficiency with which assets have been used to generate sales revenue. Most activity ratios focus on turnover. Activity can also be expressed in terms of the number of days of activity (e.g., sales) in the year-end balance (e.g., accounts receivable).

In addition to ROI and ROE based on total data, certain per share ratios are also important. The price/earnings ratio, dividend yield, dividend payout ratio, and preferred dividend coverage ratios are examples.

Leverage ratios focus on the financial leverage of the firm. Financial leverage will magnify ROE relative to ROI, and it adds risk to the securities issued by the firm.

Book value per share of common stock is frequently reported, but because it is based on the financial statement value of the firm's assets instead of their market value, book value is not very useful in most circumstances.

An effective way to compare the financial condition and results of operations of different sized firms is to express balance sheet data as a percentage of total assets, and income statement data as a percentage of sales. This process results in *vertical* common size financial statements. It is also useful to prepare *horizontal* common size financial statements that show trends in individual items over several years in comparison to a base year.

Investors, managers, employees, and others are frequently interested in other operating statistics that use data not contained in the financial statements. More than financial data are needed to develop a complete picture about a company.

Financial statement analysis ratios are summarized below by category of ratio.

I. Profitability measures

A. Return on investment (ROI)
  1. General model

$$ROI = \frac{Return}{Investment}$$ Return is frequently net income, and investment is frequently average total assets.

This ratio gives the rate of return that has been earned on the assets invested, and is the key measure of profitability.
  2. DuPont model

$$ROI = Margin \times Turnover$$

$$= \frac{Net\ income}{Sales} \times \frac{Sales}{Average\ total\ assets}$$

Margin expresses the net income resulting from each dollar of sales. Turnover shows the efficiency with which assets are used to generate sales.
  3. Variations of the general model use operating income, income before taxes, or some other intermediate income statement amount in the numerator and average operating assets in the denominator to focus on the rate of return from operations before taxes.

B. Return on equity (ROE)
  1. General model

$$ROE = \frac{Net\ income}{Average\ total\ owners'\ equity}$$

This ratio gives the rate of return on that portion of the assets provided by the owners of the entity.

2. A variation of the general model occurs when there is preferred stock. Net income is reduced by the amount of the preferred stock dividend requirement, and only common stockholders' equity is used in the denominator. This distinction is made because the ownership rights of the preferred and common stockholders differ.

C. Price/Earnings ratio (P/E Ratio)

$$\frac{\text{Price earnings ratio}}{\text{(or earnings multiple)}} = \frac{\text{Market price per share}}{\text{Earnings per share}}$$

This ratio expresses the relative expensiveness of a share of a firm's common stock because it shows how much investors are willing to pay for the stock relative to earnings. Generally speaking, the greater a firm's ROI and rate of earnings growth, the higher the P/E ratio of its common stock will be. Most of the time *diluted* earnings per share is used in this calculation.

D. Dividend yield

$$\text{Dividend yield} = \frac{\text{Annual dividend per share}}{\text{Market price per share of stock}}$$

The dividend yield expresses part of the stockholder's ROI: the rate of return represented by the annual cash dividend. The other part of the stockholder's total ROI comes from the change in the market value of the stock during the year; this is usually called the *capital gain* or *loss*.

E. Dividend payout ratio

$$\text{Dividend payout ratio} = \frac{\text{Annual dividend per share}}{\text{Earnings per share}}$$

The dividend payout ratio expresses the proportion of earnings paid as dividends to common stockholders. It can be used to estimate dividends of future years if earnings can be estimated. Diluted earnings per share is usually used in this calculation.

F. Preferred dividend coverage ratio

$$\frac{\text{Preferred dividend}}{\text{coverage ratio}} = \frac{\text{Net income}}{\text{Preferred dividend requirement}}$$

The preferred dividend coverage ratio expresses the ability of the firm to meet its preferred stock dividend requirement. The higher this coverage ratio, the lower the probability that dividends on common stock will be discontinued because of low earnings and failure to pay dividends on preferred stock.

II. Liquidity measures

A. Working capital

$$\text{Working capital} = \text{Current assets} - \text{Current liabilities}$$

The arithmetic relationship between current assets and current liabilities is a measure of the firm's ability to meet its obligations as they come due.

B. Current ratio

$$\text{Current ratio} = \frac{\text{Current assets}}{\text{Current liabilities}}$$

This ratio permits an evaluation of liquidity that is more comparable over time and between firms than the amount of working capital.

C. Acid-test ratio

$$\text{Acid-test ratio} = \frac{\text{Cash (including temporary cash investments)} + \text{Accounts receivable}}{\text{Current liabilities}}$$

By excluding inventories and other nonliquid current assets, this ratio gives a conservative assessment of the firm's bill-paying ability.

III. Activity measures

A. Turnover:
1. Total asset turnover

$$\text{Total asset turnover} = \frac{\text{Sales}}{\text{Average total assets}}$$

Turnover shows the efficiency with which assets are used to generate sales. Refer also to the DuPont model under profitability measures.

2. Variations include turnover calculations for accounts receivable, plant and equipment, and total operating assets. Each variation uses sales in the numerator and the appropriate average amount in the denominator.

3. Inventory turnover

$$\text{Inventory turnover} = \frac{\text{Cost of goods sold}}{\text{Average inventories}}$$

Inventory turnover focuses on the efficiency of the firm's inventory management practices. Cost of goods sold is used in the numerator because inventories are carried at cost, not selling price.

B. Number of days' sales in:
1. Accounts receivable

$$\frac{\text{Number of days' sales in}}{\text{Accounts receivable}} = \frac{\text{Accounts receivable}}{\text{Average day's sales}}$$

$$\text{Average day's sales} = \frac{\text{Annual sales}}{365}$$

This measure shows the average age of the accounts receivable, and reflects the efficiency of the firm's collection policies relative to its credit terms.

2. Inventory

$$\frac{\text{Number of days'}}{\text{sales in inventory}} = \frac{\text{Inventory}}{\text{Average day's cost of goods sold}}$$

$$\frac{\text{Average day's cost}}{\text{of goods sold}} = \frac{\text{Average cost of goods sold}}{365}$$

This measure shows the number of days' sales that could be made from the inventory on hand. The trend of this measure reflects management's ability to control inventories relative to sales.

IV. **Financial leverage measures**
   A. Debt ratio

$$\text{Debt ratio} = \frac{\text{Total liabilities}}{\text{Total liabilities and owners' equity}}$$

   B. Debt/Equity ratio

$$\text{Debt/Equity ratio} = \frac{\text{Total liabilities}}{\text{Total owners' equity}}$$

Each of these measures shows the proportion of debt in the capital structure. Note that a debt ratio of 50% is the same as a debt/equity ratio of 100%. These ratios reflect the risk caused by the interest and principal requirements of debt. Variations of these models involve the definition of total liabilities. Current liabilities, deferred taxes, and minority interest are excluded by some analysts because they are not interest bearing and do not add as much risk as does long-term debt.

   C. Times interest earned

$$\text{Times interest earned} = \frac{\text{Earnings before interest and taxes}}{\text{Interest expense}}$$

This is a measure of the firm's ability to earn enough to cover its annual interest requirement.

Key Terms and Concepts

book value per share of common stock (p. 387)   The quotient of total common stockholders' equity divided by the number of shares of common stock outstanding. Sometimes called *net asset value per share of common stock*. Not a very useful measure most of the time.

common size statement (p. 388)   A financial statement in which amounts are expressed in percentage terms. In a *vertical* common size balance sheet, total assets are 100%, and all other amounts are expressed as a percentage of total assets each year; for an income statement, sales are 100% each year. *Horizontal* common size financial statements are side-by-side comparisons of two or more years' data.

debt ratio (p. 385)   The ratio of total liabilities to the sum of total liabilities and total owners' equity. Sometimes long-term debt is the only liability used in the calculation.

debt/equity ratio (p. 385)   The ratio of total liabilities to total owners' equity. Sometimes only long-term debt is used for the numerator of the ratio.

dividend payout ratio (p. 382)   The ratio of the annual dividend per share of common stock to the earnings per share.

dividend yield (p. 381)   The ratio of the annual dividend per share of common stock to the market price per share.

earnings multiple (p. 378)   Another term for the *price/earnings ratio;* an indicator of the relative expensiveness of a firm's common stock.

effect of the inventory cost-flow assumption on working capital (p. 372)   When the cost of items being purchased for inventory is changing, the inventory cost-flow assumption used (e.g., FIFO or LIFO) influences the inventory account balance, total current assets, and working capital.

extra dividend (p. 382)   A dividend that is not likely to be incorporated as part of the regular dividend in the future.

financial leverage measures (p. 385)   The debt ratio and debt/equity ratio that indicate the extent to which financial leverage is being used.

number of days' sales in accounts receivable (p. 375)   An indicator of the efficiency with which accounts receivable are collected.

number of days' sales in inventory (p. 375)   An indicator of the efficiency with which inventories are managed.

preferred dividend coverage ratio (p. 383)   The ratio of net income to the annual preferred stock dividend requirement.

price/earnings ratio (p. 378)   An indicator of the relative expensiveness of a firm's common stock.

regular dividend (p. 382)   A dividend that is likely to be declared on a repetitive, periodic (i.e., quarterly, semiannual or annual) basis.

times interest earned ratio (p. 387)   The ratio of earnings before interest and taxes to interest expense. An indicator of the risk associated with financial leverage.

WHAT DOES IT MEAN?
ANSWERS

1. It means that comparing several ratio results over a period of time permits a more valid comparison of the direction of relative performance than a comparison of a single ratio. However, it is necessary to understand how alternative accounting practices have affected the financial statement amounts reported for each firm.

2. It means that working capital, the current ratio, and the acid-test ratio are calculated and interpreted to determine whether the entity is likely to be able to pay its obligations when they come due.

3. It means that to determine how efficiently the firm's assets are being used and/or managed, various turnover ratios are calculated and evaluated.

4. It means that the ratio of sales for the period to average total assets used during the period has risen, indicating that assets were used more efficiently relative to sales generated. Perhaps this was accomplished by producing more product with the same amount of plant and equipment and/or reducing inventories.

5. It means that the firm is less profitable in the sense of earnings related to assets used to generate earnings.

6. It means to break ROI into its margin and turnover components to help determine whether the decrease in ROI is due to reduced profitability or less efficient use of assets, or both.

7. It means that investors are willing to pay more for a share of the firm's common stock than for a share of common stock of most other firms. This may be caused by investor expectations for much higher growth in profitability in the immediate future for the firm relative to expectations for other firms.

8. It means that the firm is retaining and reinvesting proportionately more of its earnings than other companies. This may be because the firm anticipates needing more capital for expansion, and the board of directors prefers to retain earnings for that use rather than raise capital by selling more stock or issuing debt.

9. It means that the firm has a relatively high proportion of debt to equity in its capital structure.

10. It means that if the firm cannot earn a greater rate of return than the interest rate being paid on borrowed funds, its chances of not being able to repay the debt and of going bankrupt are greater than if it had less financial leverage.

11. It doesn't mean much at all because book value is based on balance sheet values, which are not market values or replacement values.

12. It means that instead of using currency amounts in the statements, elements of the financial statements are expressed as a percentage of total assets (for the balance sheet) or as a percentage of total revenues (for the income statement). This is an easy and effective way of making comparisons over time for a single company and of comparing one company with another—as long as consideration is given to the effects of different accounting practices that may have been used.

13. It means that other statistics, such as rate of employee turnover, market share, and/or sales per employee are frequently relevant and useful to the evaluator.

Exercises and Problems

Note: Where no specific learning objective is identified, the requirements involve calculating and using several ratios, including those discussed in Chapter 3.

11–1. **Identify information used in an investment decision.** Look forward to the day when you will have accumulated $2,000, and assume that you have decided to invest that hard-earned money in the common stock of a publicly owned corporation. What data about that company will you be most interested in, and how will you arrange those data so they are most meaningful to you? What information about the company will you want on a weekly basis, on a quarterly basis, and on an annual basis? How will you decide whether to sell, hold, or buy some more of the firm's stock?

11–2. **Obtain an annual report and discuss information sources.** If your library has a common stock investment advisory service such as *Moody's Handbook of Common Stocks,* Standard and Poor's *Corporation Stock Market Encyclopedia,* or Value Line Reports, find in one of these sources the report about a company you have heard about or in which you have an interest. Alternatively, visit a brokerage firm office and ask for a report from one of the above sources, or a report prepared by the brokerage firm's research division. Review the report and notice the analytical data that it contains. What other data besides those in the report would you like to obtain? Why do you want these other data? How would you get them?

Intel LO 9   **11–3.**   **Prepare a common size balance sheet, 1995.** Refer to the consolidated balance sheets on page 19 of the Intel Corporation annual report in the Appendix.

Required:

Prepare a common size balance sheet at December 30, 1995, using the following captions:

Total current assets
Property, plant, and equipment (net)
Long-term investments and other noncurrent assets
   Total assets
Total current liabilities
Total noncurrent liabilities
Total shareholders' equity
   Total liabilities and shareholders' equity

Intel LO 9   **11–4.**   **Prepare a common size balance sheet, 1996.** Solve the requirements of Problem 11–5 for the year ended December 28, 1996.

LO 1   **11–5.**   **Review problem—understanding liquidity measures.** Assume that the current ratio for Arch Company is 2.0, its acid-test ratio is 1.5, and its working capital is $300,000. Answer each of the following questions *independently,* always referring back to the original information.
   a. How much does the firm have in current liabilities?
   b. If the only current assets shown on the balance sheet for Arch Company are Cash, Accounts Receivable, and Merchandise Inventory, how much does the firm have in Merchandise Inventory?
   c. If the firm collects an account receivable of $100,000, what will its new current ratio and working capital be?
   d. If the firm pays an account payable of $100,000, what will its new current ratio and working capital be?
   e. If the firm sells inventory that was purchased for $50,000 at a cash price of $60,000, what will its new acid-test ratio be?

LO 1   **11–6.**   **Effect of transactions on liquidity measures.** Selected balance sheet accounts for Tibbetts Company on September 30, 1998, are as follows:

Cash	$ 32,000
Marketable securities	58,000
Accounts receivable, net	86,000
Inventory	90,000
Prepaid expenses	14,000
Total current assets	$280,000
Accounts payable	$ 98,000
Other accrued liabilities	22,000
Short-term debt	40,000
Total current liabilities	$160,000

   a. Calculate the working capital, current ratio, and acid-test ratio for Tibbetts Company as of September 30, 1998.

b. Summarized below are the transactions/events that took place during the fiscal year ended September 30, 1999. Indicate the effect of each item on Tibbetts Company's working capital, current ratio, and acid-test ratio. Use + for increase, − for decrease, and (NE) for no effect. *(Hint: It may be helpful to record the journal entry(ies) or use the horizontal model for each item before considering the effects on liquidity measures.)*

Example	Working Capital	Current Ratio	Acid-Test Ratio
Paid accounts payable, $195,000.	NE	+	+
1. Credit sales for the year amounted to $240,000. The cost of goods sold was $156,000.			
2. Collected accounts receivable, $252,000.			
3. Purchased inventory on account, $168,000.			
4. Issued 500 shares of common stock for $18 per share.			
5. Wrote off $7,000 of uncollectible accounts using the allowance method.			
6. Declared and paid a cash dividend, $20,000.			
7. Sold marketable securities costing $26,000 for $31,000 in cash.			
8. Recorded insurance expense for the year, $12,000. The premium for the policy was paid in June, 1998.			
9. Borrowed cash on a short-term bank loan, $10,000.			
10. Repaid principal of $40,000 and interest of $3,000 on a long-term bank loan.			

11–7. Effect of transactions on various financial ratios. Indicate the effect that each transaction/event listed below will have on the financial ratio listed opposite it, and provide an explanation for your answer. Use + for increase, − for decrease, and (NE) for no effect. Assume that current assets exceed current liabilities in all cases, both before and after the transaction/event.

Transaction/Event	*Financial Ratio*
a. Split the common stock 2 for 1.	Book value per share of common stock
b. Collected accounts receivable.	Number of days' sales in accounts receivable
c. Issued common stock for cash.	Total asset turnover
d. Sold treasury stock.	Return on equity
e. Accrued interest on a note receivable.	Current ratio
f. Sold inventory on account.	Acid-test ratio
g. Wrote off an uncollectible account.	Accounts receivable turnover
h. Declared a cash dividend.	Dividend yield
i. Incurred operating expenses.	Margin
j. Sold equipment at a loss.	Earnings per share

11–8.   Effect of transactions on various financial ratios. Indicate the effect that each transaction/event listed below will have on the financial ratio listed opposite it, and provide an explanation for your answer. Use + for increase, − for decrease, and (NE) for no effect. Assume that current assets exceed current liabilities in all cases, both before and after the transaction/event.

Transaction/Event	*Financial Ratio*
a. Purchased inventory on account.	Number of days' sales in inventory
b. Sold inventory for cash, at a profit.	Inventory turnover
c. Issued a 10% stock dividend.	Earnings per share
d. Issued common stock for cash.	Debt ratio
e. Sold land at a gain.	Return on investment
f. Purchased treasury stock for cash.	Debt/Equity ratio
g. Accrued interest on a note payable.	Times interest earned
h. Accrued wages that have been earned by employees.	Current ratio
i. Equipment was purchased for cash.	Plant and equipment turnover
j. Issued bonds at an interest rate that is less than the company's ROI.	Return on equity

11–9.   Comparative analysis of liquidity trends for firms in various industries. The following data were taken from the "selected financial highlights" provided in the 1996 annual reports of the companies listed below (amounts are in millions):

	1996	*1995*	*1994*	*1993*	*1992*
Working capital:					
1. La-Z-Boy Incorporated	241	237	224	202	184
2. The Sherwin-Williams Company	365	620	592	597	498
3. The Quaker Oats Company	(465)	(622)	(496)	(6)	(38)
4. Microsoft Corporation	5,414	4,273	3,399	2,287	
Current ratio:					
1. La-Z-Boy Incorporated	3.5	3.5	3.7	4.1	3.8
2. The Sherwin-Williams Company	1.3	2.0	2.0	2.1	2.0
3. The Quaker Oats Company	0.7	0.6	0.7	1.0	1.0
4. Microsoft Corporation	3.2	4.2	4.7	5.1	

a. Evaluate the working capital and current ratio trends for each company.

b. In your opinion, is Microsoft becoming more liquid or less liquid? Explain.

c. Quaker Oats reported the lowest current ratio for each of the years reported above, while La-Z-Boy reported a relatively high current ratio for each year? What industry or firm-specific characterisitcs might account for these results?

d. In your opinion, can a company such as Quaker Oats continue to survive in the long-run with negative working capital? What other information would you like to know when evaluating this company's overall liquidity?

e. Notice that working capital and the current ratio dropped significantly in 1996 for Sherwin-Williams. What do you suppose caused these dramatic changes? Use the additional information provided in the balance sheet exerpts on the next page to make an educated guess.

	1996	1995
Cash and cash equivalents	$ 2	$ 270
Accounts receivable, net	452	334
Inventories	643	463
Other current assets	319	172
Total current assets	$1,416	$1,239
Short-term borrowings	$ 168	$ —
Accounts payable	386	277
Compensation and other accruals	431	310
Accrued taxes	66	32
Total current liabilities	$1,051	$ 619

11–10. Analytical problem—comparative analysis of profitability and financial leverage measures. The annual reports of Dow Jones & Company and The McGraw-Hill Companies, two publishing and information services companies, indicate the following for the year ended December 31, 1996 (amounts in millions):

	Dow Jones	*McGraw-Hill*
Operating revenues	$2,482	$3,075
Net income	190	496
Total assets, 1-1-96	2,599	3,057
Total liabilities, 1-1-96	997	2,022
Total liabilities, 12-31-96	1,116	2,281
Total stockholders' equity, 12-31-96.	1,644	1,361

Required:

   a. Calculate ROI and ROE for each company for 1996. *(Hint: You will need to calculate some of the numbers used in the denominator of these ratios.)*

   b. Based on the results of your ROI and ROE analysis in part *a* above, do you believe that either firm uses financial leverage more effectively than the other? Explain your answer. *(Hint: Compare the percentage differences between ROI and ROE for each firm. Is there a significant difference that would suggest that one firm uses leverage more effectively than the other?)*

   c. Calculate the debt ratio and debt/equity ratio for each firm at the end of 1996.

   d. Compare the results of your analysis in part *c* to your expectations concerning the relative use of financial leverage in part *b*. Do the debt and debt/equity ratios calculated in part *c* make sense relative to your expectations? Explain your answer.

11–11. Ratio analysis—comprehensive problem. Presented on the next page are summarized data from the balance sheets and income statements of Wiper, Inc,:

WIPER, INC.
Condensed Balance Sheets
December 31, 1999, 1998, 1997
(in millions)

	1999	1998	1997
Current assets:	$ 677	$ 891	$ 736
Other assets	2,413	1,920	1,719
	$3,090	$2,811	$2,455
Current liabilities:	$ 562	$ 803	$ 710
Long-term liabilities:	1,521	982	827
Owners' equity	1,007	1,026	918
	$3,090	$2,811	$2,455

WIPER, INC.
Selected Income Statement and Other Data
For the Years Ended December 31, 1999 and 1998
(in millions)

	1999	1998
Income statement data:		
Sales	$3,050	$2,913
Operating income	296	310
Interest expense	84	65
Net income	192	187
Other data:		
Average number of common shares outstanding	41.3	46.7
Total dividends paid	$ 50.0	$ 52.3

Required:

a. Calculate return on investment, based on net income and average total assets, for 1999 and 1998. Show both margin and turnover in your calculation.

b. Calculate return on equity for 1999 and 1998.

c. Calculate working capital and the current ratio for each of the past three years.

d. Calculate earnings per share for 1999 and 1998.

e. If Wiper's stock had a price/earnings ratio of 13 at the end of 1999, what was the market price of the stock?

f. Calculate the cash dividend per share for 1999, and the dividend yield based on the market price calculated in part *e*.

g. Calculate the dividend payout ratio for 1999.

h. Assume that accounts receivable at December 31, 1999, totaled $309 million. Calculate the number of days' sales in receivables at that date.

i. Calculate Wiper's debt ratio and debt/equity ratio at December 31, 1999 and 1998.

j. Calculate the times interest earned factor for 1999 and 1998.

k. Review the results of these calculations, evaluate the profitability and liquidity of this company, and state your opinion about its suitability as an investment for a young, single professional with funds to invest in common stock.

11–12.   **Analytical problem—complete an income statement and balance sheet using financial ratio data.** Presented on the next page are partially completed financial statements for Whittaker, Inc.:

WHITTAKER, INC.
Income Statement
For the Year Ended December 31, 1998

Sales	$	?
Cost of goods sold		?
Gross profit	$	?
Operating expenses		?
Income from operations	$	?
Interest expense		?
Income before taxes	$	?
Income taxes (20%)		?
Net income	$	?

WHITTAKER, INC.
Balance Sheet
December 31, 1998

Current assets:		
Cash	$	?
Accounts receivable, net		?
Inventory		?
Total current assets		$171,000
Property, plant and equipment, net		?
Total assets	$	?
Current liabilities	$	?
Bonds payable, 15%		70,000
Total liabilities	$	?
Owners' equity:		
Common stock, $2 par value		10,000
Additional paid-in capital		15,000
Retained earnings		?
Total owners' equity	$	?
Total liabilities and owners' equity	$	?

Additional information:

- Financial ratios computed from these financial statements include the following:

Current ratio	1.9 to 1
Acid-test ratio	1.3 to 1
Debt/Equity ratio	2.0 to 1
Inventory turnover	4.0 times
Accounts receivable turnover	6.8 times
Times interest earned	4.45 times
Gross profit ratio	40%
Return on investment	12%
Earnings per share	$5.52

- All sales during the year were made on account. Cash collections during the year exceeded sales by $14,000, and no uncollectible accounts were written off.
- The balance of the accounts receivable account was $57,000 on January 1, 1998.
- No common stock was issued during the year.
- Dividends declared and paid during the year were $7,600.
- The balance of the inventory account was $48,000 on January 1, 1998.
- Interest expense on the income statement relates to the 15% bonds payable; $10,000 of these bonds were issued on May 1, 1998; the remaining amount of bonds payable were outstanding throughout the year. All bonds were issued at face amount.

    a. Complete the income statement and balance sheet for Whittaker, Inc. Show how each amount was determined.

    b. After completing part *a,* use your answers to recompute each of the financial ratios provided as additional information.

Intel   **11–13.**   **Ratio analysis—comprehensive problem, 1996 data.** This problem is based on the 1996 annual report of Intel Corporation, in the Appendix.

Required:

a. Compute the following profitability measures for the year ended December 28, 1996:

    1. Return on investment, based on net income (perform a DuPont analysis).
    2. Return on equity, based on net income.
    3. Price/earnings ratio. Use $131.00 as the year-end market price.
    4. Dividend yield.
    5. Dividend payout ratio.

b. Compute the following liquidity measures at December 28, 1996:

    1. Working capital.
    2. Current ratio.
    3. Acid-test ratio.

c. Compute the following activity measures for the year ended December 28, 1996:

    1. Number of days' sales in accounts receivable, based on a 365-day year.
    2. Number of days' sales in inventory, based on a 365-day year.
    3. Accounts receivable turnover.
    4. Inventory turnover.
    5. Turnover of net property, plant, and equipment.

d. Compute the following financial leverage measures at December 28, 1996:

    1. Debt ratio.
    2. Debt/equity ratio.
    3. Times interest earned.

e. Compute the following physical measures of Intel's profitability at December 28, 1996:

    1. Net revenues per employee.
    2. Operating income per employee.

    (Hint: The number of employees at year-end is disclosed on p. 7 of the Appendix.)

     11–14.   **Analysis of selected liquidity, activity, financial leverage, and profitability measures of Microsoft Corporation.** Presented below are summarized data from the balance sheets and income statements of Microsoft Corporation, a computer software company:

MICROSOFT CORPORATION
Condensed Income Statements and Other Data
For the Years Ended June 30, 1996, and 1997
(in millions)

	1996	*1997*
Revenue	$8,671	$11,358
Operating expenses:		
Cost of revenue	1,188	1,085
Research and development	1,432	1,925
Sales and marketing	2,657	2,856
General and administrative	316	362
Total operating expenses	5,593	6,228

	1996	1997
Operating income	$3,078	$ 5,130
Interest income	320	443
Other expenses	(19)	(259)
Income before income taxes	3,379	5,314
Provision for income taxes	1,184	1,860
Net income	2,195	3,454
Preferred stock dividends	—	15
Net income available for common shareholders	$2,195	$ 3,439
Earnings per share	$ 1.71	$ 2.63
Market price per share at year-end	$60.00	$127.50

MICROSOFT CORPORATION
Condensed Balance Sheets
June 30, 1996, and 1997
(in millions)

	1996	1997
Assets		
Current assets:		
Cash and short-term investments	$ 6,940	$ 8,966
Accounts receivable	639	980
Other	260	427
Total current assets	7,839	10,373
Property, plant, and equipment	1,326	1,465
Equity investments	675	2,346
Other assets	253	203
Total assets	$10,093	$14,387
Liabilities and Stockholders' Equity		
Current liabilities:		
Accounts payable	$ 808	$ 721
Accrued compensation	202	336
Income taxes payable	484	466
Unearned revenue	560	1,418
Other	371	669
Total current liabilities	2,425	3,610
Minority interest	125	
Put warrants	635	
Commitments and contingencies		
Stockholders' equity:		
Convertible preferred stock—shares authorized 0 and 100; shares issued and outstanding 0 and 13		980
Common stock and paid-in capital—shares authorized 4,000; shares issued and outstanding 1,194 and 1,204	2,924	4,509
Retained earnings	3,984	5,288
Total stockholders' equity	6,908	10,777
Total liabilities and stockholders' equity	$10,093	$14,387

At June 30, 1995, total assets were $7,210, total liabilities were $1,752, and total stockholders' equity was $5,458 (in millions).

Required:

a. Calculate Microsoft's working capital, current ratio, and acid-test ratio at June 30, 1997, and at June 30, 1996.

b. Calculate Microsoft's ROE for the years ended June 30, 1997, and 1996.

c. Calculate Microsoft's ROI, showing margin and turnover, for the years ended June 30, 1997, and 1996.

d. Calculate Microsoft's price/earnings ratio at June 30, 1997, and 1996.

e. Calculate the following activity measures for Microsoft for the year ended June 30, 1997:

    1. Accounts receivable turnover.

    2. Number of days' sales in accounts receivable.

f. Calculate the following financial leverage measures for Microsoft at June 30, 1997, and 1996:

    1. Debt ratio.

    2. Debt/equity ratio.

g. Microsoft did not declare or pay any dividends during fiscal 1997 or fiscal 1996. What do you think is the primary reason for this?

h. Write a conclusion about the appropriateness of an investment in the common stock of Microsoft Corporation for a young, single professional with funds to invest in common stock.

11–15. **Ratio analysis—comprehensive problem, 1997 data.** Review the accompanying financial statements (Statements 1, 2, 3, and 4) for Sample Co. Note especially the format of the balance sheet, which is Statement 3. Study the financial statements and see how they are interrelated.

Required:

a. The financial statements of Sample Co. use a number of captions and terms that may be somewhat confusing at first glance. For example, the term *consolidated financial position* is used to describe the firm's balance sheet. For each item listed below, indicate the more conventional meaning of the caption or term—as described in this text.

    1. Consolidated results of operations *(Statement 1).*

    2. Profit *(Statements 1, 2, and 4).*

    3. Profit per share of common stock *(Statement 1).*

    4. Changes in consolidated ownership *(Statement 2).*

    5. Profit employed in the business *(Statements 2 and 3).*

    6. Ownership *(Statements 2 and 3).*

    7. Net current assets *(Statement 3).*

    8. Net assets *(Statement 3).*

b. Calculate the following ratios for the year ended December 31, 1997:

    1. Return on investment, using the DuPont model, based on operating income.

    2. Return on equity, based on net income.

c. Calculate the following activity measures for the year ended December 31, 1997:

    1. Number of days' sales in accounts receivable based on a 365-day year.

    2. Inventory turnover.

    3. Turnover of buildings, machinery and equipment, and land.

d. Calculate the following leverage measures:

    1. Debt (long-term debt due after one year) to owners' equity at December 31, 1997.

    2. Debt (long-term debt due after one year) to debt (as above) plus owners' equity at December 31, 1997.

    3. Times interest earned for the year ended December 31, 1997.

e. The market price of Sample Co.'s common stock was $42 per share at the end of 1997. Calculate the following ratios at that date:

    1. Price/earnings ratio.

2. Dividend payout ratio.
3. Dividend yield.

STATEMENT 1

SAMPLE CO.
Consolidated Results of Operations
For the Years Ended December 31
(millions of dollars except per share data)

	1998	1997	1996
Sales	**$10,359**	$8,251	$7,362
Operating costs:			
Cost of goods sold	**$ 8,011**	$6,523	$6,064
Selling, general, and administrative expenses	**1,242**	1,071	980
Research and development expenses	**182**	159	178
	$ 9,435	$7,753	$7,222
Operating profit	**$ 924**	$ 498	$ 140
Interest expense	**264**	209	197
	$ 660	$ 289	$ (57)
Other income	**182**	170	160
	$ 842	$ 459	$ 103
Provision for income taxes	**262**	118	21
Profit of consolidated companies	**$ 580**	$ 341	$ 82
Equity in profit (loss) of affiliated companies	**36**	(22)	(6)
Profit—before extraordinary tax benefit	**$ 616**	$ 319	$ 76
Extraordinary tax benefit from foreign tax credit carryforwards	**—**	31	—
Profit	**$ 616**	$ 350	$ 76
Profit per share of common stock before extraordinary tax benefit	**$ 6.07**	$ 3.20	$ .77
Profit per share of common stock after extraordinary tax benefit	**$ 6.07**	$ 3.51	$ .77
Dividends paid per share of common stock	**$ .75**	$ .50	$ .50

STATEMENT 2

SAMPLE CO.
Changes in Consolidated Ownership
For the Years Ended December 31
(dollars in millions)

	1998	1997	1996
Common stock:			
Balance at beginning of year	**$ 827**	$ 714	$ 696
Common shares issued, including treasury shares reissued: 1998—1,317,485; 1997—2,601,332; 1996—452,959	**83**	113	18
Treasury shares purchased: 1998—1,326,058	**(86)**	—	—
Balance at year-end	**$ 824**	$ 827	$ 714

STATEMENT 2   *(concluded)*

	1998	1997	1996
Profit employed in the business:			
Balance at beginning of year	**$2,656**	$2,363	$2,349
Add: Profit	**616**	350	76
Deduct: Dividends paid and payable	**88**	57	62
Balance at year-end	**$3,184**	$2,656	$2,363
Foreign currency translation adjustment:			
Balance at beginning of year	**$ 82**	$ 72	$ 23
Aggregate adjustment for year	**23**	10	49
Balance at year-end	**$ 105**	$ 82	$ 72
Ownership at year-end	**$4,113**	$3,565	$3,149

STATEMENT 3

SAMPLE CO.
Consolidated Financial Position
At December 31
(dollars in millions except per share data)

	1998	1997	1996
Current assets:			
Cash and short-term investments	**$ 75**	$ 155	$ 166
Receivables	**2,669**	2,174	1,808
Refundable income taxes	**114**	130	92
Deferred income taxes and prepaid expenses allocable to the following year	**474**	224	208
Inventories	**1,986**	1,323	1,211
	$5,317	$4,006	$3,485
Current liabilities:			
Short-term borrowings	**$1,072**	$ 623	$ 696
Payable to material suppliers and others	**1,495**	1,351	1,182
Wages, salaries, and contributions for employee benefits	**485**	431	450
Dividends payable	**30**	19	12
Income taxes	**118**	48	10
Long-term debt due within one year	**235**	286	122
	$3,435	$2,758	$2,472
Net current assets	**$1,882**	$1,248	$1,013
Buildings, machinery, and equipment—net	**2,802**	2,467	2,431
Land—at original cost	**107**	96	97
Patents, trademarks, and other intangibles	**71**	47	60
Investments in and advances to affiliated companies	**288**	227	185
Long-term receivables	**902**	665	413
Other assets	**199**	123	90
Total assets less current liabilities	**$6,251**	$4,873	$4,289

STATEMENT 3   *(concluded)*

	1998	1997	1996
Long-term debt due after one year	**$1,953**	$1,287	$1,134
Deferred income taxes	**185**	21	6
Net assets	**$4,113**	$3,565	$3,149
Ownership (Statement 2):			
Common stock of $1.00 par value:			
Authorized shares: 200,000,000			
Outstanding shares (1998—101,414,138; 1997—			
101,422,711 [after deducting 23,470 and 2,961			
treasury shares, respectively]; 1996—98,832,079) at			
paid-in amount	**$ 824**	$ 827	$ 714
Profit employed in the business	**3,184**	2,656	2,363
Foreign currency translation adjustment	**105**	82	72
	$4,113	$3,565	$3,149

STATEMENT 4

SAMPLE CO.
Consolidated Statement of Cash Flows
For the Years Ended December 31
(millions of dollars)

	1998	1997	1996
Cash flows from operating activities:			
Profit	**$ 616**	$ 350	$ 76
Adjustments for noncash items:			
Depreciation and amortization	**434**	425	453
Other	**(74)**	144	86
Changes in assets and liabilities:			
Receivables	**(777)**	(699)	(765)
Refundable income taxes	**15**	(34)	1
Inventories	**(598)**	(124)	(68)
Payable to material suppliers and others	**348**	252	(14)
Other—net	**(39)**	(80)	(4)
Net cash provided by operating activities	**$ (75)**	$ 234	$(235)
Cash flows from investing activities:			
Expenditures for land, buildings, machinery, and			
equipment	**(793)**	(493)	(331)
Proceeds from disposals of land, buildings, machinery,			
and equipment	**30**	32	16
Investments in and advances to			
affiliated companies	**(24)**	(65)	(52)
Other—net	**(50)**	(25)	41
Net cash used for investing activities	**$(1,259)**	$(931)	$(637)

STATEMENT 4   *(concluded)*

	1998	1997	1996
Cash flows from financing activities:			
Dividends paid .... $	(77)	$ (50)	$ (49)
Common shares issued, including treasury shares			
reissued	4	6	3
Treasury shares purchased	(86)	—	—
Proceeds from long-term debt issued	371	503	156
Payments on long-term debt	(298)	(102)	(307)
Short-term borrowings—net	965	(91)	578
Net cash provided by financing activities .... $	879	$ 266	$ 381
Effect of exchange rate changes on cash .... $	(48)	$ 40	$ 41
Decrease in cash and short-term investments .... $	(81)	$ (11)	$(139)

11–16.   **Ratio analysis—comprehensive problem, 1998 data.** Solve the requirements of Problem 11–15 for the year ended December 31, 1998. The market price of Sample Co.'s common stock was $65 at December 31, 1998.

PART II

Managerial Accounting

CHAPTER
12

Managerial/Cost Accounting and Cost Classifications

Managerial accounting, sometimes called *management accounting,* involves using economic and financial information to plan and control many of the activities of the entity, and to support the management decision-making process. **Cost accounting** is a subset of managerial accounting that relates primarily to the determination and accumulation of product, process, or service costs. Managerial accounting and cost accounting ordinarily have an internal orientation, as opposed to the primarily external orientation of financial accounting. Much of the same data used in or generated by the financial accounting process are used in managerial and cost accounting, but the latter are more likely to have a future orientation, such as in the preparation of budgets.

As with financial accounting, managerial accounting and cost accounting have special terminology or, as many would say, *jargon*. Most of these terms relate to different types of costs. An important early lesson about managerial and cost accounting is that *there are different costs for different purposes*. When a marketing or production manager asks a management accountant what a certain item or activity costs, the accountant is not being disrespectful when asking: "Why do you want to know?" Costs used for valuing inventory are different from the costs that should be considered when analyzing a product modification or potential new product.

In this chapter, we will look briefly at the management process, identify several of the contributions that the managerial accountant makes to that process, and then focus on cost classifications and descriptions. Subsequent chapters will describe how costs are used in the planning and controlling processes.

WHAT DOES IT MEAN?

1. What does it mean to state that there are different costs for different purposes?

Learning Objectives

After studying this chapter, you should understand:

1 The major differences between financial accounting and managerial accounting.

2 The difference between product costs and period costs, and the three components of product cost.

3 The general operation of a product costing system and how costs flow through the inventory accounts to cost of goods sold.

4 The presentation and interpretation of a statement of cost of goods manufactured.

5 The difference between absorption costing and direct (or variable) costing.

6 The difference between direct and indirect costs.

7 The difference between variable and fixed cost behavior patterns, and the simplifying assumptions made in this classification method.

8 Why expressing fixed costs on a per unit of activity basis is misleading and may result in faulty decisions.

9 That all costs are controllable by someone at some time but that in the short run some costs may be classified as noncontrollable.

10 The meaning and application of the following "cost" terms: *differential, allocated, sunk,* and *opportunity.*

Managerial Accounting Contrasted to Financial Accounting

Managerial accounting supports the internal planning (future-oriented) decisions made by management. Financial accounting has more of a score-keeping, historical orientation, although data produced by the financial accounting process form some of the foundation on which plans are based. Planning is a key part of the **management process,** and although there are many descriptions of that process, a generally acceptable definition would include reference to the process of planning, organizing, and controlling an entity's activities so that the organization can accomplish its purpose. A schematic model of the process looks like this:

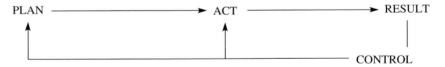

The diagram suggests that controls provide feedback. Actual results are compared to planned results, and if a variance exists between the two, then either the plan or the actions, or perhaps both, are changed.

Not all of a firm's objectives are stated in financial terms by any means. For example, market share, employee morale, absence of layoffs, and responsible corporate citizenship are all appropriate objectives that are expressed in nonfinancial terms. However, many of the firm's goals will be financial in nature (e.g., ROI, ROE, growth in sales, earnings, and dividends, to name just a few). The accountant plays a major role in identifying these goals, in helping to achieve them, and in measuring the degree to which they have been accomplished.

Objective 1
Understand the major differences between financial accounting and managerial accounting.

Emphasis on the future is a principal characteristic that makes managerial accounting different from financial accounting. Anticipating what revenues will be and forecasting the expenses that will be incurred to achieve those revenues are critical activities of the budgeting process. Another difference between managerial accounting and financial accounting that is emphasized in planning is the breadth of focus. Financial accounting deals primarily with the financial statements for the organization as a whole; managerial accounting is more concerned with units within the organization. Thus, even though an overall company ROI objective is established, effective planning requires that the planned impact of the activities and results of each unit (division, product line, plant, sales territory, and so on) of the organization be considered.

Measuring results involves using the historical data of financial accounting, and because of the time required to perform financial accounting and auditing procedures, there is usually a time lag of weeks or months between the end of an accounting period and the issuance of financial statements. However, for performance feedback to be most effective, it should be provided as quickly as possible after action has been completed. Management accounting is not constrained by generally accepted accounting principles, so approximate results can be quickly generated for use in the control process. In other words, relevant data, even though not absolutely accurate in a financial accounting sense, are useful for evaluating performance soon after an activity has been completed.

Exhibit 12–1 summarizes the principal differences between managerial accounting and financial accounting.

If time and effort have been devoted to develop a plan, it is appropriate to attempt to control the activities of the organization so that the goals of the plan are accomplished. Many of the activities of the managerial accountant are related to cost control; this control emphasis will be seen in most of the managerial accounting ideas that are explained in these chapters.

Another management concept relevant to the control process is that if an individual is to be held accountable, or responsible, for the results of

---

EXHIBIT 12–1   Managerial Accounting Compared to Financial Accounting

Characteristic	Managerial Accounting	Financial Accounting
Service perspective	Internal to managers	External to investors and creditors
Time frame	Present and future for planning and control	Past—financial statements are historical
Breadth of concern	Micro—individual units of the organization plan and act	Macro—financial statements are for the organization as a whole
Reporting frequency and promptness	Control reports issued frequently (e.g., daily) and promptly (e.g., one day after period-end)	Most financial statements issued monthly, a week or more after month-end
Degree of precision of data used	Reasonable accuracy desired, but "close counts"—relevance is often more important than reliability	High accuracy desired, with time usually available to achieve it—reliability is of utmost importance
Reporting standards	None imposed because of internal and pragmatic orientation	Imposed by generally accepted accounting principles and the FASB

an activity, that individual must also have the authority to influence those results. If a manager is to be held responsible for costs incurred by a unit of the organization, the financial results reported for that unit should not include costs incurred by other units that have been arbitrarily assigned to the unit being evaluated. In other words, the results should not reflect costs that the manager being held responsible cannot control.

Management accountants work extensively with people in other functional areas of the organization. For example, industrial engineers and management accountants work together to develop **production standards,** which are the expected or allowed times and costs to make a product or perform an activity. Management accountants help production people interpret performance reports, which compare actual and planned production and costs. Sales personnel, the marketing staff, and management accountants are involved in estimating a future period's sales. Personnel professionals and management accountants work together to determine the cost effect of compensation changes. These few examples illustrate the need for management accountants to have a breadth of knowledge and interest about the organization and its operating environment. The examples also suggest that it is appropriate for persons in other functional areas to have a general understanding of managerial accounting. Helping you to achieve that general understanding is the objective of the remaining chapters of this book. The topics to be discussed are:

Cost classifications and cost accounting systems (Chapter 12).
Cost-volume-profit analysis (Chapter 13).
Budgeting and performance reporting (Chapter 14).
Standard costs and variance analysis (Chapter 15).
Capital budgeting (Chapter 16).

 WHAT DOES IT MEAN?

2. What does it mean that managerial accounting has a different time frame from financial accounting?
3. What does it mean to have feedback for control purposes?

Cost Classifications

The term *cost* means different things to different people, and in the management planning and decision-making process, it is important to use costs that are appropriate to the situation. Likewise, management accountants should make sure that everyone involved in any given situation understands the costs being used. The cost classifications most frequently encountered are:

For cost accounting purposes:
  Product cost
  Period cost
Relationship to product or activity:
  Direct cost
  Indirect cost

> Relationship between total cost and volume of activity:
>   Variable cost
>   Fixed cost
> Time-frame perspective:
>   Controllable cost
>   Noncontrollable cost
> For other analytical purposes:
>   Differential cost
>   Allocated cost
>   Sunk cost
>   Opportunity cost

These classifications are not mutually exclusive. Thus a cost might be identified as a "controllable, variable, direct, product cost," for example.

Costs for Cost Accounting Purposes

Objective 2
Understand the difference between product costs and period costs, and the three components of product cost.

Cost accounting relates to the determination of product, process, or service costs. In addition to being useful for management planning and control, **product costs** are used by manufacturers and merchandisers to determine inventory values and, when the product is sold, the amount of cost of goods sold. This is, of course, a financial accounting use of product cost. Even though service firms do not usually produce items for inventory, their costs of providing services will also be identified and analyzed for management planning and control purposes.

The product costing emphasis in the financial accounting chapters of this book focused on the cost-flow assumption (FIFO, LIFO, weighted-average) used by merchandising firms. Although these same cost-flow issues also apply to manufacturing firms, our focus at this point is on the components of product cost for an entity that produces its own inventory. Product costing for a manufacturer is more complex than for a merchandiser because making a product is more complex than buying an already finished product. However, the accounting concepts involved are the same. The cost of the product is recorded and reported as an asset (inventory) until the product is sold, when the cost is transferred to the income statement (cost of goods sold) as an expense to be matched with the revenue that resulted from the sale. The difference between a manufacturer and a merchandiser is illustrated schematically in the following diagram:

Manufacturer
    Ingredients
        +
    Human effort   } = Manufactured product   ⟶   Sold to customers
        +
    Machine support

Merchandiser   Purchased product   ⟶   Sold to customers

The cost associated with each of the inputs of a manufactured product is classified as raw materials, direct labor, or manufacturing overhead.

Raw materials are the ingredients of the product—the materials that are put into the production process and from which the finished product is made. The cost of raw materials includes the same items as the product cost of a merchandiser. The finished product of one process or company may be the raw material of another process or company. For example, corn is the raw material of a corn processor, and one of the processor's finished products may be corn syrup. The candy manufacturer uses the corn syrup as a raw material of its products.

Direct labor is the effort provided by workers who are directly involved with the manufacture of the product. For example, workers who perform machine operations on raw materials, workers who operate or control raw material conversion equipment (e.g., melters, mixers, heat treaters, coolers, and evaporators), and workers who assemble or package the product are directly involved in manufacturing activities. Their compensation costs would be considered direct labor costs.

Manufacturing overhead, or **overhead,** includes all manufacturing costs except those for raw materials and direct labor. Overhead is an indirect cost because it is not feasible to specifically relate overhead items to individual products. Examples of overhead costs include factory utilities, maintenance and housekeeping costs (both materials and labor), depreciation expense for the factory building and production equipment, and compensation of production managers and supervisors.

As the manufacturing process becomes more complex and technologically oriented, overhead costs generally become more significant. The development of robotic production methods, for example, has resulted in increased overhead costs. Thus planning and controlling overhead has become an increasingly important activity in many firms.

Costs not included in inventory as product costs are reported in the income statement as incurred. These are the selling, general, and administrative costs (or operating expenses) of the firm that are not related to production activities. These items are called **period costs** because they are recorded as expenses in the accounting period in which they are incurred. Accounting for product and period costs is illustrated in Exhibit 12–2.

WHAT DOES IT MEAN?

4. What does it mean that a cost is a direct, product, variable cost?

5. What does it mean that product costs flow through inventory on their way to the income statement?

Cost Accounting Systems—General

Every manufacturing firm uses a cost accounting system to accumulate the cost of products made. Although some firms manufacture a single, unique product, one unit at a time, most firms produce large quantities of identical products in a more or less continuous process (i.e., production runs). As you can imagine, cost accounting systems vary considerably in terms of complexity because they are designed for the specific needs of individual companies, but virtually all systems have the general characteristics described below.

EXHIBIT 12–2   Accounting for Product and Period Costs

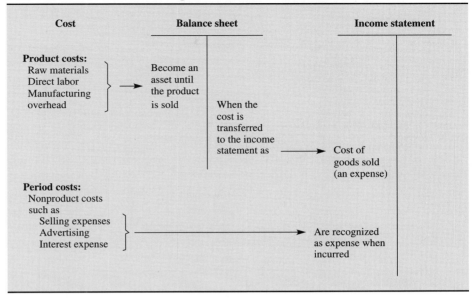

A manufacturing cost accounting system involves three inventory accounts: *Raw Materials, Work in Process,* and *Finished Goods.* The **Raw Materials Inventory** account holds the cost of parts, assemblies, and materials (e.g., for a sailboat manufacturer—glass fiber cloth, epoxy resin, wood, sailcloth, deck fittings, and rope) that will be used in the manufacturing process. The **Work in Process Inventory** account is used to accumulate all of the manufacturing costs, including raw materials, direct labor, and manufacturing overhead. When the manufacturing process is complete, the cost of the items made is transferred to the **Finished Goods Inventory** account. At the end of the accounting period, each of these inventory accounts may have a balance. For Raw Materials and Finished Goods, the balance represents the cost of the items on hand at the end of the period. For Work in Process, the balance represents the sum of the costs incurred for products that were started in production but have not been completed at the end of the period. The Work in Process Inventory account balance will be relatively small (or zero) for production processes that are of short duration or that are cleared out at the end of the period (e.g., candy manufacturing or food processing). Work in Process Inventory is likely to exist for firms that have relatively long-duration manufacturing processes, but the account balance will usually be low relative to Raw Materials and Finished Goods. For Intel, however, work in process represents the largest portion of inventory reported on the 1995 and 1996 balance sheets, which is a clear reflection of the complexity of its chip manufacturing process (see pages 22 and 10 in the Appendix). When a manufactured item is sold, its cost is transferred from the balance sheet Finished Goods Inventory account to cost of goods sold in the income statement. Exhibit 12–3 illustrates and compares the flow of product costs for a manufacturing firm and a merchandising firm.

Objective 3
Understand the general operation of a product costing system and how costs flow through the inventory accounts to cost of goods sold.

EXHIBIT 12–3   Flow of Cost Comparison—Manufacturer and Merchandiser

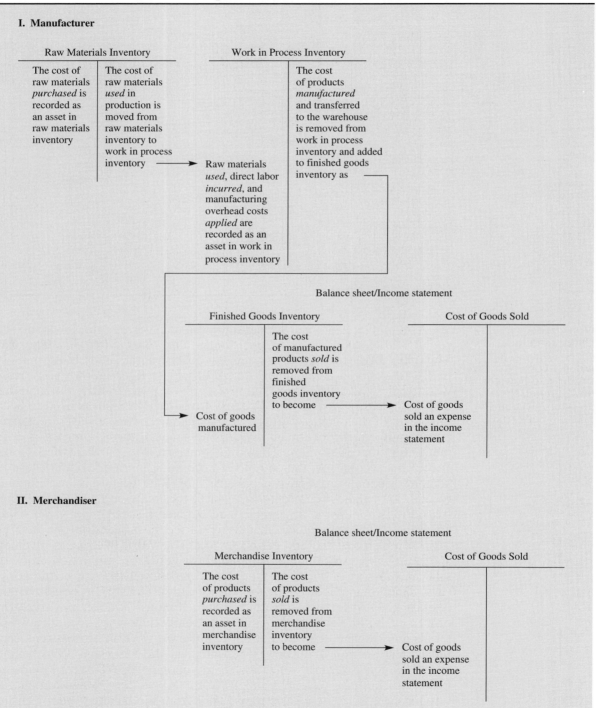

I. Manufacturer

Raw Materials Inventory

The cost of raw materials *purchased* is recorded as an asset in raw materials inventory	The cost of raw materials *used* in production is moved from raw materials inventory to work in process inventory

Work in Process Inventory

Raw materials *used*, direct labor *incurred*, and manufacturing overhead costs *applied* are recorded as an asset in work in process inventory

The cost of products *manufactured* and transferred to the warehouse is removed from work in process inventory and added to finished goods inventory as

Balance sheet/Income statement

Finished Goods Inventory

Cost of goods manufactured

The cost of manufactured products *sold* is removed from finished goods inventory to become

Cost of Goods Sold

Cost of goods sold an expense in the income statement

II. Merchandiser

Balance sheet/Income statement

Merchandise Inventory

The cost of products *purchased* is recorded as an asset in merchandise inventory	The cost of products *sold* is removed from merchandise inventory to become

Cost of Goods Sold

Cost of goods sold an expense in the income statement

The cost of a single unit of a manufactured product is determined by averaging the total material, labor, and overhead costs incurred in the manufacture of some quantity of the product (e.g., the average cost per unit in a production run). Determining the raw material and direct labor costs is usually fairly easy; raw material inventory usage records and time records for direct labor workers provide these data. It is the assignment of overhead costs that presents the challenge. Most cost systems apply overhead to production by using a single, or at most a very few, surrogate measures of overhead behavior. One of the most popular bases is direct labor hours. Other bases include direct labor cost, machine hours, raw material usage, and the number of units made. The simplifying assumption is that overhead is incurred because products are being made, and the number of direct labor hours (or other base) used on a particular production run is a fair indicator of the overhead incurred for that production run. Given this relationship, at the beginning of the year an estimate is made of both the total overhead expected to be incurred during the year and the total direct labor hours (or other base) expected to be used. Estimated total overhead cost is divided by the estimated total direct labor hours (or other base) to get a **predetermined overhead application rate** per direct labor hour (or other base). To illustrate product costing and other cost and managerial accounting concepts, the hypothetical firm Cruisers, Inc., a manufacturer of fiberglass sailboats, will be used. Exhibit 12–4 illustrates how the cost of a boat made during the month of April can be determined. Note that the first step is the determination of the predetermined overhead application rate. This is shown in Section I of Exhibit 12–4. Then overhead is assigned to specific production runs based on this predetermined overhead application rate. This is illustrated in Section II of Exhibit 12–4. If multiple overhead application bases are used, the estimated overhead cost associated with each base must be divided by the estimated usage of each base to develop the separate **overhead application rates.** For example, overhead may be applied based on 140% of direct labor cost, plus $3.10 per pound of a certain raw material used in the production process. Study Exhibit 12–4 to see how cost components are accumulated and then averaged to get the cost of a single unit.

Although the costing process involves estimates and provides an overall average, many firms do an excellent job of estimating both total overhead costs and total activity, resulting in quite accurate overhead application and product costing. Because the predetermined overhead application rate calculation is based on estimates, at the end of the year there will be a difference between the total overhead costs actually incurred and the costs applied to production during the year. This difference is called **overapplied overhead** or **underapplied overhead.** At the end of the year, if the overapplied or underapplied overhead is small relative to total overhead costs incurred, it is transferred to cost of goods sold. If it is material in amount, it is allocated between inventories and cost of goods sold in proportion to the total overhead included in each. On a monthly basis, the overapplied or underapplied overhead is carried forward in the Manufacturing Overhead account. The reason for this is that estimates for the

---

EXHIBIT 12–4   Product Costing Illustration

I. Calculation of predetermined overhead application rate:

Assumptions:

Cruisers, Inc., incurs overhead costs in proportion to the number of direct labor hours worked; therefore, the overhead application rate is based on direct labor hours.

The estimated annual production level is 1,250 sailboats, and each sailboat should require 240 direct labor hours to complete.

Estimated total overhead cost to be incurred for the year: $4,200,000.

Estimated total direct labor hours to be worked in the year: 300,000.

$$\text{Overhead application rate} = \frac{\text{Estimated total overhead cost}}{\text{Estimated total direct labor hours}}$$

$$= \$4{,}200{,}000/300{,}000 \text{ hours}$$

$$= \$14/\text{direct labor hour}$$

II. Calculation of product cost:

Assumptions:

Cruisers, Inc., produced 86 SeaCruiser sailboats during April; a total of 20,640 labor hours were worked, and the following costs were incurred:

Raw materials	$368,510
Direct labor	$330,240

The cost of each boat is determined by dividing the total manufacturing costs incurred by the number of boats produced:

Raw materials	$368,510
Direct labor	330,240
Overhead (20,640 direct labor hours × the overhead application rate of $14/hour)	288,960
Total manufacturing cost incurred	$987,710
Cost per boat ($987,710/86 boats)	$ 11,485

---

whole year were used to calculate the predetermined overhead application rate, and variations in cost and activity that occur in one month may be offset in a subsequent month. Thus, a better matching of revenue and expense usually occurs if the overapplied or underapplied overhead adjustment is made only at the end of the year.

Exhibit 12–5 illustrates the flow of these product costs through the accounts of Cruisers, Inc., for April. Note the use of the Manufacturing Overhead account—this is an account that functions as an asset-type clearing account. *Actual* manufacturing overhead costs incurred are recorded as increases (debits) in this account, and the manufacturing overhead *applied* to Work in Process is a reduction (credit) to the account. The Manufacturing Overhead account will not have any balance at the beginning or end of the year because, as already stated, overapplied or underapplied overhead is transferred to Cost of Goods Sold or allocated between inventories and Cost of Goods Sold. However, at month-ends during the year the account is likely to have a relatively small overapplied or underapplied balance. This is the case in the Exhibit 12–5 illustration.

EXHIBIT 12–5   Cruisers, Inc., Flow of Product Costs for April

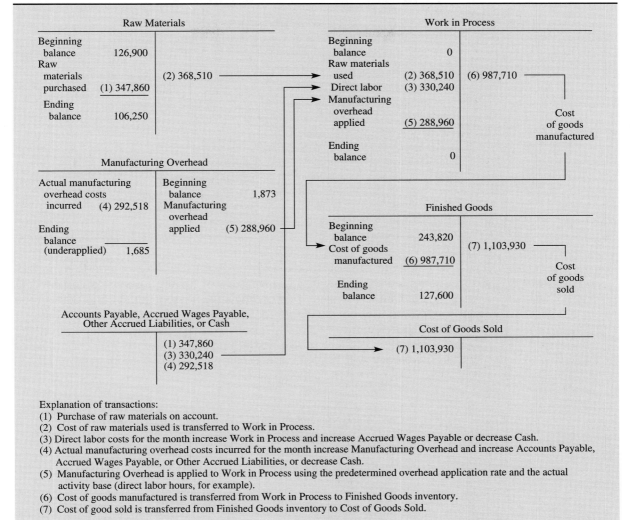

Explanation of transactions:
(1) Purchase of raw materials on account.
(2) Cost of raw materials used is transferred to Work in Process.
(3) Direct labor costs for the month increase Work in Process and increase Accrued Wages Payable or decrease Cash.
(4) Actual manufacturing overhead costs incurred for the month increase Manufacturing Overhead and increase Accounts Payable, Accrued Wages Payable, or Other Accrued Liabilities, or decrease Cash.
(5) Manufacturing Overhead is applied to Work in Process using the predetermined overhead application rate and the actual activity base (direct labor hours, for example).
(6) Cost of goods manufactured is transferred from Work in Process to Finished Goods inventory.
(7) Cost of good sold is transferred from Finished Goods inventory to Cost of Goods Sold.

WHAT DOES IT MEAN?

6. What does it mean that manufacturing overhead is applied to inventory?

7. What does it mean when there is underapplied overhead at the end of the year?

Objective 4
Understand the presentation and interpretation of a statement of cost of goods manufactured.

Manufacturing costs can be summarized and reported in a **statement of cost of goods manufactured.** Such a statement using amounts for Cruisers, Inc., for April is illustrated in Exhibit 12–6. Although it was assumed that there were no beginning or ending inventories for work in process, Exhibit 12–6 illustrates how work in process balances would be reported in this statement.

EXHIBIT 12-6 Statement of Cost of Goods Manufactured

CRUISERS, INC.
Statement of Cost of Goods Manufactured
For the Month of April

Raw materials:		
Inventory, March 31	$126,900	
Purchases during April	347,860	
Raw materials available for use	$474,760	
Less: Inventory, April 30	(106,250)	
Cost of raw materials used		$368,510
Direct labor cost incurred during April		330,240
Manufacturing overhead applied during April		288,960
Total manufacturing costs incurred during April		$987,710
Add: Work in process inventory, March 31		–0–
Less: Work in process inventory, April 30		–0–
Cost of goods manufactured during April		$987,710

To calculate cost of goods sold for April, the cost of goods manufactured is added to the beginning inventory of finished goods to get the cost of goods available for sale. The ending inventory of finished goods is then subtracted from goods available for sale to arrive at cost of goods sold.

The determination of cost of goods sold for April will depend on the type of inventory system in use. If the periodic system is used, the cost of ending inventory will be determined using the cost of goods sold model:

Beginning inventory	$ 243,820
Cost of goods manufactured	987,710
Cost of goods available for sale	$1,231,530
Less: Ending inventory	(127,600)
Cost of goods sold	$1,103,930

If the perpetual system is used, the cost of each unit of product will be calculated, and cost of goods sold is the number of units sold multiplied by the cost of each. Recall that under the perpetual system, the cost of goods sold is recorded throughout the year as sales are made, whereas under the periodic system, cost of goods sold is determined at the end of the year when a physical inventory count is taken.

To summarize, product costs are attached to the product being manufactured and are treated as an expense when the product is sold (or is lost, becomes worthless from obsolescence, or is otherwise no longer an asset to the firm). Period costs—selling, general, and administrative expenses—are reported in the income statement of the period in which such costs are incurred. *Another way to distinguish between product and period costs is to think of product costs as manufacturing costs, and period costs as non-manufacturing costs.*

In the Exhibit 12-5 illustration of the flow of product costs for Cruisers, Inc., the end result was that cost of goods sold was $1,103,930 for the

Exhibit 12–7   Income Statement

CRUISERS, INC.
Income Statement
For the Month of April

Sales	$2,012,400
Cost of goods sold	(1,103,930)
Gross profit	$ 908,470
Selling, general, and administrative expenses	(562,110)
Income from operations	346,360
Interest expense	(78,420)
Income before taxes	267,940
Income tax expense	(93,779)
Net income	$ 174,161

month of April. Revenues and nonmanufacturing (i.e., period) costs were omitted from the transaction data in Exhibit 12–5 for sake of clarity. An income statement for Cruisers, Inc., using assumed amounts, is presented in Exhibit 12–7. Notice that selling, general, and administrative expenses represent a significant amount of the total operating expenses. Nonoperating expenses reported for interest and income taxes are also significant. You should keep these relationships in mind as you study the next two sections of this chapter. Each of the alternative cost accounting systems (job order costing, process costing, and activity-based costing) described in these sections emphasize the flow of product costs and determination of cost of goods sold. Although cost of goods sold represents the largest expense for most manufacturing firms, overall profitability is dependent upon the firm's ability to control all costs.

Cost Accounting Systems—Job Order Costing, Process Costing, and Hybrid Costing

The general cost accounting system illustrated in the prior section must be adapted to fit the manufacturing environment of the entity. A **job order costing system** is used when discrete products, such as sailboats, are manufactured. Each production run is treated as a separate "job." Costs are accumulated for each job, as illustrated in Exhibit 12–4 for Cruisers' production of 86 SeaCruiser sailboats, and the cost per unit is determined by dividing the total costs incurred by the number of units made. During any accounting period, a number of jobs, or production runs of different products, may be worked on. For any job or production run, costs are accumulated, and the cost per unit of product made is calculated as illustrated for the SeaCruiser sailboat.

When the manufacturing environment involves essentially homogeneous products that are made in a more or less continuous process, frequently involving several departments, it is not feasible to accumulate product cost by job, so a **process costing system** is used. The processing of corn into meal, starch, and syrup is an example of an activity for which process costing would be applicable. The objectives of process costing and job order costing are the same: to assign raw material, direct labor, and manufacturing overhead costs to products and to provide a means to compute the unit cost of each item made. In process costing, costs are accumulated by department (rather than by job) and are assigned to the products processed through the department.

The accumulation of costs by department is relatively straightforward, but the existence of partially completed work in process inventories adds a complexity to the determination of the number of units of product over which departmental costs are to be spread. For example, assume that during the month 100,000 units were transferred from the first department in the manufacturing sequence to the next department, and at the end of the month an additional 15,000 units in inventory were 50% completed. Production during the month is stated in **equivalent units of production**—the number of units that would have been produced if all production efforts during the month had resulted in completed products. In this example, the costs incurred by the first department during the period (including costs in the beginning inventory) would be spread over 107,500 units—the 100,000 units completed plus 50% × 15,000 ending inventory units—to get the weighted-average cost per equivalent unit for this department. This is the cost per unit for items transferred to the next department, and the cost used to value the first department's ending inventory. Costs of subsequent departments include costs transferred in from prior departments. Ultimately, all production costs are transferred to Finished Goods Inventory after the final department completes the production cycle.

As manufacturing firms have sought to increase efficiency and to lower costs in recent years, production processes have been developed that mix elements of job order and continuous process manufacturing environments. Whether labeled flexible manufacturing, batch manufacturing, just-in-time manufacturing, or something else, most of these processes involve streamlined work flow, tighter inventory controls, and extensive use of automated equipment. Hybrid costing systems have evolved for these processes. Hybrid cost accounting systems mix elements of job order and process costing systems to accomplish the objective of assigning manufacturing costs to units produced. It is important to recognize that cost accounting systems will change in response to changes in the production process; the opposite should not be true.

Activity-Based Costing

In recent years, overhead costs have become an increasingly significant part of product cost, and managers have needed higher-quality cost information to permit greater control and better responses to the pressures of increased competition. Nonproduct administrative and marketing costs have become as important as product costs in this environment. As a result, the application of overhead on the basis of a few broad rates based on direct labor hours and/or machine hours has been replaced in many firms by an **activity-based costing** (ABC) system.

An ABC system involves identifying the activity that causes the incurrence of a cost; this activity is known as a **cost driver.** Examples of

---

EXHIBIT 12–8   Activity-Based Costing Illustration

I. Manufacturing overhead cost drivers, and estimated annual costs and activity levels, for Cruisers, Inc.:

Activity (Cost Driver)	Estimated Annual Cost	Estimated Total Activity	Predetermined Rate per Unit of Activity
Production order preparation	$ 135,000	180 orders	$ 750/order
Hull and deck mold setup	2,140,000	1,000 setups	2,140/setup
Raw material acquisition	650,000	2,600 receipts	250/receipt
Material handling	450,000	9,000 moves	50/move
Quality inspection	750,000	6,000 inspections	125/inspection
Clean up and waste disposal	75,000	250 loads	300/load
Total manufacturing overhead	$4,200,000		

II. Actual activity levels required to produce 86 SeaCruiser sailboats in April, and manufacturing overhead applied:

Activity (Cost Driver)	Activity Required	Rate per Unit of Activity	Overhead Applied
Production order preparation	11 orders	$ 750/order	$ 8,250
Hull and deck mold setup	86 setups	2,140/setup	184,040
Raw material acquisition	185 receipts	250/receipt	46,250
Material handling	610 moves	50/move	30,500
Quality inspection	340 inspections	125/inspection	42,500
Clean up and waste disposal	17 loads	300/load	5,100
Total manufacturing overhead applied			$316,640

---

cost drivers are machine setup, quality inspection, production order preparation, and materials handling activities. The number of times each activity is performed and the total cost of the activity are estimated, and a predetermined cost per activity is calculated. These activity-based costs are applied to products, manufacturing processes, and even administrative and marketing efforts. There are likely to be significantly more cost drivers than direct labor hours or machine hours. The development of an ABC system is a complex process involving considerable analysis and a significant investment. Comprehensive computerized databases are virtually a prerequisite to effective activity-based costing.

ABC systems have led to more accurate costing than older overhead application methods and have supported more effective management of the production, administrative, and marketing functions. Exhibit 12–8 presents an example of activity-based costing for the manufacturing overhead related to the SeaCruiser sailboats previously costed in Exhibit 12–4.

Notice that the $316,640 of manufacturing overhead applied to the production of the 86 SeaCruiser sailboats in April using activity-based costing is different from the $288,960 applied (using a direct labor hours rate) in Exhibit 12–4. The advantages of ABC are that it more clearly focuses on the activities causing cost and directs management attention to those activities. For example, in analyzing the makeup of what appears to be a very high setup cost, management of Cruisers, Inc., might develop alternative setup methods that would be less costly. It might also be fruitful to study the material acquisition system to try to make that system more efficient or reduce the number of times raw materials need to be received. To the extent that management can determine cost drivers and understand why and how costs are incurred, the effectiveness of cost controls and the efficiency with which the organization operates can be increased.

The extension of ABC beyond manufacturing overhead to administrative and marketing efforts has led to better decisions that are based on cost, such as pricing, product mix, and product development decisions.

WHAT DOES IT MEAN?

8. What does it mean when an activity-based costing system is used?

Cost Accounting Systems—Absorption Costing and Direct Costing

Objective 5
Understand the difference between absorption costing and direct (or variable) costing.

The cost accounting systems described so far are **absorption costing** systems because all of the manufacturing costs incurred are absorbed into the product cost. An alternative system, called **direct costing** or **variable costing,** assigns only variable costs to products; fixed manufacturing costs are treated as operating expenses of the period in which they are incurred. (Variable and fixed costs are described in the following section.) Absorption costing must be used for financial and income tax reporting purposes because fixed manufacturing overhead is part of the cost of a product. However, some managers are willing to incur the additional expense of using a direct (or variable) costing system for internal planning and control purposes because it results in product and inventory values that reflect the relationship between total cost and volume of activity.

The distinction between absorption costing and direct costing focuses on *manufacturing overhead* costs only. Raw material and direct labor are always product costs, and selling, general, and administrative expenses are always treated as operating expenses of the period in which they are incurred. Under absorption costing *both* variable and fixed manufacturing overhead are considered product costs and are applied to work in process. Under direct costing only variable manufacturing overhead is a product cost applied to work in process; fixed manufacturing overhead is treated as a period cost and recorded as an operating expense when incurred. Exhibit 12–9 is a schematic diagram illustrating these alternative systems.

The significance of the distinction between absorption costing and direct costing is a function of the change in ending inventory. If inventories have increased, under absorption costing the fixed manufacturing overhead related to the inventory increase is an asset in the balance sheet, but under direct costing it is an expense in the income statement. Thus when inventories increase, expenses are lower and profits are higher under absorption costing than under direct costing. The opposite is true when inventories decrease. Direct costing advocates point out that absorption costing gives an erroneous profit signal to managers. These advocates maintain that greater profits should result in periods when the firm's sales result in inventory decreases than in periods when production has exceeded sales and inventories increase.

For financial reporting and income tax purposes, firms that use direct costing must make a year-end adjustment to reclassify that part of the fixed

EXHIBIT 12–9 **Cost Flows—Absorption Costing and Direct (Variable) Costing**

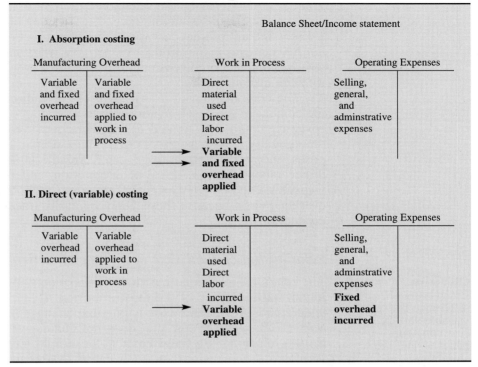

manufacturing overhead incurred during the year that relates to the ending inventory. The effect of this reclassification is to decrease the balance of the Operating Expense account on the income statement and to increase the Work in Process and Finished Goods Inventory account balances on the balance sheet. The amount of fixed manufacturing overhead to be reclassified can be calculated fairly easily based on the proportion of the variable cost of ending inventory to the total variable manufacturing costs incurred during the year.

Do not confuse the product costing procedure with what you may have experienced in a repair shop where the price you pay is based on material cost and labor hours multiplied by a rate that includes the labor cost, overhead cost, and an amount to cover administrative costs and profit. This is a technique for arriving at the price a customer is to be charged and, although similar in concept to product costing, the result is selling price, not product cost.

Relationship of Cost to Product or Activity

Objective 6
Understand the difference between direct and indirect costs.

Direct cost and **indirect cost** are terms used to relate a cost to a product or activity. Whether a cost is direct or indirect depends on the context within which the term is being used. When describing product cost, raw materials and direct labor are direct costs, and overhead is an indirect cost. However, when evaluating the profitability of a product line, the total product cost would be a direct cost, as would the specific advertising and marketing costs associated with the product. The costs of a training program designed to make the sales force more effective with all of the firm's product lines would be an indirect cost. One way of distinguishing between a direct and an indirect cost is to think of a direct cost as a cost that would *not* be incurred if the product or activity were discontinued. An indirect cost is one that would continue to be incurred even if the product or activity were discontinued.

The classification of a cost as direct or indirect is significant only in the context of the cost's relationship to a product or activity. In fact, some costs are commonly treated as indirect costs even though they could be theoretically treated as direct costs. For example, for product costing purposes, indirect materials (e.g., glue, thread, staples, and grease) and indirect labor (e.g., salaries of production supervisors, quality control inspectors, and maintenance workers) are usually treated as manufacturing overhead costs because they cannot be easily traced to individual units of production.

Relationship of Total Cost to Volume of Activity

Objective 7
Understand the difference between variable and fixed cost behavior patterns, and the simplifying assumptions made in this classification method.

The relationship of total cost to volume of activity describes the **cost behavior pattern,** one of the most important cost classification methods to understand. A **variable cost** is one that changes *in total* as the volume of activity changes. A cost that does not change *in total* as the volume of activity changes is a **fixed cost.** For example, raw material costs have a variable cost behavior pattern because the greater the number of units produced, the higher the total raw material costs incurred. On the other hand, factory building depreciation expense is a fixed cost because total depreciation expense will not change regardless of the level of production (unless, of course, a units of production method is used to calculate depreciation, in which case this cost would be variable). The distinction between fixed and variable cost behavior patterns is illustrated graphically in Exhibit 12–10.

The fixed or variable label refers to the behavior of *total* cost relative to a change in activity. When referring to the behavior of unit costs, however, the labels may be confusing because variable costs are constant per

EXHIBIT 12–10   Cost Behavior Patterns

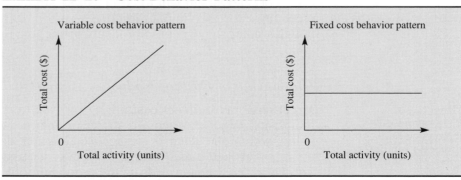

unit, but fixed costs per unit will change as the level of activity changes. Thus, it is necessary to understand the behavior pattern on both a total cost basis and a per unit basis. Variable costs change in total as activity changes but are constant per unit. Fixed costs do not change in total as activity changes but will vary if expressed on a per unit of activity basis.

Knowledge of the cost behavior pattern is important to the planning process, and several simplifying assumptions are usually made to facilitate the use of this cost characteristic. The most significant assumption has to do with the range of activity over which the identified or assumed cost behavior pattern exists. This is the **relevant range** assumption, and it is most applicable to fixed costs. Returning to the depreciation expense example, it is clear that at some point an increase in the volume of production would require more plant capacity, and depreciation expense would increase. On the other hand, if substantially lower production volumes were anticipated in the future, some of the factory would be closed down or converted to other use, and depreciation expense would decrease. To say that depreciation expense is fixed is to say that over some relevant range of production the total cost will not change. Different fixed expenses will have different relevant ranges over which they have a fixed cost behavior pattern. When a cost is identified as fixed and cost projections are made based on that cost behavior pattern classification, the limits of the relevant range assumption must be considered. The other major simplifying assumption is that the cost behavior pattern is *linear,* not curvilinear. This assumption relates primarily to variable costs. Because of economies of scale, quantity discounts, and other factors, variable costs will change slightly when expressed on a per unit basis. These changes are usually not significant, but if they are, appropriate adjustment in unit costs should be made in analyses based on cost behavior patterns. These assumptions are illustrated and described in more detail in the next chapter.

It is clear that not all costs can be classified as either variable or fixed. Some costs are partly fixed and partly variable. Sometimes costs with this mixed behavior pattern are called **semivariable costs.** Utilities for the factory, for example, have a mixed behavior pattern because when the plant isn't operating, some lights must be kept on for safety and security, but as production increases more electricity is required. Analytical techniques can break this type of cost into its fixed and variable components, and a **cost formula** can be developed, expressed as:

$$\text{Total cost} = \text{Fixed cost} + \text{Variable cost}$$
$$= \text{Fixed cost} + (\text{Variable rate per unit} \times \text{Activity})$$

This cost formula can then be used to forecast the total cost expected to be incurred at various levels of activity. For example, assume that it has been determined that the fixed cost for utilities is $350 per month and that the variable rate for utilities is 30 cents per machine hour. Total estimated utilities cost for a month in which 6,000 machine hours were planned would be:

$$\text{Total cost} = \$350 + (\$.30 \times 6,000 \text{ machine hours})$$
$$= \$2,150$$

EXHIBIT 12–11   The Error of Unitizing Fixed Costs

Assume the following university business office costs per month associated with providing a student check-cashing privilege:

Salaries	$ 900
Allocated space costs (depreciation, utilities, etc.)	300
Total per month	$1,200
If 2,000 checks are cashed in a month, the "cost" per check is ($1,200/2,000)	$ .60
If 6,000 checks are cashed in a month, the "cost" per check is ($1,200/6,000)	$ .20

How much does it cost to cash a check?

What action would students take if they learned that a check-cashing fee was being considered based on the "cost" of cashing a check during the coming month?

Objective 8
Understand why expressing fixed costs on a per unit of activity basis is misleading and may result in faulty decisions.

Great care must be taken with the use of fixed cost per unit data because any change in the volume of activity will change the per unit cost. As a general rule, *do not unitize fixed expenses because they do not behave on a per unit basis!* For example, most of the costs of a university business office—salaries, depreciation, and utilities—are fixed; to calculate the "cost" of cashing student checks by dividing a portion of business office costs by the number of checks cashed in a period of time will give a misleading result, as illustrated in Exhibit 12–11. Sometimes fixed costs must be unitized, as in the development of a predetermined overhead application rate (described earlier). It is also important to recognize that the relevant range is often quite wide, and significant increases in activity can be achieved without increasing fixed costs (i.e., there are economies of scale to be achieved that result in efficiencies and a reduction of fixed cost per unit). However, whenever fixed costs are unitized, be very careful about the conclusions that you draw from the data.

WHAT DOES IT MEAN?

9. What does it mean to say that determination of cost behavior pattern involves some implicit assumptions?

10. What does it mean to develop a cost formula?

Cost Classification according to a Time-Frame Perspective

Objective 9
Understand that all costs are controllable by someone at some time but that in the short run some costs may be classified as noncontrollable.

Frequently, reference is made to a "noncontrollable" cost, which implies that there is really nothing the manager can do to influence the amount of the cost. This may be true in the short run (e.g., for the coming quarter or year), but in the long run every cost incurred by the organization is controllable by someone. For example, real estate taxes on a firm's plant and office facilities cannot usually be influenced by management in the short run because the assessed valuation and tax rates are established by taxing authorities. However, when the decision was made to build or buy the facilities, the relative level of property taxes was established. Land in a prime location and a fancy building with plenty of space for possible expansion could be expected to result in higher property taxes over the years than more modest facilities. The point is not whether appropriate facilities were obtained, but that the decision makers (top management or board of directors) had control over the general level of property taxes when the decision was being made. It is not appropriate to think of any cost as being noncontrollable over all time frames.

To eliminate the potential for fuzzy thinking that the controllable/ noncontrollable classification may encourage, many firms use the terms **committed cost** and **discretionary cost.** A committed cost is one that will be incurred to execute long-range policy decisions that the firm has "committed" to. A discretionary cost is one that can be adjusted in the short-run (usually on an annual basis) at management's discretion. Examples are presented here.

Committed Costs	*Discretionary Costs*
Salaries of top management	Company softball team
Real estate taxes	Public relations
Advertising (especially for a consumer products company)	Charitable contributions
	Management development programs
Quality control	Internships for college students
Depreciation	
Insurance	

With respect to committed costs, the control issue for managers is focused on whether the cost is appropriate for the value received from its incurrence. On the other hand, when beginning or curtailing discretionary costs, managers do have short-term discretion about the level of cost to be incurred. As suggested by the examples above, significant nonfinancial considerations must also be made with respect to discretionary costs.

Cost Classifications for Other Analytical Purposes

Objective 10
Understand the meaning and application of the following "cost" terms: *differential, allocated, sunk,* and *opportunity.*

Differential costs are brought into focus when possible future activities are analyzed. A differential cost is one that will differ according to the alternative activity that is selected. For example, if a modification of an existing product is being considered, only the changes in cost resulting from the modification need to be considered relative to the additional revenues expected to result from the modification. Those costs that will continue to be incurred whether or not the modification is made are not relevant to the decision.

Allocated costs are those that have been assigned to a product or activity (a "cost center") using some sort of arithmetic process. For example, overhead costs are allocated to production runs using the overhead application rate, the derivation of which was described earlier. The topic of cost allocation will be covered in more detail in Chapter 14, but at this point a warning about cost allocations is appropriate. Many cost allocation methods are arbitrary and do not result in assigning costs in a way that reflects the reasons the costs were incurred. Therefore, managers must be very careful about the conclusions made from an analysis that includes allocated costs. A general rule, similar to that proscribing the unitization of fixed costs, is appropriate to learn: *Do not arbitrarily allocate costs to a cost center because the allocated costs may not behave the way assumed in the allocation method.*

A **sunk cost** is a cost that has been incurred and cannot be unincurred, or reversed, by some future action. For example, if a firm has acquired a special purpose asset that would not be useful to any other organization, the cost of the asset represents a sunk cost. If the asset is put in use, its cost will be shown as depreciation expense over its life; if scrapped, its net book value will be recorded as a loss. Either way, the cost of the asset will be reflected in the income statement. When a new car is driven out of the dealer's lot, a sunk cost has been incurred that is equal to the loss in value because the car is now "used." *Sunk costs are never relevant to the analysis of alternative future actions (i.e., they are never differential costs) because they have been incurred and will not change.*

Opportunity cost is an economic concept that is too frequently overlooked in accounting analyses. Opportunity cost is the income forgone because an asset was not invested at a rate of return that could have been earned. For example, assume that you keep a $200 minimum balance in a noninterest-bearing checking account for which no service charge is assessed regardless of balance. If your next best alternative is to invest the $200 in a 6% savings account, the opportunity cost of your decision is $12 per year (6% $\times$ $200). Because opportunity cost relates to a transaction that did not occur, no record of it is made in the financial accounting process; thus, it is often overlooked. Awareness of opportunity cost raises the question: What other alternatives are there for earning a return on a particular asset?

WHAT DOES IT MEAN?

11. What does it mean to state that a cost is a sunk cost?

Summary

Management is the process of planning, organizing, and controlling an organization's activities to accomplish its goals. Managerial accounting (sometimes called *management accounting*) supports the management process.

Managerial accounting differs from financial accounting in several ways. Managerial accounting has an internal orientation, a future perspective, and often focuses on individual units within the firm rather than the organization as a whole. Reasonably accurate data are acceptable for internal analysis, and performance reports tend to be issued on a frequent basis for managerial control and decision making.

There are different costs for different purposes. Cost terminology is important to understand if cost data are to be used appropriately.

Cost accounting systems distinguish between product costs and period costs. Product costs for a merchandising firm are the costs associated with products held for sale. Product costs for a manufacturing firm include raw materials, direct labor, and manufacturing overhead. Period costs, such as selling, general, and administrative expenses, are reported as expenses in the fiscal period in which they are incurred.

Cost accounting systems account for the flow of product costs into work in process inventory, the transfer of cost of goods manufactured out of work in process inventory into finished goods inventory, and finally to cost of goods sold when the product is sold. One of the challenging objectives of the cost accounting system is to assign manufacturing overhead to products made. The cost of a single unit of product is the sum of the costs incurred to produce a quantity of units divided by the number of units produced.

The increased significance of overhead costs has led to the development of activity-based costing as a means of more accurately assigning overhead by relating costs to the activities that drive them.

The difference between absorption costing and direct (or variable) costing is in the accounting for fixed manufacturing overhead. In absorption costing, fixed manufacturing overhead is a product cost. In direct (or variable) costing, fixed manufacturing overhead is a period cost.

Costs can be classified as direct or indirect, relative to a particular product or activity.

The behavior pattern of a cost relates to the change in total cost for a change in activity. Variable costs change, in total, as activity changes. Fixed costs remain constant in total as activity changes. Assumptions about linearity and relevant range are implicit when a cost is described as variable or fixed. Many costs have a mixed behavior pattern (i.e., they are partly variable and partly fixed). A cost formula expresses the total amount of a cost for a given level of activity by combining the fixed and variable elements of the total cost. It is inappropriate, and may be misleading, to express a fixed cost on a per unit basis because by definition a fixed cost is constant over a range of activity.

Costs that are controllable in the short run are usually called *discretionary costs.* Costs that are controllable only in the long run are called *committed costs.* However, all costs are controllable by someone over some time frame.

When an analysis of costs involved in alternative plans is made, differential costs are those that differ between alternatives. Sometimes cost allocations are made for analytical purposes. If the allocation is made on an arbitrary basis rather than by recognizing causal factors, users of the data must be very careful about the conclusions they reach because cost behavior has not been accurately reflected. Sunk costs have been incurred and cannot be reversed. Opportunity cost is not reflected in the accounting records but should be recognized when making an economic analysis.

Key Terms and Concepts

absorption costing (p. 428)   A product costing process in which both variable and fixed manufacturing costs are included in product costs.

activity-based costing (p. 426)   The process of accumulating manufacturing overhead cost by production support activity (e.g., machine setup) and then applying manufacturing overhead to production based on the activity required for each job or product.

allocated cost (p. 433)   A cost that has been assigned to a product or activity using some sort of arithmetic process.

committed cost (p. 433)   A cost that is incurred because of a long-range policy decision.

cost accounting (p. 413)   A subset of managerial accounting that relates to the determination and accumulation of product, process, or service costs.

cost behavior pattern (p. 430)   Identification of whether a cost is fixed or variable.

cost driver (p. 426)   An activity that causes the incurrence of a cost.

cost formula (p. 431)   An arithmetic expression that reflects the fixed and variable elements of a cost.

differential cost (p. 433)   A cost that will differ based on the selection of an alternative activity.

direct cost (p. 429)   A cost directly related to the product or activity under consideration; the cost would not be incurred if the product or activity were discontinued.

direct costing (p. 428)   A product costing process in which only variable manufacturing costs are included in product cost. Sometimes called *variable costing.*

direct labor (p. 418)   Effort provided by workers who are directly involved in the manufacture of a product.

discretionary cost (p. 433)   A cost that can be raised or lowered in the short run.

equivalent units of production (p. 426)   In a process costing system, the number of units that would have been produced if all production efforts during the period had resulted in completed products.

finished goods inventory (p. 419)   Inventory ready for sale to customers.

fixed cost (p. 430)   A cost that does not change in total as the level of activity changes within a relevant range.

indirect cost (p. 429)   A cost that is indirectly related to the product or activity under consideration; the cost would continue to be incurred if the product or activity were discontinued.

job order costing system (p. 425)   A product costing system used when discrete products, or "jobs," are manufactured.

management process (p. 414)   Planning, organizing, and controlling the activities of an organization so it can accomplish its purpose.

managerial accounting (p. 413)   Accounting that uses economic and financial information to plan and control many of the activities of an entity, and to support the management decision-making process. Sometimes called *management accounting.*

manufacturing overhead, or **overhead** (p. 418)   All manufacturing costs except those classified as raw materials or direct labor.

opportunity cost (p. 434)   An economic concept relating to income forgone because an opportunity to earn income was not pursued.

overapplied overhead (p. 421)   A credit balance in the Manufacturing Overhead account that results from applied overhead in excess of actual overhead costs.

overhead application rate (p. 421)   The rate used to allocate overhead to specific production runs. See *predetermined overhead application rate.*

period costs (p. 418)   Noninventoriable costs, including *selling, general, and administrative expenses,* that relate to an accounting period.

predetermined overhead application rate (p. 421)   The rate per unit of activity (e.g., direct labor hour) used to apply manufacturing overhead to work in process.

process costing system (p. 425)   A costing system used to accumulate costs for a production process that is more or less continuous, frequently involving several departments.

product costs (p. 417)   Inventoriable costs including raw materials, direct labor, and manufacturing overhead.

production standard (p. 416)   Expected or allowed times and costs to make a product or to perform an activity.

raw materials (p. 418)   The ingredients of a product.

raw materials inventory (p. 419)   Inventory of materials ready for the production process.

relevant range (p. 431)   The range of activity over which the fixed or variable cost behavior pattern exists.

semivariable cost (p. 431)   A cost that has both fixed and variable elements.

statement of cost of goods manufactured (p. 423)   A supplementary financial statement that supports cost of goods sold, which is an element of the income statement. This statement summarizes raw materials, direct labor, and manufacturing overhead costs incurred during the period.

sunk cost (p. 434)   A cost that has been incurred and that cannot be unincurred or reversed by some future action.

underapplied overhead (p. 421)   A debit balance in the Manufacturing Overhead account that results from actual overhead costs in excess of applied overhead.

variable cost (p. 430)   A cost that changes in total as the volume of activity changes.

variable costing (p. 428)   A product costing process in which only variable manufacturing costs are included in product cost. Sometimes called *direct costing.*

work in process inventory (p. 419)   Inventory account for the costs (raw materials, direct labor, and manufacturing overhead) of items that are in the process of being manufactured.

WHAT DOES IT MEAN?
ANSWERS

1. It means that cost is a very broad term that must be qualified so communication about cost is clear. It is important to understand cost terminology.

2. It means that managerial accounting is more future oriented, while financial accounting is concerned primarily with reporting events that have already occurred.

3. It means that planned results are compared to actual results, and either actions or plans are changed so future results come closer to planned results.

4. It means that the cost is either direct material or direct labor incurred in making a product; as such, total cost will vary with the quantity of product made.

5. It means that these costs are initially recorded as an inventory asset and that when the related product is sold, the cost of the product is recognized as cost of goods sold.

6. It means that a way of assigning these indirect costs to inventory has been developed and used as a means of including manufacturing overhead in product cost.

7. It means that actual overhead incurred during the year is more than overhead applied to work in process by using the predetermined overhead application rate because actual overhead and/or actual production was different from the estimates used at the beginning of the year to develop the overhead application rate.

8. It means that there has been an extensive effort to refine the method of assigning costs to products and processes so cost data are more accurate and can be used on a more timely basis than was the case with older cost systems.

9. It means that classification of a cost as fixed or variable is based on the simplifying assumptions of linearity and relevant range.

10. It means that a formula for predicting the total cost at some level of activity has been developed and that it recognizes both the fixed and variable elements of the cost's behavior pattern.

11. It means that the cost has been incurred, and nothing will happen to affect that cost.

Exercises and Problems

LO 2, 6, 7   **12–1.   Cost classifications.** For each of the following costs, check the columns that most likely apply.

Cost	Product Direct	Product Indirect	Period	Variable	Fixed
Wages of assembly-line workers	———	———	———	———	———
Depreciation—plant equipment	———	———	———	———	———
Glue and thread	———	———	———	———	———
Shipping costs	———	———	———	———	———
Raw materials handling costs	———	———	———	———	———
Salary of public relations manager	———	———	———	———	———
Production run setup costs	———	———	———	———	———
Plant utilities	———	———	———	———	———
Electricity cost of retail stores	———	———	———	———	———
Research and development expense	———	———	———	———	———

LO 2, 6, 7   **12–2.   Cost classifications.** For each of the following costs, check the columns that most likely apply.

| | Product | | | | |
Cost	Direct	Indirect	Period	Variable	Fixed
Raw materials	_____	_____	_____	_____	_____
Staples used to secure packed boxes of product	_____	_____	_____	_____	_____
Plant janitors' wages	_____	_____	_____	_____	_____
Order processing clerks' wages	_____	_____	_____	_____	_____
Advertising expenses	_____	_____	_____	_____	_____
Production workers' wages	_____	_____	_____	_____	_____
Production supervisors' salaries	_____	_____	_____	_____	_____
Sales force commissions	_____	_____	_____	_____	_____
Maintenance supplies used	_____	_____	_____	_____	_____
President's salary	_____	_____	_____	_____	_____
Electricity cost	_____	_____	_____	_____	_____
Real estate taxes for:					
Factory	_____	_____	_____	_____	_____
Office building	_____	_____	_____	_____	_____

LO 2, 7

12–3. **Cost classifications.** Knoblauch, Inc., manufactures rugby jerseys for collegiate sports teams and sells its merchandise through university bookstores.

Required:

Identify a specific item in the company's manufacturing, selling, or administrative processes for which the cost would be classified as:

a. Raw material.

b. Direct labor.

c. Variable manufacturing overhead.

d. Fixed manufacturing overhead.

e. Fixed administrative expense.

f. Fixed indirect selling expense.

g. Variable direct selling expense.

LO 2, 7

12–4. **Cost classifications.** Campus Carriers manufactures backpacks that are sold to students for use as book bags.

Required:

Identify a specific item in this company's manufacturing, selling, or administrative processes for which the cost would be classified as:

a. Raw material.

b. Direct labor.

c. Variable manufacturing overhead.

d. Fixed manufacturing overhead.

e. Fixed administrative expense.

f. Fixed indirect selling expense.

g. Variable direct selling expense.

LO 10

12–5. **Application of cost terminology.** Assume that you have decided to drive your car to Florida for the spring break. A classmate learns about your plans and asks about riding with you. Explain how you would apply each of the following cost concepts to the task of determining how much, if any, cost you would take into consideration for the purposes of setting a price to be charged for taking the classmate with you.

a. Differential cost.

b. Allocated cost.

c. Sunk cost.

d. Opportunity cost.

LO 10

12–6. **Give examples of various costs.** Attending college involves incurring many costs. Give an example of a college cost that could be assigned to each of the following classifications. Explain your reason for assigning each cost to the classification.

a. Sunk cost.

b. Discretionary cost.

c. Committed cost.

d. Opportunity cost.

e. Differential cost.

f. Allocated cost.

LO 3

12–7. **Product costing—various issues.** Gale Co. produces ceramic coffee mugs and pencil holders. Manufacturing overhead is assigned to production using an application rate based on direct labor hours.

Required:

a. For 1999, the company's cost accountant estimated that total overhead costs incurred would be $408,750 and that a total of 54,500 direct labor hours would be worked. Calculate the amount of overhead to be applied for each direct labor hour worked on a production run.

b. A production run of 750 coffee mugs used raw materials that cost $810 and used 90 direct labor hours at a cost of $9.50 per hour. Calculate the cost of each coffee mug produced.

c. At the end of April 1999, 530 coffee mugs made in the above production run had been sold, and the rest were in ending inventory. Calculate (1) the cost of the coffee mugs sold that would have been reported in the income statement and (2) the cost included in the April 30, 1999, finished goods inventory.

LO 3

12–8. **Product costing—manufacturing overhead.** Lamps, Inc., manufactures women's gloves. Manufacturing overhead is assigned to production on a machine-hour basis. For 1999, it was estimated that manufacturing overhead would total $359,520 and that 21,400 machine hours would be used.

Required:

a. Calculate the predetermined overhead application rate that will be used for absorption costing purposes during 1999.

b. During August, 3,900 pairs of gloves were made. Raw materials costing $6,240 were used, and direct labor costs totaled $9,165. A total of 780 machine hours were worked during the month of August. Calculate the cost per pair of gloves made during August.

c. At the end of August, 1,050 pairs of gloves were in ending inventory. Calculate the cost of the ending inventory and the cost of the gloves sold during August.

LO 3

12–9. **Manufacturing overhead—over/underapplied.** Hartford, Inc., produces automobile bumpers. Overhead is applied on the basis of machine hours required for cutting and fabricating. A predetermined overhead application rate of $12.70 per machine hour was established for 1999.

Required:

a. If 9,000 machine hours were expected to be used during 1999, how much overhead was expected to be incurred?

b. Actual overhead incurred during 1999 totaled $121,650, and 9,100 machine hours were used during 1999. Calculate the amount of over- or underapplied overhead for 1999.

c. Explain the accounting necessary for the over- or underapplied overhead for the year.

LO 3   **12–10.**   **Manufacturing overhead—over/underapplied.** Waite Co. makes desk accessories. Manufacturing overhead is applied to production on a direct labor hours basis. During the first month of the company's fiscal year, $56,520 of manufacturing overhead was applied to Work in Process Inventory using the predetermined overhead application rate of $6 per direct labor hour.

Required:

a. Calculate the number of hours of direct labor used during March.

b. Actual manufacturing overhead costs incurred during March totaled $49,340. Calculate the amount of over- or underapplied overhead for March.

c. Identify two possible explanations for the over- or underapplied overhead.

d. Explain the accounting appropriate for the over- or underapplied overhead at the end of March.

LO 3   **12–11.**   **Manufacturing overhead—multiple application bases.** The Regimental Tie Co. manufactures neckties and scarves. Two overhead application bases are used; some overhead is applied on the basis of raw material cost at a rate of 140% of material cost, and the balance of the overhead is applied at the rate of $7.20 per direct labor hour.

Required:

Calculate the cost per unit of a production run of 530 neckties that required raw materials costing $1,950 and 75 direct labor hours at a total cost of $840.

LO 3   **12–12.**   **Manufacturing overhead—multiple application bases.** Continental Mfg. Co. makes hand tools. Two manufacturing overhead application bases are used; some overhead is applied on the basis of machine hours at a rate of $5.60 per machine hour, and the balance of the overhead is applied at the rate of 240% of direct labor cost.

Required:

a. Calculate the cost per unit of a production run of 4,200 eight-inch screwdrivers that required:
1. Raw materials costing $490.
2. 21 direct labor hours costing $357.
3. 36 machine hours.

b. At the end of April, 3,870 of the above screwdrivers had been sold. Calculate the ending inventory value of the screwdrivers still in inventory at April 30.

LO 3   **12–13.**   **Activity-based costing.** Zukowski, Inc., manufactures and sells diagnostic equipment used in the medical profession. Its job costing system was designed using an activity-based costing approach. Direct materials and direct labor costs are accumulated separately, along with information concerning four manufacturing overhead cost drivers (activities). Assume that the direct labor rate is $20 per hour and that there were no beginning inventories. The following information was available for 1999, based on an expected production level of 400,000 units for the year:

Activity (Cost Driver)	Budgeted Costs for 1999	Cost Driver Used as Allocation Base	Cost Allocation Rate
Materials handling	$3,600,000	Number of parts used	$ 1.50 per part
Milling and grinding	8,800,000	Number of machine hours	11.00 per hour
Assembly and inspection	6,000,000	Direct labor hours worked	5.00 per hour
Testing	1,200,000	Number of units tested	3.00 per unit

The following production, costs, and activities occurred during the month of September:

Units Produced/Tested	Direct Materials Costs	Number of Parts Used	Machine Hours	Direct Labor Hours
50,000	$3,500,000	275,000	95,000	160,000

Required:

a. Calculate the total manufacturing costs and the cost per unit produced and tested during the month of September for Zukowski, Inc.

b. Explain the advantages of the ABC approach relative to using a single predetermined overhead application rate based on direct labor hours. *(Note: You do not have to calculate the overhead that would be applied for the month of September using this alternative method.)*

LO 3   **12–14.**   **Activity-based costing versus traditional overhead allocation methods.** Woodruff Industries manufactures and sells custom-made coffee tables. Its job costing system was designed using an activity-based costing approach. Direct materials and direct labor costs are accumulated separately, along with information concerning three manufacturing overhead cost drivers (activities). Assume that the direct labor rate is $15 per hour and that there were no beginning inventories. The following information was available for 1999, based on an expected production level of 50,000 units for the year:

Activity (Cost Driver)	Budgeted Costs for 1999	Cost Driver Used as Allocation Base	Cost Allocation Rate
Materials handling	$ 250,000	Number of parts used	$ 0.20 per part
Cutting and lathe work	1,750,000	Number of parts used	1.40 per part
Assembly and inspection	4,000,000	Direct labor hours	20.00 per hour

The following production, costs, and activities occurred during the month of July:

Units Produced	Direct Materials Costs	Number of Parts Used	Direct Labor Hours
3,200	$107,200	70,400	13,120

Required:

a. Calculate the total manufacturing cost and the cost per unit of the coffee tables produced during the month of July (using the activity-based costing approach).

b. Assume instead that Woodruff Industries applies manufacturing overhead on a direct labor hours basis (rather than using the activity-based costing system described above). Calculate the total manufacturing cost and the cost per unit of the coffee tables produced during the month of July. *(Hint: You will need to calculate the predetermined overhead application rate using the total budgeted overhead costs for 1999.)*

c. Compare the per unit cost figures calculated in parts *a* and *b* above. Which approach do you think provides better information for manufacturing managers? Explain your answer.

LO 7   **12–15. Estimating costs based on behavior patterns.** Ryan estimates that the costs of insurance, license, and depreciation to operate his car total $320 per month and that the gas, oil, and maintenance costs are 14 cents per mile. Ryan also estimates that, on average, he drives his car 1,400 miles per month.

Required:

a. How much cost would Ryan expect to incur during April if he drove the car 1,529 miles?

b. Would it be meaningful for Ryan to calculate an estimated average cost per mile for a typical 1,400-mile month? Explain your answer.

LO 7   **12–16. Estimating costs based on behavior patterns.** The following table shows the amount of cost incurred in March for the cost items indicated. During March 4,000 units of the firm's single product were manufactured.

Raw materials	$20,800
Factory depreciation expense	40,500
Direct labor	49,600
Production supervisor's salary	5,000
Computer rental expense	3,100
Maintenance supplies used	600

Required:

a. How much cost would you expect to be incurred for each of the above items during April when 5,600 units of the product are planned for production?

b. Calculate the average total cost per unit for the 4,000 units manufactured in March. Explain why this figure would not be useful to a manager interested in predicting the cost of producing 5,600 units in April.

LO 5, 8   **12–17. Variable versus absorption costing.** Cole, Inc., manufactures wool sweaters. Costs incurred in making 9,000 sweaters in October included $22,500 of fixed manufacturing overhead. The total absorption cost per sweater was $11.60.

Required:

a. Calculate the variable cost per sweater.

b. The ending inventory of sweaters was 1,600 units lower at the end of the month than at the beginning of the month. By how much and in what direction (higher or lower) would cost of goods sold for the month of October be different under variable costing than under absorption costing?

c. Express the sweater cost in a cost formula.

LO 5, 8   **12–18.   Variable versus absorption costing.** Conolly, Inc., manufactures pocket calculators. Costs incurred in making 9,500 calculators in May included $29,450 of fixed manufacturing overhead. The total absorption cost per calculator was $10.25.

Required:

a. Calculate the variable cost per calculator.

b. The ending inventory of pocket calculators was 750 units higher at the end of the month than at the beginning of the month. By how much and in what direction (higher or lower) would operating income for the month of May be different under variable costing than under absorption costing?

c. Express the pocket calculator cost in a cost formula.

LO 5, 8   **12–19.   Variable versus absorption costing.** Avajade Co. manufactures fishing equipment. During 1998, total costs associated with manufacturing 15,000 fly-cast fishing rods (a new product introduced this year) were as follows:

Raw materials	$62,100
Direct labor	16,500
Variable manufacturing overhead	11,250
Fixed manufacturing overhead	18,000

Required:

a. Calculate the cost per fishing rod under both variable costing and absorption costing.

b. If 300 of these fishing rods were in finished goods inventory at the end of 1998, by how much and in what direction (higher or lower) would 1998 operating income be different under variable costing than under absorption costing?

c. Express the fishing rod cost in a cost formula. What does this formula suggest the total cost of making an additional 200 fishing rods would be?

LO 5, 8   **12–20.   Variable versus absorption costing.** Swanson, Inc., manufactures cellular telephones. During 1998, total costs associated with manufacturing 32,000 of the new EZ-9801 model (introduced this year) were as follows:

Raw materials	$275,200
Direct labor	454,400
Variable manufacturing overhead	115,200
Fixed manufacturing overhead	108,800

Required:

a. Calculate the cost per phone under both variable costing and absorption costing.

b. If 4,200 of these phones were in finished goods inventory at the end of 1998, by how much and in what direction (higher or lower) would 1998 cost of goods sold be different under variable costing than under absorption costing?

c. Express the phone cost in a cost formula. What does this formula suggest the total cost of making an additional 500 phones would be?

LO 2, 3, 4   **12–21.**   **Cost of goods manufactured, cost of goods sold, and income statement.** Kimane, Ltd., incurred the following costs during November:

Raw materials used	$33,100
Direct labor costs incurred	65,200
Manufacturing overhead, actual	44,800
Selling expenses	26,700
Administrative expenses	19,400
Interest expense	9,100

Required:

During the month, 5,300 units of product were manufactured and 4,800 units of product were sold. On November 1, Kimane, Ltd., carried no inventories. On November 30, there were no inventories other than finished goods.

a. Calculate the cost of goods manufactured during November and the average cost per unit of product manufactured.

b. Calculate the cost of goods sold during November.

c. Calculate the difference between cost of goods manufactured and cost of goods sold. How will this amount be reported in the financial statements?

d. (Optional) Prepare an income statement for Kimane, Ltd., for the month of November. Assume that sales for the month were $244,800 and the company's effective income tax rate was 30%.

LO 2, 3, 4   **12–22.**   **Cost of goods manufactured, cost of goods sold, and income statement.** Zena, Inc., incurred the following costs during July:

Selling expenses	$25,340
Direct labor costs incurred	37,752
Interest expense	7,135
Manufacturing overhead, actual	32,760
Raw materials used	61,464
Administrative expenses	19,675

Required:

During the month, 2,600 units of product were manufactured and 1,450 units of product were sold. On July 1, Zena, Inc., carried no inventories. On July 31, there were no inventories for raw materials or work in process.

a. Calculate the cost of goods manufactured during July and the average cost per unit of product manufactured.

b. Calculate the cost of goods sold during July.

c. Calculate the difference between cost of goods manufactured and cost of goods sold. How will this amount be reported in the financial statements?

d. (Optional) Prepare an income statement for Zena, Inc., for the month of July. Assume that sales for the month were $138,040 and the company's effective income tax rate was 35%.

LO 3, 4   **12–23.**   **Cost of goods manufactured and cost of goods sold.** The following table summarizes the beginning and ending inventories of Gregorich, Inc., for the month of October:

	Sept. 30	Oct. 31
Raw materials	$33,500	$27,600
Work in process	71,300	64,800
Finished goods	47,200	41,900

Required:
Raw materials purchased during the month of October totaled $123,900. Direct labor costs incurred totaled $312,200 for the month. Actual and applied manufacturing overhead costs for October totaled $188,400 and $192,300, respectively.
a. Calculate the cost of goods manufactured for October.
b. Calculate the cost of goods sold for October.

LO 2, 3, 4   **12–24.** **Cost of goods manufactured, cost of goods sold, and income statement.** Bodden & Co. incurred the following costs during April:

Raw materials purchased	$44,100
Direct labor ($12.50 per hour)	57,500
Manufacturing overhead (actual)	90,300
Selling expenses	31,800
Administrative expenses	14,700
Interest expense	6,400

Manufacturing overhead is applied on the basis of $20 per direct labor hour. Assume that overapplied or underapplied overhead is transferred to cost of goods sold only at the end of the year. During the month, 4,200 units of product were manufactured and 4,400 units of product were sold. On April 1 and April 30, Bodden & Co. carried the following inventory balances:

	April 1	April 30
Raw materials	$19,600	$17,900
Work in process	53,200	57,400
Finished goods	41,800	32,700

a. Prepare a Statement of Cost of Goods Manufactured for the month of April and calculate the average cost per unit of product manufactured.
b. Calculate the cost of goods sold during April.
c. Calculate the difference between cost of goods manufactured and cost of goods sold. How will this amount be reported in the financial statements?
d. (Optional) Prepare an income statement for Bodden & Co. for the month of April. Assume that sales for the month were $272,800 and the company's effective income tax rate was 34%.

LO 2, 3, 4   **12–25.** **Product costing—various issues.** Marble Co. uses an absorption cost system for accumulating product cost. The following data are available for the past year:

Raw materials purchases totaled $240,000.

Direct labor costs incurred for the year totaled $420,000.

Variable manufacturing overhead is applied on the basis of $6.00 per direct labor hour.

Fixed manufacturing overhead is applied on the basis of machine hours used. When plans for the year were being made, it was estimated that total fixed overhead costs would be $312,000, and that 96,000 machine hours would be used during the year.

The direct labor rate is $16.00 per hour.

Actual machine hours used during the year totaled 88,000 hours.

Actual general and administrative expenses for the year totaled $320,000.

Inventory balances at the beginning and end of the year were as follows:

	Beginning of Year	End of Year
Raw materials	$ 39,000	$ 27,000
Work in process	33,000	51,500
Finished goods	104,000	122,000

Required:

Calculate the following:

a. Predetermined fixed manufacturing overhead application rate.
b. Cost of raw materials used.
c. Variable manufacturing overhead applied to work in process.
d. Fixed manufacturing overhead applied to work in process.
e. Cost of goods manufactured.
f. Cost of goods sold.

LO 2, 3, 4   **12–26.** **Cost of goods manufactured, cost of goods sold, and income statement.** Calculate each of the missing amounts.

	Firm A	Firm B	Firm C
Beginning raw materials inventory	$ 17,000	$?	$ 42,000
Purchases of raw materials during the year	?	96,000	226,000
Raw materials available for use	?	119,000	?
Ending raw materials inventory	12,000	?	51,000
Cost of raw materials used	90,000	101,000	?
Direct labor costs incurred	130,000	?	318,000
Variable manufacturing overhead applied	?	34,000	72,000
Fixed manufacturing overhead applied	100,000	60,000	?
Total manufacturing costs incurred	370,000	?	?
Beginning work in process	15,000	7,000	19,000
Ending work in process	25,000	11,000	16,000
Cost of goods manufactured	$?	$266,000	$?
Sales	$?	$410,000	$?
Beginning finished goods inventory	30,000	?	61,000
Cost of goods manufactured	?	266,000	?
Cost of goods available for sale	?	303,000	761,000
Ending finished goods inventory	50,000	?	48,000
Cost of goods sold	?	273,000	?
Gross profit	140,000	?	198,000
Selling, general, and administrative expenses	68,000	?	?
Income from operations	$?	$ 32,000	$ 89,000

CHAPTER
13

Cost-Volume-Profit Analysis

Cost-volume-profit (CVP) analysis involves the use of knowledge about cost behavior patterns to interpret and forecast the changes in operating income that result from changes in revenues, costs, or the volume of activity. One especially important application of CVP analysis is the determination of the break-even point for a company (or one of its units or products). Because CVP analysis emphasizes the cost behavior pattern of various costs and the impact on costs and profits of changes in the volume of activity, it is useful both for planning and for evaluating actual results achieved.

Learning Objectives

After studying this chapter, you should understand:

1 What kinds of costs are likely to have a variable cost behavior pattern and what kinds of costs are likely to have a fixed cost behavior pattern.
2 How to use the high-low method to determine the cost formula for a cost that has a mixed behavior pattern.
3 The difference between the traditional income statement format and the contribution margin income statement format.
4 The importance of using the contribution margin format to analyze the impact of cost and sales volume changes on operating income.
5 How the contribution margin ratio is calculated and how it can be used in CVP analysis.
6 How changes in sales mix can affect projections made with CVP analysis.
7 The meaning and significance of break-even point and how the break-even point is calculated.
8 The concept of operating leverage.

449

Applications of CVP Analysis

Cost Behavior Pattern: The Key

Recall the cost behavior patterns described in Chapter 12. Variable costs change *in total* as activity changes, but are constant when expressed on a per unit basis. Fixed costs *do not change in total* as activity changes, but fixed costs per unit decrease as the level of activity increases. However, as emphasized in Chapter 12, expressing fixed costs on a per unit basis is dangerous because they do not behave that way, and erroneous decisions or judgments could result.

Two simplifying assumptions are made in connection with the determination of cost behavior patterns. First, the behavior pattern is true only within a relevant range; if activity moves beyond the relevant range, the cost will change. Second, the cost behavior pattern identified is assumed to be linear within the relevant range, not curvilinear. These concepts were also introduced in Chapter 12.

The relevant range idea relates to the level of activity over which a particular cost behavior pattern exists. For example, if the production capacity of the plant of Cruisers, Inc., is 90 SeaCruiser sailboats per month, additional equipment would be required if production of 120 boats per month were desired. The investment in additional equipment would result in an increase in depreciation expense. On the other hand, if long-term demand for the boat could be satisfied with a capacity of only 50 boats per month, it is likely that management would "mothball" (or dispose of), some of the present capacity, and depreciation expense would fall. The graph below illustrates a possible relationship between depreciation

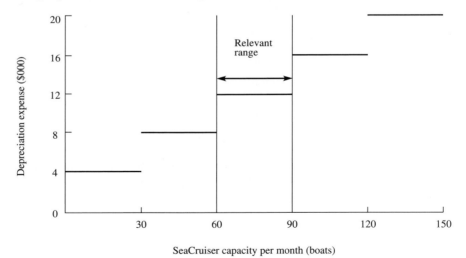

SeaCruiser capacity per month (boats)

expense and capacity. The relevant range for depreciation expense of $12,000 per month is production capacity of 61 to 90 boats. As long as capacity remains in this range, the total fixed expense for depreciation will not change, but if capacity changes to another relevant range, then the amount of this fixed expense will also change.

The linearity assumption means that the cost behavior pattern will plot as a straight line within the relevant range. Although applicable to both fixed and variable costs, the significance of this assumption is best illustrated with a variable cost like raw materials such as glass fiber cloth. Because of quantity discounts and shipping efficiencies, the cost per unit of this raw material will decrease as the quantity purchased increases. This is illustrated in the left graph below. For analytical purposes, however, it may

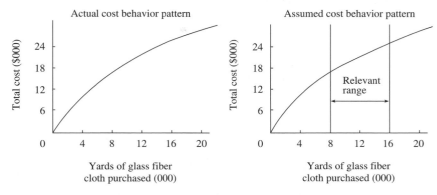

be assumed that the cost is linear within a relevant range, as shown in the right graph. Even though the cost per yard does vary slightly, for purposes of using cost-volume-profit analytical techniques it will be assumed constant per yard (variable in total) when purchases total between 8,000 and 16,000 yards per month.

It is clear that if these assumptions are overlooked, or if costs are incorrectly classified or described, the results of the analytical process illustrated later in this chapter will be inaccurate. Cost-volume-profit analysis is a valuable and appropriate tool to use in many situations, but the cost behavior assumptions made are crucial to the validity and applicability of its results, and must be kept in mind when evaluating these results.

Objective 1
Understand what kinds of costs are likely to have variable and fixed cost behavior patterns, respectively.

Generally speaking, raw materials and direct labor costs are variable costs. In addition, some elements of manufacturing overhead will have a variable cost behavior pattern. For example, maintenance and housekeeping materials used, as well as the variable portion of factory utilities, will be a function of the quantity of product made. Other manufacturing overhead costs are fixed, including depreciation expense, supervisory salaries, and the fixed portion of utility costs.

Selling, general, administrative, and other operating expenses also fit both patterns. Sales commissions, for example, vary in proportion to sales revenue or the quantity of product sold. The wages associated with those employees who process orders from customers, or who handle payments from customers, may be variable if those functions are organized so that the number of workers can be expanded or contracted rapidly in response to changes in sales volume. On the other hand, advertising costs are usually fixed in the short run; once approved, the money is spent, and it is difficult to relate sales volume changes directly to advertising expenditures.

A particular cost's estimated behavior pattern is determined by analyzing cost and activity over a period of time. One of the analytical techniques involves using a scattergram to identify high and low cost-volume data, and then simple arithmetic to compute the variable rate and cost formula. This "high-low" method is illustrated in Exhibit 13–1. More complex techniques, including simple and multiple regression analysis, can

EXHIBIT 13–1   High-Low Method of Estimating a Cost Behavior Pattern

Objective 2
Understand how to use the high-low method to determine the cost formula for a cost that has a mixed behavior pattern.

Assumption:
During the months of January through June the following utility costs were incurred at various production volumes:

Month	Total Utility Cost	Total Production Volume
January	$2,500	8,000 units
February	3,500	13,000 units
March	4,000	16,000 units
April	5,500	12,000 units
May	2,000	6,000 units
June	5,000	18,000 units

I. The Scattergram:

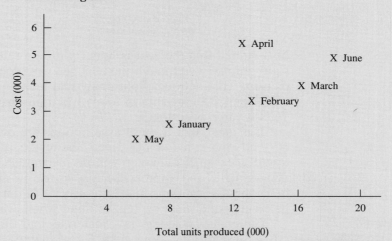

It can be observed in the scattergram that a cost-volume relationship does exist because of the approximate straight-line pattern of most of the observations. However, the April data do not fit the pattern. This may be due to an error or some unusual condition. This observation is an "outlier" and will be ignored in the calculation of the cost formula because of its variation from the cost-volume relationship that exists between other data.

II. Calculation of the Variable Cost Behavior Pattern:
The high-low method of calculating the variable cost behavior pattern, or variable cost rate, relates the change in cost to the change in activity, using the highest and lowest relevant observations.

$$\text{Variable rate} = \frac{\text{High cost} - \text{Low cost}}{\text{High activity} - \text{Low activity}}$$
$$= \frac{\$5,000 - \$2,000}{18,000 \text{ units} - 6,000 \text{ units}}$$
$$= \$3,000/12,000 \text{ units}$$
$$= \$.25 \text{ per unit}$$

III. The Cost Formula:
Knowing the variable rate, the fixed cost element can be calculated at either the high or low set of data, and the cost formula can be developed because total cost is equal to variable cost plus fixed cost.

EXHIBIT 13–1   *(concluded)*

> At 18,000 units of activity, the total variable cost is 18,000 units $\times$ \$.25 per unit = \$4,500.
>
> Fixed cost calculation:
>
> | | |
> |---|---|
> | Total cost at 18,000 units = | \$5,000 |
> | Variable cost at 18,000 units = | 4,500 |
> | Fixed cost = | \$ 500 |
>
> The cost formula for utilities is:
>
> Total cost = Fixed cost + Variable rate
> = \$500 + \$.25 per unit produced
>
> At 6,000 units of production, total cost would be:
>
> \$500 + (\$.25 $\times$ 6,000) = \$2,000
>
> Likewise, the cost formula could be used to estimate total utility costs at any level of activity (within the relevant range). Note that it is coincidence if the cost formula explains total cost accurately at points not used in the high-low calculation because the calculation assumes a linear relationship between the observations used, and in practice exact linearity will not exist.

also be used, but at some point the perceived increase in accuracy is offset by the simplifying assumptions involved in using the cost formula for planning and control purposes.

A Modified Income Statement Format

Objective 3
Understand the difference between the traditional income statement format and the contribution margin format.

The traditional income statement format classifies costs according to the reason they were incurred: cost of goods sold, selling expenses, administrative expenses, research and development expenses, and so on. The income statement format used in CVP analysis, frequently referred to as the **contribution margin format,** classifies costs according to their behavior pattern—variable or fixed. The alternative formats are:

Traditional Format *(expenses classified by function)*		*Contribution Margin Format* *(expenses classified by cost behavior pattern)*	
Revenues	\$	Revenues	\$
Cost of goods sold	_____	Variable expenses	_____
Gross profit	\$	Contribution margin	\$
Operating expenses	_____	Fixed expenses	_____
Operating income	\$_____	Operating income	\$_____

Revenues and operating income (income before interest and taxes) are the same under either alternative. The difference is in the classification of expenses: functional in the traditional format and according to cost behavior pattern in the contribution margin format. Although the behavior pattern classification could be carried beyond operating income to other income and expense, and income taxes, it usually isn't because the greatest

Objective 4
Understand the
importance of using
the contribution
margin format to
analyze the impact of
cost and sales volume
changes on operating
income.

benefits of the contribution margin approach are realized in the planning
and control/evaluation processes applied to a firm's operations.

The contribution margin format derives its name from the difference
between revenues and variable expenses. **Contribution margin** means that
this amount is the contribution to fixed expenses and operating income
from the sale of product or provision of service. The significance of this
concept lies in understanding cost behavior patterns. As revenue increases
as a result of selling more products or providing more services, variable
expenses will increase proportionately, and so will contribution margin.
However, *fixed expenses will not increase* because they are not a function
of the level of revenue-generating activity.

Use of the traditional income statement model can result in misleading
and erroneous conclusions when changes in activity levels are being considered because it is assumed that all expenses change in proportion to
changes in activity. This error is made because cost behavior patterns are
not disclosed. The error is avoided when the contribution margin model is
used correctly. For example, assume that a firm currently has revenues of
$100,000, and operating income of $10,000. If revenues were to drop by
20% to $80,000, a quick conclusion would be that operating income would
also decline by 20%, to $8,000. However, analysis using the contribution
margin format results in a much more accurate, and disturbing, result:

	Current Results	Results Assuming a 20% Decline in Volume
Revenues	$100,000	$80,000
Variable expenses (60%)	60,000	48,000
Contribution margin (40%)	$ 40,000	$32,000
Fixed expenses	30,000	30,000
Operating income	$ 10,000	$ 2,000

Because fixed expenses did not change (the firm did not move into a different relevant range), the $8,000 reduction in contribution margin result-
ing from the 20% reduction in revenues carried right through to reduce
operating income by the same dollar amount. This is an example of why it
is misleading to think of fixed costs on a per unit basis. Although fixed
costs (and especially the relevant range assumption) should not be overlooked by the manager, it must be recognized that they behave differently
from variable costs.

Objective 5
Understand how the
contribution margin
ratio is calculated and
how it can be used in
CVP analysis.

The **contribution margin ratio** is the ratio of contribution margin to
revenues. This ratio can be used to calculate directly the change in contribution margin for a change in revenues. Continuing with the same data
used above, a $12,000 increase in revenue would result in a $4,800 (40%
× $12,000) increase in contribution margin and a $4,800 increase in operating income.

**WHAT
DOES IT
MEAN?**

1. What does it mean to rearrange the income statement model from
the traditional format to the contribution margin format?

2. What does it mean to state that the contribution margin model is
more useful than the traditional model for determining the effect on operating income of changes in activity?

An Expanded Contribution Margin Model

The benefits of using the contribution margin model for planning can be best understood, and illustrated, by applying the model to a single product. For analytical purposes, an expanded version of the model, using the captions already illustrated, but adding some columns, is helpful. The expanded model is:

	Per Unit	×	Volume	=	Total	%
Revenue..........................	$					
Variable expenses	————					
Contribution margin	$———	×	———	=	$	——%
Fixed expenses.......................					————	
Operating income					$———	

The preferred route through the model is to: (1) express revenue, variable expense, and contribution margin on a per unit basis, (2) multiply contribution margin per unit by volume to get total contribution margin, and (3) subtract fixed expenses from total contribution margin to get operating income. Note that *fixed expenses are not unitized!* The contribution margin ratio is calculated (contribution margin per unit divided by revenue per unit) because it can frequently be used to answer "what if" questions that may be asked in the planning process.

To illustrate the use of the model, assume that management wants to know the operating income from a product that has the following revenue, cost, and volume characteristics:

Selling price per case...	$	15
Variable expenses per case......................................		9
Fixed expenses associated with the product..........................	$	40,000
Sales volume in cases...		8,000 cases

Using these data in the model results in the following analysis:

	Per Unit	×	Volume	=	Total	%
Revenue..........................	$ 15					
Variable expenses	9					
Contribution margin	$ 6	×	8,000	=	$48,000	40%
Fixed expenses.......................					40,000	
Operating income					$ 8,000	

Now suppose that management wants to know what would happen to operating income if a $3 per unit price cut would result in a volume increase of 5,000 units, to a total of 13,000 units. The solution:

	Per Unit	×	Volume	=	Total	%
Revenue............................	$ 12					
Variable expenses	9					
Contribution margin	$ 3	×	13,000	=	$39,000	25%
Fixed expenses........................					40,000	
Operating income					$(1,000)	

Based on the quantitative analysis, the price reduction would not be made.

Next, suppose that management proposes the same $3 per unit price cut in conjunction with a $3,000 increase in advertising, with the expectation that volume would increase to 18,000 units. The analysis of the effect on operating income is:

	Per Unit	×	Volume	=	Total	%
Revenue............................	$ 12					
Variable expenses	9					
Contribution margin	$ 3	×	18,000	=	$54,000	25%
Fixed expenses........................					43,000	
Operating income					$11,000	

Note that the advertising expense increase is reflected in fixed expenses. The analysis suggests that if the volume increase can be achieved with the price cut and increased advertising combination, operating income will increase from its present level. But watch out for the relevant range assumption: The impact on fixed expenses of such a large increase in sales volume must be questioned.

The expanded contribution margin model can also be used to calculate the volume of activity required to achieve a target level of operating income. For example, using the original data for selling price, variable expenses, and fixed expenses, suppose management wanted to know the sales volume required to have operating income of $23,000. The solution involves entering the known data in the model, and working to the middle to obtain the required volume:

	Per Unit	×	Volume	=	Total	%
Revenue............................	$ 15					
Variable expenses	9					
Contribution margin	$ 6	×	?	=	$63,000	40%
Fixed expenses........................					40,000	
Operating income					$23,000	

The required sales volume is $63,000/$6 = 10,500 units.

The contribution margin ratio is used to directly calculate the effect on contribution margin and operating income when the change in operations is expressed in terms of total revenues. For example, if the contribution margin ratio is 40%, and total revenues are expected to increase by $12,000, a $4,800 ($12,000 × 40%) increase in contribution margin and operating income would result, assuming that fixed expenses didn't change.

Another use of the contribution margin ratio is to determine the increase in revenues and sales volume that would be necessary to cover an increase in fixed expenses. For example, if fixed expenses were to increase by $9,000, contribution margin would have to increase by the same amount if operating income isn't going to change. If the contribution margin ratio is 40%, revenues would have to increase by $22,500 ($9,000/40%) to generate a $9,000 increase in contribution margin. The sales volume increase needed to generate the additional revenue is determined by dividing $22,500 by the $15 selling price per unit. (Of course, the volume increase of 1,500 units could also be calculated by dividing the increased contribution margin required, $9,000, by the contribution margin of $6 per unit.)

The contribution margin ratio is also used to determine revenue and contribution margin changes when per unit data are not available or not applicable. For example, the contribution margin model is frequently used to analyze the impact on the operating income of an entire product line (e.g., a candy bar brand) that is sold in a variety of package or size configurations, assuming that each configuration has the same, or very nearly the same, contribution margin ratio. Thus, if a product line had a contribution margin ratio of 30%, would an advertising program costing $21,000 be cost effective if it generated an additional $80,000 of revenue? The increase in contribution margin would be $24,000 (30% × $80,000), which is $3,000 more than the cost of the additional advertising; yes, the program would be cost effective. Alternatively, the increased fixed expenses divided by the contribution margin ratio ($21,000/30%) shows that an additional $70,000 of revenue would be needed to cover the increased fixed expense. Because the revenue increase is estimated to be $80,000, which is $10,000 more than required, an operating income increase of $3,000 (30% × $10,000) can be expected.

Although all of the examples used so far have expressed volume as units of product, the contribution margin model is also useful for organizations that provide services rather than sell products. For example, a day care center could identify variable expenses by type of activity and then set charges to achieve a target contribution margin ratio that would be expected to generate enough total contribution margin to cover fixed expenses and operating income. Using the expanded contribution margin model, expected variable expenses of $18 per week per child, and a target contribution margin ratio of 40 percent, the revenue needed to be charged per week per child is calculated as follows:

	Per Child	×	Volume	=	Total		%
Revenue	$?						100%
Variable expenses	18						?
Contribution margin	$?	×	?	=	$	?	40%

If the contribution margin ratio is 40%, the variable expense ratio is 60% (revenues = 100%); 60% of revenue per child = $18; revenue per child = $18/0.60 = $30. This process is virtually the same as that described in Chapter 9 to calculate a required selling price when the cost of the item and the desired gross profit ratio are known.

Multiple Products and Sales Mix Considerations

Objective 6
Understand how changes in sales mix can affect projections made with CVP analysis.

When the contribution margin model is applied using data for more than one product, the **sales mix** issue must be considered. Sales mix refers to the relative proportion of total sales accounted for by different products. Because different products are likely to have different contribution margin ratios, the average contribution margin ratio for a given mix of products will change if the sales mix of the products changes.

The effect of a sales mix change is illustrated in Exhibit 13–2. Sales mix is an important concept to understand because almost all firms have multiple products or services. When there is a range of quality to a firm's products (e.g. good, better, best), the higher-quality products generally have higher contribution margin ratios, so marketing efforts are frequently focused on those products. On the other hand, a strategy that some firms try to follow is to price their products to achieve a contribution margin ratio that is about the same for all products. A company that is able to achieve this approximate parity in contribution margin ratios among its products doesn't have to be concerned, from a product profitability standpoint, about sales mix changes. Thus marketing efforts can be more broadly based than if sales mix were a consideration.

**WHAT
DOES IT
MEAN?**

3. What does it mean to expand the contribution margin model?

4. What does it mean that fixed expenses should not be unitized because they don't behave that way?

5. What does it mean to state that contribution margin ratio is frequently a more useful measurement than contribution margin per unit?

Break-Even Point Analysis

Objective 7
Understand the meaning and significance of break-even point and how the break-even point is calculated.

The **break-even point** is usually expressed as the amount of revenue that must be realized in order for the firm (or product or activity or group of products or activities) to have neither profit nor loss (i.e., operating income equal to zero). The break-even point is useful to managers because it expresses a minimum revenue target, and managers frequently find it easier to think in terms of revenues rather than variable and fixed expenses. In addition, the amount of sales (or revenues) generated by the firm is easily determined on a daily basis from the accounting system.

The contribution margin model is used to determine the break-even point by setting operating income equal to zero and solving the model for the revenue or physical sales volume that will cause that result. The calculation of break-even point in terms of total revenues and units is illustrated at the top of page 460.

Exhibit 13–2 Multiple Products and Sales Mix

I. Assume that a company has two products. Per unit revenue, variable expenses, and product volumes for present operations are shown below:

	Product A				Product B				Total Company	
	Per Unit	× Volume	= Total	%	Per Unit	× Volume	= Total	%	Total	%
Revenue.........	$ 40	× 2,000	= $80,000		$ 30	× 2,000	= $60,000		$140,000	100%
Variable expenses...	30				18					
Contribution margin	$ 10	× 2,000	= $20,000	25%	$ 12	× 2,000	= $24,000	40%	$ 44,000	31.4%
Fixed expenses......									30,000	
Operating income									$ 14,000	

Note that fixed expenses are shown only in the total company column because they apply to the company as a whole, not to individual products.

II. Now assume that the sales mix changes and that instead of sales volume of 2,000 units of each product, sales volume becomes 2,500 units of Product A and 1,500 units of Product B. The company's contribution margin format income statement becomes:

	Product A				Product B				Total Company	
	Per Unit	× Volume	= Total	%	Per Unit	× Volume	= Total	%	Total	%
Revenue.........	$ 40	× 2,500	= $100,000		$ 30	× 1,500	= $45,000		$145,000	100%
Variable expenses...	30				18					
Contribution margin....	$ 10	× 2,500	= $ 25,000	25%	$ 12	× 1,500	= $18,000	40%	$ 43,000	29.7%
Fixed expenses.......									30,000	
Operating income									$ 13,000	

Note that even though total sales volume was the same, total revenues increased, but total contribution margin and operating income decreased. This is due to the fact that proportionately more units of Product A, with its relatively low contribution margin ratio, were sold than of Product B, which has a relatively high contribution margin ratio. As a result, the company's average contribution margin ratio also decreased.

459

Selling price per unit .... $ 12
Variable expenses per unit 8
Total fixed expenses $45,000

	Per Unit	×	Volume	=	Total	%
Revenue	$ 12					
Variable expenses	8					
Contribution margin	$ 4	×	?	=	$?	33.3%
Fixed expenses					45,000	
Operating income					$ 0	

According to the model, contribution margin clearly must be equal to fixed expenses of $45,000.

$$\text{Total revenues at break even} = \frac{\text{Fixed expenses}}{\text{Contribution margin ratio}}$$

$$= \$45,000/33.3\%$$

$$= \$135,000$$

$$\text{Volume in units at break even} = \frac{\text{Fixed expenses}}{\text{Contribution margin per unit}}$$

$$= \$45,000/\$4$$

$$= 11,250 \text{ units}$$

or

$$\text{Volume in units at break even} = \frac{\text{Total revenues required}}{\text{Revenue per unit}}$$

$$= \$135,000/\$12$$

$$= 11,250 \text{ units}$$

Most firms plan for certain desired levels of operating income and would not be satisfied to simply break even. As illustrated earlier, the contribution margin model can be used to determine total revenues, and sales volume in units, for any amount of desired operating income. The break-even formula can also be easily modified to determine these amounts by adding the desired operating income to the numerator. To illustrate, assume the same information as above, and a desired operating income of $10,000.

$$\frac{\text{Total revenues for desired}}{\text{level of operating income}} = \frac{\text{Fixed expenses} + \text{Desired operating income}}{\text{Contribution margin ratio}}$$

$$= (\$45,000 + \$10,000)/33.3\%$$

$$= \$165,000$$

$$\text{Volume in units for desired} = \frac{\text{Fixed expenses} + \text{Desired operating income}}{\text{Contribution margin per unit}}$$

$$= (\$45,000 + \$10,000)/\$4$$

$$= 13,750 \text{ units}$$

Break-even analysis is frequently illustrated in graphical format, as illustrated in Exhibits 13–3 and 13–4 with data from the above example. Note that in these graphs, the horizontal axis is sales volume in units, and the vertical axis is total dollars. In Exhibit 13–3 the horizontal line represents fixed expenses of $45,000, and variable expenses of $8 per unit are added to fixed expenses to produce the total expense line. Revenues start at the origin and rise at the rate of $12 per unit in proportion to the sales volume in units. The intersection of the total expense line and the total revenue line is the break-even point. The sales volume required to break even (11,250 units) is on the horizontal axis directly below this point, and total revenues required to break even ($135,000) can be read on the vertical axis opposite the intersection. The amount of operating income or loss can be read as the dollar amount of the vertical distance between the total revenue line and total expense line for the sales volume actually achieved. Sometimes the area between the two lines is marked as "profit area" or "loss area." Note that the loss area begins with an amount equal to total fixed

EXHIBIT 13–3   Break-Even Graph

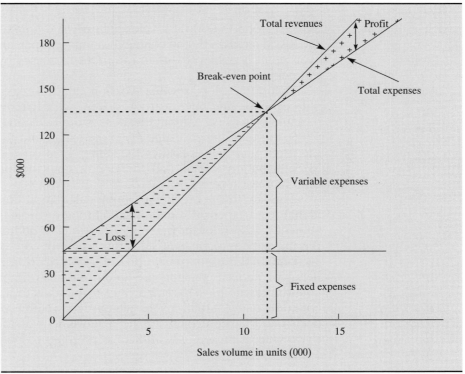

Sales volume in units (000)

EXHIBIT 13–4   **Break-Even Graph Featuring Contribution Margin**

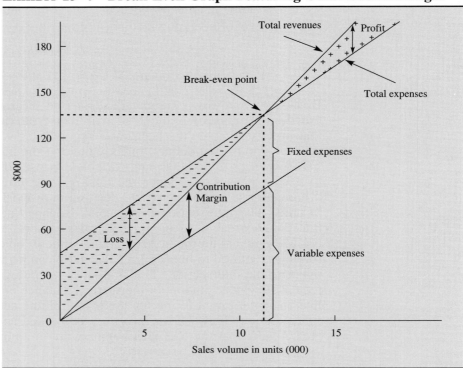

expenses of $45,000 (at a sales volume of 0 units). As unit sales increase, the loss decreases by the contribution margin per unit of $4 until the break-even point is achieved—then the profit increases by the contribution margin per unit.

Exhibit 13–4 is another version of the break-even graph. The variable expense line begins at the origin, with fixed expenses added to total variable expenses. Although expenses are rearranged compared to Exhibit 13–3, the total expense line stays the same, and the break-even point and the profit and loss areas are the same. This version permits identification of contribution margin and shows how contribution margin grows as volume increases.

The key to the break-even point calculation (and graphic presentation) is that fixed expenses remain fixed in total regardless of the level of activity, subject to the relevant range assumption. In addition to that assumption, the linearity and constant sales mix assumptions must also be considered. In spite of these simplifications, the contribution margin model and cost behavior pattern concepts are among the most important management accounting ideas to understand, and to be able to apply. The manager encounters many situations in which cost-volume-profit analysis supports decisions that contribute to the achievement of the organization's objectives. One of these applications is described in Business in Practice—The 1-Cent Sale.

> ## BUSINESS IN PRACTICE
> ## The 1-Cent Sale
>
> An understanding of cost-volume-profit relationships is shown by the manager of a fast-food and soft ice cream business operating in a midwestern city when a 1-cent sale is held in February. Ice cream sundaes are featured—two for the price of one, plus 1 cent. None of the other menu items are on sale.
>
> Those sundaes usually sell for a price of $1.25 to $1.75, but even with generous estimates, it is hard to come up with variable costs (ice cream, topping, cup, and spoon) much greater than 30 percent of the usual selling price. So even when the price is effectively cut in half, there is still a positive contribution margin. And what happens to the store's fixed costs during the sale? They are probably not affected at all. The fixed costs (including workers' wages) will be incurred whether or not extra customers come in for the sundae special. And of course, many of those customers will probably buy other items at the regular price.
>
> The net result of the special promotion is that the store builds traffic and business at a time of otherwise low activity (assuming that normal demand for sundaes is low in February). All of the additional sales volume generates a positive contribution margin, fixed expenses are the same as they would have been without the promotion, and operating income is increased over what it would otherwise have been.

WHAT DOES IT MEAN?

6. What does it mean to break even?

7. What does it mean to be aware of the effect of sales mix changes on a firm's operating income?

Operating Leverage

Objective 8
Understand the concept of operating leverage.

When an entity's revenues change because the volume of activity changes, variable expenses and contribution margin will change proportionately. But the presence of fixed expenses, which do not change as the volume of activity changes, means that operating income will change proportionately more than the change in revenues. This magnification of the effect on operating income of a change in revenues is called **operating leverage.** This was illustrated in the discussion of the contribution margin format income statement example earlier in this chapter (page 454). It showed a 20% decline in volume where revenues, variable expenses, and contribution margin all declined 20%, but operating income declined 80% (from $10,000 to $2,000). Note the similarity of operating leverage to financial leverage, explained in Chapter 11, in which fixed interest expense causes a proportionately greater change in ROE than the percentage change in ROI resulting from any given change in operating income.

Operating leverage also helps to explain proportionately greater growth in Intel Corporation's Net Income relative to its growth in Net Revenues, as shown in the example of horizontal income statement analysis on page 389 in Chapter 11.

EXHIBIT 13–5   Operating Leverage

I. Assume that two companies make similar products but that the companies have adopted different cost structures. Company A's product is made in a labor-intensive operation with relatively high variable costs but relatively low fixed costs, and Company B's product is made in a capital-intensive operation with relatively low variable costs but relatively high fixed costs. Each firm presently sells 6,000 units of product. A contribution margin model for each firm is presented below.

	Company A— Lower Operating Leverage				Company B— Higher Operating Leverage			
	Per Unit ×	*Volume* =	*Total*	*%*	*Per Unit* ×	*Volume* =	*Total*	*%*
Revenue......	$ 50				$ 50			
Variable expenses	35				20			
Contribution margin......	$ 15 ×	10,000 =	$150,000	30%	$ 30 ×	10,000 =	$300,000	60%
Fixed expenses			50,000				200,000	
Operating income			$100,000				$100,000	

II. Effect on operating income of an increase in volume from 10,000 to 11,000 units:

Contribution margin......	$ 15 ×	11,000 =	$165,000	30%	$ 30 ×	11,000 =	$330,000	60%
Fixed expenses			50,000				200,000	
Operating income			$115,000				$130,000	
Percentage change in volume			+10%				+10%	
Percentage change in operating income			+15%				+30%	

Note that Company B's operating income increased at a much greater rate, and to a considerably higher amount, than Company A's operating income. Operating leverage resulted in the operating income of each firm increasing proportionately more than the change in volume of activity. With an increase in volume, the greater contribution margin per unit and contribution margin ratio of Company B's product resulted in a greater increase in its operating income than experienced by Company A.

Just as high financial leverage increases the risk that a firm may not be able to meet its required interest payments, high operating leverage increases the risk that a small percentage decline in revenues will cause a very large percentage decline in operating income. *The higher a firm's contribution margin ratio, the greater its operating leverage.* Management can influence the operating leverage of a firm by its decisions about incurring variable versus fixed costs. For example, if a firm substitutes automated production equipment for employees, it has changed a variable cost

EXHIBIT 13–5   *(concluded)*

III. Effect on operating income of a decrease in volume from 10,000 to 9,000 units:

Contribution margin......	$ 15	× 9,000	= $135,000 30%	$ 30	× 9,000	= $270,000 60%	
Fixed expenses			50,000			200,000	
Operating income			$ 85,000			$ 70,000	
Percentage change in volume			−10%			−10%	
Percentage change in operating income			−15%			−30%	

Note that Company B's operating income decreased at a much greater rate, and to a considerably lower amount, than Company A's operating income. Operating leverage resulted in the operating income of each firm decreasing proportionately more than the change in volume of activity. With a decrease in volume, the greater contribution margin per unit and contribution margin ratio of Company B's product resulted in a greater reduction of its operating income than experienced by Company A.

(assuming the employees could be laid off if demand for the firm's products declined) to a fixed cost (the machine will depreciate, be insured, and be included in the property tax base whether or not it is being used), and has increased its contribution margin ratio and operating leverage. If the management of a firm anticipates a decline in demand for the firm's products or services, it may be reluctant to change its cost structure by shifting variable costs to fixed costs, even though productivity increases could be attained, because the equipment has to be operating in order to realize the benefits of productivity gains. The effect of different cost structures on operating leverage is illustrated in Exhibit 13–5.

WHAT DOES IT MEAN?

8. What does it mean to state that a product has a relatively high degree of operating leverage?

Summary

Cost-volume-profit (CVP) analysis uses knowledge about cost behavior patterns to interpret and forecast changes in operating income resulting from changes in revenue, cost, or in the volume of activity.

Variable costs change in total as the volume of activity changes. Fixed costs remain constant in total as the volume of activity changes. The simplifying assumptions of linearity and relevant range must be kept in mind when cost behavior pattern data are used.

When a particular cost is partly fixed and partly variable, the high-low method can be used to develop a cost formula that recognizes both the variable and fixed elements of the cost.

The contribution margin format income statement reclassifies the functional cost categories of the traditional income statement to cost behavior pattern categories. Contribution margin is the difference between revenues and variable expenses. Unless there are changes in the composition of variable expenses, contribution margin changes in proportion to the change in revenues.

The expanded contribution margin format model provides a framework for analyzing the effect of revenue, cost, and volume changes on operating income. A key to using this model is that fixed costs are only recognized in total; they are not unitized.

The contribution margin ratio can sometimes be used to determine the effect of a volume change on operating income more quickly and more easily than using unit revenue and variable expense, and volume.

Sales mix describes the relative proportion of total sales accounted for by specific products. When different products or product lines have significantly different contribution margin ratios, changes in the sales mix will cause the percentage change in total contribution margin to be different from the percentage change in revenues.

The break-even point is the total sales volume (in units or dollars) at which operating income is zero. Using the contribution margin model, the break-even point is achieved when total contribution margin is equal to fixed expenses. Break-even analysis can also be illustrated graphically to provide a visual representation of profit and loss areas, and to demonstrate the impact of the contribution margin per unit on operating income (or loss).

Operating leverage describes the percentage change in operating income for a given percentage change in revenues. Since fixed expenses don't change when revenues change, operating income changes by a greater percentage amount than revenues. The higher a firm's fixed expenses relative to its variable expenses, the greater the operating leverage and the greater the risk that a change in the level of activity will cause a much larger change in operating income. Operating leverage can influence management's decisions about whether to incur variable costs or fixed costs.

Key Terms and Concepts

break-even point (p. 458)   The amount of revenue required to have neither operating income nor operating loss.

contribution margin (p. 454)   The difference between revenues and variable costs.

contribution margin format (p. 453)   An income statement format in which variable costs are subtracted from revenues to show contribution margin, from which fixed costs are subtracted to determine operating income.

contribution margin ratio (p. 454)   The ratio of contribution margin to revenues.

cost-volume-profit (CVP) analysis (p. 449)   Analysis of the impact on profit of volume and cost changes using knowledge about the behavior patterns of the costs involved.

operating leverage (p. 463)   The concept that operating income changes proportionately more than revenues for any given change in the level of activity. Firms with proportionately higher fixed costs (and lower variable costs per unit) have greater operating leverage than firms with lower fixed costs (and higher variable costs per unit).

sales mix (p. 458)   The proportion of total sales represented by various products or categories of products.

WHAT DOES IT MEAN?
ANSWERS

1. It means that instead of using cost of goods sold and operating expense functional categories, expenses are classified according to cost behavior pattern as variable or fixed; then variable expenses are subtracted from sales to arrive at contribution margin, from which fixed expenses are subtracted to arrive at operating income.

2. It means that because cost behavior pattern classification is based on the effect on expenses of changes in activity, an accurate impact of activity changes on operating income can be more easily determined using the contribution margin model.

3. It means to express revenue and expenses on a per unit basis, multiply per unit contribution margin by volume to obtain total contribution margin, and subtract total fixed expenses to arrive at operating income.

4. It means that since fixed expenses don't change as the volume of activity changes, to express fixed expenses on a per unit basis doesn't make sense.

5. It means that because many firms have multiple products, overall planning and control are more easily accomplished by focusing on contribution margin ratio rather than the contribution margin of individual products.

6. It means that revenues equal expenses, so operating income is zero.

7. It means that because different products have different contribution margin ratios, changes in the proportion of sales of one product to total sales compared to the proportion of sales of another product to total sales—that is, a change in the sales mix—will affect operating income based on the products' relative contribution margin ratios.

8. It means that the product has a relatively high contribution margin ratio, so the effect of changes in sales volume on contribution margin and operating income will be magnified relative to the effect on contribution margin and operating income of changes in the sales volume of a product with a lower contribution margin ratio.

Exercises and Problems

LO 2   **13–1.   High-low method.** A department of Gamma Co. incurred the following costs for the month of February. Variable costs, and the variable portion of mixed costs, are a function of the number of units of activity.

Activity level in units	5,000
Variable costs	$10,000
Fixed costs	30,000
Mixed costs	20,000
Total costs	$60,000

During April the activity level was 8,000 units, and the total costs incurred were $70,500.

Required:

a. Calculate the variable costs, fixed costs, and mixed costs incurred during April.

b. Use the high-low method to calculate the cost formula for mixed cost.

LO 2   **13–2.** **High-low method—missing amounts.** The following data have been extracted from the records of Puzzle Co.:

	June	November
Production level, in units	12,000	18,000
Variable costs	$21,000	$?
Fixed costs	?	31,000
Mixed costs	18,000	?
Total costs	$70,000	$88,000

Required:

a. Calculate the missing costs.

b. Calculate the cost formula for mixed cost using the high-low method.

c. Calculate the total cost that would be incurred for the production of 20,000 units.

d. Identify the two key cost behavior assumptions made in the calculation of your answer to *c*.

LO 3, 5   **13–3.** **Understanding CVP relationships.** Calculate the missing amounts for each of the following firms:

	Sales	Variable Costs	Contribution Margin Ratio	Fixed Costs	Operating Income (Loss)
Firm A	$320,000	?	32%	?	$38,300
Firm B	?	$465,050	?	$118,000	71,950
Firm C	134,000	?	26%	36,700	?
Firm D	?	59,000	20%	?	(4,920)

LO 3   **13–4.** **Understanding CVP relationships.** Calculate the missing amounts for each of the following firms:

	Units Sold	Selling Price	Variable Costs per Unit	Contribution Margin	Fixed Costs	Operating Income (Loss)
Firm A	11,200	$24.00	?	$100,800	$41,300	?
Firm B	8,400	?	$18.20	?	64,500	$32,940
Firm C	?	7.30	4.20	10,850	?	(6,750)
Firm D	4,720	?	51.25	41,064	48,210	?

LO 3, 4, 5   **13–5.**   **Prepare a contribution margin format income statement—answer what-if questions.** Shown below is an income statement in the traditional format for a firm with a sales volume of 8,000 units. Cost formulas are also shown.

Revenues	$32,000
Cost of goods sold ($6,000 + $2.10/unit)	22,800
Gross profit	$ 9,200
Operating expenses:	
Selling ($1,200 + $.10/unit)	2,000
Administration ($4,000 + $.20/unit)	5,600
Operating income	$ 1,600

Required:

a. Prepare an income statement in the contribution margin format.
b. Calculate the contribution margin per unit and the contribution margin ratio.
c. Calculate the firm's operating income (or loss) if the volume changed from 8,000 units to:
   1. 12,000 units.
   2. 4,000 units.
d. Refer to your answer to part *a* for total revenues of $32,000. Calculate the firm's operating income (or loss) if unit selling price and variable expenses per unit do not change, and total revenues:
   1. Increase $12,000.
   2. Decrease $7,000.

LO 3, 4, 5, 8   **13–6.**   **Prepare a contribution margin format income statement—answer what-if questions.** Shown below is an income statement in the traditional format for a firm with a sales volume of 15,000 units.

Revenues	$105,000
Cost of goods sold ($8,000 + $3.60/unit)	(62,000)
Gross profit	$ 43,000
Operating expenses:	
Selling ($1,500 + $0.80/unit)	(13,500)
Administration ($4,000 + $0.50/unit)	(11,500)
Operating income	$ 18,000

Required:

a. Prepare an income statement in the contribution margin format.
b. Calculate the contribution margin per unit and the contribution margin ratio.
c. Calculate the firm's operating income (or loss) if the volume changed from 15,000 units to:
   1. 20,000 units.
   2. 10,000 units.
d. Refer to your answer to part *a* when total revenues were $105,000. Calculate the firm's operating income (or loss) if unit selling price and variable expenses do not change, and total revenues:
   1. Increase $15,000.
   2. Decrease $10,000.

LO 3, 4, 5, 7   **13–7.   Prepare a contribution margin income statement—calculate break-even point.** Presented below is the income statement for Big Wateb, Inc., for the month of August:

Sales	$65,000
Cost of goods sold	56,000
Gross profit	$ 9,000
Operating expenses	14,000
Operating loss	$ (5,000)

Based on an analysis of cost behavior patterns, it has been determined that the company's contribution margin ratio is 20%.

Required:
a. Rearrange the above income statement to the contribution margin format.
b. If sales increase by 30%, what will be the firm's operating income?
c. Calculate the amount of revenue required for Big Wateb, Inc., to break even.

LO 3, 4, 5, 7   **13–8.   Prepare a contribution margin income statement—calculate break-even point.** Presented below is the income statement for Docmag Co. for March:

Sales	$80,000
Cost of goods sold	42,000
Gross profit	$38,000
Operating expenses	32,000
Operating income	$ 6,000

Based on an analysis of cost behavior patterns, it has been determined that the company's contribution margin ratio is 30%.

Required:
a. Rearrange the above income statement to the contribution margin format.
b. Calculate operating income if sales volume increases by 8%. *(Note: Do not construct an income statement to get your answer.)*
c. Calculate the amount of revenue required for Docmag to break even.

LO 3, 4, 5, 6   **13–9.   CVP analysis—what-if questions; break-even.** Penta Co. makes and sells a single product. The current selling price is $15 per unit. Variable expenses are $9 per unit, and fixed expenses total $27,000 per month.

Required:
(Unless otherwise stated, consider each requirement separately.)
a. Calculate the break-even point expressed in terms of total sales dollars and sales volume.
b. Calculate the monthly operating income (or loss) at a sales volume of 5,400 units per month.
c. Calculate monthly operating income (or loss) if a $2 per unit reduction in selling price results in a volume increase to 8,400 units per month.

d. What questions would have to be answered about the cost-volume-profit analysis simplifying assumptions before adopting the price-cut strategy of part *c*?
e. Calculate monthly operating income (or loss) that would result from a $1 per unit price increase and a $6,000 per month increase in advertising expenses,

both relative to the original data, and assuming a sales volume of 5,400 units per month.

f. Management is considering a change in the sales force compensation plan. Currently, each of the firm's two salespersons is paid a salary of $2,500 per month. Calculate the monthly operating income (or loss) that would result from changing the compensation plan to a salary of $400 per month, plus a commission of $.80 per unit, assuming a sales volume of:

1. 5,400 units per month.
2. 6,000 units per month.

g. Assuming that the sales volume increase of 600 units per month achieved in part *f* could also be achieved by increasing advertising by $1,000 per month instead of changing the sales force compensation plan, which strategy would you recommend? Explain your answer.

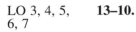

LO 3, 4, 5, 6, 7

13–10. **CVP analysis—what-if questions; sales mix issue.** Kiwi Manufacturing Co. makes a single product that sells for $32 per unit. Variable costs are $20.80 per unit, and fixed costs total $47,600 per month.

Required:

a. Calculate the number of units that must be sold each month for the firm to break even.

b. Calculate operating income if 5,000 units are sold in a month.

c. Calculate operating income if the selling price is raised to $33 per unit, advertising expenditures are increased by $7,000 per month, and monthly unit sales volume becomes 5,400 units per month.

d. Assume that the firm adds another product to its product line and that the new product sells for $20 per unit, has variable costs of $14 per unit, and causes fixed expenses in total to increase to $63,000 per month. Calculate the firm's operating income if 5,000 units of the original product and 4,000 units of the new product are sold each month. For the original product, use the selling price and variable cost data given in the problem statement.

e. Calculate the firm's operating income if 4,000 units of the original product and 5,000 units of the new product are sold each month.

f. Explain why operating income is different in parts *d* and *e,* even though sales totaled 9,000 units in each case.

LO 3, 4, 5, 6, 7

13–11. **CVP application—expand existing product line?** Campus Canvas Co. currently makes and sells two models of a backpack/book sack. Data applicable to the current operation are summarized in the columns below labeled Current Operation. Management is considering an expansion—adding a Value model to its current Luxury and Economy models. Expected data if the new model is added are shown in the columns below labeled Proposed Expansion.

	Current Operation		Proposed Expansion		
	Luxury	*Economy*	*Luxury*	*Economy*	*Value*
Selling price per unit	$20	$12	$20	$12	$15
Variable expenses per unit	$ 8	$ 7	$ 8	$ 7	$ 8
Annual sales volume—units	10,000	20,000	6,000	17,000	8,000
Fixed expenses for year	Total of $70,000		Total of $84,000		

Required:

a. Calculate the company's current total contribution margin and the current average contribution margin ratio.

b. Calculate the company's current amount of operating income.

c. Calculate the company's current break-even point in dollar sales.

d. Explain why the company might incur a loss, even if the sales amount calculated in part *c* was achieved and selling prices and costs didn't change?

e. Calculate the company's total operating income under the proposed expansion.

f. Based on the proposed expansion data, would you recommend adding the Value model? Why or why not?

g. Would your answer to part *f* change if the Value model sales volume were to increase to 10,000 units annually, and all other data remained the same? Why or why not?

LO 4, 5, 6, 7   **13–12.**   **CVP application—eliminate product from operations?** Muscle Beach, Inc., makes three models of high-performance weight-training benches. Current operating data are summarized below:

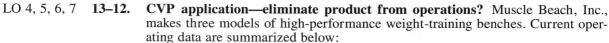

	MegaMuscle	*PowerGym*	*ProForce*
Selling price per unit	$170	$220	$310
Contribution margin per unit	$ 51	$ 77	$ 62
Monthly sales volume—units	4,000	3,000	1,000
Fixed expenses per month		Total of $468,000	

Required:

a. Calculate the contribution margin ratio of each product.

b. Calculate the firm's overall contribution margin ratio.

c. Calculate the firm's monthly break-even point in sales dollars.

d. Calculate the firm's monthly operating income.

e. Management is considering the elimination of the ProForce model due to its low sales volume and low contribution margin ratio. As a result, total fixed expenses can be reduced to $420,000 per month. Assuming that this change would not affect the other models, would you recommend the elimination of the ProForce model?

f. Assume the same facts as in part *e*. Assume also that the sales volume for the PowerGym model will increase by 500 units per month if the ProForce model is eliminated. Would you recommend the elimination of the ProForce model?

LO 4, 5   **13–13.**   **Calculate selling price of new product with a target CM ratio.** Sevprod, Inc., makes and sells a large number of consumer products. The firm's average contribution margin ratio is 35%. Management is considering adding a new product that will require an additional $15,000 per month of fixed expenses and will have variable expenses of $7.80 per unit.

Required:

a. Calculate the selling price that will be required for the new product if it is to have a contribution margin ratio equal to 35%.

b. Calculate the number of units of the new product that would have to be sold if the new product is to increase the firm's monthly operating income by $6,000.

LO 4, 5, 6, 7   **13–14.**   **Calculate selling price of new product; what-if questions; break-even.** Hancock Corp. has annual revenues of $275,000, an average contribution margin ratio of 34%, and fixed expenses of $100,000.

Required:

a. Management is considering adding a new product to the company's product line. The new item will have $8.25 of variable costs per unit. Calculate the selling price that will be required if this product is not to affect the average contribution margin ratio.

b. If the new product adds an additional $30,600 to Hancock's fixed expenses, how many units of the new product must be sold at the price calculated in part *a* to break even on the new product?

c. If 20,000 units of the new product could be sold at a price of $13.75 per unit, and the company's other business did not change, calculate Hancock's total operating income and average contribution margin ratio.

d. Describe how the analysis of adding the new product would be complicated if it were to "steal" some volume from existing products.

LO 4, 5   **13–15.**   **Special promotion—effects of a two-for-one sale.** Barb and Jan's ice cream shop charges $1.25 for a cone. Variable expenses are $.35 per cone, and fixed costs total $1,800 per month. A "sweetheart" promotion is being planned for the second week of February. During this week, a person buying a cone at the regular price could receive a free cone for a friend. It is estimated that 400 additional cones would be sold and that 600 cones would be given away. Advertising costs for the promotion would be $120.

Required:

a. Calculate the effect of the promotion on operating income for the second week of February.

b. Do you think the promotion should occur? Explain your answer.

LO 4, 5   **13–16.**   **Special promotion—effects of a 1-cent sale.** The management of Primo's Prime Pizzeria is considering a special promotion for the last two weeks of May, which is normally a relatively low demand period. The special promotion would involve selling two medium pizzas for the price of one, plus 1 cent. The medium pizza normally sells for $9.99 and has variable expenses of $3.00. Expected sales volume without the special promotion is 400 medium pizzas per week.

Required:

a. Calculate the total contribution margin generated by the normal volume of medium pizzas in a week.

b. Calculate the total number of medium pizzas that will have to be sold during the 1-cent sale to generate the same amount of contribution margin that results from the normal volume.

c. What other factors should management consider in evaluating the pros and cons of the special promotion?

LO 4, 5, 7   **13–17.**   **CVP analysis—effects of changes in cost structure; break-even.** Greene Co. makes and sells a single product. The current selling price is $32 per unit. Variable expenses are $20 per unit, and fixed expenses total $43,200 per month. Sales volume for January totaled 4,100 units.

Required:

a. Calculate operating income for January.

b. Calculate the break-even point in terms of units sold and total revenues.

c. Management is considering installing automated equipment to reduce direct labor cost. If this were done, variable expenses would drop to $14 per unit, but fixed expenses would increase to $67,800 per month.

   1. Calculate operating income at a volume of 4,100 units per month with the new cost structure.

2. Calculate the break-even point in units with the new cost structure.
3. Why would you suggest that management seriously consider investing in the automated equipment and accept the new cost structure?

4. Why might management not accept your recommendation but decide instead to maintain the old cost structure?

LO 4, 5, 7   **13–18.   CVP analysis—effects of change in cost structure; break-even.** Hucker, Inc., produces small-scale replicas of vintage automobiles for collectors and museums. Finished products are based on a 1/20th scale of originals. The firm's income statement showed the following:

Revenues (1,500 units)	$840,000
Variable expenses	462,000
Contribution margin	$378,000
Fixed expenses	290,000
Operating income	$ 88,000

An automated stamping machine has been developed that can efficiently produce body frames, hoods, and doors to the desired scale. If the machine is leased, fixed expenses will increase by $30,000 per year. The firm's production capacity will increase, which is expected to result in a 20% increase in sales volume. It is also estimated that labor costs of $28 per unit could be saved, because less polishing and finishing time will be required.

Required:

a. Calculate the firm's current contribution margin ratio and break-even point in terms of revenues.
b. Calculate the firm's contribution margin ratio and break-even point in terms of revenues if the new machine is leased.
c. Calculate the firm's operating income assuming that the new machine is leased.
d. Do you believe that management of Hucker, Inc., should lease the new machine? Explain your answer.

LO 3, 4, 5   **13–19.   CVP application—accept special sales order?** Integrated Circuits, Inc., (ICI) is presently operating at 50% of capacity and manufacturing 50,000 units of a patented electronic component. The cost structure of the component is as follows:

Raw materials	$ 1.50 per unit
Direct labor	1.50 per unit
Variable overhead	2.00 per unit
Fixed overhead	$100,000 per year

A Japanese firm has offered to purchase 30,000 of the components at a price of $6 per unit, FOB ICI's plant. The normal selling price is $8 per component. This special order will not affect any of ICI's "normal" business. Management figures that the cost per component is $7, so it is reluctant to accept this special order.

Required:

a. Show how management comes up with a cost of $7 per unit for this component.

b. Evaluate this cost calculation. Explain why it is or is not appropriate.

c. Should the offer from the Japanese firm be accepted? Why or why not?

LO 3, 4, 5 **13–20. CVP application—accept special sales order?** Foreway Manufacturing Co. makes and sells several models of locks. The cost records for Model B–603 show that manufacturing costs total $21.62 per lock. An analysis of this amount indicates that $11.90 of the total cost has a variable cost behavior pattern, and the remainder is an allocation of fixed manufacturing overhead. The normal selling price of this model is $29 per lock. A chain store has offered to buy 14,000 B–603 locks from Foreway at a price of $15.75 each to sell in a market that would not compete with Foreway's regular business. Foreway has manufacturing capacity available and could make these locks without incurring additional fixed manufacturing overhead.

Required:

a. Calculate the effect on Foreway's operating income of accepting the order from the chain store.

b. If Foreway's costs had not been classified by cost behavior pattern, is it likely that a correct special order analysis would have been made? Explain your answer.

c. Identify the key qualitative factors that Foreway managers should consider with respect to this special order decision.

LO 4, 5, 7 **13–21. CVP application—allow special discount?** Assume that you are a sales representative for Saturn Candy Company. One of your customers is interested in buying some candy that will be given to the members of a high school Substance Abuse Awareness Club. The club members will be marching in a community parade and will give the candy to children who are watching the parade. Your customer has asked that you discount the normal selling price of the candy to be given to the club by 35%. You know that the contribution margin ratio of the candy, based on the regular selling price, is 50%.

Required:

Identify the pros and cons of complying with the customer's request, and state the recommendation you would make to your sales manager.

LO 1, 4, 5 **13–22. CVP application—determine offering price.** Bill Sparks is in charge of arranging the "attitude adjustment" period and dinner for the monthly meetings of the local chapter of the Young Executives Association. Bill is negotiating with a new restaurant that would like to have the group's business, and Bill wants to apply some of the cost-volume-profit analysis material he has learned. The restaurant is proposing its regular menu prices of $1.50 for a before-dinner drink, and $16.50 for dinner. Bill has determined that on average, the persons attending the meeting have 1.5 drinks before dinner. He also believes that the contribution margin ratios for the drinks and dinner are 60% and 45%, respectively.

Required:

Prepare a memo to Bill outlining the possible offers he might make to the restaurant owner, and recommend an offer that he should make.

LO 8 **13–23. Comparison of operating leverage and financial leverage.** The concept of financial leverage was introduced in Chapter 7 and expanded upon in Chapter 11. In Problem 7–25, you were asked to describe the risks associated with financial leverage. You should now review the solution provided for this problem in the student supplement, *Study Outlines, Solutions to Odd-Numbered Problems, and Ready Notes.*

a. Describe the risks associated with operating leverage.

b. Outline the similarities and differences between operating leverage and financial leverage. *(Hint: Compare Exhibit 13–5 to the discussion and analysis in Exhibits 7–1 and 11–3.)*

LO 8   **13–24.   Understanding the effects of operating leverage.** Clarke, Inc., and Spence Co. compete within the same industry and had the following operating results in 1998:

	Clarke, Inc.	Spence Co.
Sales	$420,000	$420,000
Variable expenses	84,000	252,000
Contribution margin	$336,000	$168,000
Fixed expenses	294,000	126,000
Operating income	$ 42,000	$ 42,000

a. Calculate the amount of operating income (or loss) that you would expect each firm to report in 1999 if sales were to:
   1. increase by 20%.
   2. decrease by 20%.

b. Explain why an equal percentage increase (or decrease) in sales for each firm would have such differing effects on operating income.

CHAPTER
14

Budgeting and Performance Reporting

Planning is an essential part of the management process, and a **budget** quantifies future financial plans. *Budgeting* is the process of planning, in financial terms, the organization's activities and the results of those activities. Budgeting involves the use of financial accounting concepts because ultimately the results of the organization's activities will be reported in terms of income, cash flows, and financial position (i.e., the financial statements). Budgeting also involves using managerial accounting techniques, especially knowledge about cost behavior patterns, because the aggregate financial plan of an organization is the sum of plans for individual products and units.

Budgets are useful because:

- The preparation of a budget forces management to plan.
- The budget provides a benchmark against which to compare actual performance.
- The budget preparation process requires communication and co-ordination of activities among the different functional areas of the firm—finance, production, marketing, personnel, and so on—if organizational goals are to be achieved.

Although it may seem that these benefits should be achieved even without a budget, they are often not realized without a budgeting process because each functional area gets so wrapped up in its own activities that the impact on other functions is overlooked or given secondary significance. When budgets are properly developed and administered, they can also serve as motivational tools. Operational managers can focus on the specific goals that will help them to achieve their budget objectives, knowing that their success will contribute to the overall success of the firm.

Performance reporting involves the comparison of actual results with planned results, with the objective of highlighting those activities for which actual and planned results differed, either favorably or unfavorably, so that appropriate action can be taken. Appropriate actions may include changing the way activities are carried out or changing goals.

Learning Objectives

After studying this chapter, you should understand:

1 Why budgets are useful and how management philosophy can influence the budgeting process.

2 How alternative budget time frames can be used.

3 The significance of the sales forecast (or revenue budget) to the overall operating budget.

4 How the purchases/production budget is developed.

5 The importance of cost behavior patterns in developing the operating expense budget.

6 Why a budgeted income statement and budgeted balance sheet are prepared.

7 How the cash budget is developed.

8 How the performance report facilitates the management-by-exception process.

9 How the operating results of segments of an organization can be reported most meaningfully.

10 What a flexible budget is and how it is used.

Budgeting

The Budgeting Process in General

Objective 1
Understand why budgets are useful and how management philosophy can influence the budgeting process.

Many organizations commit substantial time and resources to the budgeting process. A useful budget is not prepared in a few hours or a few days; usually several months and the efforts of many people are devoted to the process. Once developed, a budget is not put on the shelf; it should become a useful tool to help managers accomplish the goals that were established.

How the budget is used in an organization will depend on the management philosophy of the top managers. In a highly structured, autocratically managed firm, the budget may be seen as being "carved in stone," and managers may develop dysfunctional practices to avoid being criticized for failing to meet budgeted results. For example, in such an environment, the sales force may defer entering customer orders in a month in which the sales target has already been achieved, sacrificing customer service levels and sales in order to get a head start on the next month's quota. Or a manager may commit funds for supplies that aren't really needed in order to use the full budget allowance, on the premise that doing so will facilitate justifying a budget allowance of at least that much for the next period. These and other budget "games" waste valuable time and resources.

The budget should be seen as a guide that reflects management's best thinking at the time it is prepared. However, the plan may have to change if circumstances differ from those envisioned when the budget was prepared. Otherwise, large differences between budgeted amounts and actual amounts may have to be anticipated and accepted. The objective of the organization should not be to have actual results equal budgeted results;

the objective should be to operate profitably, as expressed and measured by rate of return, growth in profits, market share, levels of service, and other measures that reflect the purpose of the organization.

Management philosophy is reflected in whether the budget is prepared using **top-down budgeting** (a dictated approach), or an interactive, participative approach in which lower-level managers provide significant input to the budgeting process. One approach is not better than the other in all situations. The **participative budgeting** approach should result in lower-level managers identifying more closely with the budget objectives, but there may be times, as when a firm is under heavy pressure to survive, that dictated objectives are appropriate.

The beginning point for most budgets is the actual performance for the current period. The manager first determines what the revenues and/or costs have been recently and then adjusts these amounts for changes that are expected to occur in the next period. The disadvantage of this incremental approach is that inefficiencies in the present way of doing things tend to be carried into the future. **Zero-based budgeting** is a technique that became popular in the 1970s. Zero-based budgeting involves identifying and prioritizing the activities carried out by a department, determining the costs associated with each, and then authorizing for the future only those activities that satisfy certain priority constraints. Some firms and organizations—especially governmental and social service agencies—embarked on a zero-based budgeting program but discontinued it because of the heavy administrative and paperwork burdens it required. An alternative zero-based approach used by some organizations involves determining budget estimates by showing the details of all amounts to be expended, rather than just showing increments from the current period's budget or actual results.

WHAT DOES IT MEAN?

1. What does it mean to have a participative budgeting process?

The Budget Time Frame

Objective 2
Understand how alternative budget time frames can be used.

Budgets can be prepared for a single period or for several periods. A **single-period budget** for a fiscal year would be prepared in the months preceding the beginning of the year and used for the entire year. The disadvantage of this approach is that some budget estimates must be made more than a year in advance. For example, a firm operating on a calendar year will prepare its 1999 budget during the last few months of 1998. November and December 1999 activities are being planned before actual results for those months in 1998 are known.

A multiperiod, or **rolling budget,** involves planning for segments of a year on a repetitive basis. For example, in a three-month/one-year rolling budget, a budget for each quarter of 1999 will be prepared late in 1998. During the first quarter of 1999, a budget for the next four quarters will be prepared. This will be the second budget prepared for each of the last three quarters of 1999 and the first budget for the first quarter of 2000. This process will continue each quarter, as illustrated in Exhibit 14–1.

The advantage of such a **continuous budget** is that the final budget for any quarter should be much more accurate because it has been prepared

EXHIBIT 14–1   Budget Time Frames

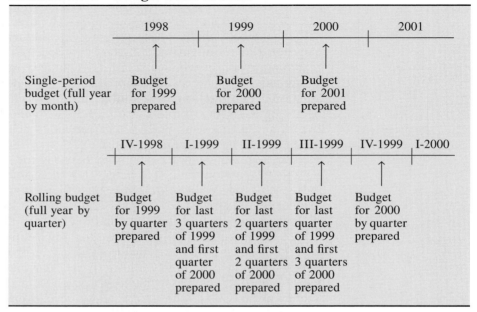

more recently. The obvious disadvantage to this process is the time, effort, and money required. However, in a rapidly changing environment, the benefit of a budget that requires frequent assessment of the organization's plans may be worth the cost. The multiperiod budget can be prepared with any reporting frequency that makes sense for the organization and for the activity being budgeted. Thus, full financial statements may be budgeted on a six-month/one-year cycle, but cash receipt and disbursement details may be budgeted on a one-week/four-week cycle, or even a daily/one-week/four-week cycle (i.e., every day a budget by day for the next several days is prepared, and every week a budget by week for the next four weeks is prepared).

WHAT DOES IT MEAN?

2. What does it mean to have a rolling or continuous budget?

The Budgeting Process

The first step in the budgeting process is to develop and communicate a set of broad assumptions about the economy, the industry, and the organization's strategy for the budget period. This is frequently done by planners and economists and is approved by top management. These assumptions represent the foundation on which the action plans for the budget period are built.

The **operating budget,** which is the operating plan expressed in financial terms, is made up of a number of detailed budgets. These include:

The sales/revenue budget (or forecast).

The purchases/production budget.

The operating expense budget(s).

The income statement budget.

The cash budget.

The balance sheet budget.

Objective 3
Understand the significance of the sales forecast to the overall operating budget.

The key to every budget is the forecast of "activity" that is expected during the budget period. This is usually a sales or revenue forecast developed using an estimate of the physical quantity of goods or services to be sold, multiplied by the expected selling price per unit. Merchandising firms may develop a **sales forecast** using expected revenues from groups of products. Commodity processing firms may forecast expected activity (e.g., bushels of corn to be processed) because revenues are based on the commodity price plus a "spread" or markup, and the commodity price can fluctuate widely. Service organizations forecast expected activity based on the expected number of clients to be served and the quantity of service likely to be required by each client. Based on these activity measures and an anticipated revenue per service, total revenues can be estimated.

The sales forecast is the most challenging part of the budget to develop accurately because the organization has little or no control over a number of factors that influence revenue-producing activities. These include the state of the economy, regulatory restrictions, seasonal demand variations, and competitors' actions. Numerous quantitative models, many of which involve computer processing, have been developed to assist in forecasting revenues. The past experience of managers provides valuable input to the forecast. Information provided by the sales force and market research studies is also important. The firm's pricing policies, advertising effectiveness, and production capacity may also be considered. But, in the final analysis, the sales forecast is only an educated guess resulting from a great deal of effort. Although the rest of the budgeting process flows from it, managers must remember that variations from the sales forecast will occur, and good managers will be prepared to respond quickly to those variations.

Once the sales forecast has been developed, the other budgets can be prepared because the items being budgeted are a function of sales (or a similar measure of activity). For example, the quantity of product to purchase or manufacture depends on planned sales and desired inventory levels. Selling expenses will be a function of sales, and other operating expenses depend on quantities sold and purchased (or manufactured). After revenues and expenses have been forecast, an income statement can be completed. Next the cash budget (or projected statement of cash flows) can be prepared, given the budgeted operating results and plans for investing and financing activities. Finally, by considering all of these expectations, a balance sheet as of the end of the period can be prepared. This hierarchy of budgets, as well as the way each budget is related to the balance sheet and income statement, is illustrated in Exhibit 14–2. Keep in mind that the key assumption of the entire budgeting process is the sales forecast.

WHAT DOES IT MEAN?

3. What does it mean to say that the key to the entire budget is the forecast of operating activity; for example, the sales budget?

EXHIBIT 14-2 Hierarchy of Budgets and Financial Statement Relationships

Budgets (in order of preparation)	Assets	= Liabilities	+ Owners' equity	← Net Income	= Revenues	− Expenses	Explanation
1. Sales forecast	+ Cash + Accounts Receivable	+ Accounts Payable			+ Revenues (i.e., sales)	− Cost of Goods Sold	Assets are increased by the difference between sales and cost of goods sold.
2. Purchases/ production	− Inventories + Inventories − Cash						Purchase/production of inventory requires the use of cash and/or incurrence of a liability.
3. Operating expenses	− Cash − Accumulated Depreciation	+ Other Accrued Liabilities				− Operating Expenses − Depreciation Expense	Examples include wages, utilities, rent, insurance, advertising, and research and development.
4. Budgeted income statement			+ Retained Earnings	← Net income	= Revenues	− Expenses	Summarizes the income statement effects caused by the above budgets.
5. Cash: (Operating)	+/− Cash	− Accounts Payable					Includes effects caused by the above budgets (i.e., cash sales and payments for operating expenses), and all other anticipated effects on cash. Broken down by categories to facilitate the preparation of a budgeted Statement of Cash Flows, if desired.
(Investing)	− Accounts Receivable − Cash + Plant and Equipment	− Other Accrued Liabilities					
(Financing)	+/− Cash	+/− Long-term Debt	+ Capital Stock − Dividends − Treasury Stock				
	Assets	= Liabilities	+ Owners' Equity				
6. Budgeted balance sheet							A detailed balance sheet is prepared based on the results of all other budgets.

482

The Purchases/Production Budget

Objective 4
Understand how the purchases/production budget is developed.

Recall that the following model was used to determine cost of goods sold under a periodic inventory system:

Beginning inventory	$
Add: Purchases.	
Goods available for sale	$
Less: Ending inventory	( )
Cost of goods sold	$

By changing dollars to physical quantities, the same model can be used to determine the quantity of merchandise to be purchased or manufactured. The captions change slightly, and the model would be revised as follows:

Beginning inventory		units
Add: Purchases (or production)		units
Goods available for sale		units
Less: Ending inventory	( )	units
Quantity of goods sold		units

To use the model, first enter the beginning and ending inventory quantities based on the firm's inventory management policies and the quantity of goods sold from the sales forecast. The goods available for sale in units is calculated by working from the bottom up (the quantity of goods sold is added to ending inventory), and then beginning inventory is subtracted from goods available for sale to get the purchase or production quantity. Of course, the model could be rearranged to permit calculation of the purchase or production quantity in a traditional equation format (Purchases or production = Quantity sold − Beginning inventory + Ending inventory), but this would require learning another model.

A firm's inventory management policies should recognize the average lead time to receive or make finished goods and/or raw materials. Likewise, these policies will ordinarily provide an allowance for forecast errors. For example, a finished goods inventory policy might be to have a desired ending inventory equal to 1.4 times the quantity expected to be sold in the subsequent month (or period). Remember that one period's ending inventory is the next period's beginning inventory. The beginning inventory for the first budget period could be estimated using the firm's inventory policy or the estimated ending inventory of the current period.

The results of the production and purchases budget model will frequently be adjusted to reflect production efficiencies or appropriate order quantities. For example, if the production budget calls for significantly different quantities of production each month for several months, management may elect to plan a constant production level and ignore the ending inventory policy because the benefits of production efficiencies are greater

---

EXHIBIT 14–3   Production Budget and Raw Materials Purchases Budget Illustration

---

I. Assumptions:

  A. Sales forecast in units per month:

      January   10,000 units
      February   12,000 units
      March   15,000 units
      April   11,000 units

  B. Inventory policy:

     Finished goods ending inventory should equal 1.4 times the subsequent month's forecasted sales. Raw materials ending inventory should equal 50% of the subsequent month's budgeted raw material usage.

  C. Three pounds of raw materials are required for each unit of finished product.

II. Production Budget Calculations:

  A. Ending inventory of finished goods required:

	December	January	February	March
Ending inventory units required (1.4 × sales forecast for subsequent month)	14,000	16,800	21,000	15,400

  B. Production budget using the cost of goods sold model (assuming that December 31 inventory is equal to that required by the finished goods inventory policy).

	January	February	March
Beginning inventory (units).	14,000	16,800	21,000
Add: Production (units)	?	?	?
Goods available for sale (units)	?	?	?
Less: Ending inventory (units)	(16,800)	(21,000)	(15,400)
Quantity of goods sold (units).	10,000	12,000	15,000
By working from the bottom up, the quantity of goods available for sale is calculated first, and then beginning inventory is subtracted from goods available for sale to get production in units of.	12,800	16,200	9,400

---

than the costs of carrying inventory. Likewise, if the purchases budget indicates that 38,400 units of raw material should be purchased but standard shipping containers contain 2,000 units each, the actual quantity ordered will be either 38,000 or 40,000 units. Inventories will absorb the difference between the budget calculation and the practical order quantity. Remember that in most cases, the budget calculations result in a guide to action; they do not produce absolute amounts to be followed at all costs.

To complete a budgeted income statement, physical quantities developed in the model must be converted to dollars. This is done by multiplying the cost of a unit by the budgeted quantity for each element of the model. (Standard costs, discussed in Chapter 15, and the use of computer software facilitate this task.)

When the number of units to be produced is known, the quantity of each raw material input to be purchased would be forecast using the same model. Of course, the quantity of each raw material used per unit of production must be substituted into the model, as follows:

EXHIBIT 14–3   *(concluded)*

III. Raw Materials Purchases Budget Calculations:

	January	February	March
A. Quantity of raw material used each month to produce the number of units called for by the production budget (3 pounds of raw materials per unit of finished product)	38,400	48,600	28,200
B. Ending inventory required (equal to 50% of next month's usage in pounds)	24,300	14,100	*

C. Purchases budget using cost of goods sold model with known data (assuming that December 31 inventory is equal to that required by the raw materials inventory policy).

	January	February
Beginning inventory (pounds)	19,200	24,300
Add: Purchases	?	?
Raw materials available for use (pounds).	?	?
Less: Ending inventory (pounds)	(24,300)	(14,100)
Quantity of materials used (pounds)	38,400	48,600
By working from the bottom up, the quantity of raw materials available for use is calculated first, and then beginning inventory is subtracted from raw materials available for use to get purchases in pounds of	43,500	38,400

Note that the purchases budget for March cannot be established until the sales budget for May is available because the inventory of finished goods at the end of March is a function of April production requirements.

*Won't be known until the April production budget is established.

Beginning inventory	units
Add: Purchases	units
Raw materials available for use	units
Less: Ending inventory.	( ) units
Quantity of materials used in production	units

Exhibit 14–3 illustrates the development of a manufacturing firm's production budget and a raw materials purchases budget to support the budgeted level of production. A merchandising firm's purchases budget would be similar to a manufacturer's production budget. The computations involved are not complex, but they are numerous, and computer programs are widely used in the process.

If quantity forecast data are not desired because the cost of using the above approach is greater than its benefit, the approach can be easily modified to provide a dollar amount forecast for purchases or production. This is accomplished by using the complement of the budgeted gross profit ratio to calculate budgeted cost of goods sold. Beginning and ending inventories can be expressed as a function of budgeted cost of goods sold, and the dollar amount of budgeted purchases can then be determined. This process is illustrated in Exhibit 14–4.

The cost of goods manufactured budget will include budgeted amounts for direct labor and manufacturing overhead. Determining these budget

---

EXHIBIT 14–4   **Budgeted Purchases Using the Gross Profit Ratio**

I. Assumptions:
Sales forecast as shown below.
Gross profit ratio budgeted at 30%.
Ending inventory planned to be 80% of next month's cost of goods sold.

II. Required:
Calculate the budgeted purchases for April, May, and June.

III. Budget Calculations:

	March	April	May	June	July
Sales forecast..........................	$85,000	$90,000	$75,000	$82,000	$92,000
Cost of goods sold (Sales × (1 − 0.3)).....	59,500	63,000	52,500	57,400	64,400
Ending inventory.....................	50,400	42,000	45,920	51,520	
Beginning inventory..................		$50,400	$42,000	$45,920	
Add: Purchases		?	?	?	
Goods available for sale		$?	$?	$?	
Less: Ending inventory		(42,000)	(45,920)	(51,520)	
Cost of goods sold...................		$63,000	$52,500	$57,400	

By working from the bottom up, the amount
of goods available for sale is calculated first,
and then beginning inventory is subtracted
from goods available for sale to get

purchases of		$54,600	$56,420	$63,000	

---

amounts frequently involves the use of a standard cost system (discussed in Chapter 15), which is based on an analysis of the labor and overhead inputs required per unit of product.

Many manufacturing firms increase the accuracy of their cost of production and cost of goods sold forecasts by using the contribution margin model for manufacturing costs. (Note that in a merchandising firm the cost of goods sold is a variable expense.) Variable costs of manufacturing (raw materials, direct labor, and variable overhead) are determined, and the variable cost ratio (variable manufacturing costs as a percentage of selling price) is calculated. This ratio is then used instead of the cost of goods sold ratio as illustrated in Exhibit 14–4. Fixed manufacturing expenses are budgeted separately because they are not a function of the quantity produced or sold.

The Operating Expense Budget

Objective 5
Understand the importance of cost behavior patterns in developing the operating expense budget.

The cost behavior patterns of selling, general, administrative, and other operating expenses are determined, and these expenses are budgeted accordingly. For example, sales commissions will be a function of the forecast of either sales dollars or units. The historical pattern of some expenses will be affected by changes in strategy that management may plan for the budget period. In a participative budgeting system, the manager of each department or cost responsibility center will submit the anticipated cost of the department's planned activities, along with descriptions of the activities and explanations of significant differences from past experience. After review by higher levels of management, and perhaps negotiation, a final budget will be established.

Operating managers have a natural tendency to submit budget estimates that are slightly higher than what the costs are really expected to be. This practice gives the manager some **budget slack** for contingencies or cost increases that may not have been planned. Adding budget slack or "padding the budget" can result in a significantly misleading budget for the organization as a whole. In spite of budget managers' pleas and/or threats that padding be eliminated, the practice probably continues in virtually all organizations. Some budget managers deal with the problem by judgmentally reducing the grand total of all departmental expense budgets when the company budget is prepared.

The Budgeted Income Statement

Objective 6
Understand why a budgeted income statement is prepared.

The sales forecast, cost of goods sold budget, and operating expense budget data are used by management accountants to prepare a budgeted income statement. This is a complex process but a necessary one if the anticipated overall results of the budget period are to be evaluated in a meaningful way.

In many cases, if the budgeted income statement shows unacceptable results, top management will request that operating departments review their budget proposals and make appropriate adjustments so that profitability goals can be achieved.

The Cash Budget

Objective 7
Understand how the cash budget is developed.

The cash budget is very much like a budgeted statement of cash flows, but with a relatively short time frame. The financial manager must be able to anticipate short-term borrowing requirements because arrangements for borrowing must be made in advance of the date the cash is needed. When considering a loan proposal, the bank lending officer will need to know how much cash will be needed, how soon it will be needed, and when the borrower expects to repay the loan. A potential borrower who cannot answer these questions because a cash budget has not been prepared may be denied an otherwise reasonable loan request or may be charged a higher interest rate because of the perceived risk caused by these uncertainties. The financial manager must also know when temporarily excess cash is available for investment, and when it will be needed, so that cash can be invested to earn interest income.

A number of assumptions about the timing of cash receipts and disbursements must be made when the cash budget is prepared. For example, how long after the sale will an account receivable be collected? The days' sales in receivables statistic will help answer this question. Again, the sales forecast comes into play. For example, assume that, based on past experience, the entity expects that 25 percent of a month's sales will be collected in the month of sale, 60 percent will be collected in the month following the month of sale, and 12 percent will be collected in the second month following the month of sale. (The last 3 percent will be collected over several months but is ignored in the budgeting process because of its relatively small amount and uncertain collection pattern. Some of these accounts may eventually be written off as uncollectible.) A cash receipts analysis for March and April might look like this:

	January	February	March	April
Sales forecast	$40,000	$50,000	$30,000	$40,000
Collections:				
25% of current month's sales			$ 7,500	$10,000
60% of prior month's sales			30,000	18,000
12% of second prior month's sales			4,800	6,000
Total collections			$42,300	$34,000

If this cash receipts forecast were being made in late December for the next four months, collections of sales made prior to January would probably be based on an estimate of when the accounts receivable at the end of December would be collected. This approach, and an alternative format for the cash receipts forecast analysis, would look like this:

	January	February	March	April
Sales forecast	$40,000	$50,000	$30,000	$40,000
Collections:				
From December 31 accounts receivable of $68,423 (amounts assumed)	$38,000	$25,000	$ 3,000	$ 1,000
From January sales	10,000	24,000	4,800	—
From February sales		12,500	30,000	6,000
From March sales			7,500	18,000
From April sales			—	10,000
Total collections	$48,000	$61,500	$45,300	$35,000

Note that the difference between the budgeted cash receipts for March and April in the two formats is the estimated collections of December 31 accounts receivable. Even though the estimated collections from sales occur over three months, the estimated collections of December 31 accounts receivable are more realistically spread over a longer period, and it has been recognized that not all of the receivables are likely to be collected.

It should be clear that the keys to an accurate cash receipts forecast are the accuracy of the sales forecast and the accuracy of the collection percentage estimates. The actual calculation is clearly an ideal computer spreadsheet application.

On the cash disbursement side, the payment pattern for purchases must be determined. If suppliers' terms are 2/10, net 30, the financial manager will assume that two-thirds of a month's purchases will be paid for in the same month as the purchase, and one-third will be paid for in the subsequent month. The format of the analysis of payments on accounts payable will be similar to that illustrated above for cash receipts. As was the case for the cash receipts forecast, the accuracy of the cash payments forecast is a function of the accuracy of the sales forecast and the payment pattern estimates. (Remember that the sales forecast impacts the finished goods budget and the raw materials purchases budget. Therefore, cash disbursements will also be impacted by the sales forecast.)

In addition to the payments for purchases, a number of other cash disbursements must be estimated. For example, the frequency with which the company pays its employees will be related to projected payroll expense to determine this significant disbursement. Capital expenditure plans and anticipated dividend payments will have to be considered. Of course, projected depreciation and amortization expenses are ignored in cash budgeting because these are not expenses requiring a cash disbursement.

Once the assumptions about the timing of cash receipts and disbursements have been made, the preparation of the cash budget is a straight-forward mechanical process. Budgeted cash receipts are added to the beginning cash balance, budgeted disbursements are subtracted, and a preliminary ending balance is determined. The organization will have an established minimum cash balance to be maintained. This "inventory" of cash serves the same purpose as an inventory of product; it is a cushion that can absorb forecast errors. If the cash forecast indicates a preliminary balance that is less than the desired minimum, temporary investments must be liquidated or a loan must be planned to bring the forecast balance up to the desired level. If the preliminary balance is greater than the minimum desired working balance, the excess is available for repayment of loans or for investment. The cash budget will be prepared for monthly periods at least; many organizations forecast cash flows on a daily basis for a week or two, and then weekly for a month or two, so optimum cash management results can be achieved. Exhibit 14–5 illustrates a cash budget format and shows sources of the budget amounts.

The Budgeted Balance Sheet

Objective 6
Understand why a budgeted balance sheet is prepared.

The impact of all of the other budgets on the balance sheet is determined, and a budgeted balance sheet is prepared. This hierarchy is illustrated in Exhibit 14–2. For example, the production and purchases budgets include inventory budget estimates. The operating expense budget is the source of the depreciation and amortization impact on the balance sheet. The budgeted income statement indicates the effect of net income or loss on retained earnings. The cash budget, with its assumptions about collections of accounts receivable and payments of accounts payable and other liabilities, purchases of equipment, and payment of dividends and other financing activities, is the source of many budgeted balance sheet amounts. All of the current assets (except inventories) are derived from the cash budget, as are the budgeted amounts for plant assets, liabilities, paid-in capital, treasury stock, and the dividend impact on retained earnings. In effect, the financial accounting process is applied using planned transaction amounts to generate an anticipated balance sheet. This balance sheet will be analyzed to determine that all of the appropriate financial ratios are within the

EXHIBIT 14–5   Cash Budget Illustration and Assumptions

CRUISERS, INC.
Cash Budget
For the Months of March and April

Date budget prepared: February 25

Activity	March	April	Source/Comments
Beginning cash balance	$ 5,000	$20,000	March: Forecast balance for March 1. April: Indicated cash balance at end of March.
Cash Receipts:			
From sales made in prior periods	60,000	50,000	Analysis of accounts receivable detail when budget prepared, and sales forecast for subsequent periods with collection estimates based on past experience.
From sales made in current period	10,000	8,000	Sales forecast and estimates based on past experience.
From investing activities	1,000	—	Plans for sale of assets.
From financing activities	5,000	—	Plans for new borrowings or sale of stock.
Total cash available	$81,000	$78,000	
Cash Disbursements:			
To suppliers for inventory purchases	$30,000	$36,000	Analysis of accounts payable detail for purchases that have been made and of purchases budget for subsequent periods with estimates based on supplier terms and past payment practices.
To other creditors and employees for operating expenses and wages	20,000	24,000	Analysis of accrued liability detail for transactions that have occurred and of production budget and operating expense budget for subsequent periods, and knowledge of past payment practices.
For investing activities	8,000	17,000	Plans for purchase of plant and equipment, and other investments.
For financing activities	3,000	—	Plans for dividend payments, debt repayments, or purchases of treasury stock.
Total disbursements	$61,000	$77,000	
Indicated cash balance	$20,000	$ 1,000	
Desired cash balance	5,000	5,000	Based on financial operating needs and amount of "cushion" for error that is desired.
Excess (Deficiency)	$15,000	$(4,000)	Excess available for temporary investment or repayment of loans. Deficiency indicates a need to liquidate temporary investments or arrange financing.

limits established by top management. The reason for any discrepancies will be determined, and appropriate changes in plans will be considered. This process can very well require modifications to some of the other budgets, and if so, the entire budgeting process may have to be repeated. Although this may seem like a tedious and frustrating thing to do, it is better done in the planning process than after the company has already acted. Recovery at that stage may be very difficult to accomplish, and the firm's financial condition may have been adversely affected.

If desired, a budgeted statement of cash flows can be prepared from the budgeted income statement and balance sheet data. The process for doing this is the same as illustrated in Chapter 9. Many organizations prepare cash budgets on a monthly basis, along with an overall annual cash budget, which serves the same purpose as a statement of cash flows.

The most challenging parts of the budgeting process are developing the sales forecast, coming up with the assumptions related to the timing of cash receipts and disbursements, and establishing policies for ending inventory quantities, the minimum desired cash balance, and other targets. The budget calculations are easily made for most organizations using computer spreadsheet models. These models make it feasible for planners to change various assumptions and quickly and easily see the effect on budgeted results.

Budgeting for Other Analytical Purposes

Although this chapter emphasizes the budgeting of dollars and units of production for manufacturing firms, many firms in the service sector of the economy also use budgeting techniques for other important resources such as personnel time or for nonfinancial measures such as the utilization of productive capacity. For example, law firms and public accounting firms are often concerned with "time" budgets and the ability of professional employees to generate "billable hours." Merchandising firms, especially large retail organizations, may be concerned with budgeted sales dollars per square foot of floor space.

Within a manufacturing firm, budgets can also be developed to meet the needs of other functional areas, such as the research and development, marketing, or customer service departments. Likewise, activity-based costing principles (discussed in Chapter 12) can be extended to the budgeting process. *Activity-based budgeting* is an attempt to relate the cost of performing each unit of activity (cost driver) to the demand for that activity. The budgeted cost per unit of activity (e.g., cost per part handled, or cost per unit inspected) can be compared to the actual cost incurred for the level of activity performed during the period, and corrective action can be taken if necessary.

Standard costs (discussed in Chapter 15) are unit budgets for product cost components (raw materials, direct labor, and manufacturing overhead). They provide benchmarks against which actual performance can be measured. Capital budgeting (discussed in Chapter 16) involves long-term strategic planning and the commitment of a significant amount of the firm's resources for extended periods of time. Whereas the operating budget reflects the firm's strategic plans to achieve current period profitability, the capital budget provides an overall blueprint to help the firm meet its long-term growth objectives.

Performance Reporting

Characteristics of the Performance Report

The **performance report** compares actual results to budgeted amounts. The performance report is an integral part of the control process because those activities that are performing differently from expectations are highlighted, and the managers responsible for achieving goals are provided with information about activities that need attention.

The general format of a performance report is:

Activity	Budget Amount	Actual Amount	Variance	Explanation

The **variance** is usually described as *favorable* or *unfavorable,* depending on the nature of the activity and the relationship between the budget and actual amounts. For revenues a **favorable variance** is the excess of actual revenues over the budget amount. An actual expense that is greater than a budgeted expense causes an **unfavorable variance.** Sometimes the favorable or unfavorable nature of the variance must be determined based on the relationship of one variance to another. For example, if a favorable variance in advertising expense resulted from not placing as many ads as planned, and this caused lower sales than were forecast, the variance is not really favorable to the company.

The explanation column of the performance report is used to communicate to upper-level managers concise explanations of causes of significant variances. Because top management probably doesn't want to be inundated with details, a system of **responsibility reporting** is used by many organizations. Responsibility reporting involves successive degrees of summarization, such that each layer of management receives detailed performance reports for the activities directly associated with that layer but summaries of the results of activities of lower layers in the chain of command.

The paramount concern of a manager should be with the actions that are going to be taken to eliminate unfavorable variances and to capture favorable ones. Performance reports should not be used to find fault or place blame; such uses are likely to result in dysfunctional behavior when developing budget amounts and/or reporting actual results.

Objective 8
Understand how the performance report facilitates the management-by-exception process.

The **management by exception** concept is frequently used in connection with performance reporting to permit managers to concentrate their attention on only those activities that are not performing according to plan. The presumption is that management time is a scarce resource and that if a thorough job of planning is done, a manager's attention need be devoted only to those areas not performing according to plan. To facilitate the use of management by exception, the variance is frequently expressed as a percentage of the budget, and only those variances in excess of a predetermined percentage (e.g., 10%) are investigated. The objective of this analysis is to understand why an unusual variance occurred and, if appropriate, to take action to eliminate unfavorable variances and capture favorable variances.

Performance reports must be issued soon after the period in which the activity takes place if they are to be useful for influencing future activity. Otherwise, it would be difficult to link results to the actions that caused those results. If there is too long a time lag, the actions are forgotten or confused with later activities. Not all performance reports need to be issued with the same frequency. Thus, production supervisors might receive weekly cost and volume reports, a supervisor responsible for the use of a high-cost raw material might receive a daily usage report, and the advertising manager might only receive a monthly expenditure report.

An issue that arises in the design of a performance report is the extent of the cost-generating activities to be listed for a particular responsibility area relative to the degree of short-term control that the manager has over those activities. For example, should the performance report for a production line show the depreciation expense, property taxes, insurance cost, and other "noncontrollable" expenses associated with that production line? Or should the performance report be limited to those expenses over which the supervisor has real short-term control? Advocates of the all-inclusive report format suggest that it is appropriate for the supervisor to be aware of all costs, even though she or he may not be able to influence them in the short run. Advocates of the limited format believe that the report should focus on those costs that the supervisor can control. They argue that the inclusion of other costs causes confusion and may focus attention on the wrong costs (i.e., those that can't be controlled in the short run). There is no "right" answer to this issue. One middle ground solution is to periodically provide the supervisor with all cost data but to focus the performance report on those costs that can be controlled in the short run. Notice that at the heart of the issue is the allocation of fixed costs, and recall the previously discussed warning not to allocate fixed costs arbitrarily because "they don't behave that way."

A performance report for the April production of SeaCruiser sailboats made by Cruisers, Inc., is presented in Exhibit 14–6. (Actual costs in this exhibit have been brought forward from Exhibit 12–4.) Note that the

EXHIBIT 14–6   Performance Report Illustration

CRUISERS, INC.
Performance Report—SeaCruiser Sailboats
April

Activity	Budget	Actual	Variance*	Explanation
Raw materials............	$370,300	$368,510	$ 1,790 F	Variance not significant in total.
Direct labor	302,680	330,240	27,560 U	New workers not as efficient as planned.
Manufacturing overhead:				
Variable	89,400	103,160	13,760 U	Related to additional hours caused by labor inefficiency.
Fixed................	193,200	185,800	7,400 F	Plant fire insurance premium credit received.
Totals	$955,580	$987,710	$32,130 U	

*F is favorable, U is unfavorable.

manufacturing overhead has been classified according to cost behavior pattern. This is appropriate because the efforts made to control these costs will be a function of their cost behavior pattern. The performance report in Exhibit 14–6, although interesting and perhaps helpful to top management's determination of why budgeted results were not achieved, is not very useful for operating managers and supervisors. Some of the questions raised by this report include:

1. Were there significant but offsetting variances in raw materials?
2. Which workers were not efficient?
3. Were the new workers being paid a lower than budget wage rate until they became proficient?
4. Is the training program for new workers effective?
5. How does the manufacturing overhead variance affect the validity of the predetermined overhead application rate used to apply overhead to production?

A method for answering these questions, and others, and for preparing a performance report that is useful for the cost controlling efforts of operating managers and supervisors will be discussed in Chapter 15.

WHAT DOES IT MEAN?

4. What does it mean to use a performance report to evaluate the results achieved during a period?
5. What does it mean to capture favorable variances and eliminate unfavorable variances?
6. What does it mean to have a favorable variance?

Reporting for Segments of an Organization

Objective 9
Understand how the operating results of segments of an organization can be reported most meaningfully.

A **segment** of an organization is a division, product line, sales territory, or other organizational unit. Management frequently reports company results by segment in such a way that the total income for each segment equals the total company net income. For example, assume that Cruisers, Inc., has three divisions: sailboats, motorboats, and repair parts. The following income statement might be prepared:

CRUISERS, INC.
Segmented Income Statement
Quarter Ended July 31, 1998

	Total Company	Sailboat Division	Motorboat Division	Repair Parts Division
Sales	$560,000	$320,000	$160,000	$80,000
Variable expenses	240,000	128,000	72,000	40,000
Contribution margin	$320,000	$192,000	$ 88,000	$40,000
Fixed expenses	282,000	164,000	72,000	46,000
Operating income	$ 38,000	$ 28,000	$ 16,000	$ (6,000)

From an analysis of this segmented income statement, management might decide to eliminate the repair parts division because it is operating at a loss. In fact, you might think that operating income would increase by $6,000 if this division were eliminated.

Now suppose that, as a result of a detailed analysis of the fixed expenses, you learn that the fixed expenses assigned to each division represent the sum of the fixed expenses incurred in each division (**direct fixed expenses**) plus an allocated share of the corporate fixed expenses (**common fixed expenses**) that would continue to be incurred even if one of the divisions were to be closed. (Would the president's salary—a common fixed expense—be reduced if one of the divisions were closed?) Your analysis of fixed expenses shows:

	Total Company	Sailboat Division	Motorboat Division	Repair Parts Division
Direct fixed expenses	$170,000	$100,000	$40,000	$30,000
Common fixed expenses allocated in proportion to sales	112,000	64,000	32,000	16,000
Total fixed expenses	$282,000	$164,000	$72,000	$46,000

Since the common fixed expenses will continue to be incurred even if the repair parts division is closed, Cruisers, Inc., would be worse off by $10,000 if the division were eliminated. Why? Because that division's contribution to common fixed expenses and profits (referred to as **segment margin**) would also be eliminated. This is illustrated clearly in a more appropriately designed segmented income statement:

CRUISERS, INC.
Segmented Income Statement
Quarter Ended July 31, 1998

	Total Company	Sailboat Division	Motorboat Division	Repair Parts Division
Sales	$560,000	$320,000	$160,000	$80,000
Variable expenses	240,000	128,000	72,000	40,000
Contribution margin	$320,000	$192,000	$ 88,000	$40,000
Direct fixed expenses	170,000	100,000	40,000	30,000
Segment margin	$150,000	$ 92,000	$ 48,000	$10,000
Common fixed expenses	112,000			
Operating income	$ 38,000			

The key feature of the corrected segmented income statement is that common fixed expenses have not been *arbitrarily allocated* to the segments. The corrected statement reflects the contribution of each segment to the common fixed expenses and company profit. Using this approach should avoid analytical errors like the one that would have resulted in closing the repair parts division.

The same statement format separating direct and common fixed expenses should be used whenever both classifications of fixed expenses exist. For example, if the sailboat division's segment margin of $92,000 were to be broken down by sales territory, that division's $100,000 of direct fixed expenses would be analyzed, and the portion that is direct *to each territory* would be subtracted from the territory contribution margin to arrive at the territory's segment margin. The division's fixed expenses that are common from a territory perspective *would not* be allocated to the territories; they would be subtracted as a single amount from the total territory segment margin to arrive at the division's segment margin of $92,000.

Sometimes the segments of an organization are referred to as *responsibility centers, cost centers, profit centers,* or *investment centers.* A **responsibility center** is an element of the organization over which a manager has been assigned responsibility and authority, and for which performance is evaluated. A **cost center** does not directly generate any revenue for the organization. For example, the industrial engineering department would be a cost center. An organization segment that is responsible for selling a product, like the sailboat division of Cruisers, Inc., could be either a **profit center** or an **investment center.** The method of evaluating the performance of each kind of center (or segment) is summarized in Exhibit 14–7.

Because individuals would like to think of their efforts in terms of profits rather than costs, sometimes an effort is made to convert cost centers to profit centers or investment centers by establishing a **transfer price** at which products, components, or services are "sold" from one segment of the organization to another. Since the revenue of one segment becomes the cost of another segment, it is difficult to establish a transfer price that is considered fair by all concerned. This issue, plus the increased bookkeeping costs, means that there have to be significant behavioral and other qualitative benefits expected to warrant transfer pricing at the cost center level of the organization. Transfer pricing is commonly applied to intersegment transactions between major divisions of a company, and to affiliates organized as separate legal entities. These transfer prices can influence bonuses, source of supply decisions, and state and national income tax obligations. The determination of an appropriate transfer price in these situations is often quite complex.

EXHIBIT 14–7   **Methods of Evaluating Responsibility Centers (Segments)**

Segment	How Performance Is Evaluated
Cost center	Actual costs incurred compared to budgeted costs.
Profit center	Actual segment margin compared to budgeted segment margin.
Investment center	Comparison of actual and budgeted return on investment (ROI) based on segment margin and assets controlled by the segment.

7. What does it mean to have a responsibility reporting system?
8. What does it mean to state that common fixed expenses should never be arbitrarily allocated to segments; for example, products or organizational units?

The Flexible Budget

Consider the following partial performance report for the hull manufacturing department of Cruisers, Inc., for the month of March:

Activity	Budget Amount	Actual Cost	Variance	Explanation
Raw materials	$ 64,056	$ 69,212	$ 5,156 U	Produced more boats than planned.
Direct labor..........	48,720	54,992	6,272 U	Same as above.
Variable overhead	10,880	12,438	1,558 U	Same as above.
Fixed overhead	36,720	37,320	600 U	Immaterial.
Total	$160,376	$173,962	$13,586 U	

Objective 10
Understand what a flexible budget is and how it is used.

Now suppose that you find out that the budget amount was based on the expectation that 100 hulls would be built during March but that 110 hulls were actually built. What could be done to make this performance report more useful for managers? Your first inclination is to recalculate the budget amount columns by increasing each of the variable cost items by 10 percent to determine how much cost should have been incurred for the activity actually performed. (Why isn't the fixed overhead budget amount also increased by 10%?) Adjusting the original budget so it reflects budgeted amounts for actual activity is called *flexing the budget*.

The performance report using the **flexible budget** would be:

Activity	Budget Allowance	Actual Cost	Variance	Explanation
Raw materials	$ 70,462	$ 69,212	$1,250 F	Immaterial.
Direct labor	53,592	54,992	1,400 U	Immaterial.
Variable overhead	11,968	12,438	470 U	Immaterial.
Fixed overhead	36,720	37,320	600 U	Immaterial.
Total	$172,742	$173,962	$1,220 U	

The variances are now relatively insignificant, and the initial conclusion made from this report is the correct one: The production manager is performing according to plan for the number of hulls that were actually produced.

Of course, there is a question about why 110 hulls were produced when the original budget called for production of 100 hulls. The answer to that question, however, is not relevant to controlling costs for the number of hulls actually produced.

Flexible budgeting does not affect the predetermined overhead application rate used to apply overhead to production. To the extent that the actual level of production differs from the activity estimate used in developing the predetermined overhead application rate, fixed manufacturing overhead will be overapplied or underapplied. However, this is not a cost control issue. It is an accounting issue, usually resolved by closing the amount of overapplied or underapplied overhead to cost of goods sold.

Flexible budgeting means that *the budget allowance for variable costs should be flexed to show the costs that should have been incurred for the level of activity actually experienced.* This is done by multiplying the variable cost per unit of *each* variable cost item (i.e., direct materials, direct labor, and variable manufacturing overhead) by the actual activity level (e.g., number of units produced in a month) to determine the *budget allowance* against which actual costs can be meaningfully compared. The variance in the level of activity should be investigated and explained so that improvements in activity forecasting can be achieved, but this is a separate and distinct issue from cost performance evaluation.

WHAT DOES IT MEAN?

9. What does it mean to do flexible budgeting?

10. What does it mean to state that budgeted fixed expenses are not flexed?

Summary

A budget is a financial plan. Many organizations have a policy to require budgets because budgets force planning, provide a benchmark against which to compare performance, and require coordination between the functional areas of the organization. Performance reporting involves comparing planned results with actual results.

To a large extent, the budgeting process is influenced by behavioral considerations. How the budget is used by management will influence the validity of the budget as a planning and controlling tool. In most instances, an interactive, participative approach to budget preparation, together with an attitude that the budget is an operating plan, results in a most useful budget document.

Budgets can be prepared for a single period or on a multiperiod, rolling basis. Which is most appropriate for any activity depends on the degree of control over the activity and the rapidity with which the environment of the activity changes. Different activities may have different budget time frames.

An operating budget is made up of several component budgets. The sales forecast (or revenue budget) is the starting point for all of the other budgets that become part of the operating budget. There is a hierarchy of budgets, and the results of one budget will provide input for the preparation of another budget.

The purchases/production budget is prepared once the sales forecast has been determined and an inventory policy has been established. Ending inventory is expressed as a function of the expected sales or usage of the subsequent period. One period's ending inventory is the next period's beginning inventory.

Operating managers have a natural tendency to build slack into their budget estimates. When budget managers combine departmental budgets into an overall organizational budget, the cumulative slack can cause the overall budget to lose significance. Budget managers must be aware of the slack issue and deal with it in ways that lead to the achievement of organizational goals.

The operating expense budget is a function of the sales forecast, cost behavior patterns, and planned changes from past levels of advertising, administrative, and other activities.

A budgeted income statement shows planned operating results for the entity as a whole. If top management is not satisfied with budgeted net income, changes in operations may be planned and/or various elements of the operating budget may be returned to operating managers for revision.

Once the income statement budget has been settled, a cash budget can be prepared. Cash flows from operating activities are forecast by adjusting net income for noncash items included in the income statement, as well as expectations about cash receipts and disbursements related to revenues and expenses. Cash flows from investing and financing activities are estimated, and the estimated cash balance at the end of the fiscal period is determined. Cash in excess of a minimum operating balance is available for investment. A deficiency in cash means that plans should be made to liquidate temporary investments or borrow money, or that cash payment assumptions must be revised.

The budgeted balance sheet uses data from all of the other budgets. Management uses this budget to evaluate the entity's projected financial position. If the result is not satisfactory, appropriate operating, investing, and financing plans will be revised.

The challenge to accurate budgeting is having an accurate estimate of activity and assumptions and policies that reflect what is likely to happen in the future. Computer spreadsheet models can make the budget calculation a relatively easy process that can be repeated many times to determine the impact of changes in estimates and assumptions.

Part of the payoff of the budgeting process involves comparing planned results with actual results. This is done in a performance report. The variance shown in the performance report is the difference between the budget and actual amounts. Management by exception involves focusing attention on those activities that have a significant variance. The objective of this analysis is to understand why the variance occurred and, if appropriate, to take action to eliminate unfavorable variances and capture favorable variances.

Segment reporting for an organization involves assigning revenues and expenses to divisions, product lines, geographic areas, or other responsibility centers. In this process, costs that are common to a group of segments should not be arbitrarily allocated to individual segments in that group.

Flexible budgeting recognizes cost behavior patterns. The original budget amount for variable items based on planned activity is adjusted by calculating a budget allowance based on actual activity for the period. This results in a variable cost variance that is meaningful because the effect of a difference between budgeted and actual volume of activity is removed from the variance. Only variable cost budgets are flexed.

Key Terms and Concepts

budget (p. 477)   A financial plan.

budget slack (p. 487)   Allowances for contingencies built into a budget. Sometimes called *padding* or *cushion*.

common fixed expense (p. 495)   An expense that is not assigned to an organization segment in a segmented income statement because the expense would be incurred even if the segment were eliminated.

continuous budget (p. 479)   A budget that is prepared for several periods in the future, and then revised several times prior to the budget period. Sometimes called a *rolling budget.*

cost center (p. 496)   A responsibility center for which performance is evaluated by comparing budgeted cost with actual cost.

direct fixed expense (p. 495)   An expense assigned to an organization segment in a segmented income statement that would not be incurred if the segment were eliminated.

favorable variance (p. 492)   The excess of actual revenue over budgeted revenue, or budgeted cost over actual cost.

flexible budget (p. 497)   A budget adjusted to reflect a budget allowance based on the actual level of activity, rather than the planned level of activity used to establish the original budget.

investment center (p. 496)   A responsibility center for which performance is evaluated by comparing budgeted return on investment with actual return on investment.

management by exception (p. 492)   A management concept that involves thorough planning and then exerting corrective effort only in those areas that do not show results consistent with the plan.

operating budget (p. 480)   An operating plan comprising the sales forecast (or revenue budget), the purchases/production budget, the operating expense budget, the income statement budget, the cash budget, and the budgeted balance sheet.

participative budgeting (p. 479)   A budgeting process that involves input and negotiation of several layers of management.

performance report (p. 492)   A report comparing planned and actual activity or costs.

profit center (p. 496)   A responsibility center for which performance is evaluated by comparing budgeted profit with actual profit.

responsibility center (p. 496)   An element of the organization over which a manager has been assigned responsibility and authority.

responsibility reporting (p. 492)   A system of performance reporting that involves successive degrees of summarization as the number of management responsibility levels being reported about increases.

rolling budget (p. 479)   A budget that is prepared for several periods in the future, and then revised several times prior to the budget period. Sometimes called a *continuous budget.*

sales forecast (p. 481)   Expected sales for future periods; a key to the budgeting process.

segment (p. 494)   A unit of an organization, such as a product line, sales territory, or group of related activities.

segment margin (p. 495)   The contribution of a segment of an organization to the common fixed expenses and operating income of the organization.

single-period budget (p. 479)   A budget that has been prepared only once prior to the budget period. This contrasts with a "continuous budget."

top-down budgeting (p. 479)   A budgeting approach that implies little or no input from lower levels of management.

transfer price (p. 496)   A price established for the "sale" of goods or services from one segment of the organization to another segment of the organization.

unfavorable variance (p. 492)   The excess of budgeted revenue over actual revenue, or actual cost over budgeted cost.

variance (p. 492)   The difference between budget and actual; variances are labeled as "favorable" or "unfavorable," usually on the basis of the arithmetic difference between budget and actual.

zero-based budgeting (p. 479)   A budgeting process that involves justifying resource requirements based on an analysis and prioritization of unit objectives without reference to prior period budget allowances.

WHAT DOES IT MEAN? ANSWERS

1. It means that the final budget results from the joint efforts of people at every level of management.

2. It means that the budget is prepared for several periods in the future, so subsequent budgeting involves refining the budgets previously prepared for subsequent periods, plus preparing the first budget for a new period added at the end of budget horizon.

3. It means that the level of planned operating activity determines the quantity of product or the capacity for services needed to fulfill the plan, and that this in turn influences the level of operating expenses and other costs that will be incurred as well as the level of cash and other resources that will be needed to support fulfillment of the plan.

4. It means that actual results are compared to planned or budgeted results, and explanations for variances are determined.

5. It means that managers should usually work to repeat activities that resulted in favorable variances and to eliminate activities that caused unfavorable variances.

6. It means that actual results are better than planned results; for example, actual sales are greater than forecast sales, or actual expenses are less than budgeted expenses.

7. It means that a performance report for a particular area of responsibility reflects those items over which the managers of that area have control.

8. It means that because these expenses would not decrease in total even if the segment disappeared, erroneous conclusions can result from an analysis that includes arbitrarily allocated fixed expenses.

9. It means that when the performance report is prepared, the budgeted amounts reflect expected costs at the actual level of activity achieved, rather than originally budgeted costs for the expected level of activity.

10. It means that because fixed expenses are not expected to change if the level of activity changes, it is not appropriate to change the budget for fixed expenses even though actual activity differs from planned activity.

Exercises and Problems

LO 3, 4   **14–1.   Production and purchases budgets.** Recognition, Inc., makes award medallions that are attached to ribbons. Each medallion requires 24 inches of ribbon. The sales forecast for February is 2,000 medallions. Estimated beginning inventories and desired ending inventories for February are the following:

	Estimated Beginning Inventory	Desired Ending Inventory
Medallions	1,000	800
Ribbon (yards)	50	20

Required:
a. Calculate the number of medallions to be produced in February.
b. Calculate the number of yards of ribbon to be purchased in February.

LO 3, 4   **14–2.   Production and purchases budgets.** Wren Co. is forecasting sales of 62,000 units of product for September. To make one unit of finished product, five pounds of raw materials are required. Actual beginning and desired ending inventories of raw materials and finished goods are:

	September 1 (Actual)	September 30 (Desired)
Raw materials (pounds)	74,700	68,200
Finished goods (units)	5,900	8,300

Required:
a. Calculate the number of units of product to be produced during September.
b. Calculate the number of pounds of raw materials to be purchased during September.

LO 4   **14–3.   Purchases budget.** Two ounces of x-scent are required for each gallon of Bracer, a popular after-shave lotion. Budgeted *production* of Bracer for the first three quarters of 1998 is:

Quarter I	10,000 gallons
Quarter II	18,000 gallons
Quarter III	11,000 gallons

Management's policy is to have on hand at the end of every quarter enough x-scent inventory to meet 25% of the next quarter's production needs. 5,000 ounces of x-scent were on hand at the beginning of Quarter I.

Required:

a. Calculate the number of ounces of x-scent to be purchased in each of the first two quarters of 1998.

b. Explain why management plans for an ending inventory instead of planning to purchase each quarter the amount of raw materials needed for that quarter's production.

LO 3, 4 **14–4. Production and purchases budgets.** Trendsetters, Inc., has actual sales for May and June, and forecasted sales for July, August, September, and October as follows:

Actual:	
May	5,900 units
June	6,200 units
Forecasted:	
July	6,000 units
August	6,800 units
September	5,600 units
October	5,300 units

Required:

a. The firm's policy is to have finished goods inventory on hand at the end of the month that is equal to 70% of the next month's sales. It is currently estimated that there will be 4,000 units on hand at the end of June. Calculate the number of units to be produced in each of the months of July, August, and September.

b. Each unit of finished product requires 6.5 pounds of raw materials. The firm's policy is to have raw material inventory on hand at the end of each month that is equal to 60% of the next month's estimated usage. It is currently estimated that 26,000 pounds of raw materials will be on hand at the end of June. Calculate the number of pounds of raw materials to be purchased in each of the months of July and August.

LO 3, 4 **14–5. Purchases budget.** Clydesdale's Furniture, a retail store, has an average gross profit ratio of 46%. The sales forecast for the next four months follows:

July	$250,000
August	220,000
September	310,000
October	400,000

Management's inventory policy is to have ending inventory equal to 300% of the cost of sales for the subsequent month, although it is estimated that the cost of inventory at June 30 will be $410,000.

Required:

Calculate the purchases budget, in dollars, for the months of July and August.

LO 3, 4 **14–6. Purchases budget—analytical.** Columbian Emeralds, Ltd. is a retail jeweler. Most of the firm's business is in jewelry and watches. The firm's average percentage markup on cost for jewelry is 150%, and for watches is 60%. The sales forecast for the next two months for each product category is as follows:

	Jewelry	Watches
May	$124,000	$60,000
June	96,000	51,000

The company's policy, which is expected to be achieved at the end of April, is to have ending inventory equal to 200% of the next month's cost of goods sold.

Required:

a. Calculate the cost of goods sold for jewelry and watches for May and June.

b. Calculate a purchases budget, in dollars, for each product for the month of May.

LO 3, 6   **14–7.   Cash receipts budget.** Fox River Center's sales are all made on account. The firm's collection experience has been that 30% of a month's sales is collected in the month the sale is made, 50% is collected in the month following the sale, and 18% is collected in the second month following the sale. The sales forecast for the months of May through August is:

May	$240,000
June	280,000
July	300,000
August.	350,000

Required:

Calculate the cash collections that would be included in the cash budgets for July and August.

LO 3, 6   **14–8.   Cash receipts budget.** Threeputt Co. had actual sales for July and August, and forecasted sales for September, October, November, and December as follows:

Actual:	
July	$ 98,000
August.	105,000
Forecasted:	
September	114,000
October	94,000
November	122,000
December	107,000

Based on past experience, it is estimated that 30% of a month's sales is collected in the month of sale, 55% is collected in the month following the sale, and 10% is collected in the second month following the sale.

Required:

Calculate the estimated cash receipts for September, October, and November.

LO 3, 6   **14–9.**   **Cash budget—(part one).** QB Sportswear is a custom imprinter that began operations six months ago. Sales have exceeded management's most optimistic projections. Sales are made on account and collected as follows: 50% in the month after the sale is made and 45% in the second month after sale. Merchandise purchases and operating expenses are paid as follows:

In the month during which the merchandise is purchased or the cost is incurred	75%
In the subsequent month	25%

QB Sportswear's income statement budget for each of the next four months, newly revised to reflect the success of the firm, follows:

	September	October	November	December
Sales	$42,000	$54,000	$68,000	$59,000
Cost of goods sold:				
Beginning inventory	$ 6,000	$14,400	$20,600	$21,900
Purchases	37,800	44,000	48,900	33,100
Cost of goods available for sale	$43,800	$58,400	$69,500	$55,000
Less: Ending inventory	(14,400)	(20,600)	(21,900)	(20,000)
Cost of goods sold	$29,400	$37,800	$47,600	$35,000
Gross profit	$12,600	$16,200	$20,400	$24,000
Operating expenses	10,500	12,800	14,300	16,100
Operating income	$ 2,100	$ 3,400	$ 6,100	$ 7,900

Cash on hand August 31 is estimated to be $40,000. Collections of August 31 accounts receivable were estimated to be $20,000 in September and $15,000 in October. Payments of August 31 accounts payable and accrued expenses in September were estimated to be $24,000.

Required:

a. Prepare a cash budget for September.

b. What is your advice to management of QB Sportswear?

LO 3, 6   **14–10.**   **Cash budget—(part two).** Refer to the QB Sportswear data presented in Problem 14–9.

Required:

a. Prepare a cash budget for October and November. What are the prospects for this company if its sales growth continues at a similar rate?

b. Assume now that QB Sportswear is a mature firm, and that the September–November data represent a seasonal peak in business. Prepare a cash budget for December, January, and February, assuming that the income statements for January and February are the same as December's. Explain how the cash budget would be used to support a request to a bank for a seasonal loan.

LO 6   **14–11.   Cash budget.** The monthly cash budgets for the third quarter of 1999 are shown below ($000 omitted) for McKenzie & Davis Mfg. Co. A minimum cash balance of $20,000 is required to start each month, and a $50,000 line of credit has been arranged with a local bank at a 15% interest rate.

	July	August	September	Total
Cash balance, beginning.	$ 26	$?	$?	$ 26
Add collections from customers	?	107	?	?
Total cash available	$ 94	$?	$156	$337
Less disbursements:				
Purchase of inventory	$?	$ 60	$ 48	$?
Operating expenses.	30	?	?	?
Capital additions.	34	8	?	44
Payment of dividends	–	–	?	9
Total disbursements.	$?	$107	$ 83	$304
Excess (deficiency) of cash available over disbursements	$(20)	$?	$ 73	$?
Borrowings.	?	–	–	?
Repayments (including interest)	–	–	?	?
Cash balance, ending	$?	$ 20	$?	$ 32

Required:

Calculate the missing amounts. *(Hint: The total cash available includes collections from customers for all three months, plus the beginning cash balance from July 1, 1999.)*

LO 6   **14–12.   Cash budget—comprehensive.** Presented below are the budgeted income statements for the second quarter of 1999 for Wutless-Bwoy, Inc.:

	April	May	June
Sales	$140,000	$170,000	$190,000
Cost of goods sold*	96,000	114,000	126,000
Gross profit	$ 44,000	$ 56,000	$ 64,000
Operating expenses**	22,000	25,000	27,000
Operating income	$ 22,000	$ 31,000	$ 37,000

*Includes all *product costs* (i.e., direct materials, direct labor, and manufacturing overhead).
**Includes all *period costs* (i.e., selling, general, and administrative expenses).

The company expects about 30% of sales to be cash transactions. Of sales on account, 60% are expected to be collected in the first month after the sale is made, and 40% in the second month after sale. Depreciation, insurance and property taxes represent $12,000 of the estimated monthly cost of goods sold, and $8,000 of the estimated monthly operating expenses. The annual insurance premium is paid in January, and the annual property taxes are paid in August. Of the remainder of the cost of goods sold and operating expenses, 80% are expected to be paid in the month in which they are incurred and the balance in the following month.

Current assets as of April 1, 1999, consist of cash of $14,000 and accounts receivable of $149,800 ($105,000 from March credit sales and $44,800 from February credit sales). Current liabilities as of April 1 consist of: $18,000 of accounts payable for product costs incurred in March, $4,600 of accrued liabilities for operating expenses incurred in March, and a $40,000, 12%, 120-day note payable that is due on April 17, 1999.

An estimated income tax payment of $40,000 will be made in May. The regular quarterly dividend of $16,000 is expected to be declared in May and paid in June. Capital expenditures amounting to $17,200 will be made in April.

Required:

a. Complete the monthly cash budgets for the second quarter of 1999 using the format shown below. Note that the ending cash balance for June is provided as a check figure.

b. Assume that management of Wutless-Bwoy, Inc. desires to maintain a minimum cash balance of $10,000 at the beginning of each month, and that a $50,000 line of credit has been arranged with a local bank at an interest rate of 10% to ensure the availability of funds. Borrowing transactions are to occur only at the end of months in which the budgeted cash balance would otherwise fall short of the $10,000 minimum balance. Repayments of principal and interest are to occur at the end of the earliest month in which sufficient funds areexpected to be available for repayment. Explain how this minimum cash balance requirement would affect the monthly cash budgets prepared in part *a* above.

WUTLESS-BWOY, INC.
Cash Budget
For the Months of April, May, and June, 1999

	April	May	June
Beginning cash balance....................	$ 14,000	$	$
Cash Receipts:			
From cash sales made in current month			
From credit sales made in:			
February			
March			
April			
May.................................			
Total cash available	$	$	$
Cash Disbursements:			
For cost of goods sold and operating expenses			
incurred in:			
March	$	$	$
April			
May.................................			
June.................................			
For payment of note payable and interest			
For capital expenditures			
For payment of income taxes			
For payment of dividends			
Total disbursements......................	$	$	$
Ending cash balance	$	$	$ 22,400

LO 3, 4, 6   **14–13.   Sales, production, purchases, and cash budgets.** Ferdi Co. is in the process of preparing the second quarter budget for 1999, and the following data have been assembled:

- The company sells a single product at a selling price of $40 per unit. The estimated sales volume for the next six months is as follows:

March	6,000 units	June	8,000 units
April	7,000 units	July	9,000 units
May	10,000 units	August	6,000 units

- All sales are on account. The company's collection experience has been that 40% of a month's sales are collected in the month of sale, 55% in the month following the sale, and 5% are uncollectible. According to budget, the net realizable value of accounts receivable (i.e., accounts receivable less allowance for uncollectible accounts) is expected to be $132,000 on March 31, 1999.
- Management's policy is to maintain ending finished goods inventory each month at a level equal to 50% of the next month's budgeted sales. The finished goods inventory on March 31, 1999, is expected to be 3,500 units.
- To make one unit of finished product, three pounds of materials are required. Management's policy is to have enough materials on hand at the end of each month to equal 40% of the next month's estimated usage. The raw materials inventory is expected to be 10,200 pounds on March 31, 1999.
- The cost per pound of material is $6, and 80% of all purchases are paid for in the month of purchase; the remainder is paid in the following month. The accounts payable for raw material purchases is expected to be $26,280 on March 31, 1999.

Required:

a. Prepare a sales budget in units and dollars, by month and in total, for the second quarter (April, May, and June) of 1999.
b. Prepare a schedule of cash collections from sales, by month and in total, for the second quarter of 1999.
c. Prepare a production budget in units, by month and in total, for the second quarter of 1999.
d. Prepare a materials purchases budget in pounds, by month and in total, for the second quarter of 1999.
e. Prepare a schedule of cash payments for materials, by month and in total, for the second quarter of 1999.

LO 3, 4, 6   **14–14.   Sales, production, purchases, and cash budgets.** Seymour, Inc. is in the process of preparing the fourth quarter budget for 1999, and the following data have been assembled:

- The company sells a single product at a selling price of $60 per unit. The estimated sales volume for the next six months is as follows:

September	13,000 units	December	20,000 units
October	12,000 units	January	9,000 units
November	14,000 units	February	10,000 units

- All sales are on account. The company's collection experience has been that 32% of a month's sales are collected in the month of sale, 64% in the month following the sale, and 4% are uncollectible. According to budget, the net realizable value of accounts receivable (i.e., accounts receivable less allowance for uncollectible accounts) is expected to be $499,200 on September 30, 1999.
- Management's policy is to maintain ending finished goods inventory each month at a level equal to 40% of the next month's budgeted sales. The finished goods inventory on September 30, 1999, is expected to be 4,800 units.
- To make one unit of finished product, five pounds of materials are required. Management's policy is to have enough materials on hand at the end of each month to equal 30% of the next month's estimated usage. The raw materials inventory is expected to be 19,200 pounds on September 30, 1999.
- The cost per pound of material is $4, and 70% of all purchases are paid for in the month of purchase; the remainder is paid in the following month. The accounts payable for raw material purchases is expected to be $75,960 on September 30, 1999.

Required:

a. Prepare a sales budget in units and dollars, by month and in total, for the fourth quarter (October, November, and December) of 1999.
b. Prepare a schedule of cash collections from sales, by month and in total, for the fourth quarter of 1999.
c. Prepare a production budget in units, by month and in total, for the fourth quarter of 1999.
d. Prepare a materials purchases budget in pounds, by month and in total, for the fourth quarter of 1999.
e. Prepare a schedule of cash payments for materials, by month and in total, for the fourth quarter of 1999.

LO 9   **14–15.** **Segmented income statement.** The president of Bookston, Inc., attended a seminar about the contribution margin model and returned to her company full of enthusiasm about it. She requested that last year's traditional model income statement be revised, and she received the following report:

	Total Company	Division		
		A	B	C
Sales	$100,000	$40,000	$25,000	$35,000
Variable expenses	60,000	26,000	15,000	19,000
Contribution margin	$ 40,000	$14,000	$10,000	$16,000
Fixed expenses	30,000	10,000	11,000	9,000
Net income (loss)	$ 10,000	$ 4,000	$ (1,000)	$ 7,000

The president was told that the fixed expenses of $30,000 included $21,000 that had been split evenly between divisions because they were general corporate expenses. After looking at the statement, the president exclaimed, "I knew it! Division B is a drag on the whole company. Close it down!"

Required:
a. Evaluate the president's remark.
b. Calculate what the company's net income would be if Division B were closed down.
c. Write a policy statement related to the allocation of fixed expenses.

LO 9   **14–16.   Segmented income statement.** Murphey Co. produces three models of calculators. The following table summarizes data about each model:

	Business	*Math*	*Student*
Selling price per unit.....................	$ 12	$ 20	$ 10
Contribution margin per unit.................	4	6	2
Units sold per month.....................	3,000	1,500	4,500
Total contribution margin....................	$12,000	$9,000	$ 9,000
Direct fixed expenses.....................	5,200	3,700	6,100
Segment margin.........................	$ 6,800	$5,300	$ 2,900
Allocated company fixed expenses.............	3,333	1,667	5,000
Operating income (loss).....................	$ 3,467	$3,633	$(2,100)

Required:

a. Criticize the above presentation. On what basis does the $10,000 of company fixed expenses appear to be allocated?
b. Calculate the effect on total company net income if the student model were discontinued.
c. Calculate the contribution margin ratio for each model.
d. If an advertising campaign focusing on a single model were to result in an increase of 5,000 units in the quantity of units sold, which model should be advertised? Explain your answer.
e. If an advertising campaign focusing on a single model were to result in an increase of $15,000 in revenues, which model should be advertised? Explain your answer.

LO 10   **14–17.   Performance reporting.** The chair of the Biology Department of Science University has a budget for laboratory supplies. Supplies have a variable cost behavior pattern that is a function of the number of students enrolled in laboratory courses. For planning purposes, when the budget was prepared in March 1998, it was estimated that there would be 200 students enrolled in laboratory courses during the Fall 1998 semester. Actual enrollment for the fall semester was 212 students.

Required:
a. Explain what action should be taken with respect to the supplies budget when the actual enrollment is known.
b. Would your answer to part *a* be any different if the actual enrollment turned out to be 182 students? Explain your answer.

LO 10   **14–18.   Performance reporting.** Dittle Co. manufactures a single product. The original budget for April was based on expected production of 14,000 units; actual production for April was 13,300 units. The original budget and actual costs incurred for the manufacturing department are shown below:

	Original Budget	Actual Costs
Direct materials........	$220,500	$216,600
Direct labor...........	170,800	165,400
Variable overhead	86,100	78,100
Fixed overhead	68,000	69,000
Total.............	$545,400	$529,100

Required:

Prepare an appropriate performance report for the manufacturing department.

LO 10   **14–19.** **Flexible budgeting.** The cost formula for the maintenance department of Hampstead, Ltd. is $19,400 per month plus $7.70 per machine hour used by the production department.

Required:

a. Calculate the maintenance cost that would be budgeted for a month in which 6,700 machine hours are planned to be used.

b. Prepare an appropriate performance report for the maintenance department assuming that 7,060 machine hours were actually used in the month of May and that the total maintenance cost incurred was $68,940.

LO 10 **14–20.** **Flexible budgeting.** One of the significant costs for a nonpublic college or university is student aid in the form of gifts and grants awarded to students because of academic potential or performance, and/or financial need. Gifts and grants are only a part of a financial aid package, usually accounting for no more than 20% of the total package. Federal and state grants, other scholarships, loans, and income from work constitute the rest of financial aid, but these funds are not provided by the institution. Assume that for the 1998–1999 academic year, Wonder College had a gift and grant budget of $900,000 and that all of these funds had been committed to students by June 15, 1998. The college had capacity to enroll up to 200 additional students.

Required:

Explain why and how flexible budgeting should be applied by the management of Wonder College in administering its gift and grant awards budget.

Standard Costs and Variance Analysis

A **standard cost** is a unit budget allowance for a component—material, labor, or overhead—of a product or service. Standard costs are used in the planning and control processes of manufacturing and service firms that perform repetitive operations in the production of goods or performance of services. Although usually associated with manufacturing, standard costs are being used with greater frequency in financial and consumer service companies.

This chapter will review the various methods of establishing standards. It will then explain how variances can be analyzed so that supervisors and managers can identify why they occurred and can plan action to eliminate unfavorable variances or capture those that are favorable.

As you study the material presented in this chapter, keep in mind that standard costs should be used in conjunction with a performance reporting system that is designed to meet the information needs of management. When appropriately developed and implemented, a standard costing system establishes performance targets and provides benchmarks against which actual results can be compared.

Learning Objectives

After studying this chapter, you should understand:

1 Why and how standards are useful in the planning and control process.
2 How the standard cost of a product is developed.
3 How standard costs are used in the cost accounting system.
4 How and why the two components of a standard cost variance are calculated.
5 The specific names assigned to variances for different product inputs.
6 How the control and analysis of fixed overhead variances and variable cost variances differ.
7 The alternative methods of accounting for variances.

Standard Costs

Using Standard Costs

Objective 1
Understand why and how standards are useful in the planning and control process.

Standard costs are used in the planning and control phases of the management process and are used in financial accounting to value the inventory of a manufacturing firm. A standard cost has two elements: the quantity of input and the cost per unit of input. The quantity of input could be weight or volume of raw materials, hours of labor, kilowatt hours of electricity, number of welding rods, or any other measure of physical input use. Standard cost systems are traditionally and most extensively used in the manufacturing environment, but their use in the service sector of the economy is growing rapidly.

Because the standard represents a unit budget (i.e., the expected quantity and cost of the resources required to produce a unit of product or provide a unit of service), standards are used extensively in the budget preparation process. Once the sales forecast has been developed and expressed in units, standards are used to plan for the inputs that will need to be provided to make the product or provide the service.

As the budget period proceeds, actual inputs used can be compared to the standard inputs that should have been used to make or service the actual output achieved. Based on these performance reports, managers can determine where to focus their efforts so goals will be achieved.

In many situations, control focuses on the quantity dimensions of the standard cost, rather than the dollar amount of the standard cost (the product of quantity multiplied by unit cost) because the supervisor responsible can relate more easily to the physical quantity than to the dollar cost. For example, the supervisor responsible for raw material usage and the supervisor responsible for order-processing activity probably relate more easily to pounds used and number of orders processed per employee, respectively, than they would to the costs of those inputs used during a reporting period.

Standard costs that have been appropriately developed (see discussion below) can be used in the cost accounting system described in Chapter 12. This results in a cost system that is easier to use than one involving actual costs, especially when it comes to valuing the inventory because the standard costs have been developed prior to the accounting period, whereas actual costs aren't known until after the accounting period has been completed.

Developing Standards

Objective 2
Understand how the standard cost of a product is developed.

Because standards are unit budgets, all of the management philosophy and individual behavior considerations identified in the discussion of the budgeting process in Chapter 14 apply also to standards. Three classifications of the approach to developing standards are:

Ideal, or engineered, standards.
Attainable standards.
Past experience standards.

An **ideal standard** is one that assumes that operating conditions will be ideal and that material and labor inputs will be provided at maximum levels of efficiency at all times. One of the work measurement techniques used by industrial engineers is called *motion and time study*. This technique involves a very detailed analysis of the activities involved in performing a task, with the objective of designing workstation layout and operator movements so that the task can be performed most efficiently. Industrial engineers recognize that individual fatigue and other factors will result in actual performance over a period of time that will be less than 100 percent efficient, as defined by motion and time study analysis. However, these factors are ignored when an ideal standard is established. The principal disadvantage of ideal standards is that unfavorable variances will almost certainly be generated, and as a result, supervisors and employees will not use the standard as a realistic performance target.

An **attainable standard** is one that recognizes that there will be some operating inefficiencies relative to ideal conditions. Actual performance will result in both favorable and unfavorable variances. Employees are more likely to try to achieve this kind of standard than an ideal standard because of the sense of accomplishment that comes from meeting a legitimate goal. There may be varying degrees of "tightness" or "looseness" in an attainable standard, depending upon management philosophy and operating circumstances. For example, some firms create a highly competitive work environment and establish tight standards that require considerable effort to achieve. Once an attainable standard is established, it is not set forever. Changes in worker efficiency and/or changes in the work environment may call for changes in the standard.

A **past experience standard** has the disadvantage of including all of the inefficiencies that have crept into the operation over the years. Such a standard does not contain any challenge, and performance is not likely to improve over time. Such a standard reflects current performance but is not likely to provide an incentive for improvement.

Establishing performance standards for an organization that has not had them before is a significant management challenge. It is only natural for workers to be uncomfortable with the idea that someone will now be measuring and watching their efficiency. The usefulness of standards for planning and control purposes will increase over time as those affected by them learn and become accustomed to how supervisors and managers use the resulting performance reports. Many organizations have experienced productivity and profitability increases, and workers have experienced increases in job satisfaction and compensation as a result of well-designed and carefully implemented standard cost systems.

WHAT DOES IT MEAN?

1. What does it mean to develop a standard cost?
2. What does it mean to have an attainable standard?

Costing Products with Standard Costs

The process of establishing a standard cost for a product involves aggregating the individual standard costs for each of the inputs to the product: raw materials, direct labor, and manufacturing overhead. Once the

Objective 3
Understand how
standard costs are
used in the cost
accounting system.

standard quantities allowed have been developed, as explained in the prior section, a standard cost for each unit of input is developed, and the standard cost for a unit of product is determined.

Developing the standard cost for each unit of input involves estimating costs for the budget period. The purchasing agent will provide input for raw material costs, the personnel department will be involved in establishing standard labor rates, and the production, purchasing, and personnel departments will provide data for estimating overhead component costs. Because of the necessity to recognize cost behavior patterns for planning and control purposes, overhead costs will be classified as variable or fixed. Variable overhead will usually be expressed in terms of direct labor hours, machine hours, or some other physical measure that reflects the causes of overhead expenditures. Fixed overhead is expressed as a total cost per accounting period for planning and control purposes, but for product costing purposes it is allocated to individual products. The allocation is made by developing a fixed overhead application rate that is established by dividing the total fixed overhead budget amount by an estimated total volume of activity (such as direct labor hours, machine hours, or some other measure of activity). This is similar to the process used for variable overhead. However, since fixed overhead does not behave on a per unit basis, this approach is not valid for planning and controlling fixed overhead; it is used only to allocate fixed overhead to individual products for product costing purposes.

The result of this process is a standard cost calculation that might look like this for a SeaCruiser sailboat hull manufactured by Cruisers, Inc.:

Variable costs:
  Raw materials:
    218 yds. of fiberglass cloth @ $2.10/yd. . . . . $ 457.80
    55 gal. of epoxy resin @ $.92/gal. 50.60
    1 purchased keel plate @ $132.16 . . . . 132.16
      Total raw materials. . . . . $ 640.56
  Direct labor:
    26 hours of "build-up" labor @ $12.80/hr. . . . . $ 332.80
    8 hours of finishing labor @ $19.30/hr. 154.40
      Total direct labor . . . . $ 487.20
  Variable overhead (based on total direct labor hours):
    34 hours @ $3.20/hr. . . . . $ 108.80
      Total standard variable cost per unit $1,236.56
Fixed costs:
  Fixed overhead (the $10.80 rate is based on total budgeted fixed overhead
    for the year divided by total estimated direct labor hours to be worked
    during the year):
    34 hours @ $10.80/hr. . . . . $ 367.20
Total standard cost per unit. $1,603.76

Note: For consistency purposes, the total variable and fixed manufacturing overhead cost equals $14 per direct labor hour, as shown in Exhibit 12–4. This is the predetermined overhead application rate used for cost accounting purposes. The fixed overhead component of that rate is determined as explained in Exhibit 12–4; the variable component is developed by building a standard based on the relationship between the elements of variable overhead (e.g., utilities and maintenance) and the chosen activity base. In this example, that activity base is direct labor hours, but it can be any other physical measure that has a causal relationship with the cost.

In a similar fashion, the standard cost of every component of the boat would be developed. The standard cost of the SeaCruiser is the sum of the standard cost for each component. The standard cost of all other models would be compiled in the same way. There is a great deal of effort and cost involved in implementing a standard cost system, but the benefit/cost ratio is positive because of the planning, control, and product costing uses of the system. Many firms revise standard quantities allowed when necessary because of performance and operating changes, and they revise standard costs per unit of input on an annual basis. However, some large firms with many products involving hundreds of raw material and direct labor inputs have adopted a different strategy. They may review and revise standards on a cyclical basis over a two- or three-year period, or they may retain standards for several years, anticipating and accepting variances that result from quantity or price changes. Managers of any firm using standards must weigh the trade-offs involved in keeping the standards current compared to revising them periodically.

Other Uses of Standards

In addition to being used for product costing in a manufacturing environment, standards can be developed and used for planning and control of period costs and qualitative goals in both manufacturing and service organizations. For example, a day care center could develop a standard cost for the food provided to its clients and/or a standard for the number of staff required for a given number of clients of a given age.

Both manufacturing firms and service organizations are seeking to respond to increased competitive pressures by becoming more efficient. One result of this has been the development of goals, which can be expressed as standards, for such activities as these:

Quality control, including total quality management programs and statistical quality control measures.

Inventory control, including just-in-time inventory management systems and flexible manufacturing systems.

Machine usage, including downtime for setup, preventative maintenance, and unscheduled repairs.

Service levels, including customer/client response times, out-of-stock frequencies, and delivery times.

Few of these standards are expressed in terms of dollars per unit of product; they need not be expressed in dollars to be useful for management planning and control.

For manufacturing firms, standards are often developed to express organizational goals based on the notion of *continual improvement* (e.g., "zero defects" or "100% on-time deliveries"). Even though absolute perfection cannot be realistically achieved, many firms use these types of standards to emphasize the importance of making progress and showing improvement rather than simply meeting standards. To monitor progress toward such goals, performance must be measured on an *on-line* basis— as production occurs—so that feedback can be provided continually. Machine adjustments and/or changes in the work flow can be made as the need arises, and many problems can be solved on the factory floor. Management's feedback loop is shortened significantly under this approach, which has the effect of increasing *throughput* (i.e., the output rate, or cycle time) in the manufacturing process and reducing machine *downtime*.

A similar approach can be taken to monitor the "quality" of production and/or customer service. For production quality, an important measure is the first-time pass rate for each process, as indicated by the number (or percentage) of defective units per batch inspected. The higher the first-time pass rate, the less rework and scrap, which in turn reduces labor and material costs, respectively. Perhaps more importantly, poor production quality leads to unhappy customers and lost sales opportunities. To monitor customer service quality, procedures must be established to ensure that immediate and appropriate actions will be taken to resolve all of those customer complaints that management deems it feasible to resolve. The true "cost" of losing a valued customer may be unknown, but it is likely to exceed many of the readily measurable costs for which standards have traditionally been developed.

Variance Analysis

Analysis of Variable Cost Variances

Objective 4
Understand how and why the two components of a standard cost variance are calculated.

To achieve the control advantages associated with a standard cost system, performance reports similar to those described in Chapter 14 must be provided to individuals responsible for incurring costs. The total variance for any particular cost component is referred to as the **budget variance** because it represents the difference between budgeted cost and actual cost. The budget variance is caused by two factors: the difference between the standard and actual *quantity* of the input, and the difference between the standard and actual *unit cost* of the input. Even if the same individual were responsible for both quantity and price, it would be desirable to break the budget variance into the **quantity variance** and the **cost per unit of input variance.** However, since different managers are usually responsible for each component of the total variance, it is essential to separate the two components so that each manager can take the appropriate action to eliminate unfavorable variances or capture those that are favorable.

As is the case with much of managerial and financial accounting, different organizations use different terms for these variances. In the discussion that follows, quantity variance will be referred to as a *usage* or *efficiency variance,* and the cost per unit of input variance will be referred to as a *price, rate,* or *spending variance.* These terms are generally, but not exclusively, used in practice. In addition, variances will be referred to here as *favorable* or *unfavorable.* In some organizations, a favorable variance is shown as a positive but otherwise unlabeled amount, and an unfavorable variance is shown as a negative amount. Whether a variance is favorable or unfavorable is determined in the context of the item being evaluated and the goals of the organization. Thus, spending less for raw materials because lower-than-specified-quality materials were purchased may give rise to an arithmetically favorable variance (actual cost was less than standard cost) that is not desirable because of the negative impact on product quality.

To illustrate the two components of the budget variance, we will focus on the "build-up" labor of the SeaCruiser hull for which the standard cost was summarized earlier. Assume that 100 hulls were made last month. The table below summarizes the actual and standard labor hours and the hourly rates for build-up labor inputs. Note that variances are also indicated (F is favorable, U is unfavorable).

Actual	2,540 hours @ $12.95/hr.		$32,893
Standard	2,600 hours @ $12.80/hr.		33,280
Budget variance	60 F	$ .15 U	$ 387 F

The analysis of the budget variance into the quantity variance and the cost per unit of input variance is:

Variance due to hours difference:	
60 hours × $12.80 (standard rate)	$768 F
Variance due to rate difference:	
$.15/hr. × 2,540 hours (actual hours)	$381 U
Budget variance	$387 F

The quantity variance (due to the difference between standard hours allowed and the actual hours worked) is called the **direct labor efficiency variance** because it relates to the efficiency with which labor was used. In this case, the efficiency variance is favorable because the 100 hulls were produced in fewer build-up labor hours than were allowed at standard. Note that standard quantities for variable cost inputs are based on the flexible budgeting concept described in Chapter 14; the standard quantity allowed is adjusted in response to the number of units produced. The cost per unit of input variance (due to the difference between the actual and standard hourly pay rates) is called the **direct labor rate variance.** In this case, the rate variance is unfavorable because workers were paid a higher rate than allowed at standard. Part of the budget variance is really a joint variance due to the fact that there was a difference between both standard and actual *hours* and the standard and actual *rate* per hour. However, rather than report three variances, the joint variance is included with the rate variance. This keeps the efficiency variance "pure," which is appropriate because efficiency is usually more subject to control than are pay rates.

The efficiency variance would be reported to the supervisor responsible for direct labor inputs to the product. The rate variance would be reported to the personnel manager or other individual who is responsible for pay rates. Management-by-exception procedures are appropriate, and, if a variance is significant, the reasons for it will be determined so that appropriate action can be taken to eliminate unfavorable variances and capture favorable ones.

The variances are labeled favorable or unfavorable based on the arithmetic difference between standard and actual, but these labels are not necessarily synonymous with "good" and "bad," respectively. This example illustrates a trade-off that can frequently be made. Even though the workers were paid more than the standard rate, the work was performed efficiently enough to more than make up for the unfavorable rate variance. If this occurred because of a conscious decision by the production supervisor, it may be appropriate to make a permanent change in the way the work is done and to change the standards accordingly. Alternatively, achieving a favorable rate variance by using less skilled employees may result in a more-than-offsetting unfavorable efficiency variance.

Objective 5
Understand the specific names assigned to variances for different product inputs.

The budget variance for raw materials and variable overhead can also be analyzed and separated into two components, as illustrated above for direct labor. The label assigned to each of the components varies from input to input, but the calculations are similar. The labels generally used are: **raw materials usage variance, raw materials price variance, variable overhead efficiency variance,** and **variable overhead spending variance.** These variances are summarized below:

	Variance Due to Difference between Standard and Actual	
Input	*Quantity*	*Cost per Unit of Input*
Raw materials	Usage	Price
Direct labor	Efficiency	Rate
Variable overhead	Efficiency	Spending

The terms *usage* and *efficiency* refer to quantity of input; from the perspective of direct labor, efficiency relates to the quantity of hours actually used relative to the quantity for which the standard calls. The variable overhead quantity variance is called the *efficiency variance* because variable overhead is, in most cases, assumed to be related to direct labor hours. The terms used for cost per unit of input variances are consistent with the way costs are usually referred to: price for raw materials and rate for employee wages. "Spending" is used for variable overhead because of the number of different costs that go into overhead; although an overall spending rate is calculated, the variance simply reflects the fact that actual overhead costs differ from the spending that was anticipated when the rate was established.

The general model for calculating each variance is:

$$\text{Quantity variance} = \left(\begin{array}{c} \text{Standard} \\ \text{quantity} \\ \text{allowed} \end{array} - \begin{array}{c} \text{Actual} \\ \text{quantity} \\ \text{used} \end{array} \right) \times \begin{array}{c} \text{Standard} \\ \text{cost per} \\ \text{unit} \end{array}$$

$$\begin{array}{c} \text{Cost per unit} \\ \text{of input} \\ \text{variance} \end{array} = \left(\begin{array}{c} \text{Standard} \\ \text{cost per} \\ \text{unit} \end{array} - \begin{array}{c} \text{Actual} \\ \text{cost per} \\ \text{unit} \end{array} \right) \begin{array}{c} \text{Actual} \\ \times \text{quantity} \\ \text{used} \end{array}$$

This model can also be expressed in the following way:

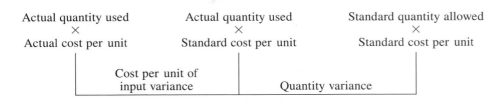

The arithmetic sign of the variance calculated using either of the above versions of the model indicates whether the variance is favorable (+) or unfavorable (−). Variance calculation examples for some of the Sea-Cruiser hull costs are illustrated in Exhibit 15–1.

Although the total budget variance of $234 F calculated in Exhibit 15–1 is easily considered immaterial, some of the individual variances are much more significant. It just happens that they are largely offsetting. This emphasizes the need to analyze the variances for each standard. Thus, although not illustrated in Exhibit 15–1, variances for the other raw material, direct labor, and variable overhead components of the SeaCruiser hulls would also be computed.

What use will be made of the information in Exhibit 15–1? Remember that the objectives of variance analysis are to highlight deviations from planned results, to capture favorable variances, and to eliminate unfavorable variances. With respect to raw materials, it is possible that the favorable price variance of $1,125 was caused by buying lower-quality fiberglass that resulted in the unfavorable usage variance of $1,470. As a result of the performance report, there should be communication between the purchasing agent and the raw materials supervisor to resolve the issue. Without this analysis and communication, the purchasing agent, not being aware that the price savings were more than offset by higher usage, might continue to buy lower-quality material. Likewise, the favorable labor efficiency variance of $768 might be the result of using more experienced and higher-paid employees this month, which in turn caused a $381 unfavorable rate variance. After analysis and discussion, the direct labor supervisor, production superintendent, and personnel manager might decide to continue this trade-off. Variance analysis information should result in actions to maintain or increase the profitability of the company. If the benefit of calculating variances is not greater than the cost of doing so, there isn't much sense in making the calculations.

As is the case with any performance reporting, variances should be communicated to the individuals responsible as promptly as feasible after the activity has occurred. This way, the causes of the variances can be

---

EXHIBIT 15–1   Calculation of Standard Cost Variances

I. Assumptions:

The following performance report summarizes budget and actual usage and costs for the items shown for a month in which 100 SeaCruiser hulls were produced.

	Budget	Actual	Variance
Raw materials:			
Glass fiber cloth:....................	$45,780	$46,125	$345 U
Budget: Standard/hull of 218 yds.			
@ $2.10/yd. × 100 hulls			
Actual: 22,500 yds. @ $2.05/yd.			
Direct labor:			
Build-up labor:	33,280	32,893	387 F
Budget: Standard/hull of 26 hrs.			
@ $12.80/hr × 100 hulls			
Actual: 2,540 hrs. @ $12.95/hr.			
Variable overhead:			
Related to build-up labor:	8,320	8,128	192 F
Budget: Standard/hull of 26 hrs.			
@ $3.20/hr × 100 hulls			
Actual: 2,540 hrs. @ $3.20/hr.			
Totals........................	$87,380	$87,146	$234 F

II. Required:

Analyze the budget variance for each item by calculating the quantity and cost per unit of input variances.

III. Solution:

$$\text{Quantity variance} = \left(\begin{array}{c} \text{Standard} \\ \text{quantity} \\ \text{allowed} \end{array} - \begin{array}{c} \text{Actual} \\ \text{quantity} \\ \text{used} \end{array} \right) \times \begin{array}{c} \text{Standard} \\ \text{cost per} \\ \text{unit} \end{array}$$

Raw materials
usage variance
$$= [(218 \text{ yds.} \times 100 \text{ hulls}) - 22,500 \text{ yds.}] \times \$2.10$$
$$= \$1,470 \text{ U}$$

Direct labor
efficiency variance
$$= [(26 \text{ hrs.} \times 100 \text{ hulls}) - 2,540 \text{ hrs.}] \times \$12.80$$
$$= \$768 \text{ F}$$

Variable overhead
efficiency variance
$$= [(26 \text{ hrs.} \times 100 \text{ hulls}) - 2,540 \text{ hrs.}] \times \$3.20$$
$$= \$192 \text{ F}$$

---

easily remembered and appropriate action can be taken. All variances need not be reported with the same frequency. In most organizations the usage of raw materials and the efficiency of direct labor are most subject to short-term control, so these variances will be reported more frequently than the cost per unit of input variances. In many situations, it is appropriate to report raw material usage variances and direct labor efficiency variances in physical terms because supervisors are more accustomed to thinking in terms of pounds, square feet, and direct labor hours than in

EXHIBIT 15–1   *(concluded)*

$$\begin{array}{c} \text{Cost per unit} \\ \text{of input} \\ \text{variance} \end{array} = \left(\begin{array}{c} \text{Standard} \\ \text{cost per} \\ \text{unit} \end{array} - \begin{array}{c} \text{Actual} \\ \text{cost per} \\ \text{unit} \end{array} \right) \times \begin{array}{c} \text{Actual} \\ \text{quantity} \\ \text{used} \end{array}$$

Raw materials
price variance

$$= (\$2.10/\text{yd.} - \$2.05/\text{yd.}) \times 22,500 \text{ yds.}$$
$$= \$1,125 \text{ F}$$

Direct labor
rate variance

$$= (\$12.80/\text{hr.} - \$12.95/\text{hr.}) \times 2,540 \text{ hrs.}$$
$$= \$381 \text{ U}$$

Variable overhead
spending variance

$$= (\$3.20/\text{hr.} - \$3.20/\text{hr.}) \times 2,540 \text{ hrs.}$$
$$= 0$$

IV. Recap of Variances:

	Usage/Efficiency	*Price/Rate/Spending*	*Total*
Raw materials	$1,470 U	$1,125 F	$345 U
Direct labor	768 F	381 U	387 F
Variable overhead	192 F	0	192 F
Totals	$ 510 U	$ 744 F	$234 F

terms of dollars. For example, using the data in Exhibit 15–1, and eliminating standard cost per unit from the model, the quantity variances would be calculated and expressed as follows:

$$\begin{array}{c} \text{Quantity} \\ \text{variance} \end{array} = \left(\begin{array}{c} \text{Standard} \\ \text{quantity} \\ \text{allowed} \end{array} - \begin{array}{c} \text{Actual} \\ \text{quantity} \\ \text{used} \end{array} \right)$$

Raw material
usage variance

$$= (218 \text{ yds.} \times 100 \text{ hulls}) - 22,500 \text{ yds.}$$
$$= 700 \text{ yds. U}$$

Direct labor
efficiency variance

$$= (26 \text{ hrs.} \times 100 \text{ hulls}) - 2,540 \text{ hrs.}$$
$$= 60 \text{ hrs. F}$$

Some organizations calculate and report the raw materials price variance at the time materials are purchased rather than when they are used. This variance is called the **raw materials purchase price variance.** This is especially appropriate if raw materials inventories are maintained, as opposed to having materials put directly into production, because it shows the purchasing manager any price variance soon after the purchase is made rather than later when the material is used. For example, if 4,000 pounds of raw material A were purchased at a cost of $3.64 per pound, and the standard cost was $3.60 per pound, the purchase price variance would be calculated as follows:

General model:

$$\begin{pmatrix} \text{Cost per unit} \\ \text{of input} \\ \text{variance} \end{pmatrix} = \begin{pmatrix} \text{Standard} & \text{Actual} \\ \text{cost per} & - & \text{cost per} \\ \text{unit} & \text{unit} \end{pmatrix} \times \begin{matrix} \text{Actual} \\ \text{quantity} \\ \text{used} \end{matrix}$$

Modification for purchase price variance:

$$\begin{pmatrix} \text{Cost per unit} \\ \text{of input} \\ \text{variance} \end{pmatrix} = \begin{pmatrix} \text{Standard} & \text{Actual} \\ \text{cost per} & - & \text{cost per} \\ \text{unit} & \text{unit} \end{pmatrix} \times \begin{matrix} \text{Actual} \\ \text{quantity} \\ \textit{purchased} \end{matrix}$$

$$= (\$3.60 - \$3.64) \times 4{,}000 \text{ lbs.}$$

$$= \$160 \text{ U}$$

WHAT DOES IT MEAN?

3. What does it mean to have an unfavorable raw materials usage variance?

4. What does it mean to analyze the direct labor budget variance to determine the efficiency variance and rate variance components?

5. What does it mean to state that a favorable usage variance may not really be favorable?

6. What does it mean to state that for variance analysis to be effective, it should result in better communication between managers?

Analysis of Fixed Overhead Variance

Objective 6
Understand how the control and analysis of fixed overhead variances and variable cost variances differ.

The fixed manufacturing overhead variance is analyzed differently from the variable cost variances because of the cost behavior pattern difference. For control purposes, the focus is on the difference between the fixed overhead that was budgeted for the period and actual fixed overhead expenditures. This difference is labeled a *budget variance* (the same term used to identify the difference between budgeted and actual variable costs). A variance also arises if the number of units of product made differs from planned production. The reason for this is that fixed overhead is applied to production using a predetermined application rate (see Exhibit 12–4) based on planned activity. If actual activity is different, the amount of fixed overhead applied to production will be different from that planned to be applied. This variance is called a **volume variance.**

It is not appropriate to make any per unit fixed overhead variance calculations because fixed costs do not behave on a per unit basis.

To illustrate the calculation of fixed overhead variances, we return to the production of SeaCruiser sailboats by Cruisers, Inc. The predetermined fixed overhead application rate shown in the standard cost calculation on page 516 is $10.80 per direct labor hour. To recap from Chapter 12, this rate would have been determined as follows:

Total estimated (budgeted) fixed manufacturing overhead for the year	$3,240,000
Total estimated (budgeted) direct labor hours for the year (1,250 sailboats @ 240 hours each)	300,000 hours
Predetermined fixed overhead application rate ($3,240,000/300,000 hours)	$10.80/direct labor hour

Now assume that the actual fixed manufacturing overhead for the year totaled $3,327,500, and that the actual level of production was 1,288 sailboats. The standard direct labor hours allowed for actual production during the year would be 309,120 hours (1,288 actual sailboats × 240 standard hours allowed per sailboat). The fixed manufacturing overhead account would appear as follows:

Fixed Manufacturing Overhead

Actual costs incurred	3,327,500	Fixed manufacturing overhead *applied* to production (309,120 direct labor hours × $10.80/direct labor hr.)	3,338,496
		Balance (overapplied overhead)	$10,996

The overapplied overhead is made up of a budget variance and a volume variance, as follows:

Budget variance:		
Budgeted fixed manufacturing overhead...........		$3,240,000
Actual fixed manufacturing overhead.............		3,327,500
Budget variance		$ 87,500 U
Volume variance:		
Budgeted direct labor hours for year.............	300,000 hrs.	
Standard direct labor hours allowed for actual production during year.......................	309,120 hrs.	
Excess of standard hours allowed for volume of production actually achieved over estimated hours ..	9,120 hrs.	
Predetermined fixed overhead application rate.......	× $10.80/hr.	
Volume variance...........................		98,496 F
Net variance (overapplied overhead)		$ 10,996 F

This is another situation in which the net variance is small, but it results from larger offsetting variances that may deserve investigation.

The above illustration uses annual data; in practice, the analysis is likely to be made monthly or with a frequency that leads to the most effective control of fixed overhead. As stated earlier, by its very nature, fixed overhead is difficult to control on a short-term basis. Yet, for many firms, it has become a significant cost that may be greater than all of the variable costs combined, so it does receive much management attention.

WHAT DOES IT MEAN?

7. What does it mean to state that the analysis of fixed manufacturing overhead variance is not likely to be done with the same frequency as the analysis of variable cost variances?

Accounting for Variances

Objective 7
Understand the alternative methods of accounting for variances.

Some interesting issues arise in connection with the accounting for variances. Usually, if the net total of all of the favorable and unfavorable variances is not significant relative to the total of all production costs incurred during the period, the net variance will be included with cost of goods sold in the income statement. Since standard costs were used in valuing inventories during the period, standard costs were also released to cost of goods sold; classifying the net variance with this amount has the effect of reporting cost of goods sold at the actual cost of making those items. If the net variance is significant relative to total production costs, it may be allocated between inventories and cost of goods sold in proportion to the standard costs included in these accounts. On the other hand, if the standards represent currently attainable targets, then a net unfavorable variance can be interpreted as the cost of production inefficiencies that should be recognized as a cost of the current period. If this is the case, none of the net variance should be assigned to inventory because doing so results in postponing the income statement recognition of the inefficiencies until the product is sold. A net variance that is favorable would indicate that the standards were too loose, and so it would be appropriate to allocate the variance between inventory and cost of goods sold. In any event, the financial statements and explanatory notes are not likely to contain any reference to the standard cost system or accounting for variances because disclosures about these details of the accounting system do not increase the usefulness of the statements as a whole.

Summary

A standard cost is a unit budget for a component of a product or service. As such, standards are used like any budget in planning and controlling. Standards can also facilitate the calculation of product costs for inventory valuation purposes.

Because a standard is a unit budget, it can be used in the process of building the various component budgets of the operating budget. Standards also provide a benchmark for evaluating performance. Standards are usually expressed in monetary terms ($/unit) but can also be useful when expressed in physical quantities (lbs./unit).

Standards are usually established on the basis of engineering studies and should be attainable. Ideal standards and past experience standards are less useful because they are not likely to serve as positive motivators.

The standard cost for a product is the sum of the standard costs for raw materials, direct labor, and manufacturing overhead used in making the product. A fixed manufacturing overhead standard is a unitized fixed expense and therefore must be used carefully because fixed expenses do not behave on a per unit basis.

Standards are useful for the entire range of planning and control activities; they are not restricted to use in product costing. Thus, many service organizations and manufacturing firms have developed standards for period costs. Standards can also be developed for qualitative goals that may not be expressed in financial terms.

Variances from standard can be caused by a difference between standard and actual quantity, and by a difference between standard and actual costs per unit of input. Variance analysis breaks the total variance into the amounts caused by each difference. This is done because different managers are responsible for each component of the total variance. The objective of reporting variances is to have the appropriate manager take action to eliminate unfavorable variances and to capture favorable variances. Communication between managers is essential to achieve this objective.

Variances can be labeled in many ways, but a generally used classification is the following:

	Variance Due to Difference between Standard and Actual	
Input	*Quantity*	*Cost per Unit of Input*
Raw materials	Usage	Price
Direct labor	Efficiency	Rate
Variable overhead	Efficiency	Spending

Quantity variances for raw materials and direct labor are frequently expressed by quantity as well as dollar amount because the manager responsible for controlling the variance usually thinks in quantity terms.

Fixed manufacturing overhead variances are analyzed differently from variable cost variances because of the cost behavior pattern difference. The fixed overhead budget variance is the difference between total budgeted and total actual fixed overhead. The fixed overhead volume variance arises because the actual level of activity differed from that used in calculating the fixed overhead application rate.

In most standard cost systems, standard costs are recorded in work in process inventory and finished goods inventory. Variances are usually taken directly to the income statement in the fiscal period in which they arise as an adjustment of cost of goods sold.

Key Terms and Concepts

attainable standard (p. 515)   A standard cost or production standard that is achievable under actual operating conditions.

budget variance (p. 518)   The difference between budgeted amount and actual amount.

cost per unit of input variance (p. 518)   That part of a variable cost budget variance due to a difference between the standard and actual cost per unit of input. See also *raw materials price variance, direct labor rate variance,* and *variable overhead spending variance.*

direct labor efficiency variance (p. 519)   That part of the direct labor budget variance due to the difference between actual hours required and standard hours allowed for the work done.

direct labor rate variance (p. 519)   That part of the direct labor budget variance due to the difference between the actual hourly wage rate paid and the standard rate.

ideal standard (p. 515)   A standard cost or a production standard that assumes ideal operating conditions and maximum efficiency at all times.

past experience standard (p. 515)   A standard cost or production standard that is based on historical data.

quantity variance (p. 518)   That part of a variable cost budget variance due to a difference between the standard and actual quantity of inputs. See also *raw materials usage variance, direct labor efficiency variance,* and *variable overhead efficiency variance.*

raw materials price variance (p. 520)   That part of the raw materials budget variance due to the difference between standard cost and actual cost of raw materials *used.*

raw materials purchase price variance (p. 523)   That part of the raw materials budget variance due to the difference between standard cost and actual cost of raw materials *purchased.*

raw materials usage variance (p. 520)   That part of the raw materials budget variance due to the difference between standard usage and actual usage of raw materials.

standard cost (p. 513)   A unit budget allowance for a cost component of a product or an activity.

variable overhead efficiency variance (p. 520)   That part of the variable overhead budget variance due to the difference between actual hours required and standard hours allowed for the work done.

variable overhead spending variance (p. 520)   That part of the variable overhead budget variance due to the difference between actual variable overhead cost and the standard cost allowed for the actual inputs used (based on direct labor hours, for example).

volume variance (p. 524)   A fixed manufacturing overhead variance caused by actual activity being different from the estimated activity used in calculating the predetermined overhead application rate.

WHAT DOES IT MEAN?
ANSWERS

1. It means that a budgeted unit cost for material, labor, and overhead is developed to facilitate the determination of a product or process cost and for use in the planning and control activities of the firm.

2. It means that barring unusual circumstances, workers should be able to acquire and use materials, perform direct labor, and support the manufacturing process at the standard.

3. It means that more than the standard amount of raw material allowed was used for the production achieved.

4. It means that the variance associated with each cost element—rate paid and hours used—is determined and reported to the individuals who are responsible for rate paid and hours used.

5. It means that the variance may have resulted from an undesirable activity, such as purposely not putting enough ingredients into a batch, that could adversely affect the quality of the product.

6. It means that responsible managers don't operate in a vacuum and that their control activities have to be coordinated to achieve optimum results.

7. It means that because costs are fixed, this type of overhead is difficult to control on a short-term—e.g., by shift or by week—basis. But because fixed costs are becoming increasingly significant to many firms, they are likely to receive a lot of attention.

Exercises and Problems

LO 1, 2   **15–1.**   **Developing direct labor cost standards.** Wood Turning Co. makes decorative candle pedestals. An industrial engineer consultant developed ideal time standards for one unit of the model 2C pedestal. The standards are given below, along with the cost accountant's determination of current labor pay rates:

Worktype 1	.15 hours @ $12.30 per hour
Worktype 2	.30 hours @ $10.90 per hour
Worktype 3	.60 hours @ $19.50 per hour

Required:

    a. Using the above data, calculate the direct labor cost for a model 2C pedestal.

    b. Would it be appropriate to use the cost calculated in part *a* as a standard cost for evaluating direct labor performance and valuing inventory? Explain your answer.

LO 1, 2   **15–2.**   **Developing raw material cost standards.** Natway Manufacturing Co. manufactures and sells household cleaning products. The company's research department has developed a new cleaner for which a standard cost must be determined. The new cleaner is made by mixing 11 quarts of triphate solution and 4 pounds of sobase granules and boiling the mixture for several minutes. After the solution has cooled, 2 ounces of methage are added. This "recipe" produces 10 quarts of the cleaner, which is then packaged in one-quart plastic dispenser bottles. Raw material costs are:

Triphate solution	$ .30 per quart
Sobase granules	.74 per pound
Methage	1.20 per ounce
Bottle	.12 each

Required:

    a. Using the above data, calculate the raw material cost for one bottle of the new cleaner.

    b. Assume that the above costs are the current best estimates of the costs at which required quantities of the raw materials can be purchased. Would you recommend that any other factors be considered in establishing the raw material cost standard for the new cleaner?

    c. Explain the process that would be used to develop the direct labor cost standard for the new product.

LO 2, 3   **15–3.**   **Standard absorption cost per unit.** Starchy Co. processes corn into corn starch and corn syrup. The company's productivity and cost standards follow:

    From every bushel of corn processed, 12 pounds of starch and 3 pounds of syrup should be produced.

    Standard direct labor and variable overhead totals $.42 per bushel of corn processed.

    Standard fixed overhead (the predetermined fixed overhead application rate) is $.35 per bushel processed.

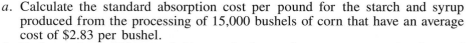

Required:

a. Calculate the standard absorption cost per pound for the starch and syrup produced from the processing of 15,000 bushels of corn that have an average cost of $2.83 per bushel.

b. Evaluate the usefulness of this standard cost for management planning and control purposes.

LO 2, 3   **15–4.   Standard absorption cost per unit.** A cost analyst for Stamper Manufacturing Co. has assembled the following data about the Model 24 stamp pad:

The piece of sheet metal from which eight pad cases can be made costs $.14. This amount is based on the number of sheets in a 3,000-pound bundle of sheet metal, which is the usual purchase quantity.

The foam pad that is put in the case costs $.02, based on the number of pads that can be cut from a large roll of foam.

Production standards, based on an engineering analysis recognizing attainable performance, provide for the manufacture of 1,800 pads by two workers in an eight-hour shift. The standard direct labor pay rate is $11 per hour.

Manufacturing overhead is applied to units produced using a predetermined overhead application rate of $16 per direct labor hour of which $7 per hour is fixed manufacturing overhead.

Required:

a. Calculate the standard absorption cost of a package of 12 stamp pads.

b. Stamper Manufacturing Co.'s management is considering a special promotion that would result in increased sales of 2,000 packages of 12 pads per package. Calculate the cost per package that is relevant for this analysis.

LO 3, 4, 5   **15–5.   Calculate variable cost variances—explain results.** The standards for one case of Springfever Tonic are:

Direct materials...............	4 lbs. @ $ 5.00/lb. = $20
Direct labor..................	3 hrs. @ $13.00/hr. = 39
Variable overhead (based on direct labor hours)	3 hrs. @ $ 6.00/hr. = 18

During the week ended April 25, the following activity took place:

7,400 lbs. of raw materials were purchased for inventory at a cost of $4.95 per pound.

2,000 cases of finished product were produced, and:

8,300 lbs. of raw material were used.

5,800 direct labor hours were worked at a total cost of $78,300.

$35,670 of actual variable overhead costs were incurred.

Required:

Calculate each of the following variances, and provide plausible explanations for the results:

a. Price variance for raw materials purchased.

b. Raw materials usage variance.

    c. Direct labor rate variance.
    d. Direct labor efficiency variance.
    e. Variable overhead spending variance.
    f. Variable overhead efficiency variance.

LO 3, 4, 5   **15–6.** **Calculate variable cost variances—explain results.** The standards for one case of Brightlites are:

Direct materials	5 lbs. @ $ 6.80/lb.
Direct labor	2.4 hrs. @ $14.00/hr.
Variable overhead (based on machine hours)	1.5 hrs. @ $ 4.50/hr.

During the week ended May 30, the following activity took place:

    2,910 machine hours were worked.

    11,400 lbs. of raw material were purchased for inventory at a total cost of $80,940.

    1,900 cases of finished product were produced, and:

        9,260 lbs. of raw material were used.

        4,420 labor hours were worked at an average rate of $14.35 per hour.

        $12,513 actual variable overhead costs were incurred.

Required:
Calculate each of the following variances, and provide plausible explanations for the results:
    a. Price variance for raw materials purchased.
    b. Raw materials usage variance.
    c. Direct labor rate variance.
    d. Direct labor efficiency variance.
    e. Variable overhead spending variance.
    f. Variable overhead efficiency variance.

LO 3, 4, 5   **15–7.** **Direct labor variances—solving for unknowns.** Goodwrench's Garage uses standards to plan and control labor time and expense. The standard time for an engine tune-up is 3.5 hours, and the standard labor rate is $15 per hour. Last week, 24 tune-ups were completed. The labor efficiency variance was six hours unfavorable, and the labor rate variance totaled $81 favorable.

Required:
    a. Calculate the actual direct labor hourly rate paid for tune-up work last week.
    b. Calculate the dollar amount of the labor efficiency variance.
    c. What is the most likely explanation for these two variances? Is this a good trade-off for the management of the garage to make? Explain your answer.

LO 3, 4, 5   **15–8.** **Direct labor variances—solving for unknowns.** Molk Industries has established direct labor performance standards for its maintenance and repair shop. However, some of the labor records were destroyed during a recent fire. The actual hours worked during August were 2,500, and the total direct labor budget variance was $1,300 unfavorable. The standard labor rate was $16 per hour, but a recent labor strike allowed the firm to hire lower-paid replacement workers for some jobs, and this produced a favorable rate variance of $3,500 for August.

Required:

a. Calculate the actual direct labor rate paid per hour during August.

b. Calculate the dollar amount of the direct labor efficiency variance for August.

c. Calculate the standard direct labor hours allowed for the actual level of activity during August. *(Hint: Use the formula for the quantity variance and solve for the missing information.)*

LO 3, 4, 5   **15–9.   Direct material variances—solving for unknowns.** Dutko, Inc., manufactures end tables, armchairs, and other wood furniture products from high-quality materials. The company uses a standard costing system and isolates variances as soon as possible. The purchasing manager is responsible for controlling direct material price variances, and production managers are responsible for controlling usage variances. During November, the following results were reported for the production of American Oak armchairs:

Units produced	1,500 armchairs
Direct materials purchased	19,000 board feet
Direct materials issued into production	17,200 board feet
Standard cost per unit (12 board feet × $8)	$96 per unit produced
Purchase price variance	$2,850 unfavorable

Required:

a. Calculate the actual price paid per board foot purchased.

b. Calculate the standard quantity of materials allowed (in board feet) for the number of units produced.

c. Calculate the direct materials usage variance.

d. What is the most likely explanation for the price and usage variances? Is this a good trade-off for management of Dutko, Inc., to make? Explain your answer.

LO 3, 4, 5   **15–10.   Direct material variances—the price versus usage trade-off.** Hosh, Inc., manufactures quality replacement parts for the auto industry. The company uses a standard costing system and isolates variances as soon as possible. The purchasing manager is responsible for controlling the direct material price variances for hundreds of raw material items that are used in the company's various production processes. Recent experience indicates that, in the aggregate, direct material price variances have been favorable. However, several problems have occurred. Direct material usage variances have become consistently unfavorable for many items, and the company's total budget variance for direct materials has been unfavorable during each of the past six months. Direct laborers have complained about the quality of certain raw material items, and major customers have cancelled purchase orders. In the meantime, the company's raw materials inventory has increased by nearly 300%.

Required:

a. Give a probable explanation of why these results have occurred. *(Hint: What might the purchasing manager be doing that is dysfunctional for the company as a whole?)*

b. How could the performance reporting system be improved to encourage more appropriate behavior on the part of the purchasing manager?

LO 4, 5   **15–11.   Performance reporting and flexible budgeting.** Presented below is a partially completed performance report for a recent week for direct labor for the binding department of a book publisher.

	Original Budget	Flexed Budget	Actual	Budget Variance
Direct labor	$1,800		$1,888	

The original budget is based on the expectation that 3,000 books would be bound; the standard is 20 books per hour at a pay rate of $12 per hour. During the week, 2,860 books were actually bound. Employees worked 160 hours at an actual total cost of $1,888.

Required:

a. Calculate the flexed budget amount against which actual performance should be evaluated and then calculate the budget variance.

b. Calculate the direct labor efficiency variance in terms of hours.

c. Calculate the direct labor rate variance.

LO 4, 5   **15–12.   Performance reporting and flexible budgeting.** For the stamping department of a manufacturing firm, the standard cost for direct labor is $12 per hour, and the production standard calls for 2,000 stampings per hour. During February, 121 hours were required for actual production of 230,000 stampings. Actual direct labor cost for the stamping department for February was $1,573.

Required:

a. Complete the following performance report for February:

	Flexed Budget	Actual	Budget Variance
Direct labor			

b. Analyze the budget variance by calculating the direct labor efficiency and rate variances for February.

c. What alternatives to the above monthly report could result in improved control over the stamping department's direct labor?

LO 1   **15–13.   Frequency of performance reporting.** If a company uses a standard cost system, should all variances be calculated with the same frequency (e.g., monthly) and should they always be expressed in dollar amounts? Explain your answer and include in it the reason for calculating variances.

LO 1, 5   **15–14.   Rank the importance of eight variances.** Assume that you are the production manager of a small branch plant of a large manufacturing firm. The central accounting control department sends you monthly performance reports showing the flexed budget amount, actual cost and variances for raw materials, direct labor, variable overhead (which is expressed on a direct labor-hour basis), and fixed overhead. The variable cost budget variances are separated into quantity and cost per unit of input variances, and the fixed overhead budget and volume variances are shown. All variances are expressed in dollars.

Required:

a. Rank the eight variances in descending order of their usefulness to you for planning and controlling purposes. Explain your ranking.

b. Given the usefulness ranking in part *a,* explain how the frequency of reporting and the units in which each variance is reported might make the performance reports more useful.

LO 1, 2, 3   **15–15.**   **Evaluate the effects of erroneous standards.** During the year ended May 31, 1999, Teller Register Co. reported favorable raw material usage and direct labor and variable overhead efficiency variances that totaled $285,800. Price and rate variances were negligible. Total standard cost of goods produced during the year was $1,905,340.

Required:

a. Comment about the effectiveness of the company's standards for controlling material and labor usage.

b. If standard costs are used for valuing finished goods inventory, will the ending inventory valuation be higher or lower than if actual costs were used? Explain your answer.

c. Assume that the ending inventory of finished goods valued at standard cost is $158,780. Calculate the adjustment to finished goods inventory that would be appropriate because of the erroneous standards.

LO 3, 7   **15–16.**   **Using standard costs to record inventory transactions.** York Co. uses a standard cost system. When raw materials are purchased, the standard cost of the raw materials purchased is recorded as an increase in the Raw Materials Inventory account. When raw materials are used, the standard cost of the materials allowed for the units produced is recorded as an increase in the Work in Process Inventory account. Likewise, the standard cost of direct labor and variable manufacturing overhead is recorded as an increase in Work in Process Inventory.

Required:

a. Explain where in the financial statements the difference between the actual and standard cost of raw materials purchased will be recorded.

b. In the above system, under what circumstances will the increases and decreases in the Finished Goods Inventory account (due to production and sales, respectively) represent the actual cost of products made and sold?

c. How does the accounting for overapplied or underapplied overhead, originally discussed in Chapter 12, differ from York Co.'s cost accounting system?

LO 2, 5   **15–17.**   **Direct labor variances—insurance company application.** The Duncan Insurance Company developed standard times for processing claims. When a claim was received at the processing center, it was first reviewed and classified as simple or complex. The standard time for processing was:

Simple claim	45 minutes
Complex claim	2.5 hours

Employees were expected to be productive 7.5 hours per day. Compensation costs were $90 per day per employee. During April, which had 20 working days, the following number of claims were processed:

Simple claims	3,000 processed
Complex claims	600 processed

Required:

a. Calculate the number of workers that should have been available to process April claims.

b. Assume that 27 workers were actually available throughout the month of April. Calculate a labor efficiency variance, expressed as both a number of workers and a dollar amount for the month.

LO 1, 2   **15–18.   Direct labor variances—banking application.** LaSalle State Bank developed a standard for teller staffing that provided for one teller to handle 12 customers per hour. During June, the bank averaged 50 customers per hour and had five tellers on duty at all times. (Relief tellers filled in during lunch and rest breaks.) The teller compensation cost is $12 per hour. The bank is open eight hours a day, and there were 21 working days during June.

Required:

a. Calculate the teller efficiency variance during June expressed in terms of number of tellers and cost per hour.

b. Now assume that during June, during the 11:00 A.M. to 1:00 P.M. period every day, the bank served an average of 80 customers per hour. During the other six hours of the day, an average of 40 customers per hour were served.

1. Calculate a teller efficiency variance for the 11:00 to 1:00 period expressed in terms of number of tellers per hour and total cost for the month.

2. Calculate a teller efficiency variance for the other six hours of the day expressed in terms of number of tellers per hour and total cost for the month.

3. As teller supervisor, explain the significance of the variances calculated in 1 and 2 above, and explain how you might respond to the uneven work flow during each day.

LO 2, 3, 6   **15–19.   Fixed overhead variances—various issues.** Revco's production budget for October called for making 40,000 units of a single product. The firm's production standards allow one-half of a machine hour per unit produced. The fixed overhead budget for October was $36,000. Revco uses an absorption costing system. Actual activity and costs for October were:

Units produced	39,000
Fixed overhead costs incurred	$37,000

Required:

a. Calculate the predetermined fixed overhead application rate that would be used in October.

b. Calculate the number of machine hours that would be allowed for actual October production.

c. Calculate the fixed overhead applied to work in process during October.

d. Calculate the over- or underapplied fixed overhead for October.

e. Calculate the fixed overhead budget and volume variances for October.

LO 2, 3, 5, 6   **15–20.   Variable and fixed overhead variances—various issues.** Presented below are the original overhead budget and the actual costs incurred during April for Compo, Inc. Compo's managers relate overhead to direct labor hours for planning, control, and product costing purposes. The original budget is based on budgeted production of 15,000 units in 5,000 standard direct labor hours. Actual production of 16,200 units required 5,600 actual direct labor hours.

	Original Budget	*Actual Costs*
Variable overhead	$21,000	$23,600
Fixed overhead	32,000	33,200

Required:

a. Calculate the flexed budget allowances for variable and fixed overhead for April.

b. Calculate the direct labor efficiency variance for April expressed in terms of direct labor hours.

c. Calculate the predetermined overhead application rate for both variable and fixed overhead for April.

d. Calculate the fixed and variable overhead applied to production during April if overhead is applied on the basis of standard hours allowed for actual production achieved.

e. Calculate the fixed overhead budget and volume variances for April.

f. Calculate the over- or underapplied fixed overhead for April.

Capital Budgeting

Capital budgeting is the process of analyzing proposed capital expenditures—investments in plant, equipment, new products, and so on—to determine whether or not the proposed investment will generate, over time, a large enough return on investment (ROI) to contribute to the organization's overall ROI objectives.

Objective 1
Understand the attributes of capital budgeting that make it significantly different from operational budgeting.

Capital budgeting differs from operational budgeting in the time frame being considered. Whereas capital budgeting concerns investments and returns that are spread over a number of years, operational budgeting involves planning for a period that is usually not longer than one year. (Even in multiyear operational budgeting, there is an opportunity to rebudget for periods beyond the current year.) Thus, the operating budget reflects the firm's strategic plans to achieve current period profitability, and the capital budget provides an overall blueprint to help the firm meet its long-term growth objectives.

Capital budgeting is an activity that involves most of the functional areas of the organization. The managerial accountant may make the mathematical calculations, but the departments affected by the proposed capital expenditure will normally have significant input to the capital budgeting process.

Learning Objectives

After studying this chapter, you should understand:

1 The attributes of capital budgeting that make it a significantly different activity from operational budgeting.

2 Why present value analysis is appropriate in capital budgeting.

3 The concept of cost of capital and why it is used in capital budgeting.

4 How the net present value technique is used.

5 Why the present value ratio is used to assign a profitability ranking to alternative capital expenditure projects.

6 How the internal rate of return technique differs from the net present value approach of evaluating capital expenditure projects.

7 How issues concerning estimates, income taxes, and the timing of cash flows and investments are treated in the capital budgeting process.

8 How the payback period of a capital expenditure project is calculated.

9 Why the accounting rate of return of a project is calculated and how it can be used most appropriately.

10 Why not all management decisions are made strictly on the basis of quantitative analysis techniques.

Investment Analysis

Investment Decision Special Considerations

Objective 2
Understand why present value analysis is appropriate in capital budgeting.

Investment decisions involve committing financial resources now in anticipation of a return that will be realized over an extended period of time. This extended time frame, which can be many years, adds complexity to the analysis of whether or not to make the investment because of compound interest/present value considerations. The time value of money can be ignored for most operating expenditure decisions because the benefit of an expenditure will be received soon after the expenditure is made, and a simple benefit/cost relationship can be determined. This is not so for capital expenditures because the benefits of the expenditure will be received over several years, and $100 of benefit to be received five years from now is not the same as $100 of benefit to be received one year from now.

The concept of present value was explained in Chapter 6 (see Business in Practice—Present Value on pages 196–203). It would be appropriate for you to review that explanation now unless you have a full understanding of present value techniques.

Most business firms and other organizations have more investment opportunities than resources available for investment. Capital budgeting procedures, especially those applying present value analysis techniques, are useful in helping management identify the alternatives that will contribute most to the future profitability of the firm. However, as is the case with most quantitative techniques, the quantitative "answer" will not necessarily dictate management's decision. The quantitative result will be considered along with qualitative factors in the decision-making process. Examples of qualitative factors include the willingness to assume competitive risks associated with expanding (or not expanding) into a new market area, the implications for keeping control of a board of directors if more stock must be sold to raise funds for the expansion, and of course, top management's personal goals for the organization. Because capital budgeting involves projections into the future, top management attitudes about the risk of forecasting errors have a major impact on investment decisions.

Most firms involve the board of directors in capital budgeting by having the board approve all capital expenditures above a minimum amount. Depending on the company and its financial circumstances, this amount may range from $5,000 to $1 million or more. High-level approval is required because the capital expenditure represents a major commitment of company resources, and it involves a multiyear period of time.

WHAT DOES IT MEAN?

Objective 3
Understand the concept of cost of capital and why it is used in capital budgeting.

1. What does it mean to have a capital budget?

Cost of Capital

The principal financial objective of a firm organized for profit is to earn a return on the assets invested that will permit payment of all borrowing costs (interest) and provide the owners a return on their investment (ROE—return on equity) that compensates them fairly for the financial risks being taken. To meet the requirements of these resource providers, whose claims are shown on the right-hand side of the balance sheet, attention must be focused on the assets that are reported on the left-hand side of the balance sheet. Thus, return on assets (ROI—return on investment) becomes a primary concern of financial managers who evaluate proposed capital expenditures.

The **cost of capital** is the rate of return on assets that must be earned to permit the firm to meet its interest obligations and provide the expected return to owners. Determining the cost of capital of a company is a complex process that is beyond the scope of this text. Suffice it to say here that cost of capital is a composite of borrowing costs and stockholder dividend and earnings' growth rate expectations. The cost of capital is most useful as a "worry point" guide to management (i.e., an indication of an approximate *minimum* ROI that creditors and owners are expecting). Most firms set a cost of capital rate for investment analysis purposes that is somewhat greater than the "true" economic cost of acquiring funds. This allows for estimation errors in the calculation and provides some cushion for estimation errors in the data used in the investment analysis itself. The cost of capital used for analyzing proposed capital expenditures is also influenced by the perceived riskiness of the proposal being evaluated. More risky proposals (e.g., new product development or expansion into a new activity) will be required to earn a higher rate of return than less risky proposals (e.g., equipment replacement or expansion of an existing activity). This risk difference is related to the uncertainties associated with operating in a somewhat different environment than that in which the firm is experienced.

The cost of capital is the *discount rate* (i.e., the interest rate at which future period **cash flows** are discounted) used to determine the present value of the investment proposal being analyzed. For most firms, the cost of capital is probably in the range of 10 to 20%. In the capital budgeting illustrations presented in this chapter, the cost of capital will be a given. However, you should recognize that in practice the development of the cost of capital rate is both complex and time-consuming.

Capital Budgeting Techniques

Of the four generally recognized capital budgeting techniques, two use present value analysis, and two do not. Because money does have value over time, the two methods that recognize this fact are clearly superior, at least conceptually, to those that ignore the time value of money. The methods are:

Methods that use present value analysis:
   Net present value (NPV) method.
   Internal rate of return (IRR) method.

Methods that do not use present value analysis:
> Payback method.
> Accounting rate of return method.

Each of these methods uses the amount to be invested in the capital project. The **net present value, internal rate of return,** and **payback methods** use the amount of *cash* generated by the investment each year. The **accounting rate of return method** uses accrual accounting net income resulting from the investment. For most investment projects, the difference between the cash generated each year and accrual accounting net income is depreciation expense—a noncash item that reduces accrual accounting net income. Again, because of their recognition of the time value of money and focus on cash flows, the NPV and IRR methods are much more appropriate than either payback or accounting rate of return.

Net Present Value

Objective 4
Understand how the net present value technique is used.

The net present value method involves calculating the present value of the expected cash flows from the project using the cost of capital as the discount rate, and comparing the total present value of the cash flows to the amount of investment required.

Based on this analysis, the following conclusions can be drawn:

If the present value of expected cash flows is: then →	*The net present value (NPV) is:* and →	*The expected rate of return on the project is:*
Greater than the required investment	Positive	Greater than the cost of capital
Less than the required investment	Negative	Less than the cost of capital
Equal to the required investment	Zero	Equal to the cost of capital

Accordingly, the discount rate used in net present value analysis is sometimes referred to as the *hurdle rate* because it represents the minimum rate of return required for an investment to yield a positive NPV. The net present value method is illustrated in Exhibit 16–1.

Objective 5
Understand why the present value ratio is used to assign a profitability ranking to alternative capital expenditure projects.

When alternative projects involving different investment amounts are being considered, the NPV approach must be carried one step further. Projects should not be assigned a profitability ranking on the basis of the dollar amount of the net present value because of disparities in the investment amounts. The ratio of the present value of the cash flows to the investment, referred to as the **present value ratio** (or **profitability index**), provides a more appropriate ranking mechanism. For example, assume the following data for the projects indicated:

Project	*Present Value of Cash Flows*	*Investment*	*Net Present Value*	*Present Value Ratio*
A	$ 22,800	$ 20,000	$2,800	1.14
B	104,000	100,000	4,000	1.04

EXHIBIT 16–1   Net Present Value (NPV) Analysis of a Proposed Investment

I. Assumptions:

A. A new packaging machine costing $100,000 installed has an estimated useful life of five years and an estimated salvage value of $6,000 after five years. The new machine will be purchased at the end of 1998.

B. Installation and use of the machine in the firm's operations will result in labor savings during each of the next five years as follows:

1999	$26,000
2000	27,000
2001	31,000
2002	35,000
2003	38,000

C. The firm's cost of capital is 16%.

II. Time-Line Presentation of Cash Flows from the Investment:

	12/31/98	1999	2000	2001	2002	2003
Cash flows from investment:						
Savings		$26,000	$27,000	$31,000	$35,000	$38,000
Salvage						6,000
Total		$26,000	$27,000	$31,000	$35,000	$44,000

III. Net Present Value Calculation at 16%:

	12/31/98	1999	2000	2001	2002	2003
Present value factors (Table 6–2, 16%)		0.8621	0.7432	0.6407	0.5523	0.4761
Present value of cash flows from investment		$22,415	$20,066	$19,862	$19,331	$20,948

Total present value of cash flows from investment	$102,622
Investment	(100,000)
Net present value at 16%	$ 2,622

IV. Conclusion from Analysis:

The net present value is positive; therefore the projected rate of return on this investment is greater than the 16% cost of capital. Based on this quantitative analysis, the investment should be made.

Even though project B has a greater net present value, it is clear from looking at the present value ratios that project A has a higher rate of return and is thus a more desirable investment. When the NPV approach to investment analysis is used, it is appropriate to take this second step and calculate the present value ratio, especially when a selection must be made from several positive NPV projects.

WHAT DOES IT MEAN?

2. What does it mean to state that present value analysis is appropriate for capital budgeting?

3. What does it mean to calculate the net present value of a proposed capital investment?

4. What does it mean if the net present value of a proposed capital expenditure is positive?

Internal Rate of Return

The difference between the NPV and IRR methods is that the discount (interest) rate—the cost of capital—is a given in the NPV approach, whereas the IRR approach solves for the actual rate of return that will be earned by the proposed investment. This is the discount rate at which the present value of cash flows from the project will equal the investment (i.e., the discount rate at which the NPV equals zero). Thus, the IRR method may require several calculations using different discount rates. Once the project's internal rate of return is known, a conclusion about the suitability of the investment is made by comparing the IRR to the cost of capital. If the IRR is greater than the cost of capital, the investment will be recommended. If the IRR is less than the cost of capital, the investment will not be recommended.

With respect to the investment proposal illustrated in Exhibit 16–1, the IRR must be greater than 16% because the NPV is positive. Determination of the actual IRR requires another set of present value calculations using a higher discount rate (18% is the next higher rate in the Chapter 6 tables) and then **interpolating** to determine the actual discount rate at which the present value of cash flows would equal the investment. The IRR method is illustrated in Exhibit 16–2.

There are some theoretical advantages to the NPV approach to evaluate proposed capital expenditures, but many managers use both approaches because they are more comfortable knowing the actual rate of return. Computer programs make the calculations easy; estimating the amount and timing of future cash flows associated with a proposal is the most challenging part of the process.

**WHAT
DOES IT
MEAN?**

5. What does it mean to state that the net present value calculation technique is easier to use than the internal rate of return calculation method?

Some Analytical Considerations

Estimates.   The validity of present value calculations will be a function of the accuracy with which future cash flows can be estimated. A great deal of effort will be expended in making estimates. When the project involves a replacement machine, the estimates of future cash flows (inflows from expense savings, and outflows for preventative and periodic maintenance) can be made relatively easily. When the project involves an investment in a new product or a major capacity expansion, the most important (and hardest) data to estimate are revenues. Most firms will require a **post-audit** of the project to determine whether or not the anticipated benefits are actually being realized. While it may be too late to affect a project already completed, knowledge about past estimating errors should permit analysts to improve future estimates. An understanding of the significance of various estimates on the results of the calculations can be obtained by changing the estimates. This process is a form of sensitivity analysis that helps identify the most significant estimates.

Cash Flows Far in the Future.   Given the challenges of estimating, many capital budgeting analysts will not consider probable cash flows that are

EXHIBIT 16–2   Internal Rate of Return (IRR) Analysis of a Proposed Investment

I. Assumptions:
Same as in Exhibit 16–1.
The NPV of the proposed investment at a discount rate of 16% is $2,622 (from Exhibit 16–1).

II. Time-Line Presentation of Cash Flows from the Investment:

	12/31/98	1999	2000	2001	2002	2003
Cash flows from investment:						
Savings		$26,000	$27,000	$31,000	$35,000	$38,000
Salvage						6,000
Total		$26,000	$27,000	$31,000	$35,000	$44,000

III. Net Present Value Calculation at 18%:

		1999	2000	2001	2002	2003
Present value factors (Table 6–2, 18%)		0.8475	0.7182	0.6086	0.5158	0.4371
Present value of cash flows from investment		$22,035	$19,391	$18,867	$18,053	$19,232

Total present value of cash flows from investment . . . . $ 97,578
Investment . . . . (100,000)
Net present value at 18% . . . . $ (2,422)

IV. Interpolation:

Discount rate	16%	17%	18%
Net present value	$2,622	$0	$(2,422)

The discount rate at an NPV of $0 is almost exactly 17%.

V. Conclusion from Analysis:
The internal rate of return of the project is the discount rate at which the NPV = $0, so the IRR is 17%. The expected IRR is more than the firm's 16% cost of capital. Based on this quantitative analysis, the investment should be made.

expected to occur more than 10 years in the future. In essence their position is that if the project will not have a satisfactory return considering the cash flows in the first 10 years, then the project is too risky to accept even if later cash flows will give it a satisfactory rate of return. For example, the present value of $100 to be received in 11 years, at a discount rate of 20%, is $13.46, so far-distant cash flows will not add significantly to the total present value of cash flows.

Timing of Cash Flows within the Year.   The present value factors in Tables 6–2 and 6–3 assume that all of the cash flow each year is received at the end of the year. It is more likely that the cash flows will be received fairly evenly throughout the year, and although present value can be calculated using that assumption, it is not uncommon for the end-of-the-year assumption to be used because it results in a slightly lower, more conservative present value amount.

Investment Made over a Period of Time.   Capital expenditure projects involving new products, new plants, and capacity expansion usually require expenditures to be made over a period of time. For example, payments are usually made to a building contractor every month during construction, and for a major project, construction may extend over several years. When this is going to occur, the investment amount used in the present value analysis should be determined as of the point at which the project is expected to be put into service. This means that interest on cash disbursements made during the construction or preoperating period should be considered, so the investment amount will include the time value of money invested during that period.

Income Tax Effect of Cash Flows from the Project.   The cash flows identified with a proposed capital expenditure should include all of the associated inflows and outflows, including income taxes. The model for making this calculation is essentially the same as that used in the statement of cash flows to determine cash generated from operating activities. For example, assume that a capital expenditure proposal for a new product reflects the following makeup of operating income, income taxes, and net income for the first year the product is sold:

Revenues	$240,000
Variable expenses	100,000
Contribution margin	$140,000
Direct fixed expenses:	
Requiring cash disbursements	85,000
Depreciation of equipment	20,000
Operating income	$ 35,000
Income taxes @ 40%.	14,000
Net income	$ 21,000

To calculate the amount of cash flow from this product, it is necessary to add back the depreciation expense to net income. Remember that depreciation is a deduction for income tax purposes but is not a cash expenditure. Therefore, the cash flow during the first year for this new product would be:

Net income	$21,000
Add: Depreciation expense	20,000
Cash flow from the product.	$41,000

In addition, any other differences between accrual basis earnings and cash flows would be recognized when using the NPV and IRR methods.

Working Capital Investment.   Capital expenditure proposals that involve new products or capacity expansion will usually require a working capital increase because accounts receivable and inventories will increase. The working capital increase required is treated as additional investment (i.e., it is a cash outflow at the beginning of the project, or later). If the new product or capacity expansion has a definite life, the investment in working capital will be recovered after the product is discontinued or the expansion is reversed. The expected recovery of the working capital investment should be treated as a cash inflow.

Least Cost Projects. Not all capital expenditures are made to reduce costs or increase revenues. Some expenditures required by law—environmental controls, for example—will increase operating costs. (The "benefit" may be the avoidance of a fine.) Alternative expenditures in this category should also be evaluated using present value analysis; however, instead of seeking a positive NPV or IRR, the objective is to have the lowest negative result. Even though the present value ratio will be less than 1.0, the most desirable alternative is still the one with the highest present value ratio.

Payback

Objective 8
Understand how the payback period of a capital expenditure project is calculated.

The payback method to evaluate proposed capital expenditures answers the question: How many years will it take to recover the amount of the investment? The answer to this question is determined by adding up the cash flows (beginning with the first year) until the total cash flows equal the investment and then counting the number of years of cash flow required. For example, using the data from Exhibit 16–1, for a machine costing $100,000, the projected annual and cumulative cash flows were:

Year	Cash Flow	Cumulative Cash Flow
1999 (1st year).......	$26,000	$ 26,000
2000 (2nd year)	27,000	53,000
2001 (3rd year).......	31,000	84,000
2002 (4th year).......	35,000	119,000
2003 (5th year).......	44,000	163,000

The investment will be recovered during the fourth year, after $16,000 of that year's $35,000 has been realized. Expressed as a decimal, 16/35 is 0.46, so the project's payback period would be expressed as 3.46 years.

The obvious advantage of the payback method is its simplicity. Present value analysis is confusing to some people, but anyone can understand payback period. There are two major disadvantages to the payback method. First, it does not consider the time value of money, and this is a fatal flaw. Second, as traditionally used, the payback method does not consider cash flows that continue after the investment has been recovered. Thus a project having a payback period of three years and no subsequent cash flows would appear to be more desirable than a project that has a payback period of four years and cash flows that continue for five more years.

In spite of its flaws, the payback method is used by many firms, especially in connection with equipment replacement decisions. The widespread use of the payback method is due to the clarity of its meaning and the fact that in a rapidly changing technological environment, the speed with which an investment is recovered is critical. Many firms require early and significant cash flows from an investment in new plant and equipment because they don't have the financial capacity to finance their activities while waiting for the payoff from an investment to begin. Some analysts report the payback period along with NPV (or present value ratio) and IRR just to answer the question, "How long until the investment is recovered?"

Accounting Rate of Return

Objective 9
Understand why the accounting rate of return is calculated and how it can be used most appropriately.

The accounting rate of return method focuses on the impact of the investment project on the financial statements. Accounting operating income (or net income) is related to the effect of the investment on the balance sheet. This is done on a year-by-year basis. The calculation for 1999, using data from Exhibit 16–1, is illustrated in Exhibit 16–3.

The fatal flaw of the accounting rate of return approach is that the time value of money is not considered. Some financial managers will make the accounting rate of return calculation, not for investment evaluation purposes, but to anticipate the effect that the investment will have on the financial statements. Large start-up costs for a new product line or new production facility may adversely affect reported results for a year or two. Management should be aware of this and should put stockholders on notice in advance in order to minimize the impact of the start-up costs on the market price of the firm's common stock.

EXHIBIT 16–3   Accounting Rate of Return Analysis of a Proposed Investment

I. Assumptions:
   Same as in Exhibit 16–1.

II. Calculation:

$$\frac{\text{Accounting}}{\text{rate of return}} = \frac{\text{Operating income}}{\text{Average investment}}$$

$$= \frac{\text{Savings} - \text{Depreciation expense}}{\text{Average investment}}$$

For 1999:

$$= \frac{26{,}000 - 18{,}800^*}{(100{,}000 + 81{,}200^\dagger)/2}$$

$$= \frac{7{,}200}{90{,}600}$$

$$= 7.9\%$$

*Straight-line depreciation expense:

(Cost − Salvage value)/Estimated life
(100,000 − 6,000)/5 years = 18,800

†Net book value at end of 1999:

Cost − Accumulated depreciation
100,000 − 18,800 = 81,200

6. What does it mean to state that both the payback method and accounting rate of return method are flawed because they do not recognize the time value of money?

The Investment Decision

Objective 10
Understand why not all management decisions are made strictly on the basis of quantitative analysis techniques.

As is the case with virtually every management decision, both quantitative and qualitative factors are considered. After the results of the quantitative models just illustrated have been obtained, the project with the highest NPV or IRR may not be selected. Overriding qualitative factors could include the following:

- Commitment to a segment of the business that requires capital investment to achieve or regain competitiveness even though that segment does not have as great an ROI as others.
- Regulations that mandate investment to meet safety, environmental, or access requirements. Fines and other enforcement incentives aside, management's citizenship goals for the organization may result in a high priority for these investments.
- Technological developments within the industry may require new facilities to maintain customers or market share at the cost of lower ROI for a period of time.
- The organization may have limited resources to invest in capital projects, and as a result of the capital rationing process, less ambitious, lower ROI projects may be approved instead of large-scale, higher ROI projects for which resources cannot be obtained.

In addition to considering issues such as these, management's judgments about the accuracy of the estimates used in the capital budgeting model may result in selection of projects for which the estimates are believed to be more accurate.

The important point to be remembered here is that although the use of appropriate quantitative models can significantly improve the management decision-making process, most decisions are significantly influenced by top management's values and experiences—qualitative factors. Whether the decision involves the use of time value of money calculations, cost behavior pattern information, analysis of variances, or other applications you have learned, all important managerial decisions involve uncertainty and require the use of judgment. This is one reason top managers receive top salaries—their job is at risk if they make the wrong decision.

Integration of Capital Budget with Operating Budgets

Several aspects of the capital budget interact with the development of the operating budget. Contribution margin increases and cost savings from anticipated capital expenditure projects must be built into the expenditure and income statement budgets. Cash disbursements for capital projects must be included in the cash budget. The impact of capital expenditures on the balance sheet forecast must also be considered. Most importantly, you should understand that capital budgeting expenditures impact the level at which the firm will be able to operate in future years. Investments in equipment, new plant facilities, and other long-term operational assets are necessary to support the firm's growth objectives. Thus, the development of the capital budget is an integral part of the overall budgeting and strategic planning process.

WHAT DOES IT MEAN?

7. What does it mean to integrate the capital budget into the operating budget?

Summary

Capital budgeting has a much longer-term time-frame perspective than operational budgeting. Capital expenditure analysis, which leads to the capital budget, attempts to determine the impact of a proposed capital expenditure on the organization's ROI.

Capital budgeting procedures should involve the use of present value analysis because an investment is made today in expectation of returns far into the future. The time value of money must be recognized if appropriate capital expenditure decisions are to be made.

In addition to evaluating the results of numerical analyses, decision makers consider qualitative factors related to the proposed investment. Most qualitative factors relate to the risks associated with the investment or with the numbers used to support the investment decision.

Cost of capital is the minimum ROI that should be earned on the proposed investment. The risk associated with the proposal will affect the cost of capital, or desired ROI, used to evaluate the investment.

Net present value and internal rate of return are two investment analysis methods that recognize the time value of money. The net present value approach uses the cost of capital as the discount rate to calculate a difference between the present value of future cash flows from the investment and the amount invested. If the net present value is zero or positive, the proposed investment's ROI is equal to or greater than the cost of capital, and the investment is an appropriate one to make. The present value ratio, or profitability index, provides a means to rank alternative proposals. The internal rate of return approach solves for the proposal's ROI, which is then compared to cost of capital. The investment is an appropriate one to make if the ROI of the proposed investment equals or exceeds the cost of capital.

Some analytical considerations related to capital budgeting include estimating accuracy, timing of cash flows within a year, and investments made over a period of time. Many firms require a post-audit of a capital project to evaluate the estimates made in the initial analysis. Some projects will require an increase in working capital, which is considered part of the investment.

Payback and accounting rate of return are two investment analysis methods that do not recognize the time value of money and are thus not appropriate analytical techniques. Nevertheless, many analysts and managers use the results of these methods along with the results of the NPV and IRR methods.

In addition to considering the results of the various quantitative models used to evaluate investment proposals, management also identifies and considers qualitative factors when deciding whether or not to proceed with an investment. These qualitative factors are frequently more significant than the quantitative model results.

The capital budget is integrated into the operating budget. Production capacity, depreciation expense, and cash outflows for purchases of new plant and equipment are directly affected by the capital budget.

Key Terms and Concepts

accounting rate of return method (p. 540)   A capital budgeting analytical technique that calculates the rate of return on the investment based on the financial statement impacts of the investment.

capital budgeting (p. 537)   The process of analyzing proposed investments in plant and equipment and other long-lived assets.

cash flows (p. 539)   In capital budgeting, the cash receipts and disbursements associated with a capital expenditure over its life.

cost of capital (p. 539)   The ROI that must be earned to permit the firm to meet its interest obligations and provide the owners their expected return; the discount rate used in the present value calculations of capital budgeting.

internal rate of return (IRR) method (p. 540)   A capital budgeting analytical technique that solves for the time-adjusted rate of return on an investment over its life.

interpolating (p. 542)   A mathematical term to describe the process of *interpreting* and *relating* two factors from a (present value) table to approximate a third factor not shown in the table.

net present value (NPV) method (p. 540)   A capital budgeting analytical technique that relates the present value of the returns from an investment to the present value of the investment, given a cost of capital.

payback method (p. 540)   A capital budgeting analytical technique that calculates the length of time for the cash flows from an investment to equal the investment.

post-audit (p. 542)   The process of comparing the assumptions used in a capital budgeting analysis with the actual results of the investment.

present value ratio (p. 540)   The ratio of the present value of the cash flows from an investment to the investment. See *profitability index.*

profitability index (p. 540)   The ratio of the present value of the cash flows from an investment to the investment; used for ranking proposed capital expenditures by profitability.

WHAT DOES IT MEAN?
ANSWERS

1. It means that there is a plan for making capital expenditures—i.e., investments in new plant and equipment.

2. It means that because expenditures and/or benefits are likely to extend over a period of several years, it is appropriate to recognize the time value of money when determining the economic viability of an investment.

3. It means that the present value of the future cash flows expected from the investment, discounted at an appropriate interest rate—i.e., the cost of capital—is compared to the present value of the investment—also discounted at the cost of capital if necessary because the investment is made over several periods.

4. It means that the present value of the future inflows is greater than the present value of the investment, and if this actually occurs, the rate of return on the investment will be greater than the cost of capital.

5. It means that in the net present value technique the discount rate—cost of capital—is given so that only one set of calculations needs to be made, but in the internal rate of return method the discount rate—actual rate of return—must be solved for, sometimes on a trial-and-error basis.

6. It means that they ignore the vital economic fact that money does have value over time and that the pattern of returns from an investment has a major effect on its real rate of return.

7. It means that the effects of additional productive capacity of new plant and equipment will affect activity and expense levels planned in the operating budget.

Exercises and Problems

16–1.   Review problem—time value of money applications. An investor has asked for your help with the following time value of money applications. Use the appropriate factors from Table 6–2 or Table 6–3 to answer the following questions.

Required:

a. What is the present value of $65,000 to be received in four years using a discount rate of 12%?

b. How much should be invested today at a return on investment of 12% compounded annually to have $65,000 in four years?

c. If the return on investment was greater than 12% compounded annually, would the amount to be invested today to have $65,000 in four years be more or less than the answer to part *b*? Explain your answer.

16–2.   Review problem—time value of money applications. Use the appropriate factors from Table 6–2 or Table 6–3 to answer the following questions.

Required:

a. Kulpa Co.'s common stock is expected to have a dividend of $3 per share for each of the next eight years, and it is estimated that the market value per share will be $92 at the end of eight years. If an investor requires a return on investment of 16%, what is the maximum price the investor would be willing to pay for a share of Kulpa Co. common stock today?

b. Vecchi bought a bond with a face amount of $1,000, a stated interest rate of 14%, and a maturity date 10 years in the future for $985. The bond pays interest on an annual basis. Three years have gone by and the market interest rate is now 16%. What is the market value of the bond today?

c. Katie purchased a U.S. Series EE savings bond for $75, and six years later received $106.38 when the bond was redeemed. What average annual return on investment did Katie earn over the six years?

16–3.   Present value analysis—effects of estimation errors. Capital budgeting analysis involves the use of many estimates.

Required:

For each of the following estimation errors, state whether the net present value of the project will be too high or too low:

    a. The investment is too high.

    b. The cost of capital is too low.

    c. The cash flows from the project are too high.

    d. The number of years over which the project will generate cash flows is too low.

LO 3

16–4. Present value analysis—cost of capital. Tibbetts Enterprises is evaluating the cost of capital to use in its capital budgeting process. Over the recent past, the company has averaged a return on equity of 15% and a return on investment of 12%. The company can currently borrow short-term money for 9%.

Required:

    a. Which of the above rates is most relevant to deciding the cost of capital to use? Explain your answer.

    b. Without prejudice to your answer to part *a,* explain why the company might choose to use a cost of capital of 16% to evaluate capital expenditure opportunities.

LO 4, 6

16–5. Calculate NPV—compare to IRR. Safehaven, Ltd. is considering the investment of $85,000 in a new machine. The machine will generate cash flow of $14,000 per year for each year of its eight-year life and will have a salvage value of $9,000 at the end of its life. The company's cost of capital is 10%.

Required:

    a. Calculate the net present value of the proposed investment. (Ignore income taxes.)

    b. What will the internal rate of return on this investment be relative to the cost of capital? Explain your answer.

LO 4, 6, 7

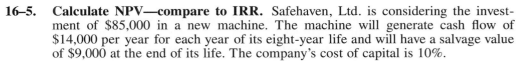

16–6. Calculate NPV—compare to IRR. The following data have been collected by a task force of capital budgeting analysts at Perona & Brolley Ltd. concerning the drilling and production of known reserves at an off-shore location:

Investment in rigging equipment and related personnel costs required to pump the oil	$5,300,000
Net increase in inventory and receivables associated with the drilling and production of the reserves. Assume this investment will be recovered at the end of the project	1,200,000
Net cash inflow from operations for the expected life of the reserves, by year:	
1998	2,000,000
1999	3,600,000
2000	1,700,000
Salvage value of machinery and equipment at the end of the well's productive life.	1,000,000
Cost of capital.	18%

Required:

    a. Calculate the net present value of the proposed investment in the drilling and production operation. Assume that the investment will be made at the beginning of 1998, and the net cash inflows from operations will be received in lump sum at the end of each year. Ignore income taxes, and round answers to the nearest $1.

    b. What will the internal rate of return on this investment be relative to the cost of capital? Explain your answer.

c. Differences between estimates made by the task force and actual results would have an effect on the actual rate of return on the project. Identify the significant estimates made by the task force. For each estimate, state the effect on the actual ROI if the estimate turns out to be less than the actual amount finally achieved.

LO 4, 5, 6, 8   **16–7.   Calculate NPV, present value ratio, and payback.** Rivara Company is considering the investment of $120,000 in a new machine. It is estimated that the new machine will generate additional cash flow of $21,000 per year for each year of its eight-year life and will have a salvage value of $15,000 at the end of its life. Rivara's financial managers estimate that the firm's cost of capital is 12%.

Required:
a. Calculate the net present value of the investment.
b. Calculate the present value ratio of the investment.
c. What is the internal rate of return of this investment, relative to the cost of capital?
d. Calculate the payback period of the investment.

LO 4, 5, 6, 7, 8   **16–8.   Calculate NPV, present value ratio, and payback.** Capper Co. is evaluating the purchase of another sewing machine that will be used to manufacture sport caps. The invoice price of the machine is $66,000. In addition, delivery and installation costs will total $4,200. The machine has the capacity to produce 10,000 dozen caps per year. Sales are forecast to increase gradually, and production volumes for each of the five years of the machine's life are expected to be:

1998	3,000 dozen
1999	4,700 dozen
2000	7,100 dozen
2001	9,400 dozen
2002	10,000 dozen

The caps have a contribution margin of $4.20 per dozen. Fixed costs associated with the additional production (other than depreciation expense) will be negligible. Salvage value and the investment in working capital should be ignored. Capper Co.'s cost of capital for this capacity expansion has been set at 16%.

Required:
a. Calculate the net present value of the proposed investment in the new sewing machine.
b. Calculate the present value ratio of the investment.
c. What is the internal rate of return of this investment relative to the cost of capital?
d. Calculate the payback period of the investment.

LO 3, 4, 8   **16–9.   Interpretation of present value analysis and payback.** The Goodwrench Garage is considering an investment in a new tune-up computer. The cost of the computer is $24,000. A cost analyst has calculated the discounted present value of the expected cash flows from the computer to be $26,220, based on the firm's cost of capital of 20%.

Required:

a. What is the expected return on investment of the machine, relative to 20%? Explain your answer.
b. The payback period of the investment in the machine is expected to be 4.6 years. How much weight should this measurement carry in the decision about whether or not to invest in the machine? Explain your answer.

LO 3, 4, 6   **16–10.**   **Interpretation of present value analysis—calculate annual cash flow.** City Hospital is considering the acquisition of a new diagnostic scanning machine. The investment required to get the machine operational will be $2,466,840. The machine will be capable of performing 7,500 scanning procedures per year, but based on the experience of other hospitals, management estimates that the machine will be used at 80% of its capacity. The hospital's cost of capital is 12%; the machine has an estimated useful life of six years and no salvage value.

Required:

a. Assuming a constant cash flow every year, calculate the annual net cash flow required from the scanner if the IRR of the investment is to equal 12%. (*Hint: The annual net cash flow requirement is an annuity.*)

b. If the direct cash costs of operating the scanner equal 50% of the annual net cash flow requirement calculated in part *a*, what price should the hospital charge per scanning procedure in order to achieve a 12% ROI?

LO 5   **16–11.**   **Present value ratios index.** Information about four investment proposals is summarized below:

Proposal	Investment Required	Net Present Value
1	$50,000	$30,000
2	60,000	24,000
3	30,000	15,000
4	45,000	9,000

Required:

Calculate the present value ratio of each proposal and indicate which proposal is the most desirable investment.

16–12.   **Calculate NPV—rank projects using present value ratios.** The following capital expenditure projects have been proposed for management's consideration at Hope, Inc., for the upcoming budget year:

				Project		
	Year(s)	A	B	C	D	E
Initial investment	0	$(50,000)	$(50,000)	$(100,000)	$(100,000)	$(200,000)
Amount of net cash return	1	10,000	0	32,000	10,000	60,000
	2	10,000	0	32,000	20,000	60,000
	3	10,000	20,000	32,000	30,000	30,000
	4	10,000	20,000	32,000	40,000	30,000
	5	10,000	20,000	32,000	50,000	30,000
Per year	6-10	10,000	12,000	0	0	30,000
NPV (14% discount rate)		$ 2,126	$?	$?	$?	$ 5,884
Present value ratio.......		1.04	?	?	?	?

Required:

a. Calculate the net present value of projects B, C, and D, using 14% as the cost of capital for Hope, Inc.

    b. Calculate the present value ratio for projects B, C, D, and E.

    c. Which projects would you recommend for investment if the cost of capital is 14%, and:

       1. $100,000 is available for investment?

       2. $300,000 is available for investment?

       3. $500,000 is available for investment?

    d. What additional factors (beyond those considered in parts *a-c* above) might influence your project rankings?

16–13.   **Case study—NPV of opening a small business.** Lorna Myers has recently retired as a flight attendant, and is interested in opening a fitness center and health spa exclusively for women in Grand Cayman, where she resides. After careful study, she is somewhat puzzled as to how to proceed. In her words, "I see my business going in one of two directions: either I open the fitness center and health spa all at once, or I start with the health spa and hold off on the fitness center for a while. Either way, it should be a success because women on this Island love to be pampered. My only concern about the fitness center is the initial cost, but if the projections look good enough, I know some investors in Phoenix who can help me get started. In any event, I plan to retire permanently in 10 years."

    The following information is available:

- Lorna has identified a suitable location for her business in a new shopping center in George Town, capital of the Cayman Islands. The developer has units of 1,000 square feet and 2,500 square feet available, and is willing to sell either unit for CI$150 per square foot (CI$1.00 = US$1.25). Alternatively, the space can be leased at a cost of CI$1.80 per square foot per month, on an annual basis.

- Commercial real estate values have more than doubled in Grand Cayman during the past ten years, with no slow-down in sight. As a result, Lorna is more attracted to the purchase option because she expects the price per square foot to be CI$300 by the time she is ready to sell her unit in 10 years.

- Exercise machines and other equipment necessary to open the fitness center would cost US$50,000. In addition, US$35,000 would need to be invested in equipment related to the health spa. The useful life for all such equipment is 10 years, and the expected salvage value is not large enough to be concerned about.

- In addition, US$8,000 would need to be invested in an inventory of cosmetics and skin care products necessary to operate the health spa. This level of inventory would need to be maintained throughout the 10 year period, and will be given away to loyal customers when Lorna retires permanently.

- The health spa can be operated in the 1,000 square foot unit. Variable operating costs would include CI$0.10 per square foot per month for cleaning, and CI$.040 per square foot per month for utilities. The 2,500 square foot unit is large enough to operate both the fitness center and health spa, and the CI$0.10 rate per square foot for cleaning would not change. However, if the 2,500 square foot unit were used, the health spa would be located in an open-spaced loft which would need to be air-conditioned at all times. As a result, utility costs are expected to be CI$0.60 per square foot per month under this option.

- Lorna is a certified esthetician and expects to do most of the makeovers, facials, and peels herself, but needs a qualified assistant for the health spa. She estimates that it will cost US$25,000 per year to hire an appropriate person. Likewise, for the fitness center, two full-time aerobics instructors would be hired for US$20,000 each per year, and a physical trainer would be hired for US$30,000 per year.

- Additional fixed costs include US$3,000 per year for advertising, and US$4,500 per year for maintenance, insurance, and other items. These costs will be incurred without respect to the size of operations.

- Annual membership fees to the fitness center will be US$300, and a preliminary market survey shows a demand of approximately 500 initial members. Although members tend to come and go, the net change in membership from year to year is not expected to be significant. No additional fees will be charged to fitness center members.

- Health spa fees are assessed on a user-basis, although the steam room facilities are available at no charge to fitness center members. The net cash inflow from cosmetics and skin care products (after deducting the cost of inventory used and sold) is expected to be CI$8,000 per month.

- Lorna's cost of capital is 12%, and there are no taxes in the Cayman Islands.

Required:

a. Calculate the net present value in US$ of an investment in the health spa *only,* assuming that the 1,000 square foot unit is purchased and then resold at the end of ten years. *(Hint: Before making your present value calculations, multiply all amounts expressed in CI$ by $1.25 to convert into US$.)*

b. Calculate the net present value in US$ of an investment in the fitness center and health spa, assuming that the 2,500 square foot unit is purchased and then resold at the end of ten years.

c. Lorna is quite concerned about possible forecasting errors, and has asked you to prepare a more conservative estimate. Repeat part *b* above, assuming that the fitness center attracts only 300 members per year (rather than 500); the net cash inflow per month from cosmetics and skin care products is only CI$6,000 per month (rather than CI$8,000 per month); and that commercial real estate values in Grand Cayman at the end of ten years are only CI$200 per square foot (rather than CI$300 per square foot).

d. Explain why it might be in Lorna's best interest to lease (rather than purchase) the 1,000 square foot unit if she initially decides to open the health spa only. Although no calculations are required, you should consider both quantitative and qualitative factors in your response.

e. What is your overall recommendation? Include an explanation of any additional factors that you would consider in making your recommendation. Keep in mind that Lorna has not given herself a salary in her projections. Assume that a reasonable salary would be CI$4,000 per month.

LO 3, 4, 5, 6, 7, 8, 10

16–14. **Comprehensive problem—quantitative and qualitative analysis.** The following data have been collected by capital budgeting analysts at Terselic, Inc., concerning an investment in an expansion of the company's product line. Analysts estimate that an investment of $150,000 will be required to initiate the project at the beginning of 1998. The estimated cash returns from the new product line are summarized in the following table; assume that the returns will be received in lump sum at the end of each year.

Year	Amount of Cash Return
1998	$42,000
1999	54,000
2000	65,000
2001	48,000

The new product line will also require an investment in inventory and receivables of $50,000; this investment will become available for other purposes at the end of the project. Salvage value of machinery and equipment at the end of the product line's life is expected to be $25,000. The cost of capital used in Terselic, Inc.'s, capital budgeting analysis is 14%.

Required:

a. Calculate the net present value of the proposed investment. Ignore income taxes and round all answers to the nearest $1.

b. Calculate the present value ratio of the investment.

c. What will the internal rate of return on this investment be relative to the cost of capital? Explain your answer.

d. Calculate the payback period of the investment.

e. Based on the above quantitative analysis, would you recommend that the product-line expansion project be undertaken? Explain your answer.

f. Identify some qualitative factors that you would want to have considered with respect to this project before management proceeds with the investment.

LO 3, 4, 9, 10   **16–15.**   **Accounting rate of return and NPV.** Spiffy Co. uses the accounting rate of return method to evaluate proposed capital investments. The company's desired rate of return (its cost of capital) is 18%. The project being evaluated involves a new product that will have a three-year life. The investment required is $100,000, which consists of an $80,000 machine, and inventories and accounts receivable totaling $20,000. The machine will have a useful life of three years and a salvage value of $50,000. The salvage value will be received during the fourth year, and the inventories and accounts receivable related to the product will also be converted back to cash in the fourth year. Accrual accounting net income from the product will be $29,000 per year, before depreciation expense, for each of the three years. Because of the time lag between selling the product and collecting the accounts receivable, cash flows from the product will be:

1st year	$14,000
2nd year	24,000
3rd year	29,000
4th year	20,000

Required:

a. Calculate the accounting rate of return for the first year of the product. Assume straight-line depreciation. Based on this analysis, would the investment be made? Explain your answer.

b. Calculate the net present value of the product using a cost of capital of 18% and assuming that cash flows occur at the end of the respective years. Based on this analysis, would the investment be made? Explain your answer.

c. Which of these two analytical approaches is the most appropriate to use? Explain your answer.

LO 4, 5, 8, 9, 10   **16–16.**   **Accounting rate of return, payback, and NPV.** Oldweigh Corp. evaluates capital expenditure proposals using the accounting rate of return method. A recent proposal involved a $50,000 investment in a machine that had an estimated useful life of five years and an estimated salvage value of $10,000. The machine was expected to increase net income (and cash flows) before depreciation expense by $15,000 per year. The criteria for approving a new investment are that it have a rate of return of 16% and a payback period of three years or less.

Required:

a. Calculate the accounting rate of return on this investment for the first year. Assume straight-line depreciation. Based on this analysis would the investment be made? Explain your answer.

b. Calculate the payback period for this investment. Based on this analysis, would the investment be made? Explain your answer.

c. Calculate the net present value of this investment using a cost of capital of 16%. Based on this analysis, would the investment be made? Explain your answer.

d. What recommendation would you make to the management of Oldweigh Corp. about evaluating capital expenditure proposals? Support your recommendation with the appropriate rationale.

Appendix

1996 Annual Report of Intel Corporation

As discussed in the text, financial statement disclosures and accounting methods are continually evolving. The presentations in this document reflect generally accepted principles of accounting as of the date of their publication. Subsequent changes in accounting principles and reporting standards will be reflected in subsequent years' reports. Visit our World Wide Web site (www.mhhe.com/business/accounting/marshall) to access current reports.

*Courtesy Intel Corporation, 1997.

Table of contents

1996

Earnings per share
(Dollars, adjusted for stock splits through 1996)

5.81
4.5
4.03
3.0
2.60 2.62
1.5
1.24

92 93 94 95 96
0

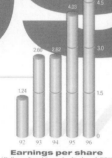

To our stockholders

Intel Corporation 1996

29%

**Increase in
net revenues.**
(1995–1996)

44%

**Increase in
earnings per share.**
(1995–1996)

36%

**Return on average
stockholders' equity.**
(1996)

2

In 1996, Intel's market value more than doubled—to $111 billion.

To our stockholders

We are pleased to report another outstanding year at Intel. Revenues totaled $20.8 billion, up 29 percent from $16.2 billion in 1995. Earnings per share rose 44 percent over last year, to $5.81.

Our performance in 1996 was driven by strong demand for our Pentium® and Pentium® Pro processors, which provide the brains for computers from servers to home PCs. We expanded the Pentium processor family in 1996 with a new 200-MHz Pentium processor and shifted the entry-level chip to the 120- and 133-MHz Pentium processors.

We continued to invest heavily in the manufacturing facilities that allow us to deliver more powerful microprocessors while keeping PC system costs low. In 1996, we announced plans for two new manufacturing sites: a new state-of-the-art wafer fab in Fort Worth, Texas, and an assembly and test facility in San Jose, Costa Rica.

Driving connected PC growth.
About 70 million PCs were sold around the world in 1996, and a substantial majority of those PCs contained Intel microprocessors. This year, one trend in particular has driven this PC market growth: the spread of networked computing via the popularity of the Internet and internal corporate networks. In fact, 1996 was the year in which PC manufacturers and users around the world embraced the concept that computing is, by definition, networked.

R&D lab to the computing industry.
We at Intel have long known that our growth depends on the continued expansion of the PC platform's capabilities. The more users demand of PCs, the more power will be required to drive them, and the more microproces-

sors will be sold. In response, we have expanded Intel's role in the computing industry over the last several years. Acting as a sort of R&D lab and strategic think tank to the industry, we work with PC makers, software developers and PC users to understand their future needs and wishes, and work intensely with industry leaders to develop products or specifications that meet those needs.

In 1996, we focused on two key initiatives that aim to solve persistent problems in computing and embody the exciting potential of a world of

networked computers: connected CD-ROMs and down-the-wire manageability.

• **Connected CD-ROMs:** Users have long been frustrated by the snail-like bandwidth performance of today's modem-and-phone-line Internet connections. We have worked with software developers to create a solution—connected CD-ROM software.

The bandwidth-hungry, multimedia environment and content of the program are delivered on a CD-ROM. These "hybrid applications" link to the Internet to provide updated content and real-time interaction with other users. We believe that connected PC software is the wave of the future for home PCs.

• **Down-the-wire manageability:** Expansion of internal business PC networks has been hindered by the high costs of establishing, maintaining and updating such networks. Indeed, network management costs have raised the total cost of ownership of a single connected business PC to more than

$7,000 annually, according to Gartner Group, a research and consulting firm.

To address this serious issue, we launched our Wired for Management initiative, aimed at reducing the total cost of ownership of business PCs. We and other industry leaders are delivering immediate hardware and software solutions to make it easier to install and maintain PC networks without sacrificing performance.

Taking responsibility for our own growth.
We know we can't wait for growth to come to us. We are responsible for our own future and work to make it as successful as possible by removing roadblocks to PC platform growth, developing preference for the Intel Inside® brand among PC users and supporting emerging PC markets around the world. Together, these strategies build value for our stockholders, which is, after all, our most important goal.

This has been an outstanding year. We have confidence in our strategies and capabilities, and we are determined to do what we can to continue expanding developments in computing and telecommunications.

As part of our continuous evolution of Intel's management team, in January 1997 we announced a realignment of titles and responsibilities in the Executive Office. Effective May 21, 1997, Craig Barrett becomes president and continues as chief operating officer. Andy Grove becomes chairman and continues as chief executive officer. Gordon Moore becomes chairman emeritus and continues, with Craig and Andy, to be part of the Executive Office. Together, we look forward to the continuing opportunities and challenges of our business in the coming year.

Gordon E. Moore
Chairman

Andrew S. Grove
President and Chief Executive Officer

Craig R. Barrett
Executive Vice President and Chief Operating Officer

Highlights of 1996

A revolution in progress

Twenty-five years ago, we introduced the world's first commercial microprocessor, the 4004. The microprocessor's invention revolutionized computing and changed forever the way people work, learn and communicate. We were proud this year when former Intel engineers and microprocessor co-inventors (left to right) **Stan Mazor, Federico Faggin and Ted Hoff** were inducted into the Inventors Hall of Fame for this remarkable contribution to technology and society.

New territory for our smartest chip

Our powerhouse Pentium® Pro processors were at the core of the growing **PC server market segment** this year. In a new breed of scalable servers, several Pentium Pro chips are combined, providing power to connect desktop systems or run large applications more effectively than traditional single-chip servers. This capability is moving the Intel architecture up into the mid-range market segment for servers and workstations, competing with traditionally more expensive, proprietary systems.

The best of the Web—without the wait

In July, Intel gathered more than 1,000 software, communications and entertainment industry representatives to share our vision of the most exciting new multimedia solution: **connected CD-ROMs**. For example, in *Monopoly* Interactive*, a CD-ROM generates an exciting animated 3D game world, while players from around the globe challenge each other over the program's Internet link. This and other connected CD-ROMs provide powerful solutions to the bandwidth-clogging frustrations of the World Wide Web.

Multimedia goes to Hollywood

In 1996 we worked with Creative Artists Agency (CAA), one of Hollywood's leading literary and talent agencies, to expose actors, directors, writers and musicians to the **potential of new media** on networked PCs. Our new CAA/Intel Media Lab in Beverly Hills, California, is a state-of-the-art multimedia facility designed to stimulate the development of compelling new electronic content, such as broadcast-quality entertainment and interactive programs.

Business PC costs come tumbling down

To help **drive down the costs of business computing**, we launched our Wired for Management initiative in September. Leading hardware and software suppliers joined us in announcing a series of specifications and products expected to make business PCs easier to upgrade, diagnose and repair remotely. For example, a new hardware monitoring chip tracks environmental conditions such as temperature and voltage, and reports to the central management software, which responds promptly to abnormal conditions.

Manufacturing records

Our manufacturing performance continues to improve, even as we add new facilities and advances to increasingly complex production processes. We built our newest factory, Fab 12 in Chandler, Arizona, in **record time**, going from ground breaking to production in 23 months. The plant also achieved record product yields on ramp-up, trimming months off time to market and validating our policy of copying new manufacturing processes exactly from development lab to production floor.

Improving tomorrow today

In 1996, we expanded our **corporate giving and community programs** in response to enormous employee enthusiasm. "Intel Involved" links employee volunteers with projects in their interest areas: building homes with Habitat for Humanity, teaching computing skills in schools, protecting local wetlands, reading to children and more. In 1996 Intel employees around the world volunteered a total of 106,000 hours of labor to help make our communities better places to live and work.

Show grandma the kids' latest artwork—over the phone

It sounds futuristic, but it's here: For the first time, a simple low-cost, PC-based video phone is available to home PC users (133-MHz Pentium® processor minimum). The Intel Video Phone with ProShare® technology, introduced to market in 1996, delivers **quality video communications over ordinary telephone lines**. Major PC OEMs have incorporated the technology into their current PCs, and developers have embraced the standards, ensuring compatibility among various video phone products.

Facts and figures

1996: the b

In 1996, PC users around the world continued to make the Pentium® processor their chip of choice. Strong sales of this processor family drove our 1996 results, returning our seventh consecutive year of both record revenues and earnings. We hit a new milestone with more than $20 billion in revenues in one year.

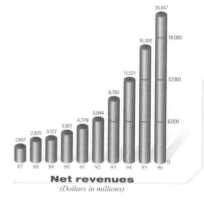

Net revenues
(Dollars in millions)

30%

Compound annual growth rate (CAGR) percent increase in net revenues over the last decade.

Earnings per share
(Dollars, adjusted for stock splits)

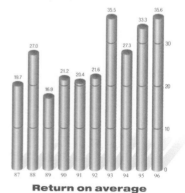

Return on average stockholders' equity
(Percent)

The fiscal year-end closing price of Intel stock has risen at a 39% CAGR over the last ten years.

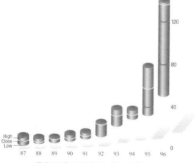

Stock price trading ranges by fiscal year
(Dollars, adjusted for stock splits)

Note: Past performance does not guarantee future results. Share and per share amounts reported herein have been adjusted for stock splits through 1996 only.

Facts and figures

Intel Corporation 1996

ottom line

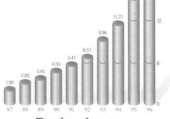

Book value per share at year-end
(Dollars, adjusted for stock splits)

30%

Ten-year CAGR percent increase in book value per share, reflecting reinvestments of profits and new infusions of capital.

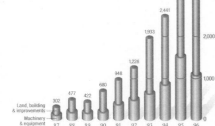

Capital additions to property, plant and equipment
(Dollars in millions)

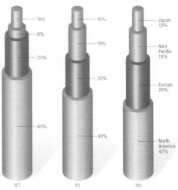

Geographic breakdown of revenues
(Percent)

More than half of Intel's 1996 revenues came from outside North America.

Employees at year-end
(In thousands)

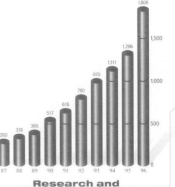

Research and development
(Dollars in millions)

24%

CAGR percent increase in R&D over the last decade.

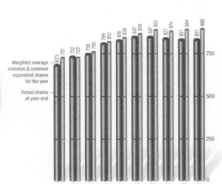

Common shares outstanding
(In millions, adjusted for stock splits)

www.intel.com

Intel Corporation 1996

For many years, we at Intel have focused our efforts around one touchstone belief: that as the PC provides more excitement and usefulness to consumers, more PCs will be sold and more Intel processors will be needed. Recently, the World Wide Web has been driving PC growth, as this easy-to-use, graphical Internet interface continues to attract

8

the technology

a strategy

the brand

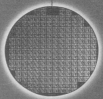

Many booming product areas rely on Intel processors. We encourage the growth with active initiatives to expand the connected PC's potential.

Our Intel Inside® program is growing internationally, continuing to make consumers aware of the benefits of genuine Intel technology.

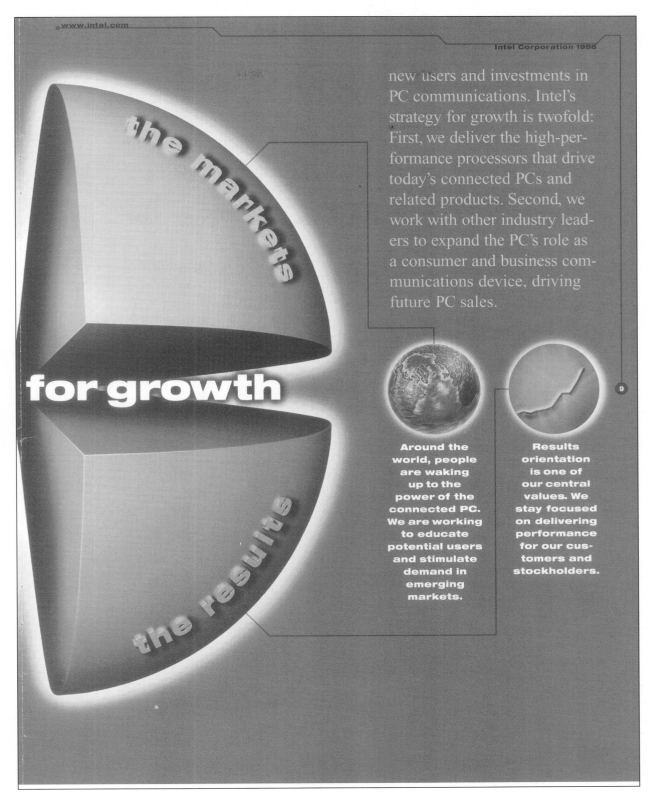

Intel Corporation 1996

the markets

for growth

the results

new users and investments in PC communications. Intel's strategy for growth is twofold: First, we deliver the high-performance processors that drive today's connected PCs and related products. Second, we work with other industry leaders to expand the PC's role as a consumer and business communications device, driving future PC sales.

Around the world, people are waking up to the power of the connected PC. We are working to educate potential users and stimulate demand in emerging markets.

Results orientation is one of our central values. We stay focused on delivering performance for our customers and stockholders.

1971 4004

2,300 transistors

60,000 instructions per second

25 process steps to
produce the 4004 chip

The microprocessor
then and now

What a difference a quarter-century makes. In 1971, **our 4004 was the world's first microprocessor**, providing astonishing performance for the time. Today, the complexity and performance of our chips have increased exponentially, continuing to power new revolutions.

Pentium® Pro processor **1996**

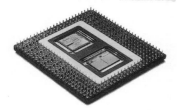

5.5 million transistors

300 million instructions per second

More than 200 major steps to
produce the Pentium® Pro processor

the tech
driving product growth

The richest PC
experience

Based on Intel's Media Benchmark, our new Pentium® processor with MMX™ media enhancement technology **boosts multimedia performance** by more than 60 percent, compared to equivalent-speed Pentium processors without MMX technology. The technology will be incorporated into Intel's new microprocessors beginning in 1997.

www.intel.com

Intel Corporation 1996

The content
users want

Intel is committed to improving the Internet experience for PC consumers. Among other efforts in 1996, we encouraged software developers to create more **connected CD-ROM** titles, giving PC users the best of both the powerful desktop and the dynamic Web. For instance, with *Frommer's Interactive Travel Guide,* users can take a 3D multimedia tour of San Francisco on CD-ROM, and then use a built-in Internet link to book hotel rooms and event tickets.

nology

11

Memories
on the move

Intel's flash-memory-based Miniature Cards open exciting doors for many digital consumer appliances. A **matchbook-sized card** can slip into a digital camera in lieu of film, and then be plugged into a PC. Users can easily edit their pictures and incorporate them into a family newsletter or Web page.

More manageable
networking

Our Wired for Management initiative aims to make network management less complex and costly. Our new LANDesk® Management Suite of software allows **remote monitoring and control** of networked PCs, and centralized distribution of software updates, making business networks much easier to manage and lowering the total costs of business computing.

Brand value
worldwide

The Intel Inside® branding program, which educates PC users about the benefits of Intel microprocessors, has played a critical role in our growth. In 1996, the journal *Financial World* designated the Intel brand the **tenth most valuable brand in the world.**

the

br

building

preference for

Prime time is
Intel time

In 1996, we launched new **TV ad campaigns** for the Pentium® processor. They highlight the processor's ability to deliver the best performance for local software and Internet applications—and for the connected CD-ROM software that brings users the best of both worlds. The ads are helping to convey the message that the Pentium processor is the chip of choice for the best PC experience.

www.intel.com

Intel Corporation 1996

International
advertising

We have worked to develop advertising messages and visual styles that will work in markets around the world. Our efforts are aimed at building a **consistent image of Intel** in the minds of PC customers everywhere.

and
the Intel Inside® brand

Growing
our brand

In 1996, more than 1,300 licensees worldwide participated in the Intel Inside program. Television advertising support for customers began in 1995 and **has grown to include more than 60 OEMs**, who use the Intel Inside logo and "bong" sound in ads for their Pentium processor-based PCs.

#10

Intel's 1996 rank among the world's most valuable brands.

www.intel.com

Intel Corporation 1996

Tapping potential
worldwide

Around the world, we are working to **stimulate demand in emerging markets** and educate potential PC users about the power of networked PCs. About 50 percent of Intel's advertising and promotion dollars are spent in locations outside the United States.

14

the m

reaching potential PC

The fastest
growing user group

Korea emerged as one of the world's most **promising consumer markets** for PCs in 1996. With children being the country's fastest growing segment of users, Intel donated Pentium® processor-based PCs and a Web server to KidNet,* an online service dedicated to Korean children.

合家欢

www.intel.com

Intel Corporation 1996

Brazil is hot

According to market research firm IDC, the Brazilian PC market segment (largest in South America) grew 42 percent in units sold from 1994 to 1995. Intel is focusing on the 70 percent of Brazilians under age 30, a **generation hungry for powerful PC technology**. Our promotional programs are having a strong effect—distributors report vigorous demand for Intel processor-based PCs.

customers worldwide

Taking it to the streets **of China**

Exciting new technology was on display in the People's Republic of China in the fall of 1996. Intel coordinated a series of PC Demo Days in the country's major cities, with one hundred PC retailers holding special events to **demonstrate PC capabilities to curious crowds**. In Beijing alone, more than 80,000 people joined in, getting a first-

电脑游园会

hand experience of the world of connected Intel processor-based computing.

The India boom

Home to one-sixth of the Earth's population, India enjoys a thriving economy, a growing high-tech industry base and a highly educated work force. Intel is establishing business and technology offices in cities throughout the country and is working directly with local PC companies, distributors and users. In 1996, to **increase computer literacy through hands-on experience**, we donated equipment and software for a new Intel Technology Lab at the prestigious Indian Institute of Technology in Bangalore.

www.intel.com

Intel Corporation 1996

Why we do
what we do

Intel is committed to building value for stockholders. We maintain a vigilant, flexible and highly strategic approach to market opportunities in order to maximize long-term results. We are pleased that our efforts have **returned significant value** for our investors. In fiscal 1996, Intel's market capitalization increased more than $64 billion, and our fiscal year-end stock price grew 139 percent.

the bottom

139%

**Increase in fiscal
year-end stock
price, 1995-96.**

Outstanding
earnings growth

For fiscal 1996, our earnings per share were $5.81, a **44 percent jump** over 1995 earnings per share.

87   88   89   90   91

Note: Past performance does not guarantee future results. Share and per share amounts reported herein have been adjusted for stock splits through 1996 only.

Customers get
more for less

Returning value to stockholders is rooted in our ability to deliver results to our customers. We have consistently generated manufacturing advances to squeeze increasing numbers of transistors onto each processor— leading to **more power on desktops for less and less money**. This trend spurs creativity among hardware and software companies, continuing to drive growth in the industry as a whole.

$225

**PC cost per
MIPS in 1991.**

(million instructions per second)

$7

**PC cost per
MIPS in 1996.**

Many happy
returns

Intel stock has **split 10 times through 1996**. A purchase of 100 shares for $2,350 at the initial public offering in 1971 would have grown to 15,188 shares worth more than $2 million by the end of fiscal 1996.

line for customers and stockholders

THE MOST ADMIRED

COMPANY	TOTAL RETURN TO INVESTORS	
COMPOUND ANNUAL RATE	1986–96	1996
Coca-Cola	29.8%	43.3%
Mirage Resorts	27.9%	25.4%
Merck	22.1%	24.0%
United Parcel Service	N.A.	N.A.
Microsoft	44.5%	88.3%
Johnson & Johnson	22.2%	18.1%
Intel	43.8%	131.2%
Pfizer	21.7%	34.0%
Procter & Gamble	21.9%	32.1%
Berkshire Hathaway	28.3%	6.2%
S&P 500	11.8%	20.3%

N.A. Not applicable.

What Intel did for
stockholders

Intel **ranked #1** in calendar year 1996 total return to investors among the top 100 U.S. companies by market capitalization. In addition, in *Fortune* magazine's annual Corporate Reputations Survey, Intel was named the seventh most admired company in the U.S. (see table at left).

Consolidated statements of income

Intel Corporation 1996

Three years ended December 28, 1996

(In millions—except per share amounts)	1996	1995	1994
Net revenues	**$ 20,847**	**$ 16,202**	**$ 11,521**
Cost of sales	9,164	7,811	5,576
Research and development	1,808	1,296	1,111
Marketing, general and administrative	2,322	1,843	1,447
Operating costs and expenses	13,294	10,950	8,134
Operating income	**7,553**	**5,252**	**3,387**
Interest expense	(25)	(29)	(57)
Interest income and other, net	406	415	273
Income before taxes	**7,934**	**5,638**	**3,603**
Provision for taxes	2,777	2,072	1,315
Net income	**$ 5,157**	**$ 3,566**	**$ 2,288**
Earnings per common and common equivalent share	**$ 5.81**	**$ 4.03**	**$ 2.62**
Weighted average common and common equivalent shares outstanding	888	884	874

See accompanying notes.

18

Consolidated balance sheets

Intel Corporation 1996

December 28, 1996 and December 30, 1995

(In millions—except per share amounts)

	1996	1995
Assets		
Current assets:		
Cash and cash equivalents	$ 4,165	$ 1,463
Short-term investments	3,742	995
Trading assets	87	—
Accounts receivable, net of allowance for doubtful accounts of $68 ($57 in 1995)	3,723	3,116
Inventories	1,293	2,004
Deferred tax assets	570	408
Other current assets	104	111
Total current assets	**13,684**	**8,097**
Property, plant and equipment:		
Land and buildings	4,372	3,145
Machinery and equipment	8,729	7,099
Construction in progress	1,161	1,548
	14,262	11,792
Less accumulated depreciation	5,775	4,321
Property, plant and equipment, net	**8,487**	**7,471**
Long-term investments	**1,353**	**1,653**
Other assets	**211**	**283**
Total assets	**$ 23,735**	**$ 17,504**
Liabilities and stockholders' equity		
Current liabilities:		
Short-term debt	$ 389	$ 346
Accounts payable	969	864
Deferred income on shipments to distributors	474	304
Accrued compensation and benefits	1,128	758
Accrued advertising	410	218
Other accrued liabilities	507	328
Income taxes payable	986	801
Total current liabilities	**4,863**	**3,619**
Long-term debt	**728**	**400**
Deferred tax liabilities	**997**	**620**
Put warrants	**275**	**725**
Commitments and contingencies		
Stockholders' equity:		
Preferred Stock, $.001 par value, 50 shares authorized; none issued	—	—
Common Stock, $.001 par value, 1,400 shares authorized; 821 issued and outstanding in 1996 and 1995, and capital in excess of par value	2,897	2,583
Retained earnings	13,975	9,557
Total stockholders' equity	**16,872**	**12,140**
Total liabilities and stockholders' equity	**$ 23,735**	**$ 17,504**

19

See accompanying notes.

580 *Appendix*

www.intel.com

Consolidated statements of cash flows

Intel Corporation 1996

Three years ended December 28, 1996

(In millions)	1996	1995	1994
Cash and cash equivalents, beginning of year	**$ 1,463**	**$ 1,180**	**$ 1,659**
Cash flows provided by (used for) operating activities:			
Net income	5,157	3,566	2,288
Adjustments to reconcile net income to net cash provided by (used for) operating activities:			
Depreciation	1,888	1,371	1,028
Net loss on retirements of property, plant and equipment	120	75	42
Amortization of debt discount	—	8	19
Change in deferred tax assets and liabilities	179	346	(150)
Changes in assets and liabilities:			
(Increase) in accounts receivable	(607)	(1,138)	(530)
Decrease (increase) in inventories	711	(835)	(331)
(Increase) in other assets	(7)	(251)	(57)
Increase in accounts payable	105	289	148
Tax benefit from employee stock plans	196	116	61
Purchase of trading assets	(75)	—	—
(Gain) on trading assets	(12)	—	—
Increase in income taxes payable	185	372	38
Increase in accrued compensation and benefits	370	170	44
Increase (decrease) in other liabilities	533	(73)	337
Total adjustments	3,586	450	649
Net cash provided by operating activities	**8,743**	**4,016**	**2,937**
Cash flows provided by (used for) investing activities:			
Additions to property, plant and equipment	(3,024)	(3,550)	(2,441)
Purchases of available-for-sale investments	(4,683)	(685)	(3,168)
Sales of available-for-sale investments	225	114	10
Maturities and other changes in available-for-sale investments	2,214	1,444	2,740
Net cash (used for) investing activities	**(5,268)**	**(2,677)**	**(2,859)**
Cash flows provided by (used for) financing activities:			
Increase (decrease) in short-term debt, net	43	(179)	(63)
Additions to long-term debt	317	—	128
Retirement of long-term debt	—	(4)	(98)
Proceeds from sales of shares through employee stock plans and other	261	192	150
Proceeds from sales of put warrants	56	85	76
Repurchase and retirement of Common Stock	(1,302)	(1,034)	(658)
Payment of dividends to stockholders	(148)	(116)	(92)
Net cash (used for) financing activities	**(773)**	**(1,056)**	**(557)**
Net increase (decrease) in cash and cash equivalents	**2,702**	**283**	**(479)**
Cash and cash equivalents, end of year	**$ 4,165**	**$ 1,463**	**$ 1,180**
Supplemental disclosures of cash flow information:			
Cash paid during the year for:			
Interest	$ 51	$ 182	$ 76
Income taxes	$ 2,217	$ 1,209	$ 1,366

Cash paid for interest in 1995 includes approximately $108 million of accumulated interest on Zero Coupon Notes that matured in 1995.

Certain 1995 and 1994 amounts have been reclassified to conform to the 1996 presentation.

See accompanying notes.

www.intel.com

Consolidated statements of stockholders' equity

Intel Corporation 1996

Three years ended December 28, 1996

(In millions)

	Common Stock and capital in excess of par value		Retained earnings	Total
	Number of shares	Amount		
Balance at December 25, 1993	837	$ 2,194	$ 5,306	$ 7,500
Proceeds from sales of shares through employee stock plans, tax benefit of $61 and other	12	215	—	215
Proceeds from sales of put warrants	—	76	—	76
Reclassification of put warrant obligation, net	—	(15)	(106)	(121)
Repurchase and retirement of Common Stock	(22)	(164)	(429)	(593)
Redemption of Common Stock Purchase Rights	—	—	(2)	(2)
Cash dividends declared ($.115 per share)	—	—	(96)	(96)
Net income	—	—	2,288	2,288
Balance at December 31, 1994	827	2,306	6,961	9,267
Proceeds from sales of shares through employee stock plans, tax benefit of $116 and other	13	310	—	310
Proceeds from sales of put warrants	—	85	—	85
Reclassification of put warrant obligation, net	—	61	(42)	19
Repurchase and retirement of Common Stock	(19)	(179)	(855)	(1,034)
Cash dividends declared ($.15 per share)	—	—	(124)	(124)
Unrealized gain on available-for-sale investments, net	—	—	51	51
Net income	—	—	3,566	3,566
Balance at December 30, 1995	821	2,583	9,557	12,140
Proceeds from sales of shares through employee stock plans, tax benefit of $196 and other	17	457	—	457
Proceeds from sales of put warrants	—	56	—	56
Reclassification of put warrant obligation, net	—	70	272	342
Repurchase and retirement of Common Stock	(17)	(269)	(925)	(1,194)
Cash dividends declared ($.19 per share)	—	—	(156)	(156)
Unrealized gain on available-for-sale investments, net	—	—	70	70
Net income	—	—	5,157	5,157
Balance at December 28, 1996	821	$ 2,897	$ 13,975	$ 16,872

See accompanying notes.

Notes to consolidated financial statements

Accounting policies

Fiscal year. Intel Corporation ("Intel" or "the Company") has a fiscal year that ends the last Saturday in December. Fiscal years 1996 and 1995, each 52-week years, ended on December 28 and 30, respectively. Fiscal 1994 was a 53-week year and ended on December 31, 1994. The next 53-week year will end on December 30, 2000.

Basis of presentation. The consolidated financial statements include the accounts of Intel and its wholly owned subsidiaries. Significant intercompany accounts and transactions have been eliminated. Accounts denominated in foreign currencies have been remeasured into the functional currency in accordance with Statement of Financial Accounting Standards (SFAS) No. 52, "Foreign Currency Translation," using the U.S. dollar as the functional currency.

The preparation of financial statements in conformity with generally accepted accounting principles requires management to make estimates and assumptions that affect the amounts reported in the financial statements and accompanying notes. Actual results could differ from those estimates.

Investments. Highly liquid investments with insignificant interest rate risk and with original maturities of three months or less are classified as cash and cash equivalents. Investments with maturities greater than three months and less than one year are classified as short-term investments. Investments with maturities greater than one year are classified as long-term investments.

The Company accounts for investments in accordance with SFAS No. 115, "Accounting for Certain Investments in Debt and Equity Securities." The Company's policy is to protect the value of its investment portfolio and to minimize principal risk by earning returns based on current interest rates. A substantial majority of the Company's marketable investments are classified as available-for-sale as of the balance sheet date and are reported at fair value, with unrealized gains and losses, net of tax, recorded in stockholders' equity. The cost of securities sold is based on the specific identification method. Realized gains or losses and declines in value, if any, judged to be other than temporary on available-for-sale securities are reported in other income or expense. Investments in non-marketable instruments are recorded at the lower of cost or market and included in other assets.

Trading assets. During 1996, the Company purchased securities classified as trading assets. The Company maintains its trading asset portfolio to generate returns that offset changes in certain liabilities related to deferred compensation arrangements. The trading assets consist of marketable equity securities and are stated at fair value. Both realized and unrealized gains and losses are included in other income or expense and generally offset the change in the deferred compensation liability, which is also included in other income or expense.

Fair values of financial instruments. Fair values of cash and cash equivalents approximate cost due to the short period of time to maturity. Fair values of long-term investments, long-term debt, short-term investments, short-term debt, trading assets, non-marketable instruments, swaps, currency forward contracts, currency options, options hedging marketable instruments and options hedging non-marketable instruments are based on quoted market prices or pricing models using current

market rates. No consideration is given to liquidity issues in valuing debt.

Derivative financial instruments. The Company utilizes derivative financial instruments to reduce financial market risks. These instruments are used to hedge foreign currency, equity and interest rate market exposures of underlying assets, liabilities and other obligations. The Company does not use derivative financial instruments for speculative or trading purposes. The Company's accounting policies for these instruments are based on the Company's designation of such instruments as hedging transactions. The criteria the Company uses for designating an instrument as a hedge include the instrument's effectiveness in risk reduction and one-to-one matching of derivative instruments to underlying transactions. Gains and losses on currency forward contracts, and options that are designated and effective as hedges of anticipated transactions, for which a firm commitment has been attained, are deferred and recognized in income in the same period that the underlying transactions are settled. Gains and losses on currency forward contracts, options and swaps that are designated and effective as hedges of existing transactions are recognized in income in the same period as losses and gains on the underlying transactions are recognized and generally offset. Gains and losses on any instruments not meeting the above criteria would be recognized in income in the current period. Income or expense on swaps is accrued as an adjustment to the yield of the related investments or debt they hedge.

Inventories. Inventories are stated at the lower of cost or market. Cost is computed on a currently adjusted standard basis (which approximates actual cost on a current average or first-in, first-out basis). Inventories at fiscal year-ends were as follows:

(In millions)	1996	1995
Materials and purchased parts	$ 280	$ 674
Work in process	672	707
Finished goods	341	623
Total	**$ 1,293**	**$ 2,004**

Property, plant and equipment. Property, plant and equipment are stated at cost. Depreciation is computed for financial reporting purposes principally by use of the straight-line method over the following estimated useful lives: machinery and equipment, 2–4 years; land and buildings, 4–45 years.

The Company adopted SFAS No. 121, "Accounting for the Impairment of Long-Lived Assets and for Long-Lived Assets to Be Disposed Of," effective as of the beginning of fiscal 1995. This adoption had no material effect on the Company's financial statements.

Deferred income on shipments to distributors. Certain of the Company's sales are made to distributors under agreements allowing price protection and/or right of return on merchandise unsold by the distributors. Because of frequent sales price reductions and rapid technological obsolescence in the industry, Intel defers recognition of such sales until the merchandise is sold by the distributors.

www.intel.com
Notes to consolidated financial statements
Intel Corporation 1996

Advertising. Cooperative advertising obligations are accrued and the costs expensed at the same time the related revenue is recognized. All other advertising costs are expensed as incurred. The Company does not incur any direct-response advertising costs. Advertising expense was $974 million, $654 million and $459 million in 1996, 1995 and 1994, respectively.

Interest. Interest as well as gains and losses related to contractual agreements to hedge certain investment positions and debt (see "Derivative financial instruments") are recorded as net interest income or expense on a monthly basis. Interest expense capitalized as a component of construction costs was $33 million, $46 million and $27 million for 1996, 1995 and 1994, respectively.

Earnings per common and common equivalent share. Earnings per common and common equivalent share are computed using the weighted average number of common and dilutive common equivalent shares outstanding. Fully diluted earnings per share have not been presented as part of the consolidated statements of income because the differences are insignificant.

Stock distributions. On June 16, 1995, the Company effected a two-for-one stock split in the form of a special stock distribution to stockholders of record as of May 19, 1995. Share, per share, Common Stock, capital in excess of par value, stock option and warrant amounts herein have been restated to reflect the effect of this split.

On January 13, 1997, the Board of Directors of the Company approved a two-for-one stock split (the "1997 stock split") to be effected as a special stock distribution of one share of Common Stock for each share of the Company's Common Stock outstanding, subject to stockholder approval of an increase in authorized shares at the Company's Annual Meeting on May 21, 1997. Because the 1997 stock split cannot be effected until there is an increase in authorized shares, none of the share, per share, Common Stock, capital in excess of par value, stock option or warrant amounts herein has been restated to reflect the effect of the 1997 stock split.

Common Stock

1998 Step-Up Warrants. In 1993, the Company issued 40 million 1998 Step-Up Warrants to purchase 40 million shares of Common Stock. This transaction resulted in an increase of $287 million in Common Stock and capital in excess of par value, representing net proceeds from the offering. The Warrants became exercisable in May 1993 at an effective price of $35.75 per share of Common Stock, subject to annual increases to a maximum price of $41.75 per share effective in March 1997. As of December 28, 1996, approximately 40 million Warrants were exercisable at a price of $40.25 and expire on March 14, 1998 if not previously exercised. For 1996 and 1995, the Warrants had a dilutive effect on earnings per share and represented approximately 19 million and 11 million common equivalent shares, respectively. The Warrants did not have a dilutive effect on earnings per share in 1994.

Stock repurchase program. The Company has an authorization from the Board of Directors to repurchase up to 110 million shares of Intel's Common Stock in open market or negotiated transactions. During 1996 the company repurchased 16.8 million shares at a cost of $1.3 billion, including $108 million for exercised put warrants. As of December 28, 1996, the Company had repurchased and retired approximately 84.9 million shares at a cost of $3.5 billion since the program began in 1990. As of December 28, 1996, after reserving 4.5 million shares to cover outstanding put warrants, 20.6 million shares remained available under the repurchase authorization.

Put warrants

In a series of private placements from 1991 through 1996, the Company sold put warrants that entitle the holder of each warrant to sell one share of Common Stock to the Company at a specified price. Activity during the past three years is summarized as follows:

(In millions)	Cumulative premium received	Put warrants outstanding	
		Number of warrants	Potential obligation
December 25, 1993	**$ 118**	**29.6**	**$ 688**
Sales	76	25.0	744
Exercises	—	(2.0)	(65)
Expirations	—	(27.6)	(623)
December 31, 1994	**194**	**25.0**	**744**
Sales	85	17.5	925
Repurchases	—	(5.5)	(201)
Expirations	—	(25.0)	(743)
December 30, 1995	**279**	**12.0**	**725**
Sales	56	9.0	603
Exercises	—	(1.8)	(108)
Expirations	—	(14.7)	(945)
December 28, 1996	**$ 335**	**4.5**	**$ 275**

The amount related to Intel's potential repurchase obligation has been reclassified from stockholders' equity to put warrants. The 4.5 million put warrants outstanding at December 28, 1996 expire on various dates between February 1997 and April 1997 and have exercise prices ranging from $56 to $69 per share, with an average exercise price of $61 per share. There is no significant dilutive effect on earnings per share for the periods presented.

Borrowings

Short-term debt. Short-term debt and weighted average interest rates at fiscal year-ends were as follows:

(In millions)	1996		1995	
	Balance	Weighted average interest rate	Balance	Weighted average interest rate
Borrowed under lines of credit	$ 30	N/A	$ 57	3.2%
Reverse repurchase agreements payable in non-U.S. currencies	263	6.4%	124	9.2%
Notes payable	3	0.7%	2	4.7%
Drafts payable	93	N/A	163	N/A
Total	**$ 389**		**$ 346**	

At December 28, 1996, the Company had established foreign and domestic lines of credit of approximately $1.1 billion, a portion of which is uncommitted. The Company generally renegotiates these lines annually. Compensating balance requirements are not material.

The Company also borrows under commercial paper programs. Maximum borrowings reached $306 million during 1996 and $700 million during 1995. This debt is rated A1+ by Standard and Poor's and P1 by Moody's. Proceeds are used to fund short-term working capital needs.

Long-term debt. Long-term debt at fiscal year-ends was as follows:

(In millions)	1996	1995
Payable in U.S. dollars:		
AFICA Bonds due 2013 at 4%	$ 110	$ 110
Reverse repurchase arrangement due 2001	300	—
Other U.S. dollar debt	4	4
Payable in other currencies:		
Irish punt due 2008–2024 at 6%–12%	268	240
Greek drachma due 2001	46	46
Total	**$ 728**	**$ 400**

The Company has guaranteed repayment of principal and interest on the AFICA Bonds issued by the Puerto Rico Industrial, Medical and Environmental Pollution Control Facilities Financing Authority (AFICA). The bonds are adjustable and redeemable at the option of either the Company or the bondholder every five years through 2013 and are next adjustable and redeemable in 1998. The Irish punt borrowings were made in connection with the financing of a factory in Ireland, and Intel has invested the proceeds in Irish punt denominated instruments of similar maturity to hedge foreign currency and interest rate exposures. The Greek drachma borrowings were made under a tax incentive program in Ireland, and the proceeds and cash flows have been swapped to U.S. dollars. The $300 million reverse repurchase arrangement payable in 2001 has a current borrowing rate of 5.9%. The funds received under this arrangement are available for general corporate purposes. This debt may be redeemed or repaid under certain circumstances at the option of either the lender or Intel.

Under shelf registration statements filed with the Securities and Exchange Commission (SEC), Intel has the authority to issue up to $3.3 billion in the aggregate of Common Stock, Preferred Stock, depositary shares, debt securities and warrants to purchase the Company's or other issuers' Common Stock, Preferred Stock and debt securities, and, subject to certain limits, stock index warrants and foreign currency exchange units. In 1993, Intel completed an offering of Step-Up Warrants (see "1998 Step-Up Warrants"). The Company may issue up to $1.4 billion in additional securities under effective registration statements.

As of December 28, 1996, aggregate debt maturities were as follows: 1997–none; 1998–$110 million; 1999–none; 2000–none; 2001–$346 million; and thereafter–$272 million.

Investments

The stated returns on a majority of the Company's marketable investments in long-term fixed rate debt and equity securities are swapped to U.S. dollar LIBOR-based returns. The currency risks of investments denominated in foreign currencies are hedged with foreign currency borrowings, currency forward contracts or currency interest rate swaps (see "Derivative financial instruments" under "Accounting policies").

Investments with maturities of greater than six months consist primarily of A and A2 or better rated financial instruments and counterparties. Investments with maturities of up to six months consist primarily of A1 and P1 or better rated financial instruments and counterparties. Foreign government regulations imposed upon investment alternatives of foreign subsidiaries, or the absence of A and A2 rated counterparties in certain countries, result in some minor exceptions. Intel's practice is to obtain and secure available collateral from counterparties against obligations whenever Intel deems appropriate. At December 28, 1996, investments were placed with approximately 200 different counterparties.

Investments at December 28, 1996 were as follows:

(In millions)	Cost	Gross unrealized gains	Gross unrealized losses	Estimated fair value
Commercial paper	$ 2,386	$ —	$ (1)	$ 2,385
Bank deposits	1,846	—	(2)	1,844
Repurchase agreements	931	—	(1)	930
Loan participations	691	—	—	691
Corporate bonds	657	10	(6)	661
Floating rate notes	366	—	—	366
Securities of foreign governments	265	14	(2)	277
Fixed rate notes	262	—	—	262
Other debt securities	284	—	(2)	282
Total debt securities	7,688	24	(14)	7,698
Hedged equity	891	71	(15)	947
Preferred stock and other equity	270	174	(3)	441
Total equity securities	1,161	245	(18)	1,388
Swaps hedging investments in debt securities	—	5	(17)	(12)
Swaps hedging investments in equity securities	—	15	(42)	(27)
Options hedging investments in equity securities	(9)	—	(16)	(25)
Currency forward contracts hedging investments in debt securities	—	5	—	5
Total available-for-sale securities	**8,840**	**294**	**(107)**	**9,027**
Less amounts classified as cash equivalents	(3,932)	—	—	(3,932)
Total investments	**$ 4,908**	**$ 294**	**$ (107)**	**$ 5,095**

Notes to consolidated financial statements

Investments at December 30, 1995 were as follows:

(In millions)	Cost	Gross unrealized gains	Gross unrealized losses	Estimated fair value
Commercial paper	$ 576	$ —	$ —	$ 576
Repurchase agreements	474	—	—	474
Securities of foreign governments	456	1	(1)	456
Corporate bonds	375	5	—	380
Bank time deposits	360	—	—	360
Loan participations	278	—	—	278
Floating rate notes	224	—	—	224
Fixed rate notes	159	1	(1)	159
Collateralized mortgage obligations	129	—	(1)	128
Other debt securities	119	—	(1)	118
Total debt securities	3,150	7	(4)	3,153
Hedged equity	431	45	—	476
Preferred stock and other equity	309	91	(11)	389
Total equity securities	740	136	(11)	865
Swaps hedging investments in debt securities	—	2	(9)	(7)
Swaps hedging investments in equity securities	—	5	(47)	(42)
Currency forward contracts hedging investments in debt securities	—	3	—	3
Total available-for-sale securities	3,890	153	(71)	3,972
Less amounts classified as cash equivalents	(1,324)	—	—	(1,324)
Total investments	$ 2,566	$ 153	$ (71)	$ 2,648

In 1996 and 1995, debt and marketable securities with a fair value at the date of sale of $225 million and $114 million, respectively, were sold. The gross realized gains on such sales totaled $7 million and $60 million, respectively. There were no material proceeds, gross realized gains or gross realized losses from sales of securities in 1994.

The amortized cost and estimated fair value of investments in debt securities at December 28, 1996, by contractual maturity, were as follows:

(In millions)	Cost	Estimated fair value
Due in 1 year or less	$ 7,005	$ 7,007
Due in 1–2 years	320	327
Due in 2–5 years	86	88
Due after 5 years	277	276
Total investments in debt securities	$ 7,688	$ 7,698

Derivative financial instruments

Outstanding notional amounts for derivative financial instruments at fiscal year-ends were as follows:

(In millions)	1996	1995
Swaps hedging investments in debt securities	$ 900	$ 824
Swaps hedging investments in equity securities	$ 918	$ 567
Swaps hedging debt	$ 456	$ 156
Currency forward contracts	$ 1,499	$ 1,310
Currency options	$ 94	$ 28
Options hedging investments in marketable equity securities	$ 82	$ —
Options hedging investments in non-marketable instruments	$ —	$ 82

While the contract or notional amounts provide one measure of the volume of these transactions, they do not represent the amount of the Company's exposure to credit risk. The amounts potentially subject to credit risk (arising from the possible inability of counterparties to meet the terms of their contracts) are generally limited to the amounts, if any, by which the counterparties' obligations exceed the obligations of the Company. The Company controls credit risk through credit approvals, limits and monitoring procedures. Credit rating criteria for off-balance-sheet transactions are similar to those for investments.

Swap agreements. The Company utilizes swap agreements to exchange the foreign currency, equity and interest rate returns of its investment and debt portfolios for a floating U.S. dollar interest rate based return. The floating rates on swaps are based primarily on U.S. dollar LIBOR and reset on a monthly, quarterly or semiannual basis. Income or expense on swaps is accrued as an adjustment to the yield of the related investments or debt they hedge.

Pay rates on swaps hedging investments in debt securities match the yields on the underlying investments they hedge. Payments on swaps hedging investments in equity securities match the equity returns on the underlying investments they hedge. Receive rates on swaps hedging debt match the expense on the underlying debt they hedge. Maturity dates of swaps match those of the underlying investment or the debt they hedge. There is approximately a one-to-one matching of swaps to investments and debt. Swap agreements remain in effect until expiration. If a contract remains outstanding after the termination of a hedged relationship, subsequent changes in the market value of the contract would be recognized in earnings.

25

Weighted average pay and receive rates, average maturities and range of maturities on swaps at December 28, 1996 were as follows:

	Weighted average pay rate	Weighted average receive rate	Weighted average maturity	Range of maturities
Swaps hedging investments in U.S. dollar debt securities	6.3%	5.7%	.7 years	0–2 years
Swaps hedging investments in foreign currency debt securities	8.7%	7.4%	.8 years	0–3 years
Swaps hedging investments in equity securities	N/A	5.6%	.4 years	0–1 years
Swaps hedging debt	5.6%	6.9%	3.9 years	2–5 years

Note: Pay and receive rates are based on the reset rates that were in effect at December 28, 1996.

Other foreign currency instruments. Intel transacts business in various foreign currencies, primarily Japanese yen and certain European currencies. The Company has established revenue and balance sheet hedging programs to protect against reductions in value and volatility of future cash flows caused by changes in foreign exchange rates. The Company utilizes currency forward contracts and currency options in these hedging programs. The maturities on these instruments are less than 12 months. Deferred gains or losses attributable to foreign currency instruments are not material.

26 **Fair values of financial instruments**

The estimated fair values of financial instruments outstanding at fiscal year-ends were as follows:

	1996		1995	
(In millions)	Carrying amount	Estimated fair value	Carrying amount	Estimated fair value
Cash and cash equivalents	$ 4,165	$ 4,165	$ 1,463	$ 1,463
Short-term investments	$ 3,736	$ 3,736	$ 995	$ 995
Trading assets	$ 87	$ 87	$ —	$ —
Long-term investments	$ 1,418	$ 1,418	$ 1,699	$ 1,699
Non-marketable instruments	$ 119	$ 194	$ 239	$ 259
Swaps hedging investments in debt securities	$ (12)	$ (12)	$ (7)	$ (7)
Swaps hedging investments in equity securities	$ (27)	$ (27)	$ (42)	$ (42)
Options hedging investments in marketable equity securities	$ (25)	$ (25)	$ —	$ —
Options hedging investments in non-marketable instruments	$ —	$ —	$ (9)	$ (13)
Short-term debt	$ (389)	$ (389)	$ (346)	$ (346)
Long-term debt	$ (728)	$ (731)	$ (400)	$ (399)
Swaps hedging debt	$ —	$ 13	$ —	$ (1)
Currency forward contracts	$ 5	$ 18	$ 3	$ 4
Currency options	$ —	$ —	$ —	$ —

Concentrations of credit risk

Financial instruments that potentially subject the Company to concentrations of credit risk consist principally of investments and trade receivables. Intel places its investments with high-credit-quality counterparties and, by policy, limits the amount of credit exposure to any one counterparty. A substantial majority of the Company's trade receivables are derived from sales to manufacturers of microcomputer systems, with the remainder spread across various other industries.

During 1995, the Company experienced an increase in its concentration of credit risk due to increasing trade receivables from sales to manufacturers of microcomputer systems. Although the financial exposure to individual customers increased in 1996, the concentration of credit among the largest customers decreased slightly during the year. The Company's five largest customers accounted for approximately 30% of net revenues for 1996. At December 28, 1996, these customers accounted for approximately 25% of net accounts receivable.

The Company endeavors to keep pace with the evolving computer industry and has adopted credit policies and standards intended to accommodate industry growth and inherent risk. Management believes that credit risks are moderated by the diversity of its end customers and geographic sales areas. Intel performs ongoing credit evaluations of its customers' financial condition and requires collateral as deemed necessary.

Interest income and other

(In millions)	1996	1995	1994
Interest income	$ 364	$ 272	$ 235
Foreign currency gains	26	29	15
Other income	16	114	23
Total	**$ 406**	**$ 415**	**$ 273**

Other income for 1995 included approximately $58 million from the settlement of ongoing litigation and $60 million from sales of a portion of the Company's investment in marketable equity securities. Other income for 1994 included non-recurring gains from the settlement of various insurance claims.

Provision for taxes

The provision for taxes consisted of the following:

(In millions)	1996	1995	1994
Income before taxes:			
U.S.	$ 5,515	$ 3,427	$ 2,460
Foreign	2,419	2,211	1,143
Total income before taxes	**$ 7,934**	**$ 5,638**	**$ 3,603**
Provision for taxes:			
Federal:			
Current	$ 2,046	$ 1,169	$ 1,169
Deferred	8	307	(178)
	2,054	1,476	991
State:			
Current	286	203	162
Foreign:			
Current	266	354	134
Deferred	171	39	28
	437	393	162
Total provision for taxes	**$ 2,777**	**$ 2,072**	**$ 1,315**
Effective tax rate	**35.0%**	**36.8%**	**36.5%**

Notes to consolidated financial statements

The tax benefit associated with dispositions from employee stock plans reduced taxes currently payable for 1996 by $196 million ($116 million and $61 million for 1995 and 1994, respectively).

The provision for taxes reconciles to the amount computed by applying the statutory federal rate of 35% to income before taxes as follows:

(In millions)	1996	1995	1994
Computed expected tax	$ 2,777	$ 1,973	$ 1,261
State taxes, net of federal benefits	186	132	105
Other	(186)	(33)	(51)
Provision for taxes	**$ 2,777**	**$ 2,072**	**$ 1,315**

Deferred income taxes reflect the net tax effects of temporary differences between the carrying amount of assets and liabilities for financial reporting purposes and the amounts used for income tax purposes.

Significant components of the Company's deferred tax assets and liabilities at fiscal year-ends were as follows:

(In millions)	1996	1995
Deferred tax assets		
Accrued compensation and benefits	$ 71	$ 61
Deferred income	147	127
Inventory valuation and related reserves	187	104
Interest and taxes	54	61
Other, net	111	55
	570	408
Deferred tax liabilities		
Depreciation	(573)	(475)
Unremitted earnings of certain subsidiaries	(359)	(116)
Other, net	(65)	(29)
	(997)	(620)
Net deferred tax (liability)	**$ (427)**	**$ (212)**

U.S. income taxes were not provided for on a cumulative total of approximately $992 million of undistributed earnings for certain non-U.S. subsidiaries. The Company intends to reinvest these earnings indefinitely in operations outside the United States.

During 1996, Intel reached resolution on all outstanding issues related to income tax returns for the years 1978–1987. Final adjustments were also received from the Internal Revenue Service (IRS) for the years 1988–1990. Neither event had a material effect on the Company's 1996 financial statements.

The Company's U.S. income tax returns for the years 1991–1993 are presently under examination by the IRS. Final proposed adjustments have not yet been received for these years. Management believes that adequate amounts of tax and related interest and penalties, if any, have been provided for any adjustments that may result for the years under examination.

Employee benefit plans

Stock option plans. Intel has a stock option plan (hereafter referred to as the EOP Plan) under which officers, key employees and non-employee directors may be granted options to pur-

chase shares of the Company's authorized but unissued Common Stock. The Company also has an Executive Long-Term Stock Option Plan (ELTSOP) under which certain employees, including officers, may be granted options to purchase shares of the Company's authorized but unissued Common Stock. In January 1997 the Board of Directors approved the 1997 Stock Option Plan, which made an additional 65 million shares available for employees other than officers and directors. Under all plans, the option purchase price is equal to fair market value at the date of grant.

Options currently expire no later than ten years from the grant date and generally vest after five years. Proceeds received by the Company from exercises are credited to Common Stock and capital in excess of par value. Additional information with respect to the EOP and the ELTSOP activity was as follows:

		Outstanding options	
(In millions)	Shares available for options	Number of shares	Weighted average exercise price
December 25, 1993	**64.8**	**83.6**	**$ 11.90**
Grants	(12.0)	12.0	$ 33.08
Exercises	—	(8.8)	$ 6.59
Cancellations	1.6	(1.6)	$ 20.63
December 31, 1994	**54.4**	**85.2**	**$ 15.28**
Grants	(14.0)	14.0	$ 48.22
Exercises	—	(10.7)	$ 8.14
Cancellations	3.0	(3.0)	$ 25.66
December 30, 1995	**43.4**	**85.5**	**$ 21.20**
Grants	(13.3)	13.3	$ 69.12
Exercises	—	(11.9)	$ 9.86
Cancellations	2.5	(2.5)	$ 34.10
December 28, 1996	**32.6**	**84.4**	**$ 29.96**
Options exercisable at:			
December 31, 1994		28.8	$ 7.54
December 30, 1995		29.1	$ 9.10
December 28, 1996		28.6	$ 11.44

The range of exercise prices for options outstanding at December 28, 1996 was $4.79 to $131.19. The range of exercise prices for options is wide due primarily to the increasing price of the Company's stock over the period of the grants.

The following tables summarize information about options outstanding at December 28, 1996:

	Outstanding options		
Range of exercise prices	Number of shares (in millions)	Weighted average contractual life (in years)	Weighted average exercise price
$4.79–$13.41	34.0	3.7	$10.26
$13.63–$36.13	25.3	6.7	$27.29
$38.91–$131.19	25.1	8.9	$59.12
Total	**84.4**	**6.1**	**$29.96**

Notes to consolidated financial statements

	Exercisable options	
Range of exercise prices	Number of shares (in millions)	Weighted average exercise price
$4.79–$13.41	25.6	$ 9.34
$13.63–$36.13	2.6	$24.92
$38.91–$131.19	.4	$55.21
Total	**28.6**	**$11.44**

These options will expire if not exercised at specific dates ranging from January 1997 to December 2006. Prices for options exercised during the three-year period ended December 28, 1996 ranged from $3.04 to $69.43.

Stock Participation Plan. Under this plan, eligible employees may purchase shares of Intel's Common Stock at 85% of fair market value at specific, predetermined dates. Of the 118 million shares authorized to be issued under the plan, 23.8 million shares were available for issuance at December 28, 1996. Employees purchased 3.5 million shares in 1996 (3.5 million and 4.0 million in 1995 and 1994, respectively) for $140 million ($110 million and $94 million in 1995 and 1994, respectively).

Pro forma information. The Company has elected to follow APB Opinion No. 25, "Accounting for Stock Issued to Employees," in accounting for its employee stock options because, as discussed below, the alternative fair value accounting provided for under SFAS No. 123, "Accounting for Stock-Based Compensation," requires the use of option valuation models that were not developed for use in valuing employee stock options. Under APB No. 25, because the exercise price of the Company's employee stock options equals the market price of the underlying stock on the date of grant, no compensation expense is recognized in the Company's financial statements.

Pro forma information regarding net income and earnings per share is required by SFAS No. 123. This information is required to be determined as if the Company had accounted for its employee stock options (including shares issued under the Stock Participation Plan, collectively called "options") granted subsequent to December 31, 1994 under the fair value method of that statement. The fair value of options granted in 1995 and 1996 reported below has been estimated at the date of grant using a Black-Scholes option pricing model with the following weighted average assumptions:

	Employee stock options		Stock Participation Plan shares	
	1996	1995	1996	1995
Expected life (in years)	6.5	6.5	.5	.5
Risk-free interest rate	6.5%	6.8%	5.3%	6.0%
Volatility	.36	.36	.36	.36
Dividend yield	.2%	.3%	.2%	.3%

The Black-Scholes option valuation model was developed for use in estimating the fair value of traded options that have no vesting restrictions and are fully transferable. In addition, option valuation models require the input of highly subjective assumptions, including the expected stock price volatility. Because the Company's options have characteristics significantly different from those of traded options, and because changes in the subjective input assumptions can materially affect the fair value estimate, in the opinion of management, the existing models do not necessarily provide a reliable single measure of the fair value of its options. The weighted average estimated fair value of employee stock options granted during 1996 and 1995 was $32.69 and $23.26 per share, respectively. The weighted average estimated fair value of shares granted under the Stock Participation Plan during 1996 and 1995 was $16.22 and $12.25, respectively.

For purposes of pro forma disclosures, the estimated fair value of the options is amortized to expense over the options' vesting period. The Company's pro forma information follows (in millions except for earnings per share information):

	1996	1995
Pro forma net income	$ 5,046	$ 3,506
Pro forma earnings per share	$ 5.68	$ 3.96

The effects on pro forma disclosures of applying SFAS No. 123 are not likely to be representative of the effects on pro forma disclosures of future years. Because SFAS No. 123 is applicable only to options granted subsequent to December 31, 1994, the pro forma effect will not be fully reflected until 1999.

Retirement plans. The Company provides tax-qualified profit-sharing retirement plans (the "Qualified Plans") for the benefit of eligible employees in the U.S. and Puerto Rico and certain foreign countries. The plans are designed to provide employees with an accumulation of funds for retirement on a tax-deferred basis and provide for annual discretionary contributions to trust funds.

The Company also provides a non-qualified profit-sharing retirement plan (the "Non-Qualified Plan") for the benefit of eligible employees in the U.S. This plan is designed to permit certain discretionary employer contributions in excess of the tax limits applicable to the Qualified Plans and to permit employee deferrals in excess of certain tax limits. This plan is unfunded.

The Company accrued $209 million for the Qualified Plans and the Non-Qualified Plan in 1996 ($188 million in 1995 and $152 million in 1994). Of the $209 million accrued in 1996, the Company expects to fund approximately $181 million for the 1996 contribution to the Qualified Plans and to allocate approximately $10 million for the Non-Qualified Plan. The remainder, plus approximately $177 million carried forward from prior years, is expected to be contributed to these plans when allowable under IRS regulations and plan rules.

Contributions made by the Company vest based on the employee's years of service. Vesting begins after three years of service in 20% annual increments until the employee is 100% vested after seven years.

The Company provides tax-qualified defined-benefit pension plans for the benefit of eligible employees in the U.S. and Puerto Rico. Each plan provides for minimum pension benefits that are determined by a participant's years of service, final average

www.intel.com

Notes to consolidated financial statements

Intel Corporation 1996

compensation (taking into account the participant's social security wage base) and the value of the Company's contributions, plus earnings, in the Qualified Plan. If the participant's balance in the Qualified Plan exceeds the pension guarantee, the participant will receive benefits from the Qualified Plan only. Intel's funding policy is consistent with the funding requirements of federal laws and regulations.

Pension expense for 1996, 1995 and 1994 for the U.S. and Puerto Rico plans was less than $1 million per year, and no component of expense exceeded $3 million.

The funded status of these plans as of December 28, 1996 and December 30, 1995 was as follows:

(In millions)	1996	1995
Vested benefit obligation	**$ (3)**	**$ (3)**
Accumulated benefit obligation	**$ (4)**	**$ (4)**
Projected benefit obligation	$ (5)	$ (6)
Fair market value of plan assets	11	8
Projected benefit obligation less than plan assets	6	2
Unrecognized net (gain)	(15)	(12)
Unrecognized prior service cost	3	3
Accrued pension costs	**$ (6)**	**$ (7)**

At fiscal year-ends, the weighted average discount rates and long-term rates for compensation increases used for estimating the benefit obligations and the expected return on plan assets were as follows:

	1996	1995	1994
Discount rate	7.0%	7.0%	8.5%
Rate of increase in compensation levels	5.0%	5.0%	5.5%
Expected long-term return on assets	8.5%	8.5%	8.5%

Plan assets of the U.S. and Puerto Rico plans consist primarily of listed stocks and bonds, repurchase agreements, money market securities, U.S. government securities and stock index derivatives.

The Company provides defined-benefit pension plans in certain foreign countries where required by statute. The Company's funding policy for foreign defined-benefit plans is consistent with the local requirements in each country.

Pension expense for 1996, 1995 and 1994 for the foreign plans included the following:

(In millions)	1996	1995	1994
Service cost-benefits earned during the year	$ 10	$ 9	$ 5
Interest cost of projected benefit obligation	7	6	5
Actual investment (return) on plan assets	(14)	(4)	(8)
Net amortization and deferral	14	(2)	3
Net pension expense	**$ 17**	**$ 9**	**$ 5**

The funded status of the foreign defined-benefit plans as of December 28, 1996 and December 30, 1995 is summarized below:

1996 (In millions)	Assets exceed accumulated benefits	Accumulated benefits exceed assets
Vested benefit obligation	**$ (43)**	**$ (9)**
Accumulated benefit obligation	**$ (46)**	**$ (15)**
Projected benefit obligation	$ (62)	$ (23)
Fair market value of plan assets	68	3
Projected benefit obligation less than (in excess of) plan assets	6	(20)
Unrecognized net loss	3	3
Unrecognized net transition obligation	2	1
Prepaid (accrued) pension costs	**$ 11**	**$ (16)**

1995 (In millions)	Assets exceed accumulated benefits	Accumulated benefits exceed assets
Vested benefit obligation	**$ (44)**	**$ (8)**
Accumulated benefit obligation	**$ (46)**	**$ (14)**
Projected benefit obligation	$ (62)	$ (22)
Fair market value of plan assets	67	4
Projected benefit obligation less than (in excess of) plan assets	5	(18)
Unrecognized net loss	4	5
Unrecognized net transition obligation	2	—
Prepaid (accrued) pension costs	**$ 11**	**$ (13)**

At fiscal year-ends, the weighted average discount rates and long-term rates for compensation increases used for estimating the benefit obligations and the expected return on plan assets were as follows:

	1996	1995	1994
Discount rate	5.5%–14%	5.5%–14%	5.5%–14%
Rate of increase in compensation levels	4.5%–11%	4.5%–11%	4.5%–11%
Expected long-term return on assets	5.5%–14%	5.5%–14%	5.5%–14%

Plan assets of the foreign plans consist primarily of listed stocks, bonds and cash surrender value life insurance policies.

Other postemployment benefits. The Company has adopted SFAS No. 106, "Employers' Accounting for Postretirement Benefits Other Than Pensions," and SFAS No. 112, "Employers' Accounting for Postemployment Benefits." There was no material impact on the Company's financial statements for the periods presented.

www.intel.com
Notes to consolidated financial statements
Intel Corporation 1996

Commitments

The Company leases a portion of its capital equipment and certain of its facilities under operating leases that expire at various dates through 2011. Rental expense was $57 million in 1996, $38 million in 1995 and $38 million in 1994. Minimum rental commitments under all non-cancelable leases with an initial term in excess of one year are payable as follows: 1997–$23 million; 1998–$18 million; 1999–$14 million; 2000–$11 million; 2001–$9 million; 2002 and beyond–$25 million. Commitments for construction or purchase of property, plant and equipment approximated $1.6 billion at December 28, 1996. In connection with certain manufacturing arrangements, Intel had minimum purchase commitments of approximately $333 million at December 28, 1996 for flash memories and other memory components and for production capacity of board-level products.

Contingencies

In March 1995, EMI Group, N.A. (formerly known as Thorn EMI North America Inc.) brought suit in Federal Court in Delaware against Intel, alleging that certain Intel manufacturing processes infringe a U.S. patent. In May 1996, the Court granted Intel's motion for summary judgment on some of the processes in issue. In November 1996, the Court granted Intel's motion for summary judgment on the remaining processes in issue and entered judgment in favor of Intel and against EMI on the claims in EMI's complaint. EMI has filed a Notice of Appeal with respect to the Court's decision. Although the ultimate outcome of this lawsuit cannot be determined at this time, management, including internal counsel, does not believe that the outcome of this litigation will have a material adverse effect on the Company's financial position or overall trends in results of operations.

Intel has been named to the California and U.S. Superfund lists for three of its sites and has completed, along with two other companies, a Remedial Investigation/Feasibility study with the U.S. Environmental Protection Agency (EPA) to evaluate the groundwater in areas adjacent to one of its former sites. The EPA has issued a Record of Decision with respect to a groundwater cleanup plan at that site, including expected costs to complete. Under the California and U.S. Superfund statutes, liability for cleanup of this site and the adjacent area is joint and several. The Company, however, has reached agreement with those same two companies which significantly limits the Company's liabilities under the proposed cleanup plan. Also, the Company has completed extensive studies at its other sites and is engaged in cleanup at several of these sites. In the opinion of management, including internal counsel, the potential losses to the Company in excess of amounts already accrued arising out of these matters will not have a material adverse effect on the Company's financial position or overall trends in results of operations, even if joint and several liability were to be assessed.

The Company is party to various other legal proceedings. In the opinion of management, including internal counsel, these proceedings will not have a material adverse effect on the financial position or overall trends in results of operations of the Company.

The estimate of the potential impact on the Company's financial position or overall results of operations for the above legal proceedings could change in the future.

Industry segment reporting

Intel operates predominantly in one industry segment. The Company designs, develops, manufactures and markets microcomputer components and related products at various levels of integration. The Company sells its products directly to original equipment manufacturers (OEMs) and also to a network of industrial and retail distributors throughout the world. The Company's principal markets are in the United States, Europe, Asia-Pacific and Japan, with the U.S. and Europe being the largest based on revenues. The Company's major products include microprocessors and related board-level products, chipsets, embedded processors and microcontrollers, flash memory chips, and network and communications products. Microprocessors and related board-level products account for a substantial majority of the Company's net revenues. No customer exceeded 10% of revenues in 1996, 1995 or 1994. Summary balance sheet information for operations outside the United States at fiscal year-ends is as follows:

(In millions)	1996	1995
Assets	$ 4,784	$ 4,404
Total liabilities	$ 1,694	$ 1,661
Net property, plant and equipment	$ 1,615	$ 1,414

www.intel.com

Notes to consolidated financial statements

Geographic information for the three years ended December 28, 1996 is presented in the following tables. Transfers between geographic areas are accounted for at amounts that are generally above cost and consistent with rules and regulations of governing tax authorities. Such transfers are eliminated in the consolidated financial statements. Operating income by geographic segment does not include an allocation of general corporate expenses. Identifiable assets are those that can be directly associated with a particular geographic area. Corporate assets include cash and cash equivalents, short-term investments, trading assets, deferred tax assets, long-term investments and certain other assets.

(In millions) 1996	Sales to unaffiliated customers	Transfers between geographic areas	Net revenues	Operating income	Identifiable assets
United States	$ 8,668	$ 9,846	$ 18,514	$ 5,255	$ 12,982
Europe	5,876	917	6,793	1,118	2,405
Japan	2,459	20	2,479	340	659
Asia-Pacific	3,844	2,004	5,848	509	1,361
Other	—	865	865	529	359
Eliminations	—	(13,652)	(13,652)	453	(3,439)
Corporate	—	—	—	(651)	9,408
Consolidated	**$ 20,847**	**$ —**	**$ 20,847**	**$ 7,553**	**$ 23,735**

1995					
United States	$ 7,922	$ 6,339	$ 14,261	$ 3,315	$ 12,603
Europe	4,560	1,190	5,750	1,383	2,517
Japan	1,737	28	1,765	353	665
Asia-Pacific	1,983	1,566	3,549	271	893
Other	—	684	684	410	329
Eliminations	—	(9,807)	(9,807)	124	(3,651)
Corporate	—	—	—	(604)	4,148
Consolidated	**$ 16,202**	**$ —**	**$ 16,202**	**$ 5,252**	**$ 17,504**

1994					
United States	$ 5,826	$ 4,561	$10,387	$ 2,742	$ 7,771
Europe	3,158	380	3,538	418	1,733
Japan	944	61	1,005	125	343
Asia-Pacific	1,593	1,021	2,614	154	540
Other	—	639	639	378	324
Eliminations	—	(6,662)	(6,662)	179	(1,878)
Corporate	—	—	—	(609)	4,983
Consolidated	**$ 11,521**	**$ —**	**$ 11,521**	**$ 3,387**	**$ 13,816**

31

Supplemental information (unaudited)
Quarterly information for the two years ended December 28, 1996 is presented on page 37.

Report of Ernst & Young LLP, independent auditors
Intel Corporation 1996

The Board of Directors and Stockholders, Intel Corporation

We have audited the accompanying consolidated balance sheets of Intel Corporation as of December 28, 1996 and December 30, 1995, and the related consolidated statements of income, stockholders' equity, and cash flows for each of the three years in the period ended December 28, 1996. These financial statements are the responsibility of the Company's management. Our responsibility is to express an opinion on these financial statements based on our audits.

We conducted our audits in accordance with generally accepted auditing standards. Those standards require that we plan and perform the audit to obtain reasonable assurance about whether the financial statements are free of material misstatement. An audit includes examining, on a test basis, evidence supporting the amounts and disclosures in the financial statements. An audit also includes assessing the accounting principles used and significant estimates made by management, as well as evaluating the overall financial statement presentation. We believe that our audits provide a reasonable basis for our opinion.

In our opinion, the consolidated financial statements referred to above present fairly, in all material respects, the consolidated financial position of Intel Corporation at December 28, 1996 and December 30, 1995, and the consolidated results of its operations and its cash flows for each of the three years in the period ended December 28, 1996, in conformity with generally accepted accounting principles.

Ernst & Young LLP

San Jose, California
January 13, 1997

32

Financial summary

Ten Years Ended December 28, 1996

(In millions)	Net investment in property, plant & equipment	Total assets	Long-term debt & put warrants	Stock-holders' equity	Additions to property, plant & equipment
1996	$ 8,487	$ 23,735	$ 1,003	$ 16,872	$ 3,024
1995	$ 7,471	$ 17,504	$ 1,125	$ 12,140	$ 3,550
1994	$ 5,367	$ 13,816	$ 1,136	$ 9,267	$ 2,441
1993	$ 3,996	$ 11,344	$ 1,114	$ 7,500	$ 1,933
1992	$ 2,816	$ 8,089	$ 622	$ 5,445	$ 1,228
1991	$ 2,163	$ 6,292	$ 503	$ 4,418	$ 948
1990	$ 1,658	$ 5,376	$ 345	$ 3,592	$ 680
1989	$ 1,284	$ 3,994	$ 412	$ 2,549	$ 422
1988	$ 1,122	$ 3,550	$ 479	$ 2,080	$ 477
1987	$ 891	$ 2,499	$ 298	$ 1,276	$ 302

(In millions—except per share amounts)	Net revenues	Cost of sales	Research & development	Operating income	Net income	Earnings per share	Dividends declared per share
1996	$ 20,847	$ 9,164	$ 1,808	$ 7,553	$ 5,157	$ 5.81	$ .19
1995	$ 16,202	$ 7,811	$ 1,296	$ 5,252	$ 3,566	$ 4.03	$ .15
1994	$ 11,521	$ 5,576	$ 1,111	$ 3,387	$ 2,288	$ 2.62	$ .115
1993	$ 8,782	$ 3,252	$ 970	$ 3,392	$ 2,295	$ 2.60	$ .10
1992	$ 5,844	$ 2,557	$ 780	$ 1,490	$ 1,067	$ 1.24	$ .05
1991	$ 4,779	$ 2,316	$ 618	$ 1,080	$ 819	$ .98	—
1990	$ 3,921	$ 1,930	$ 517	$ 858	$ 650	$ .80	—
1989	$ 3,127	$ 1,721	$ 365	$ 557	$ 391	$ .52	—
1988	$ 2,875	$ 1,506	$ 318	$ 594	$ 453	$ .63	—
1987	$ 1,907	$ 1,044	$ 260	$ 246	$ 248	$ .34	—

33

Results of operations

Intel posted record net revenues in 1996, for the tenth consecutive year, rising by 29% from 1995 to 1996 and by 41% from 1994 to 1995. Higher volumes of the rapidly ramping Pentium® microprocessor family, partially offset by lower processor prices and decreased revenues from sales of related board-level products, were responsible for most of the growth in revenues from 1995 to 1996. The Pentium® Pro microprocessor family, introduced in late 1995, also contributed to the growth in revenues from 1995 to 1996. The growth in revenues from 1994 to 1995 was driven primarily by higher volumes of the Pentium processor family and related board-level products, which surpassed sales of the Intel486™ microprocessor family in the third quarter of 1995. Revenues from the Intel486 microprocessor family declined substantially in 1995 and 1996, primarily due to this shift in market demand toward the Company's more advanced microprocessors.

Higher volumes of flash memory and chipset products also contributed toward the increase in revenues from 1994 to 1996 and also helped enable the successful Pentium and Pentium Pro microprocessor ramps. Revenues from embedded control products and networking and communications products also grew over this period.

Cost of sales increased by 17% from 1995 to 1996 and by 40% from 1994 to 1995. The overall growth in cost of sales from 1994 to 1996 was driven by unit volume growth in Pentium microprocessor and related board-level products, new factories commencing production, manufacturing process conversions and shifts in product mix. While revenues increased substantially from 1995 to 1996, growth in cost of sales was significantly less. Cost of sales in the first half of 1996 and the fourth quarter of 1995 were negatively impacted by unusually high reserves related to inventories of certain purchased components. The second half of 1996 was favorably impacted by factory efficiencies from higher volumes, as well as relatively lower new factory startup costs. In addition, in the second half of 1996 the Company sold significantly more processor products than in the second half of 1995.

The gross margin percentage was 56% in 1996, compared to 52% in 1995 and 1994. However, as a result of all of the revenue and cost factors discussed above, the gross margin percentage in the second half of 1996 was 60% (63% in the fourth quarter), compared to 50% in the second half of 1995 (48% in the fourth quarter). Gross margin for the fourth quarter of 1994 included the impact of a $475 million charge, primarily to cost of sales, related to a divide problem in the floating point unit of the Pentium microprocessor. See "Outlook" for a discussion of gross margin expectations.

Sales of Pentium microprocessors and related board-level products comprised a majority of the Company's revenues and a substantial majority of its gross margin during 1995 and 1996. During 1996 Pentium Pro microprocessors and related board-level products became an increasing portion of the Company's revenues and gross margin. The Intel486 microprocessor family contributed negligible revenues and gross margin during 1996. During 1995, the Intel486 microprocessor family represented a significant but rapidly declining portion of the Company's revenues and gross margin, while it comprised a majority of the Company's revenues and a substantial majority of its gross margin during 1994.

Research and development spending grew by 40% from 1995 to 1996 and 17% from 1994 to 1995, as the Company substantially increased its investments over this time period in strategic programs, particularly for the internal development of microprocessor products and related manufacturing technology. Increased spending for marketing programs, including media merchandising and the Company's Intel Inside® cooperative advertising program, and other revenue-dependent expenses drove the 26% and 27% increases in marketing, general and administrative expenses from 1995 to 1996 and from 1994 to 1995, respectively.

The $4 million decrease in interest expense from 1995 to 1996 was mainly due to lower average borrowing balances and interest rates in 1996, partially offset by lower interest capitalization. The decrease in interest expense from 1994 to 1995 was primarily due to lower average borrowing balances in 1995 in addition to higher interest capitalization resulting from increased facility construction programs.

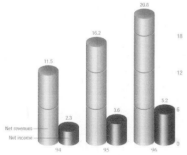

Revenues and income
(Dollars in billions)

Costs and expenses
(Percent of revenues)

www.intel.com
Management's discussion and analysis of financial condition and results of operations
Intel Corporation 1996

Although the Company had higher average investment balances in 1996, interest and other income decreased by $9 million from 1995 to 1996, primarily due to the offsetting effect of $118 million in unusual gains in 1995. Interest and other income increased by $142 million from 1994 to 1995, mainly due to the previously noted gains in 1995, in addition to higher average interest rates on investments in 1995.

The Company utilizes investments and corresponding interest rate swaps to preserve principal while enhancing the yield on its investment portfolio without significantly increasing risk, and uses forward contracts, options and swaps to hedge foreign currency, equity and interest rate market exposures of underlying assets, liabilities and other obligations. Gains and losses on these instruments are generally offset by those on the underlying hedged transactions; as a result, there was no material net impact on the Company's financial results during the 1994 to 1996 period.

The Company's effective income tax rate decreased to 35.0% in 1996 compared to 36.8% and 36.5% in 1995 and 1994, respectively.

Financial condition

The Company's financial condition remains very strong. As of December 28, 1996, total cash and short- and long-term investments totaled $9.3 billion, up from $4.1 billion at December 30, 1995. Cash generated from operating activities rose to $8.7 billion in 1996, compared to $4.0 billion and $2.9 billion in 1995 and 1994, respectively.

Investing activities consumed $5.3 billion in cash during 1996, compared to $2.7 billion during 1995 and $2.9 billion during 1994, as operating activities generated significantly more cash during 1996. Capital expenditures totaled $3.0 billion in 1996, as the Company continued to invest in property, plant and equipment, primarily for microprocessor manufacturing capacity. The Company had committed approximately $1.6 billion for the construction or purchase of property, plant and equipment as of December 28, 1996. See "Outlook" for a discussion of capital expenditure expectations in 1997.

Inventory levels, particularly raw materials and finished goods, decreased significantly in 1996. This decrease was primarily attributable to the sell-through of purchased parts inventory and lower costs of manufacturing. The increase in accounts receivable

in 1996 was mainly due to revenue growth, offset somewhat by improved receivable collections. During 1995, the Company experienced an increase in its concentration of credit risk due to increasing trade receivables from sales to manufacturers of microcomputer systems. Although the financial exposure to individual customers has increased with the growth in revenues, the concentration of credit among the largest customers has decreased slightly in 1996. The Company's five largest customers accounted for approximately 30% of net revenues for 1996. At December 28, 1996, these customers accounted for approximately 25% of net accounts receivable.

The Company used $773 million for financing activities in 1996, compared to $1.1 billion and $557 million in 1995 and 1994, respectively. The major financing applications of cash in 1996 and 1995 were for stock repurchases totaling $1.3 billion for 16.8 million shares (including $108 million for exercised put warrants) and $1.0 billion for 18.9 million shares, respectively. Financing applications of cash in 1994 included stock repurchases of $658 million and the early retirement of the Company's 8⅛% debt. Financing sources of cash during 1996 included $300 million under a private reverse repurchase arrangement and $261 million in proceeds from the sale of shares primarily pursuant to employee stock plans ($192 million in 1995 and $150 million in 1994).

As part of its authorized stock repurchase program, the Company had outstanding put warrants at the end of 1996, with the potential obligation to buy back 4.5 million shares of its Common Stock at an aggregate price of $275 million. The exercise price of these warrants ranged from $56 to $69 per share, with an average exercise price of $61 per share as of December 28, 1996.

Other sources of liquidity include combined credit lines and authorized commercial paper borrowings of $1.8 billion, $30 million of which was outstanding at December 28, 1996. The Company also maintains the ability to issue an aggregate of approximately $1.4 billion in debt, equity and other securities under Securities and Exchange Commission (SEC) shelf

35

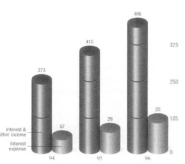

Other income and expense
(Dollars in millions)

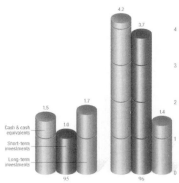

Cash and investments
(Dollars in billions)

registration statements. The Company believes that it has the financial resources needed to meet business requirements in the foreseeable future, including capital expenditures for the expansion of worldwide manufacturing capacity, working capital requirements, the potential put warrant obligation and the dividend program.

Outlook

The outlook section contains a number of forward-looking statements, all of which are based on current expectations. Actual results may differ materially.

Intel expects that the total number of personal computers using Intel's Pentium and Pentium Pro microprocessors and other semiconductor components sold worldwide will continue to grow in 1997. Intel has expanded manufacturing capacity over the last few years and continues to expand capacity. Intel's financial results are substantially dependent on this market segment. Revenue is also a function of the mix of microprocessors and related motherboards and the mix of microprocessor types and speed, all of which are difficult to forecast. Because of the large price difference between types of microprocessors, this mix affects the average price Intel will realize and has a large impact on Intel's revenues.

Intel's strategy has been, and continues to be, to introduce ever higher performance microprocessors. To implement this strategy, the Company plans to cultivate new businesses and continue to work with the software industry to develop compelling applications that can take advantage of this higher performance, thus driving demand toward the newer products. In line with this strategy, the Company has recently announced higher performance members of the Pentium microprocessor family, including the Pentium processor with MMX™ technology. Capacity has been planned based on the assumed continued success of the Company's strategy. If the market demand does not continue to grow and move rapidly toward higher performance products, revenues and gross margin may be impacted, the manufacturing capacity installed might be under-utilized and capital spending may be slowed. The Company may continue to reduce microprocessor prices aggressively and systematically to bring its technology to market.

The Company's gross margin percentage is a sensitive function of the product mixes sold in any period. Because the percentage of motherboards that Intel's customers purchase changes with the maturity of the product cycle, and motherboards generally have lower gross margin percentages than microprocessors, Intel's gross margin percentage varies depending on the mix of microprocessors and related motherboards within a product family and the mix of types of microprocessors. Various other factors, including unit volumes and costs, and yield issues associated with production at factories, processor speed mix and mix of shipments of other semiconductors, will also continue to affect the amount of cost of sales and the variability of gross margin percentages in future quarters. The Company's goal continues to be to grow gross margin dollars. Intel's current gross

margin expectation for 1997 is 60% plus or minus a few points. However, the Company believes that over the long-term the gross margin percentage will be 50% plus or minus a few points, as the Company introduces higher performance products and costs continue to increase. In addition, from time to time the Company may forecast a range of gross margin percentages for the coming quarter. Actual results may differ from these estimates.

To implement its strategy, Intel continues to build capacity to produce high-performance microprocessors and other products. The Company expects that capital spending will increase to approximately $4.5 billion in 1997 to support significant expansion of worldwide manufacturing capacity. This spending plan is dependent upon changes in manufacturing efficiencies, delivery times of various machines and construction schedules for new facilities. Depreciation for 1997 is expected to be approximately $2.5 billion, an increase of approximately $600 million from 1996. Most of this increased depreciation would be included in cost of sales and research and development spending.

The industry in which Intel operates is characterized by very short product life cycles. Intel considers it imperative to maintain a strong research and development program to continue to succeed. The Company will also continue spending to promote its products and to increase the value of its product brands. Based on current forecasts, spending for marketing and general and administrative expenses is expected to increase in 1997.

The Company currently expects its tax rate to increase to 35.5% for 1997. This estimate is based on current tax law and current estimate of earnings, and is subject to change.

The Company's future results of operations and the other forward-looking statements contained in this outlook, in particular the statements regarding growth in the personal computer industry, gross margin, capital spending, depreciation, research and development, and marketing and general and administrative expenses, involve a number of risks and uncertainties. In addition to the factors discussed above, among the other factors that could cause actual results to differ materially are the following: business conditions and growth in the computing industry and in the general economy; changes in customer order patterns, including timing of delivery and changes in seasonal fluctuations in PC buying patterns; competitive factors, such as rival chip architectures, competing software-compatible microprocessors, acceptance of new products and price pressures; risk of inventory obsolescence due to shifts in market demand; variations in inventory valuation; timing of software industry product introductions; continued success in technological advances and their implementation, including the manufacturing ramp; shortage of manufacturing capacity; risks associated with foreign operations; changes in product mixes; and litigation involving intellectual property and consumer issues.

Intel believes that it has the product offerings, facilities, personnel, and competitive and financial resources for continued business success, but future revenues, costs, margins and profits are all influenced by a number of factors, including those discussed above, all of which are inherently difficult to forecast.

36

Financial information by quarter (unaudited)

Intel Corporation 1996

(In millions—except per share data)

1996 for quarter ended	*December 28*	*September 28*	*June 29*	*March 30*
Net revenues	$ 6,440	$ 5,142	$ 4,621	$ 4,644
Cost of sales	$ 2,392	$ 2,201	$ 2,150	$ 2,421
Net income	$ 1,910	$ 1,312	$ 1,041	$ 894
Earnings per share	$ 2.13	$ 1.48	$ 1.17	$ 1.02
Dividends per share[A] Declared	$ .05	$ .05	$ .05	$ .04
Paid	$ .05	$ .05	$ .04	$ .04
Market price range Common Stock[B] High	$137.50	$ 97.38	$ 76.88	$ 61.00
Low	$ 95.44	$ 69.00	$ 56.88	$ 50.00
Market price range Step-Up Warrants[B] High	$ 98.38	$ 58.88	$ 39.31	$ 28.50
Low	$ 56.75	$ 31.75	$ 24.00	$ 21.63

(In millions—except per share data)

1995 for quarter ended	*December 30*	*September 30*	*July 1*	*April 1*
Net revenues	$ 4,580	$ 4,171	$ 3,894	$ 3,557
Cost of sales	$ 2,389	$ 2,008	$ 1,805	$ 1,609
Net income	$ 867	$ 931	$ 879	$ 889
Earnings per share	$ .98	$ 1.05	$ .99	$ 1.02
Dividends per share[A] Declared	$ .04	$ .04	$ .04	$ .03
Paid	$ .04	$ .04	$ .03	$ .03
Market price range Common Stock[B] High	$ 72.88	$ 76.44	$ 65.63	$ 44.25
Low	$ 56.75	$ 58.63	$ 42.75	$ 31.81
Market price range Step-Up Warrants[B] High	$ 39.00	$ 43.63	$ 31.88	$ 11.91
Low	$ 26.75	$ 30.44	$ 11.31	$ 6.97

[A] Intel plans to continue its dividend program. However, dividends are dependent on future earnings, capital requirements and financial condition.

[B] Intel's Common Stock (symbol INTC) and 1998 Step-Up Warrants (symbol INTCW) trade on The Nasdaq Stock Market* and are quoted in the Wall Street Journal *and other newspapers. Intel's Common Stock also trades on the Zurich, Basel and Geneva, Switzerland exchanges. At December 28, 1996, there were approximately 105,000 registered holders of Common Stock. All stock and warrant prices are closing prices per The Nasdaq Stock Market.*

37

Board of directors

Gordon E. Moore [3]
Chairman of the Board

Andrew S. Grove [3]
President and
Chief Executive Officer

Craig R. Barrett
Executive Vice President
and Chief Operating
Officer

John P. Browne
Group Chief Executive
The British Petroleum
Company p.l.c.
An integrated oil company

Winston H. Chen [1]
Chairman
Paramitas Foundation
A private foundation

D. James Guzy [4]
Chairman
Arbor Corporation
A limited partnership

Max Palevsky [2 4†]
Industrialist

Arthur Rock [1† 2 3† 4]
Principal of Arthur Rock
and Company
A venture capital firm

Jane E. Shaw [1 2]
Founder,
The Stable Network
*A biopharmaceutical
consulting company*

Leslie L. Vadasz
Senior Vice President
Director, Corporate
Business Development

David B. Yoffie [2† 4]
Max and Doris Starr
Professor of International
Business Administration
Harvard Business School

Charles E. Young [1]
Chancellor
University of California
at Los Angeles

[1] *Member of the Audit &
Finance Committee*

[2] *Member of the
Compensation Committee*

[3] *Member of the
Executive Committee*

[4] *Member of the
Nominating Committee*

[†] *Committee Chairman*

Directors emeriti

Richard Hodgson
Industrialist

Sanford Kaplan
Retired corporate
executive

Corporate officers

Gordon E. Moore
Chairman of the Board

Andrew S. Grove
President and
Chief Executive Officer

Craig R. Barrett
Executive Vice President
and Chief Operating
Officer

Frank C. Gill
Executive Vice President
General Manager,
Internet and
Communications Group

Paul S. Otellini
Executive Vice President
Director, Sales and
Marketing Group

Gerhard H. Parker
Executive Vice President
General Manager,
Technology and
Manufacturing Group

Leslie L. Vadasz
Senior Vice President
Director, Corporate
Business Development

Ronald J. Whittier
Senior Vice President
General Manager,
Content Group

Albert Y. C. Yu
Senior Vice President
General Manager,
Microprocessor
Products Group

Michael A. Aymar
Vice President
General Manager,
Desktop Products Group

Andy D. Bryant
Vice President
Chief Financial Officer

Dennis L. Carter
Vice President
Director, Sales and
Marketing Group

Sunlin Chou
Vice President
Director, Components
Technology Development

F. Thomas Dunlap, Jr.
Vice President
General Counsel and
Secretary

Kirby A. Dyess
Vice President
Director, Internet and
Communications Group
New Business
Development

Carlene M. Ellis
Vice President
Director, Information
Technology

Patrick P. Gelsinger
Vice President
General Manager,
Desktop Products Group

Hans G. Geyer
Vice President
General Manager,
European Operations

Thomas L. Hogue
Vice President
Director, Materials

Harold E. Hughes, Jr.
Vice President
Director, Planning and
Logistics

Robert T. Jenkins
Vice President
Director,
Corporate Licensing

D. Craig Kinnie
Vice President
Assistant General
Manager, Internet and
Communications Group

Edward A. Masi
Vice President
Enterprise Server Group

Avram C. Miller
Vice President
Director, Business
Development

John H. F. Miner
Vice President
General Manager,
Enterprise Server Group

Stephen P. Nachtsheim
Vice President
General Manager,
Mobile/Handheld
Products Group

Ronald J. Smith
Vice President
General Manager,
Computing
Enhancement Group

Arvind Sodhani
Vice President
Treasurer

Michael R. Splinter
Vice President
Assistant General
Manager, Technology and
Manufacturing Group

Appointed officers

Frank Alvarez
Vice President
Technology and
Manufacturing Group
General Manager,
Strategic Components
Manufacturing

Robert J. Baker
Vice President
Technology and
Manufacturing Group
General Manager,
Microprocessor
Components
Manufacturing

Edwin G. Bauer
Vice President
Sales and
Marketing Group
Director, Americas
Sales and Marketing

Louis J. Burns
Vice President
Information Technology
Director, Information
Technology

Mark A. Christensen
Vice President
Internet and
Communications Group
General Manager,
Network Products
Division

John E. Davies
Vice President
Desktop Products Group
Director, Consumer
Desktop Marketing

Richard A. DeLateur
Vice President
Finance
Intel Architecture Groups

Nobuyuki Denda
Vice President
Sales and
Marketing Group
Executive Vice President,
Japan Operations

Luther G. Disney
Vice President
Technology and
Manufacturing Group
Director,
Corporate Services

Edward D. Ekstrom
Vice President
Internet and
Communications Group
General Manager,
Systems Management
Division

Youssef A. El-Mansy
Vice President
Technology and
Manufacturing Group
Director, Portland
Technology Development

Corporate directory

Intel Corporation 1996

Michael J. Fister
Vice President
Microprocessor
Products Group
General Manager,
Microprocessor Division 6

Dov Frohman
Vice President
Microprocessor
Products Group
General Manager,
Israel Operations

William O. Howe
Vice President
Computing
Enhancement Group
General Manager,
Memory Components
Division

James W. Jarrett
President
Intel PRC Corporation

Robert M. Jecmen
Vice President
Technology and
Manufacturing Group
Director, California
Technology and
Manufacturing

James B. Johnson
Vice President
Internet and
Communications Group
General Manager,
Internet Services
Operation

Patrick S. Jones
Vice President
Finance
Corporate Controller

Claude M. Leglise
Vice President
Content Group
Director, Entertainment/
Education Developer
Relations

Bruce H. Leising
Vice President
Technology and
Manufacturing Group
General Manager,
Peripheral Components
Manufacturing

Michael C. Maibach
Vice President
Government Affairs

Sean M. Maloney
Vice President
Sales and
Marketing Group
General Manager,
Asia-Pacific Operations

David B. Marsing
Vice President
Technology and
Manufacturing Group
General Manager,
Assembly/Test
Manufacturing

Frank A. McCabe
Vice President
Technology and
Manufacturing Group
General Manager,
Ireland Operations

Steven D. McGeady
Vice President
Internet and
Communications Group
Director, Strategy

Patricia Murray
Vice President
Human Resources
Director,
Human Resources

Ikuo Nishioka
Vice President
Sales and
Marketing Group
President,
Japan Operations

Boon Chye Ooi
Vice President
Technology and
Manufacturing Group
General Manager,
Systems Manufacturing

Jacob A. Peña, Jr.
Vice President
Technology and
Manufacturing Group
General Manager,
Philippine Operations

Robert H. Perlman
Vice President
Finance
Director, Tax,
Customs and Licensing

David Perlmutter
Vice President
Microprocessor
Products Group
General Manager, Israel
Development Center

William B. Pohlman
Vice President
Computing
Enhancement Group
General Manager, Central
Logic Engineering

Pamela L. Pollace
Vice President
Sales and
Marketing Group
Director, Worldwide
Press Relations

William M. Siu
Vice President
Technology and
Manufacturing Group
Director, Assembly
Technology Development

Jon F. Slusser
Vice President
Technology and
Manufacturing Group
Director, Corporate
Quality Network

Stephen L. Smith
Vice President
Microprocessor
Products Group
General Manager,
Santa Clara Processor
Division

William A. Swope
Vice President
Desktop Products Group
Director, Business
Desktop Marketing

Kenneth M. Thompson
Vice President
Technology and
Manufacturing Group
General Manager,
Technology
Manufacturing
Engineering

Keith L. Thomson
Vice President
Technology and
Manufacturing Group
Oregon Site Manager

Earl L. Whetstone
Vice President
Sales and
Marketing Group
General Manager,
European Operations

James H. Yasso
Vice President
Desktop Products Group
General Manager,
Reseller Products
Division

Fellows

Gregory E. Atwood
Technology and
Manufacturing Group
Director, Flash
Memory Architecture

Mark T. Bohr
Technology and
Manufacturing Group
Director, Process
Architecture and
Integration

Robert P. Colwell
Microprocessor
Products Group
Director, IA-32
Architecture

Richard L. Coulson
Desktop Products Group
Director, I/O Architecture

John H. Crawford
Microprocessor
Products Group
Director, Microprocessor
Architecture

Paolo A. Gargini
Technology and
Manufacturing Group
Director,
Technology Strategy

Kevin C. Kahn
Internet and
Communications Group
Director,
Communications
Infrastructure Lab

Ellen R. Konar
Sales and
Marketing Group
Director, Corporate
Strategic Marketing

Peter D. MacWilliams
Desktop Products Group
Director, Platform
Architecture

Paul D. Madland
Microprocessor
Products Group
Director, Circuit
Technology

Eugene S. Meieran
Technology and
Manufacturing Group
Director, Manufacturing
Strategic Support

Frederick J. Pollack
Microprocessor
Products Group
Director, Measurement,
Architecture and Planning

Justin R. Rattner
Enterprise Server Group
Director, Server
Architecture Lab

Uri C. Weiser
Microprocessor
Products Group
Director, Israel
Development Center
Architecture

Richard B. Wirt
Microprocessor
Products Group
Director,
Microcomputer Labs

Leo D. Yau
Technology and
Manufacturing Group
Director, Innovative
Technology Modules

Ian A. Young
Technology and
Manufacturing Group
Director, Advanced
Circuit and Technology
Integration

39

Investor information

Investor materials

For investor information, including additional annual reports, 10-Ks, 10-Qs or any other financial literature, please contact Harris Trust & Savings Bank in the U.S. at (800) 298-0146 or (312) 461-5545; or the Company in Europe: (44) 1793 403 000; in Hong Kong: (852) 2844-4555; and in Japan: (81) 298-47-8511.

Intel on Nasdaq

Intel's Common Stock and 1998 Step-Up Warrants trade on The Nasdaq Stock Market* under the symbols INTC and INTCW, respectively.

Intel on the Internet

Intel's home page on the World Wide Web contains background on the Company and its products, financial information, job listings and our animated online annual report, as well as other useful information. Specific information of interest to investors can be found at www.intc.com.

Dividend reinvestment program

Intel's Dividend Reinvestment Program allows stockholders to reinvest dividends and contribute additional cash to purchase Intel Common Stock on an occasional or monthly basis. For more information, call Intel's transfer agent, Harris Trust & Savings Bank, at (800) 298-0146 or (312) 461-5545.

Transfer agent and registrar

Harris Trust & Savings Bank, 311 West Monroe, P.O. Box A3504, Chicago, IL 60690-3504. Stockholders and warrant-holders may call (800) 298-0146 or (312) 461-3309 with any questions regarding transfer of ownership of Intel stock and warrants.

Independent auditors

Ernst & Young LLP, San Jose, California.

Environmental, health and safety

This was an outstanding year for Intel in reducing injuries to employees in the workplace. Over the past three years, Intel has reduced the recordable injury rate 68 percent and the lost-day case rate 75 percent. Injury rates for new-construction contractors during the same period have been reduced by 80 percent.

Intel's Craig Barrett and Carol Browner, administrator of the U.S. Environmental Protection Agency, signed an agreement for Intel's Project XL (eXcellence and Leadership) for Fab 12 in Chandler, Arizona. Project XL is a key component of President Clinton's vision of "regulatory reinvention" to promote superior environmental performance with more community participation and lower administrative costs.

Please see our *Environmental, Health and Safety at Intel* report at www.intel.com/intel/other/ehs/index.htm. For a printed copy, call (800) 753-9754 extension 348, or (847) 296-9333 extension 348.

Workplace of choice

We strive to be a workplace of choice in which people of diverse backgrounds are valued, challenged, acknowledged and rewarded, leading to increasingly higher levels of fulfillment and productivity. For more information, see our *Workplace of Choice* report at www.intel.com/intel/community/workplace.

Index